THE JOHNS CONNECTIONS

With References to
Ayer, Benjamin, Browder, Cadwalader, Calhoun,
Davis, Edwards, Emanuel, Evans, Griffith, Harry,
Hughes, Humphrey, James, Janeway, Jenkins,
John, Jones, Lewis, Loftin, Lovelace, Miles, Moore,
Morgan, Nunn, Olivier, Owen, Prichard,
Pouncey, Rhys (Rhees), Rice, Richards, Roberts,
Rogers, Sides (Seitz), Thomas, Townsend, Welsh,
Wild, Williams, Wilson, Woodley, and Many
Other Related Families

Helen Sides Dye

HERITAGE BOOKS
2007

HERITAGE BOOKS

AN IMPRINT OF HERITAGE BOOKS, INC.

Books, CDs, and more—Worldwide

For our listing of thousands of titles see our website
at
www.HeritageBooks.com

Published 2007 by
HERITAGE BOOKS, INC.
Publishing Division
65 East Main Street
Westminster, Maryland 21157-5026

Other books by the author:

The Browder Connection

CD: The Browder Connection

International Standard Book Number: 978-0-7884-1218-9

DEDICATED TO
my son-in-law
GREGORY DRINKERT,
Ventura, Ca.,
whose skill and
computer expertise have provided
enormous help with
my books.

TABLE OF CONTENTS

AUTHOR'S NOTES...

Much has been written regarding the early history of the Welsh who came to America in the late 1600's and early 1700's seeking religious freedom. Our Johns antecedents were among those Welsh.

Information regarding the Johns is scattered throughout many sources. This is an endeavor to pull the available information together for genealogical analysis. Certain historical information must be digested to understand the data that is available. There is a surfeit of information, and in this case, it makes research difficult but more interesting.

Our Johns' family members have long believed the Johns family came from Wales in 1701 as part of a group of Baptists who first came to Pennsylvania, then went to Delaware. Around 1737, they went from Del. and Pa. to the Pee Dee River area of Craven Co., S. C. with a Baptist group and settled there.

They believed the first of our family to come over was Thomas John and his wife Mary. Griffith John of South Carolina was thought to be son of Thomas and Mary. Griffith John settled with his wife Margaret near Hunts Bluff in 1737. One known son was Jonathan, whose wife was Mary, and another son was Thomas John. David John, from whom our line descended, was believed to be either son or brother of Griffith.

Desiring to establish proof for these beliefs or else determining the true facts, it was necessary to go through the early records in Pennsylvania, Delaware, South and North Carolina.

The first interesting fact I learned was the way the Welsh used surnames, which was a system called "patronymics." This was still used by many Welsh until the middle of the Eighteenth Century. This consisted of taking the first name of the father as the children's surnames. Confounding this further, was the inconsistency of spelling and usage. In the same family, some children would use the same surname the father used, while others took his first name as their surname. Also, some used John or Jones interchangeably. Jones was considered the Anglicized version of John, but either usage was considered proper. This will be further explained in Chapter I. I was unaware of this, although I had read a couple of books on the Johns families.

The next problem was the large number of people who lived in New Castle County, Del. during this early time period who had the names of Griffith John, Thomas John, John or Jonathan John, and David John. In Virginia and other states were also people who had newly arrived from Wales and had these same names.

Other items necessary to be checked were the early Welsh Tract Church Minutes and records. From this source came the assumption that Thomas and Mary John were the progenitors of the Johns from whom we were connected. From these records also came the belief that they were husband and wife because they became members of the Welsh Tract Baptist Church in New Castle County, Del. at the same time.

A thorough reading of the available records indicated that Thomas John and Mary John Jr. joined this church group, along with others from the Philadelphia area, during a period of a year and a half after arrival of the 1701 group. Some of their group also joined with the Philadelphia church. This was caused by a controversy over laying-on-of-hands that divided the group of Baptists already in Pennsylvania and the newly arrived group from Wales. Also, the Keithian controversy within the Quaker religion brought in new members from that church that chose between these Baptist beliefs. Among these were the Miles family and others from the surrounding Great Valley area of Chester Co., Pa.

Some Welsh that settled in New Castle County, Del. during this early 1700's period had been here for some time. They arrived during the 1680's with the Quaker groups in Philadelphia. This necessitated researching the Quakers in order to learn, when possible, which ones were recent arrivals and which had been here a number of years. This led to finding they were mostly interrelated and came from the same areas in Wales. They continued to intermarry during the 1700's. This meant our John's connections in Pennsylvania would extend farther back than 1701 in Pa., as they also had connections with those in the Quaker and Baptist religions that had arrived earlier.

To summarize briefly, the group of people which came to Philadelphia in 1701 as the Baptist "church" were probably related to each other, as well as to people who had arrived earlier. Also, through continued marriages with families of these earlier emigrants, they became connected. The early writers of Welsh settlers stressed the close family relationships of groups arriving together. For that reason, it was necessary to collect information on all those who arrived in 1701 and earlier. Information was needed on the earlier arrivals of the Quakers.

I have endeavored to give the sources I found, in order to assist other researchers who are connected with this group of Baptists and Quakers, and with some other early Welsh settlers.

My belief is that our line descends from Griffith John (d. 1749, Del.) to David John (d. 1764, Ga.). I have not reached firm convictions as to the father of our Griffith. I do lean more towards his having lived several years in Pa. or Del. before he took out land in Del. in 1703. This is mostly caused by the witnesses to his documents tending to be from families of longer residence in this country. Most genealogists have a partiality towards these witnesses being related in some way.

As to the Griffith (d. 1765, S.C.), I feel he was our David's brother. He appears to be a contemporary of David. These are only my opinions, and I give options and available information for others to use.

It may be impossible to pin down absolutely the direct connections, but enough can be learned to get the feel of the relationships. I have endeavored to bring together as much pertinent information as possible in an effort to aid the serious researcher. Suggestions are also given for other locales to research. It is my hope that this information will aid in obtaining insight and understanding of our early Welsh ancestors.

Many thanks for help from all those involved in the search for the Johns' family history, Mary Kathryn Harris of Fort Worth, Tx.; Elbert Johns of Louisville, Ky.; Johnnie Zollinger of Carmel, In.; Virginia Smith and her mother, Lillie Prichard of Friendship, Tn.; Ellen John of Lawton, Okla.; and Sharon Rizzo of Chicago, Ill. A special thanks to those wonderful volunteers who give their time at the Mormon Family Libraries, especially Marge and Larry at the Covina Family History Center. Also, words of appreciation are certainly due Peggy Comstock for her assistance at our California State Society Daughters of the American Revolution Research Library, located at the State Headquarters House in Glendora, Ca.

Helen Sides Dye,
Glendora, Ca. 91740

CHAPTER ONE

ORIGIN OF NAME AND EARLY HISTORY...

The given name John has an ancient origin going back to Biblical times. However, the Welsh used given names or Christian names differently than the English by using them as surnames. Thus, John and Johns as used by our family as a surname is of Welsh origin.

The Welsh people were called Ancient Britons. Many folk tribes had come into the part of the country later called Wales from as far back as 2,000 B.C. Later Celtic invaders imposed their language and institutions. Wales had three centuries of Roman military rule. At that time, the coastal lowlands of the south came under the influence of the British. Migration in ca 400 resulted in a group of new tribal kingdoms in North and Central Wales. By ca 450 to ca 600, the Welsh kingdoms were actually the rear end of a loose confederation of British states which extended from Scotland to Cornwall, and which withstood the first shock of the Anglo-Saxon invasion. During this time, Welsh Wales passed through a period of intense missionary activity on the part of immigrants from other Celtic areas.[1]

By ca 800, the people began to form dynastic unions through marriage and because of attacks by the Norse. Between 850 and 1063, there was a degree of political unity under Rhodri the Great (844-878), Howel (Hywel) the Good (910-950), and Gruffydd ap Llewelyn (1039-63). Many battles were fought with the British, and several leaders such as Howel the Good formed friendships with and became vassals of the English kings. After 1066 when the Normans invaded, the country passed through several centuries of profound change. The principality of Wales was effectively united with England in 1536. The name Great Britain was not used until 1604.[2]

Although the name John pre-dates King John of England, there is also a Welsh connection with this king. He was king from 1199 to 1216,[3] and there is a connection by marriage between his descendants and those of the Princes of Wales. He was the king who granted the Magna Carta in 1215 under threat of civil war.

John was used as a Welsh surname in a way that needs explanation. Until the eighteenth century, most Welsh used their father's first, or given name as their last name, or surname. This was done by the use of "ap" meaning "son of," between their first name and their father's, and sometimes the ap was left off. [Also, sometimes "ab" was used instead of "ap."] (Example: David ap John, or just David John.) This name was used during a person's lifetime. His children would take his first name as their last. This was true of females, as well as males. Females used "verch" instead of "ap." Females did not

---

[1]Encyclopaedia Britannica, Vol. 23, Encyclopaedia Britannica, Inc. 1969, p. 155.
[2]Encyclopaedia Britannica, Vol. 10, 1969, p. 734.
[3]Merion in the Welsh Tract, Norristown 1898, Thomas Allen Glenn, pp.78-79.

customarily change their names after marriage until after the beginning of the eighteenth century. The Anglicized version of the John surname was usually considered Jones, and there are variants, such as Joanes, etc.

The way they were used now seem peculiar to us, and require some attempt to understand on our part. This lack of one family name carried down through the ages does not indicate they were not proud of their ancestry- - - - quite the opposite. From early times, their society was basically aristocratic until Henry VIII destroyed the concepts it relied on in 1526 when England and Wales were united. This caste system was based exclusively on "blood." The Welsh believed you could not own real estate, be accepted in the community, called a "gentleman," etc., until you could show at least five generations of royal connection. This idea was a vital part of Welsh life throughout the Middle Ages.

These pedigrees were retained in the family, and certain people were appointed to record them. The names of people were strung together with a series of "aps" meaning "son of" or "verch" meaning "daughter of." There is more to this, but you get the idea. (Pedigree example with explanation: John David (John son of David) ap William (meaning David was son of William) ap Evan (William son of Evan) ap, etc., etc.

After 1526 when Wales was united with Great Britain, this was gradually changed. There were many poor people in Wales, but the Welsh still followed the "blood," not a person's economic ability.[4] Hence, many were "poor but proud," as the saying goes.

When the first Welsh settlers came over to America, all you could be sure of when you saw the surname John was that this man was the son of someone with that first name.[5] However, they usually came in groups, from the same areas, which made it easier to trace the relationships. Although a few families carried the same surnames for a few generations in the English way, there was, in most cases, no direct family line of people with the surname. Even though a person used a particular surname during his lifetime, his children might use his first name as their surname, thus having a surname different from the one he used. Or as often happened with the surname John, the children took the name of Jones, which was widely regarded as the Anglicized version.

In some of the early books, when I found the surname "John", this person's father was named John [i.e., John Thomas, John William, etc.] The author would say the children of this man took the surname "Jones." Of course, we know this was not always the case, or there would not have been any "John" or "Johns" surnames. Research indicates some also kept the name John or Johns. Sometimes in the early records, it would be written either or

---

[4]"Report Prepared By Major Francis Jones On The Welsh Manuscripts Contained In The Muniments Of The College of Arms." 1957.
[5]"Merion In The Welsh Tract," Glenn, Norristown 1898.

both ways. A lot of the early records were kept in Welsh and later translated into English by the interpreter. Also, it appears that in some families, some of the children took the surname Jones and some took John. Differing versions were considered correct. Therefore, the name John in the early records was the same whether written John or Jones. During the first half of the 1700's, there was no consistency, and it was often difficult to determine if the children used the same surname as their father used, or took his first name as their surname. In most wills, the children's surname was not given.

In Wales they had lived near the land owned by the family. In most cases, you find the genealogy or pedigree in an allied family group, as they intermarried in a closely-knit group of people.

Most of these people who took the surname John /Johns/Jones were related through an allied group of names. With the John name, we often found Cadwalader, Thomas, David [Davis], Benjamin, William[s], Hugh[es], Richard[s] or Prichard, Griffith, Morgan, James, Harry, Owen, Samuel, Robert[s], Walter[s], Lewis, as well as Evan[s] and Rhys (or Rees, Reese, variants Rice, Price) in the early records.

Finding the coat of arms used by early families is also a good way to see their connections or alliances.

Heirs to even small estates were married early. As late as the Seventeenth Century, marriages of boys 14 to 16 to girls 12 to 14 were quite common.[6] By the late 1600's, girls were commonly married before the age of 20.[7] It was common for either spouse to remarry soon after the death of a partner.

A large portion of the John/Johns/Jones families who came early (1682 - early 1700) to this country through Pennsylvania and Delaware appear to have come from the counties of Pembroke, Merioneth and Carmarthen in Wales. There are several pedigree charts in early books and the Historical Society of Pennsylvania which include the John/Johns lineage among those of the founding fathers of Pennsylvania. One of the John lines goes back to Rhodri the Great (844-878), over-king of Wales.[8] This pedigree covers about 40 pages just to get up to around the year 1600, and has a lot of ancient history about battles fought, etc. It also encompasses so many names of Welsh Princes and others from Welsh history that is unfamiliar to most of us. This pedigree is interesting and should be read by Johns descendants for its historical and genealogical content. It tells of some of the bloody battles and events of importance in Welsh history.

[6]"Welsh Founders of Pennsylvania, Vol. II, Genealogical Society of Utah, Oxford; Fox, Jones & Co., Kemp Hall, High St., by Thomas Allen Glenn, 1911. P. XII.
[7]An Historical and Geographical Account of Pensilvania and of West-New-Jersey, by Gabriel Thomas, 1698, as given in Narratives of East Pa. West N.J. & Del. 1630-1707, Edited by Albert Cook Myers, Charles Scribner's Sons N.Y. 1912.
[8]Welsh Founders of Pa., V. II, Glenn, pp. 47-107.

The Welsh helped the Tudor King Henry VII on the field of Bosworth to win the English Crown for his family. The Welsh enjoyed a period of prosperity and special privileges under his reign.

However, during the reign of Henry VIII, the monasteries of the Welsh, as well as those of the Catholic religion, were destroyed. The Welsh church differed somewhat in form and belief from that of Rome. Through the years the earlier Welsh Princes had founded and endowed land and good livings on large magnificent convents and abbeys. Several Princes retreated or retired in these abbeys after losing battles. During Henry VIII's reign, the abbeys and convents that the earlier Welsh Princes had endowed were 'not left with one stone on another.' After destroying these imposing buildings, the land was sold off to the Welsh gentry for what it would bring.

The Abbey of Marcella, near Bala, in Merionethshire was sold to the Price family, who moved from Denbighshire and brought with them many of the families mentioned in the John pedigree. "Among those who settled in Penllyn at that time were the families of Owen, of Fron Goch, and the ancestors of John Cadwalader, of Philadelphia."[9]

The new churchmen who took occupancy then were completely dependent for their livelihood on the tithes they collected. As happens with the human species, these tithes were often excessive, dishonest and exorbitant. For this reason, many of the Welsh joined Cromwell's army during the English Civil War (1642-51). During the war, many of the Welsh parishes were supplied with Non-Conformist ministers.

Between 1639 and 1660, Puritan sects gained followers in the southeastern part of Wales. These dissenters were among the class of farmers that were well off, and were only a small percentage of the country.

The Quaker religion came into being because of offense caused by the British Parliament introducing the full presbyterian system (i.e., church government by a group of elders) in 1643, with its strict discipline and rigidity. George Fox was the founder of the group that became the Friends, or Quakers. In his journal he described how two members from the Parish of Wrexham in Denbighshire were sent "down among us" and one, John ap John, "abode in the truth, and received a gift in the ministry to which he continued faithful." Though he intended to, John ap John never came to America. But he was one of the primary movers of the Quaker religion in Wales, and purchased land for the early settlement from William Penn.

Quakers were known as "Friends of Truth" in the seventeenth century, and they used the term "Friend" to all that they addressed. They were later called "Society of Friends." They believed the priesthood lay in all believers, and accepted that women shared equal responsibility with men in worship and church organization. [This feeling of equality of women carried through in

---

[9]Ibid, p. 11.

4

other ways as found in the early records of Welsh settlements in this country. Women owned property, were active in the church, and occasionally voted.]

Along with the Quakers, several other religious groups, including the General Baptists, opposed the full presbyterian system, and wanted more toleration and expansion of the rights of the regular worshipers. Many believed in the immediacy [i.e., presence of knowledge in the mind] of Christ's teachings, with its application to the whole of life, and believed that the buildings where the meetings were held and the person preaching were irrelevant.

After the death of Cromwell, Charles II was restored to the throne. He had a Catholic wife, which caused distrust from those who had embraced Protestant beliefs. As well, Charles II was not overly fond of those who had beheaded his father. Those who had been prominent in the Civil War and subsequently joined other churches suffered the most under his rule and from the High Church authorities.

Special acts were passed to prevent the spread of non-conformist religions. People were forbidden to meet together, and were compelled to take the oath of allegiance and supremacy to the King. This oath went against their religious beliefs of God's supremacy. They were willing to affirm [not swear] their loyalty to the King. Persons not attending the parish church were heavily fined. They were dragged before Justices who were often their kinsmen who had been Royalists during the war. There was often pettiness and spitefulness brought into this because they could not make them yield to their will. The non-conformists were put in chains, driven many miles over muddy roads to the jails, and beaten with swords along the way. Some of the men had been ordered to be drawn and quartered, and the women burned, but fortunately these sentences were not carried out. However, many were thrown into prison, and some died there. Fines were heavily imposed and much property taken from them.

The Welsh people were descended from a race with a long history of battles, murder and sudden death. Many of their forefathers were famous soldiers, and they were not easily conquered in battles. Rejecting their often violent past history, through their religion they embraced peace and love for their fellow man. Once convinced of their call by God to His service, they did not hesitate to face danger, shunning by neighbors, or even death for their beliefs. J. J. Levick, M.D. in an address to the Historical Society of Pennsylvania early this century regarding these settlers, gave good, concise descriptions of them: 'They were humble disciples, consistent enemies of strife and oppression, intent on being followers of the truth.' "They were of the blood of heroes to which the blood of martyrs is closely akin..."

They were persecuted and imprisoned, sometimes dying in prison, for their beliefs. Many records still exist recording this persecution. (Even in this

country, the Puritans hung four Friends in Boston between 1659 and 1661. [10])
Because of their beliefs, these people adopted an extreme attitude against
taking oaths and paying tithes. These beliefs were not toned down and an
orderly system of government established within the Quaker groups until
1667-69. More than 450 had died in prison, and 15,000 had served legal
sentences by this time. This persecution was only ended in 1689 by the
Toleration Act.

By 1681, the persecution continued despite the short reign of the
Declaration of Indulgence and the repealing of the more severe acts relating to
the oath of allegiance. These people were elated when they learned that
William Penn was offering land for sale in the New World where one could
have an asylum from all religious persecution.

The earlier effects of the Reformation had been felt in other parts of the
world. People from Holland came into New York in 1608 and in 1614 and
claimed all the country from the Connecticut River to the Delaware River.
Under the auspices of the Dutch, small groups of Swedes and English came to
engage in the enriching beaver trade. In 1638, a small group of Swedes
planted the first permanent white settlement on the Delaware, where today
stands the city of Wilmington, Del. They were the first to build log cabins.

Charles II of England put in a claim prior to the Dutch that he supported by
armed forces. The Dutch kept possession until the treaty of Breda in 1667,
but the king of England gave the country to his brother, the Duke of York,
four years before this treaty, and in the same year sold the Western Jersey part
to Lord Berkley and Sir George Carteret.

There were a number of people migrating to this country from England
beginning about 1667. By 1675, there were a few Baptists from England (and
Wales) who settled along the Delaware River. A group of Baptists from
Tipperary in Ireland arrived around 1683 and then proceeded on to the
interior. Due to the religious upheavals in their homelands, most of these
early settlers came for religious freedom.

William Penn, the English Quaker and strong advocate of religious
freedom, along with eleven other Quakers in 1681, bought the proprietary
rights to East New Jersey from the widow of Sir John Carteret. That same
year, Penn applied to King Charles II for a vast province on the west-bank of
the Delaware River. This was granted to Penn in payment of a large debt
Charles II owed to Penn's father, and was named Pensylvania for Penn's
father. Penn also received a grant of the three "lower counties" (later
Delaware) from the Duke of York. Penn hoped to have a refuge for Quakers
and other religiously persecuted people in Pennsylvania, as well as having a
source of income for himself from the sales of land and quit-rents.

---

[10]Encyclopedia Britannica, Inc., 1969, Vol. 9, p. 938.

William Penn was an English Quaker, and had spent time in prison for his beliefs. Being strong in his beliefs, he sold land to English Quakers, Welsh Quakers, Germans, and other groups seeking religious freedom.

He met with leaders of the Welsh Quakers in the latter part of 1681 in London to work out an agreement with them to settle in Pennsylvania. The leaders for the Welsh were Dr. Griffith Owen, Dr. Edward Jones, Dr. Thomas Wynne, John ap Thomas, Charles Lloyd, John ap John, Richard Davies, Edward Prichard, and others.

The Welsh made an agreement for the purchase of 40,000 acres of land in Pennsylvania. This large acreage was to be resold in smaller tracts to families who settled. Another 10,000 acres was also sold to the Welsh.

During the latter part of the 1600's, beginning in 1682, a large group of Quakers came over from Wales primarily to Pennsylvania. At the same time and earlier, English Quakers and others were arriving. The Welsh came by groups, with the majority of the first groups being Quakers. The first group came from near Bala, Merionethshire. This immigration was steady until the Welsh was granted more religious freedom at home through the Toleration Act of 1689.

The first ship bound for Pennsylvania was the "Bristol Factor," which left Bristol the middle of October 1681 and reached New Castle on the Delaware 15 December 1681. The next was the "John & Sarah" from London. Then a ship arrived in Delaware that came from New England. The "Amity" of London sailed from the Downs 23 April 1682, and arrived in the Delaware 3 August 1682. The "Freeman" of Liverpool arrived the 5th or 6th August 1682. The "Hester & Hannah" arrived in Upland 8 August 1682 after a voyage of twenty weeks. The next ship to arrive was the "Lyon" of Liverpool, on 13 August 1682. This carried four families of the seventeen comprising the Edward Jones Company. This was the first group of Welsh to arrive to settle Pennsylvania.

The "Friendship" of Liverpool arrived 14 August 1682. A small ship, the "Mary," of Fowey, a small seaport of Cornwall, arrived 15 August 1682. The "Society" of Bristol arrived in the 6th month [August] of 1682. After this, there was a lull in arrivals, with the "Golden Hind" arriving in September 1682. The "Samuel" came into the Delaware on 22 September 1682. Another ship to arrive about that time was the "Friend's Adventure" of Liverpool, said to have arrived 28 September 1682 or earlier, with emigrants from Cheshire and Staffordshire.

The "Providence" of Scarborough arrived in the Delaware 29 September 1682. The next ship was variously listed by several names in the records, the "Isabella Ann & Katherine," the "Ann," and the "Elizabeth," etc. [The same master, Thomas Hudson, was given for each, and obviously all were the same ship.] Penn's records gave it as the "Elizabeth Ann & Catherine" of London. It arrived 29 September 1682, the same day as the "Providence." The "Hopewell," with Michael Yoakley, master, sailed up the Thames during the first week or so of October, 1682, for Pennsylvania, Maryland, Virginia and Carolina, but the date of arrival in the Delaware is not known. The "Lamb" of Liverpool arrived 22 October 1682.

By this time, the "Bristol Factor" had returned to England with a load of tobacco from Virginia. The last load was put on it for Virginia 2 September, but the sailing date is unknown. A letter from Evan Oliver mentions their child who was born "within sight of the Capes of Delaware" on 24 October 1682 and it was said to have been on this ship.[11]

The most famous of all these ships, the "Welcome," which carried William Penn and his party, arrived at New Castle 27 October 1682, and sailed on to Upland the next day, the 28th.

Before the end of October, the next ship the "Jeffrey" arrived, having made the trip in 29 days. The next ship that arrived in December was the "Antelope" which came from Belfast, Ireland and brought Irish passengers. Record of this was not found in the English port books, but from some of the passengers who registered their arrival as being on the 9th or 10th of December 1682.

The next ship that arrived in the Delaware was the "Unicorn" which contained goods both for Pennsylvania and Virginia. On 5 October 1682 the London Impartial Mercury [newspaper] noted this ship in Bristol "was fitting out for Pensylvania on board which 40 Quakers together with their families will imbarq." This paper also reported "tis said they carry over with them 300 pounds-worth of Half-pence, and Farthings which in that Collony go current for twice their value and 'tis added that some discontented Presbyterians will Likewise accompany them." This ship arrived before the end of December 1682.

The last ship to arrive from England before the year's end was the "Submission." This voyage was very stormy and the passengers landed at Choptank on the Eastern Shore of Maryland on November 2, 1682. These passengers were set down and made their way to Appoquidimink Creek, twenty miles south of New Castle, by mid-February 1683. The passengers were naturally annoyed at being uncomfortably set down on the wrong side of the peninsula in the winter. In writing of this in "Passengers and Ships Prior to 1684," author Sheppard defended the Captain as having to do this as he had to sail up the Chesapeake if he wanted to sell and trade his goods for Maryland and Virginia tobacco. During this first year, twenty three ships brought passengers to Penn's Colony.

The early Welsh settlers were well equipped by birth and fortune to make this move and cope with the many problems involved. No other group that settled in Pennsylvania was as well endowed. They were freeholders or heirs

---

[11]"Passengers and Ships Prior to 1684," Walter Lee Sheppard Jr., Heritage Books, Inc., Bowie, Md. Reprinted 1992, p. 54.

to comfortable estates. Many of their fathers, or they themselves, had fought bravely under Cromwell in the Civil War.

The group of allied Welsh families that showed pedigrees back to Rhodri Mawr (Rhodri the Great) are recorded as "Owen, Evans, and Allied Families. Genealogy of the Princes of South Wales, families of Cadwalader, Edward (Edwards), Foulke, George, Griffith of Cefn Amwlch, Hugh, John, Jones, Llewelyn, Lewis, Morgan, and others."[12]

John's or Jones' were among the founding families of Pennsylvania and Delaware. One of the large groups of acreage, 5000 acres, was purchased by Dr. Edward Jones and seventeen others, and became the first group of Welsh Quakers to settle in Pennsylvania. "The seventeen persons concerned in this purchase had their homes in the neighbourhoods of Bala and Dolgelly, Merionethshire, Wales, and besides being neighbours and friends, were more or less connected by ties of blood and intermarriage."[13] These were John Thomas, Hugh Roberts, William ap Edward, Edward Rees, Edward Jones, Edward Owen, John ap Edward, Robert David, Rees John William, Thomas Prichard, Gainor Robert, Cadwalader Morgan, Thomas Lloyd, William John, John Watkin, Hugh John and Evan Rees.

The first settlement in Merion was made by Dr. Edward Jones, Edward Reese, William ap Edward, and a few others from near Bala, Merionethshire. They set sail from Liverpool in the ship "Lyon" and arrived in the landing place of Upland (now Chester) on the 13th of 6mo. 1682. [This was the way dates were written then, as March was the first month of the year.] From there, they went on to what was the beginning of the city of Philadelphia.

The Welsh wanted and had assumed their land would all be laid out in one place, with the plantations adjacent to each other, located near the city of Philadelphia (supposedly already laid out), so as to constitute a separate Barony. Their desire was to carry on their freedom to worship, and to be governed by people elected by themselves with like values and blood. A conference was held with the Proprietor William Penn by the Drs. Griffith Owen, Edward Jones, Thomas Wynne and their group on behalf of the Welsh Nation in the latter part of 1681 to ascertain this. William Penn professed great kindliness towards the Welsh, and those Welsh attending this meeting were under the impression this was granted. However, they neglected to get this in writing.

Writings of William Penn indicate he wanted settlements closer together and did not want to leave large tracts of adjoining land unsettled. He sold 15,000 acres to a Frankfort, Germany, group in 1681. Francis Daniel Pastorius was their agent. The Germans began settling in 1683, and they ran into similar problems.

---

[12] Welsh Founders of Pa., Glenn, Vol. I, p. 14.
[13] Ibid, p. 73.

Upon arrival the Welsh Quakers found many difficulties. They were forced to spend days in the Land Office trying to get their land surveyed. They were compelled to have the tracts that they had purchased divided. Part was surveyed to them near Philadelphia and part in the area afterwards called Goshen (Chester Co.), and part in the lower counties of New Castle, Kent and Sussex, now Delaware.

A letter written to Hugh Jones of Bala, in Wales, about 1708, by John, the son of Thomas John, told of the hardships endured by these first settlers. They had arrived in a place of wilderness, knowing no one. Thomas John arrived alone in April 1682 and had to go looking for any assistance he could find, and was offered assistance from a kind Swedish family. He was allowed to move in with this family and received much kindness and help from them. There was no land to be had within twelve miles of Philadelphia. [He later purchased 300 acres in the southern part of Radnor Township in Chester Co. More on him later.]

Other Welsh settlers arrived in the fall. Because of the slowness in getting located and settled, many of the first settlers were forced to live in caves and dugouts in the banks of the Delaware during their first winter. "If we have bread we will drink water and be content," they said; yet no one was in want, and all were much attached to each other; indeed much more so, perhaps, than many who have every outward comfort this world can afford." They were used to servants and comfortable homes in Wales. Yet they did not let this get them down.

The division of their land and the long wait to get it surveyed caused some ill feelings toward William Penn that never abated. He had made agreements with people of other races whose voices he also had to consider, and he also had problems caused by his indebtedness and high living. It was maintained by several early settlers that the purchasing of the land from Penn was one thing, and getting the warrant of survey was another.

Despite these hardships, there actually was a lot to be thankful for. Many Quakers chartered ships and sailed in independent groups on vessels already in the colonial trade. They were able to pay their own way and were not responsible to any financing company; the Indians were peaceful; other white people had already settled in the Delaware Valley; and they had not sailed into a great unknown. The English port books indicate they took an enormous amount of supplies with them.

They found the land was desirable in many ways. It had streams of water and a lot of timber and fieldstones for building. Plus, the rolling hills reminded them of home. The Swedes were the first to build log cabins and showed the Welsh how to built these. However, most Welsh preferred and built stone houses as soon as they could. The townships of Merion, Radnor and Haverford were soon established.

Disputes between the Welsh and the English began by 1684 when parcels and lands that were located within the bounds of the Welsh holdings were laid out to English settlers. The Welsh were not using all their land, holding it in reserve for other kinsmen to come, but other settlers, especially the English, desired to use it then. Penn required they have the land surveyed in order to obtain title. Some had not been surveyed before settling, and some land was surveyed several times.

In 1689, the Chester County line was in dispute. A petition by the Justices of Chester County was put before Governor John Blackwell with the purpose of putting about sixty Welsh voters into Chester County who had previously voted in Philadelphia County. The Welsh considered themselves a separate Barony, with election purposes only in Philadelphia County. Using this dissension among the Welsh as an excuse, the Justices wanted to exclude their vote in Philadelphia County for political reasons. Radnor and Haverford townships would be moved to Chester County. Despite protests, the Welsh lost, and the townships became part of Chester County. (This part is now in Delaware County.) This ended the growth of the "Welsh Tract" as such. This dispute continued for a long time, but the three townships continued to be known as the "Great Welsh Tract" on into the early part of the 1800's.

By 1691, a religious difference among the Quakers surfaced in belief regarding "The sufficiency of what every man naturally has within himself for the purpose of his own salvation." They set up separate meeting houses in different parts of the country, with a general one at Burlington in opposition to that of Philadelphia.[14] George Keith, a Quaker from Scotland, and others signed and published a "Confession of Faith." Keith became their leader. This group was called "Keithians" and "Keithian Quakers." Apparently the Quakers took them to court, but were unable to act against them. The Keithians soon declined in numbers and some returned to the Quaker religion. Many became "Keithian Baptists." A large group of the Quakers later joined the Baptist and Presbyterian churches, and some returned to the Church of England. George Keith was originally a Presbyterian, and later he became Church of England.

Some of the Welsh names, using the "ap," became different, such as Price from "ap Rhys," Prichard from "ap Richard,"and Bevan from "ab Evan." Some Welsh lived in England before immigrating, or came via London or Liverpool, but most came directly from Wales.

Although Welsh members of the Quaker religion came first into the Welsh Tract in the Province of Pennsylvania and were joined by Quakers from other countries, by 1700 the influx of Quakers had almost ended. The Baptists and members of other religions from Wales followed. They came to a place already occupied by members of their own and related families. Three other townships, Newtown, Goshen (on Chester Creek) and Uwchland were soon settled.

---

[14]"Materials Towards History of the Am. Baptists in XII Volumes," Morgan Edwards, Philadelphia, 1770.

Early records of the Baptists maintain they comprised the largest religious group to arrive in Pennsylvania. Perhaps this was counting those arriving after 1700. In books written by the antecedents of Quakers, the earlier Baptist influx was downplayed.

* *

CHAPTER TWO

WELSH QUAKERS.
Arrival in Pennsylvania in 1682.

There were a number of Johns and Jones from Wales that settled in Pennsylvania and Delaware as part of the Quakers religious groups beginning in 1681. Some of these Quakers later became members of other churches and/or married into families of other religions.

After meeting with William Penn in London in 1681 to work out conditions, these Welsh Quakers purchased land from him. An account of the purchasers of the Welsh Tract, as set forth in "D. Powers Acct of ye Welch Purchasers in Genl," showed the following purchasers and the amounts of their acreage.

Purchaser	Acreage
Charles Lloyd and Margaret Davis	5,000
Richard Davis [Davies]	5,000
William Jenkins	1,000
John Poy [Poyer]	750
John Burge	750
William Mordant	500
William Powell	1,250
Lewis David	3,000
Morris Llewlin	500
Thomas Simons	500
John Bevan	2,000
Edward Prichard	2,500
John ap John, and Thomas Wyn	5,000
Edward Joanes, and John Thomas	5,000
Richard Davis	1,250
Richard ap Thomas	5,000
Daniell Hurry [Harry]	300
Mordicia Moore in Right of	500
John Millington	500
Henry Right	500
Daniell Med_____	200
Thomas Ellis	1,000
Tho. Ellis for B. Roules	250
Th. Ellis on ac't Humph. Tho.	100
David Powell	1,000
Burke and Simson	1,000
John Kinsy	200
John Kinsy	100

Dave Meredith	250
John Day	300
David Davis	200
Henry Joanes	400
Thomas John Evan	250
John Evans	100
John Jormon	50
David Kinsy	200
Evan Oliver	100
Samuel Mills	100
Thomas Joanes	50
David Joanes	100
John Ffish	300

"The whole Compl'nt 50,000 acres."
* *

William Penn originally intended to sell his land in America in blocks of 5,000 acres or more. He proposed shares of 5,000 acres at 100 Pounds per share, and for those unable to buy, he offered land at a nominal quitrent. He also offered those who bought the first 100 shares (of 5,000 acres each share), a share in a city lot proportionate to the size of each individual purchase. Those who purchased land from William Penn before he left for America were designated as First Purchasers.

Of the Welsh purchases, 30,000 acres were purchased in amounts of 5,000 acres each. Another 10,000 acres they conditionally purchased was later sold by Penn or his agents in small lots to actual settlers and to parties who bought for speculation. An additional 10,000 acres reserved in the "Welsh Tract" was taken up in a few years by Welshmen. Some Welsh arrived in Pennsylvania before making their purchases.

Most of these purchasers were from the ancient Welsh shire of Merioneth, and Bala was one of its chief towns. Their parishes were:
1. Llanykil, which was in the hundred of Penllyn, had town of Bala.
2. Llanvawr (or Llanfor) was due north of Bala. It comprised the townships of Tre'r Llan, Rhiwaedog Uwch Avon, Rhiwaedog Is Avon; Nant Lleidog, Penmaen, Ciltalgarth (or Kiltalgarth, Garth, Ucheldref, and Llanwry Bettws; also included the church lands of Trinity and Fron Goch. [Township of Llaethgwm, which was formerly in Llanvawr, was later in Llandderfel.]
3. Llangower, south of town of Bala and east of Bala Lake.
4. Llandderfel, east of Bala Lake, included township of Llan, Nant Ffreiar, Tref Gynlas (Cynlas), Selwern, Crogan, Dol Drewyn, Llaethgwm and Caergeliog. In Llanderfel was farm of Gwern y Brechtwn or Owl's Brindle Bush (Lloyd and Foulke Families); Fron Goch, home of Owens, Evans, Johns, etc. of Gwynedd & Philadelphia (also partly in Llanfor Parish for

church purposes; Rhiwlas, Plasynghrogen (another Lloyd family); and Palau.

5. Llanuwchllyn, [anciently Llanuwchllyn Tegid,] was located southwest of Llyn Tegid; contained townships of Pen Aran, Tref Prys, or Brysg, Pennant, Llivr, Tref Gastell and Cynllwd.

These five parishes were all in the old hundred of Penllyn, and within five miles of Bala.[1]

The large Welsh purchasers of land from Penn consisted of seven groups [companies,] with buyers purchasing in their names, then selling off in smaller parcels. They were in effect real estate brokers for Penn. These seven Welsh companies were:

1. John ap Thomas, of Llaithgwm, Merionethshire, and Dr. Edward Jones, of Bala, Merionethshire.   5,000 acres.
2. Charles Lloyd, of Dolobran, Montgomeryshire, and Margaret Davies, widow, of Dolobran.   5,000 acres.
3. John Bevan, of Treverigg, Glamorganshire.   2,000 acres.
4. John ap John, of Ruabon, Denbighshire, and Dr. Thomas Wynne, of Caerwys, Flintshire.   5,000 acres.
5. Lewis ap David, of Llandewy Velfry, Pembrokeshire.   3,000 acres.
6. Richard ap Thomas, of Whitford Garne, Flintshire.   5,000 acres.
7. Richard Davies, of Welshpool, Montgomeryshire.   5,000 acres.

* *

Most of the emigrants to Penn's Colony sailed from London and Bristol. The voyage was long and tiring, seldom taking less than two months. They were required to pack food and drinks to last the duration of the voyage. Furniture, household goods, bricks, glass and even grist mills were brought. Some of the port records are still extant, showing the enormous amount of goods brought by these emigrants.

The first Welsh "Company" to arrive and have land laid out in the Welsh Tract was that of John ap Thomas and Dr. Edward Jones. Four of the seventeen families in this first company made the voyage. Their number, including children and servants, was forty. They arrived 13 August 1682 on the "Lyon" of Liverpool, a ship of only 90 tons. They made the voyage in eleven weeks.

Various records of the people who arrived at the same time as Penn in 1681 have been published, some of which were inaccurate. Investigation of the port books, and other published records now give a clear record of those who arrived on the "Welcome" with William Penn.[2]

---

[1]Merion in the Welsh Tract, Glenn, pp. 57, 58, 59.
[2]Passengers and Ships Prior to 1684, Sheppard Jr., Heritage Books Inc., 1992.

FIRST WELSHMAN TO ARRIVE IN PHILADELPHIA:

THOMAS SION [JOHN] EVAN: The first Welsh colonist to arrive in Philadelphia was Thomas John Evan who later purchased 250 acres of land. He was of the Church of England, but joined the Quakers after he settled in Radnor Township. [I believe Browning erroneously conjectured that Thomas John Evan might have been a son of John Evan Edwards who also lived in Radnor Township.[3]] Thomas John Evan was from the Comot of Penllyn, near Bala, which was also the home of Griffith, William and Robert John. For this reason I <u>speculate</u> he may have been a brother or step-brother to them. He arrived in April 1682, before the arrival of the Edward Jones Company. A letter written by his son John Jones, to his cousin Hugh Jones in Wales ca 1725, was twice printed in Wales [1806 and 1831] and several times in this country. This was 18 years after the death of Thomas John Evan. It contains an interesting account of his father Thomas John's experiences when he first arrived in Pennsylvania:

"I received a letter from you, dated May 8 last; and I was glad to find that one of my relatives, in the old land of which I have heard so much, was pleased to recollect me. I have heard my father speak much about old Wales; but I was born in this woody region, this new world.

I remember him frequently mentioning such places as Llanyeil, Llanuwehllyn, Llanfor, Llangwm, Bala, Llangower, Lyn Tegid, Arenig Fawr, Fron Dderw, Brynllysg, Phenbryn, Cyffdy, Glanllafar, Fron Goch, Llaethgwm, Hafodfadog, Cwm Tir y Mynach, Cwm Glan Lleidiog, Trawsfynydd, Tai Hirion yn Mignaint, and many others. It is probably uninteresting to you to hear these names of places; but it affords me great delight even to think of them, although I do not know what kind of places they are; and indeed I long much to see them, having heard my father and mother so often speak in the most affectionate manner of the kind-hearted and innocent old people who lived in them, most of whom are now gone to their long home. Frequently, during long winter evenings, would they in merry mood prolong their conversation about their native land till midnight; and even after they had retired to rest, they would sometimes fondly recall to each other's recollection some man, or hill, house, or rock. Really I can scarcely express in words how delighted this harmless old couple were to talk of their old habitations, their fathers and mothers, brothers and sisters, having been now twenty-four years in a distant and foreign land, without even the hope of seeing them more. I fear this narrative will be irksome to you; but I cannot forbear when I think of these innocent artless old people.

And now, my kinsman, I will give you an account of the life and fortunes of my dear father, from the time when he left Wales to the day of his death.

---

[3]Browning, Welsh Settlement of Pa., Reprint Gen. Publ. Co., Inc., Baltimore, 1967, p. 231.

Three weeks to the time when he first heard tell of Pennsylvania, at St. Peter's Fair in Bala he took leave of his neighbors and relatives, who were taking account of his departure for London. He was waiting three months for a ship; after boarding the first ship he set out from England by [or upon] the name of William Penn.[4] He had a very tempestuous passage for several weeks; and when in sight of the river [Delaware], owing to adverse winds and a boisterous sea, the sails were torn, and the rudder injured. By this disaster they were greatly disheartened, and were obliged to go back to Barbadoes, where they continued three weeks, expending much money in refitting their ship. Being now ready for a second attempt, they easily accomplished their voyage, and arrived safely in the river [Delaware] on the 16th of April, being thirty weeks from the time they left London. During this long voyage he learned to speak and real English tolerably well.

They now came up the river a hundred and twenty miles, to the place where Philadelphia is at present situated. At that time there was, as the Welsh say, na they nac ymogor (neither house nor shelter), but the wild woods; nor any one to welcome them to land. A poor outlook, this, for persons who had been so long at sea, many of whom had spent their little all. This was not the place for remaining stationary. My father therefore went alone where chance led him, to endeavor to obtain the means of subsistence. He longed very much at this time for milk. During his wanderings he met with a drunken old man, who understood neither Welsh nor English, and who, noticing the stranger, invited him to his dwelling, where he was received by the old man's wife and several sons in the most hospitable manner. They were Swedes. Here he made his home, till he had a habitation of his own.

As you shall hear, during this summer [1682] our governor, William Penn, Esquire, arrived here, together with several from England, having bought lands here. They now began to divide the country into allotments, and to plan the city of Philadelphia, (which was to be more than two miles in length), laying it out in streets and squares, etc., with portions of land assigned to several of the houses. He also bought the freehold of the soil from the Indians, a save race of men, who have lived here from time immemorial, as far as I am able to understand. They can give no account of themselves, not knowing when or whence they came here; an irrational set, I should imagine; but they have some kind of reason, too, and extra-ordinary natural endowments in their peculiar way; they are very observant of their customs, and more unblamable, in many respects, than we are. They had neither towns nor villages, but lived in booths or tents. [As translated.]

---

[4]The name of the ship here might have been incorrect due to the literal Welsh translation and obscure meaning. A probable account was that it was one of William Penn's ships that sailed under his orders.

In the autumn of this year several from Wales arrived here: Edward ab Rhys, Edward Jones of Bala, William ab Edward, and many others. By this time there was a kind of neighborhood here, although as neighbors they could little benefit each other. They were sometimes employed in making huts beneath some cliff, or under the hollow banks of rivulets, thus sheltering themselves where their fancy dictated. There were neither cows nor horses to be had at any price. "If we have bread, we will drink water, and be content," they said; yet no one was in want, and all were much attached to each other; indeed much more so, perhaps than many who have every outward comfort this world can afford.

During this eventful period, our governor began to build mansion-houses at different intervals, to the distance of fifty miles from the city, although the country appeared a complete wilderness.

The governor was a clever intelligent man, possessing great penetration, affable in discourse, and a pleasant orator; a man of rank, no doubt, but he did not succeed according to his merit; the words of the bard Edward Morys might be applied to him:

> The old person did not keep a fragment of his sense;
> He fell away to the pursuit of wealth.

At this time my father, Thomas Sion Evan, was living with the Swedes, as I mentioned before, and intending daily to return to Wales; but as time advanced, the country improved. In the course of three years several were beginning to obtain a pretty good livelihood, and my father determined to remain with them. There was by this time no land to be bought within twelve miles of the city; and my father, having purchased a small tract of land, married the widow of Thomas Llwyd [Lloyd] of Penmaen.

> You have heard tell in Dyffryn Clwyd
> Of Thomas Lloyd of Penmaen.

He now went to live near the woods. It was a very rare but pleasing thing to hear a neighbor's cock crow. My father had now only one small horse; and his wife was much afflicted with the tertian ague. We might suppose that many things would be revolved in the mind of a man in such a situation as this; but I never heard him complain of the difficulties under which he labored. Everything was agreeable to these innocent people; although in want of some present necessaries, yet they were peaceable and friendly to each other. In process of time, however, the little which he had prospered, so that he became possessed of horses, cows, and everything else that was necessary for him, or even that he wished; indeed he never coveted much. During the latter years of his life, he kept twelve good milch cows. He had eight children, but I was the eldest. Having lived in this manner

18

twenty-four years, he now became helpless and infirm, and very subject to difficulty of breathing at the close of his day's labor. He was a muscular man, very careful and attentive to his worldly occupations. About the end of July [1707], eighteen years to last July, he became sick, and much enfeebled by a severe fever; but asthma was his chief complaint. Having been thus five weeks indisposed, he departed this life, leaving a small farm each for my brother and myself, a corresponding portion for my sister, and a fair dower for my mother. My sister married Rhisiart ab Tomas ab Rhys, a man whom I much respected prior to his marriage, and still regard. My brother and I continue to live with my mother, as before, endeavoring to imitate our father in the management of his affairs; but we are in many respects unequal to him. Our mother is seventy-three years old, somewhat infirm, but enjoying pretty good health, considering her age.

And now, my kind kinsman, I have given you the history of my father and myself, and I hope you will be pleased with it. Do send me some news; if you should have anything remarkable to mention I should be glad to hear it.--I must conclude my letter. Your kinsman,...["5]

Walter Lee Sheppard Jr. critiques this letter in "Passengers and Ships Prior to 1684 Penn's Colony: Vol. I," (Heritage Books, 1992). He wrote many of these statements were inaccurate. He surmised Thomas John Evan sailed to Barbados and awaited transportation from there in the spring. The trip itself would not have taken thirty weeks, the name of the ship was incorrect, and he would not have had to go to London to learn of William Penn's proposed settlement. My thoughts regarding this are: 'With the length of time passed after his father's death and when John wrote the letter, there were undoubtedly a few inaccuracies in his memory of what his father had told him and an opportunity to confuse his story with others told by early settlers. As well, the family probably enhanced the story through retelling it through the years. The actual length of the trip and where his father learned of Penn's colony are of minor importance.'

After Thomas John Evan arrived from near Bala, Merionethshire in Wales in April 1682, he married Lowery Jones of Merion, widow of

Thomas Lloyd in 1686. Thomas Lloyd, of "Penmaen," a township in the parish of Llanvawr, Merionethshire, Wales, was a well known bard before

[5]Printed in Welsh July 1806, in Welsh magazine published in London called Y Greal (The Historical Magazine), no. V., pp. 210-213. Printed in Welsh magazine Y Gwyliedydd (The Sentinel), Jan 1831, VIII. 15-17. In April 1831, English translation in London in Cambrian Quarterly Magazine, III. 141-144. Reprinted with omissions in the Pennsylvania Magazine of History, XIII.227-231, and in Thomas Allen Glenn's "Merion in the Welsh Tract", Norristown, 1896, pp. 41-44. In Narratives of Early Pennsylvania, Edited by Albert Cook Myers, Charles Scribner's Sons, 1912, Facsimile Reprint 1989 by Heritage Books, Inc., pp. 454-459.

he became a Quaker. Thomas John Evan died in 1707, and was buried in the Friends' Burial Ground near the Radnor Meeting House. His will was dated 31 March 1707. He left his farm of 300 acres equally to his two sons John and Joseph; his daughter Elizabeth 50 pounds; and to his wife Lowry 6 pounds per annum with the right to reside on the farm. He appointed as Guardians and Overseers, friends Rowland Ellis Sr., Joseph Owen, and Rowland Ellis Jr. Lowry John Evan, his wife, proved his will. He only named children John, Joseph and Elizabeth, but the above letter mentioned that he had eight children, some of whom died early. John mentioned in his letter that his mother was then 73 years of age, making her birth around 1652. John was probably in his 60's when the letter was written, and he would have had grown children and grandchildren by that time.

Thomas John's farm of 300 acres was located in the southern part of Radnor Township, in Chester Co., now Delaware Co., about midway between Bryn Mawr and Newtown Square. Ithan Creek flowed through the eastern part, and Darby Creek through the western part, per Glenn.

Most of the early deeds in Radnor had the same witnesses: Edward Jones, Thomas Davies, David James, Richard Jones, Daniel Morris, Samuel Miles, John Evans, and Daniel Meredith. Some others living there were Richard Price, Henry Price, Richard Moore, George Painter, William Howell, Lewis Harry, Benjamin Humphrey, David Lewis, and Benjamin Lewis.

Many of these inhabitants of Radnor became associated with the Baptists in the Welsh Tract Baptist Church in New Castle Co. The Miles were among the founders of the Great Valley Baptist Church. Some of the Miles purchased land in the Welsh Tract of New Castle Co.

JOHN JOHN, or JONES, who wrote the above letter, was born ca 1687 in Radnor, Pa. He had a brother, JOSEPH JONES, b. 2mo. 28. 1695 in Radnor, Pa. Joseph married Sarah Morgan in 1727. She was born in 1698, the daughter of John Morgan, of Nantmell, County Radnor, gentleman. Their child Hannah married Nathaniel Miles. More research should be done on this family. The farms of these two brothers were located not far from the Baptist Church in New Castle County, Del. There are indications that these brothers and their families were affiliated with the Baptists. One of the John Jones mentioned in a deed there might have been this one.

A survey in New Castle Co. for a Joseph John was made 6 June 1748, Survey J, Vol. 2, #29, St. George's Hundred, for 100 acres of land and improvements adjoining the land formerly granted to Percus and Jacob Hyats. A Joseph John died intestate in New Castle Co., Del. David John was Executor of his estate. (Will Book G, p. 424, 2 Oct 1750.)

David Miles and Alice Miles came from the Miles family in Radnor. They joined the Baptist church in New Castle County, from the Pennepek church by letter in 1709. Nathaniel Miles became a Keithian Quaker, and he and many from this group became Keithian Baptists. Richard Miles, of

Radnor, brother of Nathaniel, was a prominent Baptist, and was a member of the Great Valley Church. See chapter on Baptists.

James Miles was from the Friends' monthly meeting in the parish of Llanfihangel Helygen, Radnorshire, Wales, and entered in Philadelphia Monthly Meeting records 27 5mo. 1683. He was afterwards baptized in the Baptist Church, per the Pennepek Church records. He was the father of Samuel Miles, Richard Miles, David Miles, Ann Miles and Griffith Miles. Samuel Miles married Margaret James, spinster, 24 4 mo. 1682, who was a purchaser of 200 acres from Richard Davies.

David James was a weaver from Llandegley and Glaseram and was believed to have sailed on the "Bristol Factor" which arrived in October 1683. His name was included with Evan Oliver on the Certificate of Removal, obtained at the last moment before the ship sailed from Bristol, dated 26 August 1682. However, Margaret James, his wife, and daughter Mary had to write back to Wales for theirs. Another account says David James' Certificate was temporary, and he also had to write back to obtain one. He appears to have been related to the Olivers. Evan Oliver and wife Jean (Jane) came originally from Glascombe, Wales, with their six children, David, Elizabeth, John, Hannah, Mary and Evan. Another child, Seaborn was born within sight of land in Pa. They purchased part of the Richard Davies land before leaving Wales.

Philip James, cooper, received warrant for a city lot on rent 6. 8mo. 1683. (Warrants and Surveys, III, 241.) His wife Sarah died in 1698 and he married second, Esther Willcox Freeland, daughter of Barnabas Willcox and widow of William Freeland. (James will in Will Book B, 200, #74, 1702.) The Willcox family were connected with the family of Griffith Jones, merchant, who will be discussed later. Jones had goods on the "Bristol Factor."
* *

COMPANY NO. 1:

The first large group of Welsh Quakers that arrived in Pennsylvania was part of the Edward Jones and John Thomas Company. They were from Merionethshire, and were members of the Penllyn Monthly Meeting. They arrived on the ship "Lyon," with John Compton, Master, which left Liverpool in May 1682, and arrived 13th of 6mo. [August] 1682. This was a year after the first ship load of settlers for Penn's colony had arrived, and two month's before Penn arrived for his first visit. First Purchasers are those who purchased land from Penn in London before he sailed for his Colony in 1682.

These Welsh families came from five parishes in Wales that are located within five miles of Bala, in the shire of Merioneth. They were from the neighborhoods of Bala and Dolgelley. They were related, and most had pedigrees showing royal blood. Most of the "Certificates of Membership and Dismissal" brought with them were signed by the same group. Some of

21

these signers were: Robert Owen; Evan Owen; Richard Price, Cadwalader Ellis; Evan Rees; Rees Evan; Ellis David; Thomas Ellis; Rowland Ellis; Hugh Griffith; Edward Griffith; Morris Humphrey; Thomas Prichard; David Jones; William Morgan; Griffith John; Roger Robert; and Owen Humphrey.

EDWARD JONES AND COMPANY was also called "The Merioneth Adventurers," or Dr. Edward Jones and John ap Thomas and Company. Edward Jones and John ap Thomas were Trustees chosen to purchase the land from William Penn for distribution to the group. The group had subscribed one hundred pounds for the purchase of 5,000 acres, and consisted of seventeen landowners with their family members and servants.

Four of these families arrived on the "Lyon" on 13 August 1682, after a journey of eleven weeks. These families were:

1. Dr. Edward Jones, wife Mary (dau of Dr. Thomas Wynne), children Martha and Jonathan Jones.
2. Edward ap Rees, (whose descendants took the name of Price,) wife Mably, and children Rees and Catherine.
3. Robert ap David, (took name Davis), wife Elizabeth and small child.
4. William ap Edward, (whose descendants took name Williams,) with second wife Jane, and children Elizabeth and Katherine.

DR. EDWARD JOHN or JONES was referred to as Edward Jones, chyrurgion, of Bala. He was son of John Lloyd, and brother-in-law of John Thomas, of Llaithgyn. Edward Jones was born in Merionethshire ca 1645. Remaining records show he was "of ancient and honorable family," and connected with the gentry of Wales. His wife was Mary, the daughter of Dr. Thomas Wynne who was the leader of Company No. 4 of Welsh settlers. Mary had this written about her in "The Philadelphia Friend, XXIX, 396": "She was an approved minister among Friends, and zealous for the promotion of the truth."

John ap Thomas and Dr. Edward Jones were among the most distinguished members of their community in Wales. Edward Jones was known as a skillful physician. He and John ap Thomas suffered a great deal from persecution for their religious beliefs. Records show the humiliation, fines and imprisonment suffered by many of these people for following religions other than the ones proscribed for them by the government. After hearing of Penn's offer of land and religious freedom in America, they determined to leave their country and go to Pennsylvania to seek freedom to practice their religion.

They were among the group of Welsh that visited William Penn in London to see about purchasing land in Pennsylvania. This group consisted of Dr. Edward Jones, John ap John, Dr. Griffith Owen, Dr. Thomas Wynne, John ap Thomas, Thomas Ellis, Hugh Roberts, Charles Lloyd, Richard Davies, John Bevan, Edward Prichard, William Jenkins, John Burge, and others.

Dr. Edward Jones and John ap Thomas were selected to become leaders and trustees for a group of friends and relations who together formed a company. They organized the Company and collected the necessary 100 pounds. John ap Thomas intended to settle in Pennsylvania, but he became very ill and was unable to leave as planned. As a partner with John ap Thomas in the trusteeship of this purchase, Edward Jones came over with the first group and led them in settling in.

An account of those subscribing to the 100 Pounds purchase price for these first 5,000 acres in the Welsh Tract was found written by John ap Thomas:

"An account of wt sum of money every ffriend in Penllyn hath Layd out to buy land in Pensylvania & wt quantity of Acres of Land each is to have and wt sum of Quit Rents falls upon every one."

	Pounds			Acres	Quit Rent		
John Tho	25	0s	0d	1250	12s	6d	
Hugh Robt	12	10	0	625	6	3	
Edd Jones	6	5	0	312 1/2	3	1	1/2
Robt Davis	6	5	0	312 1/2	3	1	1/2
Evan Rees	6	5	0	312 1/2	3	1	1/2
John Edd	6	5	0	312 1/2	3	1	1/2
Edd Owen	6	5	0	312 1/2	3	1	1/2
Will Edd	3	2	6	156 1/4	1	6	1/3
Edd Rees	3	2	6	156 1/4	1	6	1/3
Will Jones	3	2	6	156 1/4	1	6	1/3
Tho Rich	3	2	6	156 1/4	1	6	1/3
Rees John W	3	2	6	156 1/4	1	6	1/3
Tho lloyd	3	2	6	156 1/4	1	6	1/3
Cadd Morgan	3	2	6	156 1/4	1	6	1/3
John Watkin	3	2	6	156 1/4	1	6	1/3
Hugh John	3	2	6	156 1/4	1	6	1/3
Gainor Robt	3	2	6	156 1/4	1	6	1/3
	P 100	0	0	5,000	P2	10	

**

In the records they often used their parish and profession or status to differentiate themselves from others of the same name, and were great at abbreviating words:

John Tho was John ap Thomas, of Llaithgwm, gentleman.
Hugh Robt, [was] Hugh Roberts of Kiltalgarth, gentleman.
Edd Jones, Edward Jones, chyrurgion [surgeon], of Bala.
Robt Davis, Robert ap David, of Gwern Evel Ismynydd, yeoman.
Evan Rees, Evan ap Rees, of Penmaen, grocer.
John Edd, John ap Edwards, of Nant Lleidiog, yeoman.
Edd Owen, Edward ap Owen, late of Doleyserre, gentleman.

Will Edd, William ap Edward of Ucheldre, or Ueneldri, yeoman.

Edd Rees, Edward ap Rees, of Kiltalgarth, gentleman.

Will Jones, William ap John alias Jones, of Bettws, yeoman.

Tho Rich, Thomas ap Richard alias Prichard, of Nant Lleidiog, yeoman.

Rees John W, Rees ap John ap William, alias Rees Jones, of Llanglynin, yeoman.

Tho lloyd, Thomas Lloyd, of Llangower, yeoman.

Cadd Morgan, Cadwalader Morgan, of Gwernevel, yeoman.

John Watkin, John Watkins, of Gwernevel, bathilor [batchelor?].

Hugh John, Hugh ap John alias Jones, of Nant Lleidiog, yeoman.

Gainor Robt, Gainor Roberts, of Kiltagarth, spinster.

After their arrival in August 1682, they settled on the west side of the Schuylkill River, in Lower Merion. [In 1896, the land was described as 'lying north of the Pennsylvania Railroad, near Philadelphia.'][6] As all of these subscribers came from the hundred of Penllyn in the shire of Merionethshire, the area was first called Merioneth in honor of the shire from which they came. Then it was called "Merioneth Town" or "Merion Town," and later separated into Upper and Lower Merion.

Several of the purchasers of land did not come over, but their land was laid out and surveyed with the rest. Subsequently, some of these purchasers sold out to others. The surveyors were not too accurate, and other surveys were made later.

A letter written by Dr. Edward Jones dated "Skoolkill River, ye 26th of ye 6mo. 1782" mentioned 2,500 acres on the Schuylkill as "ye Country lots." The earliest document showing the location of this land was found on a map of Pennsylvania made by the surveyor-general, Thomas Holmes, which he began to compile after Penn's first departure from America, but it was only a general outline. Next, there was an original draft of the lands included in the Welsh Tract, which designated the land of "Edward Jones and Company, containing 2,500 acres, being 17 devisions." Surveyor David Powell left a rough draft of the 2,500 acres on the "city liberties's" line and the Schuylkill river. This was preserved at Harrisburg, and Powell has written on the survey that it was made by Charles Ashcom, on warrant from Mr. Powell, dated 24. 6mo. 1682, and that another rough survey was made on warrant "from ye Gov'r, date 22d 1 mo. 83."

"Mr. Powell's mem. on the final and extant plot, dated "20th of ye 3d mo. 84" says, "According to a War't from Capt. Thomas Holmes, Survey'r Genrall, Bearing dat the 24th of ye 1st mo. 84, directed unto me for the Subdiving of 2,500 Acres of Land for Edward Joans & Company upon the west sid of Skoolkool above fals Contageous unto the City Liberty. I therefor Laid out and Subdivided the said quality of Land, 25th of 1st mo. at

---

[6]Merion In The Welsh Tract, Glenn, p. 57.

the befor mentioned place, and unto every man by proportion as by these sevrall figure doth now at large Apeer with their bounds and courses entered in ye sd figur by a skale of 80 perch in an inch. Da Powell." The first 2,500 acres had boundaries as follows: North, "Vakant Land," East "Skoolkool" river South, "The Citty Libarty," and West, two tracts of Charles Lloyd and Thomas Lloyd, or Company No. 2."[7]

About 1,884 acres of the first company's patent was located in Goshen Township. Goshen was in Chester Co., now Delaware Co., where the city of West Chester is now located. Chester Creek ran through the area. This was near the border of New Castle County, De. [One of the land surveys for New Castle Co., De. has a "tract of land called Goshen", Thomas Ogle's land of 222 acres in New Castle Co." This was land on Christiana Creek, which divided the two counties.]

A letter from Dr. Edward Jones to John ap Thomas, was dated "Skoolkill River ye 26th of ye 6 mo 1682" and refers to the first survey of this land:

"Ye name of town lots is called now Wicoco; here is a Crowd of people striving for ye Country land, for ye town lot is not divided, & therefore we are forced to take up ye Country lots. We had much adoe to get a grant of it, but it Cost us 4 or 5 days attendance, besides some score of miles we traveled before we brought it to pass. I hope it will please thee and the rest yt are concerned, for it hath most rare timber, I have not seen the like in all these parts, there is water enough beside. The end of each lot will be on a river as large or larger than the Dye [Dee] at Bala, it is called Skool Kill River."

Their deeds were copied into Books C I and C II, located in office of the Recorder of Deeds, Philadelphia, dated between 28 February and 1 April 1682; recorded 22nd of 3 mo. 1684. The surveyors were very inefficient and several surveys were made through the years. Confirmative patents were not granted until 1702/3, when a resurvey was done.

Mention was made in the deeds of "The Liberty Land." This 2,500 acres of land was laid out adjoining the city of Philadelphia, and a small acreage of this was given in proportion to the amount of land purchased, for use as city lots, with most being in small parcels. This was surveyed according to a warrant from Thomas Holmes, Surveyor, "ye 1st mo. 84", and accomplished by Deputy Surveyor David Powell according to a memo dated "20th of ye 3d mo. 84." This practice was soon stopped for the individual purchasers, since Penn had only intended this for holders of 5,000 acres and not individual purchasers within a group.

---

[7]Welsh Settlement of Pensylvania, by Browning, Reprint 1967, pp. 51, 52.

The three original townships in the Great Welsh Tract were Merion (Lower), Haverford and Radnor.

"The original lines encompassed eleven and a half of the present contiguous Pensylvania townships, in counties of Montgomery, Delaware and Chester, these being Lower and Upper Merion, Haverford, Radnor, Tredyffrin, East and West Whiteland, Willistown, East and West Goshen, East Town, and a part of West Town. The north and west lines of Whiteland township, are the old Welsh Tract lines. The Welsh Tract's north line separated Tredyffrin tp. and Whiteland tp. from Schuylkill, Charleston, and Uwchland townships, and the west line of the Welsh Tract separates West Whiteland, West Goshen, and the borough of Westchester from East Caln and East Bradford townships. Its northwest corner being the northwest corner of West Whiteland township."[8]

In Merion, there were no members of religions other than Quakers until after 1700. Later on, two other areas which consisted mostly of Baptists were also called Welsh Tract, one being "Gwynedd" in Philadelphia County, and the other in New Castle County.

* *

Dr. Edward Jones used a seal on his will with a lion rampant. This was found in the coat of arms in most genealogies of these settlers. This is not surprising, as most were related to each other. The author Thomas Glenn wrote that a descendant of Dr. Jones indicated that the arms used in the Jones family for many years were:

"Or, within a burdure, a lion rampant azure. Crest, a lion rampant azure, having in his sinister paw a harp or."

He stated these were the arms of a family of Jones anciently of Merionethshire, and are given in Burke's General Armory. The letter indicated they were used by the family a long time prior to their appearance in Burke.[9] Thomas A. Glenn wrote of finding a record of the same coat of arms in Philadelphia with minor differences, and containing a motto in three languages, thus:

"Coat of Arms of Griffin Jones, of Merionethshire, A. D. 1569, and of Flintshire, South Wales, A. D. 1584." ARMS; Or, within a burdure a lion rampant azure. CREST; A lion rampant azure holding in his sinister paw a harp or. MOTTO: "Vulgar, Foremost yet Steady." "Classic, Progressus Sed Firmus." "Barbaric, "Blaenaf etto yn anhyblygg." The paper has this

---

[8]Ibid, p. 488.
[9]Narratives of Early Pa., Myers, pp. 315-316.

26

endorsement: "Done by Henry Salt, Heraldic Engraver, No. 9, Great Turnstile, Lincoln's Inn, London."

In the book "Merion in The Welsh Tract" by Thomas Allen Glenn, pedigrees were shown of many of these early Welsh settlers, who were nearly all related in various ways. The "lion rampant, azure" was in several. Marchweithian, Lord of Is Aled who had his castle at Llyweni, had as his arms: Gules, a lion rampant, argent, armed and langued Azure." (Pp. 252, 253.) Descendants of Marchweithian are entitled to use this coat of arms.

Edward Jones kept only 312 1/2 acres of the land from the large original 5,000 acres purchased. This came out to be only 306 1/4 after survey. He sold two acres, his "Liberty lands," [to Edward ap Rees, Rhys, or Price], leaving 151 1/4 acres in Merion, and 153 acres in Goshen Township. Edward Jones later purchased 200 acres in Goshen from Richard Thomas. He later owned other acreage which he purchased.

Dr. Jones was one of the organizers and first members of the Merion Meeting. He was a Trustee of the Merion Peculiar, or Preparative Meeting, along with Robert Owen, Cadwalader Morgan and Thomas Jones.

Dr. Jones died at his Merion home February 1737, and his burial was recorded in Merion Meeting records: "Edward Jones, Doctor, aged 80 years," 12mo. 16. 1737. He signed his will 27. 3mo. 1732, and it was proved at Philadelphia 2 Aug 1738. Witnesses were John Roberts and Esther Thomas. He named sons Jonathan, Edward, Evan, Thomas and John Jones, the youngest son, and desired that John should continue to feed, clothe, and support his brother Thomas. [An indication he was ill or infirm.] His wife Mary was to have the estate during her lifetime, then it was to go to son John. He gave John Cadwalader, his son-in-law, land in the center of Philadelphia, and gave negroes to each of the Cadwalader girls, Mary, Rebecca and Hannah, and one to each grandson, and to Thomas Cadwalader and Martha Roberts. Named daughters Martha, Elizabeth and Mary, and appointed his wife and sons Jonathan, Edward and Evan, and John Cadwalader, as executors.

Thomas Chalkley in his journal wrote that he was "a man much given to hospitality, a lover of good and virtuous people and was beloved by them...There were many hundreds at his funeral."[10]

The children of Edward Jones and Mary who were named in his will:

1. MARTHA JONES, b. Wales; m. 1699, John Cadwalader.
2. JONATHAN JONES, b. Wales, 1680; d. Lower Marion Township, 1770; m. Gainor Owen.
3. EDWARD JONES, b. Merion.
4. THOMAS JONES, b. Merion.

---

[10]The Philadelphia Friend, Vol. 29, p. 396.

5. EVAN JONES, b. Merion; m. (1) Mary Stephenson, N.Y., and (2) dau of Col. Mathews of Fort Albany, N.Y.
6. JOHN JONES, or as found in records, Jon., (Jonathan) b. Merion.
7. ELIZABETH JONES, m. Rees Thomas, Jr.
8. MARY JONES.

* *

MARTHA JONES, eldest child of Dr. Edward and Mary, was born in Wales and was a small child when they arrived. She and Jonathan were mentioned in a letter, which has been preserved, written by her father to John Thomas. He asked John Thomas to send several things, among them "2 paire of shoes for Martha, and one paire for Jonathan, let them by strong and large..." Martha was married at the Merion Meeting House on 26. 10mo. 1699, seventeen years after arrival.

She married John Cadwalader, a young schoolteacher who lived with her family for two years. John Cadwalader was born ca 1677/78 at Ciltalgarth, Llanvawr, Merionethshire. He brought his Certificate of Removal from the Pembroke Quarterly Meeting, bearing date in 1697, and stating he had attended school there. He was a teacher in the Friends' Public School in Philadelphia. He received his appointment as assistant in the school and moved into town in July 1705. In 1718-33, he was chosen a member of the City Council, and in 1729 was chosen to serve as a member of the Pensylvania Assembly. He served there until his death 23 July 1734. He purchased 100 acres in Chester County 22. 9mo. 1715.

* *

JONATHAN JONES, second child of Dr. Edward Jones, was born in Bala, Merionethshire, North Wales, 3rd day of 11mo. 1680. He came to Pa. in 1682; married at Merion the 4th day of 8mo. 1706, Gainor Owen, dau of Robert and Rebecca Owen. Gainor Owen was born 16th of 8mo. 1688. Many church members attended their wedding and signed the Certificate. Attendees surnamed Jones and those with first names of John who signed the marriage certificate were: Jane Jones; Anne Jones; John Moore; Robert Jones; John Owen; John Jones; John Williams; Richard Jones; Robert John; Gainor Jones; John Griffith; Ellen Jones; Catharine Jones; Edward Jones; Mary Jones; Griffith John; Edward Jones Jr.; Evan Jones; Eliza. Jones; John Owen; John Jones; John Owen; and John Cadwalader.

Shortly after they married, Jonathan purchased the plantation called Wynnewood and St. Mary's from Gainor's brother, Evan Owen. It had 451 acres. Jonathan died the 30th day of 7mo. 1770 and was buried at Merion 8th of 8mo. 1770. Their children were:
1. MARY JONES, m. Benjamin Hayes.
2. EDWARD JONES, b. 1708; d. unmarried.
3. REBECCA JONES, b. 1709; m. John Roberts, of Pencoyd, son of Robert Roberts; grandson of John Roberts of Penllyn, Caernarvonshire.

4. OWEN JONES, b. 1711; m. Susanna Evans, dau of Hugh & Lowry Evans of Merion, 30 3mo. 1740.
5. EZEKIEL JONES, b. ca 1712, believed to have died without issue, as his father did not know if he was living in 1768 [per Thomas A. Glenn].
6. JACOB JONES, b. 1713.
7. JONATHAN JONES, b. 1715; died 1747; m. _____, and had two daughters, Gainor and Mary Jones. Received 101 acres of land from deed of his father; left this to his two daughters by will dated 11 of 5mo. 1747, proved 1 Nov. 1747. They sold this to their uncle Owen Jones.

* *

OWEN JONES, 2nd son of Jonathan and Gainor, was b. in Merion 19th of 9mo. 1711; d. 9 Oct 1793. Married 30 May 1740, Susanna, second dau of Hugh Evans, of Merion, by his third wife, Lowry, widow of Robert Lloyd, of Merion, and daughter of Rees John William of Merion. Owen Jones was Provincial Treasurer of Pa. His will was dated 11 Oct 1791; proved at Phila. Left 350 acres of land to son Owen, and the 101 acres purchased from nieces to son Jonathan.

Owen and Susanna Jones had the following children:
1. JANE JONES, b. 5th 1mo. 1740/1; m. Caleb Foulke.
2. LOWRY JONES, b. 30th 10mo. 1742; m. Daniel Wister.
3. OWEN JONES, b. 15th 1mo. 1744/5; m. (1) Mary Wharton; (2) Hannah Smith. No children survived.
4. SUSANNA JONES, b. 4th 7mo. 1747; m. John Nancarro.
5. HANNAH JONES, b. 28th 10mo. 1749; m. Amos Foulke.
6. ANN JONES, b. 13th 3mo. 1752; d. unm.
7. MARTHA JONES, b. 10th 3mo. 1754; d. unm.
8. REBECCA JONES, b. 3d 7mo. 1757; m. John Jones, who d.s.p.
9. SARAH JONES, b. 30th 5mo. 1760; m. Samuel Rutter.
10. JONATHAN JONES, b. 15th 7mo. 1762; m. (1) Mary Potts; (2) Mary McClenaghan. Died prior to 1822; will signed 15 Mar 1821.

[Owen Foulke, tanner, of Bettws-y-Coed, Carnarvonshire, Wales, who had purchased land from the John ap Thomas and Dr. Thomas Wynne Company was also on this ship. He had land surveyed in Philadelphia and in New Castle Co.]
* *

EDWARD JONES, [Jr.], son of Dr. Edward and Mary, was of Blockley Township, and received some of the land owned by his father. His will was signed in presence of Martha Palmer, John Wynne and Jonathan Hood. It was dated 14 Nov 1730, proved 30 Sept 1732 by wife Mary. He named children: Aquilla, Penelope, Salvenas, Beula, and Prudence; his brothers Jonathan and John; his father-in-law, William Palmer; brother-in-law John

Cadwalader. Trustees named were Jonathan and John Jones, William Palmer, and John Cadwalader.
* *

JOHN JONES, or Jon. JONES, son of Dr. Edward and Mary Jones, received 188 acres from his father's estate. By deed dated 15 Oct 1741, he and wife Mary conveyed "to Anthony Tunis, late of township of Germantown, now of Lower Merion," 402 acres of land, "late estate of Dr. Edward Jones," for 812 Pounds of Pensylvania money. He was described as "John Jones, late of Lower Merion, and of Philadelphia, yeoman, (youngest son of Edward Jones, late of Merion, Chyrurgeon, deceased)." The land was described as abutting properties of John Roberts, Hugh Evans, Rees Price, Richard George, and Thomas David. Joseph Tunis (second son of Anthony Tunis) gave a portion of this land in 1763 to the Merion Preparative. It was adjoined on the eastend by the graveyard land given in 1695 by Edward Rees.

John Jones moved to Philadelphia after he sold his land in 1741. His wife was Mary Doughty of New Jersey. John died in 1743. Their children were:

1. DEBORAH JONES, m. John Price in 1743.
2. THOMAS JONES.
3. ISRAEL JONES.
4. DOUGHTY JONES, m. Hannah Gardiner in 1747.
5. EDWARD JONES.
6. JOHN JONES.
7. WHITEHEAD JONES, m. Ann Johns in 1762.
8. SAMUEL JONES.
9. AMY JONES.
10. MARY JONES.
11. MARTHA JONES, m. John Brook 1761.[11]
* *

REES JOHN WILLIAM, b. ca 1620, one of the original purchasers of the first company, was generally known as Rees Jones, and was son of John ap William, a farmer in Llangelynin parish, Merioneth. His father was a Quaker who was persecuted because of his beliefs. John William was born ca 1590, and was living in the Parish of Llangelynin in Merionethshire in 1661. He had three children, Evan John, Rees John and Margaret John.

Rees John married Hannah Richards or Price about 1678. She was b. in 1656, sister to Jane, wife of Cadwalader Morgan of Merion, and to Edward ap Rees [later Price] who came on the "Lyon" on 13 August 1682. She was daughter of Richard Gryffyth ap Rhys or Prees, [known as Richard Price], of Llanvawr, or Lanfor parish, in Merioneth. Her pedigree (as others)

---
[11]Welsh Founders of Pennsylvania, by Thomas Allen Glenn, p. 183.

showed Royal Descent back to John, King of England. Her father was a member of the Friends' Penylln Monthly Meeting, near Bala, and his name was often found on the Certificates of Membership and Removal from the Penllyn Meeting.

Rees, though one of the seventeen original purchasers of the Jones tract, did not come over until 1684. He arrived on the ship "Vine" of Liverpool, on 17. 7mo. 1684, accompanied by his wife and three children, Richard, Lowry and Evan Jones.

Rees Jones [John] and his wife Hannah brought their Certificate of Membership and Removal from the Quarterly Meeting near Dolgelly, dated 4. 1mo. 1684. He was described as "of Llwyn Grevill, Clynn parish, Merioneth."

MARGARET JOHN WILLIAM, of Llangyllynin, widow, came with the Hugh Roberts party, the second large group to arrive, in November 1683. In her own name, she obtained patent for 400 acres of land on a branch of French Creek 18th 1mo. 1717/8.

Their brother EVAN JOHN WILLIAM, or EVAN JONES, also came over at that time, with his son ROBERT JONES, who resided at Gwynedd. [Gwynedd was the area of Philadelphia County that was called the second Welsh Tract, and mostly settled by the Baptists, and Robert was possibly a Baptist.] Evan died soon after and was buried in the Merion Meeting grounds 11 mo. 1688. He bequeathed some land in Goshen (Chester Co.,) to his nephews, RICHARD and EVAN JONES. Evan Jones and wife Hannah, mother-in-law Mary Ellis, and her other daughter Gemima, brought certificate from the Meeting held at Tyddier y Gareg in Garthgunfawr, near Dolegelle, Merioneth, to the Haverford Monthly Meeting. This was signed by Humphrey, John, Robert and Rowland Owen; Owen, Robert, and Howell Lewis; and Hugh Rowland.

Rees Jones purchased the original right of Thomas ap Richard or Prichard, of Nant Lleidiog, to his share of 156 1/2 acres of the Thomas & Jones Co. tract before leaving Wales. This adjoined the back of Rees' land in Merion. He was disappointed with his land, which was laid out on a narrow strip. Only about 66 feet was on the river, and extended the full length of the other lots, to Charles Lloyd's land. There, it was only about 264 feet wide, in all being 76 1/2 acres, with the balance of his land in Goshen. The present settlement of Merion, or Merion Station, on Pennsylvania Railroad was on his land, and his dwelling house was near it. He sold 76 1/2 acres, his original purchase, to Cadwalader Morgan, whose land adjoined, on 8. 4mo. 1694.[12]

Rees Jones was designated as "husbandman." He died 26. 11 mo. 1697/8, and was buried at the Merion Meeting House. His will was witnessed by GRIFFITH JOHN and Abel Thomas, dated 24. 11 mo. 1697/8,

---

[12]Welsh Settlement of Pa., by Charles Browning, Baltimore, 1967, p. 132.

and proven at Philadelphia 4 Mar 1702/8. He named sons Richard, Evan and John; and overseers were: Cadwalader Morgan, Abel Thomas, Edward Jones, Griffith John and John Roberts. After Rees died, Hannah married again on 22. 2 mo. 1703, Ellis Davis of Goshen, a widower. Davis was buried 17. 1 mo. 1720. She married for the third time Thomas Evans of Gwynedd township, on 14. 1 mo. 1722.

Children of Rees and Hannah were:

1. RICHARD JONES, b. ca 1679. Came over with his parents, and filed as a member with the Merion Preparative Meeting on 2. 12 mo. 1704/5. He inherited about 100 acres, and then increased his holdings to around 293 3/4 acres altogether. He sold to Hugh Evans on 26 June 1729 his 156 1/4 acres in Merion, and moved to Goshen. He and his brother Evan Jones there bought 153 1/4 acres, which was 178 acres on resurvey. He died in Goshen 16. 7 mo. 1771, aged 92 years. He was married twice. He had three children by each wife. He married (1) Jane Evans, 6. 4 mo. 1705, and she died 27. 1 mo. 1711.
Children:
   1) REECE JONES, b. 2. 4mo. 1707.
   2) ANN JONES, b. 11. 11mo. 1707.
   3) HANNAH JONES, b. 11. 8mo. 1709/10.
He married (2) Rebecca Vernon, widow of Thomas Garrett in 1718. She died 23. 12 mo. 1748. Children:
   1) REBECCA JONES, b. 21. 7mo. 1719, m. William Rettew.
   2) DEBORAH JONES, b. 13. 7mo. 1721, m. John Cheyney.
   3) NEHEMIAH JONES, b. 21. 7mo. 1723.

2. LOWRY JONES, b. ca 1682. Died 25. 11 mo. 1762 at Phila., aged 80 years. Married (1) Robert ffloid or Lloyd, at Merion Meeting 11. 8 mo. 1698. He came over with Hugh Roberts in 1683 and bought 400 acres. He died 29. 3 mo. 1714, aged 45.
They had eight children.
   1) HANNAH LLOYD, b. 21 Sept 1699, d. 15 Jan 1773. Married 1st John Roberts, 23 Sept 1720, son of John Roberts and Elizabeth Owen v. Owen Humphrey. He died in 1721. M. 2nd William Paschall 22 Sept 1722, , d. 1732. M. 3rd Peter Osborne 6 Apr 1734, d. 1765.
   2) GWEN LLOYD, b. 20 Aug 1701, d. 1783, unmarried.
   3) SARAH LLOYD, b. 19 May 1703, d. 5 Jul 1739, m. Garrard Jones 5 Oct 1729 at Merion. He d. 21 Mar 1765.
   4) GAYNOR LLOYD, b. 5 Feb 1705, d. 3 Sept 1728, m. 26 Mar 1727, Mordecai James, who d. 15 Dec 1776.
   5) DAVID LLOYD, b. 27 Apr 1707, m. Anna ____. Moved to North Carolina.
   6) REES LLOYD, b. 25 Apr 1709, d. 5 Feb 1743. m. 12 Dec 1735, at Phila., Sarah Cox, d. 4 Nov 1775.

7) ROBERT LLOYD, b. 25 Aug 1711, d. 27 Aug 1786. m. 21 Jun 1735, at Gwynedd, Catharine Humphrey, d. 13 Oct 1782.

8) RICHARD LLOYD, b. 15 Jan 1713, d. 9 Aug 1755. M. 24 Sept 1736, at Darby, Hannah Sellers, d. 12 Apr 1810, had Samuel, d. infancy, Isaac, Hugh.

Lowry Jones married 2) Hugh Evans, 13. 12 mo. 1716/7, at Merion Meeting. Hugh b. 1682, d. 4 6mo. 1772, Phila. Had three children: (1) Ann, m. 1745, Samuel Howell; (2)Susanna m. 1740, Owen Jones; (3) Abigail.[13]

3. EVAN JONES, b. about 1682/3, never married. Buried at Merion Meeting 7. 1 mo. 1708. He and brother John inherited 158 1/2 acres of land in Goshen on Chester Creek from their father. Resurveyed 17. 10 mo. 1701. Was partner with brother Richard in some Goshen land. Will signed 28. 7mo. 1708, witnessed by Rowland Ellis, Richard Jones, and Robert Lloyd; was proved 25th 1mo. 1708. Mentioned mother and brothers and sisters, Lowry Lloyd; Richard; John; Edward; Jane, Sarah and Margaret Jones; overseers, Cadwalader Morgan and Abel Thomas.

4. JANNE, or JANE JONES, b. Merion 15. 9 mo. 1635; d. 17. 8 mo. 1764; buried at Goshen Meeting. Married David Davis and had nine children; four married into Ashbridge family.

5. CATHERINE JONES, b. 4. 6mo. 1688; twin, d. infancy.

6. JOHN JONES, b. 4. 6mo. 1688; twin; died, 30. 12mo. 1774. He lived at Gwynedd, and was known as John Jones, carpenter. Was a Friend. Married at Gwynedd, Jane Edward, 4. 9mo. 1713. She died 5. 11mo. 1758.

Children:

1) HANNAH JONES, m. William Foulke.

2) CATHARINE JONES, d. infancy.

3) MARGARET JONES, d. 1745.

4) PRISCILLA JONES, m. 20. 3mo. 1740, Evan Jones of Merion.

5) EVAN JONES, m. Hannah Lawrence.

6) JESSE JONES.

7) KATHARINE JONES, d. 1741.

8) JANE JONES, d. 1806.

9) BENJAMIN JONES, d. infancy.

10) RUTH JONES, d. infancy.

7. SARAH JONES, b. 25. 7mo. 1690, d. 28. 3mo. 1758. Married (1) Jacob Edge 2. 8mo. 1712, at Merion; and (2) Caleb Cowpland 10. 11mo. 1721 at Chester.

8. EDWARD JONES, believed to have died in infancy.

---

[13]Merion in the Welsh Tract, by Glenn, pp. 81-82.

9. MARGARET JONES, b. 20. 6mo. 1697. Married (1) Thomas Paschall 16. 10mo. 1716, at Merion. Married (2) George Ashbridge 6. 1mo. 1729/30.

**

JOHN ap EDWARD: Son of Edward ap John of Cynles, Llanddervel Parish, Penllyn, Merionethshire, who was member of Church of England. Purchased 312 1/2 acres, of which half surveyed in Marion, half in Goshen (Chester Co.) Arrived in August 1682. Moved from Nant Lleidiog Township, Merionethshire. Was a member of the Society of Free Traders of London. This was a trading company set up by William Penn to initiate commercial and industrial ventures in the province. Brought at least four servants with him. Died soon after arrival, buried at parish church on 1 Mar 1667. JOHN ap EDWARD had brother WILLIAM ap EDWARD, yeoman, who owned lands in Blockley township.

In "Merion in the Welsh Tract," Glenn wrote that sons took surname Edwards. However, he changed this in "Welsh Founders of Pennsylvania." Also, in the "Welsh Settlement of Pensylvania" by Robert Browning, pp. 88-89, an account of John ap Edward stated his children used the surname Jones. He wrote John Edward's son Edward was called Edward Jones, Jr. in a deed to distinguish him from Dr. Edward Jones.

John Edward's will, dated 16. 8mo. 1683 was witnessed by Gabriel Jones and William Morgan, and proven 8. 2mo. 1686 by his brother William Edwards, of Merion. [Gabriel Jones seems to have been a servant, and later lived in New Castle Co.] Left all land purchased to son Evan Jones. Left headright land (for bringing over servants, 200 acres), and his shares "in the Society Trade of Pensylvania," to his youngest son Edward Jones. Gave 15 pounds, etc. to daughter Elizabeth Jones. Made other bequests. Copies of the will are on file, along with the inventory and other papers. (Will Book A, 37, #27a, and Will Book B, 270, #101.)
John Edward's children:

1. EVAN JONES: Eldest son, b. 2. 2mo. 1677, died young, apparently unmarried before 3mo. 1684.
2. EDWARD JONES, second son, and youngest, b. 5. 8mo. 1681. He conveyed all his lands which he inherited to Dr. Edward Jones by deed dated 12. 2mo. 1702/3, which stated: "Receipt of Edward Jones, of Philadelphia, only son of John ap Edward, deceased, and nephew of William ap Edward, of Blockley" dated 23 January 1702, recorded in Philadelphia Co. deed Book C II, Folio 198. Early writers said he was believed to have moved to Virginia. His Merion tract of land extended from about the old Lancaster Road (Montgomery Avenue), across the Pensylvania Railroad between Merion station, and the borough of Narberth. There were at least a couple of Edward Jones' in Philadelphia in the early 1700's. One was a chemist and one was a merchant. [See Phila. Wills.] He probably moved to New Castle Co.

An Edward Jones was mentioned in New Castle Co. Deed Book K, Vol. 1, pp. 257,8.

3. ELIZABETH JONES: b. 18. 12mo. 1671. Married John ap Robert ap Cadwalader, called John Roberts of Gwynedd. They were founders of the Roberts family of "Woodlawn Plantation" in Whitpain township, Montgomery Co., Pa.

4. SARAH JONES, b. 8. 11mo. 1673, not named in her father's will. Writer Browning gives her as daughter; also given as daughter in "Passengers and Ships Prior to 1684" by Sheppard.

* *

Others who were part of the Edward Jones and John Thomas group came over in the ship "Morning Star" of Chester, Thomas Hayes, master, which sailed from Mosson in September 1683. Included with this group was the Robert's Party, mentioned before. They arrived in the Delaware and at Philadelphia the following November 16-20. Those aboard who were purchasers in this group were: Hugh Robert, Edward Owen, William Jones, Cadwalader Morgan, Hugh John, Katherine Thomas, and Gainor Roberts.

In addition to these, there were over fifty others, including their families and servants who settled in the Welsh Tract. Among them were John Bevan; John Roberts; Thomas Owen; Rees Thomas; Ralph and William Lewis; Richard Humphreys, John Humphreys, and Samuel Humphreys; Griffith John ap Evan; Robert ffloid; William Morgan, and Evan John [brother of Rees John William].

Another John who arrived in 1683 was John Jones, yeoman, carpenter, who was from Card. Co. in Wales. He went to Barbadoes, then to Pa. in 1683, per Glenn. He was a Quaker, and a carpenter by trade. He purchased land in Philadelphia jointly with John Jennings of Barbados, apothecary. A warrant for a city lot was granted to Jones 13 7mo. 1683, that was at the southwest corner of Second and Mulberry. (Myers, Quaker Arrivals, 3.)

* *

JOHN AP THOMAS: Among the first group to settle with Edward Jones & Co. was Katherine Roberts, the widow of John ap Thomas, who was the partner with Dr. Edward Jones in purchasing land for the first company. John ap Thomas was of Llaithgwn Township in the Parish of Llanvawr (Llanfor) in the County of Merioneth, Wales. He was designated as "gentleman," and "was the son of Thomas ap Hugh ap Evan ap Rhys Goch [a gentleman farmer, of Wern Fawr] ap Tudor ap Rees ap Evan Coch, of Bryammer, in the parish of Gerrig y Drudion, Denbighshire, derived from Marchwerthian, Lord of Issallt, who bore Gules, a lion rampt., arg., armed and langued azure."[14] John Thomas' brother, Cadwalader Thomas, predeceased his father. Cadwalader Thomas had resided on a farm at Kiltalgarth in Merioneth, and his wife was a sister of Robert Owen, and his

---

[14]Merion in the Welsh Tract, by Glenn, pp. 130-131.

son John Cadwalader was the founder of the family of Cadwalader of Philadelphia and Trenton.

John Thomas' first wife was Anna Lloyd, buried at Llandderfel 31 Aug 1665. They had two children: Elizabeth John, who married Rees Evan of Fron Ween, Penmaen, Parish of Llandor [Griffith John's pedigree also in this line]; and Thomas Jones [John]. [Cadwallader Thomas was brother of John Thomas, and his pedigree is on pp. 130-1 of "Merion in The Welsh Tract." by Glenn.]

John Thomas died at Llaithgwm, Llanfor 3 May 1683. His allotment of land in Pennsylvania was 1250 acres. He became ill from persecution and did not live to make the trip to Pennsylvania. His plans were made to leave Wales, but his illness and his death prevented this. His widow (and second wife) Katherine Robert, and their sons Robert, Evan and Cadwalader John, or Jones, were awaiting the ship to leave when he died. They, along with Katherine's stepson, Thomas, sailed for Pennsylvania on the "Morning Star" about four months after the death of John Thomas. The voyage was long and harsh and two of Katherine's young children died and were buried at sea. They arrived 16 November 1683. They brought over the will of John Thomas, which was proved at Philadelphia in 1688.

He left his 1250 acres to his sons, share and share alike. Half of this was surveyed in Merion, and the rest in Goshen Township. Money was left to his daughters. Thomas and Katherine's daughters were Mary and Sidney who died at sea, and Katherin and Elizabeth. Katherin married Robert Roberts, and Elizabeth married Rees Evan of Fron Ween, Penmaen, Penllyn, Merionethshire.

They first called their plantation Geilli yr Cochiaid, or "Grove of Red Partridges." Thomas Jones called the home he built for himself Llaethgwm (Llaithgwm) House after his previous home.

Katherine Robert purchased 612 acres of land adjacent to the Merion land. Records indicate her husband had planned ahead for her, and had a small log cabin built awaiting her arrival. They lived in this for awhile. Her sons appear to have held her in high esteem and were extremely helpful in looking out for her. She had several slaves, and was shrewd in managing her land. The following summer she purchased 150 acres on the river between the lands of Barnabas Wilcox and Joseph Harrison, on which there was "a dwelling house lately erected." Other accounts state this was a small stone house where they lived for awhile. On 10 Dec 1689, she and her sons took title for a tract of 500 acres north of her first land on the river, called "Glanrason," from Joseph Wood, and a tract of 500 acres on the river called "Mount Ararat." Robert Jones obtained an additional 165 acres in 1704. Resurveys were later made of their land, with the Merion land shown to contain 679 acres, the Goshen land 635 acres, for a total of 2,129 acres of land in the family at the beginning of the 18th century.

Katherine Robert brought a Certificate from the Friends' Penllyn Monthly Meeting, of which she was a ten-year member, dated 18th day of 5mo. 1683. This was very praiseworthy, and was signed by Robert Owen, Edward Griffith, Elizabeth & Wm. Bowen, Richard Price, Cadd Lewis, Elizabeth John, Margaret Cadwalader and others. Katherine was of gentle birth and fine breeding. She brought numerous letters and family documents that were preserved and passed down in the family. John Thomas had an impressive pedigree, and the Arms of John Thomas were "Gules, a lion rampant, argent, armed and langued azure." Katherine Thomas died 18. 11mo. 1697. A month later, 12mo. 1697, her son EVAN JOHN died.

*

THOMAS JONES, of Merion, "yeoman," eldest son of John ap Thomas, born at Llaithgwm, Merionethshire, Wales; died at Llaithgwm House in Merion Township, Phila. Co., 6th 8mo. 1727. He carried on correspondence with relatives in Wales, and these letters were also preserved. He married Anne, daughter of Griffith John, of Merion. Griffith John was a cousin of Robert Owen of "New Merion," and also of Royal descent, his line being shown in the same pedigree for Robert Owen in "Merion In The Welsh Tract," pp. 112-150. Thomas John's will was dated 31st 6 mo. 1727; proven 5 Aug 1728. Children mentioned in will: Evan and Elizabeth. The family papers of his father and mother were passed to his possession, and he was diligent in preserving them. His brother Robert was one of the witnesses to his will. Trustees were "cousins, Robert Roberts and Jonathan Jones." The family papers were passed to his brother ROBERT. Family manuscripts are now at Library of the Historical Society of Pa.

* *

ROBERT JOHN or JONES, 2nd son of John ap Thomas, b. Llaithgwm, Merionethshire, Wales,; died in Merion Township, Philadelphia Co. in 1746. He married Ellin, sister of David John or Jones of Blockley Township, 3. 11 mo. 1693, at his mother's house. Ellin probably arrived before David and Katharine John, as records show they emigrated around 1699. Robert was a Justice of the Peace for Merion, a member of the Provincial Assembly, and a very prominent man among Friends.

He purchased plantation called "Mount Arrarat" from David Hugh; was owner of "Glanrason" which contained 189 acres, and purchased from David Hugh, 20. 4mo. 1699, 150 acres (surveyed), 165 acres of Sharlow's "Mt. Ararat," confirmation deed, 12 Feb 1704, and at one time owned 1,000 acres in Merion and 426 acres in Goshen, Chester Co. Robert John's will dated 24. 12mo. 1746; proven at Philadelphia, 17 Oct 1746. He was buried at the Merion Meeting House.

Children:
1. ELIZABETH JONES, b. 6. 9mo. 1695.

2. JOHN JONES, b. 29. 10mo. 1697; d. infant.
3. JOHN JONES, b. 20. 11mo. 1698; d. infant.
4. KATHERINE JONES, b. 12. 11mo. 1700; m. Thomas Evans.
5. ANNE JONES, b. 14. 7mo. 1702; m. James Jones of Blockley, son of David Jones and Katherine.
6. GARRAD JONES, b. 28. 12mo. 1705/6; m. (1) Sarah Lloyd, and (2) Ann Humphrey. Inherited "Glanrason;" had 8 children.
7. ROBERT JONES, b. 3. 6mo. 1709.

* *

CADWALLADER JOHN or JONES, son of John ap Thomas, known as of Llaithgwn, gentleman, was in the shipping trade. He made voyages to Barbadoes and elsewhere, and appears to have prospered. Cadwalader and Thomas were granted power to take up 100 acres of land that they had laid out in Merion on 11mo. 1712/13 adjoining lands of Mordecai Moore, John Havard, James Atkinson and Owen Roberts. They procured grant and survey of a 34 foot lot on Second street, and a 20 foot lot on Third street, in place of one whole lot of 51 feet, on Second street, "of which they have been disappointed." Cadwalader Jones of Gwynedd married Martha Thomas in 1719, dau of David Thomas of Radnor, Pa.[15]

* *

COMPANY NO. 2:

The second Welsh Company to come over, as grantees under the patent for 5,000 acres obtained by Charles Lloyd, gentleman, and Margaret Davies, widow, both of Dolobran, Meifod parish, Montgomeryshire, arrived in 1683 or 1684. They had deeds dated 24 April 1683, recorded at Philadelphia 15. 5mo. 1684. They were:

Joseph Harris, "late of Wallbrook, Middlesex Co."	1,250	acres.

From Montgomeryshire, Wales:

Thomas Jones, of Llanwthin parish, yeoman.	156 1/4 acres.
Edward Thomas, of Llanwthin parish, yeoman	312 1/2 acres.
Margaret Thomas, of Garthlwlch parish, widow	156 1/4 acres.
John Humphrey, of Llanwthin parish, gent	312 1/2 acres.
John Rhytherch, of Hirnant parish, yeoman	156 1/4 acres.
Thomas Morris, of Marchnant Issa parish, gent	156 1/4 acres.
	2,500 acres.

The only John or Jones among them was:
THOMAS JONES or THOMAS JOHN THOMAS, of parish of Llandwddyn [or Llanwthin], county Montgomery, yeoman; son of John Thomas, of same place. Came to Merion, Pa. 1683/4. Entered in Radnor Monthly Meeting Records 31. 5mo. 1683. Friend. Was Freeholder of 156 1/4 acres in Merion. Died unmarried 1723.

---

[15]Welsh Founders of Pa., by Glenn, p. 213.

Margaret Thomas, of Garthlwlch, Montgomeryshire, widow, who bought 156 ¼ A from Charles Lloyd appointed Thomas Jones of Lanwithin, yeoman, on 14 Aug 1683, to act as her attorney to take possession of her grant and look after the land. He had certificate, dated 31. 5mo. 1683, from the Quarterly Meeting at Dolobran, signed by John ap John, Charles Lloyd, Richard and Evan Davies and Sampson Lloyd. After her death, the Commissioners released him from this.

Thomas Morris, of Marchantissa, Montgomery, yeoman, a purchaser of 156 1/4 acres also gave him a power of attorney, from which he was also released after Morris' death.

Thomas Lloyd, of Dolobran Hall in Montgomeryshire, b. 17 Feb 1640/41, died 10 Sept 1694. He never resided in the Welsh Tract, but was closely associated with the Quakers. He was a lawyer, a Quaker, and a minister. He was a deputy of William Penn in his Province, and was Presiding Officer of the Council. He succeeded Blackwell as Governor. His tract of land was located next to, and west of the tract taken up by the Jones and Thomas Company.
* *

COMPANY NO. 3:

Comprised the 2,000 acre patent of John ab Evan, yeoman [John Bevan] of Trefyrhig, or Trevorrigge, Llantrissent parish, Glamorganshire. His wife was Barbara. He brought Certificate of Removal, and came over on the "Morning Star" at the same time as the Hugh Roberts' party in Nov 1683. This group consisted of:

Charles ab Evan (Bevan), of Trevorrigg, and Llantwit Vardre parish, Glamorganshire, brother of John.

John Richard, of Trevorrigg, tailor.

Elizabeth Prichard and Katharine Prichard, of Telcha, Llantrissent, spinsters, whose deed for 250 acres was dated 8 May 1682, and witnessed by Barbara Awbrey, John ab Evan, Jun'r, Evan John, and John Richard.

Matthew Jones, of Carmarthen, Carmarthenshire, Mercer, whose deed, dated 1 Aug 1682 for 125 acres was witnessed by Will Broadber, Children: Evans, Ebenezer, David, Ann Buckley and Jane Miller. Daughter Ann married 1.) Samuel Buckley at Center Meeting House in Phila. 12. 2mo. 1693, and m. 2.) Joseph Gowden, widower, in 1704.

David Jones, of Carmarthen town.

Ralph Lewis, of Eglwysilan.

In Chester Co. Land records:
David Jones had draught for 150 acres as part of John ap Evans purchase of 2,000 acres…by the widow Preece her land…by Mathew Jones land…by Wm. Thomas' land.

David Jones had grant for 125 acres of land 1 Aug 1682.

Warrant for 125 acres to David Jones…in Radnor Township in Co. of Chester…part of John ap Evan purchase 13 Mar 1684.

Robert Jones 300 acres…for Daniel at request of his father Robert Jones. Dated 2. 9th 1683.

Warrant for 500 acres to Indians…formerly laid out to Griffith Jones.

John Bevan later bought back the lands taken by John Richard, the Prichards, and Ralph Lewis. No outstanding information was found regarding these two and their antecedents.

* *

COMPANY NO. 4:

This group was the purchasers of the 5,000 acres of land issued to John ap John and Dr. John Wynne. This was in two parcels of 2,500 each between John ap John and Dr. Wynne.

John ap John sold his land to:

Thomas Taylor	500 acres.
John Roberts	500 acres.
Treial Reider	400 acres.
Mary Fouk	200 acres.
Richard Davies	250 acres.
Owen Parry	150 acres.
Reserved for myself	500 acres.

"Be it remembered also yt I rebought from Trial Reder afsd 400 acres."
"So wt remains for me unsold is 900 acres."

John ap John sold the remainder of 900 acres to Hugh Roberts of Merion. Hugh Roberts had 200 acres laid out in Merion, which he sold to Robert Owen, who then sold 100 acres of same to Daniel Thomas of Marion, and after Robert died, the other 100 was sold to Thomas Rees in 1700.

The Proprietor, William Penn, sailed on the same ship as this group. They departed from England in the Sixth month, 1682, on the ship "Welcome." They landed at New Castle on the 24th of October, and at Upland, now Chester, on December fourth. Dr. Wynne immediately became involved in the welfare of the colony. At the preliminary Legislative Assembly held at Chester December 4, 1682, Thomas Wynne, along with Thomas Holmes, Surveyor General, William Clark and Edward Southbrin, were appointed a committee to desire the Governor to transmit a Constitution. At the first regular meeting in March 1682/3, he was chosen Speaker.

Dr. Wynne was the first to build a brick house. This was located on the west side of Front Street, above Chester Street. He left no memorandum of his land sales. His land operations were complicated, and later his son Jonathan applied for 400 acres on his father's account, and received it in the "Great Valley" or Chester Valley, but had to surrender 100 acres of this to make up for 100 acres which were not accounted for. Jonathan Wynne settled in Blockley township, that was formerly a part of the Liberty Lands of Philadelphia Town.

In Patent Book A, Vol. 2, p. 239, Phila., Recorded 8th of 3rd month 1701, is a Greeting filed by William Penn regarding the disposition of this land. He lists some of the above, and in addition, 500 acres to Edward Jones; 200 acres to Isaac Wheeler & William Johnson, who sold same to Owen Fowke [Foulke]. He also had 250 acres to Owen Fowke instead of the 200 acres listed above to Mary Fouk. He also listed the owners and amounts of the Liberty Lands they received. In this same paper, he had sale to John Thomas and Dr. Edward Jones, and the disposition of that 5,000 acres.

There were no John's who arrived with this group, but many who were already here intermarried with the Wynne's and the Wister branch, as well as the Foulke's and others.
* *

COMPANY NO. 5:

This group were purchasers of the 3,000 acres subcibed to Lewis David, husbandman, of Llandewy Velfry, Pembrokeshire, for which deeds were granted May 1682 to:

William Howell, Castlebigch, Pembroke, yeoman, 500 acres.

Henry Lewis, Narbeth, Pembroke, yeoman, 1000 acres.

Rees Rothers [called Protheroe and also Rhydderach], Lanwenog, Cardigan, yeoman, 500 acres.

Evan Thomas, Lanykeaven, Pembroke, yeoman, 250 acres.

Lewis David, 750 acres. [He was buried at the Merion Meeting 2. 1mo. 1707/8.]

This group had their land resurveyed 16. 12mo. 1701, and it was confirmed to them as follows:

Henry Thomas, 400 acres, and 180 acres, in Haverford tp.

John Lewis, Sen., 350 acres in Haverford tp.

John Lewis Jr., 100 acres in Haverford tp.

Richard Hayes, 260 acres in Haverford tp.

John David Thomas, 210 acres in "Duffein Mawr' tp.

Maurice Llewellyn, 420 acres in Haverford.

David Rees, 260 acres in Haverford.

Nathan Thomas, 81 acres in Haverford, and 100 acres in the upper end of the Welsh Tract.

HENRY LEWIS: Henry Lewis was probably the best known of this company, according to Browning. His wife was Margaret; he was a carpenter by trade. He owned a house and two lots in Philadelphia. Bought 1,000 acres by deed dated 10 May 1682; sold his 20 acres of "Liberty land" [bonus land] to John Ball. He sold by deed 6. 12mo. 1684, 250 acres to

John Lewis in Haverford. John Lewis also had 100 acres purchased from William Rowe. Henry's son, Henry Jr. conveyed by deed 8. 1mo. 1694/5 100 acres to John Lewis Jr. Henry Jr. also conveyed on 12. 1mo. 1694/5, 50 acres to Richard Hayes, Sr.

Henry Lewis resided at "Maencoch," as he called his plantation, which consisted of 250 acres in Haverford. He was from Narberth, in Pembroke, and he arrived in 1682 as a purchaser of Company No. 5. He was a Friend. He held office of 'peace maker' for county of Philadelphia, and was foreman of the first Grand Jury for that county. His will, signed 6mo. 14. 1688, witnessed by Lewis David, Griffith Owen, and Thomas Ellis; proved in Phila. on 8. 8mo. 1705. Sons: Henry Lewis Jr.; Lewis Lewis, Samuel Lewis, daughter Elizabeth, who married Richard Hayes Jr. Richard Hayes Jr. had daughter Hannah Hayes who m. James Jones, 10. 8mo. 1727.

HENRY LEWIS JR. Had right to 180 acres in the Welsh Tract on his father's account, and bought 79 acres from John Burge, which he had laid out in the Great Valley, now of Chester Co. Resurvey showed this 259 acres to be 352 acres; he also had 50 acres overage in Haverford, which he purchased. His sons were the Lewis' who purchased land in the Welsh Tract in New Castle Co.
* *

Rees Rothers, above, was also Rhys Rhydderach. This spelling of the name various ways, such as Rothers, Rothero, and Prothero, was found in the records with people named Rhydderach [reason unknown to me.] In 1701 Rees Ryddarch and in 1702 Catharine Ryddarch were added to the Baptist church in New Castle as members coming to them as they were dwelling near Pennepek. This Rees might have been the same, or at least a connection. He might have been the brother of John Rhydderach and Morgan Rhydderach who were listed as Baptists.

Rees purchased 500 acres located in Haverford Township. He sold 120 acres by deed dated 12. 10mo. 1692 to Thomas Rees. The next day, he transferred the same to William Lewis. William Lewis gave this 120 acres to his son David Lewis by deed dated 6 Jan. 1700/1, along with 125 acres that he had purchased from John Bevan. David Lewis also bought 100 acres from Morris Llewelly [sic] in Haverford. Rhyddarch also sold 100 acres to George Painter, and conveyed 30 acres to Maurice Llewellen by deed 6. 8mo. 1695. The balance of his land was in Dyffrin Mawr tp., and of this, he sold 210 acres to John David Thomas.[16]
* *

COMPANY NO. 6:

This consisted of the purchasers of 5,000 acres of land for which Richard ap Thomas, of Whiteford Garne, subscribed. He was described as

---

[16]Welsh Settlement of Pa., by Browning, p. 199.

'gentleman.' He was owner of a freehold of 300 Pounds per annum, and resided in Flinshire at "Whitford Garden". He was one of the early converts to Fox's teachings. His wife refused to come with him and remained at home with their daughter. He came over with his only son, Richard Thomas Jr., aged about ten years, along with some servants. He joined the Hugh Roberts party and sailed in the ship "Morning Star" of Liverpool in September 1683, arriving at Philadelphia 16 Nov 1683.

Richard Thomas arrived in ill health and died without having had an opportunity to locate his land. His will was made 18 Nov 1683, probably just before he died. It was not proven until 15 Jan 1695/6 when Richard Jr. was of age. Richard lived at the home of his guardian, Dr. Thomas Wynne, at Lewes, in Sussex County, [Delaware], until Dr. Wynne died in 1692.

Richard ap Thomas' heirs, like Dr. Wynne's heirs, also had difficulty getting their father's land. Penn conveyed 5,000 acres to Richard ap Thomas by deed dated 24th July 1681 for 100 Pounds, which was supposed to be laid out in the Welsh Tract. The Minutes from the Commissioners' dated 2. 12mo. 1701, state "of which none has been laid out Saving 600 acres on part of 1,300 Acres laid out to [William] Wood and [William] Sharlow." [William Wood's eldest son[17] Joseph Wood was a Baptist. He inherited land from his father.] This was "not approv'd of by the Commis'rs and the "100 Acres of Lib. Land [due, was] taken up by Hugh Roberts." At this Meeting "his Son and Heir, Richard ap Thomas, therefore requests Warr'ts to take up the said Land in the Welsh Tract."

"The said Richard haveing been a Verry great Sufferer by his Father's embarquing for this Province, and deceasing before, or upon his Arrival, by which means he has been reduced to great hardships, 'tis Ordered that a War't be forthwith granted to take up 2,000 A's of Vacant land where to be found in the said Tract, and that War'ts be also Issued for the remainder as fast as he can be accommodated." This was done, but he was assessed the quit rents from the date the Welsh Tract was first laid out.

On 3. 2mo. 1704, Richard Thomas Jr. made returns of the following sales "of his 5,000 acres Purchased by his Father":

Philip Howel, 700 acres.
Robert Williams, 500 acres.
Edward Jones, 200 acres.
Hugh Roberts, 100 acres Liberty Land.
David Howel, 200 acres.
Robert David, 861 1/4 acres.

---

[17]Phila. Adm. Book A, 1683-1702, p. 93, (Will of William Wood; wife Susanna, 4. 9mo. 1689.)

"In all 1,786 1/4 acrs. [He] has taken up and Patented 1,665 acrs, which Make 3,451 1/4, and there remains 1,548 3/4. To which 320 being added, allowed to him (for which he is to Pay Rent for the whole 3,200 from the first Location of the Welsh Tract as well P'r agreement), for the 1,665 acres already Patented as for the Rem'd, makes 1,868 3/4 to be Confirmed forthwith, he Paying the said arrears."[18]

All this was not settled until 1717.

* *

COMPANY NO. 7:

This group were the purchasers of the 5,000 acres which "Richard Davies, of Welshpool, gent." subscribed. The following lists those who purchased land from him, with their parishes, occupations and station in life. Their deeds were dated 19 June and 30 July 1682:

Merionethshire:	Acres
Rowland Ellis, gent, Bryn Mawr	1100
Richard Humphrey, gent, Llan Glynin	150
Ellis Maurice, gent, Dolgun vcha	78
Lewis Owen, gent, Gwanas	183
Evan John William, gent, Llangylynin	156 1/4
Evan ap William, gent, Llanvachreth	156 1/4
David ap Evan, gent, Llanvachreth	156 1/4
Edward Owen, gent, "Late of Dalserey"	
Carmarthenshire:	
James Price, gent, Mothvey	300
Caernarvonshire:	
John Roberts, gent, Llangian	150
Unknown:	
Ellis ap Hugh, [Pugh], [possibly of Merioneth]	160
Petter Edwards	100
Radnorshire:	
David Kinsey, carpenter, Nantmele	100
John Evans, gent, Nantmele	350
Ellis Jones, weaver, Nantmele	100
Margaret James, spinster, Newchurch	200
Richard Miles, weaver, Llanvihangel Velgyen	100
Roger Hughes, gent, Llanvihangel Rhydyithan	250
David Meredith, weaver, Llanbister	100
Richard Corn, glover, Langunllo	50
Richard Cooke, glover, Langunllo	100
Thomas Jones, gent, Glascombe	100
Evan Oliver, gent, Glascombe	200

---

[18]Welsh Settlement of Pa., Browning, p. 208.

John Lloyd, glover, Dissart	100
Edward Jones, gent, St. Harmon	250
David James, mariner, Glascram	100

Their purchases were laid out in Merion, Radnor, Goshen, and New Town townships, in the Welsh Tract. Several from this group later became Baptists.

Richard Davies left an account entitled "Rich'd Davies Purchase & Alienation of 5,000 acres pr Rowl'd Ellis." [Owned by Historical Society of Pennsylvania] of these purchasers which show some of the land was sold to others, and the original purchasers did not come over:

Evan John Williams died, and by his will bequeathed the land to Evan ab William. He also died, and bequeathed the land to his son Philip Evan, who also died and his brother David Evan inherited.

Edward Jones purchased 250 acres, which was sold to James Morgan. James Morgan's son & heir John Morgan later became possessor.

Ellis Jones, 100 acres, assigned right & title to William David, and William David to John Morgan.

Thomas Jones, 100 acres, title of which was made to William Davies by his heirs.

"To David Kinsey 100 acres, the Execut's of the deceased Kinsey sold the tract to James James, & ye sd James to Lewis Walker, who possesseth ye same."

"To John Evans 350 acres--out of s'd tract he sold 100 acres to John German now deceased--his widow in possession. Another pt thereof he sold vizt: 100 to John Roberts, the sd John sold the same to John Morgan who has it in possession--the remaining pt ye sd John Evans hath in's possession, all in Radnor."

"John Evans 100 acres, took up att rent, in his possession."
* *

This John Morgan, later called John Sr., was brother of Cadwalader Morgan of the Thomas & Jones Co. He came over with father, James Morgan, from Vaenor, Radnorshire; took up land in Radnor. John's daughter Hannah Morgan, married James Hunter of Radnor, and their daughter, Marby, 1757-1820, married Hugh Jones, 1748-1796, of Radnor, [and had Mary, who married 1804, Nathan Brooke of Gulph Mills 1778-1815]. The said Hugh Jones was son of Hugh Jones, 1705-1790, who with his father owned at one time 700 acres, part of it the farm land called "Brookfield", North of Bryn Mawr.[19]

The Thomas Jones who purchased the 100 acres apparently did not come over, and his heirs sold the land back to William Davies.

---

[19]Ibid, p. 216.

JOHN EVANS was of the Parish of Nantmell or Nantmele, in Radnorshire, and was a "gentleman." He was a freeholder of 350 acres of land. He later purchased much more land. He came over in 1682/3, and was a member of the Church of England. He was born ca 1640, per Thomas Allen Glenn. His wife was Delilah, and he had several children who took the surname Evans and Jones. They were:

1. SARAH, married John Morgan Sr. See below.
2. MARY, m. David Evan.
3. JANE.
4. MARGARET, m. Hugh Samuel.
5. PHOEBE, m. Edward David.
6. REES JONES.
7. THOMAS JONES.
8. DAVID JONES.
9. Child who died in infancy.

WILL of JOHN EVANS, of Radnor, [from Nantmele, Radnor], signed in the presence of Abel Roberts, John Jarman, Evan Rees, David Lloyd, and Philip Howell 17. 6mo. 1703; proved by wife Deliah, 22 Nov 1707. Named daughters Mary, wife of David Evan; Sarah, wife of John Morgan; Margaret, wife of Hugh Samuel; Phebe, wife of Edward Jones David, (and "her three children"); and Jane Jones' sons, Rees Jones and Thomas Jones. Brother Edward Evans, and his daughter Elizabeth. Overseers: David Evan and John Morgan.
* *

John Morgan Sr. was from Vainor, parish of Nantmele, county Radnorshire, also, and was listed as a "gentleman." He was a kinsman of Sarah Jones. John Morgan Sr. was born 22 Nov 1669. He came to Pennsylvania in 1691, and was a freeholder in Radnor, and a member of the Church of England. He acquired three plantations in Radnor which he called "Nantmell Hall," "Vainor," and "Brui Lion." The area where he lived was called "Morgan's corner." He died about Dec. 1744. (Will recorded in Philadelphia, Will Book G, p. 153, proved 9 Dec 1744.)

His father was James Morgan, b. ca 1645, of same place, gentleman, who had wife Jane. She died on the way to Pennsylvania on shipboard 9 Sept 1691. He died on their arrival 14 Nov 1691, and was buried at the head of Bohemia Bay, Bohemia Manor, on the Chesapeake, Md. (P. 132, Welsh Founders..., Glenn. Morgan Family Bible.)

He and Sarah Jones had children:

1. JOHN MORGAN, b. 1695.
2. HANNAH MORGAN, b. 1697.
3. SARAH MORGAN, b. 1698, m. Joseph Jones, or John, son of Thomas Sion Evan, 1727 (first Welshman to arrive in Pa.) Their dau Hannah m. Nathaniel Miles.

4. JAMES MORGAN, b. 1700, d. 1701.
5. JAMES MORGAN, b. 1702, d.s.p.
6. EVAN MORGAN, b. 1704.
7. THOMAS MORGAN, b. 1706.
8. MARY MORGAN, b. 1708.
9. SAMUEL MORGAN, b. 1709.
10. MORDECAI MORGAN, b. 1713.
* *

John Morgan, Jr., their son who was born in 1695, also married a Sarah who was a daughter of another John Evans, in 1717. This John Evans had wife Mary Hughes, and was son of Evan ap Edward, of Nant-lleidiog, Pennlyn, Merionethshire, Wales. The Evans lived in Merion township, near Philadelphia. John Morgan Jr. married secondly, Patience _____. He died in 1731, will proved 4 Mar 1731, Will Book E, p. 180, Phila.

Information from will of JOHN EVAN of Merion: Will probated at Philadelphia, of Radnor, marked in presence of William ap Edward and Hugh William, 19. 11. 1707/8, proved 19 Jan. 1708, by his wife Mary. Named brother Edward Evan. Appointed John Roberts, William ap Edward, Edward Rees, and Hugh William guardians to his children: Evan, Edward, Mary, and Sarah Johnes.
* *

Thomas Jones, son of John Evans, gent, of Nantmele, lived near Richard and Samuel Miles in Radnor. His name was also found in the records as Thomas John and Johns. His father was a member of the Church of England, per Glenn. He might have been the Thomas Jones or John who joined the Welsh Tract Baptist Church at New Castle around 1702. [Thomas John had resurvey for 600 a. in New Castle Co. in 1701.] He had a sister named Mary Jones who married David Evan. She was possibly the Mary John Jun. who joined the church at the same time. He also had a sister name Phoebe Jones who married Edward David, and a brother named David Jones.

In a tax assessment made for Chester Co., Radnor Township, in 1693, were the following names of owners, with assessment of property value in pounds (actual tax was one penny per pound):
John Evans, 45 pounds
David Meredith, 70 L.
John Evans, 30 L.
John Jarman, 44 L.
John Morgan, 32 L.
Philip Evan, 43 L.
David Evan, 41 L.
William Davis, 31 L.
Samuel Miles, 33 L.
Richard Miles, 34 L.

William David, 31 L
Richard Armes, 42 L
Matthew Joanes, 30 L.
Howell James, 44 L.
Evan Prothero, 43 L.
John Richard, 33 L.
Stephen Bevan, 45 L.
Thomas Johns, 32 L.
* *

Thomas Johns given as the taxpayer, above, might have been Thomas Sion Evan, the first Welshman to arrive in Pennsylvania. He purchased land in this area in 1683. The Thomas John who was son of the above John Evans of Nantmele probably farmed with his father at first, and might have later taken out land in New Castle Co., Del.

DAVID MEREDITH, weaver, was of Parish of Llanbister, Radnorshire, Wales. With him was wife Katherine, stepchildren Richard Moore, John Moore, and Mary Moore; and their children Meredith and Sarah. He received a warrant for a city lot 22. 9mo. 1683. His Certificate of Removal was entered in Radnor Monthly Meeting Records 20. 5mo. 1683.

Some of these people were later members of the Baptist Church in New Castle County, or had family members who intermarried with members of the Baptists there. They were affiliated also with the Great Valley Baptist Church of Chester Co.

RICHARD MILES had an additional purchase of 20 acres from Ellis Jones, "the Govern's miller."* He purchased his excess land from Penn, and had a total of 325 acres.

*ELLIS JONES, William Penn's miller, aged 45, from Denby, or Flint, arrived on the "Submission" in 1682, with his wife Jane, aged 40, children Barbara, 13, Dorothy, 10, Isaac 4 mos., and Mary Jones, 12. He lived in Chester Co. and also Bucks Co.

There were also several Jones' from England who were First Purchasers of land from William Penn. They were:
John Jones, of Parish of St. Andrews, Holbourne, London; Glover, 500 acres.
Griffith Jones, of Parish called Mary Magdalens Bermondsey in County of Surrey: Glover, 5,000 acres.
Charles Jones Senr., of the City of Bristoll 'Sope boyler' and Charles Jones Junr., the same place, Merchant, 2,000 acres.
John Jones of the City of Bristoll, Linnen Draper, and Michael Jones of the same place, Grocer, 1,000 acres.
[Taken from info in George Smith's History of Delaware Co., Pa., 1862; W. W. H. Davis's History of Bucks Co., 1876.]

* *

William Penn put a 'safe-guarding clause' in all his grants so they were guaranteed protection against Indian claims to their land. Soon after his arrival in October 1682, he began to enter into treaties with the Indian chiefs for the purchase of their domains. The chiefs claims were nebulous and vague, but there were few problems with the Indians, possibly because of this, and the honesty and peacefulness of the Quakers.

* *

The Board of Property convened at Philadelphia in 1701. They ordered a resurvey of all the land in the Welsh Tract. This stated that in pursuance of an order of the Board issued the 1st instant "for taking some Measures to regulate the Welsh Tract, some of the Chiefs of that Nation in this Province having met and concerted the Methods to be taken..."

It in effect stated that the deeds had been issued to one person for certain quantities of land, but so much of the land had changed hands several times without filing the proper papers, that the person or persons who now had a share in these was unclear. William Penn needed all the fees he could collect from the land buyers, as well as the quit-rents that he was to collect for each parcel of property let out in this way. He was deeply in debt, and it was important to have a proper accounting from the person having the land. He began to change the dates when the payments for quit-rents were to begin, and was anxious to have an accounting that would enable him to do so. The Welsh weren't too anxious to pay for another survey and the extra amounts he was asking, but wanted to keep their titles to the land. Many paid an extra fee and obtained Patents on their land.

* *

RESURVEYS OF COMPANY NO. 1:

The re-survey of the Merion tract in 1703 of the Jones' land [heirs of John Thomas] showed 679 acres, and it was confirmed to the brothers, Thomas, Robert and Cadwalader on 19. 2mo. [April] 1703.

As recorded in the minutes of the Commissioners of Property 22 December 1701, the members of the John ap Thomas and Dr. Jones Company were the first of the Welsh to have their deeds resurveyed and confirmed to them. They show warrants of resurvey issued at the time of 1701, 2, 3 for the following:

"To Hugh Roberts for 549 3/4 acres in Goshen, 482 thereof of Jno. ap Jno's."

"To Robert Roberts and Own Roberts 200 acres each, in Meirion."

"To Edward Reese 205 1/4 acres, in Meirion."

"To Edward Jones' Survey on 200 acres in Goshen, and a Resurvey on 151 1/4 in Meirion, and 153 in Goshen."

"To Edward Jones, Jun'r, 306 1/4 acres, half in Meirion, 1/2 in Goshen."

"Robert David, 274 1/4 acres in Meirion, and 234 1/2 in Goshen."

"Richard Walter 100 acres in Meirion."

"Richard Rees als Jones, 137 1/2 in Meirion, and 75 in Goshen."

"To Cadwallader Morgan 202 acres and 1/2 in Meirion."

"To John Roberts, malter, 306 acres and 1/2, 3/4 thereof in Goshen, 1/4 in Meirion."

"To Hugh Jones 768 and 1/4 acres in Meirion."

"To Griffith John 194 acres."

"To Rob't William 76 1/4 acres in Goshen."

"To Ellis David 151 acres and 1/2."

"To Thomas Jones, Robert Jones and Cadwallader Jones, 1335 acres, 1/2 thereof in Meirion, and 1/2 in Goshen, left them by their father, John Thomas, the original Purchaser."

"To John Roberts, Cordwainer, of Goshen, 78 1/4 acres in Goshen."
* *

HUGH JOHN: Lived at Nantileidiog, in Llanvawr Parish, Merioneth; was a widower, farmer and miller when he bought 156 1/2 acres of land, deed dated 18 March 1681. Came over with Hugh Robert's party in 1683. Had 156 1/4 acres in Goshen on Chester Creek, of which he sold half to John Roberts, malter, 7th day of 7mo. 1687. He lived on his Merion land with his son, Hugh. This land was resurveyed in 1703. It showed 92 acres, and he paid for the balance and received patent 8 Nov 1703. By deed dated 19 Jan 1707/8, he conveyed his Merion land to Cadwalader Morgan, whose land adjoined his. He and his son held the rest.

He sold his Goshen land to John Roberts of Pencoid, and removed to Welsh settlement at Plymouth. He had four wives. He m. (2) at Merion Meeting 16. 5mo. 1686, Margaret David, and m. (3) at Radnor Meeting 18. 11mo. 1693, and m. (4) Margaret Edwards at the Merion Meeting 22 9mo. 1703. One of his daughters married Rowland Richard. He died in Plymouth in 1727. His son HUGH JONES died in Plymouth in 1739, unmarried. Nothing is known of his son JOSEPH JONES, except birth date of 12th day 4mo. 1697.
* *

WILLIAM ap JOHN, yeoman, of Bettws, near Bala, Merionethshire; son of John _____, also had children who took the surname of Jones. He came over on the "Morning Star" with the Hugh Roberts group in 1683. He purchased 156 1/2 acres of land. He found 76 1/2 acres laid out for him on the Schuylkill River and about that amount in Goshen. He died 20. 9mo. 1683, shortly after coming over, and was buried at Merion. His noncupative will sealed and proven at Philadelphia on 1. 1mo. 1684/5, left his lands to his son "John William." [Will Book A, 37, #24, 1685/76.] His wife was mentioned as "Ann Reynald, deceased."

His other children, minors at the time, took the name Jones. They were Alice, Katherine and Gwen. His son John William sold all his land. He sold 76 1/2 acres to Cadwalader Morgan and the balance to Edward Rees, who sold to Ellis David. William Jones or John of Bettws is the same person who witnessed deeds in Wales of the John Thomas and Edward Jones Co.

* *

GAINOR ROBERTS: She was daughter of Robert ap Hugh, or Pugh, of Llyndeddwydd, near Bala, in Merioneth, whose wife was Elizabeth, daughter of William Owen of Llanvawr, and a sister of the Friends' Minister Hugh Roberts. She was a spinster of about thirty when she purchased the tract of land and came over to Pennsylvania with her brother, with whom she made her home in Kiltalgarth. They came on the ship "Morning Star" in 1683. She married John Roberts, who came over on the same ship, at the Merion Meeting 10. 1mo. 1683-4. She died 10. 12mo. 1722, aged 69 years. Both she and her husband were buried at the Merion Meeting House. They were founders of the Roberts family of "Pencoyd," Merion.

John Roberts was not one of the Thomas & Jones Co. purchasers, but he was the earliest Welsh purchaser of adjoining land, on the river. Gainor took the lands of 156 1/2 acres she had obtained, half in Merion and half in Goshen, as a marriage portion. Their wedding was the first at the Merion Meeting House.

John was known as John Roberts, the maltster, from his occupation, and he later designated himself as "of Pencoyd" to differentiate from other John Roberts who were in Merion. He became a Quaker in 1677, when he was about 29 years of age.

His will, signed 3. 7mo. 1722, was witnessed by Edward George, Gainor Jones, and Thomas Jones, and was proved at Philadelphia 31 August 1724. Overseers appointed were Robert Jones, Robert Evans and Thomas Jones.

Their children were:
1. ELIZABETH ROBERTS, b. 21. 1mo. 1692, d. unmarried, 9. 7mo. 1746.
2. ROBERT ROBERTS, b. 15. 12mo. 1685. Inherited all his father's real estate and half his personal estate. He died 17 March 1768. He married at the Merion Meeting 17. 4mo. 1709, Sidney Rees, daughter of Rees Evan of Penmaen in Merionethshire. Her mother was a daughter of John ap Thomas of Llaethgwm who died in 1683. Robert left his homestead farm of about 180 acres on the City line to JOHN ROBERTS, his eldest son, b. 26. 4mo. 1710. He married at Merion Meeting on 4. 3mo. 1733, Rebecca, daughter of Jonathan Jones, son of Dr. Edward Jones, of Merion. This John Roberts had his will proven 7 Feb 1776. Children mentioned were Algernon, Jonathan, Benjamin, John, Robert, and daughters Elizabeth, wife of Thomas Palmer, and Tacy, wife of John Palmer. He named as Trustees, "loving brothers Owen Jones, Jacob Jones, and kinsman James Lewis Jones, Jr.

* *

CADWALADER MORGAN, who purchased land in the Jones & Company group and who also came over, married Jane Price, who was sister of Rees Jones' wife. He was of Gwernfel, Merionethshire, and brought Certificate dated 8. 5mo. 1683 from Penllyn Meeting for himself, wife Jane, and at least two children, Morgan and Edward Morgan.

* *

Many children died on this trip. Penn wrote that 22 out of 100 children died of "the bloody flux" which resulted from taking on a person sick of it at Dublin.

* *

Some relationships of others in this group:

JOHN THOMAS: Had son Thomas who married GRIFFITH JOHN'S daughter, Anne. Had daughter who married a son of HUGH ROBERTS.

DR. EDWARD JONES: Son married a daughter of ROBERT OWEN. Dr. JONES married Dr. WYNNE'S daughter.

HUGH ROBERT'S son married a daughter of JOHN BEVAN. His first wife was sister to ROBERT OWEN.

REES JONES married a sister of CADWALADER MORGAN'S wife.

WILLIAM EDWARD married a sister of HUGH ROBERTS.

EDWARD REES was brother-in-law to CADWALADER MORGAN and REES JONES.

JOHN ROBERTS married a sister of HUGH ROBERTS.

ROBERT OWEN and HUGH ROBERTS were brothers-in-law.

ROBERT OWEN was brother-in-law to CADWALADER THOMAS.

JOHN CADWALADER was nephew of JOHN THOMAS and ROBERT OWEN. He was son-in-law of DR. EDWARD JONES.

Both REES JONES and his wife were related to JOHN BEVAN. Their son married a daughter of Dr. EDWARD JONES. REES JONES' daughter married ROBERT LLOYD, and was niece of HUGH ROBERTS.[20]

GRIFFITH JOHN was a cousin of HUGH ROBERT'S wife, and of ROBERT OWEN, etc.

* *

---

[20]Ibid, p. 156.

CHAPTER THREE

WELSH QUAKERS, Continued...
GRIFFITH JOHN,
gentleman, b. ca 1635, lived in Merion, and later owned land in Gwynedd. He came over on the ship "Morning Star" of Chester, Thomas Hayes, Master, sailing from Mosson in Sept 1683. Arrived in the Delaware 16-20 November 1683. He did not purchase land until after his arrival, and thus would not be considered a First Purchaser. He was a planter. His family was of Royal Descent. He was son of John ap Evan ap Robert ap Lewis ap Griffith ap Howell Goch ap Einion ap Deikws Ddu ap Madog ap Ievan Goch ap David Goch, of Penllech, ap Trahnarn Goch, of Madoc ap Rhys Gloff, Lord of Cymytmaen, ap Rhys Vaughan ap Rhys Mechyllt ap Rhys Grug ap Rhys ap Griffith ap Rhys ap Tewddur Mawr ap Einion ap Owen ap Howel dda ap Cadelh ap Rodri Mawr ap Mervyn Vrych.[1]

Cae Fadog was a farm in the township of Ciltalgarth (anciently written Kiltalgarth), in the parish of Llanfor (otherwise Llanvawr) in the comot of Penllyn, near Bala, Merionethshire. Citalgarth was also the name of a farm in the same township.[2]

Glenn, who wrote of the early Quakers, wrote he was called Griffith John and Griffith Jones. However, I believe at least part of the records regarding Griffith Jones which have been written as referring also to this Griffith John are incorrect. There was a Griffith Jones, glover, of Mary Magdalen Bermondsey, Surrey, who became a very prominent merchant in Philadelphia. He was probably originally from Wales. He was about the same age, etc., and arrived in 1682 on the "Amity" and took out land during the same period. They died within a few years of each other. Their wills shed light on their real estate holdings. Griffith Jones of Surrey was a First Purchaser of land from William Penn in the amount of 5,000 acres, and his will mentioned a sister living in Ireland. He was re-married to a lady named Joan (possibly nee Wilcox) who was apparently a widow when he married her, with grown children whom he mentioned in his will. More on him later. Glenn seemed unaware of Griffith Jones, the merchant, who was a First Purchaser.

Griffith John was from Penllyn, Merionethshire, Wales, and was brother of Cadwalader John, Robert John, Margaret John, Gwen John and Catharine John. Griffith was the younger son. His father also had children by his second wife. Those known were William John, Rowland John and Gainor John.

---

[1]Welsh Founders of Pa., by Thomas Allen Glenn, Vol. I, p. 143, Oxford, 1911.
[2]Welsh Founders of Pa., Vol II, by Glenn, p. 102.

Griffith's father, John ap Evan of Penmaen in the parish of Llanfor, left a will naming his sons Cadwalader John, Griffith John, and Rowland John. Another son Robert, who also went to Pennsylvania, was not named. Daughters named were Margaret John, Gwen John and Catherine John. Griffith brought with him a certificate from Hendre Mawr dated 6mo. 8. 1690, the same date as the one of Robert Owen. (Recap of this information on Griffith's father below.)

Griffith John was first cousin to Robert Owen, and related to many other prominent early settlers. Thomas Foulke was also related. (See Foulke Pedigree in Glenn's Welsh Founders of Pa.) Griffith had a tract of 194 acres (later survey changed this to 192) northwest of where Bala station now is (per Glenn.)

An interesting thing regarding this Griffith John that might relate to our connection is that a survey of his land which was in Philadelphia County is in with the records of the surveys in New Castle County for the John's there, and the mystery of why it was there. In his will, he left 600 acres in Gwynedd to his son Evan, and also left 300 acres to his son John in Gwynedd. There was a survey for 300 acres for a Griffith John in New Castle Co. in 1703/4. Griffith John of Merion had son named John, who was said by Glenn to have used the surname Griffith. There were several John Griffith's in New Castle Co.

Griffith's son John inherited the plantation which had been originally surveyed as 194 acres, and which was described by Griffith as having about 180 acres. He also gave John one half of the crops.

The description of this land was:

"Situate in the Welch Tract layd out in Right of John Thomas and Edward Jones their original purchase of 5,000 acres Resurveyed unto the said Griffith John the said tract of land seitus at & in Merion in the Welch tract beginning at a stake in ye line of the City Liberty land and at the corner of John Robert's land Thence by the said line of the Liberty Land west West south West five hundred and sixty six perches to a stake & then by Abel Thomas his land North 32 deg: west twenty eight perches to a stake thence by Richard Jones Land east North east sixty two perches to a stake then Richard Jones his land north thirty two degrees west twenty eight perches to a post then by Richard Walling Land north seventy degrees east two hundred and ten perches to a hickery sapling at the corner of Cadwallader Morgans land then by the same South twenty five degrees east twenty six perches to a stake at the corner of the said Morgan land and the corner of Hugh Jones his land then by the said John his land South 26 degrees east thirty perches to a stake then by John Roberts land South 30 degrees east 40 perches to the beginning containing one hundred and ninety two acres Resurveyd by David Powel and Returned into the Genl. Surveyers Office the 7th of 7mo. 1702."

His will indicated he had a daughter named Anne, and he probably had other children not mentioned. He only mentioned two sons, Evan and John in his will. He was elderly when this will was made, and would not have mentioned all his children if they were already provided for. His children were said to have assumed the surname of Griffith, according to Glenn. It is possible he had sons who also took the surname John. Glenn thought Griffith's grandsons, children of John Griffith, took name of John or Jones. Griffith's son-in-law Thomas Jones, husband of Anne, was left the balance of his estate not given to Evan and John, and was appointed sole executor. Thomas and Anne were Quakers and probably not the Thomas and Anne John of New Castle Co., who were Baptists. (Will proven at Philadelphia 30 January 1707/8. Will Book C, pp. 55 & 56. See Below.)

Griffith John was quite a prominent Welshman, and probably was well educated. There was a Griffith John who was one of the signers of the certificates of removal from the Pennlyn Men's Meeting, but Griffith's Certificate was from Hendre Mawr. A Griffith John and Elizabeth John, possibly his wife, were among the people who were persecuted and fined in Wales for belonging to the Friends. He was said to be a widower when he came to Pennsylvania.

JOHN AP EVAN: [Father of Griffith John]

The Pedigree of Roberts of Gwynedd and the Pedigree of Owen & Evans Families shown in Part II of "Welsh Founders of Pennsylvania" by Thomas Allen Glenn gives a glimpse of the close relationships of these families. The latter encompasses Griffith John's father, JOHN ap EVAN of Penmaen. John was son of Evan Robert Lewis, whose wife was Jane, heiress of Fron Goch and descended from Rhirid Flaidd, Lord of Penlynn. John's siblings were Cadwallader ap Evan [surnamed Cadwallader]; Owen ap Evan [surnamed Owen]; Griffith ap Evan [surnamed Griffith]; and Evan ap Evan, father of the Evans brothers of Gwynedd. There were people descending from each of these lines who went from Wales to Pennsylvania.

John ap Evan's will showed he was of the Township of Penmaen in the parish of Llanfor, Merionethshire, Wales, and it was proven at St. Asaph 24 April 1697. He mentioned sons Cadwalader John; Griffith John; William John who settled at Gwynedd in 1698; and son Rowland. [Records indicate Dr. Rhees Jones in New Castle Co. was son of a Rowland John.] Another son, Robert, not mentioned in will, also went to Pennsylvania. He settled in Gwynedd in Philadelphia Co. In the will of John ap Evan, he mentioned daughters Margaret John [who died on voyage to Pennsylvania]; Gwen John [widow, who died at Gwynedd]; and Catherine John. Robert Cadwalader who moved to Gwynedd married Jane, ca 1672, who was the elder daughter of John ap Evan of Penmaen.

There seemed to be a relationship between David John, of Ciltalgarth and Griffith John. Pedigree II[3], the pedigree of the Rhees brothers who moved to Pennsylvania, shows some of David John's connections. The Rhees' grandfather was Evan Rhees [or Price], Penmaen, parish of Llanfor, who did not go to Pennsylvania. He issued a deed dated 28 June 1683 to Robert David and Griffith John, for the same 312 1/2 acres. [Recorded at Philadelphia; "Penna. Mag.," xxvi., 56.] Evan Rhees married a daughter of David John, of Ciltalgarth, parish of Llanfor. His son, Rees Evan, was witness to deed to Robert David, for land in Pa. 18 Mar 1681/2. [Deed Book C I, Phila.]; he also was witness 1 Apr 1682 to deed to William ap Edward for land in Pa. [Deed Book C 1, Phila.] In his will, dated after 1690 and bef 1699/1700, he named as Executors, his "cousin" David Jones of Ciltalgarth, in the county of Merioneth, gentleman, and "cousin" Thomas Cadwalader of Hendre Mawr. Overseers included his brother [in-law] Thomas Jones [of Merion.]

Griffith John signed as witness to a number of deeds, wills, etc., and was appointed as overseer and trustee in wills. Some of the books about the Quakers state that he was sometimes called Griffith Jones, but in documents he always signed Griffith John. However, some grants issued in the name of Griffith Jones were obviously Griffith John's, as shown from his will. Patent Book A, Vol. 2, Philadelphia, has several grants to Griffith Jones, some of which were for the merchant. But from his will we know the grants in Gwynedd and some of the other grants were for this Griffith John. One of the city lots was his also.

Griffith John owned 192 acres in Merion Township. He had received one moiety [half] of the 312 1/2 acres purchased originally by Evan Rees, of Penmaen, 28 July 1683. In addition, he purchased 37 1/2 acres from John Roberts, the nephew of Thomas Lloyd. He obtained a patent for the whole in one tract of 192 acres 8 Nov 1703. This land was on the old Lancaster Road, next to the city line, and included the easterly ends of the allotments of Thomas Lloyd and John Watkin and part of the west half of that of Evan Rees.[4] Browning stated he later moved to Gwynedd, but according to his will, he describes himself as of Merion, and his plantation was there, and it is doubtful if he lived in Gwynedd. In his will, he describes himself as "of Merion," but he apparently had about 900 acres in Gwynedd, 600 acres being purchased through an agreement between William John, John Humprey, and Edward Foulke of one part and himself of the other part.

Land owned by William Edwards, Edward Jones, and Abel Thomas was located near the land of both David John and Griffith John, as shown in the following:

---

[3]Ibid, Vol. I, p. 38.
[4]Welsh Founders of Pa., by Glenn, Vol. 1, 1911, p. 89.

"WILLIAM EDWARDS, in Right of John Ap John and Thomas Winn 100 Acres, John Thomas and Edward Jones 100 Acres, William Jenkins 20 Acres, Joshua Hastings 20 Acres, Thomas Simmons ten Acres, beginning at a White Oak, being the Corner dividing it from other Land of said Edwards, then by a Line E. N. E. 267 Perches to a Black Oak at the Corner dividing it from Abel Thomas's Land, then S. S. E. by a Line and vacant Land 113 Perches, then W. S. W. a Line partly by vacant and partly by David Jones's Land 267 Perches to a Black Oak, then N. N. W. by a Line to the Beginning, containg 286 Acres and three Quarters..."

"EDWARD JONES, bought of the Proprietor, beginning at a Post at the Corner of William Edwards's Land, then by the same W. S. W. to a Corner of David Jones's Land, then by the same S. S. E. 82 Perches, then E. N. E. 118 Perches, then N. N. W. 57 Perches, then W. N. W. 8 Perches, then 16 Degrees E. 60 Perches, then E. S. E. 30 Perches (the five last Courses running by Edward Robert's Land) then by Jonathan Winn's Land N. 7 degrees E. 30 Perches, then N. 4 degrees E. 46 Perches, then N. 20 degrees W. 10 Perches, then N. N. W. 34 Perches, then by Griffith John's W. S. W. 154 Perches, then by William Edward's S. S. E. 115 Perches and a Half to the Place of Beginning, containing 165 Acres."[5]

Other records concerning Griffith John:

Several records in Wales regarding the persecution of Quakers have Griffith John and wife Elizabeth.

In an undated paper estimated to be of 1693, the name was given in "The Valuation of the Estates of the Inhabitants of the Township of Merion": Griffith John   100 Pounds.

"Griffith John, widower, was among the earliest settlers in Welsh Tract who brought certificates from meetings in Wales and England to the Haverford (Radnor) monthly meeting." (Browning, "Welsh Settlement of Pensylvania" p. 498.)

When the Philadelphia monthly meeting first took up the matter of erecting a permanent meeting house on 9. 11mo. 1682, Thomas Wynne and Lydia Griffith Jones were appointed to the building committee.

Petition addressed to Penn dated 15. 3 mo. 1691 stated Penn made certain promises to Hugh Roberts, Quaker minister, of Merion: Among signers was Griffith Jones. [Since this was signed Griffith Jones, it was probably the Griffith Jones, merchant.]

From minutes of the Merion Men's Monthly Meeting:
1702-3, 4. 12mo. Records called for cash contributions to pay for an addition to the meeting house: "Griffith John is continued [as collector] to speak to those that have not paid their subscriptions towards building the addition to the meeting House, and to receive it, and to bring account thereof to the next meeting."

---

[5] Pa. Old Rights, Property Rights, Virginia Entries, Pa. Archives, Series 3, p. 371.

1704, 9mo. (Nov.), 3. "The workmen employed by this meeting to dig stone, desiring to be paid, Edward Rees, and Griffith John are desired to answer them untill friends have an opportunity to collect them."

Witnesses for wedding of Jonathan Jones and Gainor Owen at Merion meeting house in 1706, included: Griffith John and Robert John. They were both found as witnesses to numerous documents, and this Robert was probably the brother of Griffith. In most instances where their names were signed, their surname was spelled "John." Some names were written into the records by clerks, etc., so that doesn't always apply.

ROBERT OWEN, eldest son of Owen ap Evan Robert Lewis, of Rhiwlas, who resided on the "Fron Goch" plantation near Bala in Merioneth, was a minister who had been severely persecuted for being a Quaker. He arrived in Pa. in 1691. He was related [i. e., their father's were brothers] to Griffith John and settled near him. He was a justice in Merion and was chosen twice as a member of the Assembly, 1695-1696, and was a trustee of the Merion Meeting. His will was signed 2nd of 10mo. 1697, and was witnessed by John Owens, Rowland Ellis and Robert Jones, and proved at Phila. 16 May 1705. He left his plantation to his eldest son, Evan Owen. He named Hugh Roberts, John Humphreys, John Roberts, Griffith John, Robert Jones, Robert Roberts, Robert Lloyd and Rowland Ellis as Overseers. He appointed his cousin, Griffith John, as sole Executor.

Children of Griffith John and wife, possibly named Elizabeth: (children surnamed Griffith, per Glenn, but surname not given in will):
1. JOHN GRIFFITH, of Merion, m. Grace Foulke, 3mo. 6, 1707, dau of Edward Foulke of Gwynedd.
2. EVAN GRIFFITH, of Gwynedd, m. Jane Jones, his first cousin, dau of John Humphrey of Gwynedd, 3mo. 29. 1707.
3. ANN GRIFFITH, m. Thomas Jones, of Merion, s. John ap Thomas, of Llaithgwm, County Merion.
Probably others. Several Jones and John's lived in area near Griffith John.

Commissioner's "Minutes of ye Welsh Purchasers", shown on p. 54, "Welsh Settlement..." by Browning, had a record of Hugh Roberts having sold 100 acres to Edward Griffith, 100 acres to Robert William and 100 acres to Thomas Griffith, as well as 74 acres to Abel Thomas. Hugh was related to Griffith John [his wife was cousin to Griffith], and his land was located near Griffith's. Abel Thomas' land was near Griffith John's land, and perhaps this Edward Griffith and Thomas Griffith were also Griffith's sons. Griffith was apparently old enough by the time he arrived in Pa. to have grown sons and grandsons. They would have obtained their own land, and therefore were not left land in his will. He had a wide range of family members in the area.

Griffith John died in Merion, 1707/8. His will has date 26 June 1707; proved at Philadelphia 31 Jan 1707/8 [Will Book C, 69.]:

WILL OF GRIFFITH JOHN:

"Know all men by these presents I Griffith John of Merion in the Province of Pensilvania being weak of Body yet of a Sound and perfect memory (praise therefore be given to Allmighty God) Do make & ordain this my present last Will & testament In Maner and form as followeth. Ffirst I will that all my Debts & ffuneral Expenses be paid and discharged. Also I give devise grant & bequeath unto my <u>Son John</u> and to his heirs forever my now Dwelling house and Plantation with the appurtenances thereunto belonging reputed to contain abt one hundred & Eighty acres of Land seituate in Merion aforesd together with one half of the wheat rye & Barley that is now standing or being upon the aforesd plantation with all the oats growing upon the same also one half of ye cattle yt I have not already disposed of ranging abt the sd plantation. And one half of the Sheep. Also I give devise & bequeath unto my son Evan & to his heirs forever six hundred acres of Land Lying & being in the Township of Gwynedd according to the Tenour & true Intent of a Note of agreemt. made upon my sd <u>Son Evan's</u> marriage between John Humphrey, William John & Edward ffo[u]lk[e]of the one part & myself of the other part. Also I give & bequeath unto my sd Son Evan the other half or moiety of the wheat rye barley & cattle aforesd bequeathed unto my son John. Also one half of the sheep that is upon the plantation. Also I bequeath my said son Evan the sume of one hundred pounds and one ffeather bedd and beddcloths belonging to the same provided always that if my said son Evan do oblidge my Executors hereafter named to fullfill & perform ye Contract mentioned in the note of agreement afore mentioned made between John Humphrey etc. in relation to building & clearing of land that then its my will yt my son Evan do allow my Executor out of the one hundred pounds here before bequeathed to him the full value or worth for doing the same. Also I give & bequeath unto my son John & to his Heirs for ever all the Remainder of my land in Gwynedd (Six Hundred acres herein bequeathed to my son Evan to be first laid out to his Conveniency) Reputed to Contain three hundred acres. Also one large brass pan and the sum of fifty pounds. Also I give & bequeath to the use of frds. of Merion Meeting the sum of five pounds. Also I give & bequeath unto my son in Law Thomas Jones the rest & residue of my estate Goods Chattels Bills Bonds ready money & Accots. due to me who I do also nominate & appoint to be Executor of this my last Will & Testament. And do hereby Revoke Disannull and Declare Void All fformer Wills & testaments by me made & Declared. IN WITNESS WHEREOF I have herunto putt my hand & Seal this Twenty Sixth day of the fourth month called June Anno Dmi 1707. Griffith John (Seal)

Sealed acknowledged Published & declared in the presence of John Roberts, Robt Jones - Philadelphia Jan. 31, 1707/8. Then personally appeared the above named John Roberts & Robert Jones the witness to the above & within written Will & on their Solemn attest acons according to Law did declare they saw the above named Griffith John Sign Seal Publish & Declare the within & before writing as his Last Will & testamt. & that at the doing thereof he was of sound mind & memory & understanding to the best of their knowledge. Coram Pet. Evans D. Regr.

Be it remembered that the 30 Jan 1707/8 the last will & testament of Griffith John decsd. was proved in due form of Law and Probate & Ltres. of Ammnon. was granted to Thomas Jones Sole Excr. therein named being first attested well & truly to Admr. & to bring all Inventory of the Decsds. estate unto the Regr.'s office at Phila. on or before the 31 Jan. 1708/9 and also to render a true & just acct of his adminon. where required. Given under the seal of this office. Pet. Evans Dept. Regr."

* *

There was a patent for 376 acres of land, Patent Book A, vol. 2, p. 495, dated 8th of 2mo. 1703 to Hugh and Evan Griffith, yeomen.

* *

Griffith John was one of the people who subscribed to a scheme by William Penn to obtain more land on the Susquehannah River from the Indians. Appararently nothing came of this, although money was subscribed and given to William Penn. Some of the above patents may have been given in lieu of this investment, or they could have been the results of the land taken out by his brother William.

Thomas Allen Glenn wrote in Welsh Founders of Pa., Part II, p. 45, about Griffith John having a bond dated 1 Nov., 1679, that was between Gainor Jones of Llangower in the County of Merioneth, widow and executrix of the will of Humphrey Jones of Llangower, deceased, Robert Cadwalader of Llangower, yeoman, and Evan Cadwalader of Llanyckill, yeoman. Witnesses were Cadwalader Jones, Robert Vaughan, Lewis Williams. This further illustrated the close relationship of many of these early Pennsylvania settlers. This was in the possession of Griffith John at his death, having been brought to Gwynedd by Robert Cadwalader [who married Jane John] and passed to his brother-in-law Griffith. At Griffith's death, it came into the possession of his son-in-law and executor Thomas Jones, of Merion, and is now among the Levick MSS. in that family's possession.

Close Relations of Griffith John:

MARGARET verch JOHN, of parish of Llanfor, county Mererioneth, widow of John Evan (John ap Evan), of Penmaen, Llanfor (d. 1697). Came to Gwynedd, Pa. about 1698-1700 with others of her family. She was the second wife of John ap Evan, and mother of William John, Rowland John, and Gainor John. She was stepmother of Robert John, who settled at Abington, Cadwalader John, Margaret John, Gwen John, Catharine John, and stepmother of Griffith John, who settled in Merion.

Her husband was a freeholder in the township of Penmaen, in the parish of Llanfor (adjoining Fron Goch). He had an impressive pedigree, as shown under the one for "Owen, Evans, and Allied Families" by Thomas Allen Glenn.[6]

John ap Evan's parents were Evan Robert Lewis [ca 1584] and his second wife Gainor. Evan Robert Lewis was born in the parish of Yspytty Evan, Denbighshire. [Evans MS. ped.; Dwnn, ii., 278] "...He removed from Rhiwlad [or its neighbourhood], in Merionethshire to Vron Goch, [Merionethshire], and there passed the remainder of his life. He had five sons, all taking for themselves, in the Welsh manner, the surname ap Evan." ["Historical Collections of Gwynedd," H.M. Jenkins, 1st ed., 144; from Evans MSS.]

John ap Evan's siblings were Cadwalader ap Evan, of Coed Foel, Llanfor, gentleman; Owen ap Evan, of Fron Goch, gentleman; Griffith ap Evan, of Ucheldre, yeoman; Evan Lloyd Evan, of Uchtldre, yeoman; and Alice, who married 8 Dec 1624 Thomas John of Llandderfel.

He was a staunch member of the Llanfor Church. His second wife Margaret became a devout member of the Society of Friends, as did some of their children, and this caused John Evan much anxiety. "Margaret John, of Penmaen in Llanfor" was one of those fined [along with Robert, although he was a child] for being present at a meeting at Llwyn y Braner, in Llanfor, 16 May 1675, and she was subsequently frequently prosecuted.

John ap Evan had previously provided for most of his children, so when he made his will, it was said by Glenn in "Welsh Founders...," [p. 90] "to have been made mainly for the purpose of barring his wife's right of dower, and cutting off those of his children already fully provided for. The residue of his personal estate would thus go to those children not named."

In his will, under designation of "John Evan of Penmaen, in the parish of Llanfawr (Llanfor) in the County of Merioneth, yeoman," dated 4 Aug 1696, proved 24 April 1697 [Reg. 1694/1699, folio 165, Probate Registry, St. Asaph; original in bundle for 1697.] are the following bequests:

To son Cadwaladr John, 10 shillings.

To son Griffith John, 10 shillings.

To daughter Margaret John, 10 shillings.

To daughter Gwen John, 10 pounds.

To son William John, 10 shillings.

To son Rowland John, 10 shillings.

To daughter Catherine John, 5 pounds.

Item, "whereas I see the condition of Margarett John my wife to be Reasonable and good, having a competency of a joynture for her subsistence, I give and bequeath unto the said Margarett my wife in lieu and

---

[6]Welsh Founders of Pa., Vol. II, by Glenn, pp. 47-107.

in barr of the moiety of my Personal estate the summ of ten shillings, her Dissent from the Communion of ye Church of England and vaine opinion having occasioned my frequent Disturbances and trouble."

"I appoint my daughter, Gwen John, widow, and my son-in-law, Robert Cadwalader of the parish of Llanuwllyn [Llanuwchllyn] in the County of Merioneth to be joint executors."

Witnesses: John Owen [his mark], John Jones [his mark], Margarett William [mark], Row. Price."

The known children omitted from the will were son Robert John and Jane, eldest daughter, wife of Robert Cadwalader [the Executor], and Gainor [by second wife]. Robert was named as a trustee in will of his cousin, Robert Owen of Merion, 1697; was a witness to will of half-brother William John, of Gwynedd in 1712. Robert John came to Pa. and lived at Abington.

Children of John Evan of Penmaen and his first wife:

1. CADWALADER JOHN.
2. WILLIAM JOHN, moved to Pa. 1698, settled at Gwynedd.
3. GRIFFITH JOHN, moved to Pa. in 1690, settled in Merion.
4. JANE JOHN. Married Robert Cadwalader and moved to Gwynedd, Pa. ca 1700. Children surname of Roberts.
5. MARGARET JOHN. Married David Evans. She died on voyage to Pa. in 1698; David and their children settled in township of Radnor. Children: (1) GWEN, m. Thomas Foulke, son of Edward, of Gwynedd, and (2) MARGARET, m. Robert Humphrey, of Gwynedd, 1. 9mo. 1705.
6. GWEN JOHN. Was widow when she came over, then married John Humphrey, of Llangower. She had daughter (1) JANE JONES, who m. 29. 3mo. 1707 her first cousin, Evan Griffith [Son of Griffith John], then of Merion, afterwards of Gwynedd. Her other children who came over with her were (2) CADWALADER JONES, (3) DAVID JONES, m. Loury Roberts 1707. [There was a land grant for a lot in the City Liberties, see below, dated 25. 7mo. 1701, Recorded in Patent Book A, Vol. 2, p. 80 for David Jones, late of Merioneth. Glenn wrote this was David Jones of Ciltilgarth, but it seems more likely to be this David.]
7. CATHERINE JOHN, was unmarried in 1696.

* *

WILLIAM JOHN, yeoman, Griffith's half-brother, of parish of Llanfor, county Merionethshire; son of John Evan of Penmaen, Llanfor, and Margaret, above. Came to Gwynedd, Pa. 1698. Friend. He and Thomas Evan had a grant from Robert Turner, dated 10 day 1mo. 1698, for 7,820 acres of land in Gwynedd. Did not take out patent for all of this, but had one patent for 322 acres [Patent Book A, Vol. 2, p. 472, Phila., 29. 1mo. 1703], in which description mentioned land of Edward Foulkes, land of Evan Roberts, and land of John Hughs. He also had one for 2,866 acres

[Patent Book A, Vol. 2, p. 495, recorded 29. 1mo. 1703.] This was by land of Griffith Jones. His wife was Jane, daughter of Hugh Cadwaladr ap Rhys of parish of Yspytty Evan, county Denbighshire.

Children took surname Jones or John, per information Thomas Allen Glenn received from Charles Roberts, of Phila., and quoted in Part Two of "Welsh Founders..." p. vii. William and Griffith John were both mature men when they came to Pa. and probably had other children than the ones mentioned in their wills. In "Merion In The Welsh Tract," the first book he wrote on these Welsh, Glenn stated William John's children used the surname Williams, so obviously his first information was incorrect, as it could have been for Griffith's children. William's will indicated his children used the surname John, as he named his wife Jane and his son as Executors, and their surnames were recorded as "John."

Known children of William and Jane:

1. GWEN JOHN, m. William Lewis, of Newtown, Chester Co., 1704. He was son of William Lewis from Parish of Llantrisant, Glamorganshire Co., Wales, who came to Pa. in 1686.
2. MARGARET JOHN, m. (1) Robert Ellis of Merion, 1705, (2) David Llewelyn of Haverford, widower, 1709.
3. GAINOR JOHN, m. Abraham Musgrave 1714.
4. KATHERINE JOHN, m. Humphrey Jones, son of John Humphrey, 1719.
5. ELLIN JOHN.
6. JOHN JOHN, of Gwynedd. Was left the home place by William.

* *

William John was baptized at Llanfor Church, 10 Aug. 1673, when he was several years old. This was done late by his father because his mother had joined the Friends. William was named in the will of his uncle Cadwalader Evan of Coed y Voel, dated 25 Dec 1688, as follows: To my "nephew Wm. Jon. Evan" 5 pounds "upon condition yt his father in law Hugh Cadder shall likewise give him" 5 pounds.

William settled at Gwynedd (Northern Philadelpha), and died there in 1712. His will was dated 11 Aug 1712, proved at Philadelphia 1 Nov 1712. (Will Book C, 321, Philadelphia.) He bequeathed 1400 acres of land to son John. He also had 322 acres of land in Gwynedd. One of his daughters married William Lewis of Haverford, and another married David Llewelyn of Haverford. Mention of wife Jane in will; and one of the witnesses was Robert Jones [said to be his stepbrother]; other witnesses were: Edward Foulke [brother-in-law], Thomas Jones, and Evan Griffith, [son of Griffith John]. [See will below.]

In Scharf's "History of Delaware," Vol. II, p. 950, he wrote regarding the land in the Welsh Tract in Delaware that William Jones took up "1368 acres, and in 1702, 1379 acres." We are not sure if this was William John, but because of the amount of land it would appear that it was.

63

early Welsh settlers in Pennsylvania as relatives of Griffith John and William John.

FRON GOCH in Merionethshire was described was follows:[7]

"Fron Goch, which gave its name to the present ecclesiastical district of the same name, is a large farm partly in the parish of Llandderfel, to which it still pays tithes, but mostly in the township of Ucheldre, in the parish of Llanfor, Merionethshire. It was formerly of much greater extent than at the present time, several parcels of land having been cut out of it, and appears to have extended into the township of Cynlas, formerly part of Llandderfel, but now locally in Llanfor. The principal residence was in Llanfor, near the present Fron Goch Station, but there were other tenements, some of them on detached parcels, belonging to Fron Goch. The tenants have of late times always baptized and buried at Llanfor Church, but in earlier days they occasionally buried at Llandderfel, especially if residing at the time in any of those tenements belonging to Fron Goch which lay within the latter parish. There is evidence to show that Fron Goch was sometimes considered to be a township of itself."

* *

WILL OF WILLIAM JOHN of Gwynedd, Will book C, Philadelphia, pp. 321-322:

[321] "Be it known unto all whom it may concern by these presents that I William John of Gwynedd in the county of Philadelphia & province of Pensilvania being weak of body yet of sound and perfect mine & memory praise therefore be given to almighty God do make & ordain this my present last will & Testament in manner & form following first principally I remand my body soul & spirit unto my savioure & redemters hands for all is his & my body to be decently interred according to the direction of my Executors hereafter named and as concerning what temporall estate it hath pleased God to bestow on me I dispose thereof as followeth viz: ffirst I will that all my debts & funeral Expenses be paid & discharged Also I give devise & bequeath unto my daughters Gainor Ellin & Katherine a tract of land situate lying & being in the aforesaid township containing by estimation three hundred twenty two acres of Land with the appertenances thereunto belonging bounded southward with the land of John Hughs on the eastside with the lands late of Ellis David & Evan Robert westward with the land late of Edward ffolk [Foulke] to be equally divided between them to have & to hold unto my sd. daughters Gainer, Ellen & Katherine & to their heirs forever Also I give devise & bequeath to my son John & to his heirs forever my dwelling house & plantation building improvements & appurtenances thereunto belonging containing by estimation about one thousand & four hundred acres of Land excluding always one moity or halfe of the aforementioned premises to the use & maintenance of my well beloved wife

[7]ibid, Vol. II, p. 85.

Jane during such time as she remains a widow or untill she marys and afterwards one third thereof [322] During her naturall life my son John paying to my daughter Gainor the sum of twenty pounds within one year after my decease, And to my daughter Ellin the sum of twenty pounds within two years after my decease & also my daughter Katherine the like sum of twenty pounds within three years after my decease. Also I give & bequeath unto my son in law William Lewis the sum of two pounds ten shillings & to my son in law David Lywillin [Llewellyn]] the sum of two pounds & ten shillings, Also I give & bequeath unto my son John my cart Tethre & harness belonging to the same & a horse called Buck & what stuff or materials is provided towards building a new house & as much money as will finish the Wall the wall thereof & cover it Also I give devise & bequeath all there is & residue of my personall estate goods chattells & chattled household stuff Bills Bonds & ready money as followeth one third thereof to my well beloved wife Jane & the other two thirds to be equally divided between by daughters Gainor, Ellin & Katherine & do hereby constitute nominate & appoint my well beloved wife & my aforesaid son John to be Executrs. of this my last will & testament hereby revoking discharging void all former wills & Testaments heretofore by me made In Witness whereof I have hereunto set my hand seal this Eleventh day of the month called August Anno dmi. 1712. William [mark] John {Seal}. Signed sealed acknowledged published & declared in the presence of us Robert Jones, Edward ffoelke, Thomas Jones, Robert Jones, Evan Griffith. Philada. the 1st Novembr. 1712 then personally appeared Edward ffoekle [Foulke], Thomas Jones & Robert Jones, three of the Witnesses to the within written will & on their solemn affirmation according to law did declare they saw the testator William John sign seal publish & declare the within writing to be his last will & testament & that at the doing thereof he was of a sound disposing mind & memory to the best of their knowledge. Coram Benjamin Mayne Reg. Gen.
Phila. the 1 day of Novem. 1712 Be it remembered that the last will & testament of William John was proved in due form of law & probate & letters of Administration was granted to Jane John and John John executors therein named being first   will and to administer & to bring in Inventory of the cited sd. estate into the Reg. Gen. office at Phila. on or before the 1 day of Feb. next as also to render amount when required. Given under the seal of the said office. Benj. Mayne Reg. Gen."
* *

ROBERT JOHN,

was brother of William John and Griffith John, et al. He signed various documents as a witness. He is said to have arrived in 1696, and lived in Abington, Chester Co.

It is difficult to tell if documents having Robert Jones are his, as they are said to be. There were several Robert Jones in the Phila. Co. area.

Sometimes two of them would sign as witnesses to a single document, which indicates there were two Robert's. [He married Ellin, sister of David Jones of Ciltalgarth.]

Browning in "Welsh Settlement of Pensylvania", p. 444, mentioned the General Wayne Inn located along the old Lancaster Road in the Welsh Tract, as being a landmark in Merion at the time he wrote his book. He stated it was in a stone house that was built by Robert Jones, son of John ap Thomas, sometime after he purchased the lot [one acre] in 1709 from Edward Rees.

He also referred to the blacksmith shop located near the stone house, which was also owned by Robert. He stated the stone house became an inn about 1776. For many years, it was only the home of the blacksmith whose shop was across the road. This was located very close to the Merion meeting house, with the church land surrounding three sides of it. This Robert died in 1746, will dated 21. 7 mo. 1746. He gave the stone house and lot to his grandson Silas Jones, plus ten acres "where the hempmill stood." Silas Jones, of Darby, grazier, sold this house and lot to Benjamin Jones, of Philadelphia, blacksmith, by deed dated 25 Mar. 1768.

For other information, see account of John ap Thomas, previously given.

One Robert Jones, of Gwynedd, yeoman, wife Gainor, left will signed 9th mo. 1732 [Will Book E, Phila., No. 281]. Named son John Jones, to receive plantation Robert lived on, which contained 300 acres; also to receive 185 acres recently purchased from Cadwalader Foulke. Mentioned daughter Ellin, with a money bequest and 150 acres to her, purchased from Cadwalader Foulke. Mentioned wife Gainor. Nominated "my loving uncle Cadwalader Evans, my cousins Evan Evans, Owen Evans & John Jones, Carpenter, & John Evans to be overseers." Thomas Allen Glenn in Welsh Founders of Pa., p. 186, stated this Robert was of parish of Llanfor, county Merioneth, son of John ____, and Ellin, daughter of Evan Lloyd Evan of Ucheldre. Came to Gwynedd, Pa. in 1698, was a Magistrate at Gwynedd for many years. Married Gaynor Lloyd, of Merion, wid., in 1706.
* *

GRIFFITH JONES, MERCHANT:

Griffith Jones, Glover, was a First Purchaser of 5,000 acres of land from William Penn. He arrived in Pennsylvania aboard the "Amity" with his second wife Joan, his son Joseph Jones, and stepdaughter Ann Powell, from Mary Magdalen Bermondsey Parish, Surrey, England. Servants who arrived with him were Ellinor Barber, Jeremiah Osbourne and Elizabeth Day.[8] Port records for the "Amity" show Griffith Jones loaded 15,000 bricks and tiles for this journey.[9]

---

[8]Walter Lee Sheppard Jr., Passengers and Ships Prior to 1684, Penn's Colony: Volume I, Heritage Books Inc. 1992, p. 36.
[9]Ibid. P. 35.

Robert Hopper, master "of ye Providence of Scarbrough" witnessed a money order executed by Griffith Jones 18 Oct. 1682.[10] An account of John Lowe and his wife stated they were deceased by 1. 9mo. 1685, and their children were brought to Philadelphia from the Lower Counties by the Philadelphia Meeting [Friends] and placed with various families. Griffith Jones took "the middle Girl."[11] James Atkinson, with certificate of removal from Drogheda Meeting dated 23. 8mo. 1681, lived with Griffith Jones in Philadelphia in 1683.[12]

In an account of John Swift, Glazier, one of the First Purchasers who came over on the "Alexander" of Inverness in 1682, he took as his second wife Elizabeth, who was widow of Patrick Robinson and Griffith Jones.[13]
*

Deed Book B, Vol. 1, 1664-1686, New Castle Co.:
P. 229. Joseph Moore & Anna Maria - dau of Cornelius Yoras.--Release of lands to James Sinexan & Dorcas. Wit. Jos. Wood & Griff Jones, 1 Jun 1702/3. Joseph Moore might have been son of one of the stepsons of David Meredith, a Quaker.
Joseph Moore's land, as shown in Deed Book A, p. 125:
"Whereas there is a certain tract of land in the county of New Castle called Oake Hole Situate lying & being on the West side of Delaware River and on the Noreth Side of Duck Creek next adjoining to Joseph Moore's land named Bristol Beginning at a corner marked white oak of said Moore's land standing by the side of Duck Creek...
*

In the Tax Assessments of Estates Assessed in 1693 in New Castle Co., for Little Creek Hundred was this assessment: "Thomas Gennefells for Griffith Jones, 200 L."

In the patent for 600 acres of land, Philadelphia Patent Book A, Vol. 2, p. 372, Griffith Jones was granted 5,000 acres of land in this province. Under warrant dated 18th day of Feb. last, he was granted 2,920 acres of land. In right of his purchase there was surveyed a certain tract of land, mentioned by land of James Claypoole, land of James Peters and land of William Jones [John] containing 600 acres, which was confirmed unto Griffith Jones 17. 8mo. 1702.

A couple of deeds recorded in New Castle County in 1701 designate him as "Merchant, " from Philadelphia, and show he secured a debt for 52 accounts of other people to merchants in London, agreeing to pay it in tobacco, even if he was unable to collect the amounts owing. He paid this off, as a subsequent deed shows. [Deeds in Book A, pages 126 and 157,

---

[10]Ibid. P. 49.
[11]Ibid. P. 61.
[12]Ibid. P. 62.
[13]Ibid. P. 102.

New Castle Co., Del.] Witnessed by Saml. Land, Henry Jones*, and
Reynus Vandenoolen.

[*One Henry Jones was a merchant. His will probated Mar 19, 1727, Will
Book E. Phila., #34. Children: Tamar, Rachel, Henry & Thomas Jones. A
Henry Jones was a tailor, and a Baptist. His will was probated 8 Jan 1731,
Phila. Will Book E, # 286.]

Griffith Jones and Ebenezar Empson were witnesses to a deed 18 Aug
1697 (Deed Book B, Vol. 1, p. 151) between John Moll of Bohemia River
in Province of Maryland and John Donaldson of the Town of New Castle.
Griffith had a grant for a lot on Front St. that he obtained in order to build a
wharf and houses thereon, dated 26. 2mo. 1690. [Patent Book A, Vol. 2, p.
261.] He died in 1712, and his will was probated 27th October 1712 (Will
Book C, pp. 319-321, Philadelphia.) He named son Joseph Jones as
Executor. We are not sure of his religion.

An interesting deed was found in Deed Book H, Vol. 1, p. 47, made 13th
Nov 1725, between Isaac Norris of Fairhill in the County of Philadelphia,
and Edward Lowder of Apoquinimick Hundred in the County of Newcastle.
Under the Whereas regarding this land was the statement that William Penn
granted Anthony Thomkins of New York, Merchant, a Tract of Land called
Penn--- consisting of 315 acres with its appurtenances, etc. dated 30th July
1684, recorded in Book (A), folio 28. The usual consideration for the grant
was mentioned, i.e. one good bushel of winter wheat payable each year for
each one hundred acres. The name of this tract of land was difficult to read,
but it might be "Pennset." It was located on the "north side of Duck Creek
bounded and limitted as in the same Patent is sett forth..."

This deed stated 'Anthony Thomkins died and under his will appointed
Richard Hambley Executor. Griffith Jones of Philadelphia reserved
judgment against Richard Hambley for a debt of sixty pounds which
Anthony Thomkins owed him, plus fees, so the Court at New Castle ordered
Sheriff Edward Gibbs to turn over one moity or one full half part of this
tract of land with the plantation and appurtenances on the 20th day of June
1692, to Griffith Jones in full satisfaction of this claim. Then under an
Indenture of Lease and Release, dated 4th day November 1715 between
Joseph Jones, only son and Executor of the last will and Testament of
Griffith Jones, and Isaac Norris of the other part, Joseph Jones for the
consideration therein mentioned did '(by the Tenor & Direction of the said
Griffith Jones's last Will... bearing date the 4th day of October 1712 and
remaining in the Register Generals office in Philadelphia)' released and
confirmed to Isaac Norris all the said full moity of the said Tract of Land
plantation and premises with the appurtenances...'

Then by another indenture dated the 14th day of September 1716,
between Joshua Tomkins, only son and heir at law of Anthony Thomkins,
deceased, of the one part and Isaac Norris of the other part, did release,
devise & confirm by Quit Claim all that land, etc. which Isaac Norris

received from Joseph Jones. Then by this [present] indenture, Isaac Norris and his wife Mary for the consideration of sixty pounds paid by Edward Lowder, sold and confirmed this aforesaid land to Edward Lowder, etc. This was recorded the 19th of October, 1726.

Other records show Isaac Norris signed land records in New Castle Co., Del. He was one of Penn's Land Commissioners, a Judge, and very prominent in early affairs. His wife was the daughter of Lt. Governor Thomas Lloyd. She was a minister in the Society of Friends.

"Passengers and Ships Prior To 1684" by Sheppard, p. 86, lists a deed, Deed Book E-1-5, 588: 21 4mo. 1687, Anthony Thompkins to Griffith Jones.

Thomas Allen Glenn gave an account[14] of the fight in 1689 between the Welsh and the Governor and English Justices of Chester Co., Pa. to make part of their land located in Philadelphia Co. become part of Chester Co., so as to dilute the vote of the Welsh. He stated: "Lloyd [of the Welsh group] then asked for a further hearing, which request was seconded by Samuel Carpenter, but was vigorously opposed by Griffith Jones, a Welshman in the pay of the Governor." I found nothing to ascertain the veracity of this statement by Glenn that either of the Griffith Jones or John's was in the pay of the Governor, and do not believe there was anything to indicate this part of the statement was true. I believe the Griffith Jones who was on this Council was the one who was a merchant, and he was probably a Quaker. Even though he came from England, he was probably of Welsh descent. Later records show he was on the Council when Representatives were chosen from New Castle Co., Del. Thomas Allen Glenn did not seem aware that there was another prominent person by this name.

At any rate, a more extended account of this fight was given by Browning in "Welsh Settlement of Pensylvania" from which information I'll attempt to give an abbreviated version:

'Three years after the settlement of the Great Welsh Tract, the English became jealous of its advancement and did things to slow this. The first attempt was by the people of Chester who wanted to extend their boundary and increase their tax revenue by taking part of the Welsh Tract. They wanted a new boundary line for Chester County located between the counties of Philadelphia and Chester. That would place the "towns" of Haverford and Radnor within Chester County, etc. This was introduced before the Provincial Council April 1, 1685. At this time no Welsh Quaker was a member of the Council. This Resolution was properly passed in the Executive Council, but it could not take effect until it had the sanction of William Penn or his Deputy Governor. Mr. Holme, Surveyor, who was Acting President, would not take the responsibility for putting this into

---

[14]"Merion in the Welsh Tract" by Thomas Allen Glenn, pp. 50-52, Reprinted 1970, Genealogical Publishing Co.

effect. The President of the Council Lloyd, was absent, and it is intimated that they chose this time to bring it up because he was absent.

This was again brought up at the next meeting a week later, but the Welsh Quakers had been alerted and used their efforts and influence against this. They asked instead for the bounds of all counties to be adjusted and determined for tax purposes, etc., before sending this to Penn. At the next meeting, Lloyd presided and the matter was dropped. However, Thomas Holme sent the resolution on to Penn when Lloyd declined to confirm it.

Up to March 1689/90, the Welsh Tract was put in a peculiar position as its large "towns" of Haverford and Radnor had been transferred from Philadelphia Co. to Chester Co. by the resolution of April 1, 1685. This was acknowledged by the Philadelphia Co. authorities, which made no attempt to collect taxes in these townships for Philadelphia Co. use. The Welsh would not pay any taxes to Chester Co., as they did not consider this agreement binding as it had not been sanctioned by Penn.

But on 25. 1mo.* 1689/90, the Chester line and the assignment of Haverford and Radnor was brought up in the Executive Council, with Captain John Blackwell, Deputy Governor, presiding. The news of this soon reached Thomas Lloyd, the attorney and champion for the Welsh in this matter, so he went to the Chamber and inquired of the [Deputy] Governor as to the rumor. He was assured it hadn't been brought up, and if it was to be brought up, they would be notified. That afternoon, the justices and some inhabitants of Chester Co. did appear by appointment and presented a petition to confirm this previous resolution. [*Under the calendar then in effect, March was the first month.]

Governor Blackwell demanded the Chester County committee put this matter into writing and submit it to the Council, and show proof that the Proprietor said that Radnor and Haverford townships should be included in Chester Co., as there was no documentary proof of it. Several residents wrote statements that Penn had told them he favored this.

But the clinching "proof" was a map of Philadelphia presented by Holme, which was supposedly made for the Governor by Surveyor Holme sometime after it was voted in 1685 at the Council meeting over which Holme presided, that showed Haverford and Radnor should be included within Chester Co. The map showed these two townships located in Chester Co., with the lines the way the Council wanted them. After looking at this, the President [Deputy Governor Blackwell] decided that it was Penn's desire for it to be done, although the map was not dated and there was no evidence that Penn had confirmed the resolution.

Friend Thomas Lloyd and others were very angry over this, but were unable to do anything about it. The first attempt to organize the townships with officers came when the Court made the order appointing as constables, John Lewis for Haverford, and John Jarman for Radnor. They declined to appear at Court and qualify, and warrants of contempt were put out for them, with orders for the Sheriff to bring them in. Lewis never surrendered, but Jarman was attested constable for Radnor by the Court a few months later. Several were fined for not serving as jurors. William Howell was appointed the justice of the Court in Haverford, but would not accept the commission at that time, although he did later.

After about a year, the jurisdiction of the Chester court was recognized and the Welsh 'towns' had the proper officers in 1690. Up until this time, no Welsh Quakers would accept appointments from the Chester County Court, else it would be construed as an acknowledgement by the Welsh that Haverford and Radnor were parts of the county of Chester. This forced the Court and inhabitants to bring the line matter up again before the Executive Council. Neither Penn nor Lloyd would give confirmation to the resolution, so they wanted the new Governor to confirm it.

In 1690, there was an election due for Councillors and Assemblymen, and there was to be returned for Philadelphia Co., where the Welsh Tract lay, one Councillor and six Assemblymen. Two slates of candidates were presented, one the Governor's and one the Quakers. Since they knew the Quakers could win if they voted solidly in the election, it was the scheme of the political supporters of the administration to force the acceptance of Holme's Chester County line before the election.

The Welsh refused to vote in Chester County. They cast their votes in Merion Township in Philadelphia Co. for their candidate, John Eckley. The administration candidate was defeated. The Deputy-Governor and the Council considered this illegal and reported it to the Sheriff, 1 Sept 1689, and threw out the entire Welsh Tract vote for Mr. Eckley, and ordered a new election.

"Then arose a momentuous question. The Council debated the proper manner of choosing the candidate, and conducting the election, as all were not of one main, and the "Form of Government," and the "Charter" were ambiguous and uncertain on this subject, so "the usual custom" had to be considered as the rule, whether the election must be "by vote or by ballot," a distinction being made in these methods, that is, "by vote" the expression of choice was viva voce, and "by ballot" the proceeding was comparatively secret."

In the second election, the Welsh freemen were uncertain of which method to use, and voted both ways, so the manner of voting and the result of the election was the same.

This election was voided, another election was held, and the Welsh of the three Welsh townships voted together again, this time viva voce, and again elected Mr. Eckley unanimously.

But this election was not accepted by the Deputy-Governor and the Executive Council. They said the people voted in the wrong county, and the votes were not taken uniformly, so a new election was ordered.

"This brought up again the discussion between the freemen and the Council, over the manner and method of choosing at a poll. It was on this occasion that Griffith John, or Jones (the father-in-law of Thomas Jones, of Merion, son of John ap Thomas), deserted the Welsh column, and took side against the views of the Welsh Quakers beyond the Schuylkill.

One Mr. Curtis claimed, in the debate, "it was a very fayre Election. In other places we are generally chosen by the Vote." Another gentleman said, "the balloting box is not used in any other place but this country." And Griffith Jones replied, "this was a mistake, for it is used at Upland [Chester], and all the Lower Countyes, by black and white beans put into a hatt, wch is a ballotting in my sense, and cannot be denied by the Charter when it is demanded." [Pa. Col. Rec. I. 282.]

When Captain Blackwell's tenure of office was over and he was ordered home, he thanked God for his removal, for "he was sick of the Pensylvania mess."

* *

Penn's high living caused him to continuously have money problems. This caused the Welsh to have problems with the various ways Penn devised to obtain money from them. A petition by the Welsh was addressed to Penn himself dated 15. 3mo. 1691, regarding Penn's request that they pay quit-rent from the date of the purchase of their property, instead of the time it was surveyed, as well as several other things. The difference in this petition was that they mentioned their celebrated Friends minister, Hugh Roberts, of Merion, as a person to whom Penn had made certain promises before the Welsh Friends would buy and leave their native country. This petition was signed by:

> Lewis David, John Bevan, John Humphreys, Francis Howell, William Howell, David Lawrence, John Lewis, David Meredith*, Stephen Evans, Ellis ap Hugh, John Gorman, Griffith Owen, Robert Owen, Hugh Roberts, John Roberts, Robert Davies, Cadwalader Morgan, Will Edward, Edward Jones, Thomas Jones, Rees Jones, Hugh Jones, Edward Jones, Jun., Robert Owen, Griffith Jones, Abel Thomas.

*David Meredith, son of this David, later lived in New Castle County. David Meredith, weaver, of parish of Llanbister, Radnorshire, Wales, his wife Katherine and step-children Richard Moore, John Moore, Mary Moore, and children Meredith and Sarah Meredith, had their Certificates of Removal entered in the Radnor Monthly Meeting Records 20 5mo. 1683. David's son Meredith used the name Meredith David, and his children then took the surname Meredith.

Proud, in his History of Pennsylvania, named these Welsh as being the most prominently active in public life, and in the affairs of the Province, as well as in those of the Friends: Rowland Ellis, Robert Owen, Hugh Roberts, and Ellis Pugh. But Browning wrote "there were ...others...who were quite as prominent in the affairs of Philadelphia county, and who represented it in the assembly, before 1709, namely Thomas Lloyd, Griffith Jones, David Lloyd, Griffith Owen, John Bevan, Thomas Wynne, Rees Thomas, John Roberts, etc."

Records show that Griffith Jones was chosen Mayor of Philadelphia in 1703, but he declined to serve, and was fined 20 pounds, which he did not pay. He was again chosen for the mayoralty on 3 Oct 1704. He started to decline again, but was threatened with a like fine for a total of 40 pounds, so he accepted. They were so glad he accepted, the first fine was remitted.

Several Jones and John's were merchants in Philadelphia. But William Trent had the largest store in Philadelphia ca 1700, and he left account books showing that the country people brought him peltry of all kinds and exchanged it for dry goods and groceries. Among his Welsh customers with accounts were: John Jones Sr. and Jr., Nicholas Thomas Jones, Griffith Jones, Edward Jones, Samuel Jones, Moses Jones, and Richard Jones, John Thomas "ye tailor," and others.

William Penn wrote a long letter dated London, 16. 1mo. 1684/5, to his Deputy, Thomas Loyd, a Merion Welshman, and concluded his letter with "Dearly salute me to dear friends, particularly Thomas Ellis, G. Jones, H. Lewis, T. Howel, J. B., [John Bevan] and the rest of the Welsh Friends, Captain Owen, etc., with their families."
* *

WILL OF GRIFFITH JONES.
Philadelphia Will Book C, pp. 319-321.
"I Griffith Jones of the city of Philadelphia in the province of Philadelphia Merchant being sick and weak in Body but of sound mind memory & judgment thanks be to God calling to mind the uncertainty of my continuance in this life have thought fitt & do hereby make this my last will & testament in manner & form following that is to say First I recomend my Soul & Spirit to the Mercifull protection of God that gave it & my body to the Earth to be decently interred by my loveing wife at the charge of my Executor herein after named when it shall please the Lord so to dispose of it And as touching my outward Estate I will that the same be disposed of as is herein after declared: Imprimis I will that all my just debts & funerall charges be paid as soon as possible by my said Executor. Item I give devise & bequeath unto Joseph & Ann Wilcox & unto William Chancellor & Roberta his wife & unto Sarah & Ann Wilcox daughter of the said Joseph & Ann to every & each of them a pistole of Gold. Item I give devise & bequeath to my sons' in laws Peter Robinson, Livewell Robinson & Septimo Robinson to each of them a pistole of Gold. Item I give devise & bequeath unto Sarah Evans her sister Mary both of the province of Western Jersey to each of them the sum of five pounds current money. Item I give devise & bequeath unto Joseph Willcox the sum of five pounds for the

paking in of that part of ground in the old burying ground where his family & my former wife are intered & where also I desire to be buryed & It is also my request that this said piece of ground may be enlarged if it can be conveniently be done. Item I give devise & bequeath unto the said Joseph Willcox for the former trouble in stating thereon unto & informing the auditors in the business between the widow Barker & myself the sum of twenty pounds current money. Item my will is that all the legacies hereby given & bequeathed shall be paid by my Executor within twelve months after my decease. Item I give devise & bequeath unto my loving wife Elizabeth Jones & to her heirs & assigns forever all & singular the dwelling house messuage or tenement wherein I now live with all the outhouses garden orchard fences & allso all the lotte of ground thereunto belonging which I purchased of Peter Robinson together with the hereditaments appurtenances belonging to the same provided she my said wife pay unto her son Septimus Robinson allsuch sums of money as are incumbent on me to pay unto him on account of his share of the Estate of his late father Patrick Robinson deceased & that my Executor be sufficiently discharged from the said Septimo for the same within six months after my decease. But in case my said wife shall not ffind fitt to accept the said bequest on the terms before expressed then I give devise & bequeath the said dwelling house Lotte & all & Singular the above mentioned premises unto my said wife for & during the term of her natural life & no longer she keeping the said house In tenentable repair. Item I give devise & bequeath unto my said loving wife the sum of twenty pounds per annum for & including the term her naturall life to be paid for by my Executor hereafter named in such currency of money as the rents shall be received in from my tenents. Item I give devise & bequeath unto my Granddaughter Elizabeth Jones my English chest of drawers & unto my granddaughter Ann Jones my great Bible. Item my will is that all & singular my personall Estate shall be disposed of as soon as the same can conveniently be done by my Executor for the most it will yield & the money arising thereby as also all out standing debts owed to me shall by my said Executor be received & applyed to the payment of my debts & legacies as far as the same will extend & I do hereby empower my said Executor to grant alien sell enfeoff & confirm by good proficience reconveyance as one well learned in the law shall advise & direct any part of my real estate of houses land & tenements & hereditaments ground rents or profits thereof for the most profit yield do forebare & no farther so as will be sufficient to make [indecipherable] personal Estate shall fall short to discharge my just debts & legacies & that the lotte of land & ground Rents in the City of Philadelphia excepting the bank & water lotte at the upper end thereof shall not be sold after the said debts & legacies are discharged but that my said Executor shall have full power to sell & lett out the said lotts upon ground rent for the most they will yield all which sd. ground rents & all other my ground rents which shall not be aliened & sold for the payment of my sd. debts & legacies as also all other my real Estate of what nature leins or quallity soever wheresoever lying or being not herein before given & bequeathed I give devise & bequeath unto my son <u>Joseph Jones & Margaret his wife</u> & the longest hier of them for secureing their naturall hier & from & after their decease my will is that the same shall go to the children of the said Joseph lawfull begotten & to be begotten upon the body of the sd. Margaret or any other Wife which he may happen hereafter to have to be equally devided between them & to the survivors & survivor of them but in case all the said children shall happen to dye without issue then my will is that two thirds of my sd Estate shall go to the grand chilldren of my sister Jone living in Ireland & the other third to the children of the said Joseph Willcox & to the survivor & survivors of them & lastly I do hereby constitute nominate & appoint my said son Joseph Jones Executor of this my last will & testament thereby revokeing all former & other Wills heretofore by me made & declaring this & no other to be my last Will & testament. In Wittness thereof I have hereunto sett my hand & seall this fourth day of October in the twelfth year of the reign of our sovereign Lady Ann Queen of Great Brittain viz Annoq Domini 1710. Griffith Jones [Seal] Signed sealed published & delivered by the said Griffith Jones to be the last Will & Testament in the presents of us after the word (of my sister Jone) in the second line of this side was underlined H Graham Saml. Powell William Jones

Philadelphia the 27 of October 1712 Then personally appeared Hugh Graham Samuell Powell & William Jones the three Witnesses to the within written Will who on their solemn affirmation according to law did declare they saw the testator Griffith Jones sign seal publish & declare the Within Writing to be the last will & testament & that at the doing thereof he was of sound & disposing mind & memory to the best of their knowledge. Corum. Benjamin Mayne Reg. Genl.

Be it remembred that on the 27th of 8ber 1712 The Last Will & Testament of Griffith Jones deced. was proved in due form of law & probate & letters' of Administration was granted to Joseph Jones Sole Executor therein named being first attested well & truely to administer & to bring an inventory of the deced. Estate into the Reg. Gen. office at Philada. on or before the   & also to rendr. auo. when required given undr. the seal of the sd. office. Benj. Mayne Reg. Gen.

* *

DAVID JONES, of Ciltalgarth, parish of Llanford, county Merioneth; son of John David, was referred to earlier as he seemed to have been related to Griffith John and closely connected with the early Quaker Welsh settlers. He and his wife and two children came over about 1699 and settled on their purchase of 350 acres in Blockley Township at Haverford Road and 63d Street. He was a Friend.

A land warrant issued by Penn on 19. 12mo. 1700/1, stated

DAVID JONES, of Ciltalgarth, parish of Llanford, county Merioneth; son of John David, was referred to earlier as he seemed to have been related to Griffith John and closely connected with the early Quaker Welsh settlers. He and his wife and two children came over about 1699 and settled on their purchase of 350 acres in Blockley Township at Haverford Road and 63d Street. He was a Friend.

A land warrant issued by Penn on 19. 12mo. 1700/1, stated

"Warrant to survey unto David Jones, late of Merionethshire, 250 acres of my land on the west side of Schuylkill within the bounds of the liberties of Phila., to be bounded to the eastward with the land seated to Hugh Roberts, to the northward with William Edwards, to the south'd with the line of William Warner, and to westward with my vacant land, reserving 50 acres on the northeast corner, adjoining to Jonathan Wynne and Hugh Roberts."

They brought certificate from the Monthly Meeting at Hendri Mawr, dated 24. 12mo. 1699/00, signed by Robert Vaughan, Cadwalader Ellis, Evan Rees, Thomas Richards, Rowland Owen, Edward David, Owen Lewis, Thomas Cadwalader and John Robert. This was from the same meeting place as those who signed Griffith John's Certificate. David John also had certificate from the men's meeting in Haverford West, dated 4. 1mo. 1699/00, and among signers were Andrew Llewellyn, James Lewis, Peregrine Musgrave, Evan Bowen and John Roger. Records of the Haverford Monthly Meeting show he was one of the first persons appointed an Elder in the Haverford Meeting. He died 27. 6mo. 1725, and was buried at Merion Meeting House.

David Jones had sister named Ellin, who married Robert John, son of John ap Thomas of Company No. 1. In his will he mentioned brothers John Jones and Robert Jones. They probably were brothers-in-law.

David's wife was Katherine, daughter of James Lewis, of Llandewi Velfrey, S. W.; whom he married in 1693. Katherine was an active member of the Haverford Monthly Meeting, being "an inspector of conversation," and a "visitor," and represented Haverford in the Quarterly Meeting. Katherine appears from the minutes of the Haverford Monthly Meeting to have been 'called into active service in the Meeting almost immediately after arrival in this country.' After David's death, she moved to the Philadelphia Monthly meeting, with certificate from the Radnor Monthly Meeting. She died 23. 5mo. 1764. Their Bible, "printed yn Llundian," 1678, records the births of James Lewis, on 8th mo. 10th, 1638, and "Katerin Lewis, ye 25th of 12th month 1640." They may have been Katherine's parents, as she had a brother James Lewis, of Llanddewy, known from letters she had.

Children of David and Katherine [two born in Wales]:
1. JAMES JONES, eldest son, b. 5mo. 31, 1699; m. Hannah Hayes at Haverford Meeting 10th 8mo. 1727 and had son Isaac; d. 27th of 3mo. 1791, aged 92 years.

SUSANNAH JONES. Living 16 Jul 1725, named in will.

Did not find any definite information regarding these children, other than
listed above.

* *

WILL OF DAVID JONES of Blockley:
[Book D, Phila., pp. 146-147.]

"I, David Jones of Blockley in the County of Philadelphia in the Province of
Pensilvania, yeoman, Considering the uncertainty of my time in this world,
Do Dispose of what has pleased God to Bestow on me in maner and form
following Viz first I will all my debts and funerall Charges be paid and
Discharged Also I give Devise & Bequeath unto my Eldest Son James one
Hundred acrs of Land Including the Messuage bought of John Warner To be
Laid out Regular out of that side of my tract situate next to Warners Land to
have and to Hold to him his heirs & assigns forever conveying to my
Daughter Susanah the Sum of tenn pounds within one year from my
Decease and the Sum of Tenn pounds to my Son Isaac within two years
after my decease Also the Sum of Tenn pounds to my Daughter Ellin within
four years after my Decease Also I Give Devise and Bequeath my Dwelling
House the rest of my Land and Plantation & Apurtenances Together with
the proffits thereof to my well beloved wife for the maintenance of her self
and our youngest children for the space of two years and it is my will and
mind that my son Lewis assist his mother to manage the same during the
time aforesd. and after the Expiration of the sd. Two years I give Devise and
Bequeath unto my sd. son Lewis my Dwelling House plantation &
apurtenances aforesd. by estimation one Hundred & ninety acrs or
hereabouts be the same more or Less To Have and to Hold to him & to his
Heirs for ever allways Reserving unto my well beloved wife one half of all
the premises and the proffitts thereof during the term of her naturall Life
and after the Decease of my well beloved wife My will is that my Son
Lewis pay to my Son Jacob the Sum of fiffteen pounds within one year after
his mothers Decease or after that moity of the Land The Holds Comes to
him, And to my children John, Isaac, David, Susanah, Ellin the Sum of Six
pound Each within two years after the time aforesd. Also I give one Loome
with the Appurtenances to my Son John. All the Rest and Residue of my
Estate goods cattel and chattels whatsoever I give and bequeath one third
thereof to my well beloved wife and the other two thirds to be Equally
Divided between my children John, Susanah, David, Isaac, Ellin & Jacob
Share & Share alike. And do nominate and appoint my well beloved wife
Katherine & my son Lewis to be Joynt executrs of this my Last will &
testament & do Revoake & Declare void all other wills & Testaments by me
made and do nominate and Appoint <u>my Brethen John Jones & Robt Jones</u> &
my freinds Robt Robts and Edward William to be Overseers to see this my
will pformed. and to assist my wife to advise and settle my children to

Divided between my children John, Susanah, David, Isaac, Ellin & Jacob Share & Share alike. And do nominate and appoint my well beloved wife Katherine & my son Lewis to be Joynt executrs of this my Last will & testament & do Revoake & Declare void all other wills & Testaments by me made and do nominate and Appoint <u>my Brethen John Jones & Robt Jones</u> & my freinds Robt Robts and Edward William to be Overseers to see this my will pformed. and to assist my wife to advise and settle my children to trades or otherwise and to take care of what belongs to my children that are under age. In Witness whereof I have hereunto to this my Last will & Testament put my hand & Seal the Sixteenth day of the fifth month anno dmi. 1725. David Jones [Seal] Signed Sealed published acknowledged & delivered by the Testator in the presence of John Coppock, George Plim, Ed Williams, Robt. Jones.

Philada. 22d. Septbr. 1725. Then personally appeared Edward Williams & Robert Jones two of the Witnesses to the aforegoing Will and upon their Solemn affirmations according to Law did Declare they saw & heard David Jones the Testator therein named Sign seal publish & declare the same to be his Last Will & Testamt. And that at the Doing thereof he was of Sound mind Memory & Understanding to the best of their Knowledge. Coram Moore Registr.

Be it remembered that on the 22d day of 7br 1725 the Last Will and Testament of David Jones deced was proved in due form of Law and probate & Letters Testamentary were Granted unto Katherine Jones & Lewis Jones Joynt Executors therein named being first Solemnly affirmed well and truly to administer the sd. deced. estate and bring an Inventory thereof unto the Register General's Office at Philadelphia at or before the 22nd day of Decbr. next and also to render an Accot. when thereunto lawfully required Given under the Seal of the said office. Moore Register."

* *

His Pedigree was shown on p. 40 of "Welsh Founders of Pa." by Glenn, Pedigree III. It was short, and just had "John" and his son David ap John, of Ciltalgarth, Taxed in the parish of Llanfor 1636. Then John David, of Ciltalgarth, living 16 May 1675. He joined Society of Friends. John David had David John, of Ciltalgarth, who married Katherine, dau of James Lewis of Llanddewi, So. Wales. They moved to Pa. ca 1699, and purchased land in Blockley Township. Will proved 22 Sept. 1725; Will Book D, Folio 430, Phila.

Siblings of David John of Ciltalgarth were:

(1) JOHN JONES, , of Ciltalgarth, parish of Llanfor, county
Mererioneth.; s. John ap David, of same place, gentleman. He was a Friend when he came over. Came to Pa. abt 1700; liv. 16 Jul 1725.

later it was called "Great Valley." It was organized abt 1707. The tax list for 1715 had these Welsh land owners: Thomas Jarman, Sr. and Jr., Stephen Evans, Rowland Richard, Griffith John, John Roberts, James David, Margaret Walters, John David, John David Howell, Thomas Rees, Owen Gethen, John David Griffith, Llewellyn David, James Parry, Henry John, David Evan, Thomas David, Thomas Martin, Thomas Godfrey, Thomas Hubbert, and Lewis Walker. Non resident land owners included Benjamin Davies, Mordecai Moore and William Evans.

Among the landowners in the Great Valley in 1722: James Abraham, Morris David, Hugh David, James David, Sr., John David, Henry David, Thomas David, James Davies, William Davies, Timothy Davies, Stephen Evans, Lewis Evans, William Evans, John Howell, Griffith Jones, Sr. and Jr., Thomas Jermon, Thomas James, Jenkin Lewis, James Parry, John Robert, Thomas Martin, Thomas Godfrey, Samuel Richard, John Richard, etc. Griffith John was Constable between 1707-1758. Among earliest road supervisors: David John.[16]

Clark E. John wrote about the John family of Griffith John and Samuel John who arrived in 1709, who were sons of John Phillip John ["History & Family Record of the John Family 1683 to 1964."]. They lived in Chester Co. The Binkley papers by Georgiana Holland Binkley also cover these, and both are available on microfilm at The Family History Centers of the Mormon Churches.

Several records regarding a Griffith John of Great Valley state he arrived either in 1710 or 1712. He was the Baptist minister, Rev. Griffith John who died around 1723. He had son Griffith Jr. See later. There were two other Griffith John's associated with the Great Valley Baptist Church in the early 1700's.

Some other settlers listed by author Glenn in "Merion In The Welsh Tract" with Jones name:

CADWALADER JONES, of parish of Llanfor, Merioneth Co.; son of John _____ (d. before 1698), and Ellin, daughter of Evan Lloyd Evan of Ucheldre. Moved to Pa. 1698. Died at sea on voyage. Wife: _____ Jones (b. in Wales). Children (surname Jones): 1. Robert; 2. _____; 3. _____. Brought up in Gwynedd.

ANN JONES, of Carmarthen Co., widow. Came to Pa. in 1684 with daughter Ann Jones.

CADWALADER JONES; son of John _____. Came to Pa. abt 1700. D. in Uwchllan, county of Chester, Pa. 1758. Wife: _____. Children: 1. Evan (Jones); 2. Rebecca, m. John Thomas; 3. Cadwalader; 4. _____, m. _____

---

[16]Welsh Settlement of Pensylvania, by Charles Browning, p. 491, Reprinted 1967, Gen. Publ. Co.

Pugh. Cadwalader Jones, Sr. had a sister Gwen John, liv. 1758. [This might have been the John's related to Griffith John of Merion.]

GRIFFITH JOHN, of Pembroke County, b. 1683; son of John Phillips and Ellen. Came to Chester Co., Pa. 1709. Friend. Freeholder of abt 100 acres in Chester Co. Died 1778. Wife: Ann, daughter of Robert and Gwen Williams. [Mentioned above.]

MARGARET JOHN, of parish of Llangelynin, Merioneth Co.., widow. Moved to Pa. 1683. Friend.

MARGARET JOHN, sister to one William John (not of Gwynedd), who having no issue, bequeathed her his land. She probably came to Pa. after 1700. Her will proved at Phila.

WILLIAM JOHN, of North Wales [Phila. Co.] Came to Pa. probably after 1700, and acquired land, which, dying without issue, he left to sister Margaret John, who died in Pa. per will.

CADWALADER JONES, of parish of Llanfor, Merioneth Co., yeoman; son of John Jones, of same place, decd. Came to Gwynedd, Pa. before 1719. Wife: Martha, daughter of David Thomas of Radnor, Pa.; m. 1719.

DAVID JONES, of near Haverfordwest, Pembroke Co., husbandman. Came to Pa. 1699-1700. Friend.

EDWARD JONES, of parish of St. Harmon, Radnor Co., gentleman. Had deed, dated 1682 for 250 acres land surveyed to him in Radnor. Sold his rights by deed executed in Wales to James Morgan, and probably did not move to Pa. per Glenn. However, an entry in the shipping records for the "Morning Star" listed several items shipped by Edward Jones. A lot was surveyed at the corner of Fifth and Chestnut for Edward Jones, also.

ELIZABETH JONES, of Blackpool, Montgomeryshire Co., spinster, daughter of David Jones, of same place. Moved to Pa. "with the consent of her parents," 1699. Friend.

ELLIS JONES, of parish of Nantmell, Radnor, weaver. Moved to Radnor, Pa. abt 1685. Church of England. Freeholder of 100 acres in Radnor, that he sold to William David, who resold to John Morgan. Was living in Merion 1696.

EVAN JONES, of parish of Llanfihangel, Merioneth, yeoman; son of John Pugh, of same place. Came to Pa. before 1712. Friend. Wife: Hannah, daughter of Hugh David of Gwynedd. M. 1712.

EVAN JONES, of Llaithgwm, parish of Llandderfel (now in Llanfor), Merioneth Co.; son of John Thomas of Llaithgwm, gentleman. Came to Merion, Pa. 1683. Friend. Died young, 1697, unmarried.

EVAN JONES, of near Dolgelley, Merioneth Co., yeoman; but not a native of that country. Came to Pa. about 1683. (Certif. undated). Friend. Wife: Hannah _____. Her mother was Mary Ellis of Dolgelley.

FLORENCE JONES, of Glamorgan. Co., a kinswoman of John Bevan. Came to Pa. probably 1683. Married Lewis David of Radnor, Pa.

EVAN JONES, of Llaithgwm, parish of Llandderfel (now in Llanfor), Merioneth Co.; son of John Thomas of Llaithgwm, gentleman. Came to Merion, Pa. 1683. Friend. Died young, 1697, unmarried.

EVAN JONES, of near Dolgelley, Merioneth Co., yeoman; but not a native of that country. Came to Pa. about 1683. (Certif. undated). Friend. Wife: Hannah _____. Her mother was Mary Ellis of Dolgelley.

FLORENCE JONES, of Glamorgan. Co., a kinswoman of John Bevan. Came to Pa. probably 1683. Married Lewis David of Radnor, Pa.

FRANCIS JONES, of near Redstone, Pembroke Co., husbandman. Came to Pa. 1711.

HENRY JONES, probably of South Wales. Came to Pa. before 1700. Had warrant for 500 acres to be surveyed in Welsh tract. [Possible connection: Rachel Jones, widow of Henry Jones of Phila., merchant, decsd., died intestate and administration of her estate was granted 6th of June 1700 to her son John Jones. [Adm. Book A, p. 324, Phila.] In an account of Philip Alford or Oxford, p. 50, "Passengers & Ships..." by Sheppard, he stated Alford m. 8 Dec 1686 Sarah Jones, dau of Henry Jones of Moyamensing (Davis, Bucks Co., 163.) Probably the Henry Jones whose will showed he was a Baptist.

HUGH JONES, probably of Bala, Merioneth Co., husbandman. Came to Merion, Pa. abt 1700. Freeholder near Bryn Mawr, Merion. Wife: _____
_____. Children: (surname Jones) 1. Hugh, b. 1705; owner of farm now called "Brookfield," north of Bryn Mawr; and probably others.

MARGARET JONES, of Holywell, Flint. Co., aged 16 yrs. Transported to America to serve 7 yrs., 1706. No crime, but without support. Cleared for Bohemia River. Had relatives in Pa.; probably kinswoman to Dr. Thomas Wynne or to Richard Thomas of Whitford, these places being adjacent to Holywell.

PETER JONES. Resident in Merion 1696, and a man of considerable means.

ROBERT JONES, supposedly brother of Hugh Jones, and uncle of Hugh Jones of "Brookfield." Came to Merion, Pa. abt 1700. Lived with Hugh Jones near Rowland Ellis's home.

ROBERT JONES. "Was in Merion and Gwynedd, abt 1690 to 1700, and his signature indicated he was not identical with any of the others of the name mentioned."

ROBERT JONES, b. 1690, of Denb. Co., yeoman. Came to Gwynedd, Pa., abt 1710. Died 1773. Wife: Ann Coulston; m. 1717; d. 1772. Children:
1. WILLIAM.
2. MARGARET.
3. ANN, m. Jacob Bell.
4. ELIZABETH.
5. ROBERT.
6. JOSIAH.

Was maid in family of Edward Roberts, and afterwards in that of Thomas Jones of Merion, 1708, and was related to both families. "It was then the custom to take poor relations as servants."

THOMAS JONES SR., was living in Merion 1696. Not same person as son of John Thomas, and was evidently a man of property.

THOMAS JONES, living in Merion abt 1700; perhaps son of Thomas Sr. of Merion 1696. Moved from Merion to Cheltenham. Probably same person who married Catherine Arrets.

JOHN THOMAS, of parish of Llanwddyn, Montg. Co.; son of Thomas Morris, of same place. Came to Pa. abt 1708. Living in 1723. Children probably assumed the surname of Jones.

* *

LEWIS' of interest in Philadelphia area:

RALPH LEWIS, of Eglwysilan; wife, Mary. Eventually John Bevan, who was a relative, bought back lands taken up by Ralph Lewis, [as well as 200 acres he had sold to John Richard, and the 250 acres in Haverford which he had sold to Katherine and Elizabeth Prichard of this group.] Ralph Lewis sold part of his 250 acres to David Lewis, who appears to have been his son or nephew. Purchased 250 acres from Owen Thomas 15. 11mo. 1701. Will of Hugh David of Haverford, signed 27 Apr 1709, named among overseers father-in-law Ralph Lewis, cousins David Lewis and William Lewis, and Lewis David.

WILLIAM LEWIS, of Eglwysilan, parish of Llantrisant, Glam. Co., brother of Ralph Lewis, arrived in Philadelphia 11. 5mo. 1686. Friend. Purchased plantation of 120 acres adjoining his brother Ralph's land, but which had been a portion of Lewis David tract of 3,000 acres. Browning described this as located in Haverford south of settlement of Wynnewood, near old Haverford Road. He bought 50 more acres in Radnor and in 1698, purchased 300 acres in New Town township, Chester Co. He d. 1707/8. His will was proved 12 Mar 1707/8. Wife Ann, children: 1. David, m. 1695, Ann Jones of Merion; 2. Lewis, m. Mary Howell, of Bristol; 3. Evan, m. Mary Hayes; 4. William, m. 1704 Gwen, dau of William John of Gwynedd; and 5. Nathan Lewis. [Coat of arms given on p. 190, Welsh Founders of Pa.]

CHAPTER FOUR

BAPTISTS IN PENNSYLVANIA & DELAWARE.

Establishment of Churches:

A few Protestants other than Quakers left Wales for Pennsylvania in the 1680's. Early records of the Presbyterian Church in Pennsylvania[1] refer to the Presbyterian congregation in the Great Valley (Chester County) as being made up of Welsh. Non-Quaker Welsh religious meetings were held in Davis' Queen's Head tavern on Water Street in Philadelphia, where they were conducted in the Welsh tongue.[2]

English religious refugees had settlements about the same time as the Welsh in Penn's colony in the New World. Scharf wrote in his History of Delaware, Vol. II, of the different clothes the Quakers and Baptists wore, as compared to the English. But he stated this: "From Wales, however, the Thomases, Rees, and Griffiths came, with red, freckled faces, shaggy beards and pedigrees dating back to Adam."

John Holm[e]s, a Baptist and very prominent Englishman who was Judge of Salem court when he died, arrived in 1691 and settled in the neighborhood where the Philadelphia Baptist Church was later located. The records of the Pennepek Church have the birth dates of his children. Some others were John Farmer and his wife, Joseph Todd and Rebecka Woolencroft. Early ministers were John Rumsey, Samuel Jones, Thomas Killingsworth, Elias Keach, John Watts, Joseph Wood, and Evan Morgan. Howen [Howell] [E]mannuel was baptized by Joseph Wood in 1697.

There were not enough of either Baptists or Presbyterians to make up a regular congregation with a minister at this early date, so the two shared ministers. John Watts, who was a taxpayer in New Castle Co., was a Baptist minister and preached every other week to a combined group in Philadelphia until 1698. They held their services at a storehouse in a place called Barbados Lot, which had originally been used by the Barbados Company. This was the corner of Second Street and Chestnut Street. The Presbyterians had a minister named Jedediah Andrews, whom the Baptist maintain drove them out.

At any rate, the churches then had a "misunderstanding" and the Baptists withdrew and worshipped in the brewhouse of Anthony Morris, located near the drawbridge. They continued there until they were invited by the Keithian Quakers to meet with them at Second Street in a small wooden building erected in 1692. During the Keithian controversy[3], many left the Quaker religion. Many Keithian Quakers later became Keithian Baptists.

---

[1]Presbyterians in Colonial Pa., by Guy Souilliard Klett, University of Pa. Press, 1937.
[2]Welsh Settlement of Pensylvania, by Browning, Heritage Books, p. 308.
[3]George Keith was leader of a controversy within the Quaker Church, which led to their setting up separate places of worship in 1691.

Quaker religion. Many Keithian Quakers later became Keithian Baptists.

There is a Baptist Church record of "Baptist Church Lower Duplin Twp 1689 to 1763." The records are of 'Pennepek' and Philadelphia Churches. Pennepek was also located in Philadelphia County. Many of the Quakers had land surveyed in Chester County, now Delaware County, and this was also referred to as the Welsh Tract. The Welsh called this area "Goshen." West Chester grew out of "Goshen." The early church records extant for Pennepek[4] and Philadelphia are somewhat faded and blurred, too much so for some parts to be deciphered.

The records of the Baptist Association have the dates of churches organized in the general area. Others in the Philadelphia area were Piscataway, organized in 1686; Pembroke in Philadelphia in 1687; and Pennepek in 1689.

The Lower Duplin church records give Baptism dates of families of Watts, Griffiths, Samuel Jones ("Baptized by Hen. Gregory 1683 [or '88,] dyed 1722"), Masons, Miles, Bibbs, Harts, Holmes, Waters, Eatons, and other families. Henry Gregory, Samuel Jones, John Watts, John Hart, Elias Keach, Thomas Killingsworth, Evan Morgan, and Thomas Griffith are given as doing the baptizing. Nothing was given of the parents of this Samuel Jones who was then in Philadelphia.

'Joseph Wood Baptized by Elias Keach in Burlington. 4.14.1691,' was found in these records, and Joseph Wood later was shown to have baptized others. He was the son of William Wood, a Quaker who was co-purchaser with William Shardlow of 5,000 acres. He came in 1683 on the "Jeffrey" from London. William Woods' wife was Susanna, and his children were Joseph, John, Jonathan and Susanna.[5]

Katharine, wife of John ap Thomas, of the first Quaker Company to arrive in Pennsylvania, purchased the 500 acre tract of land called "Glanrason" from Joseph Wood in 1689. He witnessed a deed in New Castle Co. with Griffith Jones 1 June 1702/ 03. Joseph Wood[6] was also a merchant as well as a speculator in land and a Baptist minister. There were indentures (in deeds) regarding him and John Jones, innkeeper, whom it appears was bound for certain sums of money, possibly for merchandise for his business.

There were two John Jones' listed with Penn's First Purchasers. One John Jones was a linen draper from Bristol who purchased 1,000 acres jointly with Michael Jones of Bristol. Another John Jones was of the Parish of St. Andrews, Holbourne, London. He was a Glover, and a First

---

[4]This was spelled Pennepek, Pennypack, and several ways in the records.
[5]Chester Court Records, 122, 230. For administration of estate, see PGM, XIX, 256, Administration Book A, 93, #99:1689.
[6]His parents were William Wood & Susanna Wood, of Darby, Chester Co. Wm. died intestate, eldest son Joseph of Mt. Wood appointed Executor 4 9mo. 1689. Phila. Adm. Book A, p. 93.

Purchaser of 500 acres. He took a patent out for his 500 acres in Philadelphia Co. This assured his ownership.

A John Jones had goods on the "Bristol Factor," [Roger Drew, Master] when she made her second trip to Pennsylvania and Virginia, arriving in October 1682. She was the first ship to sail to Pennsylvania carrying William Penn's colonists. She sailed from Bristol about the middle of October 1681 and arrived in New Castle 15 December 1681. Since he had goods on this ship, this John Jones was probably the one who was an Innkeeper.[7]

Griffith Jones who was a merchant in Philadelphia arrived on the "Amity" in August 1682 from London. He owned a wharf lot and might have been the owner of the property where the Baptists had their house of worship. He came over with the Quakers, but he seemed to have a lot of interaction with Joseph Wood and the Welsh who were Baptists. He was a witness with Joseph Wood on several documents, and probably the deed mentioned above. One of the deeds he witnessed:

New Castle Co. Deed Book B, Vol. 1, P. 151. John Moll of Bohemia River in Prov. of Md...sum paid by John Donaldson of Township of New Castle, 18 Aug 1697. Wit. Griffith Jones & Englethorp Empson.
* *

WELSH TRACT or Gwynned in Pa.:

In addition to the Quaker Welsh Tracts of Merion and Goshen, there was another Welsh Tract in Pennsylvania that consisted mainly of people who were Baptists. This was a large tract of land located in the upper part of old Philadelphia County. The first Welsh there were from North Wales, and afterwards the area in Pennsylvania was known as "North Wales" and the "Gwynedd Settlement." Some records state that the first Baptists arrived in this area in 1698, due to the influence of Robert Turner, the Irish Quaker minister, who was in Wales in 1697. They settled on land purchased from Robert Turner. However, other records indicate there were Baptists in the general area as early as 1686 who worshiped at the churches called Pennepek and Philadelphia.

Robert Turner, a merchant, was a Quaker from Dublin, Ireland who had been severely mistreated there for his religious beliefs. Possibly because of his real estate ventures, Turner was a wealthy man by 1683. When he arrived in Philadelphia on the "Lion" of Liverpool on 14th of 8mo. 1683, he had with him his daughter Martha and seventeen servants.[8]

In 1675, he and Robert Zane and other friends from Dublin were grantees for tracts of West Jersey land purchased from Friend Byllings and

---

[7]Sheppard, Jr., Passengers and Ships Prior to 1684... pp. 30, 56.
[8]Arrivals in Phila. in Pa. Magazine Historical & Biographical, VIII, 304.

they started a settlement of English speaking people there.[9] This settlement gave Penn the idea for a similar settlement.

Turner increased his land purchases by obtaining 10,000 acres in Pennsylvania. Penn confirmed 7,800 acres to him that was laid out in Philadelphia County. Turner sold this acreage to William John and Thomas Evan of Philadelphia 10. 1mo. 1698/9. They in turn sold this land to others, but retained some for themselves. The land was resurveyed as ordered on 25. 11mo. 1702. The 7,800 acres was found to contain an "overplusage" of 11,436 acres! This was said to have shown the inefficiency of the surveyors. These Welsh grantees, heirs, etc. were allowed to purchase 2,846 acres of the overage, and set up a payment schedule to Penn.

The record showing the purchasers, their acreage and overage was as follows:

	Acres	Overage
Ellis, or Da'd Pugh.	220	231
Evan Hugh.	100	110
John Hugh.	500	648
John Humphrey.	450	561
Rob't ap Evan	5,005	1,034
Edward Faulk.	400	712
Robert Jones.	500	720
Robert Evan	200	250
Evan ap Hugh.*	400	1,068
David Pugh.*	200	
Edward Pugh.*	100	
Cadwall'dr ap Evan.	500	609
Owen ap Evan	400	538
Rob't ap Hugh	200	232
William John	1,900	2,866
Thomas Evan	700	1,049
William John	150	322
Evan Robert	100	110
Hugh Griffith	200	376

* "(Brothers, Evan holds all, other two dead.)"

By the end of the year of 1698, these purchasers began to move onto their land in "North Wales." William John and Robert John of Philadelphia Co. [brothers of Griffith John] and Thomas Evan were already settled in Philadelphia Co., but moved to this area. Hugh Griffith was the son of Griffith John. They had ties with the Quakers, either through membership or marriages. Some of their descendants became Baptists.

---

[9]Welsh Settlement of Pensylvania, by Browning, Heritage, p. 266.

Many second and third generation descendants of Welsh Quakers joined other churches. The counties of Kent, Sussex and New Castle were first referred to as the "lower counties" or "territories" of the Province of Pennsylvania. After much wrangling with Maryland, these counties were annexed to the province in 1682.

When William Penn arrived on the "Welcome" in 1682, he stopped first in New Castle Co. on 27 October and visited with some of the people there. Then he re-boarded the ship, which docked at Upland the next day, at what is now Chester, Pa. At that time, most of the settlers in the New Castle area were Swedes.

On 14 June 1683, Penn issued orders to all the old settlers who had not yet received deeds to their land but only had the surveyor's certificate to make their survey, to send these certificates in and to take out deeds for their land.[10] Those who sent in their certificates never received them back again, and when they filed for new surveys and deeds, they were charged higher prices.

Large tracts of flood land that were marshy and sometimes covered by water had not been filed on, but were in use as commons. Penn later took these and sold them to others. Most of those affected were the Swedes, but others also received the same treatment. Needless to say, these people never thought highly of William Penn.

An interesting geologic feature was Cypress Swamp, located in the southern line between Delaware and Maryland, and lying in both states. The remains of huge trees, mostly cypress, were sunk under water. The description given by Thomas Scharf in the "History of Delaware," p. 2, reminded me of Reel Foot Lake in Tennessee, a sunken lake caused by the Great Earthquakes of 1811/12. The Johns Family Reunion has been held near Reel Foot Lake for the past seventy years.
* *

NEW CASTLE COUNTY:

An Assessment made in New Castle County in 1693 showed these inhabitants: George Moor[e], John Watts, Peter Alrichs, Sigfrydus Alrichs, Hermanus Alrichs, another Hermanus Alrichs, John Ogle, Joseph Moor[e], Thomas Moor[e], Valentine Hollin[g]sworth, Thomas Hollin[g]sworth, Thomas Jones, Henry Hollin[g]sworth, Hans Hanson, and Casparus Herman.

This Thomas Jones was of Brandywine Hundred and had a wife named Margaret. Many of his neighbors such as the Hollingsworth's and Moore's later went to Virginia, then North Carolina. Jones' children probably went also.

---

[10]Biography & Gen. History of the State of Del., Vol. 1, 1899. Publishers: J.M. Runk & Co., Chambersburg, Pa.

Edward Lillington was Collector for the town of New Castle and Christiana Creek in 1696/7. Others mentioned in the 1696/7 Assessment were Francis Land, Thomas Bedford, Nathaniel Morgan, Edward Land and "Widdow Samples' Estate."

Lord Baltimore of Maryland did several things to stir up trouble between the lower counties and the Province. Jealousies and other factors also entered into the situation. In one controversy in 1690 regarding the way the officials in the lower counties performed their duties, six Council members from Pennsylvania appointed and commissioned judges without the knowledge and consent of the other members of the Council.

The six members of the Council were William Clark, Luke Watson, Griffith Jones, John Brinkloe, John Cann* and Johannes D'Haes. When the other Council members found out this was done, they declared it illegal and reprimanded the six who did this.[11]

*John Cann was listed as a passenger on the ship "Griffin" which transported the first English colonists to New Jersey in the present site of the city of Salem 5 Oct 1675. (Sheppard's Passengers and Ships..., p. 137.)

Scharf wrote John Evans arrived in 1703 with commission from Penn as Lt.-Governor. A large faction wanted the lower counties to be separated from Pennsylvania. Gov. Evans tried to resolve the differences and held meetings with the concerned parties.

After a series of conflicts, these counties seceded from the Province in 1704. They were governed by their own separate Assembly consisting of representatives from the three counties, but still acknowledging the authority of the Provincial Governor of Pennsylvania.

During the summer of 1704 Gov. Evans had a lot of trouble with the Quakers because of their pacifist views against bearing arms. He tried to organize a militia for their protection on account of the war then occurring between England and France and Spain, but was only able to organize three companies from New Castle Co., two in Kent and two in Sussex. He then tried to frighten the people into taking up arms by telling them there was an impending danger of being attacked by hostile vessels that had come up the bay. This was a fabrication that became known to the people, and caused an intense dislike of the Governor.

Later, in November 1704, the Assembly of the Lower Counties authorized the erection of a fort at New Castle for Her Majesty's service. A duty was proposed on each vessel and the commander was to go ashore to get a pass before continuing. This angered the people in Philadelphia as it infringed on their freedom to travel as well as being a tax. Nevertheless this

---

[11]Scharf, History of Delaware, Vol. I, p. 124.

passed, but a provision regarding vessels owned on the river and bay was omitted.

The fort was erected in the winter of 1707. Richard Hill of Philadelphia decided to test the 1704 law and did not stop at the fort for a pass when he left for a voyage to the Barbados. He took with him Samuel Preston and Isaac Norris who were part owners of the vessel. They passed the fort safely although under fire. John French, the commander of the fort, took off after them in a boat, and they let him aboard. However, he was then taken prisoner. They delivered him to Lord Cornbury, the vice-admiral of the Queen's fleet at Salem.

The people objected to the infringements on their liberties by the measure, although they did not object to the fort per se. After protests and meetings with the citizens, the Governor promised a suspension of the objectionable features of the act. The people disliked Governor Evans and complained.

Evans was replaced by Charles Gookin in 1708. Evans had just purchased a farm at Swanhook near New Castle, and was indignant at his removal.

In 1709, some of the most prominent men of the territory sent an address to the Lords of Trade and Plantations, managers of all the British colonies, complaining about Penn's management of the three counties on the Delaware. Their leader was Jasper Yeates. The complaint was signed by nine members of the Assembly that included James Coutts, Jasper Yeates, Richard Halliwell and Robert French. Yeates wanted to make New Castle the capital of a new Province consisting of the three lower counties. But nothing happened regarding this. At this time, the estimated population of each county was from one hundred to a hundred and twenty families, not enough for an independent colony.

William Keith succeeded Charles Gookin as Governor in 1717.

There is a "Day Book" left by a blacksmith, Ellis Robert, whose little shop was located on an abandoned road near Norristown [mentioned in 1912 by Charles Browning in "Welsh Founders..."] which was a short cut between the two Welsh settlements of Merion and Goshen. It lists work that Ellis Robert did for the people from both communities. In [1703] 5th month next, "For soying with Griffith Jones 12 hundred of Oak & Poplar, L1, 15s. 6d." "ye 18th day of ye 3 month, 1703, Cadwalader Jones dr. for 2 days' work, 3s. 4d."

Other customers from this time up to 1705 were Richard Pugh, Edward Jarman, John Williamson, Thomas Craffot, Samuel Brockes , Jacob Cofing, Hernell Cassel, John Good, Morris Roberts, the widow Clancy, John Michinar, Richard Blackham, Matthew Jones, David Hughes, John Meredith, Evan Griffith, William Thomas, John Welles, William Robert Ellis, Thomas Griffith, Rowland Richard, John Morgan, Thomas David, of the Valley, John Evans, John Roberts, David Howel, Thomas Louis, John

David Thomas, David Harvey Rees, William Thomas Hugh, Robert Williamson of Goshen[12], Edward Watkin, John Davis of ye Gule, and John Cadwalader.

* *

WELSH TRACT BAPTIST CHURCH:

In 1701, a group of members of the churches of Jesus Christ in the counties of Pembroke and Carmarthen, South Wales, decided to move to Pennsylvania. This group consisted of sixteen persons with a minister, considered a sufficient number to form themselves into a church. They obtained commendatory letters from their churches, and determined to set out to the new land.

These sixteen church members were: Thomas Griffith "minister"; Griffith Nicolas*; Evan Edmond; John Edward; Elizeus (Elisha) Thomas; Enoch Morgan; Righart (Richard) David; Elizabeth Griffith: Lewis Edmond; Mary John**; Mary Thomas; Elizabeth Griffith; Shonnet (Jennet) David; Margaret Matheas; Shonnet (Jennet) Morris; and James David.[13] The group of church members consisted of nine men and seven women. Others came with them who were not church members. Most were related, as was the case with most of these groups.

*Griffith Nicholas, as well as Mary Griffith, Mary Evan, Thomas John and Jane his wife, all of Landilo Parish were listed in the Rhydwilim [Wales] records in 1689.

**The Rhydwilim records have a Mary Jones of Llanllwru who was a member in 1667. This might not be the same Mary, as married women used their father's name as their surname at this time. Two Mary John's were found in the Welsh Tract records, one was wife of Harry, and one was wife of Griffith.

A will in Book D, No. 300, for a Griffith John of Tredyfyn [Great Valley] in Chester County, proved Jan. 11, 1723, named wife Elizabeth, daughter Mary, granddaughter Christian David, daughter Prissile, 'her children from the body of Lewelin David,' daughter Martha, and son David John. Witnesses were Griffith John, John George and William Davis.* The church at Great Valley and the people there were very closely associated with the ones at the Welsh Tract Baptist Church. He was probably the Griffith John who arrived in 1710 from Rhydwilim and settled in the Great Valley of Chester Co. The witness Griffith John was probably his son Griffith Jr.

This Griffith who died would not be the Friend Griffith John who was son of John Phillip John, of Uwchlan Township, Chester Co., who was

---

[12]In Index to Surveys for New Castle Co., Del.: "Tract named "Goshen," New Castle O 2, #17, under Ogle, Thomas, Dec. 6, 1686. Near White Clay Creek; 222 acres."
[13]Records of the Welsh Tract Baptist Meeting, Pencader Hundred, New Castle County, Delaware, 1701 to 1828. The Historical Society of Delaware, Wilmington, 1904.

written about by Clark E. John of Long Beach in his book on The John Family.

*William Davies was husband of Ann Miles, daughter of James Miles. He was also probably the William Davies who was one of the people who received the grant for the 30,000 acres in the Welsh Tract of New Castle, Del.

This group of Baptists gathered at Milford-Haven, the shipping port. It was the month of June, and they sailed on a ship named "James and Mary." They landed in Philadelphia the 8th of September 1701. They were received "in a loving manner (on account of the gospel) by a group meeting in Philadelphia and Pennepek who held the same faith with us..."[14]

With this group of church members came their extended families. Many of their names were not found in the church records.

There is a scarcity of information on relationships. The church Minutes gave brief notes and names only. Relationships can mostly be gleaned from various deeds, wills, and public records, with few books written about them. Old shipping records are just beginning to be published.

During the year and a half after their arrival, the Baptists were able to add twenty members to their group who felt as they did:

(1701) Rees Ryddarch; (1702) Catharine Ryddarch; Easther Thomas; Thomas Morris; Hugh Morris; Peter Chamberlain; Mary Chamberlain, Junior; Mary Sorensee; Magdalen Morgan; Henry David; Elizabeth David; Samuel Griffiths; Richard Seruy; Rebecca Marpole; John Grinwater; Edward Edwards; John James; Mary Thomas; Thomas John; Judith Griffith; Mary John, Jun.; and Thomas Thomas.

The records here do not state when they were baptized. Some family researchers have written that Thomas John was husband of Mary John who was with the 1701 Church group, and Mary Jr. was their daughter, which appears possible.

However, the church records indicate only that Thomas and Mary Jr. joined the church during this period around 1702. It stated "Added to during the year and a half we abode at Pennepek." Among these names are some that were baptized at Pennepek or earlier in Wales, people known to have already been in this country for several years. Most were living in Radnor Township. The Pennepek records that are now too faded to read might have shed light on this.

With no proof otherwise, there must be shown the possibility of a Thomas John who was not husband of Mary John being the Thomas John who joined the Church in 1701/2. Among the possibilities would be Thomas John of Brandywine Creek, or the grandson of John Evans from Nantmele and then of Radnor, or the grandson of John Thomas Evan (the

---

[14]Ibid.

first Welshman who arrived). John Evans from Nantmele left a will[15] that mentioned Jane Jones' sons Rees Jones and Thomas Jones. Jane was probably his daughter, or daughter-in-law. His family was closely connected with the Miles and Morgan families. There are other possibilities.

Some of the records for these new members were found with the records of the Welsh and English Quakers who arrived earlier, showing they were not all newcomers from Wales. A Rhys Rydderch came in with Quaker Company No. 5 around 1683. He transferred 120 acres to William Lewis in 1692. William Lewis gave this land to his son David Lewis in 1701. The Baptist writers wrote that this Rhys Rydderch and his wife had recently arrived from Wales, and were quite elderly when they came over.

Griffith John and wife Margaret probably arrived with this first group. Records from the Parish of Mathery and Rhydwilm Church show a Griffith was baptized in 1700, and Margaret in 1701. This was probably the Griffith John who died intestate in 1719. Margaret, his wife, settled his estate. The record of this settlement was found. This did not provide much information, as he died intestate. Debts were settled to several people from this church.

There were other family members and close relations who arrived from Wales with this group who did not have their names in the Welsh Tract Minutes. It is possible Thomas John and his daughter Mary Jr. arrived with them.

The newly arrived Baptists were happy to find the Baptists in the area held the same faith as they, except the ones in Philadelphia did not believe in the ordinance of "laying-on-of hands on every particular member." Records show the newly arrived Welsh desired "very much" to hold communion with these people, but they believed they could not be in fellowship with them because of this difference in belief. They found some that believed as they did, but this was not preached or practiced in the Philadelphia church.

The Minutes state they kept themselves separate from these people, but met with them several times trying to resolve their differences. Morgan Edwards' records indicate most of them stayed near the Pennepek Church for the first year and a half. Their church records state they lived 'much scattered about for about a year and a half' and continued to hold their own weekly meetings in the homes of fellow members.

The Welsh Tract Baptist Church records indicate the church members, along with other Welsh, purchased a tract of land containing 30,000 acres the 15th day of October 1701 in New Castle County which was called Welshtract, later spelled "Welsh Tract." William Davies and David Evans, two of the three who made this purchase, seem to have been closely

---

[15]Proved by wife Deliah 22 Nov 1707 at Philadelphia.

associated with the Miles families. They received a land grant from William Penn to obtain land and settle as follows:

"Pensilvania]

William Penn Propr and Governr of the Province
of Pensilvania and Country annexed

At the Request of William Davies David Evans & William Willis on behalf of themselves and Company of new Welsh Purchasers That I would grant them to take at & in ye County of New Castle thirty thousand acres of Land or so much as there will be [Symbol] Beginning at a line distant w=/S s/w from Newcastle Seven Miles and from there extending Northwd and Southwd by streight lines at or near as may be sufficient to comprehend the said number of acres upon the terms already agreed on under their hands. These are to require thee forthwith to survey or cause to be surveyed to them the sd number of acres in the sd place and make particular Returns of the Subdivisions to each man under his proper name into any surveylance office. The whole to be laid out according to the method of Townships bef. me appointed. Given under my hand and seal at Phila. the 15th day of October 1701."

The larger portion of the Welsh Tract was located in Pencader Hundred, with the remainder in Cecil County, Md. The distinguishing feature of this land was the Iron Hill, known by that name as early as 1661. It was possibly because of this Iron Hill and the iron ore that this land was sought. Christiana Creek was the boundary of Chester (now Delaware) and New Castle Counties.

This grant was ordered by William Penn, and stated that subdivisions were to be laid out to various people and resurveys made of these. A 'resurvey' was necessary because it was now under the control of William Penn, and some of the land was settled before his arrival. [The date used on the individual grants stated that
"By Virtue of a warrant from the Proprietary and Governor dated the 15th of the 5th month 1701 for laying out unto Wm. David & David Evans 30,000 acres, etc."]

It was from this Company led by William Davis and David Evans that the Baptists purchased land in New Castle Co. William Davis appears to have been a member of the Presbyterian Church and lived in Chester Co. Before 1701 there were Welsh settlers already in New Castle Co., as well as English, Swede, and Germans. Thomas John and Margaret had already lived there for a number of years. Many of the Welsh who had land surveyed in this Welsh Tract did not belong to the Baptist religion.

After recording those who joined during the year and a half they were in the Pennepek area, this entry was made:

"After our removal down to New Castle County in the 1703 were added to the church by a letter from Wales:

Thomas John.

Rebecca John."

* *

LAND SURVEYS IN NEW CASTLE CO. RECORDS:

The first land survey found in the New Castle records to anyone surnamed John in New Castle Co. was to Thomas John and it was dated March 17, 1701/2. This stated:

"This may certifie into the Generall Survey:es office that I have surveyd and layd out of the aforesaid Tract unto Thomas John 632 a:140 perches this 17th day of March 1701/2 and being also a second purchaser from the first; Beginning att a corner marked dogwood sapling in the first Dividening Line, being also a Corner tree for Elisia Thomas, thence by his line west 610 perch to a corner marker black oake in the second Dividening Line being also a corner line for Elisia Thomas Land; then by the second Dividening Line south 166 to a now corner gum tree in the same line thence by an east line 610 perches to a new corner white oak in the first dividening line thence by the said line north 166 to the first mentioned dogwood and place of beginning; Survey'd and cut off from the whole Tract this day and year above written." George Dabeyns, Surveyor of New Castle County.

This survey also had a map showing Elisha Thomas' land lying side by side with the land of Thomas John. Since it was located near Elisha Thomas' land, this appears to be for the Thomas John who joined the Welsh Tract Church. Elisha Thomas was a very prominent member of this church.

After this reached the office of Jacob Taylor, a Certification was sent out by him stating

"Survey of a piece of land Surveyd to Thomas John the 17th day of the first month 1701/2 which being examined and revised in the said office is and followeth viz...The said land situate in the County of Newcastle Beginning at a corner marked white oak at the corner of Elisha Thomas' his land from thence extending South one hundred sixty six perches to a new corner gum tree thence by an east line six hundred and ten perches to a white oak thence north one hundred sixty six perches to a corner dogwood from thence by the said Elisha Thomas's land west six hundred and ten perches to the place of beginning containing six hundred and thirty two acres and one hundred fourty perches."

A survey dated 15th of the 5th mo. 1701 showed this land to be six hundred acres. Signed by George Dabeyne, Surveyor and Jacob Taylor.

This resurvey description only cited Elisha Thomas' land. Later surveys showed the land of Thomas Griffith and Henry Davis as being near this. Griffith John's survey of 1703/4 also joined Thomas John's land. Some family historians believe this first survey was made for Thomas John who was husband of the Welsh Tract Church constituent member Mary John. Thomas Griffith was the first Pastor of this church, but Henry Davis came from a family that arrived earlier with the Quakers.

A Welsh Tract Church record indicated there was a Thomas John, wife unknown, who moved to Philadelphia in September 1733, then returned to Welsh Tract Jan 8, 1736/7.

The next resurvey for a Thomas John in New Castle Co. in 1703 seemed to be for the one that had wife named Anne, and who died in 1726:

"This may certify into the Genll. Surveyrs: office that I have this 6th of Sept: 1704 Divided this Land for Thomas John. Beginning att an old Corner Black oake of David Price and Running west 146 pchs. to a new corner Black oake Sapling then by an old Line North: 348: pch: to a new Corner Gum then by a new Line of marked trees: East: 146: pch: to a new Corner Black oake in David Price Line then with his Line: South: 349: pchs: to the place of Beginning Containing: 318: acres Resurveyed and Divided the Day and year above written. G: Dabeyne, Surveyr."

This one only cited David Price's land, and had dividing as well as resurveying the land. The first resurvey cited Elisha Thomas' land, but also adjoined Henry Davis' and Griffith John's land. The belief that this resurvey that alluded to David Price's land was for the Thomas John with wife Anne is based on the descriptions of the land for which Anne John later gave a deed. Of these three mentioned, Price, Thomas, and Davis, only Thomas was affiliated with the Welsh Tract Baptist Church.

A survey taken 4th March 1703/4 for Griffith John, indicated he had 300 acres of land from the Welsh Tract next to that of Thomas John:

"This may Certifie into the Counsell Surveyr. Office that I have this fourth day of March 1703/4 Divided this tract of Land from the body of the Welch Tract for Griffith John beginning att a new Corner white oake standing in the said Line of Henery Davis' Land, and Running by a new Line of marked trees west 320:pch. to a new Corner Spanish oake bank in the woods from thence by a new Line of marked trees north 150:pchs. to a new Corner Red Oake bank in the woods in from thence east 320:perch. to a new Corner Hickery Standing in the land Line of Thomas John Land and Running with the land Line South: 150:pch. to the first mentioned Corner white oake and place of beginning Containing 300 acres of Land Divided from the great tract the Day and year above written. G. Dabeyns, Survey:r of New Castle County."

* *

Many of the Welsh from the nearby Welsh settlement of Goshen immediately made application for land in the Welsh Tract soon after it was surveyed. We do not know if Griffith John had arrived with the Baptists or came from the surrounding area. It would seem possible that he was Thomas John's son.

John Welsh was one mentioned by Scharf as moving there immediately after the surveys began. When it was completed, he took out 561 acres and a short time later, took out 851 acres. He sold 500 acres of the latter to Thomas Lewis 17 Aug 1727. [William Lewis had land in Newtown Tsp. in Chester Co. that he sold to his son David Lewis.] Under a survey for John Welsh was a notation that it was 'filed under John Morgan.' This might indicate that John Morgan also used the name John Welsh.

One of the first to select land in this area was James James, yeoman, of 'Bristol Township in the County of Philadelphia,' who received 1244 acres[16] and obtained a patent for this land from William Penn. He arrived earlier during the time the English and Welsh Quakers arrived. He was probably the son of David James of Radnor, an early Quaker settler. The James family was descendants of the Earls of March and always held vast estates in Wales. James became a family name in a branch of the Mortimer family.[17] The Bristol Township probably meant the one in Philadelphia Co.

There were James' who were Baptists from as early as 1667, as shown in the Rhydwilim records in Wales.

James James selected land on Iron Hill and northward to the Christiana Creek. A survey for Howel James [perhaps a brother] for 1040 acres was made the 3rd of the 4th mo. 1702, and James James' land adjoined this and William James' land. William James also took up land that year. When Howel James died, by his will dated 17 Aug 1717, he left 250 acres to his son Howel and 200 acres each to his other sons, James and Philip. Howel Sr. also devised an annuity of ten pounds to be paid to his [second] wife out of his mills and plantation. Some difficulty arose over this, and Alexander Hamilton was consulted, in which he advised her to notify the possessor of the land as it would be a charge against it.[18] Howel's son James [known as James James Jr. and James James Gent.] sold his portion to his brother Philip 12 May 1735. Philip conveyed 200 acres on which a mill was located to John Jones, bolster, of Philadelphia, 10 May 1737, and 210 acres lying on the north side of Christiana Creek to Samuel Allen, 8 Nov, 1737.

Among those receiving land here in 1702 were Thomas James, David Price, John Morgan, John Thomas, William Jones, and John Griffith. David Price took up 1050 acres 5 June 1702.

---

[16]Land Warrants of New Castle Co., signed by James Logan for William Penn, Recorded 11: 10mo. 1705, Philadelphia.
[17]Glenn, Welsh Founders of Pa., Vol. I, 1911, p. 42.
[18]Scharf, History of Delaware, V. II, p. 951.

Phillip James had survey for 525 acres the 4th of 4mo. 1702, beginning at a stake in the line of James James' land:

Survey for Philip James...five hundred and twenty five acres, being part of 30,000 acres of land surveyed to William Davis, David Evans & Co. 4 day of 4mo. 1702. Beginning at a stake in the line of James James his land... Also cited the line of Thomas James's land.

Thomas James had survey for 1250 acres of land 4. 4mo. 1702. Attention should be paid to these names as they have close connections with the Johns.

David James was listed in Sheppard's "Passengers and Ships Prior to 1684" as having arrived and was living in Radnor in 1682. There were a number of James' who took out surveys in New Castle around these dates of 1702 to 1704. Samuell James, son of James James Sr. had a survey made 6th of Sept.1704 for 455 acres, which description mentioned Thomas John's land and David Price's line.

Added to the Baptist Church by Baptism from 1703 to 1708 were John Wild*, Thomas Wild, James James, Sarah James, Shuan (Jaen) Morgan, Samuel Wild, Mary Nicholas, Richard Boen, David Thomas, Mary Bentley and Jaen Edwards. Let me stress, these added by baptism were mostly people who had arrived several years earlier. Some broke with the Quakers during the Keithian controversy.

*John Wild was baptized by Henry Gregory in Radnorshire in Wales 1 mo. 25 1697, dyed 1715, per Pennepek Church records. This would indicate he was a Baptist when he arrived.

A deed dated Oct 1724 for land that Hugh Morgan sold to Philip David had a description of land near David Price's land. This was part of Samuel James' land, deeded to James Morgan, then to Hugh Morgan. It had other interesting information:

Deed Book H, 1, pp. 565, 566, Year 1724:
Indenture made the sixth day of October 1724 between Hugh Morgan of the Welsh Tract...and Philip David of the sd. Place, farmer...for and in consideration of sixty two pounds 20 shillings...by him paid...grants bargains...unto Philip David ...all that messuage and tenement of land Situate lying ...being in the Welsh Tract aforesaid beginning at a corner Black Oak of Griffith Nicholos's Land, Running thence East one hundred forty and six perches to a corner Hickery of David Prices Land, thence South one hundred sixty & four perches to a stake thence West thence west one hundred and forty five perches thence north one hundred and sixty four perches to the place of Beginning Containing and Resurveyed for one

hundred and fifty acres of land more or less being part of a tract of land granted unto William Davies and David Evans by a certain Articles of Agreement ... and since Resurveyed and made over viz the quantity of four hundred acres by or from the sd. William Davies and David Evans unto Samuel James by a Deed of feofment of fee simple and since made over viz the fol. quantity of one hundred and fifty acres being resurveyed of or from the sd. Samuel James unto James Morgan by a like deed as aforesd. and since made over of or from James Morgan unto Hugh Morgan in like manner as is aforesaid which sd. one hundred and fifty acres together with all houses edifices buildings barns stables and houses orchards meadows profits comodities emoluments hereditments and appurtenances whatsoever thereunto belonging or in any wise appurtaining and all the Reversions and ...the said one hundred and fifty acres of land...'
* *

A survey for Samuell James taken 6th day of Sept 1704 had this Certification:
"Divided this Land for Samuell James beginning att a Corner Gum by Thomas John Corner gum tree and Running by a line of trees north; 451: pchs: to an old Cor: Black: oake in the west line then by the old Line east: 146: pch: to an old corner Hickery of David Price Land then with David Price Line: S: 451: pchs: to a corner Black oake in the said Line being a Corner of Thomas John Land then by Thomas John Land west 146: pch: to the place of Beginning Containing: 411: acres. Divided the Day and year above written."
* *

Deed Book L, Vol. 1, page 205, 17__ : John Price of tnship Nottingham in Chester Co., blacksmith, son & heir of David Price of Pencader decsd...Mother Mary Price, Admin...parcel of land 500 acres being part of a tract of 1050 acres formerly bought by my grandfather David Price...500 acres which was bequeathed to David Price by my grandfather David Price...
Note: A John Price was believed to have been a passenger on the "Endeavor," also called "Comfort," which arrived in 1683.

These deeds appear to have reference to the land sold to Thomas John in the first resurvey [618/600 acres] in 1701/2:
Deed Book H, Vol. 1, p. 184, 1729/:
Indenture between John Willson, yeoman and Edward Edwards, yeoman, for payment of 20 Pounds...land Situate lying & being in the Welsh Tract being part of a great tract of land taken up by William Davis & Co. in behalf of the possessor thereof by virtue of a warrant from the Proprietor & Governor of the Province of Pa. & territories thereunto the said land hereby granted ...as followeth, Viz: Beginning at a corner marked Persimon tree of Thomas Griffiths & running thence along the land of Henry Davis by a line

of marked trees East 48 perches to a corner stake in the ground in the line of
Henry Davis's land then running northward by a line of marked trees
dividing this from Thomas John's land 163 perches to a corner stake in the
ground in the land and line that was once John Wild's & running between
said line West 48 perches to a corner marked black oak belonging to
Thomas Griffith's line then by Thomas Griffith's land South 163 perches to
the said mentioned corner persimonn tree surveyed and rated out 50 acres
but is was found by the measure to contain within these bounds no more but
forty eight & one hundred & forty four purches being cutt of that tract of
land whereon Thomas John now Dwelleth being his lott of land in the
aforesaid great tract now called Pencader and to have and to hold...
Signed John Willson.
Witnesses: Edmund Shaco; Isaac Willson; Josiah Willy. Third Tues. Feb.
1729.

NOTE: Records show two of the Thomas John's died before this time, one
with wife Anne and the one with wife Rebecca.
* *

Deed Book I, P. 234. Another deed dated 10 Feb. 1729/30:
'John Wilson in consideration of Twenty pounds to me paid by Donald
Edwards -- sold a tract of land ... in the Welsh Tract ... taken up by
William Davis & Company...the said land ... is butted & bounded as
followeth viz. Beginning at a corner marked perssimon Tree of Thomas
Griffiths & running thence along the land of Henry Davis by a line of
marked trees east fourty eight perches to a corner stake in the ground in the
line of Henry Davis land then running northward by a line of marked trees
Dividing this from Thomas Johns Land one hundred & sixty three perches
to a corner stake in the ground in the land and line that was once John
Wilson's & running by the sd. line west fourty eight perches to a corner
marked black oak belonging to Thomas Griffith's then by Thomas Griffith's
land south one hundred & sixty three perches to the first mentioned corner
perssimon tree surveyed & laid out ffifty acres but it is found by the
measure to contain within the bounds no more but forty eight & one
hundred & fourty four perches it being cutt of that Tract of Land whereon
Thomas John now Dwelleth being his Lott of Land in that great afd. great
Tract now called Pencader. TO HAVE AND to hold ...'
* *
Note: Griffith John's land was also near Henry Davis' land.

NEIGHBORS AND CONNECTIONS.
Land mentioning David Price's land:
A deed from Isaiah Phipps & wife Elinor dated 1730:
Deed Book I, Vol. 1, pp. 288-290:

Sold to Francis Land of Christiana Creek, yeoman, for the sum of 20 pounds---situate and being in Penkader Hundred...Beginning at a corner oak of David Price's land thence by an old line of marked trees north to a new corner hickery of 200 acres of land lately sold by the said Isaiah & Elinor Phipps to David Merrick thence West by a line line dividing this from Merrick's land 150 perches to a new corner stake thence South by a line of marked trees to an old corner black oak thence East by a line of marked trees 150 perches to the first mentioned black oak to place of beginning containing 127 acres...
*

Survey made by virtue of a warrant dated 15th of 8th mo. 1701 to Thomas James for 1250 acres...to a black oak then by the line of David Price's land north 800 perches to a white oake thence Eighty two hundred & fifty perches to a white oak Then by the lands of Philip James and...
*

Survey dated 6th of Sept 1704 showed land divided for Samuell James beginning at a corner gum by Thomas John corner gum tree and running by a line of trees north... Also mentioned David Price land.
*

A survey taken for Howell James the 3rd of the fourth month 1701 for 1040 acres of land had another survey just below his for Thomas James dated 15th of 8mo. 1701 for 1250 acres which stated "Then by the line of David Price's land North 800 pchs.* to a white oake thence 825 pchs. to a white oak then by the lands of Philip James and The /Proprietary South..."
* *

NOTE: *The perch used in measurement is described as a linear or square rod or 30 1/4 square yards.
* *

Survey for 200 acres of Land on Christina Creek 21 day of Sept 1715 to Enoch Jinkins...Beginning at a new corner white oake and running by a line drawn north 30 perches to an old corner Hickery of Howell James's Land...
* *

Henry Davis received his warrant for 316 acres and 70 perches beginning at a new marked white oake at the corner of Thomas John's land. "I do hereby certify that by virtue of a warrant under the hand and seal of Edward Pennington Surveyor Genll. George Daheyns directed bearing date the 18th day of the 8th month [October] 1701. ...survey'd to Henry Davis the 17th day of this first month 1701/2 which being examined and revised in the said office is followeth viz:

"This said land situate in the County of Newcastle Beginning at a now marked white oak at the corner of Thomas John's land from thence extending east by the said Thomas John's Land six hundred and ten perches to new corner marked gum tree thence south eighty three perches to a stake from thence east six hundred and ten perches to a stake from thence north

100

eighty three perches to the first mentioned white oak Containing three
hundred sixteen acres and seventy perches. Jacob Taylor."
* *

Deed Book H, Vol. 1, p. 189: John Thomas released claim against John
David for 25 pounds...claim on 118 acres of land...now in occupation of
John David. Land description had Evan David on South; S., David Evan;
West, David Price; on North Richard Thomas.
3 day June 1727. Wit: David Evan, Thomas Evans.
* *

NOTE: The above showed John David's land as being west of David
Price's; therefore near Thomas John and Anne's land.

Thomas Griffin & Thomas Griffith: Survey G 2, #1, 3. Mar 16 1701/2, on
Seven Mi. Run, Welsh Tract; and G 2 #12, 85 acres, plot only not to be
recorded; and G 2, #13, Apr 2, 1720, 97 acres.

Book I, Vol. 1, pp. 106, 107. 17 June 1729.
James James Jr. & Henry Snicker recovered against Wm. James, yeoman,
sum of 8 pounds 16 shillings & 8 pence in debts, and 5 pounds 19 shillings
& ten pence for damages. To pay this, the Sheriff John Gooding was
ordered to seize William James' lands. Sheriff John Goodings was no
longer Sheriff, so the High Sheriff William Read was ordered to have two
people of good standing appraise this land for sale. Appraised & valued by
William Wooleston & John Lewis, then sold to highest bidder. Bought by
William Parsons, farmer, of New Castle Co. for 84 pounds.
    Land described as 150 acres and one hundred & 36 perches:
 Beginning at a Splash & small bridge on White Clay Creek Road at the
south side of the aforesd. Bridge & runns thence by a new line dividing this
from John Henreys land; South 24 degs. & a half Easterly 201 perches to a
new made corner white oake, thence by a line Dividing this from Evan
Morgan's land North 85 degs. Westerly 133 perches to a corner hickery
stump by a corner white oak saplen on the brow of a Hill by a branch
running into White Clay Creek & over against Morgan Morgans Island
thence along the aforesaid branch & below the hill north 56 degs. Easterly
16 perches North 16 perches North 34 degs. Westerly 22 perches to a corner
white Hickery by White Clay Creek thence along said Creek & bending on
the same by the several courses thereof North 22 poles, North 43 degs.
Easterly 8 perches North 30 degs. Easterly 16 perches to William
Wollastons fiord, thence still along the Creek north 75 degs. Easterly 24
perches South 34 degs. Easterly 6 poles south 25 degs. Easterly 24 poles
over against Wm. Canns house & plantation thence South 82 degs. Easterly
32 poles North 63 degs. Easterly 30 poles to John Lewis's fiord & to an old
corner Spanish oak by the creek, then leaving the creek & by a line Dividing

this from John Henery's Land South 67 degs. Easterly 12 poles to the
Splash & Small Bridge afsd. & place of Beginning...
*

Note: Some names are of people who were Quakers. However, Evan
Morgan was listed in the Pennepek Baptist records as baptizing a lot of
people.
* *

THOMAS JOHN and ANNE:

One of the Thomas John's in the Welsh Tract Baptist Minutes of 1716
was written as "Thomas Shonn Rhys." This showed he had a father who
was named John Rhys. In the chronological order of names, "Rebecca
Shonn" was written before "Ann Shonn." If this can be taken as an
indication, then the Thomas John married to Ann would have been the one
who was son of a John Rhys. This entry was in the Rhydwilim church
records in Wales:

'1693 John Rees of Nachlog Ddu and Griffith John of ye same yish [parish]
were both baptized ye 20th day of ye 3d Moneth att ynis vach and the next
day submitted to ye ordinance of Laying on of hands.'

Morgan Edwards wrote that Griffith John came to the Great Valley in
Chester Co. in 1710 from Rhydwilim. It is possible John Rees (Rhys) of
Nachlog Ddu was the father of the Griffith John who died in Great Valley,
Radnor in 1723, as well as father of David John and Rees John, who all
arrived around this time. We know some in the Great Valley were very
closely connected with those at Welsh Tract Baptist Church. There were
signatures of John Rhys as a witness on several deeds in the Chester Co.
records.

The Griffith John who took out resurvey for 300 acres in New Castle Co.
seemed to be more involved with the people who arrived earlier in
Philadelphia Co., per the names witnessing his land transactions, etc.
However, his land adjoined the Thomas John who had the first survey for
600 acres, and he could have been his son.

The following shows deed for land that belonged to Thomas John who
had wife Ann. Note it mentioned David Price's land.

Deed Book H, Vol. 1, 26 December 1728.

"Whereas there is a certain tract of land situate lying & being in New
Castle County afsd. Beginning at an old corner black oake of David Price's
land & runs by his line north 350 perches to an old corner hickery in David
Price's land thence along Samuel James' line west one hundred & fifty
perches to an old gum being a corner of Samuel James' land also
thence...being part of a larger tract of land taken up by William Davies &
David Evans...& afterwards sold by the sd. William Davies & David Evans

unto Thomas John <u>lately Decd</u>. & afterwards sold by the sd. Thomas John in his lifetime unto the sd. Izaiah Phipps & whereas there was a Deed given by the sd. Wm. Davies & David Evans unto the sd. Thomas John and also another given by the sd. Thomas John in his Life Time unto the sd. Izaia Phipps (both which sd. deed being in the custody of the said Izaia Phipps were accidentally destroyed by fire therefore the said Izaiah Phipps carefully Desiring Anne John sole Excutrix of the sd. Thomas John Decd., And the sd. Ann John Desiring the sd. William Davis and David Evans to make a new Deed...of their right & title in the sd. Land unto the sd. Izaiah Phipps which was accordingly conveyed...and Anne John unto the aforesaid Iziah Phipps by a certain deed bearing date the fourteenth day of February in the year of our Lord one thousand seven hundred and twenty seven for the consideration therein mentioned...NOW KNOW YE that the aforesaid Elioner Phipps ...in consideration and on the conditions herein after mentioned hath given granted ...unto the aforesaid David Merrick...all the right...which the aforesaid Izaiah Phipps ever had or now hath...to a certain piece or parcel of the aforesaid Three Hundred Twenty Seven acres above mentioned...Beginning at a stake in David Price's line thence along by Samuel James' line west one hundred & fifty perches to an old corner Gumm being a corner of Samuel James' land allso thence by an old line of marked trees south six hundred fourteen perches to a stake near a black oake, thence East to a corner hickory tree one hundred & Fifty perches, thence north by a line of marked trees two hundred & fourteen perches to a place of Beginning containing two hundred acres of land..."

Signed by Elioner E. Phipps, with witnesses: Thomas Evans; Thomas James; William Davies.

There was a Memorandum attached which stated parcels of "land upon the north end bordering upon Batchelor's Hope were in debate being Surveyed by Virtue of Several Warrants the one from Pa. & the other from Maryland which ...three acres are Excepted out of the aforesaid two hundred acres of land within mentioned..."

The gist of this is Thomas John sold land to Isaiah Phipps and gave him a deed for it, but the deed was lost in a fire by Isaiah Phipps. They applied to Ann John, widow of Thomas John, lately deceased, to have a new deed made. She received approval to do this on 14th day of February 1727 in Chester Co.

Church records indicate 'Thomas John, Christeen,' died 7mo. 23 day 1726. I believe this was to indicate he lived on Christiana Creek. This was the dividing line between Chester County and New Castle Co.

This deed dated 26 Dec 1728 was for 200 acres, but there was another one from the Phipps later for 118 acres, which indicated Thomas John sold them the complete amount of 318 acres which was resurveyed and divided.

The Thomas John who had the 318 acres resurveyed which had a land description that referred to David Price's land, died in 1726. So the land mentioned later in a 1729/30 deed as being 'land where Thomas John now dwelleth" and 'dividing this from Thomas John's land' would not have been the Thomas who had wife named Ann.

An account in the Welsh Tract Baptist Minutes for 1716 reported Griffith Nicholas was turned out of the church for breaking his promise that he had made regarding a business matter between him and "Brother Thomas John from Bryn." Since Bryn is the Welsh word for hill, it is possible that this referred to Thomas John of Iron Hill, who was married to Rebecca. But it could have been either Thomas John who was married to Anne, or the Thomas who was married to Susanna, as they were all living in 1716 and all had land in the Welsh Tract. The church was asked to settle the dispute by both men, but their decision apparently angered Griffith Nicholas and he said the church was "unrighteous." In 1726, Griffith Nicholas "repented and fulfilled his obligation."

In Deed Book H, Vol. 1, p. 62, dated 29 April 1723 between John Kyle and Sir William Keith, Baronet, mention was made of Griffith Nicholls [Nicholas] exchanging a small portion of land with John Devonald and with Thomas John for like quantities of land. The land which he exchanged with Thomas John was ten acres two quarters and thirty perches, and seemed to contain a grist mill, bolting mill with the mill stones, bolting cloth, running geer [gear], furniture & apparel, etc. which was included in the deed.

Perhaps the disagreement was over the payment for this additional property, or the gristmill, etc., located on it.
* *

THOMAS JOHN AND REBECCA:

Thomas John of Iron Hill who had wife Rebecca gave a vague description of his land in his will, but there does not seem to be enough land to be the first survey of 600 acres. It appears he wanted some of his land left to his children and not sold at this time.

He left an interesting will dated 7th of May, 1720, Will Book C, p. 253. It is endearing to read of the animals left to his children and Rebecca, all of whom had names. Thomas John wrote he was of White Clay Creek Hundred in his will and also mentioned his plantation on the Iron Hill. The 250 acres he purchased from James James was sold, and this probably was the plantation where he lived.

Will Book, P. 253, 1721.

THOMAS JOHN'S WILL:

In the name of God Amen I Thomas John of <u>White Clay Creek Hundred</u> in the County of New Castle, being Sick and weak in Body, but of Sound and perfect Mind and Memory praised be Almighty God therefore Doe

Make and Ordain this my present last Will and Testament in Manner and Form following. (that is to say) First & principally I commend my Soul [p. 254] into the hands of God Almighty and hoping that after my Death and [wisdom] of my Saviour Jesus hereafter to have full and free pardon and forgiveness of all my sins and to inherit everlasting Life, and my Body I commend to the Earth to be decently buried, at the Descretion of my executrix hereafter named, And as touching the Dissafection of all Such Temporale estate, as it hath pleased Almighty God to bestow upon me, I give and dispose thereof as followeth:

First I will that all my debts and funeral charges shall be paid and discharged.

Then I give unto my dear and well beloved wife Rebecca all that certain tract of Land, situate, lying and being in Pen[n]'s Manner [Manor] in the County of New Castle Containing Two hundred Acres of land together with all the appurtenances thereunto belonging To have and To hold the same during her Life Time, And in Consideration that the purchase & Money of the Said Land is not paid, I give unto my said Wife the sum of Forty Five pounds in cash, to [have] out of a Bond of Fifty Five Pounds, which is due to me from John Evans of North Wales in the County of Philadelphia. But in case the said land should prove to be rent land, and no purchase Money to be paid, then my will is that the said [fifty five] pounds, be divided betwixt my children as followeth, (Viz) Thirty five pounds equally divided betwixt them all, and the other [   ] pounds to be equally divided between my sons, Thomas & Benjamin.

I also Give unto my said Wife two horses, Known by the Names of Buck and Prince, also a Mare called Bunny, also three Cows, known by the Names of Gentle, Bossy and Blossom, also a Cart, Pair of plow Irons, and a Sett of harrow tines & [   ] fifth all my household goods.

Item I give unto my well beloved son John the sum of sixteen pounds, to be paid him, when he comes to the Age of twenty one years, Moreover if my said son be alive, after my said Wife's Decease, I give unto him my said son John the above mentioned tract of Land together with all the appurtenances there unto belonging, viz but in case that he my said son should dye before he comes to inherit the said plantation then I give the same to the eldest of my sons that shall be alive after their Mothers decease on Condicon that he my said son John or either of my sons, that comes to inherit the said plantation, shall pay unto the rest of my children, the sum of Three pounds a piece as if in case that eigther of my sons shall live to enjoy the said plantation, that then the Eldest of my daughters shall inherit the same, on the same condition before express'd. I also Give unto my said son John a Two year old Colt called Dick.

Item I give unto my well beloved Son Enoch, the sum of Sixteen pounds, to be paid him when he comes to the Age of twenty one years. I also give my said son Enoch a year old Colt, known by the nayme of Robin.

Item I give unto my well beloved Son Thomas the sum of Sixteen pounds, to be paid him, when he comes to the age of Twenty one Years.

Item I give unto my well beloved son Benjamin the sum of Sixteen pounds, to be paid him when he comes to the age of twenty one years.

Item I give unto my well beloved daughter Sarah the sum of Sixteen pounds, to be paid her when she comes to the Age of eighteen years. Also a Mare called Bonny, with a young Foal and a Two year old Colt, called Tobey, also a cow known by the name of Nutty, also a two year old heifer called Dasey, also a year old Steer and a young Calf.

Item I Give unto my well beloved Daughter Mary the sum of Sixteen pounds, to be paid her when she comes to the Age of eighteen years, also a cow called Padey, and a two year old heifer called Starry, also a Mare called Tibb and two sheep.

Item I Give unto my well beloved Daughter Ruthe the sum of Sixteen pounds, to be paid her when she comes to the Age of eighteen years.

Item I will that my plantation on the Iron hill, be Sold at the descretion of my Executor and whatever it amounts to above Fifty pounds, what I have valued it unto and have already divided, I give the over [   ] of the same, to be divided equally between all my children.

Item the rest and residue, of my personal Estate, Cows and Chattells whatsoever, I doe give to be equally divided, betwixt my two sons, Thomas and Benjamin. And I doe hereby make and ordain my loving Wife Rebecca full and Sole executor of this my last Will and Testament.

I doe also make and ordain my too dear friends James James and Howell James to be Executors of this my Last Will and testament and [Guardians] over all my children.

Item I doe hereby revoke, disanull and make void all former Wills and Testaments by me heretofore made.

IN WITNESS whereof I the said Thomas John - this my last Will and Testament, witnessed on the pages of one sheet of paper, set my hand unto, the bottom of the last page, thereof Set my Seal the Seventh Day of May, in the year of our Lord, one thousand Seven hundred and Twenty. T J Seal Sealed and Delivered in the presence of us

Thomas Edmund

David "His D" Thomas

"J Mark" Howell James.

Be it Rememberd that the _____ Day of October in the year of our Lord one thousand seven hundred and Twenty Anno Anni, _____ Septimo David Thomas and Howell James, subscribing Witnesses to the said Will appeared before me Register of the Sd. County of New Castle & declared upon oath that they saw the within named Thomas John, sign, seal, deliver, pronounce and Declare the within written Instrument, to be his last Will and testament, and that att the time of his executing the same, he appeared to them to be of sound judgment and memory and that they and Thomas

Edmund therein named Subscribed as Witness to the Same. Certified under my hand. John French Regr.

PROBATE of Thos. John's Will

In the Tenour of the presents I John French Esqr. Register for the probate of Wills and Granting Letters of Administration for the County of New Castle by Virtue of a Comicon. from the Honable. William Keith Lt. Govenour of the County of New Castle Kent & Sussex upon Delaware and Province of Pensylvania Doe & Make Known unto all Men, That on _____ Day of October in the year of our Lord, one thousand Seven hundred and Twenty before me register as above was proved, Approved and Insineated the Last Will and testament of Thomas John late of New Castle County Yeoman Deced. to these presenes annexed HAVING Whilst he lived and att the Time of his Death Goods Rights and Credits, within the said County, By means whereof the full disposetion of all & singular the Goods, Rights and Credits of the said deceased and the Granting the Admineon. of them as also the hearing accounts, calculation or Reckoning of the Said Admtion. and the final Discharge and Difussion from the Same unto me, are manifestly known to belong, NOW the Administration of all and Singular the goods, Rights and credits of the said deceased, and his Last Will and Testament any manner of ways concerning was Granted unto Rebecca John Widow and Relict of the said Decd. Sole executrix in the Same testament named. CHIEFLY of well and truly administering the same, of making a true and complete Inventory and conscionable, Appraisement of all & Singular the Goods, Rights and Credits of the sd. deceased, and exhibiting the Same into the registers office att New Castle, att or before the twenty third day of March next ensueing, and rendering upon your oath or Solemn affirmation a just and true Account of the Said Administration when there unto required. IN TESTIMONY whereof I have caused the Seal of the said office to be hereunto affixed. Dated att New Castle the _____ day of October in the seventh year of the Reign of King George over Great Britain etc. and in the year of our Lord, one thousand, Seven Hundred and Twenty. John French, Regtr.
* *

In addition to selling this land to Thomas John, deeds were made by James James Sr. to his sons James, Samuel and Daniel, who were all referred to as "heir apparent" in their individual deed. One supposition for the sale of this 250 acres to Thomas John would be that Rebecca was his daughter. [Daniel's deed for 153 acres 77 perches, dated 26 Mar 1723, in Deed Book L, V. 1, p. 28. Witnesses: Enoch Morgan, Howell James, Hannah & James Armitage. James' deed was for 143 acres, witnessed by Elisha Thomas, Enoch Morgan, Hugh Morris, Howell James, Samuel James, Thomas James, and Daniel James. Deed to Samuel James dated 28 May 1726.]

Since Thomas John seems to have died while his children were young, and the will possibly having been made early in life, it could indicate he knew he was dying when he made the will. He might have died from an injury or some illness. Or he might have been elderly, with this being children of a later marriage. Their children, being underage in 1720, probably were born in the ca 1714 to 1729 era. It is possible Rebecca was a second wife with young children.

The children of Thomas and Rebecca were:

1. JONATHAN or JOHN JOHN. He must have been the eldest son, as he was to be given the 200 acres of land after the decease of his mother.
2. BENJAMIN JOHN. Second son mentioned, and records show he was baptized in 1739. He probably was the Benjamin John in Kent Co.
3. THOMAS JOHN.
4. ENOCH JOHN.
5. SARAH JOHN.
6. MARY JOHN.
7. RUTHE JOHN.

*

The 200 acres of land that Thomas John first mentioned and gave to Rebecca was located in Penn's Manor, probably Rockland. The land in Penn's Manor was not part of the Welsh Tract, but was nearby. Manor land was sold or let out for quit-rent by Penn's Land Commissioners.

Land was sold by Rebecca, her new husband Lewis David [Davis], and James James to John Evans by deed dated 18th day of May 1725 for 50 pounds. This deed stated the amount of land sold was 250 acres. John Evans was mentioned in Thomas' will as owing him 55 pounds, and as living in the "North Wales" area of Philadelphia County.

Book G, Vol. 1, 1725 , Pp. 489-491.

Deed dated 18th day May 1725 between James James Sr., Esqr., Lewis David, and Rebecca his wife, all of Pencader, of the first part, and John Evans of the Iron Hill of the second part, has the following information:

William Penn granted by patent 20th day of Feb. 1703, recorded in Rolls office at Philadelphia, Pattent A, Vol. 3, p. 174, to James James 1244 acres of land. James James "conveyed 250 acres of said land to Thomas John of Pencader aforesaid deceased being former husband to the said Rebecca, and the said Thomas John did by his last will and testament ordain that the said 250 acres of land should be sold by the said Rebecca as being executrix of his last will & testament together with the said James whom he nominated a Trustee to his said will..."

This above land was situated [excerpt] "on or near the Rose Hills within Pencadder aforesaid being part of the said one thousand two hundred and fourty four acres of land beginning at a corner marked Spanish oak being a corner of the land of one John Jones then west by the same land two

108

hundred and twenty one perches and one half of a perch to another Spanish oak, thence north by the lands of the said <u>James James</u> two hundred and eighteen perches and one half of a perch to a part thenceforth by the land of the said <u>James James</u> one hundred and seventeen ...thence south three degrees East by the Land of Mr. William Keith..."

* *

The description of this land had "beginning at a corner marked Spanish oak being a corner of the land of one John Jones..."[19] [This John Jones was probably the one who purchased land from Phillip James.] The rest of the description referred to James James' land. The land sold was that which was purchased from James James.

This deed stated William Penn granted this land to James James by patent A, Vol. 3, p. 174, Philadelphia, confirmed 20 Feb 1703, as part of a parcel of l244 acres. The survey stated this was part of the Welsh tract land from Davis & Evans Company. In the patent, James James, yeoman, was 'of Bristol Township of the county of Philadelphia.' An account of David James who came over in 1682[20] says the James' had to live in Bristol [England] while waiting for their ship to be ready. They were from Radnorshire in Wales.

Rebecca John remarried soon after Thomas' death in 1720 to Lewis David, probably son of Henry David [or Davis] who lived nearby.

* *

The Baptist Welsh in their Minutes stated they began to get their living from this land purchased from Davies and Evans and set their meetings in order by beginning the building of a place of worship in 1703. This was completed in 1706. Their place of worship was commonly known by the name of "The Baptist Meeting House by the Iron-hill," because of the place of location. It was located at the foot of Iron Hill, and stood on high ground on the banks of Christiana River. It contained six acres which was a gift from Hugh Morris, and formed into an angle by "the running of Ironhill brook into Christiana river." In a region otherwise flat, something in that hill reminded them of the mountains of their Native Land. The church has ever since been known as the "Welsh Tract" Baptist Church."[21]

THOMAS GRIFFITH: The minister Thomas Griffith and his family settled in the Welsh Tract at Christiana, New Castle Co. where he held land and was Pastor. Records indicate he baptized many people at the Pennepek and Philadelphia churches, and also ministered at other churches in the area.

"Rev. Thomas Griffith was born in 1645 in Lanvernach parish and county of Pembroke; took on him the care of the church ... in 1701, and was

---

[19] John Jones purchased [by mortgage deed] some land of Phillip James'.
[20] Passengers and Ships Prior to 1684, Sheppard, p. 15.
[21] Pa. Materials towards a History of Baptists in Pa. in the American Baptist Historical Society, Chester, Del. Co., Pa., Morgan Edwards.

himself one of the constituents: arrived in Philadelphia with his church Sep. 8, 1701; died at Pennepek, and was there buried Jul. 25, 1725; his children were Elizabeth, Samuel, Isaac, Mary, Judith; these married into the Truax, Goodings, Morgans, and Fulton families; and raised him 18 grandchildren, most of whom were alive in 1770, under the names of Loyds, Wards, Holmes, Halls, Lilings, Morgans, Howells, Griffiths. Mr. Griffiths visited the Jersies in 1706 and 1711 and was of great service in instructing the people in the ways of the Lord ... encouraging young men to use their gifts, whereby their churches were soon supplied with ministers of their own raising."[22]

*

Records show the three branches of the Welsh Tract Church at Christiana met the first Sunday in the month to celebrate the Lord's Supper. One branch resided near "the other in London-britain township 9 miles off. The third at Littlecreek hundred in the county of Kent, about 32 miles distant; in each of which places is a meeting house."[23] A record of Chester County indicated that the Welsh rapidly filled the land in the Great Valley area in the early 1700's.

A survey for the land of Griffith John, the Quaker farmer who owned land in Merion [Phila. Co.], was included with the surveys in New Castle Co. for the Johns. I do not know why it was included in the New Castle Co. surveys. I have puzzled over this, wondering if he was any connection of these Johns. His son was John Griffith, and he had children who took the surname John. He had a daughter named Anne, who married Thomas Jones or John. [See chapter on Quakers.] This Thomas John died a Quaker and was buried in the Quaker cemetery, according to Glenn and other early writers, so he would not have been the one in the Welsh Tract Baptist Church.

* *

THOMAS LEWIS:

In Survey L 2, #16, dated March 3 1703/4, same date as the one for Griffith John for 300 acres, was a survey for 'Thomas Lewis' land ...tract of land from the body of Welsh tract...beginning...in line of Elisha Thomas' land...John Thomas' land...Thomas Griffith's land...containing 200 acres.'

He purchased 500 acres from John Welsh in 1727. He had sons named Evan, Alexander, James, David, and a daughter named Elizabeth who married Rees Thomas per his will of 1749. He was probably a relation of the John Lewis who married Elizabeth John, daughter of Griffith John, as shown later in his will in 1748. The William Lewis mentioned earlier had sons who lived in Chester Co. Thomas appears to be descended from these earlier Lewis'.

---

[22]Ibid.
[23]Morgan Edward's Materials.

110

Emphasis: Thomas Lewis' land was taken out the same date as Griffith John's and was located very close. David John and David Lewis apparently went to North Carolina together later, so it seems obvious they (John's and Lewis') were related.

Several of the Welsh Quakers were already settled in this area, especially on White Clay Creek, when the Baptists arrived. Henry Lewis, a Quaker, took out land on which a Quaker Meeting House was built. Thomas John and Margaret were in the area. Earlier records indicate some Quakers took some of their land in Chester County.

* *

JOHN LEWIS:

John Lewis, the Quaker, had a survey made Dec 1, 1705, [Survey L 1, #8, 9], near the Quaker Meeting House between Duck Creek & Appoquiniminck in New Castle Co. It was for 200 acres, with Certif. Copy. Also, he had survey B 2, #95, on King's Road, Mar 21, 1705/6, 212 acres, Cert. Copy 1746, filed under Bert, Humphrey. 10 acres of tract "belongs to the meeting house."

Another survey dated 4th day Dec 1705, stated "John Lewis of Md. for 200 acres of land...where nearest to the meeting house of the people called Quakers between Duck Creek & Aqqopuntick Hundred in Co. of New Castle."

A deed dated 17 May 1724, Deed Book G, Vol. 1, p. 82, mentioned John Lewis' will of 1 Sept 1708. Sarah Lewis was Executor. In his will, he ordered 250 acres out of his 550 acres to be sold by his executors to pay his debts and the rest set aside for the education of his children, indicating he had younger children. This deed recorded the sale of the remaining 250 acres to Edward Gray and mentioned a continuing need for money to carry out his wishes.

The Welsh Quakers already had settlements in New Castle Co., and it is impossible to tell anyone's religion from the land records. Records from the Survey Index of New Castle Co. indicate that 220 acres of land for Thomas Ogle was surveyed in this area, and state it was called "Goshen." This was the name of the land described as being on Chester Creek which the Quakers had, and might have included this. West Chester is in the area that the first Welsh settlers referred to as "the wilds of Goshen." The Ogles went back to the first land grantees in Philadelphia County.

Rees Jones, practitioner, purchased land near the Christiana Bridge called Eagles' Point which had previously been surveyed to John Ogle, Sr., deceased. This was part of land William Penn granted to Thomas Pierson 5th day of 5th mo. 1683.

In 1706 after the Baptist meeting house was finished, the congregation of Welsh Tract and those of Philadelphia and Pennepek agreed to set up a meeting once more to try to come together in their beliefs. As they met together for yearly meetings, they desired that they might have a "general union at the Lord's table."

They met at the house of Richard Miles in Radnor, Chester County, 22 Jul 1706 where this agreement was written down. Rev. Thomas Griffith was in charge of the group, which had recently been under the care of "brother John Watts meeting at Pennepak"...

* *

RICHARD, SAMUEL & GRIFFITH MILES:

RICHARD MILES, weaver, of Llanfihangel Helygen, Radnorshire, and his brother Samuel had taken land with the earlier Welsh Quaker Company No. 7. They were sons of James Miles of Radnorshire. They came with William Penn in October, 1682, on the "Welcome." Richard Miles had 100 acres in Radnor, and Samuel Miles purchased 100 acres there. James Miles, of the parish of Llanfihangel Helygen, Radnorshire, weaver, was born ca 1622. He was a Friend, and a freeholder of 100 acres of land in Pa. He moved to Radnor in 1693. James brought Certificate from Montgomery-llainhangel meeting in Radnorshire, dated 27. 5mo. 1683.

James was later baptized in the Baptist Church, as shown in the Pennepek Records.

James Miles' children were:
1. SAMUEL MILES, wife Margaret.
2. RICHARD MILES.
3. GRIFFITH MILES.
4. DAVID MILES. [He and wife Alice joined from Pennepek in 1709.]
5. ANN MILES. [24]

*

RICHARD MILES, son of James, purchased 100 acres in Wales from Richard Davies, deed dated 19 Jun 1682, recorded Phila. 12 1mo. 1684.

When Richard Miles had his land resurveyed, it amounted to 233 acres. His 50 acres purchased from brother Samuel resurveyed at 72 acres, and he purchased the overage from William Penn. He also purchased 20 acres from Ellis Jones, "the Govern's miller." . Richard owned a front lot on south side of Chestnut Street in 1683.

He was a Quaker, became one of the Keithian Quakers, and meetings were often held at his house. William Beckingham baptized Richard Miles and his wife in the Baptist faith in 1700 in Upper Providence. Richard and his wife, plus daughters Joan and Jane, were constituent members of the Great Valley Baptist Church that was started in April 1711.

The group of Baptists under the care of Thomas Griffith and John Watts of Pennepek met at his house in Radnor, July 22, 1706. They worked out their disagreements on conversing together on the "subject of union and

---

[24]Welsh Founders of Pa., Glenn, p. 194.

brotherly love, and occasional communion." Griffith and David Miles were also at this conference.

Richard's wife was Sarah Evans, daughter of John Evans of Radnor, whom he married in 1688. [This John Evans was possibly the one that purchased the land Rebecca John sold.] Their five sons-in-law were Baptists. Richard's will was dated 29 Aug 1713, proved 23 Dec 1713. Witnesses: Thomas Thomas, husband of niece Tamar, Ruth Miles, niece, and William Meredith. Richard's brother-in-law William Davies*, and John Powell "my daughter's father in law" were to be Tutors and Guardians over the children until they became of age.

About 1734, his widow Sarah moved to Plymouth township and lived with her daughter and son-in-law John Davis. Her will was dated 6 Oct 1750, proved 25 Aug 1756.

[*William Davies was one of the purchasers of the 30,000 acres of land in the Welsh Tract.]

Children of Richard Miles and Sarah were:

1. RICHARD MILES, m. Phebe Davis.
2. JAMES MILES, m. Hannah Pugh, dau of David Pugh and Catherine of Radnor. Constable in Radnor in 1701; Supervisor 1702; Pat. 174 acres land 26 Oct 1703. Children: Emos, m. Sarah Pugh; others.
3. EVAN MILES, m. Mary ____.
4. JOHN MILES, m. Rebecca James, dau of David James of Radnor.
5. JANE MILES, m. John Davis of Plymouth.
6. SARAH MILES, m. Rev. Benjamin Griffith, of Llanllwny. He was b. 1788, Llanllwny, Wales, came to Pa. in 1710; half-brother of Rev. Abel Morgan. He was a Baptist pastor and the son of John Griffith, Elder.
7. HANNAH MILES, m. Jonathan Pugh, brother of Hannah, above.
8. ABIGAIL MILES, m. John Davis. See more on Rev. John Davis in "Great Valley Baptist Church." Second Pastor there.
9. JOANNA MILES, m. Joseph Powell, son of John Powell. He and Joanna were constituent members of the Brandywine Baptist Church.
*

SAMUEL MILES, a Quaker, brought Certificate of Removal to the Philadelphia Monthly Meeting from Redstone Meeting, Radnorshire, Wales, dated 27 5mo. 1683. He married Margaret James, spinster, by Friends' ceremony at the house of Ann Thomas in New Church parish, Radnorshire, 25 June 1682. The record of their marriage was given in "Merion..." by Glenn, p. 362. Margaret James had a deed dated 20 June 1682 for 200 acres of land. They settled in Radnor, and bought 150 acres more from Thomas Lehnman. They sold 50 acres to Richard Miles. Their 258 acres was resurveyed in Sept. 1705, and found to contain 352 acres, which they purchased. They became Keithian Quakers and were later baptized at Seventh Day Baptist Church of Providence, 9. 6mo. 1698. They settled first in Philadelphia and later moved to Radnor. Samuel Miles' wrote will; was proven by his wife, 28 April 1708. His children named were Tamar, Phoebe and Ruth [m. Owen Evans.] He named Richard Miles, Stephen Bevand and Edward Reece as overseers.

Samuel and Margaret Miles' children were:[25]

1. TAMAR JAMES MILES, b. 27 8mo. 1687; m. Thomas Thomas, son of William Thomas of Radnor 6 3mo. 1708. She d. in 1770. Their daughter m. Nathan Lewis.

2. PHEBE MILES, b. 20 4mo. 1690; m. Evan Evans of Haverford 13 2mo. 1715.

3. RUTH MILES, b. 28 1mo. 1693; m. Owen Evans 3 11mo. 1715/16. Died bef. 1736.

*

Tamar James Miles was born 21 8mo. 1687, the first Welsh child born in Radnor Township. She married Thomas Thomas of Radnor, and died Oct. 28 1770. "Merion..." by Glenn, pp. 361-2, gave an account of the way she would milk her cows at 5 in the evening, then walk three miles to visit friends. This mentioned her daughter Margaret was wife of Nathan Lewis; had grandson Eli Lewis, who was a miller at his grandfather Thomas' mills (afterwards known as Levi Lewis' mill.)

*

At Richard Miles' home in 1706, they made the following agreement, per the church minutes: 'That those who believed in the ordinance of laying-on-of hands on every believer were to enjoy all liberty, within the bounds of brotherly love, to preach and practice this according to their belief. And those who did not believe in this were left to their liberty. It was further agreed that neither parties were to make opposition in mixed assemblies, and that members of either church might enjoy communion with each other.'

Those who subscribed to the Agreement were: Thomas Griffith; Samuel Griffith [son of Thomas]; Samuel Jones; Richard David; Elisha Thomas; Hugh Morris; Enoch Morgan; William Bettridge; James James; John Snowden; Peter Chamberlain; John Wilds; Joseph Hart; Thomas Morris; Joseph Wood; Griffith Miles; John Freeman; John Swift, Jr.; Evan Edmond; Joseph Todd; John Edward; John Osisson; Thomas John; Edward Church; and David Miles.

Some of these people who signed were associated with the Pennepek and Philadelphia Churches. Samuel Jones was among those signing this, and he might have been the one who was a Pastor at this time at Pennepek. He remained there until his death, and never was associated with the church in New Castle Co.

*

[25]Ibid, p. 195.

GRIFFITH MILES, son of James, was born in Wales ca 1670. He married Bridget Edwards, daughter of Alexander and Bridget Edwards of Radnor, 20 8mo. 1693 at the house of David Price* of Radnor. Witnesses were 30 in number, among them were James, Richard, Samuel and Margaret Miles, and Ann Davis. He became a member of the Pennepek Church, being baptized in 1697. His wife Bridget was baptized there in 1709. His will was proved in Philadelphia 13 June 1719.

Their children were:
1. HESTER MILES, b. 28 Sept 1693.
2. MARTHA MILES, b. 12 Oct 1695.
3. MARGARET MILES, b. 9 Apr 1698, m. John Carl.
4. GRIFFITH MILES, b. 3 Dec 1700, m. Sarah _____ in 1721; d. June 1727.
5. SAMUEL MILES, b. Sept 1703.
6. JOHN MILES, b. 26 Mar 1699. Married Ann Davies, daughter of Mirick Davies**. He d. June 1747. Will dated 28 Mar 1719, in which he described himself as Yeoman of the township of Bristol, in the county of Philadelphia. His branch first settled in Lower Dublin Township, Phila. Co., but moved to Bucks Co. about 1800.

*Had land in Del. in Welsh Tract.
**A Myrick Davies was later in Ga.
*

DAVID MILES:
Son of James, was baptized at Pennepek, 9. 7mo. 1697. He and wife Alice Miles joined Welsh Tract Church in 1709. Her name appeared as a witness to marriage of Phebe Miles (dau Samuel and Margaret) with Evan Evans 13. 2mo. 1716. No record that he owned land. He apparently died in 1710 per Welsh Tract Church records and was buried at Pennepek. Alice was among the signers 4 Feb 1716 of a Confession of Faith at Welsh Tract Church. She probably remarried, as no further record was found. Their daughter Sarah Miles was mentioned in Richard Miles' will.
*

ANN MILES:
Daughter of James, married William Davies of Radnor Township. He came to Phila. ca 1685. He purchased a lot on Walnut Street, Phila., from John Jones. He bought a plantation in Radnor, and was probably the William Davies who was co-purchaser of the large tract of land for the Welsh in New Castle Co. He was originally a member of the Society of Friends, but later became a member of the Church of England. The first English services in the vicinity were held in his house. He built a log cabin where services were held until it burned in 1700. St. David's Church of Radnor was built on this land. He was a member of the Pa. Assembly in 1712 and 1714. He later moved to Caernavon township, now Lancaster Co. The

records of the Bangor Church show numerous descendants. Ann died in 1734, and he died in 1739.

* *

THOMAS JONES AND MARGARET:

A THOMAS JONES had 100 acres of land which he had purchased from Ollie Olson confirmed by William Markham and John Goodson, two of Penn's Land Commissioners at Philadelphia on "the Sixteenth Day of the third Month fourth year of ye Reign of James the Second over England...1688." This land was described as being a Tract of Land called Goodspring situate lying and being on the outside of Delaware River and on both sides of Shillpott Creek in the County of New Castle beginning att a corner marked Chestnut tree standing by the side of a small Runn call Goodspring..."

Thomas and his wife MARGARET bought 100 acres of land from Henry Hollingsworth on Brandywine Creek in New Castle County in 1694. [Henry Hollingsworth, indentured for 2 years, was son of Valentine Hollingsworth, who came over in 1682. See below*.][26] Thomas and Margaret as a couple were not mentioned in the Welsh Tract Baptist records. They could have been members of the Brandywine Baptist Church. Thomas was later referred to in deeds as "of New Castle County" or as "of Brandywine Creek." There were land transactions dated May 25, 1727, 20th Aug 1734, and February 17, 1738/9 regarding their land, with descriptions mentioning Good Spring Runn.

An early list of passengers on the "Welcome," the ship on which Penn arrived, had a Thomas Jones who was a servant.[27] Sheppard later wrote Thomas Jones was probably the servant left to Dennis Rochford in Thomas Heriott's will. Dennis Rochford arrived about 24th 8mo. 1682. Rochford was a grocer from Brighthelmston, Sussex, and his second wife was Marie, daughter of John Heriott. Rochford died in Philadelphia Co. in 1693. This [being a servant] was sometimes done as a way to pay passage over, and they often worked for people related to them. He was probably quite young at the time he arrived, and could have been the one with land on Brandywine Creek.

Most of the deeds signed by Thomas and Margaret include his distinctive mark that looks like T. I., with a slash across the I, probably meaning a J. Deed Book E, Vol. 1, p. 316, dated 1739, the deed from Thomas and Margaret to Zacharias Derrickson was difficult to read. It was witnessed by Edward Philpot and <u>John Reese.</u> [Note: Would be same as Rees or Rhys]. The date witnessed seemed to be March 30th, 1739. A John Rees came from Wales in 1710, about the same time as many who became

---

[26]Sheppard Jr., "Passengers and Ships Prior to 1684...", Heritage Books, Inc. 1992, p. 98.
[27]Walter Lee Sheppard Jr., Passengers and Ships Prior to 1684, p. 7.

involved with the Welsh Tract Church. His children probably took the name Jones or John.

John Rees of Radnor Co. had wife named Hannah, [28] but not much else was found regarding him. He might have been the John Rees of the Rhydwilim church records in Wales. John Rees of Radnor was also one of the witnesses to David Meredith's Will. (Phil. Admin. Book C, p. 79, will dated 28th 10 mo. 1723, proved 13 May 1727.)

One transaction referred to Thomas Jones as being "of New Castle County upon the Delaware and Manor of Rockland in the said county, yeoman." This Manor was where William Penn maintained a Manor House. His Land Commissioners distributed land to purchasers in return for the payment of quit-rents.

Another deed to William Derrickson and John Wilder was made the 17th day of August, 1734. This was signed in presence of George Robison [Robinson] and Valentine Robinson.

Please note that many of the names associated with these deeds made by Thomas and Margaret were of people who later went to the Pee Dee area of South Carolina.

The Thomas John who had wife Rebecca stated he owned land in "Penn's Manor" in his will. Thomas and Rebecca were said to have joined the Welsh Tract Baptist Church by letter from Wales in 1703.

*Valentine Hollingsworth of Ballenisckcrannel, parish of Sego, Armaga, with wife Ann, daughter Mary and her husband Thomas Conway of Lisburn, Antrim; daughter Catherine, who m. in 1688 George Robinson; probably sons Thomas and Samuel, and an indentured servant, John Musgrave, were probably on the "Antelope" which arrived the 9th or 10th of December 1682 with passengers from Ireland. A Valentine Hollingsworth was found later in Lunenberg Co., Va. in 1752, and then a few years later in the Welsh tract in S.C.
*

Land Records from New Castle regarding Thomas and Margaret:
Deed Book E, 1, p. 316, 1719.
Thomas Jones and Margaret Jones to Zecherias Derreckson:
THIS INDENTURE made the first day of March ... anno domini one thousand seven hundred and nineteen BETWEEN Thomas Jones of Brandiwine Hundred in the County of New Castle upon Delaware and Margaret his wife of the one part and Zacharias Derrickson of the hundred and county aforesaid, Yeoman of the other part WHEREAS one Mr. Hollingsworth by the name of Henry Hollingsworth ... by his Deed ... dated the fifteenth day of October anno Dom. one thousand six hundred and ninety four for the considerations therein mentioned did warant and devise

---

[28]Philadelphia Families, p. 470.

unto the said Thomas Jones... a certain parcel or tract of land SITUATE lying and being in the said Brandiwine County Beginning at a marked white oak standing by _____ _____ side and thence extending south east by a line of trees one hundred and twenty perches to a bounded hickory standing in the line of the [bought?] land and extending thence by the said line south east two hundred and five perches to a corner marked black oak thence running west south [west?] to a line dividing the land from <u>the meeting house land</u> one hundred and fifty perches to a bounded maple standing in the line of a Good Spring Run thence extending by the said line South & N East eighty four perches to a round oak tree standing upon Good Spring Run then down the said Run to the Philpot Brook then along the said Brook...all courses thereof to the first mentioned white oak tree place of Beginning containing by estimation one hundred acres of land...

bounded south by & with the marsh of Peter Thomas and William [John?] easterly with...in consideration of the sum of twelve pounds ten shillings lawful money of his majesties plantations...

*

H , 1, p. 150, 1726/7:

TO ALL CHRISTIANS to who these presents shall come Know ye that I Thomas Jones of New Castle County upon the Delaware and the <u>Manor of Rockland</u> in the said County Yeoman for and in consideration of seven pounds of New Castle currencey & in hand paid by Jacob Weldin ...Have give granted bargained sold ... and confirm unto the said Jacob Weldin his heirs & assigns forever ... tract of land SITUATE and lying in the above manner beginning at the said Thomas Jones' black oak _____ adjoing to the said Jacob Weldin & running thence thirty eight perches and a half sit. be Est to another black oak corner tree thence forty perches Est to No. [ ] to a white oak corner tree thence thirty eight perches and a half & N: th be So:th to the first named black oak TO HAVE AND TO HOLD the said granted premises...Whereof I have hereunto set my hand and seal this 20th day of February 1726/7 and in the thirteenth year...THOMAS JONES T I or T J, [slash through second letter] his mark, Margaret Jones M her mark. Witness Valentine Robinson, John Green.

* *

K 1, 276, 277, 1734:

...Thomas Jones of Brandywine Hundred...for the sum of Forty pounds...well & truly paid by William Derrickson & John Wilder...one tract of land situate...in the Brandywine Hundred in the County of Newcastle containing ninety one acres be it more or less butted & bounded Beginning at a corner marked Chestnut Tree standing by the side of a small run called Good Spring from thence N:e by W: 100 pches. by a line of marked trees to a corner marked Hickere from thence west by S:by a line of marked trees perches to a corner marked black oak from thence & by E:by a line of marked trees 100 Perches to a corner marked white oak from thence E:& by

N: Line of marked trees to the first mentioned Chesnut Tree containing one hundred acres nine excepted being sold before to Jacob Weldin TO HAVE & TO HOLD...Thomas Jones, T I [slash through latter], his mark.
Deed was signed in presence of George Robinson & Valentine Robinson. Deed executed, proved by George Robinson in the Court of Common Pleas...August term 1734. David French Proton.
Also has statement by Thomas Jones giving his friend Andrew Hudson the power to act as his & his wife's attorney in this sale.
*

NOTE: The name Wilder might have been changed to Wilde later.

L, 1, pp. 31, 32, 13th Sept 1736. Between George Robinson of Brandywine Hundred...& Catharine his wife of the one part & Valentine Robinson of Brandywine Hundred...yeoman...Whereas...William Penn...did...by this Warrant under his hand...dated the 12th day of March...1682...grant unto Valentine Hollingsworth...400 acres of land...surveyed...27th day of Sept 1683 & called Newark...Beginning at a line of the Marsh layed out for Thomas John: running along Delaware River 60 perches to a line dividing this from the marsh laid out for Henry Hollingsworth & running...to a creek called Bland Creek containing...40 acres...
* *

M 1, p. 225, 1738:
...Thomas Jones of Brandywine Hundred ...for & in consideration of 40 pounds...paid by Elias King & Elias Tussey 91 acres...small runn called Good Spring...containing one hundred acres excepted being sold before to Jacob Weldin ...with 10 acres of marsh joint to Valentine Robinsons marsh...signed 8th day of October 1738. Thomas Jones [T J,] Margaret Jones [M mark.]
*

Thomas Jones and his wife Margaret appear to have sold all their land with the sale of this 91 acres to Elias King and Elias Tussey in 1738.
* *

CHURCHES:

Other churches were established in New Castle Co. In 1705, in the town of New Castle, Rev. George Ross was appointed missionary. The church established was called Emmanuel or Immanuel Presbyterian Episcopal Church. Marriage records for many of the Welsh Tract Baptists can be found in this church's records. Many Baptists were also married at the Old Swede's Church located in New Castle County, and also at the Quaker Church. If any were married at the Welsh Tract Baptist Church, we did not find any records of this.
* *

OTHER THOMAS JOHN'S & JONES':

The marriage records of New Castle Co. have the marriage of Thomas John and Hannah Green, Jan. 13, 1718/9, by the Minister Geo. Ross of Immanuel P. E. Church.

There was an account in the Church Minutes of Welsh Tract regarding Thomas Jones and his wife Eleanor. They had 'improper conduct towards each other' and were excommunicated by the church on February 6, 1724.
* *

[NOTE: An interesting deed dated 19th August 1726 between Andrew Ellis of Red Lyon Hundred and John Hooeuson, Weaver, of New Castle Hundred for part of a tract of land of three hundred eighty five acres was noted. John Hooeuson might be the antecedent of Ruth Huson (or Husong) who married Edmund Browder of McMinn Co., Tn. in 1814. See "The Browder Connections."]
* *

The Pennepek church records show the birth of Isaac Jones, b. 17. 5mo. 1710, to Henry Jones and Elinor Jones. Henry Jones lived in Philadelphia Co.
* *

ROBERT JONES:

ROBERT JONES, Millright, purchased 258 acres of land 27 Mar 1707 in New Castle Co. from John Guest of Philadelphia & wife Susanna Guest (Deed Book B, Vol. 1, p. 623.)

The deed, between John Guest of the City of Philadelphia Esqr. and Susannah his wife of the one part, and Robert Jones of the County of Chester, millright, dated 20 Aug 1707, mentioned Joseph Moore's land. "Whereas there is a certain tract of land situate on the North Easterly side of White Clay Creek in the County of New Castle in the Territories of the said Province Beginning at a corner Spanish Oak standing on the side of a great hill neare the side of White Clay Creek being allso a corner Tree of Joseph Moore's land, thence up the said creek north Sixty three Degrees westerly twenty seven perches North Eight Degrees Easterly twenty two perches North fforty three degrees westerly one hundred twenty four perches north eight degrees westerly fforty perches and north eight perches to a corner maple tree standing close by the creekside then by a line of marked trees dividing it from other land of the said John Guest south twelve degrees easterly two hundred twenty perches to a corner white oake sapling then by the said John Guests land South seventy nine degrees westerly seventy two perches to a corner white oake standing in a line of the said John Guests - Land thence by the said Joseph Moores land north sixty seven degrees westerly one hundred and eight perches to the place of beginning containing two hundred ffifty eight acres part of a certain tract of land called the Hopyard which the present commissioners of William Penn Proprietary and Governor of the said Province by a certain grant or patent under their hands and the said proprietary's great Seal dated the nineteenth day of Aprill anno

Dui 1703 ffor the consideration therein mentioned Did Grant and confirm unto the said John Guest to hold to him his heires and assignes forever as by the same Patent Recorded in the Rolls Office at Philadelphia in Patent Book A Vol. 2 page 506 may appear now this Indenture...
John Guest, Susanna Guest.
Sealed and delivered in the presence of John Ffrogg Henry Lewis John Powell.
Acknowledged in the court of common pleas at New Castle the twentieth day of Aug...1707...William Tonge...
Recorded the 14th Oct 1707.
* *

NOTE: Deed Book I, Vol. 1, p. 442, (deeds recorded May Term 1731.) mentioned Susannah Guest, wife of John Guest, was only daughter and heir of William Welsh, who was granted land 11th day of 12th mo. 1683 by William Penn. Susannah sold 400 acres & 1,000 acres to John Campbell. In Book I, P. 446, Joseph Moore sold land to Joseph Wood. A Susannah Welsh married Thomas John in 1719.
* *

Henry Lewis and John Powell were Quakers, but might have been among the Keithian Quakers who became Baptists. One of the Miles married a son of John Powell. The early Welsh writers were mostly Quakers, and sometimes did not mention when these people changed religions.

There were several records that showed Robert Jones owned land on which there was a blacksmith shop in Philadelphia County. He was said by Browning to have been the Robert Jones who was brother of Thomas Jones who married Anne John, daughter of Griffith John, the Quaker. The Quakers had a Meeting House in this area of New Castle Co.

A Robert Jones of Cholesbury, Bucks, malster, was shown as owning 500 acres in the "Second Catalogue" of names which were taken from John Reed's Map of the City and Liberties of Philadelphia, & inserted at the end of Volume IV of The Pa. Archives, Third Series.[29]

A LATER JONES IN WHITE CLAY CREEK HUNDRED with possible connections:

In "Biography & General History of the State of Del., Vol. 1, 1899, Publishers: J. M. Runk & Co., Chambersburg, Pa." page 464, [Mormon film #1000155] is a brief biography of Thomas Jefferson Jones, born Stanton, De. Jan 23, 1853, son of late Thomas W. & Rebecca Ann Barton Jones. It stated Thomas W. Jones was a miller and farmer of White Clay Creek & Mill Creek Hundred and owner of the Red Mills. Thomas Jefferson Jones married Adelaide, daughter of John R. & Eliza McFarland Lyman, Oct 24,

---

[29]Sheppard Jr., "Passengers and Ships Prior to 1684...", p. 196.

1888. She was educated at schools at Christiana Hundred. He died at White Clay Creek Dec. 6, 1895. He was a member of White Clay Creek Presbyterian Church and was buried in their graveyard. These might be descendents of Thomas and Rebecca John.

* *

Early Welsh Tract Baptist history continued to show the GRIFFITH, JOHN, and MORGAN Connections.

In 1709, there were others added by letter to the Church from a church in Pembrokeshire: (Samuel John, Minister), John Devonallt, Mary Devonallt, Lewis Philip and Catharine Edward.

The "Register of the Baptist Church at Rhdwilym, Carmarthenshire - Wales, Extract of Entries 1667-1745" had a Samuel John first listed in 1689 under "1689 A Record of the names of the Members whose Princeples are already inserted in this book": '[From] Manerdivi, Samuel John.' Later listings showed he baptized a number of people. The Devonallts were also from Rhdwilym, as were many previous members.

Also listed in 1689 in Wales were Thomas Griffith & Elyzabeth, his wife, Millyne Pist [Parish] Kilivawer; George John and Gaynor his wife, of Llandyssillio Pish, Thomas John and Jane his wife, of Landilo. Pish [Parish]; Morgan Jenkin and Elizabeth his wife, of Prendergast Pish; John David and Jenet his wife, Llangolman Parish; William Jones and Katherine Jones, of Eglwys Vayr; and John Griffith & Jane his wife, from Llanllwni parish, county Carmthen; et al.

This Baptist parish Register of Rhydwilym had the names of many of the Baptists who left Wales and settled in Chester Co., Pa. and New Castle Co., Del. The Rev. John Jenkins was first listed in 1677: "Upon ye 12th day of ye 3d Month 1677 our Bro: John Jenkins of ye Pish of Spittle and our sister Jane Meridus [Meredith] ye wife of Thomas John, taylor submitted to believers Baptysme & after to Laying on of hands." Beginning in 1677, on the first page, " Cout. Cardigan 15th day of ye tenth moneth 1667. Morgan Rytherch, Lewis Thomas, Evan David, Gwen Llian John, Elizabeth Reed, Caterin Evan, Jane Evan, Yngharad John [Harry John Jr.?] were all baptized."

In 1668, there were two entries for a Jane John who was baptized. The first one was from Llandyssil County of Cardigan, 'ye 5th of ye 2d moneth 1668'; and the second one was Jane John Lewelin.. 'the 10th day of ye fift Moneth 1668.' The 13th day of ye fift moneth 1668, "Morgan Rhytherch & Llewelin John were chosen to be deacons and they both to be set ayte for biabl."

In 1677: "Upon ye 12th day of ye 3d Month 1677 our Bro: John Jenkings of ye Pish of Spittle and our sister Jane Meridus ye wife of Thomas John, Taylor, submitted to believers Baptysme & after to Laying on of hands." Then in 1689: "A Record of the names of the Members whose Princeples are already inserted in this book" included "Landilo Yish. Thomas John and Jane his wife. Griffith Nicolas. Mary Griffith. Mary Evan."

In 1709 from East Jersey, Philip Truax and Elizabeth Tilten joined the Welsh Tract church. By a letter from Pennepak, David Miles and Al[i]ce Miles. [Mentioned above.]

These Baptists had further trouble regarding their feelings about the laying-on-of-hands because in 1709 'some new brethren arrived in the country, along with one already there, [John Devonallt, per Morgan Edwards] "who had doubts that the agreement was agreeable to the will of God." But they visited the congregation, and another in West Jersey which had come under the care of John Watts, and they were soon rewarded by 55 persons having hands laid on them since the agreement.'[30]

Baptists were still arriving from Wales. In 1710, from Rydwilin church in Wales were added Lewis Philip; Rees David (Deacon); Thomas Evan; Thomas Edmond; Arthur Edward; Eleanor Philip; Susanna David; and Mary Wallis. From Kilcam came Samuel John, Pastor; John Philip (Elder); Jenkin John (afterwards Minister of Philadelphia); John Harry; John Boulton; Richard Edward; Eleanor Philip; Mary William; Elizabeth Harry; Susanna Owen; Mary Bowen; and Elizabeth John [sister of Jenkin John.]

Many of the familes who arrived around this time from Wales settled in the east end of the Great Valley in Chester Co. and soon began meeting there. There was a lot of interaction between these Baptist groups as some of their names were included in the early Welsh Tract records.

That same year [1710] others came from Lantivy (James James, Pastor), [was in church register of Rydwilin], John Griffith [Elder]; Rees Jones; Hugh Evan; Samuel Evan; David Lewis; Rachel Griffith; Easter John [Esther John]; and Mary Evan. From Langenych where Morgan Jones was Minister, came Hugh David (afterward Minister of the Great Valley); Anthony Mathew; Simon Mathew; Simon Butler; Arthur Melchor; Hanna Melchor; and Margaret David.

From this group from Lantivy church, John Griffith, Elder, was very highly esteemed, as were the Morgans [from Morgan Rhydderch] and John's who accompanied them. Some of their family connections had already arrived in this area earlier. As was usually the case, many family members with this group were not actually listed as church members at this time. Some baptized before in Wales might not have been recorded again.

From this early Baptist group were descendants who later settled and established the Baptist Church in the Pee Dee area of South Carolina. Many of these same names were later found there, and included the James', Miles', Wild's, Lewis' and others mentioned in earlier church records in Pennsylvania.

---

[30]Minutes of the Welsh Tract Baptist Meeting, p. 11.

David John, husband of Esther Morgan John, who came over with them in 1710, was apparently not a member of the church then. In Morgan Edward's notes in "Materials..." either he or historian Benedict wrote that this David John was baptized in 1714. He was born ca 1669, and already had children when he arrived. Some of his descendants went to the Pee Dee in South Carolina in 1738. Abel Morgan and other relations went there to begin a church in Nov. 1735, but Abel Morgan returned to Pa. From these early Welsh Tract settlers came many that settled in South Carolina.
* *

MORGAN ap RYDDERCH (Rhydderch) ap David ap Griffith, was born ca 1620 to 1630, and lived at Alltgoah, parish of Llanwenog, Cardiganshire. He had at least two brothers, Rhees Rhydderch and John Rhydderch. John was a printer, almanac maker and poet. [A John Rhydderch of Hirnant, Montgomeryshire, entered in 1683.][31] Morgan married Jane _____ about 1670. He was baptized 15th day of tenth month 1667, and began preaching, not as an ordained preacher, but as an assistant preacher in 1669. "On ye 27th day of ye 9th Moneth 1669 or [our] Br. Thomas David Rees was both chosen & ordained elder Amongst us in ye church & on ye same day also or Bren Morgan Ryther and Llyweline John were ordained Decons in our said congregation."[32]

Morgan Rhydderch was persecuted by the King's officers and ordered not to preach anymore, although he continued to do so. He never came to America, but had children who did. He died about 1680. His widow Jane also had Griffith children who came to Pennsylvania.

There were Rhydderch's who arrived earlier with the Quakers, and were written about in the books on the Quakers. John Rhydderch died intestate and David Rydderch was appointed to administer his estate on the 4th of the 11mo. 1688. (Adm. Book A, p. 52, Philadelphia.) There was a Rhees Rhydderch who had arrived with one of the earlier companies.

Rhees Rhydderch and Catharine Rhydderch joined the Baptist Church in 1701 during the period when church members "tarried about" in Philadelphia County before starting the church at Welshtract. Catherine died 12th of 10mo. 1701 and Rees died 10mo. 1707. An early Baptist record stated Rhees came to America in 1701 when he was 81 years old. But I noticed in Morgan Edward's writings, one was given the impression that these Baptists all just arrived from Wales when they joined the Baptist church.

Morgan Rhydderch (ca 1620-1630) and Jane's children took the surname of Morgan, and were:
1. THOMAS MORGAN, b. ca. 1670/71.

---

[31]Sheppard Jr., "Passengers and Ships Prior to 1684...", p. 119.
[32]Register of the Baptist Church at Rhydwilym, Carmarthenshire - Wales. Extract of entries 1667-1745.

2. ABEL MORGAN, b. 1673.
3. ENOCH MORGAN, b. 1676.
4. ESTHER MORGAN, b. 1678.
* *

THOMAS MORGAN,

1-son of Morgan Rhydderch (ca 1620-1630) and Jane, was b. ca 1670/71, of
Trewen Hill, Brengwyn parish, Cardiganshire. He was the eldest son, and
was a miller. He was a Baptist and brought his family to Pennsylvania
several years after siblings Abel, Enoch and Esther came. Wife's name
unknown, but she later married William Melchion and lived in New Castle
County. Most of Thomas' children are unknown, except his son, the Rev.
Jenkin Thomas, who was born ca 1690 and died in 1765. He was a well
known poet, and twelve of his poems were published in "Flowers of
Dyved," a collection of Welsh poetry in 1824.

The profession of miller proved to be a profitable one, as good flour and
other mills sprang up in the area. At first William Penn tried to control all
the mills, and had his own miller. This outraged the people who tried
several ways around his orders. He even stopped their building windmills
that ground their flour. After much controversy, he had to stop his control
and other mills soon came into existence.
* *

ABEL MORGAN,

son of Morgan Rhydderch (ca 1620-1630) and Jane, was b. 1673, Alltgoch
(Red Forest), parish of Llanwanog, Cardiganshire, S. Wales. He was a
member of Glandwr branch of Rhydwilin Baptist Church, later Rehoboth.
He began to preach in 1692 when he was age 19; he became an ordained
Baptist Minister ca 1698. He was pastor of the church at Blaenan Gwent,
from which he left for America 28 Sept 1711 with wife Priscilla Powell and
two children. His wife and little son died on this voyage, 17 Dec 1711. He
arrived at Philadelphia 14 Feb 1712. He became pastor of Pennepek or
Lower Dublin Baptist Church with its Philadelphia Branch, where he
became quite well known. He had translated the Century Confession into
Welsh before he left Wales, and added two articles, one on singing of
Psalms and one on Laying on of hands. His greatest literary work was his
Welsh Concordance of the Bible that was prepared by him but not
published until 1730 after his death.

He married (2) Martha Burrows 11 Nov 1714. She died in October
1715. He married again (3) Mrs. Judith Gooding 7 May 1717. She was
daughter of the Rev. Thomas Griffith of the Welsh Tract church, who came
over in 1701. Records show Judith was received into First Baptist Church
Philadelphia from Pennepek Feb. 14, 1768. His will was proved March 25,
1723.
Children of Abel and Priscilla:

1. JANE MORGAN. Married John Holme Jr. of Holmesburg, City of Philadelphia, 1728 or 1729. Eight children.
2. Son who died at sea.

Children of Abel and Judith:
1. RACHELL MORGAN.
2. ABEL MORGAN. Married 4 June 1746, Elizabeth Howell, at the Old Swedes Church in June 1746. [Ref. Vol. 36, p. 14, New Castle, Old Swedes, p. 397.]
3. SAMUEL MORGAN.
4. ENOCH MORGAN.
* *

ENOCH MORGAN,
son of Morgan Rhydderch (ca 1620-1630) and Jane, was b. 1676 at Alltgoch in parish of Lanwennog in the county of Caerdigan. Arrived with the Welsh Tract church group in 1701. Wife Jane Morgan, added to church by baptism in 1703. He was minister after Rev. Elisha Thomas died, and one of the constituent members of the church at Iron Hill, Pencader Hundred, in New Castle Co. Died 25 Mar 1740, buried at Welsh Tract cemetery. [He had sons who moved to Va. and the Carolinas, according to Benedicts History of the Baptists. Son Abel returned from S. Carolina and was minister at Middletown.]
Children:
1. ABEL MORGAN, was minister of Middletown, N. J., and never married. He was born at Welsh Tract 18 Apr 1713. Died at Middletown 24 Nov 1785. Was trained in the ministry at an Academy kept by Rev. Thomas Evans in Pencader and ordained at Welsh Tract in 1734.[33] Was recommended as a teaching elder to Charlestown, S.C. to preach, from which he soon returned. Became pastor of Baptist Church at Middletown, Monmouth Co., N.J. in 1738. His mother Jane kept his house until she died at an advanced age. He was buried in the Presbyterian Church graveyard in Middletown, as there was no Baptist cemetery there. Inscription on slab marking his grave: "In memory of Abel Morgan, pastor of the Baptist Church at Middletown, who departed this life Nov. 24, 1785, in the 73 year of his age. His life was blameless; his ministry powerful; he was a burning and shining light, and his memory is dear to the saints." His nephew Samuel Morgan was his successor there.
2. ESTHER MORGAN. Born at Welsh Tract 1706, d. 1732, aged 26 yrs. Married a Douglass.

---

[33]Morgan Edwards, in "Materials..."

3. ENOCH MORGAN. Morgan Edwards wrote he believed that Enoch Morgan's wife was a Howell. One of Enoch's sons was Rev. Samuel Morgan who became pastor of the Baptist Church at Middletown, N. J. about ten days after the death of his uncle, Abel Morgan. Another son was Enoch Morgan, Jr., who was baptized 3 May 1740 at Welsh Tract. Another Enoch Morgan, possibly a grandson, was baptized 2 May 1772 at Welsh Tract. A letter in the files of Welsh Tract, dated 6 Sept 1772, indicated Enoch Morgan was then in New Valley, London Co., Va.

* *

The successor of Enoch Morgan as Pastor of the Welsh Tract Church was Rev. Owen Thomas. He was born in 1676 at a place called Georgodllys in Cilmanllwyd Parish, County of Pembroke. He arrived in Del. in 1707. On May 27, 1748, he resigned to go to Yellow Springs. He died there 12 Nov 1748. His children were Elizabeth, Morris, Rachel, Mary, Sarah, and Owen.

* *

JOHN GRIFFITH:

After the death of Morgan Rhydderch in Wales, his widow Jane, who was probably less than 30 years of age, was left with four children. About 1685/86, she became the second wife of John Griffith. Both were listed in Rhydwilym [Wales] Church Register in 1689. [The 16th day of the 4th month 1689 had an account of the baptizm of John Griffith and George Griffith. There was a Morgan Griffith at their church in Wales who was baptizing people there in 1701.]

John and Jane had several children who came to America. Jane Rhydderch Griffith died, and John Griffith was said to have married again to Rachel _____.

These earlier records show Elder John Griffith, wife Rachel, daughter Sarah Griffith, son Benjamin Griffith, his other sons and daughters, stepdaughter Esther Morgan John, along with other family connections, came to America from Wales in 1710. Benjamin and Sara were born in parish of Llanllwyni, Caermarthenshire, Wales. It was written Rhees Rhydderch and Catherine came from Wales at this time. Benedict mentioned daughter or daughters of Rhees Rhydderch who came to America. They probably took the surname Rhees. Some Rhydderchs and Morgans arrived before John Griffith, and some after.

Elder John Griffith and Rachel joined the Welsh Tract Church in 1710 upon arrival. John Griffith, Elder, was buried 12 Nov 1735, when 80 years of age. He was born ca 1655. There was another Rachel Griffith who was a widow 33 years before she died, the 12th day of June 1782.[34] She was

---

[8] Welsh Tract Baptist Meeting, New Castle Del., Bk. 3, p. 6.

Rachel Thomas, daughter of Elisha Thomas, the daughter-in-law of this John Griffith, and widow of his son, John Griffith, Jr.

JOHN GRIFFITH'S WILL:

John Griffith's will was dated 28 Oct 1735, [taken from New Castle Co. Court House, Wilmington, Del., Register of Wills, Vol. 1, 1727-1776]:

"Item. I give unto my son Daniel the sum of twenty pounds.

Item. I give unto my son Benjamin the sum of ten pounds.

Item. I give unto my grand daughter Jane the daughter of Benjamin the sum of two pounds ten shillings.

Item. I give unto my son Samuel the great chest and a little iron pot during his life and two yew and chaff bed and bed cloathes and sixty acres of land more or less in ye [east] and of ye southend of my land during his life upon condition that he doth not wast the timber.

Item. I give unto my daughter Sarah one feather bed and two sheets.

Item. I give unto my daughter Sarahs children four sheep.

Item. I give unto Owen Thomas ye sum of one pound.

Item. I give unto Enoch Morgan ye sum of one pound.

Item. I give unto my son Daniel an iron pot but next the biggest.

Item. All the rest of my Houses, Lands, Bills Bonds Goods Whatsoever I give unto my son John upon condition that he shall pay all my debts and Legacies and make him sole Executor of this my last will and testament revoking all other wills and Testaments.

...in the presence of us

Samuel Wild

Mary Wild   JOHN GRIFFITH [seal]"
* *

This will had some of John Griffith's children, but probably not all of them. Listed in his will were:

1. DANIEL GRIFFITH.
2. BENJAMIN GRIFFITH.
3. SARAH GRIFFITH.
4. SAMUEL GRIFFITH.
5. JOHN GRIFFITH. Married (2) Rachel Thomas, daughter of Elisha Thomas.

We cannot be sure that all of John Griffith's children took the surname of Griffith, as these apparently did. Some undoubtedly used John, in the Welsh way. John Griffith was married three times and probably had children by all three wives. He was quite elderly when they came over and some of his children were married in Wales.
*

BENJAMIN GRIFFITH:

He was son of John and Jane Griffith. He was born 16 Oct 1688 in Parish of Llanllwyni, Carmarthenshire. He came to America in 1710; baptized at Pennepek 11 May 1711; transferred to Welsh Tract Church in 1714. Ordained pastor of Montgomery Baptist Church 23 Oct 1725. Remained there until he died 5 Oct 1768. Married Sarah Miles, daughter of Richard Miles, of Radnor, Delaware Co., Pa.

Children:

1. JANE GRIFFITH, b. 1721. Married an Evans.
2. ABEL GRIFFITH, b. 25 Dec 1723, Montgomery Township, Montgomery Co., Pa. Ordained in 1761. Pastor of the Brandywine Church. In March 1788 settled in Salem, N. H. and was pastor of Baptist Church there. He returned to Brandywine to preach six Sabaths a year until Feb. 1791, when he went to Ky. Married (1) Sarah Coffin of Philadelphia, who d. April 1764 in childbirth of twins. She was buried with one of them on each arm in the cemetery of the Brandywine Church. Had eight children. He married (2) Rebecca Miles. They had three children. She d. Aug. 1779. Abel Griffith died 19 May 1793. Abel's daughter Rachel m. John Powell, d. Jan. 24, 1856.
3. SARAH GRIFFITH; b. 1732. Married a Roberts.
4. JOSEPH GRIFFITH; b. 1733; d. 1773. Married Mary Jones.
5. RACHEL GRIFFITH. Married Abel Davis, a member of Welsh Tract Baptist Church. Had at least one child.

* *

The Welsh Tract Baptist Church was considered the "Mother Church," and several other churches were established in surrounding areas. John Griffith and Jane's son, Benjamin Griffith, became Pastor of Montgomery Baptist Church. Other churches were Great Valley, London Tract, Duck Creek, Willmington, Cowmarsh, Montgomery, Mispillion, Brandywine, etc. More will be given on these churches later.

Statements from Samuel Jenkins, third great grandson of Morgan ap Rhydderch, showed the following were related to Morgan Rhydderch:

Rev. Griffith Jones, of Rehoboth Church in Wales [one Rev. Griffith Jones arrived in Great Valley in 1712*, and one arrived in 1749].

Rev. David Davis, of Baptist Church near New Castle.

Rev. Evans of Rock Church, Baptist, near New Castle Emlyn (Del.)

Rev. John Jones, Baptist, son of Rev. Griffith Jones, above mentioned.

Rev. Jeremiah Davis, of Independent Church.

Rev. John Jones, of Llwafydd.

Rev. John Williams, etc.[35]

---

[35]Materials Towards History of the American Baptists in XII Volumes, Philadelphia, 1770, Morgan Edwards.

*Other records have arrival date of 1710.

CHAPTER FIVE

ESTHER MORGAN JOHN and DAVID JOHN:

Esther, daughter of Morgan Rhydderch and Jane, born at Alltoch (or Alltogeh) Wales in 1678, was stepdaughter of John Griffith. She married David John in Wales. They came to Delaware in 1710. She died in Welsh Tract 2 Oct 1754.[1] Benedict in his History stated after writing that the sons of Rev. Enoch Morgan moved Southward into Va. and the Carolinas that "this is true also of a portion of the descendants of Father Morgan and David Jones."[2]

I will refer to him as David John as that was the way his name first appeared in the Church Minutes, although most of his descendants eventually used the surname Jones. Documents for him were found with both Jones and John as surname.

David John was born ca 1669 in Wales, and was buried at Welsh Tract 20 Aug 1748.[3] Rees Jones, tanner, probably was related as they arrived at the same time. David and Rees Jones came to Pennsylvania in 1710 from Wales, along with Esther John and John Griffith. Enoch and Abel Morgan, brothers of Esther, arrived in 1701 and 17ll, and all were closely connected. There is also the possibility that Thomas John who had wife Rebecca was related.

ESTHER JOHN joined the Welsh Tract Baptist church by letter from "Llantivy, James James pastor." David was not a member when they first came to Pennsylvania, and joined by baptism in 1714. He possibly was excommunicated later, as there was a David John written in the records with "Ex" written alongside, but nothing else, which was rare. [Another "Ex" was erroneously written by another name for a person that only left to go to another church.] Since there were several David John's there, it is impossible to be sure now.

His will indicated DAVID JOHN was a prosperous farmer and a large landowner. Numerous land records were found for David John, and they appeared to be his.

Children of David John [ca 1669] and Esther John [ca 1678]:

1. JOHN JONES, b. ca 1695. Moved to South Carolina. [Named in will.] Died 1759 in Welsh Neck, S.C.
2. MORGAN JONES, b. ca. 1697 in Wales. [In will.]
3. _____ JONES, m. George Brown. Children Thomas, William and George Brown. [Deceased at time will written.]

---

[1]Cemetery tombstone has "In memory of Ester Jones who Departed this live October 2, 1754, aged 76 years."
[2]Mormon Church Microfilm #0839693, Delaware History of Baptist Families.
[3]Tombstone inscription "David Jones Departed this life August the 20 1748 aged 80 years."

4. DANIEL JONES. [In will.]
5. RACHEL JONES, m. Richard Williams. [In will.]
6. MARY JONES, m. _____ Beal. [In will.]
7. DAVID JONES, b. ca 1716; died 2 Dec 1758, unmarried. Buried
    Welsh Tract Cemetery, Del. [In will.]
8. JANE JONES, m. John Passmore. Born ca 1720, d. 20 Jul 1764, Del.
    [In will.]
9. JAMES JONES, b. ca 1719. [In will.]
Probably others.

SURVEYS using Jones:
   "At the Request of David Jones of the County of New Castle that we
would Grant him to take up Two Hundred acres of vacant land joining on
Simon Thomas' land near the Welsh Tract in the said County for which he
agrees to pay to the proprietors use fifty pounds whole for and the yearly
quitrent of one bushell of good winter wheat for each Hundred acres These
are to authorize and Require thee to Survey or cause to be Surveyed unto
the said David Jones the said parcel of vacant land including within the
Same the Improvement where he Dwells Provided it be Clear of all other
Surveys and Lawfull claims and make a Return thereof into the Secretarys
office which Survey in case the said David Jones fulfill the above
agreement within three months after the date hereof shall be called
otherwise the same is to be void as if it had never been made nor this
warrant ever granted. Given under our hands and Provincial Seal at
Philada. ye 2d Day of 7mo. A.D. 1715.
Attested by: Richd. Hill; Isaac Norris; James Logan*."
* *

NOTE: *These were Penn's Land Commissioners. It appears this land was
taken out under the quit-rents, after David had lived there long enough to
make improvements.

Survey Index for New Castle Co.:
David Jones, J 1 , #12, near Welsh Tract. Warrant 2 Sept 1715. 200 acres.
New Castle Co., David Jones, J 2, #19, near main branch of Christiana
Creek. Old survey Surveyed 16 Aug. 1682 for John Ogle.
David Jones, Ref. J 2, #20,21. Near Welsh Tract, 260 acres surveyed June
28, 1717; #21 plot drawn at Phila. 1718.
Map and Statement:
"The Draught of a Tract of Land Situate Near the Welsh Tract in the
County of Newcastle Containing Two hundred and Sixty Acres Surveyd,
and Laid out to David Jones of the afsd. County on the 28th of June Anno
1717 by a Warrant from the Commissioners of Property dated the 21st of
Sept in the Year 1715.
Drawn at Phidea. December the first Day 1718. Jacob Taylor."

In center was a map on which was written "Rees Jones Decd's Land by him purchased of Alexr. Fraiser. 125 1/2 acres clear of..."
To right was Benj. Gibb's land. To left was David John's land. At bottom was Benjamin Gibbs'. He was in the Pennepek Church records.

"By virtue of a Copy of a Wart. From the Comissrs. of Property bearing date the 26 day of the 7th Mo. Anno Domi. 1715 for to Survey to Alexander Fraiser 100 acres of land hereby directed on the 24th day of Decr. 1739 by Benj. Eastburn Survr. Genl. of the Province of Pennsylvania & Countie on Deleware for Executing the same.

I have Survd. the above described Tract of Land Situate in White Clay Creek Hundred & County afsd. near the Northside of Christiana Creek now found to contain clear of ___ 125 acres of Land & Swamps being now bounded as the same was reputed to be heretofore & sold by the sd. Alexr. Fraiser to Rees Jones Tanner deced. by information & now claimed by Rachel Jones widow & Admrs. of the sd. Rees Jones tanner deced. Surveyed the 23 Febry. 1739.'   Thos Noxon Dep. Survr. Of New Castle Co.

Sworn Chambrs. Davd. Johns & Saml. Griffith.
Land shared by Jno. Griffith in behalf of Rachel Jones widow. [Rees Jones' widow m. John Griffith Jr.]
*

Under David Jones:
"David Jones Land being off an old corner black oake off Reese Jones Land and Runs by his line south: 434: perches to a corner maple standing in a marsh then east 2 perches to a corner stake in the sd. marsh then south 45 perches to a marker corner from a corner east 82 perches to a corner white oake then north 120 perches to a corner white oak then by an old line N 28 Degrees west: 44 pch. N: 33 degrees West 60: perches to a corner white oake then by a line off marker trees north 53 Degrees East 158: perch. to an old corner black oake then by an old line of Marker trees: north 33: Degrees west 214: perches to an old corner Hickory then by an old line off oake trees west 38 perches to the first mentioned corner Black oake and then off beginning Containing within these bounds 1250: acres Surveyed the 28th Day of June 1717.
George Dabeyne, Surveyr."

A statement signed by John Mandy.
Underneath:
"This land was confirmed by Patent to John White in the year 1684 described according to the within Draught reciting Ogle & Mandy's assignment to sd. White underwhom D. Jones holds the same."

A statement of John Ogle purchasing this Nov. 8, 1683 was very faint. Witness: James William & Tho: Pierson. Confirmed "this eight and twentieth day of November 1683."

Another item shown, which probably indicated it was on back of above, had: David Jones New Castle Co. formerly [land of] John Ogle & John White. Recorded in page 316 Book of Surveys.
At side of page: John White.
Under it written: Now David Jones' land in 1740.
Next was a map of John Ogle's 200 acres.
* *

The Draught of a Tract of Land Situate Near the Welch Tract...containing 260 acres Laid out to David Jones of New Castle County on the 28 June 1717, by Warrant from Commissioners of Property Dated 21 Sept 1715.
* *

'BY THE COMMISSIONERS OF PROPERTY
At the request of John Griffith of the County of New Castle that we would grant him to take up a certain parcel of vacant Land near to the land lately laid out to David Jones on the South Side of Christiana Creek Supposed to contain between one and two hundred acres for which he agrees to pay to the Proprieters. use [from crossed out] of two and twenty pounds ten Shillings Money of Pensilvania and the yearly quitrent of one bushell of good winter wheat for one hundred acres and in like proportion for the rest These are to authorize and require thee to Survey or cause to be Surveyd unto the said John Griffith the said parcel of vacant land contiguous to the lands already laid out provided the same be clear of all other surveys and lawful claims of other persons and make a Return thereof into the Secretarys office which Survey in case the said John Griffith fulfil the above agreement within three months after the date hereof Shall be called otherwise the same is to be void as if it had never been made nor this Warrant ever granted given under our hands and Seal of the Province at Philadelphia the 9th day of the 1st Month Anno Dim 1716/7. To Jacob Taylor Survr. General. Richd. Hill; Isaac Norris; James Logan.'

Under JOHN:
Map showing David John's land, Benj. Gibbs land, Saml. and James Steward, Jos. Peace [Pierce?], Robt. Meers, Jno. Hill, Sam. Allen.
* *

A Survey made for Benjamin Eastbarn, Gentl., dated 8th Nov 1739 has map showing a branch of Christiana Creek (on opposite side says Barrat's Run) running southeast to north, and has Benjamin Gibbs' land and Sam Allen's land to right of Christiana Creek; then to their right is David John's land. A square map, with David Johns on one side, Joseph Ogle on another, Hugh Huchison, then James Williams.

"Pursuant to a Warrt. from the Proprietor to me Directed bearing Date ye 22d of ye 6mo. August 1733 there of showd. Resurvey unto John Faires a certain peice or parcell of Land Situate near Cristiana Creek on sd. north side thereof 150 acres being part of a tract of Land formerly belonging to James Williams of Cristiana aforesaid Deceased Cot. 300 a. These we therefore do certifie that I have accordingly Resurveyed unto ye said said John Faires ye said quantity of 150 acres as followeth - - Beginning at an old corner Hickery Tree Standing by ye Kings Road on ye E side hereof & is also a corner of Joseph Ogles & Hugh Huchisons land, thence by an old line of marked trees of Jo. said Huchisons Land South 33 Degrees Ely 152 1/2 perches to a new made corner W: _____ in Said Huchisons line being a corner of James Williams Land also, thence by a new line of marked trees dividing this from the said James Williams Land S: 56 Deg. Wly 158 per. to a corner Stake by a new made corner. B. O. in sd line of David Johns Land thence by ye said David Johns line being an old line of marked trees N 33 Deg. Wly 152 per. to an old corner Hickery thence by an old line of marked trees of Joseph: Ogles land N: 56 Deg. Ely. 158 perches crossing the Kings Road to the first mentioned corner Hickory and..."

*

- Note: This James Williams was probably father of the Richard Williams married to David's daughter Rachel.

Another map in the surveys showed David John's land in relation to Rees Jones' land, and "land of Rees Jones & claimed by Jno. Griffith." In center was Benj. Gibbs land.

* *

Survey had a map with David John's Land. Shown North was Benja. Gibbs Land, which was joined by James Read's land on the east. Directly east of David John's land was John Griffith's land, 167 acres [on a Branch of Christiana Creek. Also directly south was John Griffith's Plantation Tract. Below this was written "Land in the Welsh Tract."

[NOTE: John Griffith's Plantation Tract probably indicated the land that was his when he acquired Rees Jones' land.]

" BY VIRTUE of a copy of a wart. from the Comissors. of Property bearing date the 4th day of the first mo. in Anno Domi. 1716/17 to Survey to John Griffith between one & two hundred acres of land [marks] newly to me directed on the 24th day of Decr. 1739 by Benja. Eastburn Survr. Genl. of the Province of Pennsylva. & Countie on Delaware for Executing the same. I have Survd. the above described Tract of Land situate in White Clay Creek Hundred & County afd. on the northside of Christiana Creek thro. W [symbol] bra. of the sd. Crk. parsell now found to contain clear of [symbols] 167 acres of Land & Swamps being now bounded as the same was reputed

135

to be heretofore by the adjacent Lands & now Surveyed to John Griffith son
of John Griffith to whom the wart. was first granted. Sworn & Brs. Survd.
the 23 Febr 1738/9. Thos. Noxon Depte. Survr. of N.C. County."
David Johns & Samuel Griffith
Land shared by
Jno. Griffith.
* *

Map made 8th Nov. 1739. Showed a branch of Christiana Creek. On north
side was written "Barrat's Run a" - To left of this was written Jos. Pearce's
Land. Back right of Christiana Creek was written "Saml. Allens' Land 194
acres...", Samuel & James Stewarts Land coming to a "V" in the corner,
then some surveyor's symbols...of David John's & Benj. Gibbs Land
beginning...Below this map was written "Benj.a. Gibbs's Land.
'BY VIRTUE of a copy of the ____ Wart. to me directed by Benj. Eastburn
Surv. Genll. of the Province of Pennsylvania & Counties on Dela. dated the
8th day of November 1739 &
I have Survd. to Saml. Allen of the afd. County the above described Tract of
Land Situate in White Clay Creek Hundred & Cty. afd. on both sides of the
road leading from the Welsh Tract to Christiana Bridge & on a branch of
Christiana Creek called Barrats Run conta. clear of [symbols] for roads &
194 acres of Land including ____ or Improvemts. wch. by the best
information I could get has been settled 18 or 20 years Surv. the 19th day of
December Ano Domi 1739 being all the baroney there. Thos. Noxon
Depty. Surv. of New Castle County.
Mathew Patton & James Boyls.'
* *

Deed Book G, Vol. 1, Pp. 285, 286, 1723:
'THIS INDENTURE made the eighth day of February...one thousand seven
hundred and twenty three Between Rees Price of White Clay Creek
Hundred in the County of New Castle upon Delaware yeoman one of the
sons of Rees Thomas late of the hered. and County aforesaid Yeoman
deceased and Catharine Thomas widdow and Relict of the said Rees
Thomas of the one part and David Jones of Penkader Hundred in the said
county yeoman of the other part whereas the said Rees Thomas by virtue of
a warrant under the hand of Edward Pennington Hon. surveyor Generall ...
bearing date the seventh day of the fourth month June anno one thousand
seven hundred one ... tract of Land situate and being in New Castle County
aforesaid. Beginning at an old Corner Chestnut tree and Extending thence
South Fifteen degrees East Eighty Two perches to an old corner hickery tree
of the tract of land commonly called the London Tract thence by the line of
the said London Tract west forty eight perches to Christianah Creek thence
west twenty four perches to a corner white oak standing by Christianah
Creek aforesaid thence along the Courses of the said Creek South thirty
eight degrees east tenn perches then South Fiffty Eight degrees east twenty

Eight perches then South thirty degrees east Fiffty Eight perches to a Corner hickory by Christianah Creek aforesaid thence by a line dividing the same from Abraham Brewsters land Houses Seventy eight degrees east one hundred and eighty five perches to an old corner white oak standing on John Reynolds line thence by the said Reynolds line North one hundred and twenty eight perches to an old corner poplar thence north forty four perches to an old corner maple tree of the said Reynold's line thence North Forty four perches to an old corner hickery tree thence by another line North fforty degrees west one hundred and fourteen perches to an old corner hickory by the fence thence by another line North forty degrees west one hundred and fourteen to an old corner hickory tree thence South Sixty degrees west one hundred and forty five perches to the Place of beginning Containing ... did grant the said three hundred acres of land with the Appurtenances unto the said Rees Price his heirs .. as by a Certain instrument in writing under the hand ...of Rees Thomas dated the third day of September anno one thousand Seven hundred and Eighteen ... This Indenture Witnesseth that the Said Rees Price and Catharine Thomas for and in Consideration of the Issue of Fiffty seven Pounds ten Shillings lawful money ... in hand paid by Said David Jones the Receipt whereof they do hereby acknowledge...and the said Rees Price and Catharine Thomas for their selves their heirs...do Covenant...and agree to and with the said David Jones...in manner and form following (viz.) that he the said David Jones his heirs and assigns Shall ... at all time forever here after quietly and peaceably have ... the said premises hereby granted with the appurtenances and shall receive the Rents and profits thereof to his and their own proper use...without ... Disturbance of the said Rees Price or Catherine Thomas...have hereunto sett their hands and seals dated the day and year first above written. Rice Price (Seal); Catharine Thomas (Sealed and Delivered) in the Presence of Elisha Thomas; Rees Jones; James James. Acknowledged in open Court of Common Pleas...the twentyth day of February one thousand seven hundred and twenty three...John Drury. Recorded the 4th day of March 1723/4.'
* *

K, 1, p. 439, 1735:
'Indenture Between John Perry of Pencader Hundred...Taylor & Sarah his wife of the one part and David Jones of Pencader afsd...Yeoman of the other part...WHEREAS William Penn late Proprietor of Pensilvania...by his Warrant bearing date the Eighteenth Day of the Eighth Month Anno Dom. was granted to one William Davies & David Evans the Quantity of Thirty Thousand Acres of Land comonly called the Welsh Tract ... and the said William Davis &...conveyed Two hundred & Nine Acres part of the said Tract unto one Thomas Watson decd. as by his Deed of the same appeareth and the said Watson conveyed the same again to Richard Seren [Sorency?] which said Seren died intestate so that Said Sarah Seren (alias Perry) party

to these presents became Sole Heirs thereof as sd. Proceedings upon Record in the Court of orphans in said County more fully appeareth NOW THIS INDENTURE FURTHER WITNESSETH that the said John Perry together with Sarah his said wife for and in Consideration of the Several sums of one Hundred & Twenty nine pounds & Fifteen Shillins (present currency) and likewise the sum of five Shillings of like money to them in Hand paid or Secured to be paid before the ensealing & Delivery of these presents by the said David Jones the receipt whereof they do hereby acknowledge & thereof & of every part and parcel thereof do clearly acquit and discharge the said David Jones...have Granted...& absolutely confirm unto the said David Jones (in his actual possession more being by virtue of a Bargain & Sale to him thereof made for one whole Year of Indenture bearing Date the Day before the date hereof and by fforce of the Statute for transferring uses into Possession) all that Tract of Land & Plantation now in Possession of said John Perry together with all Houses Barns orchards Garden Plotts woods underwoods Land arable Meadows Pastures Swamp waters water Courses Ways easments & Conveniences usually belonging to the same as it is there well known & distinguished by its meets & Boundaries following (viz) BEGINNING at a Persimon Tree the north corner of said Land in Howell James' Line running west one hundred & ninety nine perches to a corner black oak Saplin thence South one Hundred & Sixty Eight perches to a Corner white oak in James Reads Line thence East one hundred & ninety nine perches to a corner Hickery Saplin in David Evans' Line thence north one hundred & sixty eight perches by John Porters Line to the place of beginning Containing in the whole Two Hundred & Nine Acres as above & Situate in Pencader afsd. And in as large & ample manner as the said Richard Seren lately held the same together with all the Right Title Interest Possession...which the said John Perry now hath or ever had by Right of Sarah his said wife to the said Plantation or to any part or parcel thereof and the Reversons & Remainders yearly and the Rents & Profits of the premises and of every part thereof...the said Plantation & all singular other the premises...to be hereby granted...unto the said David Jones...
Signed by John Perry and Sarah Sery.
Recorded Apl. 30th 1736. In presence of David Ffrench & William Shaw.'
* *

Deed Book K, Vol. 1, p. 464, 1736:
"TO ALL CHRISTIAN PEOPLE to whom these presents shall come I Elizabeth Serey late of Pencader Hundred in the County of New Castle upon Delaware and Province of Pennsylvania widow and Admrs. Of Richard Serey decd. Do send Greeting WHEREAS I the said Elizabeth Serey by a certain writing Executed under my Hand and Seal for the Consideration therein mentioned have assigned and Set over unto John Perry my son in law the Administration of all and singular the Estate of my late Husband the said Richard Serey decd. & in & by the said writing

reserved unto myself the Dower of Three pounds per annum during the Term of my natural life in lien of my third of a certain Plantation belonging to the Estate of my Husband decd. AND WHEREAS the said John Perry hath lately granted conveyed & confirmed the said Plantation unto David Jones of Pencader afsd. Yeoman under the said Yearly payment of three pounds per annum to me payable as above NOW KNOW YE that I the said Elizabeth Serey for and in consideration of the sum of twenty pounds lawful current money of Pennsylvania to me in hand paid by the said David Jones the Receipt whereof I do hereby acknowledge & myself therewith satisfied and paid HAVE granted remised released and quit claimed and by these presents do grant remise release and forever Quit Claim unto the said David Jones...all and all manner of Dower Annuity or the said Yearly Rent of Three pounds per annum & all my Right and Titles of Dower annuity or Yearly Rent whatsoever which before sealing and Delivery hereof I had might should could or of Right ought to have or Claim of in or out of the Plantation abovesd. Situate in Pencader aforesd. now in the possession of the said David Jones so as the sd. David Jones his Heirs and Assigns Shall or lawfully may have and hold the said Plantation without suit or Trouble of me or any other person in my name to claim or demand any manner of Dower annuity on the said Rent whatsoever...NOW KNOW YE that I the said Elizabeth Serey for and in consideration of the sum of Twenty pounds lawfull current money of Pennsylvania to me in hand paid by the said David Jones the Receipt whereof I do hereby acknowledge...have granted...released and quit claimed...unto the said David Jones... Signed Elizabeth Seres E her mark."
Note: This name was probably Elizabeth Sorency.
* *

M 1, 89, 1738, 14 Aug. 1738:
'This Indenture made the fourteenth day of August in the Twelfth Year of the Reign of King George the Second over Great Brittain and in the Year of our Lord one thousand seven hundred & thirty eight Between John Allen of the County of New Castle on Delaware fuller of the one Part & David Jones of the place aforesaid Yeoman of the other part WITNESSETH that whereas the said John Allen now is and standeth rightfully & lawfully seized in his Demesne as of ffee Simple of & Into all that Tract or parcel of Land called Norhampton Situate lying & being on the North Side of Christiana Creek in the County aforesaid Beginning at a Corner Gum tree standing at the north side of the said Run and from thence North east by a Line of marked trees one hundred and sixty perches to a corner marked white oak and from the said white oak north west by a Line of marked trees two hundred perches to a corner marked red oak thence south west by a line of marked trees one hundred & sixty perches to a corner marked poplar standing by said runside & from the Poplar down the said Run side bounding therewith two hundred perches to the first mentioned gum tree

containing two hundred acres of thereabouts be the same more or less NOW
THIS INDENTURE WITNESSETH that the said John Allen for & in
consideration of the sum of one hundred & twenty pounds lawfull money of
America to him in hand paid by the said David Jones...JOHN ALLEN.
Sealed & Delivered in the Presence of John Griffith, Josiah Lowden, James
Armitage.'
* *

WILL of DAVID JOHN:
Will Book G, pp. 187,8,9. 8th Aug 1748.
"IN THE NAME OF GOD AMEN ye Eighteenth day of Aug. one thousand
seven hundred and forty Eight, I David Jones of Pencader hundred in ye
County of New Castle upon Dellaware Yeoman being weak in body but of
perfect mind & memory Thanks be given unto God: Therefore calling unto
mind ye mortality of my body and knowing that it is appointed for all men
once to die, Do make & ordain this my last Will & Testament, That is to say
principally & first of all I give & recommend my Soul into ye hand of God
that gave it & my body I recommend to ye Earth to be buried in decent
Christian burial at ye discrection of my Executors And as touching such
worldly Estate wherewith it hath pleased God to bless me in this life I give
devise and dispose of the same in the following manner & form Viz:
Imprimis I give and bequeath to Esther my dearly beloved wife one third
part of all ye proffits of all my lambs during her natural life, and all my
household goods except what shall be after Excepted & ye half of all ye
grain in and about ye Barn and ye half of ye proffits of my orchard and all
remainder of my Estate after [after] all my debts & legacies paid. Item I
give to my son Morgan Jones ye sum of ten pounds to be paid to him out of
the Eighty pound that is in his own hand due to me ye remainder being
seventy pounds, I order him to pay ye same to his brothers and sisters that is
to say ten pounds to each & every one of them & likewise I give and
bequeath to my sd. son Morgan ye land & Plantation where Thos. Nelson
lately lived to him his heirs & assigns for ever, Item I give & bequeath to
my *son James Jones the land and Plantation where he now liveth being two
hundred & forty acres, or as it is spc. Mentioned to him his heirs & assigns
forever on condition that he pays ten pounds to Ester Jones daughter of
John Jones. Item, I give to my Son John Jones ye sum of five pounds
besides ye ten pounds that I ordered my son Morgan to pay as above
mentioned. Item; I give & bequeath to my Son Daniel Jones ye land and
places where I now live, to him his heirs & assigns forever & one Cow, &
one axe, ---Item I give & bequeath unto my Son David Jones ye new
Plantation on ye south end of my land, and ye improvements* thereupon,
being one hundred acres of land to be surveyd out of ye south end of my
land to him his heirs & assigns for ever upon Condition that his sister Jane
shall live along with him while she continues unmarried, and otherwise I
give him my sd. son one bay mare and a filly besides ye ten pounds which I

ordered his brother Morgan to pay him as above, But if my sd. son David dies without issue that ye sd. land & premises shall go to ye use of David Jones son of ye above mentioned Morgan Jones his heir & assigns for ever upon Condition that ye sd. Morgan Jones, or sd. David Jones his son shall take care of and assist ye sd. David Jones ye Elder, in bargain making or ye like, when need requires by reason of his noncomsiments and likewise I give ye least cart & one plow to my sd. son. Item, I give & bequeath to my daughter Jane ye fivety pounds bond due to me from William Addlar and twenty pounds in Cash beside ye ten pounds I have ordered my son Morgan to pay her as above and one Chest wth. drawers that is now on her name & one mug and one blanket & one sheet & one horse named Roben. Item; I give to my daughter Rachell Williams the sum of ten pounds besides ye ten pounds that I ordered my son Morgan to pay to her as before mentioned and likewise I give and deliver or cause to be delivered to my sd. daughter Rachell all ye deeds & writings that it is in my custody belonging to her husband Richd. Williams being ye writings of his hand, Item, I give to my Daughter Mary Deal ye sum of ten pounds besides ye sum of ten pounds that I have ordered my son Morgan to pay her as before mentioned, Item, I give to

Item; I give to each of George Browns Children)
to Thomas Brown ye sum of ten Pounds.   ) Viz. To be Paid to each of
to John Brown ye sum of ten pounds--   ) them when they arrives to
to William Brown ye sum of ten pounds.   ) full age by my Executors.
To George Brown ye sum of ten pounds.   )

Item, I give and bequeath to my grand Son Benjm. Jones son of John Jones the land and the Improvements thereon Christiana Creek in White Clay Creek Hundred where widow Helpatrick now liveth to be delivered him when he arrives to ye age of twenty five years to him & his assigns forever, But if he dies before he arrives to good age, ye said land and premises shall be for ye use of his brother Enoch Jones his heirs and assigns forever to be delivered him when he arrives to ye age of twenty five years.

LASTLY, I constitute make and ordain my said wife Esther and my three sons Morgan, James, & Daniel to be Joint executors of this my last will & Testament AND I do hereby utterly disallow & _____ & disanule all & every other former Testaments, wills legacies & bequests & Executors by me in any ways before named willed & bequeathed Resolving & Confirming this & no other to be my last will & Testament, IN WITNESS whereof I have hereunto set my hand & Seal ye day & year above written---

To him & his assigns forever was underlined in Benjm. Jones paragraph before signing---

[Signed] David Jones (Seal)

Signed Sealed published Pronounced & declared by ye sd David Jones as his last will & Testament in ye presence of

Daniel Griffith, Thomas James, Cathirne Bloyls. [Her mark.]

[189] County of New Castle

Thomas James & Cathirne Bloyls two of ye Subscribing Evidences to be annexed Testament on their oathes do say that they were present & saw David Jones ye Testator sign & Execute the Anexed Instrument writing & acknowledged it to be his last will & Testament, he being then of perfect sound mind & memory, and that they subscribed their names as Evidences to ye same together with Daniel Griffith the other, subscribine Evidence given under my hand this 27th day of August 1748.
John Curtis Register.

By the Tenor of these Presents, I John Curtis. Esqr. Register for ye probate of wills & granting letters of Administration for ye County of New Castle upon Dellaware by virtue of a Commission from ye Honourab. George Thomas Esq. Lieutenant Governor & Commander in chief of ye Counties of New Castle Kent & Suffex upon Dellaware and Province of Pennsylvania---
DO MAKE KNOWN UNTO ALL MEN, that on the 27th day of Augst. 1748 at New Castle, in ye County of New Castle aforesd. was proved approved & insinuated the last Will of Testament of David Jones late of ye County aforesd. Deceased haveing while he lived and at the time of his death goods & Chattles rights & Credits in divers places within sd. County by means whereof ye full disposition of all & singular ye goods & Chattles rights & Credits of ye sd. Deceased & ye granting of Administration thereof as also the hearing the Acco. Calculations & reckonings of ye sd. Adminr., & ye final dischare & dismission therefrom unto me personally known to belong: And the Administration of all & singular the goods & Chattles Rights & Credits of sd. Deceased his last will & Testament any manner of way concerning was granted unto Ester Jones & sd. Executors in ye same Testament named chiefly of of well & truly Administering ye same & makeing a true & perfect Inventory & Conscionable Appraisement of all & Singular ye Goods & Chattles rights & Credits of ye sd. Deceased & Exhibiting ye same unto ye Registers office at New Castle on or before the 27th day of February next ensuing ye date hereof as also of rendering a Just & true Account of ye Administra: when thereunto required being solemly Sworn IN TESTIMONY, whereof, I have caused ye seal of ye sd. Office to be hereunto Affixed at New Castle aforesd. This 27th day of Augst. In ye 22d year of his Majestys Reign Anno Domini 1748."
* *

This was the land distributed in the above will:
1- 'I give and bequeath to my sd. son <u>Morgan</u> ye land & Plantation where Thos. Nelson lately lived...'
2- 'to my son <u>James Jones</u> the land and Plantation where he now liveth being two hundred & forty acres, or as it is spc. mentioned...'
3- 'to my son <u>Daniel Jones</u> ye land and places where I now live...'

4- 'unto my son David Jones ye new Plantation on ye south end of my land, and ye improvements thereupon, being one hundred acres of land to be surveyed out of ye south end of my land.' This had a condition that if David died without issue, this land was to go to David Jones, son of his son Morgan Jones. (Note: His son David died in 1758, unmarried.)

5- 'give & bequeath to grandson Benjamin Jones son of <u>John Jones</u> the land and the improvements thereon Christiana Creek in White Clay Creek Hundred where widow Helpatrick now liveth' This had a condition that it be given to his brother Enoch Jones if he should 'die before he arrives to a good age.'

David's son John Jones was already living in South Carolina at this time, so no land was left to him.
* *

JOHN JONES:

1-son of David [ca 1669] and Esther John [ca 1678], was b. ca 1695. Married Ann _____. They were both baptized in the Welsh Tract Baptist Church; John on December 4, 1736, and Ann, September 3, 1737. They were both dismissed to go to Pee Dee in South Carolina by a letter March 11, 1738.[4] They are the John Jones and wife Ann who were found in the list of church members in the minutes there. Apparently his descendants continued to use the name Jones. John died in 1759 in South Carolina, and Ann died in 1765[5]. She married Phillip Douglass after John died, per South Carolina Welsh Neck church minutes. Both died shortly thereafter.

Children of John Jones and Ann:

1. BENJAMIN JONES. Was left land on Christiana Creek, White Clay Creek Hundred by grandfather David John, and apparently remained there.
2. ESTHER JONES. [Mentioned in David John's will.]
3. ENOCH JONES. [Mentioned in David John's will.]
4. DAVID JONES.*
5. EDWARD JONES.*
6. THOMAS JONES.*
7. JOHN JONES.* Probably the John with wife Elizabeth.

*[Mentioned in Welsh Neck Baptist Church Minutes.]

John had other children. More will be given on this family in later chapter on South Carolina. There is also a possibility that John Jones and Ann were parents of the Griffith John who went to the Pee Dee area in S.C. in 1737 or 1738.
* *

---

[4]P. 85 of Welsh Tract Baptist Meeting, Book 5, Page 2.
[5]In Welsh Neck Church Minutes, S.C.

MORGAN JOHN,
2-son of David and Esther John, was born about 1697 in Wales. Records have his name both as Morgan John and Morgan Jones. He had a son and grandson also named Morgan. He died 4 June 1760, aged 63 years, and was buried at Welsh Tract Cemetery. He came to Pennsylvania with his parents in 1710. He married ELEANOR EVANS 17 Dec 1724 at Old Swedes Church in New Castle County.[6] She was born ca 1700, and died 7 Sep 1759, aged 59 yrs., and was buried at Welsh Tract Cemetery. They lived at White Clay Creek Hundred.

His will was recorded from a copy as late as 5 Sep 1791. It was dated 10 Dec 1759. It directs the sale of plantation at Forks of Delaware; to son JOSHUA, an allotted portion of plantation in White Clay Creek Hundred and adjacent to Christiana Creek. To son ZACKARIAH the residue of said plantation as alloted, he to pay 50 pounds to JOSHUA and to LETTICE. To son MORGAN plantation on which testator lived; should he died without issue, plantation to go to grandson MORGAN, son of Zachariah; also two working horses. To son JOHN 50 pounds; to son ABEL 100 pounds. To son DAVID 100 pounds. To daughter ANN, wife of Peter Delap, the interest of 50 pounds during marriage; if she became a widow to be absolutely hers. To daughter ESTHER, 60 pounds. To daughter LETTICE, 40 pounds. All residue to be divided between children except ANN. Sons ZACHARIAH and DAVID executors.

Children of Morgan [ca 1697] and Eleanor [ca 1700]:
1. JOSHUA JONES.
2. ABEL JONES.
3. ANN JONES, m. Peter Delap.
4. LETTICE JONES.
5. MORGAN JONES, JR.
6. JOHN JONES.
7. ZACHARIAH JONES, b. 1735; d. 3 Jul 1768. Had sons Morgan & Zachariah Jr.
8. DAVID JONES, b. 12 May 1736.
9. ESTHER JONES.

Some of Morgan Jones' Land Records:
'Resurvey of Tract of 300 acres of land adj. the London Company land on the Eastern Branch of Christina in White Clay Creek Hundred...belonging to Morgan Jones by Regular Conveyances from Rees Thomas to whom it was first surveyed by Warrant...31st Mar. 1701...The said Morgan Jones agreeing to pay the Quit Rent due from the first Survey thereof and for so doing this shall be your sufficient warrant given unto my hand and the Seal of the Land Office by Virtue of Certain Power from the said Proprietaries at

---

[6]New Castle Vol. 36, p. 7, Old Swedes, p. 288.

Philadelphis this 11th day of April 1744. Signed George Thomas. ' (Other records show he used name Morgan John.)
*

Morgan Jones, J. V. 1, #24, White Clay Creek Hundred, c. 300 acres, Apr. 17, 1744, resurvey named Rees Thomas.
Morgan Jones, J, 1, #30, E. bank of Cristiana Creek, White Clay Creek Hundred, 300 a. Surv.
Also J, 2, #37, rough draft.
* *

DAVID JONES,
8-son of Morgan and Eleanor John, was born 12 May 1736 in White Clay Creek Hundred, New Castle Co. He studied at Hopewell Academy, N. J. He was baptized 6 May 1758 by Rev. David Davis at the Welsh Tract Church. He was licensed by it to preach in 1761. He then went to Middletown, N. J. where he studied under the guidance and instruction of his cousin, the Rev. Abel Morgan. There he married 22 Feb 1762 Anne Stillwell, who was daughter of Joseph Stillwell and Sarah Shepard Stillwell, with Rev. Abel Morgan officiating. Anne Stillwell was the great, great granddaughter of Nicholas Stillwell, who came to America in 1638 and settled at Gravesend, Long Island; and died at Staten Island 23 Dec 1671. She was also great, great granddaughter of John Throckmorton, who came over with Roger Williams in the ship "Lyon" in 1631, and of John Stout who emigrated about the same time. On 12 Dec 1766, he was ordained pastor of the Free Hold Baptist Church, Monmouth Co., N.J., where he remained until 1775.

He became interested in doing missionary work among the Indians, and made two trips to the Ohio region in 1772 and 1773. There he preached to the Delaware and the Shawnee. He kept a journal of this trip that he published in 1774 (Pub. by Joseph Sabin, N.Y.)

About 1775, he began to express his strong feelings against the British actions, and show his desire for resistance to their actions. This irritated some of the apolitical members of the congregation. He packed up his family and moved to Chester County, Pa., where he became pastor of Great Valley Baptist Church. He preached before the regiment of Col. Devees that was organizing for war against the British, and in the autumn of 1775, he published the sermon that he gave. The title of this sermon was "Defensive War In a Just Cause Sinless." This was widely circulated and helped to prepare the minds of the people for the coming war.

In 1776, Rev. David Jones was appointed Chaplain of a Pennsylvania regiment raised for the war. He served under Gen. Horatio Gates in the Northern Department. He often spoke before the troops. One of his addresses, given before the Battle of Ticonderoga on 20 Oct 1776, was printed and read extensively. It was reprinted in "Lossings Field Book of the Revolutionary War." He served with Gen. Anthony Wayne, who was his neighbor in Chester Co. He was at the Battle of Brandywine; the battle at Germantown; was with the army at White Marsh and at Valley Forge in the winters of 1777 and 1778. He was almost killed at the Proli massacre. He was present when Cornwallis surrendered. He was intense and involved during the entire Revolutionary struggle. He had a reputation with the army itself "as possessing the fighting fervor of the true soldier."[7]

After the war was over, he again returned to his interest in missionary work with the Indians in the region of the Ohio. He continued to visit that country on horseback until he was well over seventy years of age.

In 1786, he became pastor of the Southhampton Baptist Church in Bucks County. He remained there until 1792, when he returned to the Great Valley Church in Chester Co. His neighbor, old commander, and friend Gen. Wayne was sent to the north west in 1796 after the defeat of Gen. St. Clair. Rev. David accompanied him as Chaplain to the troops.

In 1812, when the war with England was revived, he volunteered again as Chaplain. He served under Gen. Brown and Gen. Wilkinson until peace in 1815. His last public address was given 20 Sept 1817 at the dedication of the Paoli Monument.

Rev. David Jones died 5 Feb 1820. Anne Stillwell Jones, his wife, died 16 May 1809. They were both buried in the graveyard attached to the Great Valley Church, Chester Co.

They had eight children.
* *

JAMES JONES,
9-son of David [ca 1669] and Esther John [ca 1678], born _____, died 26 May 1786. He married Susanna _____, born 1717; d. 3 Jun 1787, at aged 70 years. Both buried at Welsh Tract Baptist Cemetery. His will was dated 19 Jan 1783; proved 7 Jun 1786. He described himself as of Pencader Hundred. Gave wife, in lieu of dower, 150 pounds and certain personal property. Gave son ENOCH plantation on which he now lived in Pencader, he to pay his brother ABEL JONES 10 pounds and to make certain yearly payments of wheat etc. to Abel, and to Susanna, the widow. To son DANIEL, gave plantation on which testator lived containing 200 acres and also certain negroes. Placed certain burdens regarding this granted estate. To son JAMES, 10 pounds; to son ABEL, 150 pounds; to daughter MARY GRIFFITH, 35 pounds; to daughter HANNAH SHIELDS, negro wench Dorcas and 80 pounds in currency. To daughter ESTHER 80 pounds, one cow, and bed and furniture and negro wench Sarah. To daughter SUSANNAH JAMES, Negro wench Heiris, and 8 pounds. To daughter MARGARET negro child Venue and bed and furniture, and new saddle and 70 pounds. SUSANNA, widow, and sons ENOCH and DANIEL appointed executors. Susanna, widow, remained administrator.

---

[7]Inf. taken from account by Morgan Edwards.

Children named in will:

1. ENOCH JONES, died 1788. Married Jane Boggs, dau of Rev. John Boggs of the Welsh Tract Church. They had four children. Letters of admission granted on his estate in New Castle 19 Dec 1788 to widow Jane, Daniel Jones and Joseph Boggs. Jane later married a Mr. Redmond. (Surname given as Jones in estate settlement.)

2. ABEL JONES, b. 1757; d.1 Sept 1831.

3. DANIEL JONES.

4. JAMES JONES.

5. MARY JONES, m. Joseph Griffith. Joseph was b. ca 1733; baptized at Welsh Tract Church 5 Oct 1764; d. 9 Sept 1775 in 40th year. His will dated 7 Sept 1773; proved 5 Oct 1773 at New Castle. Left wife Mary one third of real estate and all personal estate until son John arrived of age, provided she continued a widow. To son John, left all his lands except 100 acres. Left son James 100 acres off the south end of his land "to wit; the tract deemed to be the property of Samuel Griffith deceased," together with as much of his land then leased to James Porter as would make up 100 acres. Son John to pay each of his daughters 50 pounds when he arrived at 21 years, viz: Catherine Griffith, Susanna Griffith and Rebecca Griffith. Testator's brother Benjamin Griffith and Andrew Fisher appointed guardians of his children. Wife Mary and her brother Enoch appointed executors. Mary and Joseph had five children. Joseph had a son, Caleb Griffith, by a prior marriage.

6. JANE JONES, m. William Buchingham.

7. HANNAH JONES, m. Robert Shields.

8. ESTHER JONES, b. ca 1752; d. 10 Jan 1800, unmarried. Buried at Welsh Tract. Left will dated 8 Oct 1788, proved 7 Apr 1800. Divided her wearing apparel between her four sisters' children, viz. Mary Griffith's, one fourth; Jane Buckingham's, one fourth; Hannah Shield's, one fourth; Susanna James', one fourth; saddle to niece Susanna Griffith, etc. Brother Daniel appointed executor.

9. SUSANNA JONES. Born ca 1752. Married John James, who died 19 Jan 1811, aged 59 years. She died 8 Mar 1812.

10. MARGARET JONES.

* *

MISCELLANEOUS:

An Assessment List of Pencader Hundred, New Castle Co., Del. with assessment made by Thomas James, not dated:

David John 18 L; David John, smith 8 L; Rachel Griffith, widow 8 L; John Griffith 8 L; Richard Griffith 20 L: John Griffith 10 L; Thomas Lewis 14 L; Daniel Griffith, 8 L; Jonathan John 8 L: Jacob John 8 L: David John 8 L; et al. (Scharf, History of Delaware, Vol. II, p. 952.)

Note: The above assessment list showed three David John's as owning land and being of age to be taxed. David Sr., husband of Esther Morgan, had a son David, and David Sr.'s son Morgan had a son named David, as shown by David Sr.'s will above. The Griffith John who had the 300 acres had a son named David. Griffith's and Morgan's both had blacksmith's in the family.

Probably David John (ca 1669) was assessed for all his land at this time, as he had not yet left it to his sons. The second 'David John, smith' could have been son and heir of the Griffith John who died in 1749. Griffith John's name was not on this.

* *

DAVID JOHN'S GRIFFITH CONNECTIONS:

David Griffith late of the Welsh Tract...died intestate...17th Aug 1717...John Griffith weaver, appointed Administrator.
John Griffith, of Brandywine Hundred, will dated 25 Dec 1739. 'Estate be sold...Loving wife Caterin Griffith have it...My friend Adam Buckley...Executor.
Witness: Wm. Cloud, Henery Griffith. Proved Jan 24, 1739.

John Griffith Will of 1749, G, p. 295: John Griffith died Intestate; Rachell Griffith, appointed Administrator. 18th day of April 1749. No info given other than usual wording.
Note: This will and the following was for John Griffith Jr., son of Esther John's stepfather. He married Rachel, widow of Rees Jones.
G, 301: Rachell Griffith, adm. for John Griffith, intestate. 18 Apr 1749.

John Griffith's will 27 Nov 1753...
"In the name of God Amen I John Griffith of Pencader Hundred in the Co. of New Castle upon Delaware Weaver being sick in body but of sound & disposing mind & memory do constitute and appoint this my last Will & testament in manner following Viz...
Item To my son David I give & bequeath my Cart now in his use hereby enjoining him to pay his two brethren Thomas & John the sum of 20 shillings each..
Item To my daughter Mary now wife of Roger Williams...40 shillings.
My daughter Sarah 40 shillings, daughter Elizabeth...sum of 20 shillings, daughter Hannah, third part of all my personal estate after above distribution.
And to my son Griffith I give and bequeath all the Residue of my personal estate whatsoever to whom I also give and Bequeath Demise and confirm my Plantation that I now live upon to be possessed and Injoyed by him his Heirs & Assigns forever.
Lastly I constitute and appoint said son Griffith & my brother in law Thomas Lewis executor of this my last Will & Testament hereby Revoking

& Repealing all other Wills by me heretofore made Ratifying and Confirming this and none else for my last Will & Testament In Witness whereof I have hereunto Set my Hand & Seal this twenty seventh day of November in the year of our Lord God one thousand seven Hundred & fifty three.

John Griffith (his mark)

Wit.: Simon James, Benj. Rowland. Proved by Simon James and Henry Rowland."

NOTE: An interesting fact about this John Griffith was that in the Welsh manner, his children might have taken the surname John. He was a weaver who owned real estate which was left to son John. However, the following will referred to David Griffith, Thomas Griffith and John Griffith, and they seem to be the children of the John above. Since Evan Lewis mentioned nephews, and John Griffith mentioned brother-in-law Thomas Lewis, the Lewis' sister must have married John Griffith of the above will.
* *

Will of Evan Lewis of New Castle Hundred, March 18, 1753, named nephew Griffith, son of John Griffith; niece Hannah Griffith; friend Rachel Evans; brother Thomas Lewis; three nephews David Griffith, Thomas Griffith, and John Griffith; niece Mary dau of John Griffith, now wife of Roger Williams; niece Sarah Griffith; niece Elizabeth Griffith; nieces Hannah Lewis, & Amy Lewis, daus of brother David Lewis.; nephew John, son of brother David, deceased; bequest to his brother Joel; mentioned David, his deceased brother; nephews John & Isaac, sons of brother Thomas Lewis.
*

One Roger Williams, wife Margaret, who were probably parents of the Roger mentioned above:
Jul 12, 1741. Will of Roger Williams of Pencader. Son William Williams; son Maurice; son Roger; dau Martha W.; dau Mary Rees; dau Margaret Williams; grandson John Rees. Servant Sarah Emerson. Rest to Margaret, my dearly beloved wife. Said son Thomas... Wit: Natl. Evans, Henry Rowland, Thomas Evans.
*

Benj. Griffith (Griffie) of Brandywine Hundred, will...dated 3 day Jan 1740/41. Wife Mary Sole Executrix. Wit: Benjn. Ford, Lachus Peterson, Jno. Riley. Probated Jan 4, 1740/41.

Register of Wills: Will of David Griffith of Pencader Hundred...will signed 1 April 1747. Left residue of his goods, chattels, etc. after debts paid to his well beloved wife. Sums of money to daughter Mary John; grandchildren David, Joseph, Cathrine, Mary, Thomas, Sarah, and Dinah John. Also Elinor Williams, his maid, to receive one ewe and lamb when she reaches 18. Executors daughter Mary John and son David John. Witnesses Evan Lewis, Morris Evan, Nathanl. Williams.

<u>David Griffith's widow:</u> Book G, p. 459. Will of Cathrine Griffith, Widdow. Dated 10th day September 1750...
"Item I give devise & Bequeath to my grandson David John the sum of five pounds in Curt. Lawful money of Pa. to be paid to him within six months after my decease.
Item I will Devise & Bequeath to my Grandson Thomas John the sum of five pounds of the above like money to be paid to him when he comes to the age of twenty one years. I will Devise & bequeath to my Granddaughters Catherine Thomas the full sum of five pounds of the above money to be paid to her within six months after my decease. Item I will devise & Bequeath to my Granddaughters Mary John, Sarah John & Dinah John, the full sum of five pounds to be equally divided between them or the Survivor of them & to be paid to them as they accomplish the age of eighteen years. Item After my Debts be paid funeral charges performed and these my Legacies Contained in this my present Testament fullfill'd, I wholely give & further Bequeath to my daughter Mary John all the Residue of all my goods chattels & credits to her proper use & behoof forever; Item I also devise & Bequeath to my sd Daughter the Plantation that I am Seized of & now personally reside to her & her heirs & assigns forever. Item I make Constitute & Ordain my aforesaid Daughter my Sole Executor of this my last will & testament, Revoking all other former wills & Testaments Legacies...In witness whereof I have hereunto set Signed Sealed & delivered in sd. Presence of us, John Williams, Rees Griffith, Nathl. Williams.

Catherine Griffith (her mark C)"
Subscribing witness statements dated 27th Feb 1750.
*
<u>Will of William Griffith of Duck Creek Hundred, Kent Co., 21 day Aug 1771.</u> Son David Griffith --land situated at Appoquidick Hundred; son Daniel; Grandaughters Mary & Elizabeth Jones; dau Mary; granddaughter Martha Ashford; granddau Eleanor Griffin; son Charles.
<u>Will Book G, p. 311</u>: Benjamin Elder, wife Mary, son John, son Alex, dau Hannah, dau Margaret. Wit: Timothy Griffith, James James & Thomas James. Prob. 23 Apr. 1749.
<u>Will Book G, p. 459. Gideon Griffith, Adm. of estate of Wm. Keith, Barrister.</u>
<u>Will of Samuel Griffith - Dec 7, 1729.</u> Mormon Film #0006545, Will Record V 1-2. See Deed 21 May 1729 regarding the sale of Samuel's land due to a judgment by Isaac Miranda. Deed Book I, 1, PP. 311, 312, 313, 314, 315, 316.

Will Book G, p. 167, 7 Mar 1746. David Howell, Pencader, yeoman. Wife 1/3; Son Daniel; son David; dau Rachel Rees, wife of Rees Rees; dau Sarah Williams, wife of John Williams; sons Daniel & David, Executors. Witnesses: David John, Griffith John & Jacob Van Bibber. Jacob attested to signature. Stated David & Griffith John too sick to come in.

*

Surveys:

JOHN GRIFFING, G 2, #2, 2a, 83. Main branch of Duck Creek, Appoq. Hd., Jun 11, 1736. 200 acres, with rough plot.

Also, Surv. Gen. ret., G-L. #61, Main Branch of Duck Creek, Appoq. Hund., Aug. 16, 1747, 200 acres.

JOHN GRIFFITH, M 2, #10, on Norman's Road, Welsh Tract., Apr. 28, 1702. Filed under Morgan, John.

Also, G1, #58, south side of Christiana Creek, Mar. 4, 1716/7. 100-200 acres.

JOHN GRIFFITH, John, son of John - G, Vol. 1, #14, on a branch of Christian Creek, Feb. 23, 1739/40, 167 acres.

THOMAS GRIFFIN, on 7 mi. Run, Welsh Tract, G2, #1, 3. Mar 16, 1701/2.

THOMAS GRIFFITH, G, 2, #12, 85 acres. Plot only, not to be recorded.

THOMAS GRIFFITH, G, 2, #13, Apr. 2, 1720, 97 acres.

* *

SAMUEL GRIFFITH DEEDS & SURVEYS:

(Note: This Samuel Griffith was probably son of Thomas Griffith, the minister with the group in 1701. He was also a minister.)

Book I, Part 1, Pp. 311-316.

"The Sheriff William Read states that he has been ordered to sell the land of Samuel Griffith, dec'd., which was now in the possession of Jerome Dushene and his wife Mary of George's Hundred, because of a judgment obtained by Isaac Miranda in the Court of Common Pleas against Samuel Griffith, Merchant, Dated 21 day of May 1729: for the amount of one hundred thirty nine pounds, & thirteen shillings & nine pence. This land was sold to Anthony Dushene, of George's Hundred, being the highest bidder, for Twelve pounds Two shillings & Sixpence. This land consisted of two parcels, one for 39 acres and one for three acres, situated in Georges Hundred:

"Beginning at an old corner Hickery late of John Jills Land by ye Kings Road & runs along the road north sixty perches to a black oak corner tree by ye Dragon Bridge Then up Dragon Creek seventy seven degrees west forty pches to a corner chestnutt by ye marsh late of the sd Samuel Griffith thence up the sd Marsh south fifteen Degrees west fifty five pches to a white oak by the Marsh then cross the marsh norty seventy degrees west eight pches to a corner Spanish oak on ye North side of ye Marsh then south seventy seven Degrees west sixteen pches to a new corner Hickery in ye

line late of Thomas Morgan then up by ye sd Morgan's Line north Thirty eight degrees east forty pches to another corner tree in sd Morgan's Line then south east four pches to ye upper corner Hickery late of John Jill then by sd Jills Line north sixty degrees east eighty two pches to the first mentiond corner hickery containing in these bounds about thirty nine acres of land as also the sd piece or pcel of marsh situate lying & being in Georges Hundred in the County of New Castle & butted & bounded as followeth viz. Beginning at a new corner black oak standing on ye south side thereof & running down the same North ten degrees east eight pches north seventy two degrees east four pches north twenty degrees east seven pches north east seven pches north eight degrees west eight pches north seventy eight degrees east four pches south eighty degrees east ninteen pches to a new corner chestnut of ye marsh side then cross the marsh north thirty three degrees west eight pches to a spanish oak by Dragon Run then up Dragon Run north Eighty degrees west eight pches north thirty five degrees west seven pches crossing a small run of Dragon then up ye north side of the marsh south west eleven pches south thirty five degrees west twenty four pches south twenty nine degrees west eight pches to a corner Spanish oak by ye marsh side then cross the marsh south seven degrees east eight pches to ye before mentiond corner black oak and place of Beginning containing these bounds about three acres of marsh together with all & singular ye improvemts. Hereditamts. & Appurts. to ye sd. land & marsh hereby granted or mentiond to be granting belonging as amply & fully as the same have at any time been held used accpied. & enjoyd. by ye sd. Samuel Griffith in his Life Time or by the sd. Jerome & Mary or eighter of them of any other since ye death of ye sd. Saml. …
Acknowledged in the court of Common Pleas held for ye county of New castle in August Term 1730...David French pro tem."

Another document followed saying Isaac Miranda did recover from Jerome and Mary Dushene the lands owned by Samuel Griffith at the time of his death. Mentioned their undertenants Hesther Glen and others. This land was described as follows 'Viz Two pieces or pcls of Land Situate lying & being near George's Creek in the county afsd. ye one containing about one Hundred & Fifty Acres the other fifty three acres with ye Appurts. & likewise one other piece or pcl of land near Georges creek in ye county of New Castle afsd. containing thirty nine acres of thereabts. & one piece or pcl. of marsh containing three acres or thereabts. as also certain messuages or Tenemts. being of late dwelling houses of the sd. Saml. Griffith & a lott or pice of ground to ye sd. messuages belonging together with all & singular ye buildings & appurts. etc. situate lying & being in New Castle afsd. Containing in breadth forty five feet & half & in length three hundred feet to ye value of three hundred & thirteen pounds and that there were found in my Bailywick no more or other goods or chattells Lands or Tenemts. wch.

were of ye afsd. Samuel Griffith at ye time of his death of wch. I could cause to be made the damages in the hereunto anexed.'

Writt mentioned '& the residue of ye execion. of ye sd. writt laid in two schedul's thereunto annexed whereby it appeared as well by ye oaths of twelve honest & lawfull men of ye county afsd. that ye sd. Saml. Griffith in his life time & at ye time of his death was seized of & in the herein before mention'd lands marsh messuages & lott or piece of ground etc. by me taken in Execuion. as afsd. as also that ye rents profits of ye same lands marsh messuages and lott or piece of ground were not found by ye valuation of two petitions. & substantial freeholders of the sd. County upon oath of a clear yearly value beyond all reprize sufficient within ye space of seven years to satisfie ye Demand. afsd. in ye last recited writt mention'd And Whereas afterwards by a Writt of vendieoni cep. dated the twenty first day of February last it was remanded that ye lands marsh messuages & Lott or piece of ground afsd. I should expose to sale & have that money before the Justices of the Court of Comons. the third Tuesday in May inst. to render to ye sd. Isaac Miranda for his Damages afsd. as in & by ye Record of Proceedings of the sd. court between them had May fully appear and Whereas pursuant to ye Tennets. the same last mention'd writt & ye Laws of this Govermt. In such cases provided I have at publick vendue sold to Nicholas Vandike of Georges Hundred in ye county of New Castle afsd. yeoman being ye highest bidder all ye abovemention'd one hundred & fifty acres of land wth. ye Appurts. Thereunto belonging situate in georges Hundred in the County of New Castle afsd. for the sum of ninety pounds lawfull money of America after I had caused publick notice to be given of ye sd. sale Now Know Ye that I ye sd. William Read Sheriffe of ye County afsd. pursuant to the Tenor & Comand of the sd. writt of vendiconi expond. & the Laws afsd. in such cases provided & by virtue of the power thereby granted to me & by the Asent of ye Plts. in the sd. writt named for & in consideration of ye sum of ninety pounds of lawfull money of America being the most advantage that the sd. land & premises could in any wise be sold for to the in Hand paid by the sd. Nicholas Vandike the receipt whereof I do hereby acknowledge & thereof & of every part thereof do for ever requitt release & discharge the sd. Nicholas Vandike his Heirs Excrs. & Admrs. & every of them by these presents have granted bargained sold & delivered & by these presents do grant bargain sell & deliver unto ye sd. Nicholas Vandike all ye above mentioned Tract or pcl. of land situate lying & being aforementioned Beginning..."

NOTE: There was another document following this, apparently containing another sale of land that was Samuel Griffith's. There were several in all.

Deed Book I, p. 123: The deed concerning land which Griffith John purchased from John David Rees on 21 Aug 1729 was 50 acres which had belonged to Samuel Griffith, deceased.
* *

REES JONES, tanner:
Deed Book L, Vol. 1, p. 9, 1736:
Indenture dated 27 Sept 1736 between Evan Edmond yeoman of Pencader Hundred & Rees Jones, tanner, for sum of 120 pounds...for 200 acres of land...SITUATE lying and being in Pencader Hundred and County of New Castle aforesaid Beginning at a corner stake of the land formerly belonging to Lewis David and thence North 225 perches thence East 136 perches thence South 235 perches thence West 136 perches to the place of Beginning containing 200 acres of land...being part of a larger tract sold to the same Evan Edmond by Howell James as appears by deed the 7th day of Sept. 1712 and relation being hereto had may more fully appear together with all woods underwoods ground and soil of the same with all buildings and improvements in and upon the same or any part or parcel...
Signed Evan Edmond.
In Pres. of Hannah Armitage, Sam'l. Wild, James Armitage.
Appr. & recorded Nov. Term 1736.
*

Deed Book L, Vol. 1, p. 135: dated 29th Dec 1736..Rees Jones tanner & wife Rachel...Samuel Kerr, farmer...situate...White Clay Creek, Pencader...200 acres land & plantation...being part of four tracts of land reference being had to the deeds of the said tracts may at large appear together with... Signed by Rees & Rachel. Proved by James Armitage & Wm. Eyerson, Feb 10, 1736/7.
*

M 1, p. 216, 3 Feb 1738. Deed between Catherine Lewis, widow, and Rees Jones, tanner...land situated in Mill Creek Hundred...on west side of Red Clay Creek being a corner tree of Edward Philpots land...containing 200 acres...formerly belonging to Abraham Man and conveyed to Griffith Lewis late husband of Catherine, by Edward Philpot & William Huells as of deed dated 17 May 1726...Griffith Lewis bequeathed same to Catherine Lewis by will dated 31 day Dec 1730. Witnesses: David Lewis & James Armitage.
*

M 1, p. 422, 19th Nov 1739. Deed between Cathrine Leoline of Pencader Hundred, widow, and Rees Jones, tanner... recently purchased of Nicholas Roger and Reynold Howel ...19 day of Nov 1739... 248 acres of...Patent land & 40 acres of warrant land not included in said Patent and in as large and ample manner as one Daniel James late Posser. thereof ever held. ...In consideration of 50 pounds current lawfull money of Pennsilvania to her in hand paid by the said Rees Jones...does convey...all and singular the said Tract of Land and Plantation Together with all the Edifices & Buildings

thereon Orchards & gardens platts lands arrable meadows and pasture and all other conveniences usually belonging or appertaining to the same with the reversions & remainders rents issues & profits annually arising or accruing from the same...the said two hundred & eighty eight acres...
Cathrine Leoline (her mark) SEAL
...Signed in presence of Evan David & Reyd. Howell.
She appoints well beloved friend Thomas James Esq. for me & in my name to acknowledge...
*

Rees Jones, tanner, decd., F2, #17, White Clay Creek Hundred, near Christiana Creek, 125 1/2 acres; Feb. 23, 1739/40, mentioned widow Rachel & Alex. Fraiser.
*

Deed Book N 1, 1, 18th Aug 1740:
Between Naphtalia Johnston, yeoman, and Rachel Jones, widow. Situate...on the South side of White Clay Creek...being the end of a tract formerly Samuel Johnson's Deceased, ...by the mouth of a small Runn...dividing the said tract from Dan Johnsons...in the line of Nathaniel Bryans...containing 56 acres...with the grist mill & all the apparel and ...
*

L, 1, pp. 9, 10. Evan Edmond to Rees Jones for 120 pounds...200 acres of land situate...Pencadder Hundred...Beginning at a corner stake of the land formerly belonging to Lewis David & thence North 225 perches thence E 136 perches thence South 235 thence West one hundred thirty six perches to the place of beginning...being part of a larger tract Sold to the said Evan Edmond by Howell James as appears by Deed dated the 7th day of Sept 1712...   Signed Evan Edmond.
Wit.: Hannah Armitage
Saml. Wild & James Armitage.
Note: Rebecca John, widow of Thomas John, married Lewis David.

Deed Book L, 6 Aug 1738. Deed from Arthur Haires of New Castle Hundred, blacksmith, Dorothy, & John Haires of Whitecreek. Wit: Jno. Richardson, Robert Haires, Thomas John, 3 Feb 1738.
* *

DR. REES JONES:

Another Rees Jones was also in this area. He was a Physician, and was not Rees Jones, tanner. Filed records after his death indicated his father was Rowland Jones. He was a member of the Welsh Tract Baptist Church. He purchased land once owned by John Ogle Sr., one of the early settlers around 1680's or earlier. In "History of Delaware," p. 414, Scharf wrote the Sixth District embraced the territory westward from New Castle to White Clay Hundred, Mill Creek Hundred and Christiana Hundred. John Ogle then resided at Swart Nutten Island, later known as Lewden Island in the Christiana River, in New Castle Hundred. He also owned large tracts of land in White Clay Creek Hundred, located from White Clay Creek to Christiana Creek, embracing Christiana Village and Ogletown. The bridge that had recently been ordered over "Christina head," the head of navigation of the stream, was called the Christiana Bridge. Later the village clustered around the Bridge.

*

Deed Book K, Vol. 1, p. 385:

Indenture...Rees Jones, Physician, of Christiana Bridge and Benjamin Cook...Whereas Wm. Penn granted to Thomas Pierson...5th day of 5th mo. 1683...Eagle's Point was surveyed to John Ogle Sr., decd...25 acres...John Ogle conveyed in year 1696 to John Latham & his son & heir reconveyed same to Anne Margaret Letort on 21st Oct 1706...& Anne Letort for non payment of debt then due owing to one John French, then Shff...obtained a writ & directed to George Delayn Survyr. ...By sd. Writ seized sd. Land. then Deed of Convey. made to John Ogle Jr. 17 May 1711...John Ogle & Elizabeth to Francis Land...who with wife Christian sold land to Rees Jones...Rees Jones & Sarah his wife for 70 pounds sold to Benjamin Cook. Description mentioned garden pales of Lewis Howell.
Signed by Rees Jones & Sarah Jones. Wit: Joseph Welden & Andrew Culbertson. Aug. Term 1735.

* *

Survey Map: Showed Christiana Creek north and south, with a branch from east side. Bridge across south end. John Gooding land, called Goodings Chance. South of Creek branch was written. "Doct.r Jones," then to the east was written "Doctr. Rees Jones."
"By virtue of a copy of the Pptaries. Wart. to me Devised by Benja. Eastburn Survr. Genl. of the Province of Pennsylvania & Counties on delaware dated the 5th day of June 1739 for to Survey to John Gooding of the County of New Castle at Delaware of Land in the above Represented place & I have surveyd. for the afsd. John Gooding the above Described parcel of Land situate in White Clay Creek Hundred & County afsd. on the Northside of Christiana Creek near the Bridge Adjoining the south side of the road leading from Christiana bridge up into the County towards the Welsh Tract & is Bounded as Followings (to wit) Beginning at a corner Black Oak standing in the afsd. road & is a line tree of the Land of Doctr. Rees Jones's formerly John Ogle's & branching Thence up the sd. road bending therewith N 64 degrees W 20 pchs. N 70 deg. W 52 pchs. N 60 deg. W 40 pchs. N 41 deg. 75 pchs, N 30 deg. W 16 pchs to an old corner white oak of a Tract of land called [S or L] Longshaws Lott. standing on the South side of the afsd. Thence W of the sd. Longshaws Lott chossing a branch of Lathums run S B ___ 230 pchs. to a stake standing at the intersecting with the line of a tract of Land called Rahastraws Land late the Estate of Aisher Clayton Decd. now belonging to Joseph Peace thence with

the line thereof S 82 deg. E 140 pchs to a corner white oak sapling standing on the South east side of the Millrow to the afsd. bridge & in a line of a small Tract of Land claimed by Lewis Howell Senor by the line thereof [symbols] the afsd. run N. 53 deg. 39 pchs. to Runn branch [symbols] runs in the afsd. Creek Thence up the sd. Branch bounding thereon N 34 deg. w. 6 perches N 55 deg. W 24 pchs. N 33 deg. W. 24 pchs thence crossing the sd. Branch N. 15 deg. 10 pchs to a Co: given of the Land of Doctr. Rees Jones formerly John Ogles thence therewith N B W 50 pchs to the Beginning containing within these Bounds clear of ____ for _____ 136 acres of land or swamps...Survd. the 12th day of July ano. Domi. 1739.
*

Resurvey requested by Rees Jones, Practitioner in Physick...of about 74 acres called Eagles Point, first surveyed to John Ogle under whom the said Rees Jones claims Title thereunto. Situate on the north side of Christina Creek near the Bridge over the same ...10day of July 1741.
*

Survey for John Gooding 5th June 1739..situate in White Clay Creek Hundred...on the northside of Christianna Creek near the Bridge adjoining the southside of the road leading from Christiana Bridge up into the country towards the Welsh Tract & is bounded as follows (to wit) Beginning at a corner Black Oak standing in the aforesd. road & is a line tree of the Land of Doctr. Rees Jones's formerly of John Ogle's & running Thence up the sd. Road winding therewith N. 64 degs. W 28 forty N 70 degs. W. 52 pchs. N 60 degs. W. 40 pchs. N. 41 degs. W 75 pchs. N. 30 degs. W 16 pchs. to an old corner white oak of a Tract of Land called Longhaws Lotte standing on the South side of the afsd. Road Thence w.__ the sd. Longshaws Lotte Chassing a Branch of Lathams Run S E & 230 pchs. to a stake standing at the intersecting with the line of a Tract of Land called Rakeshaws Land late the Estate of Asher Clayton Decd. now belonging to Joseph Peace [sic] Thence with the line thereof S 82 degs. E 140 pchs. to a corner white oak sapling standing on the South East side of the Mill row to the afsd. Bridge & in a line of a small Tract of Land claimed by Lewis Howell thence by the line thereof NWQ the afsd road N 53 degs. E 39 pchs to River Branch which rams into the afsd Creek Thence up the sd. Branch bounding thereon N 34 degs. W 6 pchs. N 55 degs. W 24 pchs. N. 35 degs. W 24 Pchs. thence crossing the sd. Branch N 15 degs. E. 8 pchs. to a Co: gum of the Land of Doctr. Rees Jones formerly John Ogles thence therewith N B W 50 pchs to the Beginning...Containing within these Bounds clear of _____ for roads 136 acres of Land & Swamp ____ and now called Goodings Chance Survd. The 12th day of July Ano. Domi 1739. Thos. Noxon Dept. Ye Survr. Of N. C. Cty.
Map showed this adjoining land of Doctr. Rees Jones.
*

July 10 1741. Warrant to resurvey to Dr. Rees Jones from the Hon. Thomas Penn:

By The Proprietaries___

Whereas at the Request of Rees Jones of the County of Newcastle Practitioner in Physick that we would be pleased to grant him a Resurvey on a Tract of about Seventy four Acres of Land called Eagle's Point first surveyed to John Ogle under whom the said Rees Jones claims Title thereunto Situate on the North Side of Christina Creek near the Bridge over the same in the said County the better to regulate and fix the Lines Bounds and Quantity thereof; These are to authorize and require thee to resurvey or cause to be resurveyed unto the said Rees Jones according to the known Lines & Bounds thereof and of the adjoining Lands and also to bound the same on the Edge or bank of the said Creek and on the Water courses of Run branch the aforesaid Tract of Land and make return thereof into our secretary's office in Order for Confirmation and in so doing this shall be they sufficient Warrant. Given under my Hand and the Seal of our Land office at Philadelphia, this tenth day of July Anno Domini 1741. Thos. Penn.

Benja. Eastburn Survr Genll. A true Copy. Nichl. Scull.

*

Rees Jones, physician, J, 1, #31, n. side of Christina Crk. near bridge, July 10, 1741, resurvey C. T4.

Rees Jones, deced., paper concerning Dr. Rees Jones, J, 2, #52.

*

1754. Dec. 1. 5. Dr. Rees Jones died intestate & without issue. Evan Morgan as Heir at Law enters & takes possession of the premises, etc.

1759, Apr 9. 7. John Emms, other Heir, etc.

A slate of David Morgan's Claim. Etc.

Evan Morgan, Catharine, his wife. Another spelling has Kathryn Morgan, wife of Evan Morgan, son David.

*

Extensive letters, etc. about Dr. Rees Jones estate: One attested to says Rowland Jones had 3 children, Dr. Rees, Lewis Jones & Eliz. Jones. Heirs were Kathryn Morgan, wife of Evan Morgan. Had son David Morgan.

* *

WELSH TRACT CHURCH:

To continue with the church records after David John and Esther arrived in 1710:

The church at Welsh Tract continued to grow as new members were added to the rolls. In 1711, from Lanwennarth, Wales, where Timothy Lewis was Pastor, came James Jones and Ann Jones. From Blaeney-Gwent, Abel Morgan, Pastor, and Joseph James. Also in 1711 several were added by baptism: Thomas Rees; Thomas David; Margaret Evan; Sarah Emson

[Empson]; Rachel Thomas; Daniel Rees; William Thomas; John Thomas; Martha Thomas; John Evans; and Lydia Evans.

In 1712 were added several from Pennepek (Philadelphia) by letter: Nicholas Stephen, Mary Stephen, John Paine, and Elizabeth Paine.

In 1713, John Eaton, Juan Eaton, Joseph Eaton, Gwenllian Eaton, George Eaton, and Mary Eaton were accepted into membership by letter from the Pennepek Church in Philadelphia. The Eatons were listed early on in the Pennepek records. More who arrived from Wales became church members. From Lantivy (James James, Pastor) came Elias Thomas (brother of Elisha Thomas), Thomas Evans and Ann Evans. From Pembrokshire, (Samuel John, Pastor), came Philip Rees. James James' name was written in parenthesis, but it is possible he came over at this time.

John Bentley, James James, Jun., Eleanor David, Mary Thomas, Ann Thomas, David John, Richard Lewis, Sarah Nicholas and Mary Lewis were added by baptism in 1714. This David John was the husband of Esther John.

In 1714, were added by letter from Philadelphia: [Abel Morgan, Pastor], Benjamin Griffith, Emly Davis, and Catherine Hollin[g]sworth. In 1715, were added by letter from Shiregar (Pa.), Mary Robinet; by baptism were added Thomas James* (aged 16), John Jones, and Richard Witten. By letter from Rydivilim, Wales, [John Jenkin, Pastor] came Griffith Thomas.
*A Thomas James, possibly this one, had land adjoining Griffith John's in South Carolina.

In 1716 were added by baptism: Elizabeth John (Jenkin Jones's sister), David Davis, Thomas Richard and wife, and Mary Prys (Price). In 1717, Cornelius Vansant and Richard Herbert were added by letter; and Sarah Herbert was added by baptism.

The church apparently kept close tabs on the behavior of members, and at their monthly meeting 2 February 1716/17, a list of objectionable behavioral problems of Philip Truax were considered, and he was "dismembered Jan. 6, 1721-2."

The laying on of hands, singing of Psalms, and several other beliefs seem to have still been questioned. This caused the Rev. Abel Morgan, minister of the gospel in Philadelphia, to feel the necessity to translate into Welsh a statement of their faith and beliefs for the members to sign. They continued to meet with this church once a year, and appeared to have contact with both it and Pennepek. The "Confession of Faith" was presented to them at a meeting held Feb. 4, 1716.

According to the records kept, this "Confession of Faith" was signed by the following members: Thomas Gryffth, Elizabeth Gryffyth, Elizous [Elisha] Thomas, Mary Thomas, Enoch Morgan, Shunan Morgan, Shon Gryffyth [John Griffith], Rachel Gryffyth, Shon Phylips, James James, Sara James, Joseph Eton [Eaton], Guoullian Etton, Rhys Dafydd, Susana Dafydd, Shon Doufnallt [Devenault], Mary Dofnallt, Anthony Mathew, Robecca

Shonn [John], Dafydd Thomas, Ann Shonn, Thomas Shonn or Cryn, Mary
Walis, Thomas Shonn Rhys, Elinor Moris, Hugh Morys [Morris], Lidia
Efans [Evans], Shon Efans, Shan Mathow, Shons Etton, Mary Wiliana,
Elias Thomas, Mary Etton, Thomas Weild [Wild], Mary Thomas, Samuol
Weild, Mary Weild Ros, John Pain, Elizabeth Pain, Thomas Rhichart,
Elizabeth Rhys, Edward Edwards, Shywan Rhichart, Thomas Edmond,
Shan Edwards, William Thomas, Mary Prys, Simon Mathou [Mathew],
Elizabeth Thomas, Simon Butler, Mary Edmund, Thomas Efan, Ann
Rhichart, Thomas Moris, Ann Buttler, Rhys Jones, Ann Efan, Shonn Jones,
Hana Shon, Rhichart Whitin, Elinor Thomas, Samuel Efans, Ann Lowis
[Lewis], Shon Butler, Mary Lowis, Richart Goary, Sara Nigolas [Nicholas],
Shon James, Joanna Milor [Miller], Shon Grinwator, Mary Robinot,
Rhichart Dafydd, Dathoring Holinsworth, Samuel Gryffyth, Elizabeth
Tilton, Owon Thomas, Sara Harbort, Shoncin Shon [Jonathan John], Sara
Curd, James James, Mary Bontler, Thomas James, Emlon Dafis [Emily
Davis], Shonn Thomas, Rachel Thomas, Dafydd Shon [David John], Estor
Thomas, Abel Nigolas, Estor Shon [Esther John], Arthyr Edward, Mary
Shoncins, Gryfyth Thomas, Margaret Wiliam, Shon Milor, Lyns Edmond,
Benjamin Gryfyth [Griffith], Elizabeth Harry, Cornolius Fomsand,
Elizabeth Shion [John], Richart Harbert, Elizabeth Truwax, Shion Harry
[John Harry], Martha Dafis [Davis], Shion Boulter, Als Mils [Alice Miles],
Phylip Trywax, Elonor Phylip, Thomas Dafydd, Mary Rhys, Hugh Efan,
Margaret Moris, Dafydd Thomas, Shusan Etton, Shion Wilian, Susana
Dafydd, Samuell Philip, Elizabeth Dafydd, Thomas Rhys, Mary Thomas,
Mary James, Daniol Rhys, Cathring Thomas, Philip Rhys, Margaret
Robinott, Dafydd Lewis, Elonor Griffyth, Dafydd Efan [David Evan],
Hanah Philip, Shion Dafydd, David Davis, Sara Milchor, John Holinsworth,
Mary Jones, [1712 written at side], Garls Milor, Sarah James, William
Denn, Sara Griffith, John Evans, Morgan John, Danioll James [Daniel
James], Phillip James, [1719 written at side], Hugh Lewis, Richartt Lewis,
Griffydd Lewis, William Truax, Thomas Jones, Choffry Bontley, John
Stoutt, Wiliam Truax, Thomas Hodchoson, Richart Barow [Richard
Barrow], Thomas David, Philip David, Barnott Young, Carnolius Truax,
Margaret James, Cathrin Lewis, Sarah Edward, Jann Edward, Margaret
James, Rebekah Truax, Ann Pirce, Chathoring Roos, Rachol Milos [Rachel
Miles], Mary Truax, Elizabeth David, Abigal Thager, Elinor Jones [wife of
Morgan John], Widow Forman, [1720] Elizabeth Thomas, Sara Thomas,
Phebeh Bruor, Jane Miles, Lidia Osboorn [Osborn], Cathoring Evan Harry,
Philipp Duglass [Douglass], Joshuia Dugless, Joshua Edward, [1722]
Elizabeth Milchor, Mary Edwards, Mary Harry, Mary Nicholas, Thomas
Harry, [1723] Osboorns dater, Janott Davis, [1724] William Parson, Rinall
Howoll [Reynald Howell], Thomas James, Lewis Jones, Thomas Bowan,
Elizabeth Roger, Mary Howol [Howell], Lottie Bowon; [1725] Nathaniel
Wilds, John Rontfro, Susanah William, Margaret Rontfro [Renfro].

CHAPTER SIX

GRIFFITH JOHN and Wife MARGARET:

A Griffith John died intestate in 1719, and his widow Margaret was appointed Executor to administer his goods, chattels and credits in divers places within the County, 1 Oct 1719. The Welsh Tract Minutes show a Margaret John was buried Sep. 22, 1744 [p. 69.] There was also a Griffith John or Jones who arrived in 1710 from Rhydwilim in Wales, and was an Elder at the Great Valley Church.[1] However, records indicate he died there. He had sons who were ministers, named Samuel, Griffith and Thomas.

This was excerpt from Deed Book C, V. 1, p. 144 to 146 in New Castle Co.:

"Margaret John her Letter of Adm. exc. on the Estate of Griffith John. John French Ellym. Register for the Probate of Wills and Administration, Letters of Admiteon. for the County of New Castle on Delaware, by Virtue of a Comeon. from the Hon. William Keith esq. of Exc. Senr. and Governor [p. 145] of the Counties of New Castle, Kent & Sussex
Upon Delaware and Province of Pensylvania
For Margaret John, Widow of Griffith
John, late of the County of New
Castle upon Delaware, Yeoman Dec'd.
Greeting
Whereas the said Griffith So as afsd. decd. dyed Intestate as is affirmed having whilst he lived and att the time of his death, goods, Chattells and Credits, in Divers places within this said County... And doe hereby ordain, Dispute and Constitute you the said Margaret John, Admin. of all & Singular the goods, Chattels and Credits of the sd. decd., within the Limits afsd...dated att New Castle, the first day of October in the Sixth year of the Reign of King George over Great Britain ... Anno: Dmi. one thousand seven hundred and nineteen. Inventory returned November 1719. John French, Reg.
*

Bk. C, Vol. 1, p. 144:
Administrator's Bond for estate of Griffith John---Oct 1, 1719
Administrator: Margaret Johns
Margaret John her Letters of Administration on the Estate of Griffith John. Margaret John widow.
Died intestate.
Debts to be deducted out of estate:
J. K. Gardner   Elexander White
Andrew Wallace   Phillip James

---

[1] Morgan Edwards, Materials... [Pa.] 1770, p. 27.

161

Lewis David*	William Rees
Rees Jones	William J. Cugh (Pugh?)
Thomas David	Evan Lewis
David Evan	Rees David
David Thomas	Elias Thomas
Thomas Griffith	
David Price	
William Bakell (?)	

Appraisers: David Price, John Thomas.

AUTHOR'S NOTE: Many of those named above were Baptist Church members. This settlement does not say Griffith owned any land. He might have lived on land that was in his father's name.
*Lewis David married Rebecca John after her husband died.
* *

WILLIAM JONES.
These records indicate he was living in New Castle Co. in 1715 to 1720.
Deed Book E, Vol. 1, 1715/1720:
P. 69: "Jacob Gooding & Abraham Gooding John Hansson and Mary Hanson intermarried with William Jones their and Every of their Heirs & Assigns the said share parts or portions of Right belonging to them or any of them their or any of their heirs or assigns of the said Grand tract of Land & Marsh whether divided or undivided to his & their proper use...or any title claim or demand arising therefrom thence & will warrant & forever defend by these presents In Witness whereof the said John Hanson his hand & seal...put this 13th day of Feb...1715/16..."
Deed dated 20th day Aug. 1722. 75 acres of land; William & Mary Jones; of St. George's Creek in Red Lion Hundred.
*

The other names in this deed were people who arrived during the 1680's, and were in the Brandywine area. Gooding was also mentioned in one of Thomas and Margaret Jones's deeds.
Deed dated 20th day Aug 1722: 75 acres & 45 acres of land; William & Mary Jones; of St. George's Creek in Red Lion Hundred. Mary was daughter of William Hanson, late of Reeden Island, yeoman, deceased, and granddaughter of John Hanson. This might have been the William Jones who took out grants for land in the Welsh Tract.
* *

Morgan Edwards wrote in his "Materials Towards Baptist Church History..." that Rev. Thomas Griffith's successor in 1725 was "REV. ELISHA THOMAS.

His name is written Eliseus in the first records of this church; but on his
tomb Elisha. He was born in the County of Caermarthen, in 1674; arrived
in this country with the church: ... was one of the first members; he died
Nov. 7, 1730, and was buried in this churchyard, where a handsome tomb is
erected to his memory: the top stone is divided into several compartments,
wherein open books are raised, with inscriptions and poetry both in Welsh
and English: he had two daughters, Rachel and Sarah. Rachel's first
husband was Rees Jones, by whom she had children, Rees, Mary, Deborah.
Rees and Deborah died childless. Mary married the honourable John Evans,
and is dead with her four children. Her aunt Sarah (the other daughter of
Rev. Elisha Thomas) married Daniel James and went with him to Peedee in
the year 1736; she had a son of the name of Elisha James to whom Rees
Jones devised a plantation in Newcastle county in case issue should fail in
the line of said Mary, and in case issue should fail in his line, Rees Jones
devised the same plantation to trustees chosen by the ministers of the
Philadelphian Association for the educating of Baptist youth of promising
parts and genius: it is supposed that heirs have failed in the lineage of Elisha
James; upon that supposition two grand-children of Elias Thomas (brother
of Rev. Elisha Thomas) took possession of the said plantation, but they
soon quitted their claim and the trustees of the Baptist Association
demanded possession, but the Evans have hitherto refused, tho they have no
more right to the plantation (by Rees Jones will) than the man in the Moon
has..."[2]
[Author's Note: The Cemetery had a marker for Rees Jones, Jun., who
departed this life September the 27th, 1757, aged 25 years. Another has
tombstones for two of Rees Jones' daughters Sarah and Susanna Jones,
twins, Oct. 7, 1737.]
* *

Land Records for Thomas':
Elisha Thomas, Welsh Tract, Surveys T2, 16, 16a, 17, Mar. 16, 1701/2, 526
a., with Draught.
Elias Thomas Will, 2 Jan 1737, of Pencader. Dau Sarah; mentioned Enoch
Morgan Sr.; wife Mary; son Zachariah. Wit. Hugh Evan, Rachel Jones,
Mary Evan. [Elias was brother of Elisha Thomas, the Baptist Minister.]
John Thomas, Will Book A, p. 234, 8/9 day Oct 1711...Eldest son David
Thomas, 250 acres whereon I now dwell; to two sons Thomas Thomas &
Will Bk. G, 204, David Thomas Will. 29 Sept 1748. Mother Cathrine;
sisters Rachel Griffith, Sarah Thomas, & Mary Thomas, also sister Ann
Bush. Brothers Lewis Thomas & Richard Thomas Excrs. Mentions 1
negro. Wit.: John Thomas, Ric'd. Thomas & Timothy Griffith.

---

[2]Materials Towards History of the American Baptists....

Will Bk. G, 166, Zachariah Thomas Will--Cousin Mary Evans; sister Sarah; James James brother in law, Exec. Wit: John Steel, Lewis Thomas & Enoch Morgan, 1 Aug 1748.

Will Bk. C, Pp. 171, 1719: Elizabeth Thomas, probate of John Thomas, yeoman, estate. 1719 Apr 15th.

Will of Joseph Thomas of Pencader Hundred...15th June 1762. Joseph Thomas 300 acres of land...lying upon White Oak Swamp whereon they are now settled...Eldest dau Mary Thomas,..dau Sara Thomas, ...son Benj. Thomas 150 acres.

Will Bk. C, P. 130--Lewis Thomas will. Witnesses Phillip David, Thos. David & Thomas John. [Date?]

Richard Thomas Will, 7th Aug 1753. Son Richard Thomas; dau Rachel Griffith; dau Ann Bush; dau Sarah McMechan; dau Mary Thomas; son Lewis Thomas.

Joseph Thomas of Pencader, yeoman; 15th day June 1762. Wife Jane; grandchildren Joseph Thomas, son of son Benjamin; grandsons David Howell & Enos Howell, sons of dau Dinah Howell, wife of David Howell. Son in law James James. Five children viz Benjamin Thomas, Josop Thomas, John Thomas, Elinor the wife of Joseph Jacobs, & Prisilla the wife of William Buchannon.

* *

Surveys:

Rees Thomas: (Rice) filed under Ogle, Thos., 02, #17, near White Clay Creek Hundred . ("Thos. Ogle's tract called Goshen.")

Also (Reece) on Christiana Creek, T2, #10, May 22 1706, 300 a. Resurvey.

Reece Thomas: Pencader, T1, #3, May 8, 1748, 170 a., mentioned Abr. Miller.

Reece Thomas; T2, #11, 11a, head of Long Creek, Pencader Hundred, Apr. 10, 1751, 245 1/3 a.

Reece Thomas, T2, #15; on Elk River Road, Welsh Tract, Jan. 5, 1703/4; 320 a. joint with Joseph Thomas.

Thomas Thomas, T2, #13, near Elk River Rd., Welsh Tract, Jan. 5, 1703/4, 212 a. joint with Joseph.

Griffith Thomas, S2, #67, near main Branch of Duck Creek, Nov. 14/15, 1746; 44 a., Rough draft.

John Thomas, near Elk River Rd., Welsh Track; 2/1, #6, 7, Mar 16, 1701/2; 682 a.; Survey, Gen. Ret.

John Thomas, W, 3, #64, n.d., c. 1703, see Welsh Tract.

T, 2, 1, #4, 4a, b, 5, 8, 14, Oct. 18, 1704, 36 1/4 a., Survey drau. for Wm. Thomas, Grandson of John, and survey Gen. Ret., 1752, mentions John Jr., father of William.

John Thomas, T, 1, #2, near Appoq. Hundred, Feb. 12, 1708, Cert. copy 1747.

John Thomas, St. George's Hundred, Surv. Gen. ret. #156, 158. Dec. 13, 1753, 36 1/4 a.
#158 showed date Dec. 18, 1752, and mentions Chris Byran.
Joseph Thomas, see Thomas Thomas, Jan. 5, 1703/4, Survey T2, #15.
P. 30. Agreements signed by: Elisha Thomas, Enoch Morgan, Hugh Morris, Howell James, Samuel James, Thos. James, James James Jr., Howell James, Daniel James.
* *

History of area continued:

Governor Keith was in charge until June 22, 1726, when he was suceeded by Patrick Gordon. At a meeting of the Council on July 25th, commissions were issued to David French as Attorney General for the three lower counties, and to John French and Samuel Lowman in New Castle County, as well as others in Sussex and Kent. The Justices appointed for New Castle County were John French, Robert Gordon, Joseph England, Charles Springer, John Richardson, James James, William Battell, David Evans, Andrew Peterson, Ebenezer Empson, Hans Hanson, James Dyre, Samuel Kirk, Richard Grafton and Simon Hadley.

During the latter part of 1726 and early 1727, the Assembly passed several important measures. The most important was the establishment of a regular system of law and equity courts. The first court was styled the General Quarter Sessions of the Peace and Gaol Delivery, and was held four times in each county. This court was presided over by three of the Justices. Cases not in their jurisdiction were taken to the Supreme Court of Oyer and Terminer. There was also a court of record held twice each year in each county, which was known as the Supreme Court of the Counties of New Castle, Kent and Sussex upon Delaware.

In April 1727, the Council commissioned David Evans, Richard Grafton, Robert Gordon, Benjamin Shurmer, Henry Brooke and Jonathan Bailey as judges of the Supreme Court of the lower counties. The justices of the peace for New Castle for 1727-28 were Robert Gordon, John Richard, Joseph England, Charles Springer, Andrew Peterson, Hans Hanson, Simon Hadley, William Read, Thomas January, James James Jr., Richard Cantwell, Joseph Robieson and James Armitage.

The Welsh Tract Church continued to have members sign the "Confession of Faith." '[1726] John James, Sarah James, Griffyth Nicholas, Elizabeth Thomas, Joseph Thomas, Jane Howol, Moris Howel, Rebeka Jonkin, Thomas Jonkin, Francis Boulton, Stephn Holinsworth; [1727] Elinor Johns, Mary Lewis; [Augt 1727] William Evan, James Howoll; [1728] Sara Jonkin; [1728 Epril] Elizabeth Jones, Gownllian Hugh, Richart Thomas, Simon Parson; [Augt 1728] Mary Hugh, Margaret Edward, Mary John, William Hugh, David Harry, Hary Howoll, Mary Underwood; [Sept 1 1728] Aboll James, Lewis Jorman; [Sept 1728] Sarah Edward, Margaret Forman, [Dec 1728] Benjamin Underwood; Jane Evans [1728];

165

[Sep 7 1729] John Bowen, Elizabeth Edward, William Griffith, Elizabeth Evan; [Jan 1729] David Davis, Elanor Stephen [1729].
* *

Deed Book H, page 239. 27 day Oct. 1727. Joseph Meredith of Pencader, husbandman, and his wife Elizabeth, David Meredith, his father...and Philip David, husbandman...Land Situated in Pencader Hundred Beginning at a corner Spanish oake by Thomas Griffith's fence thence along ye said line to Thomas Griffith's & thence to a post 14 perches and 1/2 thence West 95 purchases to a black oak to ye corner of Samuel James thence N. 26 to a post thence W. N. W. To a black oak in all 186 purches then N. and by east 194 to a black oak then East S. E. 40 purches to a black oak thence E. S. E. 130 to another corner tree W. then S. And by E. 100 & 55 to a corner white oak by Thomas Griffith's fence then S. & by W. 40 perches to ye place of Beginning containing 212 acres of land together with all ye houses, borns, stables orchards meadows & all ye appurtenance named hereof...Wit. Evan Rice, Griffith James, James Armalay [Armitage ?], William Williams.
*

GRIFFITH JOHN:
The only land records found prior to 1729 for Griffith John was for the 1703/4 land grant for 300 acres, and mention of his land in other deeds. There were no records for him in the Welsh Tract Church minutes. This deed for a Griffith John was made 21st day of August 1729 between John David Rees of New Castle Co., Millwright, on the one part, and Griffith John of sd. county, Farmer, of the other part, with the property being sold to Griffith John. This fifty acres was taken from the corner adjoining Thomas John's land and seemed to join Griffith John's land, per this deed.
*

Book I, p. 123, 21 day Aug. 1729.
"WHEREAS Samuel Griffith late of New Castle afsd. was lawfully seized in his lifetime of & in a certain piece or parcele of Land situate lying & being in New Castle Co. afsd. laid out for fifty acres butted & bounded as is in these presents hereafter settforth ......did sell & dispose of the sd. Fifty acres of land unto the sd. John David Rees of sd. County Millwright as afsd... & afterwards dyed and WHEREAS Mary Griffith widdow & admr. of the goods & chattels which were of the sd. Samuel Griffith at the time of his death by her Petition to the worshipful Justices of the Peace for sd. County holding in orphans court at Newcastle afsd. in & for the sd. County the twenty second day of August in the year one thousand seven hundred & twenty eight setting forth that Samuel Griffith late decd. her husband did sell & dispose of Fifty acres of land unto John David Rees millwright part of the payments for which he had made in his life Time & dyed without making the sd. David any title or otherwise empowering his wife so to do and therefore prays the Court for an order by which she might be enabled to convey the sd. Land unto the sd. John David Rees according to the bargain

made by her said Husband in his Life Time & thereby receive the sum of money yet unpaid in order to satisfy the Debts of her aforesd. husband AND WHEREAS the Court were of opinion & did order according to the motion & prayer of the aforesaid Mary Griffith the aforesd. John David Rees the forece of the above ord. did become lawfully & Rightfully seized of & in all that the above mentioned piece or parcel of lands containing Fifty acres as above mentioned which sd. piece of land is butted or bounded as followeth Viz. beginning at a corner marked gum tree standing in the line of Griffith John's land and being bounded with a line of marked trees directly north to another corner marked white oake being the farthest boundary tree in that course then altering its course by a line of marked trees Easterly to a corner marked red oake & altering its course again & running by a line of marked trees South to a corner marked tree standing in the corner of the sd. Thomas Griffiths fence running along the fence west to the first mentioned corner gum tree laid out for Fifty acres of land being part of the Tract of Land whereon Thomas John now liveth and whereas ye sd. John David Rees by certain articles of agreement duly Executed and or seal did covenant grant & agree to & with the sd. Griffith John his heirs & assigns that he the sd. John David Rees & all & every other person & persons whatsoever of in or to the sd. Fifty acres claiming or to claim any right to the same should on or before the third Tuesday in August next being this Instant August convey unto the sd. Griffith John his heirs or assigns all the present etc. by such deed and or other conveyance as should by the aforesd. Griffith or his Council required NOW THIS INDENTURE WITNESSETH that the sd. John David Rees for & in consideration of the sum of Thirty Pounds current money of America to him in hand paid & secured to be paid before the sd. Griffith John the receipt whereof is hereby acknowledged Doth grant Bargain sell Alliene Enfeoff & Confirm And by these Presents have granted bargained sold enfeoffed & confirmed unto the sd. Griffith John his heirs & assigns forever all that the above mentioned parcele of land butted & bounded as above sett forth with all & singular the appurtenances thereto belonging of what name or nature soever the same be with all & singular the writings thereto belonging in like manner afsd. TO HAVE & TO HOLD the sd. Fifty acres of Land & premises hereby granted or intended to be hereby granted & sold & every part thereof unto the sd. Griffith John his heirs & assigns to the only purpose use & behoof of the sd. Griffith John his heirs & assigns forever & the sd. John David Rees for himself his heirs Excrs. & Admrs. Doth grant & agree to & with the sd. Griffith John his heirs & assigns by these presents in the following manner that the sd. John David Rees his heirs Excrs. & Admrs. the above mentioned & sold premised with the whole appurtenances against him the aforesd. John David Rees his heirs & assigns & against all & every other person & persons whatsoever shall & will warrant & Defend forever by these presents & the same likewise free & clear & freely & clearly acquitted from all encumbrances of what name or

nature soever the lands which or be to become due only excepted & fore perused & the sd. John David Rees doth further agree for himself his heirs Excrs. & Admrs. with sd. Griffith John his heirs & assigns to make & acknowledge cause to be made & acknowledged such further deed & Conveyance of the premises to the sd. Griffith John & his assigns & shall be by him his heirs or Assigns or their or either of their Council shall be devised or required IN WITNESS WHEREOF the sd. John David Rees hath thereby set his seal the day & year first above written.
John David Rees
Mary David Rees. [Their marks.]
Sealed & Delivered before us: James James Junr.; R. Robertson.
To all Christian People to whom these presents shall come I <u>Griffith John</u> do fully clearly & absolutely for me my heirs Excrs. Admrs. & assigns revise release forever Quite Claim unto the within mentioned John David Rees his heirs Excrs. Admrs. & Assigns all such right Title or interest claim & demand as I my heirs Excrs. admrs. can or may have possess enjoy or claim for or by reason of the General Warranty within settforth and do hereby accept & acknowledge myself content and do for my heirs Excrs. & Admrs. to and my self them to acquitt the sd. John David Rees his heirs Excrs. and admrs. from any claim or title In them may have hereafter thereto any otherways than by a Speciale Warantee from John David Rees him the sd. Griffith John his heirs Excrs. & Admrs. & that on Pain of Thirty Pound Confederation money [p. 125] within mentioned Witness my hand & Seal the Day & year allso within mentioned the words "John David Rees' were sett in the margin by & Insert before Signing.
Witness present. James James Junr. Robert Robertson.
ACKNOWLEDGED in open Court of Common Pleas held at New Castle for the County of New Castle the third Tuesday in August in the third year of his Majs. Reign. Witness my hand & Seal of the County this twenty third Day of August Anno Dei. 1729. David French prothon."
* *

Will Book G, p. 167, 7 March 1746, David Howell, Pencader, yeoman. Left wife 1/3; mentioned son Daniel, son David, dau Rachel Rees, wife of Rees, dau Sarah Williams, wife of John Williams, sons Daniel & David, executors. Wit: David John, <u>Griffith John</u> & Jacob Van Bibber. Jacob attested to signature. Stated David & Griffith John too sick to come in.
* *

In Deed Book C, V. 1, p. 6, dated in 1702, there were recorded indentures given by John Jones, Gent., of Philadelphia, for certain sums of money to Matthias Vanbibber. One document was witnessed by William Hinton, Jacob Isaac Vanbibber, and Francis Jones. Another was witnessed by Joseph Wood, Adam Baldridge, and William Jones.
*

The next record for Griffith John was his will written in 1748, which will be given later.

THOMAS JOHN AND WIFE, SUSANNAH:

The Marriage Records for New Castle County have the following: "Thomas John and Susannah Welsh. Ref. Vol. 87, p. 95, Holcomb, Immanuel Church, p. 217, Welsh Tract, Jan. 27, 1715, Minister John Ross." It appears that this was the same Thomas John who had the first survey for 618 acres, which was later found to be 600 acres. There was a Susannah Welsh who married John Guest, and John Guest died. This was probably Thomas John's second marriage. Mary, who was one of the constituent members of the Welsh Tract Church, could have been his first wife.

In 1723, Deed Book G, 1, pp. 303-304:

This Indenture made the Twelfth day of November in …one thousand seven hundred and twenty three Between Simon Hadley of Mill Creek hundred in the County of New Castle upon Delaware, Yeoman, and Ruth his wife of the one part and Thomas John of Pencader Hundred in the said County Yeoman of the other part Witnesseth that the said Simon Hadley and Ruth his wife for and in consideration of the sume of one hundred and twenty five pounds lawfull money of America to them or one of them in hand by the said Thomas John well and truly paid…Receipt whereof …acknowledge …have granted…unto the said Thomas John his heirs and assigns forever all that Tract or parcell of Land Situate and being in the County of Chester and New Castle aforesaid Beginning at a Post in a Line of Beginning Trees and thence Extending South by the Mannor Line one hundred and Eighty four perches to an post thence north by the land of William Roe thirty four perches to a post thence east by the land of William Holliday twenty one perches to a black oak thence North by the same land one hundred and fifty perches to a post thence east by the Land of Benjamin Freed two hundred and forty nine perches to the place of beginning Containing by Estimation three hundred acres it being part or parcel of a greater Tract or parcell of Land granted and conveyed unto the said Simon Hadley…
Signed by Simon Hadley and Ruth Hadley. Witnesses: Richard Thomas and Cornelius Toby. Acknowledged 22 day of May 1724, Entered in the Records of Said Court in Court Dockett page 294…

NOTE: Thomas John purchased 300 acres in above deed, in the area where Chester Co. and New Castle County joined, near Penn's Manor [Rockland?] Which Thomas John was of Pencader Hundred? The only one who described himself this way was the one married to Susannah. The one with wife Rebecca was described as being of Pencader in a deed after his death, but he described himself as of White Clay Creek Hundred.

Deed Book I, Vol. 1, P. 179, 1729: A deed dated <u>Sixth day of November, 1729</u>, between William Davis of Radnor, Chester Co. and David Evans of Pencader Hundred parties for the first part, confirmed 1156 acres of land conveyed to Thomas John of Pencader Hundred, yeoman, party of the other part. This land was described as:

"Situate lying & being in New Castle County bounded as followeth Beginning at a black oak by the road thence on a straight course south to a corner gum of Henry Davids land thence East six hundred & ten perches to another corner black oak of Henry Davids thence along the Line Jonathan Morgan to a corner white oak three hundred & four perches thence west three hundred & ten perches to the place of beginning being part of a Tract of land granted unto us by William Penn Esqr..."

Witnesses were Thomas Evans, William Williams, Daniel James and John Lewis.
* *

This appears to include the 600 acres first surveyed, which was lying next to Elisha Thomas' land, and had a description of Griffith John's land adjoining. Daniel James, the witness above, was the husband of Sarah Thomas, who was daughter of Elisha Thomas. Elisha's other daughter Rachel was first married to Rees Jones, then to John Griffith Jr. Sarah and Daniel James went to the Pee Dee in South Carolina in 1736. Griffith John Sr. (will of 1748) had a daughter married to John Lewis, who was probably a brother or son of Thomas Lewis who had land nearby. David Lewis and David Johns had land side by side several times in North Carolina and Georgia.
* *

Deed Book M, Vol. 1, p. 75, 1736:

This deed dated 16 day Feb. 1736, from Thomas John, Gent., and Susanna his wife, of Pencader Hundred to John Devor of the township of Lancashire in the Co. of Lancashire and George Moore...five hundred & fifty three acres and sixty eight perches of land situate...in New Castle Co. bounded as followeth: Beginning at a Stake North ...it being a part of that 1156 acres of land which the said Thomas John enjoyed and had a Deed of the same from William Davis and David Evans according to the Articles of Agreement assigned by the Proprietors bearing Date the 15th day day of October 1701...Now this 553 acres of land and 68 perches being legaly surveyed...according to the Articles of a Bargain made and concluded between Thomas John of the one part and John Reynolds and George Moore of the other part bearing date..13th Oct 1736...Reference thereunto being had now know yee that I Thomas John...do by these presents grant...unto the said John Devor and George Moore..."
Signed by Thomas John .
Susanah John [her mark];

Witnesses: Thomas James; George Reynolds; John Evans. Susannah attested to signing of her own free will before Thomas James.
* *

NOTE: One or more of the following surveys could have been for the Thomas Jones who had wife Margaret, as they sold off their land in 1738, and moved elsewhere also. Also note, the Quaker David Meredith had Moore sons-in-law, but George Moore was not one of them. This George Moore was from Ireland.
*

Survey dated 23 day of 7mo. 1737 "I have survd. for Thomas Jones the above described tract of land situate in Appoqk. Hundred & County afsd. Bounded as follows: beginning at a corner Blazed [standing near a Branch of Duck Creek] W. O. sd to be a corner of sd Thos. Jones Duckling plantation running thence up the afsd. brch N. 32 deg. w 85 pchs. unto sd Branch thence No 50 deg. to nd afsd. to a corner Black Oak by a pond side thence s 32 deg. East 100 pchs. to a _____ side near a corner B _____: Thence S 28 degrees 1/2 W 108 ps. to a point where two Branches unite & draining thence into the main branch of Duck Creek thence up the largest Branch above Described & binding thereof West 36 pchs. N. 20 deg. W. 42 pchs. to the Beginning Containing within these bounds (w sd appear to have been formerly marked) clear of allowannce for roads. 90 acres Survd. this 1-3 _____ anno domi 1737. Thos. Noxen."
*

NOTE: This had a map of the land showing it was apparently called "Without Doubt" and "Thos. Jones Duckling Plantation." There were 95 acres 19 perches, with 5 acres 19 perches for roads - - clear 90 acres.

There was also a map of a tract of land of Thomas Jones' of 153 acres, and what appeared to be a couple more parcels of his land. One part of his land joined Thos. Moore's land. This latter map had notation "I have survey'd unto Thomas Jones the Tract of Land described by the above Figure situate in Apoqk. Hundred Newcastle County on the 23 & 24th days of January 1744. Geo. Stevenson, Dep. Surv. of Newcastle Co."
* *

P. 454. Deed dated 23 Nov 1738 between John Devor and Robert Aikin. John Devor sells his half of 553 acres & sixty eight perches of land which the two purchased from Thomas John, "beginning at a Staik North one hundred and sixty perches to a corner white oak, East one hundred & Eighty five pearches, North Eight degrees, east east fifteen degrees north north twenty five degrees, east east again thirteen degrees, south south again six degrees west, east again three hundred pearches to a doggwood corner tree, south one hundred & forty pearches to a black oak corner, West five hundred & eighteen perches to a place of Beginning..."
* *

Another Survey dated 27th Feb. 1739 for Thomas Jones for 150 acres of land situated "in the forrest of Appoquink. Hundred adjoining his other Land in the county aforesaid."

* *

To continue with Thomas and Susanna's land sales:
Deed Book N, Vol. 1, Pp. 163, 164, 1740:

Deed dated 11th day of May 1740 between Thomas John of Pencader Hundred, Yeoman, and Susanna his wife, of first part and Evan David, Farmer, of the other part. Sold 50 acres for 15 pounds, it being part of the larger tract he originally owned. "Beginning at a corner dogwood tree in the southeast corner of said land running thence north one hundred and thirty perches to a corner white oak thence west sixty two perches to a corner white oak standing in a little swamp thence south one hundred and thirty perches to a corner stake thence east sixty two perches to the place of Beginning containing fifty acres one rood and twenty perches..."
Signed by Thomas John and Susanna John [her mark]. Witnesses: David John & John Thomas.

* *

Deed Book N, Vol. 1, p. 413, 1742:

Deed dated 19th day August 1742 between Thomas John of Pencader Hundred, yeoman, and Susanna his wife, first party, and John Henderson of White Clay Creek, Taylor, for 50 pounds, for which he sold 217 acres of land, being part of the larger tract he originally owned. "Beginning at a corner stake standing in a line of George Moore's land thence extending east sixteen perches, North Eight dgrs. east Fifty one pchs. North seventy five Dgrs. west six pchs., north twenty five Dgrs. east Seventeen pches. south Seventy Seven Dgrs. fifty one pchs. South Six Dgrs. west Fifty Six pchs., East Two hundred and fifteen pchs. to a corner stake of Evan David's land thence north one hundred thirty four pchs. & a half to a corner white oak of ye afsd. Evan David's land, Thence west two hundred eighty two pchs. & a half to a corner Black oak near William Evans's line thence South one Hundred and thirty four pches. and a half to the beginning containing within these bounds Two hundred & seventeen acres of land being part of a larger tract formerly purchased by the afsd. Thomas John of William Davis & David Evans..."
Signed by Thomas John and Susanna John [her mark].

* *

N, 1, 479, 1742:

Deed dated 13 Nov 1742 between Thomas John late of Pencader Hundred but now of <u>Appoquidick Hundred</u>, yeoman, & Susannah his wife, parties of first part, and John Johnson of Pencader Hundred, of the second part: they sold 228 acres of land [in Pencader, New Castle Co.] for 50 pounds. "Beginning at the westernmost corner of John Henderson's land

being originally part of the afsd. tract & in a line of William Evan's land, thence running with the sd. John Henderson's Division line to his most south east corner of his land & to the line of the land of George Moore & Robert Eakins (also part of the afsd. Tract) thence by their line to the line of the afsd. John Johnson's dwelling Plantation & therewith to the line of Griffith John's land & therewith to the line of the land late of David Thomas Deced. thence Extending therewith & the line of the afsd. William Evans land to the place of beginning containing within the before described limits two hundred & twenty eight acres of land, meadow & Swamps..."
* *

This appears to be a total of 1,038 acres of land Thomas and Susannah sold out of his 1,156 acres in Pencader before his death.
*

WILL Book G, p. 337, 2 Oct 1749:
County of New Castle on Deleware ---

"To Susannah John Administratior of all & Singular the goods & Chattels Rights & credits which were of Thomas John late of the County aforesaid Deceased - -
WHEREAS THE SAID Thomas John so as aforesd. deceased died intestate as stated having while he lived & at the time of his death goods & Chattles Rights & Credits in divers places within ye sd. County...I designing that the goods & Chattles Rights & Credits of the deceased may be well & faithfully Administ. & Converted & disposed to pious uses do grant unto you the sd. Susannah John in whose credility in this behalf I very much confide full power by the tenor of these presents to administer all ye singular the goods & Chattles frr. which were of the sd. deceased at the time of his death and faithfully to dispose thereof, as also to receive collect & recover all the debts whatsoever to the sd. deceased, ... & making a line & perfect inventory & Conscionable Appraisement of all & Singular ye Goods & Chattles afsd. of the sd. deceased & Exhibiting the same into the registers Office at New Castle in sd. County aforesd. on or before the 2d day of Aprill next ensuing the date hereof, & rendering a Just & true Account of yr. Administration on or before the 2d. day of October which shall be in the year of our Lord 1750 being solemly sworn, And I ordain & constitute you the said Susannah John Administratrix of all & Singular the goods & Chattles & etc. ...In testimony whereof I have caused the seal of office to be hereunto affixed at New Castle this 2d. day October in the 23d year of his Majestys Reign Anno Domini 1749."
* *

JAMES JAMES ESQR.

James James, Esqr. was considered one of the prominent citizens of New Castle Co. and was actively involved with community affairs. He might be the James James who was son of the Sr. who had the grant for 1244 acres of land. However, in 1713, it appears the Welsh Baptist Pastor James James arrived from Lantivy. A James James Jr. was baptized in the church in 1714. James James and several others were appointed as Justices of the Peace on 5th Aug 1726:

John Richardson, James James, William Battell, David Evans, Andrew Peterson, Ebenezer Empson, Hans Hanson, James Dyre, Samuel Kirk, Richard Grafton, Simon Hadley. [Deed Book H, Vol. 1, p. 71.]
*

Deed Book L, 1, P. 28: James James to son James James Jr...Land bounded on E. by Rees Jones land...on N. by James Armitage land...143 acres and 77 perches...Signed James James.
Wit: Elishia Thomas, Enoch Morgan, Howell James, James Armitage, Daniel James. 3 day June 1723.
There were deeds also for land to his sons Samuel and Daniel, all referred to as "heir apparent."
* *

SAMUEL JAMES
IRON ORE IN NEW CASTLE CO.:

Samuel James was a millwright and the person who began the first iron works in New Castle County. He was son of James James. Some of the James family went to the Pee Dee in South Carolina at about the same time as Griffith John and his family, and some of their land was adjoining his in South Carolina. They were undoubtedly related to the John's through intermarriage, and went to South Carolina together.

Samuel James lived in Pencader Hundred. His wife was named Sarah. He appears to be son of James James Sr. of Wales, Bristol, England and Philadelphia Co. who took out 1244 acres on 27 June 1702, and had this confirmed by William Penn on 21 Feb 1703. Samuel received land from his father by deed of gift 24 Jan 1709. [This was recorded 7 Feb 1727.] He erected a successful forge on this property and having plenty of iron ore, was able to interest the leading iron masters of Philadelphia in this locality. On 3 June 1723, he made a deed to Evan Owen and William Branson, merchants from Philadelphia, for one acre and three quarters of land for the sum of 30 pounds.

Samuel, being a millwright, had noticed the iron ore in New Castle County, and was interested in mining the ore and setting up a forge to process it. Records indicate there was knowledge of this ore from an early date, and it was mentioned in official papers of New Castle Co. in 1661.
*

Some of the deeds pertaining to Samuel James:
Deed Book H, Vol. 1, p. 565, 6th Oct 1724. Deed between Hugh Morgan of the Welsh Tract, farmer, and Philip David, farmer, sells "all that messuage and tenement of land Situate ...in the Welsh Tract...beginning at a corner

black oak of Griffith Nicholas's land, Running thence East 155 pchs. to a corner hickery of David Price's land thence 164 pchs. to a stake thence west thence west 145 pchs. thence North 164 pchs. to the place of Beginning containing...150 acres of land...sold to William Davis and David Evans...and sold by them to Samuel James...who sold unto James Morgan...and since made over to Hugh Morgan... Signed in pres. of Hugh Morgan, Evan David Jun. and Thomas Evans.
*

Deed Book H, Vol. 1, pp. 246-250, Year 1727:
Samuel James of Pencader Hundred, Millright, and wife Sarah, Evan Owen of City of Philadelphia, Mcht., & William Branson, of same place, Mcht. WHEREAS James James of Pencader Hundred yeoman by his patent dated 24 Jan 1709 did grant & convey by virtue of his patent of Deed of gift to Samuel James...Beginning at N. Side of Christiana Creek lying or being in ye Hundred & county whereso said out of a greater Tract of land belonging to ye sd. James James Beginning at ye N. Side of Christiana Creek at a persimon Tree standing by ye sd. Creek & from thence by ye line of land late belonging to James James ye East side next Thirty Nine Degrees east sixteen perches to a stone set for a corner & from thence South 39 degrees west 21 perches to ye sd. Creek & by several courses of ye sd. Creek 16 perches to ye first mentioned persimon tree & place of beginning Containing one acre & three quarters of land or thereabouts as by ye said Indenture Relation being had thereto it at large appear by force & virtue whereof or some good & effectual grants & assurances...now this Indenture witnesseth that ye Samuel James by virtue of this deed of gift...date 3 June 1723 & Sarah his wife for & in consideration of 30 pounds lawfull money...pd. by sd. Evan Owen & William Brandon.
Signed Samuel James & Sarah James.
Witnesses: David Davis, Charles Branest, James James Jr., dated 7 Feb 177.
*

In Deed Book H, Vol. 1, pp. 222-226, an Indenture Octopartite dated 21 Oct 1727 was made. This was a lengthy agreement. Here is a summary: The first parties mentioned were William Branson of City of Philadelphia; Thomas Rutter of said City, Smith; and Gabriel Goldney of City of Bristol in Great Britain, Merchant. The next eight mentioned as parties to this were Samuel James, of Pencader, millwright; Reece Jones of Penkadder Hundred, tanner; Samuel Nutt, County of Chester, Iron Monger; Evan Owen, City of Phila., merchant; William Branson of City of Phila., merchant; John Rutter, City of Philadelphia, Smith; Casper Wisler, City of Philadelphia, Brass Button maker.
This stated the eight parties mentioned intended to make and build one furnace for melting and casting of Iron in Penkadder [sic] Hundred at their own expense, and had then purchased several tracts of land towards that end, to wit:

Reece Jones & Samuel James had purchased two hundred & fifty acres of land or thereabouts from Richard Owen.

Of Thomas Rutter and Samuel James four hundred & fifty acres or thereabouts.

Of one Thomas Kitchen, Evan Owen & Reece Jones a certain messuage or tenement plantation & three hundred acres thereto, belonging of one James James, Esquire.

The parties had agreed for one acre and three quarters of one acre of land with Samuel James erecting the furnace, one with 'free liberty & privileges to digg & carry away ore of any part of ye said Samuel James land where he then did live for ye use of sd furnace.'

They had all agreed to be copartners in purchasing several parcels of land, in defending the same in making and building the furnace, digging and preparing the ore, casting the iron in the furnace, and in providing coal ore and other materials, etc.

The parties all agreed to pay their proportion of the moneys agreed upon which would be necessary for supporting the works, paying for servants, cattel [cattle], carriages, instruments, wages, etc.

Evan Owen & William Branson, by a certain deed poll dated 15th of March last past, published & declared that one acre and three quarters of one acre of land was purchased by monies of Casper Wister, John Leacock, William Fishbourn, Thomas Rutter, Edward Bradley, William Monington, Samuel Nutt & Reece Jones. As of them, Evan Owens, William Branson, John Leacock, William Wishbourn, Edward Bradley & Wm. Monington had bought shares of other of the parties to the Indenture Octopartite. This gave each a sixteenth of a share, etc. Then mention was made of purchases started and not yet finished. Other names involved were Thomas James and Philip David.

Money mentioned in this indenture was two hundred & thirty five pounds nineteen shillings to Thomas Rutter paid by Gabriel Goldney; five shillings Gabriel Goldney paid to William Branson. It appeared this gave Gabriel Goldney, merchant, of Bristol, England, one full sixteenth part.

This forge was to be called Abington Furnace and the business was The Abington Iron Works. It is not certain how long this business operated with all the people involved. It seems, however, that it was continually operated by Samuel James until 1734, and was commonly called "Samuel James or the Abinton Iron Works."

There followed another Indenture made by Thomas Rutter & William Branson; which sold one sixteenth part in this furnace & company to Gabriel Gouldney of ye city of Bristol in Great Britain merchant, for the sum of 5 shillings lawfull money.
*

Deed Book I, Vol. 1, P. 102, Year 1729.

This Indenture made 10th day June...1729 BETWEEN Samuel James of Penkader Hundred...Gent. of the one part & James White & Abraham Taylor both of the City of Philadelphia...Merchants, of the other part WITNESSETH that the sd. Samuel James for & in consideration of 400 pounds lawfull money of Pensilvania...HATH granted Bargained Sold...unto the sd. John White & Abraham Taylor all that parcel or Tract of land of 201 acres & 126 perches Situate in Pencader Hundred...with the messuages & plantation hereon and a forge thereon erected, almost finished for the forging of Iron Bars out of the grosser metals the land Beginning at a Black oak in the line of Thomas Watts & Elishia Thomas & being a corner also of James James Junr.'s land & running by his line 37 perches to a Spanish Oake at another corner thence Extending to Elishia Thomas' House & thence by a line of James James Senr. near the road 41 perches to a black oake stump on the S. side of a small runn that crosseth the same road thence upon a straight line following James James' land and crossing Cristiana Creek one hundred forty seven perches to a stake on the North East end of Chestnutt Hill being a corner of Thomas James' land thence by the sd. Thomas James' line two hundred & Eighteen perches to a stake neare a black oake on the north side of the Iron Hill thence East by a line of Thomas John Sixty two perches to a chestnut tree in the line of Hugh Morris' Land Thence by a Line of sd. Hugh Morris' one hundred thirty To a stake near a hickery tree thence east by a line of sd. Hugh Morris sixty two perches to a corner Spanish oak near the Anabaptist Meeting House thence north thirty six perches to an old rotten Black Oak thence east crossing Christiana creek twenty Two perches to a poplar tree in Philip James' land thence north by his line thirty four perches to a stake thence continuing the same course by the sd. Thomas Watts's line one hundred ninety two perches to the place of Beginning...

Signed Samuel James

Sealed & Del. In presence of us Richard Grafton, Thomas Crowder, J. Hopes Junr.

*

The next deed, in 1735, seemed to indicate that the above was not an actual sale of the land, but a mortgage taken out on it. He must have continued to have financial difficulties and borrowed even more with the land and forge as security. Please note that neither David John, Thomas John or Griffith John had land involved with this forge, although they were nearby.

*

Deed Book K, Vol. 1, Year 1735, p. 427:
Samuel James Jr., yeoman, also known as Samuel James Jr., Gent., owed 852 pounds and was assessed damages of 83 shillings & 8 pence to John White & Abraham Taylor as assessed in Feb. Term on behalf of that suit...expended of the lands & tenements goods & chattels...this 24th day of

May...200 acres., etc. and also eighth part of furnace commonly called Samuel James' or [Abington] Iron Works, together with 1/8 part of lands and tenements & their appurtenances to the said furnace building & the same did sell unto the said John White & Abraham Taylor...all that the afsd. Plantation & tract of land butted & bounded as followeth viz.:
Same as given before in Deed Book I, Vol. 1, p. 102 in indenture to James White & Abraham Taylor. Signed Henry Newton, Sheriff.
Received on the within mentioned John White and Abraham Taylor the within mentioned sum of 125 pounds in full of the...money within written. Henry Newton.
*

Thomas Scharf in his History of Delaware mentioned that the ore beds in New Castle and Sussex Counties were entirely bog ores. He specifically mentioned the ore found in the vicinity of White Clay Creek, Pencader Hundred. He stated there was a forge and furnace built, and ore mined and smelted for about ten years, then abandoned. This was undoubtedly the forge established by Samuel James, as these records indicate. Samuel James' land lay next to one of the Thomas John's. The John's and James' land was in the vicinity of Iron Hill.

In an account of the sale of the forge and furnace building, p. 954, Scharf stated it was purchased by Andrew Fisher, Miller. He stated the land was owned at the time he wrote his history (1888) by William McConaughey. "A part of the old wall and a heap of embers on land now owned by Cooch Bros. marks the site of the old forge." After purchasing this, Fisher erected a gristmill and a sawmill on the property. This sawmill burned in July 1883.

In Scharf's account of the iron ore, he mentioned that this was purchased by David Wood, an iron master of Philadelphia, and was operated for many years and known as "Woods' Ore Pits." They were still operating when Scharf's book was written in 1888. Scharf also mentioned iron ore being mined in Sussex Co. 1763 to 1776, with the iron shipped to England. When the Chesapeake was blockaded, they had to abandon the furnaces.
* *

DANIEL JAMES:
Book l, Vol. 1., p. 28. James James to his son & heir apparent Daniel James...153 acres 77 perches...bounded on E. by James James Jr...on north by James Armitages...144 acres. 23 Mar 1723. Wit: Elisha Thomas, Enoch Morgan, Howell James, Hanah Armitage & James Armitage.
*

Deed Book L, Vol. 1, p. 18, 24 Sept 1736:
Daniel James yeoman & Allan Delap Gent., Wm. Penn by patent to Daniel [should be James] James father of said Daniel James...for 1,244 acres of land...and James James did convey of the aforesaid tract unto two of the sons viz James James Jr. and Daniel James 248 acres & 40 acres more

adjoining being North in the said patent...Daniel James and wife Sarah sell...land Beginning at a corner black oak thence by Rees Jones' land North 221 perches to a stake by James Armitages land thence West by the said Armitages land 210 perches to a corner stake thence south 29 perches to a corner stake thence South 94 perches to a corner stake thence E. 84 perches to a corner stake thence E. 20 degrees South 120 perches to a corner swamp oak thence South 55 degrees East 98 perches to a corner black oak Sapling thence North 60 degrees East 36 perches to the first mentioned corner black oak and place of beginning containing 288 acres be the same more or less together with all ... Signed Daniel James & Sarah James.
In Pres. of: Thos. Allison, Tho. Pagert, James Armitage.
* *

PHILIP JAMES, MILLER:
William James obtained a warrant for a tract of land 25 October 1701 containing 1200 acres which was surveyed 3 June 1701. This was located in the Welsh Tract, and obtained from Davis, Evans and Willis. In 1707, he apparently had financial problems after erecting a grist mill and a saw mill. These mills and two hundred acres were seized by the Sheriff and sold at public sale. Howel James Sr. was the purchaser. He was probably the brother of James James Sr. and father of William James.

In Will Book C, p. 91, Howell James Sr., on 17th Aug. 1717, in his will mentioned sons Howell Jr., James James & Phillip James --- owned a grist mill and boulting mill. Grandson James James, son of William James. Witnesses: Enoch Morgan, Richard Owen, David Jones. Names sons James, Phillip & Howell Excrs.

Howell James was a Quaker, and possibly always remained one. He took as his second wife Phebe Evans Phillips Moore 27th 8mo. 1715 at Radnor Meeting House. She was daughter of Stephen Evans of Radnor, and married first Phillip Phillips, who died. Her second husband was Richard Moore, stepson of David Meredith. He died and she married the widower Howell James.

Some of the land sold by Phillip James was land inherited from his father. In father Howell's will, 250 acres of land was left to son Howel, and 200 each to his other sons, James and Philip. James sold his portion to his brother Philip on 12 May 1735. Philip James ran the mills, and dated 2 December 1725, was a record requesting that P l be recorded as his brand mark.

Deed Book I, Part 1, p. 177, 7th day Jan 1729, showed Philip James, Yeoman, sold to Frances Land for 78 pounds real estate described as: Eastward 1/2 of two tracts of land situated on Christiana Creek...by land of Thos. Watts'...to East of land late of Howel James...land late of James James...by David Thomas's fence...Howel James's fence...Southeast side of Iron Hill...contains 200 acres...east side of whole tract of 400 acres. Signed

Philip James & Anna James. Wit. James James Jr. & Frances James. Third Tues in Feb 1729 in Court of Common Pleas.

Philip sold 200 acres of land on which the mill was located to John Jones, Bolster of Philadelphia, as shown in Deed Book I, Vol. 1, Dated 8th Apr 1730. 'Indenture between Philip James and Ann his wife, and John Jones of Philadelphia, Bolster.' Philip and Ann sold the other 1/2 of the above described land [200 acres more] to John Jones for 98 pounds. Recorded May 10, 1731.

Philip sold 210 acres lying on the north side of Christiana Creek to Samuel Allen 8 Nov 1737.[3]

*

This pertained to Howell James Jr.:

Will Bk.G, p. 134, Manken James Admin. for Howell James, 30 May 1748. Also mentioned grandson James James, son of William James. Witnesses: Enoch Morgan, Richard Owen, David Jones. Named sons James, Phillip & Howell excrs.

G, 154, Howell James settlement---To mother Ann James; brother Mankin James...Mary Robinson's daughters Ann & Rebecca; brother Phillip James.

*

James James Jr., brother of Philip:

Will Bk. L., V. 1., p. 15: 16 Aug 1736: James James Jr. gent., and wife Francis...to George Hillis for 55 pounds...Situate near Lott of Robert Millers...adj. to John Perry's land...then Lott of John Harris'...2 1/2 acres & another lott...

Wit: Benj. Cooke, John Herbert.

*

G, p. 172, Edw. Robinson Adm.for James James, 21 Aug 1748.

G, p. 137, Simon Hadley Adm. for Joseph James, 1 Jun 1749.

* *

---

[3]Scharf, "History of Delaware," p. 950.

CHAPTER SEVEN

WELSH TRACT CHURCH and MEMBERS:

Other signers of the Welsh Tract church's "Confession of Faith:"
'[Oct 4 1730] James Hiatt, Elanor Jonkin, Elanor Jonkin [1729], Mary
Nicholas; [Miscellaneous statements attached to this: 'Sept 4 1731 then was
William Nicholas received by vertue of a letter from Wales. June 3, 1732
Thomas Underwood was Bapt. September 6, 1732 then was John Jones
Bapt. Sept 30, 1732 then was Mary Jones Bapt. On November 5, 1732, ...
Hugh Jones Bapt. November 5, 1732 then was Thomas Jones Bapt.']
Continuation of signatures [1739]: Sara Barrow, Rachel Bomish, Mary
Jones.'

During the first thirty or so years, the following were taken from them by
death: [Members who were of the church's original sixteen underlined.]
"Jan'th Dafydd wife of Richard Dafydd [David], 6. 10mo. 1701.
Catherin Rhyddarch, 11. 12mo. 1701.
John Edward, in 1706.
Lewis Philip (Deacon) 26. 10mo. 1710.
Nicolas Stephen, 20. 3mo. 1712.
William Mirick, 1712.
Jamos Jonos, 5mo. 1713.
Mary John, wife of Hary John, 8mo. 1713.
Dafydd Miles, 1710.
Arthyr Milchor, 6mo. 20th day 1714.
Thomas Efan, 1mo. 1714.
John Wild, 2mo. 1715.
Mary John, wife of Griffyll [Griffith] John, 2 mo. 1715.
Mary Stephen, 22. 3mo. 1715.
Rebecka Edward, 5mo. 1715.
Lewis Phillip, 24. 2mo. 1715.
John Etton, 3mo. 1717.
Juan Eatton, 10mo. 1717.
Samuel Philips, 11mo. 1717.
Mary Bowen, 22. 1mo. 1718.
John Philips, 6. 3mo. 1718.
Edward Edwards, 26. 7mo. 1718.
John William, 30. 9mo. 1718.
Elizabeth Truax, Daniel Howlands wife, 5. 11mo. 1718.
Elizabeth Rees, Daniel Rees wife, 10. 1mo. 1719.
Richard Dafydd [David], 16. 1mo. 1719.
John Thomas, 7mo. 5. 1719.
Joana Miller, 8mo. 1719.
Thomas John Iron hill, 4mo. 17. 1720.

Sarah James, 2mo. 10. 1721.

Mary Evans (wife of John Evans, Junr.), 6mo. 2. 1721.

Mary Wallis, 8mo. 1721.

John Greenwator, 9mo. 1. 1721.

Jane Edwards, 11mo. 11. 1721.

Ellizabeth Griffith, 9mo. 1721.

John Hol[l]in[g]sworth, 6mo. 1722.

Arthyr Edward, 7mo. 5. 1722.

Garlls Miles, 6mo. 6. 1722.

Thomas Griffith (Minister of the Gospel), 6mo. 25. 1725.

Thomas John Cristeen, 7mo. 23. 1726.

Aboll Nicholas, 9mo. 27. 1726.

Griffith Nicholas, 10mo. 9. 1726.

Joshua Duglas, 11mo. 11. 1726.

Richart Lewis, 1mo. 1727.

Emling Davis, 2mo. 20. 1727.

Rachel Miles, 11mo. 10 1727.

Samuel Griffith, 11mo. 26. 1727.

Lidia Osborn, 11mo. 29. 1727.

Elizabeth Lewis, 12mo. 1728.

John Boulton, 3mo. 1729.

Lewis Jones, 7mo. 7 1729.

Hugh Lewis, 20mo. 1 1739. [Probably 1mo. 20th day.]

Cornelius Truax, 6mo. 1730.

William Truax, 1729.

Elisha Thomas (Paster), 9mo. 1. 1730. His wife Mary Thomas also died, but there was only a "D" by her name and no date.

John Paine, 9mo. 1730.

Elinor Philips, 9mo. 27. 1730.

Susana David, 10mo. 13. 1730.

Griffith Lewis, 11mo. 10. 1730.

Lyws Edmond, 9mo. 1731.

Thomas Moris, 11mo. 1731. His wife was Jennet Morris.

Perry Thomas, 11mo. 24. 1731.

Leffiis Bowen   Died Nov. 1732.

Sarah Vanholan, Died Nov 1732.

Thomas Jenkins, 1732.

Elizabeth Davis."

*

Several of the above had surnames found in the Pennepek records: the Duglas', Morris', Greenwater's, Eaton's, John Wild, etc. Of the above, Jennett Morris, a constituent member, and her husband Thomas Morris moved to Pennepek. James David, also an original member, moved to the Radnor (Chester Co.) meeting house. Enoch Morgan, another original member, preached at the Philadelphia meeting house and lived in Philadelphia Co. Evan Edmond, another original member, was excommunicated from the church in 1714. The other two original members, Elizabeth Griffith and Margaret Mathias were unaccounted for. [Probably Elizabeth was Thomas Griffith's wife.] A Griffith John who died intestate in 1719 had a wife named Margaret. The only time a Griffith John's name was in the church records was as husband of Mary John when she died.

There was another Thomas Jones with wife Elinor who belonged to this church. The Minutes indicate the church received complaints about their improper conduct towards one another. They were summoned by the church and questioned regarding their 'minor improprieties' and placed out of communion for awhile to try to reform them by words of council and advice. After awhile they took their case under consideration, and got testimony against them, so they left them out of the church. Then at their monthly meeting February 6, 1724, they excommunicated them "as fruitless branches and degenerate persons."

Beginning March 13, 1733, an attempt was made to organize the Minutes of the Welsh Tract Church. Certain books were set up for a specific purpose. For example, the church minutes were organized in such a way as to put members leaving to attend another church in certain books, the ones who died in certain books, etc. However, some later were just listed with a "D" by their name with no dates. 'D' only, designation for Died, "See Book ye third, page the _____." However, in books before the third one, are designations that the following died, [D written in] and have no notations putting them in the third book:

'David Thomas; William Thomas; Hugh Evan, Deacon; Morgan, John [sic]; David Lewis*; David Evan; William Denne; William Truax, John Renfro; Moris Howel; William Evan; James Howel; Richard Thomas, Ruling Elder died Nov 1753; Benjamin Underwood; David Davis, Minister; James Hyatt; William Nicholas; Hugh Jonos; John Watson Deacon died Nov 12, 1735; John Griffith, was baptized Aug 4, 1739, Ruling Elder; David Thomas and Enoch Morgan was baptized May 3, 1740; Thomas Howell restored; Lewis Thomas; Joseph Brown; Rees Jones Doctor; William Starkey; Jane Hyatt and Mary Watson; and Sarah Jones the wife of Dr. Jones."
*It appears David Lewis died at New Castle Co.
*

In records regarding members dismissed to other churches:
"Our brother Thomas John was recommended unto the care of the church at Philadelphia by virtue of a letter being dated Sept. 8, 1733."
"Brother Thomas John is returned and recommended by vertue of a letter from ye church in Philadelphia, dated Jan. 8, 1736/7."
No mention was made of his wife, if any.
*

Deaths in Book 3, P. 1:

"Philip Nicholas, bu. Sept. 9, 1733.

William Peerson bu. Jan. 31, 1734.

David Thomas bu. May ye 6, 1734.

Cornelius Vansant bu. May ye 9, 1734.

John Dovenald, Elder, bu. March ye 9, 1735.

Joanna Richard bu. Aug. 28th, 1735.

Ann John, bu. Oct. 29, 1735. Aged 48.

John Griffith, Elder, bu. Nov. 12, 1735. Aged 80.

Lydia Evans bu. Dec. 25th, 1735.

Thomas Richard bu. Jul. 1, 1736. Aged 83.

Nathaniel Wild bu. _____."

*

There were records of the baptisms of many, as well as others that were received by letter from other churches, scattered throughout. Among them:

September 6, 1732 John Jones bapt.

Sept. 30 1732 Mary Jones bapt.

November 5, 1732 Hugh Jones bapt.

November 5, 1732 Thomas Jones bapt.

Abel Morgan, bapt 31 of March 1733. *

Samuel Nicholas, bapt April 28, 1733.

John Harry, bapt. Sept 1, 1733.

Feremia Rees, same day.

David James and his wife Elinor, received by letter from Mountgomarin [Montgomery] Nov 3, 1733. [Note: This David James was in South Carolina in 1743.]

William Lewis, bapt August 3, 1734.

Thomas John and Zacharies Thomas, bapt Oct 4, 1735.

Thomas Money, bapt 1735. [Thomas Mauney?]

John Jones, bapt December 4, 1736.

June ye 4, 1737, John Thomas received into full communion by letter from Great Valley, dated May 22, 1739.

Deacon. March 31, 1739, John Morgan and Benjamin Jonos [Jones] baptized.

John Griffith, bapt Aug. 4, 1739. Ruling Elder.

David Thomas and Enoch Morgan, bapt May 3, 1740.

Lewis Thomas, Deacon, bapt July 5, 1740.

Jacob Jones, bapt August 2, 1740.

Jacob Jones, restored May 5, 1770 ; received into full communion.

James Jones and James James, bapt May 2d, 1741.

Daniel John, bapt September 14, 1742.

Rees Jones Doctor, bapt September 30, 1743.

John Hughes, 'received to the full communion of the church Dec 31, 1743, by vertue of a letter from the church on P. D. in South Carolina bearing date October 1, 1743. He was excommunicated July 1747.'

*

Some other John or Jones church members in Welsh Tract were disowned for doing various things against the beliefs of the Baptists: "Daniel John was disowned first for being guilty of ye sin of drunkenness, and for his application to such as is said had curious arts."

"The causes apearing against Jacob Johns, first his breaking his covenant with ye church by neglecting his pleace and it for a long time. 2ly His immoral life by drinking to excess to ye hurt of his family. 3ly Great reason to fear he has been guilty of speaking untruths was executed January 1766." Jacob John was restored May the fifth 1770.

"John Jones was disowned." [No date.]

Ex for "excommunicated" written by David John, no date or description. This might have been an error in recording that he moved.

* *

JOHN JONES, Gent. & Innkeeper:

Deed Book C, Vol. 1, p. 6, 1 Mar 1702.

John Jones of Philadelphia, Gent., "am hold and firmly bound unto Matthias Vanbibber, [Van Bibber] Merchant, for two hundred and twenty pounds... Bound to Matthias Vanbibber of Phila., merchant, in six hundred pounds of current money...

THE CONDITION of the obligation is such that whereas the above named Matthias Vanbibber at the speciall instant and request and for the prospect of the above boundon John Jones together with the said John Jones is and standeth bound in to one Joseph Woods of New Castle in the Territories of Pensilvania Gent. in the sum of two hundred pounds current silver money of Pensilvania in and by one obligation bearing even date with the forprocents with condition for the true payment of the sum of one hundred pounds of silver money of Pensilvania upon the twenty ninth day of September next ensuing ... and whereas also the said Matthias Vanbibber at the like instante and request and for the proper debt of the said John Jones together with the said John Jones is and standeth bound unto the said Joseph Wood in the sume of one hundred and six pounds current money aforesaid in and by out other obligation bearing even date with these presents with condition for the true payment of ffifty three pounds like silver money on the twenty ninth day of September herewith shall be in the yeare of our Lord one thousand seven hundred and ffoure as in and by the oath aforesaid obligation and condition ... the said John Jones his heires Executors or Administrators or any of them as well absolutely part or cause to be paid unto the said Joseph Wood his heirs Executors Administrators ...the severall and ressortive sums and sums of one hundred pounds and of fifty three pounds on the severall days and times above mentioned according to the --essertive conditions...and ...save keep harmeless and indemnified the said Matthias Vanbibber his heirs executors and administrators...and that ...the said

Joseph Woods his Heirs Executors Administrators and assigns of and from the payment of the same or any part thereof ...

(9) and in whereas the said John Jones his heires -- inheritors and Administrators and every of them shall .. at the cost and ___ in the law of the said John Jones his Heires Executors and Administrators and at the request of the said Matthias Vanbibber his Heirs Executors and Administrators by such lawfull art and arts ... conveyances and assurances in the land whatsoever as by the said Matthias Vanbibber his heirs and assigns or his or their counsell learned in the law shall be lawfully devised ... give Grant and assave unto the said Matthias Vanbibber his heirs or and assigns all that Tract of Land called Woltum Island situate in New Salem in West ner Fortie lately purchased by the said John Jones of and from Adam Baldrige of New Castle aforesaid Innholder containing five hundred acres of land clearly acquitted and discharged of ... all manner of former ...sales charges Titles troubles and Encumbrances whatsoever has made committed or done by the said John Jones or by any other person or persons whatsoever that them all and every the covenant herein before mentioned also the above written obligation shall be paid or else remaine in full force.
J. Jones
Sealed and delivered in the presence of Joseph Wood Adam Baldridge William Jones.
*

Deed Book C, Vol. 1, 1706-1709: P. 30. John Jones of Phila., Gent. & Matthias Van Bibber, Mcht., bound to Joseph Wood. 9th Mar 1702. Wit: Joseph Hamilton, Antho. Houstowne [Houston], James Van Bibber.
Deed Book H, Vol. 1, 1726-28: Pp. 41,42: John Jones, Innkeeper 28 Mar 1702, as Lawful Atty. Thos. Robins, Robert Grunny, witn.

Deed Book I, Vol. 1, p. 10: Joseph Wood by his will dated 12 Dec 1721...unto his wife Anne Wood...of Peter Jacqueth's land.
*
NOTE: The deeds regarding John Jones, Mathias Van Bibber and Joseph Wood seem to show Jones mortgaging 500 acres of land called Woltum Island in New Salem that he purchased from Adam Baldridge, Innkeeper. Jones probably became innkeeper as result of purchasing this property. William Jones had connections with Woltum Island. Perhaps John Jones was his son. William Jones was also a witness to above deed- mortgage. Please note the Van Bibber's signed as witness to several of the above for John Jones. Jacob VanBibber signed as a witness with David John and Griffith John to a will, as will be shown later. They all seem to be very closely connected.
In the records of the Quakers, Jonathan Jones, son of Dr. Edward Jones of the First Company in Philadelphia, was referred to as "Gent." and "of Philadelphia."

*

This was in the Welsh Tract.:

Deed Book I, Part 1, pp. 467-469, Year 1730:

Dated 8th Apr 1730. Indenture between Philip James of Pencader Hundred & Ann his wife, of first part, and John Jones of Philadelphia, Bolster, of second part. For the sum of 98 pounds, Philip James and wife Ann sold 200 acres of land to John Jones. Land situated: Upon Christiana Creek...land being eastward part of two tracts of land...butted on north by land late of Thomas Watts...to south by Christiana Creek...to East by land of Howell James...to West by land late of James James...The other tract begins at a corner white oak by David Thomas's fence & running by a line of trees North 58 perches to a corner stake standing by Howel James's fence thence by a new line of marked trees Northwest 292 perches to a new corner black oak standing on South side of Christiana Creek, crossing said creek four times ... by an old line of trees standing 260 perches to a corner black oak on Southeastern side of Iron Hill, then by a line of trees east 210 perches to first mentioned white oak East of said tract 'containing 200 acres as above stated the half whereof wch. is hereby contained being on ye East side of the whole 400 acres divided from ye West part of ye same by a line run between 'em together with & singular the houses buildings & mills on ye sd. land erected & all & every the ways waters watercourses timber & trees fencing Easemts. etc...Afsd. piece of land was formerly mortgaged (not yet released, to Francis Land of New Castle Co. afsd. Yeoman...by the adsd. Philip James & Ann his wife...by a certain Instrument of writing under their hands and seals

(468) dated 7 Jan 1729...that it may be lawfull to and for ye John Jones...to pay or cause to be paid unto the said Francis Land...yearly & as often as the same becomes due the several sumes mentioned in ye above recited mortgage untill the same shall be cleared & also to...'

Signed Philip James and Ann James.

(469) Delivery of deed to John Jones, and certification that Ann James signed of her own free will, etc. May 10, 1731.

*

Book L, Vol. 1, P. 136, 1737: John Jones, yeoman, of City of Phila. sold this land to Joseph Brown, yeoman, of County of New Castle, for 63 pounds:

'John Jones, yeoman, of City of Phila. sells to Joseph Brown, yeoman, of County of New Castle, for 63 pounds, "fully clearly & absolutely Remise, release & for ever quit claim unto the said Joseph Brown...all such Rights Estate...which of the said John Jones now have or had or which my Heirs...or Admrs. at any time hereafter shall or may have...in or to a Tract of land & plantation now in the full & peaceable possession...of the said Joseph Brown Situate lying & being Christeen Creek in Pencadder Hundred and County of New Castle aforesaid being the plantation formerly of Philip

James and mortgaged to me by the said Phillip James containing about 200 acres as the Butts & Boundaries are Sett forth in the Said Mortgage Deed with all the Buildings Improvements & Appurtenances to the same belonging or any ways appertaining and all writings touching remaining the same...May the 14 1737.'
Signed: John Jones
Wit: Ja: Carter, James Steel.
*

The above John Jones, here called yeoman, previously called Bolster, lived in Philadelphia. The Delaware Valley became a center of shipbuilding by 1725. I don't know what a bolster was. Sounds as if it was some job making bolts, or something to do with shipbuilding. There were three steel mills and other manufacturing companies by this time in Philadelphia.
*

JOHN JONES mentioned in a WILL, Year 1746/7:
Will Book G, pp. 458, 459: Will of Charles Patterson of New Castle Co., Innkeeper...Funeral charges & just debts be paid & ye Residue and remainder of my whole Estate be divided between my loving wife Mary Patterson & her young Daughter not yet christen'd & further I do hereby nominate Constitute & appoint my loving wife Mary Patterson & my loving Brother-in-law John Jones to be my whole Executor to this my last will & Testament Revoking hereby all former wills & legacies. In witness whereof I have hereunto set my hand & seal this 9th day of March Anno Domini 1746/7. Chas. Patterson (Seal)
Certified by Peter Noxon 10th day of Obr. 1750. Attested to by James Day & Peter Noxon.   A. Gooding.
Book G, p. 491, John Jones Administrator for Solomen Demsee, or Demrce, who died Intestate. 20th day of Sept. 1751.
Probate Court: G, 387. John Jones made Administrator for Mary Jones, who died intestate. Dated 20th March 1749. Was widow of Edward Jones. On 20th day of March 1749, James Vance gave deposition that he was at home of Mary Jones, widow & relict of Edwd. Jones of St. George's Hundred, when she gave verbal deposition for will. Mentioned son in law John Jones, his [John's] son Evan Jones, Mary's daughter Mary, wife of John Jones.
*

Will of Daniel Oborn of Pencader Hundred: Son John; dau Rachel Fairis; dau Mary Brown; grandchildren Elishea David & Susannah David; dau Sarah Oborn in her bros. hand (James Oborn)...son James Oborn sole Excr. After signing, another bequest to John John for 20 pounds when he reached age 21. Of White Clay Creek.
* *

EDWARD JONES:

<u>Deed Book K, Vol. 1, 1734-1736</u>: P. 257. Mentioned Richard Davis' will dated 9 Apr 1719; Richard left his land in three equal parts to sons Philip Davis, now deceased; Peter Davis; and Richard Davis, now deceased. Peter Davis & wife Hannah sold land to Abraham Gouldon.

P. 258. Stated Philip Davis, deceased, owed Edward Jones 20 pounds debt, with damages obtained of 104 shillings 8 pence dated 22 Feb 1730. Son Peter Davis, Excr. Ordered to sell part of 200 acres of land owned by Philip Davis to pay debt, land which he received in will of his father Richard Davis. 65 acres sold to Abraham Goulden. Signed Henry Newton Sheriff. Wit: Thomas Noxon & Peter Davis. Certif. 17th day May 1734.
* *

By 1737, a number of people had lost their farms through indebtedness to the Loan Company of New Castle County. Many became disenchanted for various reasons with the living conditions in Pennsylvania and Delaware. In many of the deeds in Philadelphia County at this time were statements by the heirs of William Penn that William Penn had granted the land for a period of 51 years under the quit rents & various agreements, which had expired, etc. Penn's two sons, as his heirs, then sold this land to others. Historians say the Welsh exodus from Pennsylvania and this area actually began in 1735.

In 1737 a group of Welsh from the Welsh Tract Church moved to the Pee Dee area in South Carolina and set up the Welsh Neck Church there in what was then Darlington Township, and Craven County.

According to the Church Minutes, these members moved to the Province of South Carolina:

"Our sister Sarah Mitcher now Sarah James is removed to Carolina and was recommended to ye care of ye church of Christ usually meeting at Charles Town, South Carolina."

"Our brothron and sisters whose names are as followeth Abel Morgan, teaching elder (Abel Morgan is returned); James James, Ruling Elder, Thomas Evan Deacon; Daniel James; Samuel Miles; John Harry; John Harry Junior; Thomas Harry; Jeremiah Rowel [Howell]; Richard Barrow; Thomas Money; Nathaniel Evan; Mary James; Annie Evan; Sarah James; Mary Wilds; Elizabeth Harry; Eleanor Jenkin; Sarah Harry; Margaret William; Mary Rowel; Sarrah Barrow, are removed to Carolina and was recommended by a letter to ye church of Christ in Charles Town or elsewhere in South Carolina, or they might constitute themselves into a church, form us Nov 1735.

Our brother Samuel Evan and his wife Mary Ann Evan was recommended unto our christian friends on pedee in South Carolina April 30, 1737.

Our brethren and sisters whose names are here set down, were recommended unto the care of our christian friends on pedee in South

Carolina: Daniel Devonald, Thomas James, David Harry, Phillip James, David James, Abol James, Simon Pirsons, Mary Boulton, Catherine Harry, Elizabeth James, Elizabeth Jones, Elinor James, Mary Hugh, November, 4, 1737.

Our brother John Jones and his wife Ann Jones who were members of our communion are removed and recommended to our christian friends on Pedee in South Carolina by a letter March 11, 1738.

Our sisters Ales Thomas and Jane David and Mary Dovenald [Devenald] are recommended by a letter to our christian friends on Peedee in South Carolina November 3rd, 1739.

John Jones, Phillip Douglass, Oliver Alison and Walter Down, Elizabeth Jones, Lettis Douglas, Rachel Alison, Rachel Downs was recommended and dismissed by a letter to our sister church on Pee Dee river in South Carolina Nov ye 1st 1741." [Taken from Church Minutes of Welsh Tract Church in Delaware. I make a point of this because some authors have omitted some of the names of those listed in the church records that went in 1741.]

Please note, of the group in 1741, Lettice Douglas was wife of Phillip Douglas, Rachel Alison was wife of Oliver Alison, and Rachel Downs was wife of Walter Downs. So it would be very probable that Elizabeth Jones was wife of John Jones. In other places, the church records also indicate that there were two John Jones' who were Removed, meaning they both left this particular church. Since the John Jones who had wife named Ann was the son of David and Esther John, we are unsure who the second one was, although we feel he probably was a son of John Jones and Ann, and therefore grandson of David.

Although his name was not in with the Baptist group in Delaware, there was a land record of Griffith John taking out land in the first area in South Carolina, and again in the second. He and his wife, with John Jones and Ann, etc., were mentioned as members of Welsh Neck (S.C.) in 1759, and later. The John's or Jones were said to have gone to the Pee Dee and were said to be descendants of David John who died in 1749. Later Griffith Jones was written Griffith John.

There was a Griffith John who settled in the Great Valley in Chester Co., Pa. who came from Wales in 1710. The records of Great Valley have Griffith John and Griffith John Jr. as taxpayers in 1722. Rev. Griffith John was pastor there, and records show he died and was buried there; perhaps Griffith Jr. was his son. Another Rev. Griffith John came to Great Valley from Wales in 1739. There is always the possibility that a Griffith John who was descended from one of the John's in the Great Valley or Montgomery churches went to the Pee Dee area.

* *

NOTE: Remember, the Thomas Jones and wife Margaret, who had land on Brandywine Creek, made the final sale of their land in October 1738, and we do not know where they went. Most probably, he was one of the

Thomas Jones who had land in Appoquidiminck Hundred. Also, the Thomas Jones who purchased land in 1688 would have been in his 70's at this time.

* *

To put names of those going to the Pee Dee where information can be gleaned:

[ABEL MORGAN can be eliminated. He went to South Carolina, but soon returned to Pa. & Delaware.]

JAMES JAMES, Ruling Elder, wife Sarah James. Was a Justice of the Peace.

PHILIP JAMES, son of James James Esqr. above; was first pastor of the new Welsh Neck Church which was established in Pee Dee area of South Carolina.

THOMAS JAMES, son of James James Esqr. James females included Elizabeth James, Elinor James, Mary James. Elinor was wife of David James who came from Montgomery Church in 1733.

ABEL JAMES, son of James James Esqr.

DANIEL JAMES, probably the son of James James Esqr.

DAVID JAMES, son of James James Esqr. Wife Elinor. [Had joined Welsh Tract church from Montgomery Church in 1733.]

SAMUEL WILD, wife Mary Wild.

JOHN HARRY, Elizabeth Harry.

JOHN HARRY, JR.

THOMAS HARRY.

DAVID HARRY. Wife Catherine Harry. Dau Mary Harry born 1751, d. 1817. She was last wife of Tristram Thomas, see his later exploits during Revolutionary War. Buried at Old Saw Mill Baptist Church.[1]

JOHN JONES, and wife Ann Jones; son of David John.

JOHN JONES, wife ELIZABETH JONES. Probably son of John & Ann, above.

ELIZABETH JONES. [Another one in records; might have been sister of Rev. Jenkin Jones.]

THOMAS EVAN, Deacon.

SAMUEL EVAN, and wife Mary Ann Evan.

NATHANIEL EVAN. Annie Evan.

JEREMIAH ROWEL (HOWELL), wife Mary.

RICHARD BARROW, with wife Sarah Barrow.

THOMAS MONEY [Mauney?].

MARGARET WILLIAM.

ELEANOR JENKIN.

SIMON PERSONS (Pierson?)

MARY HUGH.

---

[1]Sketches of Old Marlboro, p. 54, by D. D. McColl.

DANIEL DEVONALD.

PHILLIP DOUGLASS, and wife Lettice Douglas.

OLIVER ALISON, and wife Rachel Alison.

WALTER DOWNS, and wife Rachel Downs.

* *

Those who arrived in South Carolina and petitioned for land 8th Feb. 1737 were:

DAVID LEWIS.

SAMUEL WILDE.

DANIEL JAMES.

Those who established the Welch Neck Baptist Church in 1738, or 1741 per Morgan Edwards:

PHILIP JAMES and his wife. His father was James James Jr., as shown in records in Del., who was a Justice of the Peace. Philip was first Pastor of Welch Neck Church. Previously lived near Welch Tract Church on Christiana. Born ca 1701 near Pennepek Church in Pa.* Ordained 4 Apr 1743, S. C. Married Elizabeth Thomas. Children: Daniel, James, and Philip. Died 31 Jan 1754.

[*This record indicates the James' were already there before 1713 when James James, Pastor of Lantivy was mentioned.]

ABEL JAMES and his wife. Brother of above.

DANIEL JAMES and his wife. Brother of above.

DANIEL DEVONALD and his wife. [John Devonallt and Mary Devonallt were added to Welsh Tract Del. Baptist church from Kilcam in Pembrokeshire in 1709.]

THOMAS EVANS and his wife. [Thomas Evan added to church from Rydwilim in 1710.]

THOMAS EVANS JR. and his wife.

SAMUEL EVAN and his wife. [Samuel Evan and Mary Evan added to church in 1710 from Lantivy.]

THOMAS HARRY and his wife. [John Harry added from Kilcam in 1710.]

DAVID HARRY and his wife.

SAMUEL WILDS and his wife. Samuel Wild, John Wild and Thomas Wild added by baptism in 1708. [James James and Sarah James added by baptism at same time.] The Pennepek Church records had a John Wild who was 'baptized by Henry Gregory in Radnorshire in Wales, dyed 1715.'

[Nathaniel Wild was one of the people who left Welch Neck Church around 1733 and settled in Duck Creek Hundred. They started the Duck Creek Baptist Church in 1737, per account by Morgan Edwards. Records state he died, but no date written in.]

JOHN JONES and his wife, probably Elizabeth.

GRIFFITH JONES and his wife, who was probably Margaret.
DAVID JONES and his wife. [Some accounts have David James and wife.]
THOMAS JONES and his wife.
* *

Others from Del. who went to the Pee Dee:
Samuel Hollingsworth, son of Samuel Hollingsworth who owned land
before 1746 in Pee Dee. Samuel Jr. had dau Mary who was first wife of
Tristram Thomas.[2] Valentine Hollingsworth, either the one or his son who
lived on Brandywine Creek near Thomas John and Margaret, went to
Bladen Co., [then Anson Co.] N. C. See journey by John Townsend later.
* *

Records from Welsh Tract in Delaware are given covering a few years,
in order to show events taking place there after the removal of some of the
Baptist church members to South Carolina. Also, the first record of David
John in North Carolina was found in 1754. I believe he was the David John
who was son of Griffith John who died in 1749, and probably was not a
close connection of the David John who had wife Esther Morgan John.
Most if not all of the John/Morgan line seem to have taken the name Jones.
Griffith John [in S.C.] could have been the son of the John Jones who went
to the Pee Dee. A reason to believe otherwise was because his name
appears as John when others of that line were using Jones as a surname. He
only signed with an X on his will, however.
*

Record of some of the Baptizms, continued:
Elizabeth Jones was baptized October 4, 1735.
Sarah and Mary Jones baptized June 5, 1736. Also Sarah Thomas and
Elizabeth Jones, bapt.
Margaret Miles, bapt. Oct. 2, 1736.
Ann Jones, bapt. Sept 3, 1737.
Rachel Griffith and Elenor James, bapt August 4, 1739.
Lettice Douglass, Annie Jones, Mary Hugh, Judith Devonald, Elizabeth
Jones; bapt August 2, 1740.
'Mary Price was received to ye Communion of the church June ye 4, 1743.
The said Mary Price for sum time was in communion among ye
Presbyterians, but on her confession of her falt was received to her place
again, the time before mentioned.'
Sarah Jones, wife of Dr. Jones, baptized September 30, 1743.
Following persons baptized in Kent County by ministry of Rev. Mr. Jones:
Rachel Davis, Deborah Evans, Hanah Rees and Hester Rees August 2,
1752. (Others also shown as baptized by Rev. Jones.)
Daniel Griffith, received into communion by virtue of a letter from
Montgomery, April 30, 1748.

---

[2]Ibid.

The Rev. Mr. Griffith Jones, received by virtue of a letter from Wales, Jan 2, 1750.

Morgan Jones, baptized May 6, 1750. [Note: Morgan John Sr. had a son Morgan Jones.]

People who died, continued:
'Elias Thomas, bu. Jan. 10, 1738. Aged 70.

Elizabeth Pain, bu. Apr. 22, 1738.

John Evans, Elder, bu. Apr. 16, 1738.

Margaret Morgan, bu. Sept. 16, 1738.

Rev. Mr. Enoch Morgan, minister of the gospel, died Mar. 25, 1740. Aged 64.

John Evans, bu. Apr. 28, 1740.

Mary Jones, bur. April 7, 1740.

Rees Jones, Elder, bur. Nov. 25, 1739.

Philip Rees, died in South Carolina, Oct. 1739.

Rees David, Deacon, bur. Jan 1740.

Catherine Thomas, bu. May 25 1741.

Mary Thomas, bu. July 26t 1742.

Thomas Hutchinson, died in Oct. 1741.'

Book 3, Page 2:
'Richard Whitten, Ruling Elder, bu. Jan 1742.

William Nichlas, bu. Apr 18, 1743.

Mary Davis, wife of David Davis, teaching elder, bur. Jul 24, 1743.

Sarah Underwood, bu. Aug. 8, 1743.

Hugh Marice bu. Nov. 19, 1743.

Mary Thomas, widow of Mr. Elisha Thomas teaching elder, D. August 24th, 1744.

Margaret John, bur. Sep 22, 1744.

Catherine Lewis, bu. Nov. 1746.

Ann Clement, bu. Dec 1746.

Joseph Brown, bu. Mar 1st 1747.

Thomas Griffith, Ruling Elder, died.

John Thomas, Ruling Elder, died.

Elenor, wife of Morgan Jones, died.

Mr. Griffith Jones, Minister, died. [Arrived in 1739 from Wales.]

Zachariah Jones died.'
*

Baptizms, continued:
Isaic Lewis, received into full communion by virtue of a letter from Montgomery, April 6, 1754.

Thomas Robinson, and David John, Morgan Johns son, were baptized May 6, 1758.

194

John Jones, the son of Rev. Mr. Griffith Jones, was baptized Oct. 4, 1761. He was at the same time added to the church.

Zachriah Jones, baptized Oct. 6, 1764.
Sarah James, the wife of William James, was baptized April 2, 1756.
Mary Morgan, wife of John Morgan, received by letter from Great Valley 3 July 1757.
Sarah Milles [Miles], wife of David Milles [Miles], baptized Sept 3, 1757.
Hannah Bonham,* received to communion of church August 3, 1760, by virtue of letter from the church of Kingswood dated Oct 16, 1757.
Jane Thomas, the wife of Thomas Thomas was baptized July 2, 1763.
Mary Lewis, the wife of Isaiah Lewis and her sister Johanna Jones, the wife of Zachrias Jones, baptized and added to the church Nov. 3, 1769.
Sarah Smith the daughter of Lewis Morgan, baptized Aug 31, 1765. 'The next meeting she was dismissed to one of our churches in Carolina.'
Mary Price, Mary Griffith and Hanah Jones, baptized and added to the church Oct. 4, 1767.
May the second, 1772, Enoch Morgan, Junior, baptized and received into full communion.
At the same time, Joseph Griffith restored.
April 6th, 1776, James Jones, Junior received by baptizm into full communion of church.
February 28, 1778, Samuel Morgan received into full communion 'by virtue of a letter from a church at Diffical, Fairfax County in Virginia.'
April meeting of business 1781, Joanna Jones restored into full communion.
*

*Hester Bonham left will, New Castle Will Book L, p. 93, dated Oct. 10 1767. Proved Oct. 13, 1778. Was widow of Malakiah Bonham of Kingswood, West New Jersey; had dau. Elizabeth John, wife of Jacob John of Mill Creek Hundred. Grandchildren: Enoch John, Heath John, Thomas John, Jacob John and Ann John, children of dau. Elizabeth. Exec. John Evans and Evan Rice.
*

In his History of Delaware, Scharf wrote that "the present church" was built in 1746 on a lot which contained four acres given by James James and two acres purchased from Abraham Emmet. The church was a neat brick building, thirty feet square. The first pastor was Rev. Thomas Griffith (1701-1725), next was Rev. Elisha Thomas (died 1730). Rev. Enoch Morgan (d. 1740) suceeded Rev. Thomas, followed by Rev. Owen Thomas (resigned in 1748 and moved to Yellow Springs.) Next was Rev. David David (d. 1769.) His successor was Rev. John Sutton, who resigned in 1777 to go to Virginia.
*

In 1747 and 1748, the lower counties were kept in a state of anxiety due to the attack of privateers. Several pirates operated in the area, and were thought to be doing business with local merchants.

In 1747, a number of commissions were issued to officers of the militia in New Castle County. Various counties of the province began to organize small companies for defense. From New Castle County, the officers were: Capt. William McCrea, Lt. Alexander Moody, Ensign Francis Graham, Capt. Henry Dyre, Lt. Paul Allfree, Ensign Jerrard Rothwell, Capt. David Steward, Lt. Jerome Dusheene, Ensign Isaac Dusheene, Capt. George Gano, Lt. James Egbertson, Ensign Thomas Bennett, Capt. David Bush, Lt. John McKinley, Ensign Charles Bush, Capt. John Vance, Lt. John Vandyke, Ensign William Harraway, Capt. Alexander Porter, Lt. James King, Ensign Samuel Allricks, Capt. Edward Fitzrandolph, Lt. Alexander Chance, and Ensign Joseph Hotham.

Next year were added: Capt. William Patterson, Lt. John Read, Ensign Thomas Montgomery, Capt. William Danforth, Lt. Henry Colesbury, Ensign Peter Jacquet, Capt. David Witherspoon, Lt. Alexander Armstrong, Ensign Anthony Golden, Capt. James McMeehen, Lt. Abel Armstrong, Ensign Thomas Ogle, Capt. William Armstrong, Lt. James Morris, Ensign Thomas Philips, Capt. Jacob Gooding, Lt. Jacob Vanbibber and Ensign David Howell.

In May 1748, Commissions were issued to Capt. David Finney, Lt. Francis January, Ensign French Battle, Capt. Evan Rice, Lt. James Walker, Ensign Charles Bevan Sr., Capt. James Almond, Lt. Luhaff Peterson, Ensign Luke Munfee, Capt. Timothy Griffith, Lt. William Faries, Ensign David Rowland, Capt. Archibald Armstrong, Lt. Thomas McCullough, Ensign Robert Pierce. Commissions as Colonels were issued to John Gooding Sr. and William Armstrong; Thomas James and William Patterson, as Lt. Colonels, and Jacob Vanbibber and William McCrea as Majors, as two regiments were organized.

In August 1748, New Castle added Capt. John Edwards, Lt. David Johns and Ensign Robert Stewart. As an example of the way these people had moved to adjoining counties, in 1748, from Kent Co. were added Capt. James Edwards, Lt. James Lewis, Ensign James James, among others.

By 1754, the French and Indian War seemed to be only a matter of time. The Assembly of the lower counties on Delaware provided for raising a thousand pounds for His Majesty's use, and the following year passed an act for establishing a militia. The war was declared in 1756, and preparations began in earnest.

By November 1756, the three counties organized their militia in accordance with the acts of the Assembly. These Commissions were issued for the Upper Regiment of militia in New Castle County, New Castle Hundred:

North Division: Capt. Richard McWilliam, Lt. Nathaniel Silsby, Ensign Zachariah Luwaniah.

South Division: Capt. Alexander Porter, Lt. Samuel Aldricks, Ensign John Bryan.
White Clay Creek Hundred, West Division: Capt. Rees Jones, Lt. Samuel Platt, Ensign Thomas Williamson.
East Division: Capt. Samuel Patterson, Lt. Thomas Dunn, Ensign William Reid.
Miln Creek Hundred, North Division: Capt. Evan Reese, Lt. James Walker, Ensign William Ball.
South Division: Capt. Thomas Gray, Lt. William McMehan, Ensign Alexander Montgomery.
Christiana Hundred, Southwest Division: Captain James Latimer, Lt. Empson Bird, Ensign Thomas Duff.
Southeast Division: Capt. Andrew Trauberg, Lt. William Hay, Ensign Robert Robinson.
North Division: Capt. Thomas Ogle Jr., Lt. John Armstrong, Ensign John Hendrickson.
Brandywine Hundred, Southwest Division: Capt. William Empson, Lt. Thomas McKim, Ensign John Elliot.
Northeast Division: Capt. Emanuel Grub Jr., Lt. Benjamin Ford Jr., Ensign Benjamin Kellam; Field Officers, Col. William Armstrong, Lt. Colonel John Finney, Major John McKinley.

In the Lower Regiment of New Castle County were the following officers:
St. George's Hundred: Captain John Jones, Lt. Jerome Dushane, Ensign Isaac Gooding, Capt. John Vance, Lt. John Vandyke, Ensign John Anderson, Capt. Adam Peterson, Lt. William Whittle, Ensign Alexander Bryan.
Appoquinimink Hundred: Capt. William Williams, Ensign Garrett Rothwell, Capt. Alexander Chance, Lt. Charles Carson, Ensign Daniel Weldon, Capt. George Ganz, Lt. Matthew Rhea, Ensign Thomas Bennet.
Red Lion Hundred: Capt. Jacob Gooding, Lt. Thomas Tobin, Ensign David Howell.
Pencader Hundred: Capt. Lewis Thomas, Lt. David Barr, Ensign William Mitchell, Capt. Thomas Cooch, Lt. Alexander Porter, Ensign David Rowland.
Field Officers, Colonel Jacob Vanbebber, Lt. Col. David Wetherspoon and Major Thomas James.

Because of the Quakers' scruples against bearing arms, several incidents occurred in 1757 where men were seized, thrown into jail and some property seized as fines. This was brought to the Governor's attention; he said it would be taken into consideration, but nothing was done.
*

Another minister whose history was given by Morgan Edwards in the early Baptist church history was Rev. David Davis who took over the ministry at New Castle when Rev. Owen Thomas resigned to go to Yellow Springs in 1748. He wrote some of the Welsh Tract Church Minutes. Rev. Davis "was born in the parish of Whitechurch and county of Pembroke in the year 1708: came to America when a child in 1710. Was baptized Jan. 1729; and ordained in this church in 1734: at which time he bacame its pastor: he continued in the pastorship to Aug. 19, 1769 when he died: he was buried in this graveyard where a handsome stone covers his remains: He was an excellent man! And is held in dear remembrance by all that knew him! His children were: Rees, Jonathan, (late minister of the Seventh Day Baptist church at Shiloh), John, Susanna, <u>Mary</u>, Margaret: John was some time minister of the second church in Boston and died childless at the Ohyo; the rest married into the families of the Miles, Bonhams, Bentleys, Parrs or Barrs, Thomas and Booths, and have raised him many grandchildren. Contemporary with him was Rev. Griffith Jones: he officiated at Duckcreek."

*

In 1740, a market place was laid out in New Castle, with regulations for its conduct. Regular market days of Wednesday and Saturday were selected and no one was allowed to buy or sell provisions other than fish, milk and bread anywhere but at the marketplace on those days, etc. This proved such a success that other counties set up similar ones. They built a market house in the courtyard square. Officers from the three counties were appointed for the markets, with duties to supervise the new issue of money.

In the years 1751 and 1752, the Assembly of the lower counties became more active. Steps were taken to better maintain the highways and bridges. Every man paying taxes was also required either to perform or have a substitute do a day's work repairing the roads.

*

The Welsh Tract Church in New Castle County was considered the Mother Church, with other churches growing in the surrounding areas, and some members left to these churches. People also arrived at Welsh Tract from these other churches.

Information follows on some of these churches:

GREAT VALLEY

The Great Valley Meeting House was located on a long bottom of land reaching from Schuylkill to Susquhanna. It was located in the east end, in what they called the township of Tredyffryn, Chester Co., eighteen miles from Philadelphia. Two acres for this purpose was obtained partly by a gift from William George, and the rest was purchased. This bordered on a small brook that they called Nant yr Ewig. This church consisted of two branches, with the other one located about twelve miles away at Yellowspring in the township of Vincent. This had four acres of land donated by a Mr. Cox, and the buildings consisted of a meeting house, a school house, and a stable.

Settlement by the Welsh in the east end of Great Valley in Chester County began in 1701 and 1702, when several families from Wales settled there. James Davis, a member of the Baptist church of Rydwilin in Carmarthenshire, Wales, was among them. Nearby lived Richard Miles and

198

his wife in Radnor Township, which was established by Quakers. They were baptized as Baptists by William Beckingham in Upper Providence. It was at the Miles house that the agreement was reached regarding laying-on-of hands and other minor things in 1706.

There were no Baptist churches where they lived, but they desired to continue their religious fellowship and learning, so they met together and invited ministers to preach. These meetings attracted others in the neighborhood and several were baptized. In 1710, Rev. Hugh Davis, an ordained minister, William Rees, Alexander Owen, John Evans and wife Margaret arrived, increasing their number. Rev. Hugh Davis was born in 1665 in Cardiganshire, and was baptized and ordained at Rydwilim.

On April 22, 1711, they became incorporated and chose Rev. Hugh Davis as their minister. Alexander Owen and William Rees were chosen as Elders, and they joined the Association. Griffith John arrived from Rydwilim in 1712 and became an Elder of the church. [Note: Some accounts have 1710.] The membership increased fast as new arrivals came from Wales, and others joined due to Rev. Hugh Davis' influence.

Rev. John Davis arrived in America July 27, 1713. He assisted Hugh Davis in the ministry. Hugh Davis died in 1753, having served this church for 42 years, 5 months, and 21 days. Then John Davis took over as minister. He was born 1 Nov 1702 in Llanfernach parish, county of Pembroke, and married Abigail Miles.

Legacies of a certain number of pounds were given to Great Valley by William George, Thomas Rees, John Phillips, Edward Mathews, Richard Owen, William Morgan, Thomas Jenkins, Sarah Miles, Griffith Jenkins, Griffith Philips, David Rees, William Rees, Hugh Wilson, Owen Phillips, and Henry Davis. A plantation of fifty acres with a house and outhouses was the gift of Henry Davis.

BRANDYWINE

This church was located near the Brandywine River. It consisted of two branches, one in Birmingham Township, Chester Co. [now Delaware Co.], about thirty eight miles west of Philadelphia. The other was located in Newlin Township, twelves miles away.

A group of Keithian Baptists was formed in the neighborhood about 1697. They broke up in 1700 because of a difference over the day of the Sabbath. Those preferring the first day of the week were organized through visits of the pastor Abel Morgan. On June 14, 1715 these 15 persons formed the church: Jeremiah Collet, Edmund Butcher, John Powell, Richard Buffington, John Beckingham, Joseph Powell, David Roberts, Thomas George, Elizabeth Powell, Hannah Beckingham, Margery Martin, Hannah Hunter, Mary Robinet, Mary Powell, Joan Powell. They met first at the home of John Powell at Upperprovidence, but in 1717 agreed to hold their worship at Birmingham, where they built a house of worship. They built another meeting place in Newlin township within the forks of Brandiwine in 1741. Several of these people have their names listed in the Pennepek records.

There was a Thomas John and wife Margaret from Brandywine in the Deed records of New Castle Co. but no record was found of a Thomas and Margaret together. Separately there was another Thomas John, and a Margaret who died in 1744 in the Welsh Tract records.

By 1770, no one of a John surname was listed, and the only two with John as a first name were John Powell and John Beckingham.

MONTGOMERY

This church was located in the township of Montgomery in Philadelphia Co., about twenty miles from the city. John Evans gave one acre with a stone building, school house and stables in 1731. He was probably the John Evans who arrived in 1710 in the Great Valley. This church had three branches, with the second at Perquesy, which had a house erected in 1737 by William Thomas on four acres. The third was at Upperperquesy eight miles from the mother church of Welsh Tract. There seemed to be a lot of interaction between this church and Welsh Tract.

In 1770 per Morgan Edwards, ninety families belonged to the church, with ninety nine members. There was a number of John's who belonged to this church. The John and Jones were: Samuel Jones, Edward Jones, Thomas Jones, another Thomas Jones, Martha Jones, Leah Jones, Margaret Jones, Elizabeth Jones, Hester Jones, Margaret Jones, and Ann Jones. John Thomas was the minister. The Rev. John Thomas was born 9 Dec 1703 in Radnor tsp., county of Chester. He married Sarah James, and their children were Ann, Rebecka, Lea and Rachel.

TULPEHOKON

This was located about sixty five miles from Philadelphia in the township of Cumry, Berks Co., and was named from the river which runs through the neighborhood. This was started in 1738, and was made up of people who moved from Great Valley and Montgomery. They were Thomas John and wife, David Evans and wife, James James and wife, Evan Loyd and wife, George Rees and wife, John Davis and wife, Thomas Nicholas and wife, James Edwards and wife, Rees Thomas and wife, Henry Harris [Harry], David Lewis and Thomas Loyd. [This is interesting, as many with these same names went to the Pee Dee, S.C. area.]

The minister was Rev. Thomas John or Jones, who was born in 1703 in the parish of Newtowncottage in Glamorganshire. He arrived in America July 22, 1737, and was ordained in 1740. He married Martha Morris, and their children were Martha, Thomas, Samuel (who was a minister of Pennepek), GRIFFITH*, Elizabeth and Sarah.

In 1740, Hugh Morris, Evan Lloyd and Evan Price gave three acres for this church. Other gifts were given to the church, but there were not many wealthy people in the congregation.

In 1770, there were about twelve families belonging, with nineteen persons baptized. Members then were: Thomas Jones and wife, Thomas Jones Jr., John Davis, another John Davis, Thomas Nicholas, John Edwards, David Evans, Nathan Evans, Mary Jones, Martha Davis, Mary Davis, Mary Nicholas, Mary Harris, Sarah Beramfield [?], Ester Lloyd, Hannah Evans, Margaret Davis, Sarah Connog [?].[3]

[NOTE: *This Griffith Jr. appears to have been too young to be the one who went to S. Carolina.]

SOUTHHAMPTON

This was located in the township of Southampton, in Bucks Co., about eighteen miles from Philadelphia. The meeting house was erected in 1731 on a lot donated by John Morris, who also donated a plantation with 112 acres to the church. It was formed by members who lived in this neighborhood, but had been attending church at Pennepek. Some of these were former Keithian baptists. Among members forming this church were John Jones and his wife, Mary.

When Morgan Edwards reported on this church in 1770, he stated the pastor was Erasmus Kelly, [an Irishman,] who was not yet ordained in 1770. Among the members then were John Hart, John Eaton, John Morford, John Harrison, John Shaw and John Gilbert. The Rev. Samuel Jones of Pennepek, whose father Rev. Thomas John was minister of Tulpehokon, had joint care of this church from 1763 to 1770. [Hart's and Eaton's were in early Pennepek records.]

PHILADELPHIA

This church was located in Philadelphia and was one year younger than Pennepek. It was considered a center to all the associating churches. It was near the center of the city, located in a neat brick building, with burying grounds in the back. Part had belonged to the Keithians, and some was given by John Holme. A parsonage house was erected by Rev. Jenkin Jones at the expense of himself and John Swift. Several other nice endowments were received.

The Philadelphia Church was incorporated in 1746, with 56 members. Among the members were Jenkin Jones, Hannah Jones, and John Lewis.

The first Meeting House was located at the corner of Second Street and Chestnut Street, and was known by the name of Barbados lot. After the Barbados Company left the place, the Baptists held their meetings there. So also did the Presbyterians. Which group met depended on whether a Baptist

---

[3]Materials...by Morgan Edwards.

or Presbyterian minister happened to be in town. A rift developed between the Presbyterians and the Baptists, and it was written "they in a manner drove the baptists away." This was of particular interest to me because of having found records of several John's being married in the First Presbyterian Church in Philadelphia, possibly the same building. They were:

> 9, 28, 1740. David John and Mary David.
> 3, 10, 1745. Joshua John and Rachel David.
> 8, 26, 1742. Martha John and Daniel Rees.
> 11,17, 1736. Joseph John and Joanna Brightwell.
> 12,17, 1734. Martha Hutton and Reese Jones.
> 8, 24, 1734. John Johnson and Margaret Jones.
> 10,18, 1736. Mary Johnson and Isaac Jones.

The pastor of this church was the Rev. Jenkin Jones, who was born ca 1690 in the parish of Llanfernach, county of Pembroke. He arrived in America about 1710. He married the widow Melchier, and had no children. He died at Philadelphia 16 Jul 1761.

The records of "Baptist Church Lower Duplin Twp 1689 to 1763," previously mentioned, though having parts sometimes obliterated and difficult to read, have some of interest. The records contain quite a bit of information on the "teacher" Samuel John and his family, and also on the baptisms there and at Pennepek. This Samuel John was a member in the 1690's, and married Catherine _____ on 12th of 2mo. 1699. Several of their children died in infancy. Records state Samuel was buried at "Pennepak, Radnor, Feb. 3, 1721/2.", which seem to indicate that Pennepek was in Radnor, which was in Chester Co. I'm still not sure of the exact location of the Pennepek church.

Among the first records regarding the Philadelphia church are some for the family of John and Sarah Watts, the family of Thomas Bibb, Nathaniel Duglas, Edward Doyle, David Marple, Mary Shepherd, Matthew and Sarah Harbert, the Waters family, John and William Collett, Samuel John and many others. There are records on the John Holme family, the Harts, Eatons, Elias Keach at Burlington, and baptisms by Thomas Griffith at Pennepak. [Several of these men died without wills and their appointments of administrators to settle their estates are in Adm. Book A, Philadelphia.]

PENNEPEK
This church, [spelled several ways in records, Pennypak, Pennepack, Pennepek, etc.] located in Philadelphia Co. or lower Chester Co., seems to have been in existence in the 1680's and 1690's. This seems to have been close to the New Castle County line. Abel Morgan was 'Pastor of the Congregation at Philadelphia Pennepak,' and a record is found there of his

death 16th Dec 1722. Jenkin Jones was also a Pastor there. John Jones and Mary, his wife, were baptized by Rev. Jenkin Jones Nov 6, 1726. Numerous records show baptisms by Evan Morgan in 1707 and 1708. Elizabeth Jones was dismissed from the Pennepek church to go to Welsh Tract in 1715. She was the sister of Rev. Jenkin Jones, and was probably one of the Elizabeth Jones' who went to the Pee Dee in 1741.

NEW BRITAIN

This was located in the township of New Britain, in Bucks Co., about twenty five miles from Philadelphia. The church building was erected in 1744 on two acres given by Judge Growden. It consisted of two branches, with the other on the border of the Great Swamp, which was fourteen miles away and commonly known by Rockhill. There were endowments given by Thomas Jones, William George, and Simon Matthews.

Until 1743, the people here were a branch of Montgomery. They divided when a Meeting House was proposed on Leahy Hill which would be central for all the people. There were also differences on the "sonship of Christ." 'Some grounded the character of son on an eternal generation and others on mediation only.' 'The New Britainers disavowed the notion of a mediatorial sonship.' The report regarding this was dated Nov 7, 1744, and signed by Nathanial Jenkins, Owen Thomas, Benjamin Stell and Thomas Jones. Afterwards, they acted as two churches, sometimes under the same roof. The New Britainers were formally incorporated Nov. 28, 1754, and were not received in the Association until 1755. Their number was 23. This included Joshuah Jones and Thomas Jones.

DUCKCREEK

About the year 1733, eight or nine families that were chiefly members of the Welsh Tract Church, made a settlement at Duck Creek in Kent Co. From there, Morgan wrote 'the same religion spread southward to Cowmarsh and Mispellin; westward to Georgetown in Maryland; and eastward to Fastlanding.'

The Rev. Griffith Jones settled at Duck Creek. He was born Oct 8, 1695, at a place called Alltfawr, in the parish of Llanon and county of Marmarthen. Entered on the ministry in the 19th year of his age. Settled first at Penyfai and afterwards at Cefenbengord. Came to America in 1749. He died 4 Dec 1757, according to one account, and another account read Dec. 4, 1764. He was buried at Pencader. He had two wives, by whom he had children: Mary, Samuel, Morgan (minister of Hempstead in England), John, Benjamin, Robert, and Rachel.

MIDDLETOWN

This church was located 79 miles east northeast of Philadelphia. There was a history of a church on this location from the year 1667. At that time, twelve men purchased the property from the Indians. It was then located in Monmouth and Sussex counties. Some of these early members were Baptists. Some were of other denominations. Morgan Edwards gave a rather rambling account of this church that was difficult to follow.

Apparently in 1711, the church members had a falling out, and one party excommunicated the other. Silence was imposed on "two gifted brothers that preached to them, viz. John Bray and John Okison." In order to solve the dispute, a council was appointed from neighboring churches. The council met May 25, 1712. This council consisted of Rev. Timothy Brooks, of Cohaney; Abel Morgan and Joseph Wood, of Pennepek; Elisha Thomas, of Welsh Tract, with six elders, viz. Nicholas Johnson, James James, Griffith Miles, Edward Church, William Bettridge and John Manners. [Author's observation: The Rev. Morgans seemed to spend a lot of time conciliating members of various congregations.]

They were able to solve the problem, apparently. Morgan Edwards has the first minister of Middletown as Mr. John Brown; then contemporary with him was Rev. James Ashton, whose successor was Rev. John Burrows. Then apparently there was Bray and Okison. Another was George Eaglesfield.

Rev. Abel Morgan appears to have been the first Welsh minister there. He was born in Welsh Tract, April 18, 1713, the son of the Rev. Enoch Morgan, and grandson of the Rev. Abel Morgan who wrote the Welsh Concordance. He died at Middletown Nov. 24, 1785. He was never married, and was said to have looked after his mother, who lived with him. He had many publications and was an esteemed minister.

* *

Other Welsh Tract church records included these disciplined by the church:
'Joseph Griffith was disowned for being guilty of great and heinous crimes contrary to ye moral law. It was executed October ye 4th 1769.'

'Elizabeth Pritchard was disowned for the following crimes. 1st For swearing and cursing, being bitter malitious not bridling her tongue, ye Apostle James informs us w[h]ere enving and strife is there is coruption and every evil work---James. 3. 14. 15. And after repeated endeavors to reclaim her, all proving fruitless--she refusing to hear ye church, contrary to her covenant and ye rules of ye Gospel Matt 18. It was executed February ye 6th, 1773.'

'Joanna Jones was disowned for being guilty of fornication to ye great dishonour of ye holy religion of Jesus Christ. Executed March ye 6, 1773.'

'December 2, 1786.
Then was Benjamin Jones (formerly of Kent County) disowned for his long absence in a disorderly way and 2ly We have reason to believe he lived several years in Adultery and had some children by a woman, even in his wifes life time. As these are heineous crimes directly against ye moral law, we thought it our indespesible duty to cut him off from all ye special privileges of Christ church.'
* *

WELSH TRACT BAPTIST CHURCH TODAY

Joada John Cole wrote in the John Journal of the worn and deteriorated old stones in the Welsh Tract burying grounds which surround the Meeting House at the foot of Iron Hill near Newark, Del. which consisted of one with this engraved:
Thomas John. D: December 20 Aged [obliterated]; NO 1720.
    I T Died 1760   Aged 51.

Mary Kathryn Harris (Mrs. William) of Fort Worth, Tx., whose husband is a John connection, has worked on the history of the Johns family for over fifteen years. She has written and published her family's history. She has been most generous in sharing her information and research on the Johns family.

In the fall of 1997, she and her husband made a brief trip to Delaware, and she did as much research as she had time for. One of her desires was to visit the old Welsh Tract Baptist Church and cemetery. She was finally able to find it after much difficulty. It seems the people at the Visitor Center there had never heard of the Welsh Tract, much less the church. But being very nice people, they made a number of calls and located it on the outskirts of Newark. However, they warned that it was unlikely that it was still there as it was located in an area that was near some freeways and large commercial shopping centers, etc.

In Mary Kathryn's words, the map they were given "showed the cemetery to be located on the southern fringe of Newark very close to the freeway that runs east and west through Newark. Iron Hill starts right there at the freeway. It showed plainly on the map. When we got there we kept driving around trying to locate it, but saw nothing but filling stations, restaurants, etc. We were almost ready to give up when we passed the police station. I went in and explained what we were looking for. The policeman was very nice and said he knew exactly where it was and gave us very specific directions. We retraced our route back to one block from the freeway to a little side street. Sure enough, not more than a block or two off the main street into Newark, there it was.

We got out and walked around, and I was amazed at how old some of the stones are, especially the ones on the left side of the church. Several go back to burial dates in the 1730's. The church itself was locked. There is one tombstone for a Mary John who died Dec. 2, 1794, age 78...As far as I can see, no other traces of the old Welsh Tract are left."

* *

The following was information taken from "COPY OF INSCRIPTIONS Which Appear On The Tombstones In the Graveyard Surrounding The Welsh Tract Meeting House. Copied by Miss Winny Jones." Undated, but appeared to be published originally with the Minutes of the Welsh Tract Baptist Meeting by the HISTORICAL SOCIETY OF DELAWARE, WILMINGTON, 1904:

(Information from only a few deemed pertinent taken from this account.)

'..Sarah The wife of James James who died Aprel ye 10 1721 aged 56... Riceus Rythrough, natus apud Llanwenog, In Comitatu Cardigan, at his sepultus fuit An dom 1707 Aetatis suai 87.'

David Price, d. 1722.

Eliz Price, 1712.

'In memory of Mary, relict of John Thomas, afterwards of David Clark...July 14th 1775, aged 61 years.'

'John Griffith, ...12th of April 1720, aged 23 years.

Catherine Griffith, Feb. Th 20 1755 aged (obliterated).

In memory of Jane Passmore, Daugh David & Esther Jones, who departed this life July 20, 1764, aged 44 years.

In memory of Eleanor Jones, who departed this life Sep 7, 1759, aged 59.

In memory of Morgan Jones, who departed this life June 4, 1760, aged 63 years.

In memory of David Jones, Jun. who Deceased. Decem 1, 1758. Aged 42 years.

In memory of Ester Jones, who Departed this Life October 2, 1754, aged 76.

David Jones Departed this Life Aug the 20 1748 aged 80 years.

In memory of Esther Jones, who departed this life January the 10th 1800, aged 48 years.'

'In memory of John James, who died January 19th, 1811, aged 59 years.

Susanna, his wife, who died March 8th, 1812, aged 60 years.

In memory of James James, who depd. This life March ye 8, 1755, aged 36 years.'

'In memory of Sarah, wife of James Jones, who departed this life May 4th, 1827, in the 37th year of his age.

With above stone: Frank Goudy, son of Calvin & Philo Jones, b. August 27th, 1857.

In memory of Morgan Jones, who departed this life August 25th, 1820, aged 62 years, 1 month and 18 days.

Deborah James...Decr. 1, 1731, aged 4 y. Near unto her own grandfather lies Daniel James his daughters in a dark earthy womb here underneath this side the tomb. ' (Scratched in side of tablet. At top of tablet is an open Bible, with obliterated inscription. At the left side of Bible appears letter E, and at the right, the letter T.)

Notation that under tombstone, Reverand M. E. Thomas, minister of the gospel and pastor of the church of Christ in the Welsh Tract, who d. November 7, 1730, aged 56 years, was buried.

Revd. David Davis, minister of the gospel of Christ...for near 40 years, who departed...August 19, 1769, aged 62 years.

Zachariah Jones, November 1st, 1834, aged 66 years, 1 month and 16 days.

Zachariah Jones, July 3rd, 1768, aged 33 years.

Morgan Jones, April 24th, A. D. 1851, aged 44 years, 1 month and 1 day.

Zachariah Jones, Jr., Feb. 26, 1856, aged 43 years, 11 months and 9 days.

Elisha, the son of Daniel James, Novr. 23, 1728, aged 3.

Sarah James, daughter of John & Susanna James, Feb. 17, 1819, aged 41 years.

James James, December 11th, 1829, aged 42 years.

Mrs. Margaret Booth, Relict of Major Thomas Booth of St. George's Hundred, and youngest daughter of Rev. David Davis....born June 28, 1743..departed..December 2nd, 1820, aged 77 years, 5 months and 4 days.

Rees Davis, Novem (07) 1756, aged 24 years.

James Miles, b. March 13th, 1746, d. June 14, 1797, aged 51 years and 3 mos.

Rachel Miles, his wife, b. Jan. 7, 1755, d. Sept. __th, 1797, aged 42 years and 8 mos.

Mary John, d. December the 2nd, 1794, aged 78 years.

Thos. John, d. June The 27, 1720.

Philip Lewis, May 1st, 1804, aged 57 years and 7 mos.

Revd. John Boggs, Minister...for 23 years...December 9th, 1802, in the 63rd year of his age.

David Price, Sen., Sep. Ye 26, 1736, aged 50 years.

Rees Jones, Jun., who departed this life September the 27th, 1757, aged 25 years.

Sarah, wife of [Dr.] Reece Jones, who departed this life Aug. 11, 1747, aged 68 years.

Rees Jones, who departed this life Novemr. 23, 1739, aged 4 (*) years.

Under these tombstones are two of Rees Jones Daughters, Sarah and Susanna Jones, twins. Departed this life Oct 7, 173(07) aged 6 mon.

"In memory of Rev. Enoch Morgan, late minister of the gospel at the Welsh Tract M. Morgan Rhyddarch, minister Domeneinne since in South Wales and B. of Mr. Abel Morgan Jun. Pastor of Philadelphia OBYT Mch. 25, 1740 His last text was John 17. He kept the faith and run his race.

David Thomas, Sept 29, 1748, aged 33 years.

Richard Thomas…Novbr the 20th, 1753, aged 75 years.
Catherine Thomas, wife of Richard Thomas, May the 10, 1761, aged 40 years.
Mary Thomas relict of Capt. Lewis Thomas, Sept. 9, 1774, aged 6 [days or months] 51 years.
Richard Thomas Junr., January 15th 1762, aged 37 years.
Mary Thomas, Jan. 20th, 1762, aged 45 years.
Thomas Jones, July 19, 1764, aged 24 years.'
* *

GRIFFITH JOHN of New Castle Co.:

Griffith John left this will. He had 300 a. of land surveyed in 1703/4. It was probably he for whom the deed for 50 acres of land was made in 1729.
New Castle Will Book G, p. 295, 1748.

In the name of God Amen I Griffith John of the Hundred of Pencader in the County of New Castle upon Delaware Yeoman being sick & weak in Body yet thru divine mercy of perfect mind & memory and calling to mind the mortality of my body do make & ordain this my last will & testament in manner & form following Viz. Imprimis I recommend my Soul unto the hands of Almighty God who gave it and my Body to the dust to be interred after a Christian like & decent manner at the desrecion of my Excutrs. hereinafter named and renouncing my worldly Goods & possessions, I give and dispose of the same in ye following manner & form Viz

To my daughter Ann I give & bequeath the sum of Eighteen pounds Currency to be paid her out of my personal estate within the space of one year after my Decease also a mare a cow & a heifer her bed her furniture & chest.

ITEM To my daughter Elizabeth the now wife of John Peirce I give & bequeath the sum of eighteen pounds in ye manner directed in the above Article.

ITEM To my daughter Sarah I give & Bequeath the sum of Eighteen Pounds as above Directed, also her bed & furniture, and a mare a cow & a heifer & her chest as above.

ITEM To my Grand Daughter Susannah the daughter of John Lewis I give and bequeath the sum of twenty shillings to be paid her when she is of full age.

ITEM To my Grand daughter Ann sister of the late mentioned, I give the sum of forty shillings as above directed.

ITEM To my grandson David ye Brother of the last named I give the sum of twenty Shillings in manner aforesaid.

ITEM To my son David I give and bequeath all the residue of my personal estate - whatsoever, to whom I also give devise & confirm all my real estate Viz the Plantation whereon I now dwell with all the appurtenances belonging thereunto and all my lands & tenements of what degree kind or

Quality the same be off or wheresoever it may be found to be enjoyed by him his heirs or assigns forever.

Finally I constitute appoint & ordain my son David to be sole Executor of this my last Will & Testament thereby revoking & disanulling all former wills by me heretofore made, Ratifying & confirming this & none else to be my last Will & Testament In Witness whereof I have hereunto set my hand & Seal this twenty first day of Decber. in the year of our Lord God one thousand Seven hundred & forty Eight. GRIFFITH JOHN, his mark. Signed Sealed Published Pronounced & declaring in Presence of Nathl. Evans, Henry Rowland, Hugh Haughley.

The will was approved 4th day April 1749. David John appointed Executor; ordered to make a full accounting of all the goods, chattels, etc. unto the Registers Office at New Castle on or before the 4th day of October next ensuing.

Children of Griffith mentioned in will:

DAVID JOHN.

ANN JOHN.

SARAH JOHN.

ELIZABETH JOHN, wife of John Pierce.

_____ JOHN. Wife of John Lewis. Their children Ann Lewis, Susannah Lewis, and David Lewis.

* *

David John, probably the youngest son, was the only son mentioned in Griffith's [d. 1749] will. David was probably a blacksmith and did not previously own any land, unless it was one of the deeds attributed to David John who arrived in 1710 and was husband of Esther Morgan.

Griffith mentioned his grandson David Lewis, son of John Lewis. One of the things first noticed in researching the David John line in North Carolina and Georgia was that David Lewis and David John took out land several times near each other. Other Lewis' also remained near the David John family; they had same names as children of Thomas Lewis of Pencader.

In Will Book G, p. 310, dated 13th day of Nov. 1749, was an entry appointing Elizabeth Lewis Administrator of the estate of John Lewis, late of New Castle County, deceased. He died intestate. She was ordered to return an Inventory & appraisal of all his goods, Chattles, [sic] etc. before the 13th day of May next ensueing [sic] and to render a full account of the estate by 13th of Nov. 1750.

There are several possibilities regarding this Griffith John's [d. 1749] parents. His land was located adjoining the land of the Thomas John who had the first grant for 600 plus acres. We have not been able to ascertain for sure which Thomas John owned this land, but the descriptions closely match land sold by Thomas John and wife Susannah. Thomas John and wife Anne lived close to Griffith's land. Griffith John mentioned his daughter Ann first in his will. She might have been named for his wife or his mother. We found no record of his name in the Welsh Tract Church. He and possibly his parents were already in Pennsylvania and Delaware when David John and Esther's family arrived.

The Thomas John who married Susanna Welsh in 1719 was probably a father, brother or some relation of this elder Griffith. The land of that Thomas John had some of the references found in the first survey. Susannah might not have been Thomas' first wife. Thomas died right after he & Susannah completed selling their land and moved to Appoquidiminck County. [Appoquidiminck is spelled so many ways in the records that I'm not sure of the proper spelling.]

There is a possibility that Griffith John was grandson of John Evans of Nantmele, who was written about in the Quaker chapter. John Evans owned land nearby in Chester Co. and his sons took the surname John. They were close associates of the Miles family.

Another possibility is that he was grandson of Griffith John, the Quaker. Griffith John, the Quaker, had two sons named in his will, Evan and John. His son John was said to have taken the surname Griffith, but he had children who took the surname John. The land survey for land in Merion owned by the Quaker Griffith John was also in with the surveys for the John's in New Castle County.

Because of the scarcity of journals or books telling of the literal connections and inaccuracies found in those written, it is very difficult to ascertain relationships with any degree of certainty.

* *

JOSEPH JONES:

Survey made for Joseph Jones, Survey J, Vol. 2, #29, St. George's Hundred, June 6, 1748, for 100 acres. Granted survey to Joseph Jones for 100 acres of land & improvements adjoining the land formerly granted to Percus and Jacob Hyats in St. George Hundred. 6th day of June 1748.

*

New Castle Co. Will Book G, p. 424, David John, adm. of estate of Joseph John, who died intestate 2 Oct 1750.

* *

Our David John who was in North Carolina and Georgia named a son Joseph, possibly after his brother Joseph, above. We believe David did not go to the Carolines until 1754, at which time we found his land grant.

One Griffith John went to the Pee Dee area about 1736 or 1737 and settled there. We have not yet found proof of his parentage. He could have been a son of David John (d. 1748), but he seemed to be young enough to be son of Jonathan, and grandson of that David. He retained the surname John in his line, unlike John Jones who had wife Ann, and others related to David and Esther.

*

Information on Lewis' in New Castle Co. Del.:

There was no survey in New Castle Co. for a David Lewis until 1739, when there were two surveys, L 1, #10, south side of main branch of Drawyers Creek, St. George's Hundred, June 2, 1739, 180 acres. Also L 2, #15, on Road to New Castle, main branch of Second Drawyer Creek, St. George's Hundred, Nov. 24, 1739, "Davids Departure," 152 acres. One David Lewis came over from Wales in 1710, but he might be the David Lewis who died, per Church Minutes.

*

DAVID LEWIS, son of Richard Lewis:

Deed Book G, Vol. 2, P. 567, 1725:

Indenture made 1st day January 1725 Between Wessel Alricks of City of New Castle, Jeweller, of the one part, and David Lewis of White Clay Creek, farmer, of the other part...WITNESSETH that the sd. Wessel Alrichs for...the sum of 150 pounds...lawful money...to in on hand payed ...by the said David Lewis...the sd. Wessel Alrichs hath given granted...sold aliened...all that tract or parcell of land SITUATE and being on the North side of Second Drawyers Creek in St. Georges Hundred...beginning at an old corner white oak standing by the Bridge and Runs one hundred and one perches to an old corner white oak in the swamp then north by an old line one hundred and fourteen perches to an older corner black oak then east by an old line thence by an old line south one hundred thirty four perches to an old corner black oak thence by an old line south six degrees west thirty perches to an old corner maple standing by the Branch side then: After the Branch north seventy five degrees west Sixty three perches & North fifty degrees West twenty four perches West sixty four perches South west sixty perches...

*

Deed book H, Vol. 2, pp. 228-230, 20th day of Nov. 1727:

Indenture between David Lewis of St. Georges Hundred yeoman & Marey his wife of one part and Hugh Morrison of London Grove in Chester Co., yeoman of other part...WHEREAS James Anderson late of Red Lyon Hundred...by virtue of patent grant or conveyance...of a certain piece or parcel of land Situate ...on both sides of White Clay Creek in ye Hundred of Mill Creek & White Clay Creek...containing by estimation one hundred & seventy acres with ye appurtenances...sd James Anderson by certain Indenture conved unto Richard Lewis late of White Clay Creek Hundred yeoman aforesd. ...One hundred and seventy acres of Land...BEGINNING at a corner marked white oak standing on a hill on ye South side of sd Creek being corner of ye land of John Land & running hence by a line of trees north twenty perches to a marked gume standing on the Bank of ye said Creek & thence starting over ye sd Creek by a line North Seventeen Degrees easterly thirty eight perches to a corner marked maple tree standing

on an high bank being a corner tree of Thomas Woolastons late land thence by a line of marked trees Northwest & by North one hundred fifty eight perches to a corner marked hickery thence by a line of marked trees south west and by west one hundred and thirty two perches to a corner stake being a corner of James Claypools late land thence by a line of marked trees Dividing ye same land from ye other land late of ye sd. James Claypoole but now in ye tenure of a certain Richard Wooleston South East & by South two hundred perches to a corner stake being allso another corner of Land formerly belonging to ye sd James Claypoole & thence by a line of marked trees north east & by East ninety perches to ye first mentioned white oak containg as aforsd. By estimation one hundred & Seventy acres...AND ye sd. Richard Lewis being so as aforsd. Seized of ye said one hundred & Seventy acres of land & appurtenances made his last will and testament in writing under his hand & seal duly Executed & hereby [p. 129] in these words to wit 3ly I give & bequeath to my beloved son David Lewis all that tract of land he now dwelleth upon with all priviliges & appurtenances appurtaining or any wise belonging thereof to be held by him his heirs & assigns forever and afterwards sd. Richard Lewis dyed sized of ye premises & ye sd. Will was duly proved and registered as in & by ye said will dated ye twenty fourth day of Aprile in ye year of our Lord one thousand seven hundred & twenty five Recorded in Registers office in New Castell aforesd. Relation thereunto being had it doth & may more fully and at large appear NOW THIS INDENTURE WITNESSETH that ye said David Lewis & Marey his wife for & in consideration of ye sum of one hundred & thirty three pounds of good currencey money of America to them in hand paid by he said Hugh Morison at or before ye sealing & delivery of these presents & Receipt whereof they ye said David Lewis & Marey his wife doe hereby acknowledge & thereof ...grant bargain...unto ye said Hugh Morrison...ye above rented piece of land containing one hundred & seventy acres as above desscribed...   Signed David Lewis & Marey Lewis.
In presence of Alexn. Armstrong & Andrew Patterson. Recorded Dec 1, 1727.
*
Deed Book H, p. 218. 500 acres of land sold by John Welsh, Gent. to Thomas Lewis of Pencader Hundred, yeoman. Whereas John Wolfe paid the sd. Thomas Lewis...461 acres. Wit. William Williams & Thos. Smith. 1727.
Deed Book L, 1, #10. David Lewis, of New Castle 180 acres...survey on...situate south side of main branch of Drawyers Creek adj. land of Francis King in St. George's Hundred. 2 Jun 1739.
Deed Bk. L, 2, #15 David Lewis, on Road to New Castle, main branch of Second Drawyer Creek, St. George's Hundred, Nov. 24, 1739. "Davids Departure", 152 acres.

212

<u>Deed Bk. L 1, #46 David Lewis</u>, grandson of Lewis, decd., Mill Creek Hundred, Jun 14, 1773, 11 a. Resurvey to confirm title.

<u>2d day June 1739 for David Lewis</u> 156 acres of land.

<u>Will Book G, 323, 324.</u> Will of Thomas Lewis - June 13, 1749. Probated Jun 27, 1749: ...Thomas Lewis of Pencader Hd. ...Yeoman...

Item...bequeath to my eldest son Evan Lewis ye full sum of five shillings of good & lawfull money of Pensylvania for to be paid at ye Expiration of one year after my Decease & also an old gray horse called Gray to be delivered Immediately after my Decease & being now in ye tenur of my son David Lewis---

Item...Bequeath to my Second Son Alexander Lewis one gray mare called Benny for to be delivered to him Immediately after my Decease or whenever
she is demianded---

Item...bequeath to my third son James Lewis the full sum of forty pounds good & lawfull money as aforesd. for to be paid to him at ye expiration of one year as beforesd...also one black mare called Bonny to be delivered to him Imediately after my Decease now in the tenure of my son David aforesd.---

Item...Bequeath to my fourth son David aforesd. two horses one called Buck the other called Rock & now in his Tenure and as such to be enjoyed without any delivery from ye Executor.

Item...Bequeath & devise to my son in law Rees Thomas whom I Constitute appoint & ordain my Executr. of this my last will & Testament, & to my Daughter Eliza. his wife all & Singular my rights Titles Interest & Estate whatsoever over & above what is above mentioned--specified & Bequeathed to be enjoyed by them their heirs & assigns for ever, Revoking all other former wills Testaments & Executors both in law and in deed.

Thomas Lewis his mark [Written TO]

Abraham Miller
John Miller
Nathll. Williams.
* *

<u>Thomas Lewis, "Welsh Tract", L2, #16, Mar. 3, 1703/4</u>, 200 a.
Survey of Thomas Lewis' land 3rd of 1 mo. 1703/4...Tract of land from the body of Welsh Tract...beginning...in line of Elisha Thomas' land...John Thomas' land...Thomas Griffith's land...200 acres.

   [John Lewis, father of David Lewis who was mentioned in Griffith John's will of 1748, was probably a connection of this family. Richard Lewis had son David and also a brother named David.]
*

<u>Thomas Lewis, Appoq. Hundred., L1, #12, Jul. 7, 1740</u>, 100 a.
<u>Thomas Lewis</u> ---100 acre land & cedar swamp in Appoq. Hundred next adj. Thomas Ward & Thomas Collins. 5th Jul 1740.

Thomas Lewis, Appoq. Hd., Surv. Gen. G-L #93, Oct. 7, 1741, 198 acres, surv. for John Plaice.

Thomas Lewis 100 acres adj. land of John Harman sit. in Thoroughfare Appoq. Hundred 16 Aug 1746.

Thomas Lewis, L1, #11, Thoroughfare Neck, Appoq. Hd., Aug. 16, 1746, 100 a.

Also, L1, #18, 18 acres, on a drain of Duck Creek, Appoq. Hd., Sep. 29, 1747; "The Paralel", 198 acres, with rough drau; mentioned John Plaice.

Will Book C, P. 121. Thomas Lewis, wife Mary --- Thomas died intestate---Mary Lewis, Admin. 26th day March 1718/19.

*

Deed Book H, p. 141. 4th Nov 1720. William Farson late of Newcastle Co. but now of Kent Co., yeoman, & Rachell Ellis, widow of Thomas Lewis late of New Castle Co...that the sd. Wm. Farson [or Parson] for condition of the sum of 50 pounds, sold to Rachell Lewis 200 acres of land. Situate: on each side the King's Road near the head of Duck Creek in the County of New Castle Co...Signed William Farson. Wit: Joseph England; John Cowgell Thomas; Richard Empson. 20th day of Apr 1727 in Court of Common Pleas. [In several places in this deed, she was referred to as Rachell Ellis.]

* *

P. 358. 20 Aug 1724. Richard Lewis of White Clay Creek, yeoman, and Nathaniel Wainford, carpenter. 30 a. in Mill Creek Hundred. Wit: John Hole & Richard McDaniel.

Richard Lewis Will, 24 Apr 1725, p. 287. Wife Hellen; sons Jno. Lewis & David Lewis. Dau Jane Cann, wife of William Cann; grandchildren, ch. of Wm. Cann - - Hellin, William & Mary. Ann Reese, dau of Evan Reese. Wife Hellin & son John Lewis Excrs. Wit: David Lewis, John Medellin Jr., James Cooper, Atty.

31 Dec 1730: Will of Griffith Lewis, Mill Creek Hundred, wife Catharin, Excr. Left 3 pounds to two Baptist meeting houses in Welsh Tract and London Tract. Witnesses Jas. Kelly; Isaac Gefereson [Gifferson], David Lewis, probated 15 Jan 1736/37.

11 Feb 1731/32, Evan Lewis, wife Ann Lewis. Stepson David David and step dau Rachel David. Wit: James Morgan, Roger Williams, Rees Lewis. NOTE: There was a David Davis living close to the Lewis' in the 1750's and 1760's in North Carolina.

8 Nov 1746, Catharine Lewis of Mill Creek Hundred. Left Rev. Owen Thomas 10 pounds; Rev. David Davie 2 pounds, Phillip Thomas 5 shillings. Bequests to children of Phillip Thomas (Sarah Thomas); trusty friend Sarah Thomas to be sole Excr. Wit: Jonathan Evans, John Lewis, John Gillahan.

18 Mar 1753: Evan Lewis of New Castle Hundred. Bequests to nephew Griffith, son of John Griffith; niece Hannah Griffith; brother Thomas Lewis; 3 nephews David Griffith, Thomas Griffith, John Griffith; niece

Mary, dau of John Griffith, now wife of Roger Williams...and to brother Joel, plantation that my said brother David lived upon at time of his death. Nephews John & Isaac, son of brother Thomas Lewis. Nephew Isaac, son of bro Thomas, Execr.

Nov 8, 1757 will of David Lewis of Mill Creek Hundred. Brother James, son David Lewis...I now live on in Mill Creek Hundred & all utensils belonging to sd. Mill. Son James Lewis. Dau in law Eliz., wife of son James Lewis; son William's son Benj. Lewis; Grandson David Lewis; granddau Mary Lewis; grandson Enoch Lewis. Wit.: Elinor Poulston, Peter Poulston, Wm. Latimor.

Richard Lewis, 1727, Book G, p. 289. 21 day March. Dau Anne; wife Elizabeth. Daughter Esther; an unborn child; Elisha Thomas 20 pounds; Enoch Morgan 20 shillings; Owen Thomas 20 shillings. Wit: John David, John Morris, Richard Grafton.

Will Book G, 474. Josiah Lewis, adm. for Sarah Lewis, 29 Apr 1751. 2 Apr. 1761. Josiah Lewis, wife Mary; brother Philip Lewis; cousin Josiah David & Sarah David. Cousin John Moor.

Will Book G, 463: Lydia Lewis, Administrator for estate of David Lewis, who died Intestate. 25th day of March 1751. This was probably the brother of Evan Lewis mentioned in Evan's will.

Deed Book H, pp. 228 to 230...Richard Lewis by his will left to David Lewis...

Deed Book N, p. 504: David Lewis, wife Mary, of St. George's Hundred, and James Norris. 1742/3.

Deed Book G, p. 398. Stephen Lewis, tanner, to Benj. Stout Jr., yeoman. William Lewis, L2, #17, Elk River Rd., Welsh Tract, Jan. 6, 1703/4, 151 acres.

Survey 6 day Jan 1703/4 ---cut off tract of land from Welsh Tract for William Lewis...off Jenkin Evans...north side of Elk River...in John Rowlands line...151 acres.
* *

JOHN LEWIS, the Quaker:

[He does not appear to be connected with the Baptist Lewis family.]
Info from will of Philip Price of Merion, yeoman, marked 11 Dec 1719, proved 22 Nov by wife Margaret, Philadelphia. Named daughter Sarah Lewis, grandchildren, "children of John Lewis of New Castle, Del. Co.", Elizabeth Stout, Philip, Stephen, Josiah, Sarah, Mary and Ann Lewis.

Several deeds in Deed Book G, Vol. 1:

P. 93, Sarah Lewis, relict of John Lewis 1723.

P. 228. Indenture between Sarah Lewis, relict of John of Red Lyon Hd., & George Weaver.

Deed Book G, P. 519. Granted 1 day of Dec. 1705 to John Lewis of Md. & conveying to Wm. Horn, county of Chester, cooper, by [   ] Mason late widow of the sd. John Lewis by release bearing date 15 May 1718, etc. Wit: Isaac Griffith & Elinor. 13 Jan 1725.

P. 465. Rees Evans to Evan David. John Lewis died & Sarah relict, & Phillip his son, sold 125 a. to Rees Evans from est. of 550 a. left by John Lewis---now sold to Evan David. 20 Feb 1724.

P. 481. Mentioned late Samuel Griffith's land---Stephen Lewis, Cornelius Kettle---by Geo. Dakeyne's land. Mentioned John Lewis & Sarah 150 acres.

Deed Book K, Vol. 1, 12 day Aug 1734, P. 266: Richard Smith of Ceceil Co. in Province of Maryland yeoman and wife Margaret, to James Creager, of Red Lyon Hundred, Farmer...Whereas Joseph Wood, Gent., by his Indenture...dated 19th & 20th days of Feb 1707 ...to John Lewis...550 acres of land in Red Lyon Hundred...in his last will dated 1 day Sept 1708 ...among other things, his Excrs. bargained & sold toward the payment of debts, etc., 250 acres ...Sarah Lewis relict & Excr. of said John Lewis ...release by date 23 & 24 days Dec 1724...sell grant convey unto Geo. Williams yeoman, lately decd., 125 acres of afsd land...Situate...by Georges Creek...being a corner of Benj. Stouts lands...Richard Smith & wife, heirs of Geo. Williams...Aug. 22, 1734.

* *

CHAPTER EIGHT

WELSH IN SOUTH CAROLINA
Establishment of Welch Neck Baptist Church:

For various reasons, many of the Welsh people of Pennsylvania and Delaware became disenchanted with their places of abode by 1734. Many had borrowed on their land, and were beginning to lose it. There were several records of David French and Andrew Petterson, Trustees of ye General Loan Office of the County of New Castle, taking the people into court and the Sheriff ordering the sale of their land to pay off their debts with damages for same.

Phillip James had a mortgage deed made against his land, to John Jones of Philadelphia. About this time, after possessing the land for several years, John Jones sold it. The Welsh people learned of offers for free land in South Carolina, and hoped to make a new start under better conditions.

The first permanent settlement by the English in S. C. was in April 1670. This was at Albemarle Point on the west bank of the Ashley River. This area proved unfavorable, so in 1680 the people and the government moved over to the site of present day Charleston.[1] This settlement gradually spread along the coast, but did not spread into the interior until after 1730.

The Province of Carolina, as it was first called, was not divided until July 1729 into North Carolina and South Carolina. A 1730 order for a survey of part of the boundary was carried out in 1735, but the whole boundary survey was not completed until 1815. The boundary line was unclear between them and caused several disputes through the years.

In 1730, in order to encourage more settlement, eleven townships were marked out, with one of them on the Pee Dee River. One of the Indian tribes that dwelled along the Pee Dee was the Seraws, later called Charraws and Cheraws. The line between South and North Carolina bounded Craven County on the north and northeast.

Land for the new settlement was to be available in plots of fifty acres each for each man, woman, and child who agreed to occupy and improve them. From this amount, it is possible to determine the number of children each settler had. The first ten years of land use would be rent free, with a fee of four shillings per one hundred acres per year thereafter.

Pennsylvania and Delaware Welsh Baptists learned of this land and paid a visit in the latter part of 1735, or early the following year. They wanted to settle in a body and have ample room for expansion. Samuel Wilds, David Lewis, and Daniel James of New Castle Co., Del. petitioned the Government for a large tract of land for the exclusive use of the Welsh people on August 13, 1736. This was agreeable with the controlling Council, and a plot

---

[1]Encyclopaedia Britannica 1969, Vol. 20, p. 1007.

containing 173,840 acres was approved and ordered laid out on 16th November 1736.

In Benedict's account of the Griffith's, was this regarding John Jones and Ann:

"In this party were John Jones and Ann his wife. (See records of Welsh Tract Church; Morgan Edwards, "Materials" and Penn. Mag., and Rev. Jonathan Davis' History of Welsh Baptists, P. 125.) It will be noticed that David John or Jones who was married to Esther Morgan and was father of John Jones, gave him only 10 pounds in his will and did make provision for certain of John's children. It is certainly very probable that the John Jones of Welsh Neck was the son of David John. The Welsh Neck Church until the year 1744 met at the house of John Jones. The records of Welsh Tract Church show that John Jones and Ann his wife, were recommended to Pee Dee, March 11, 1738. They also show that John Jones was dismissed to Pee Dee (Dec.) Nov. 1, 1741."[2]

There were two John Jones' dismissed to go to the Pee Dee. The latter John Jones was the one with wife Elizabeth. Records regarding John Jones with wife Elizabeth were found in the New Castle Welsh Tract Church Minutes, Book 1st showing "Rm" for Removed, and "See book ye 5, page ye 3," where the records for 1741, above, were given. The other John Jones with wife Ann Jones was listed as being removed in book 5, page 2. [I give these records to show that there were two John Jones who were dismissed to go to the Pee Dee.]

John Jones who had wife Elizabeth was most probably the son of John Jones and Ann. From the context of the will of David John in New Castle who died in 1749, his son John had adult children, as he left land to two of John's children. Leah Townsend in giving the description of one of the John Jones' land[3] refers to him as John Jones Jr. Apparently he was a member of the Lynches Creek Church organized in 1755, which was said to have been begun by former Welsh Neck Church members.

We estimated the age of David's (d. 1748) son John as ca 1700, but he could have been born as far back as ca 1689 or a few years earlier. He might have been a son of an earlier wife of David's, given the Welsh propensity for marrying early.

A few of the "Minutes of the Welch Neck Baptist Church 1737-1841" (located at Society Hill, Darlington Co., S. C.) are extant. A large number of them were lost to fire and some are indecipherable due to age. The "names of

---

[2]In Pa. Notes Towards a History of Baptists in Pa. in the American Baptist Historical Society, Chester, Dela. Co., Pa., by Morgan Edwards.
[3]South Carolina Baptists, Townsend, P. 96.

the individuals who composed this party which was embodied into a church" were:

"Philip James and his wife; Abel James and his wife; Daniel James and his wife; Daniel Devonald and his wife; Thomas Evans and his wife; Thomas Evans, Jr. And his wife; John Jones and his wife; Thomas Harry and his wife; David Harry and his wife; John Harry and his wife; Samuel Wilds and his wife; Samuel Evans and his wife; Griffith Jones and his wife; David James and his wife; Thomas Jones and his wife."

I found no record of Griffith Jones or John being a Church member in the New Castle Co., Del. Welsh Tract records. He might have belonged to one of the Baptist churches associated with Welsh Tract, such as Montgomery or Great Valley.

It appears that he probably was a son of Griffith John who died in 1749, and was a brother of the David John who came to North Carolina in 1754. Griffith would not have been named in his father's will if he was already settled in South Carolina.

It is possible that he was the son of John Jones, grandson of David John [d. 1748] and Esther. The only reference found to the John's that went to the South Carolina area to establish a church was the written note by Benedict in with Morgan Edwards' "Materials…" that said David John and descendants of Morgan Rhydderech (Morgan) went there. Griffith was part of the Welsh Tract Group who went there to establish a church. He was with others from this family, and his name was written both as Jones and John for awhile. His will was signed with an X, indicating he probably could not write English. He seemed to have close connections with the James and Miles families. However, most of the known descendants of David John and Esther took the surname Jones while he used John.

This group of names of the founders of Welsh Neck Church does not include all the Welsh who received grants for land. As was true when the group of Welsh came into Pennsylvania, all names of those arriving together were not carried on the church rolls. And many soon arrived that were members of the Presbyterian and other churches.

David Lewis was not on the list of Welsh Neck Church founders, and he seems to have settled away from the main group of Baptists. There was an early grant for a David Lewis for 500 acres on the Broad River. That was probably for the David who was one of those mentioned as requesting the land for the Welsh. We believe he was a different David Lewis than the one found later living near David John in North Carolina, and cannot tell if they were related.

The group of Welsh Baptists settled in the tract first assigned to them on Cat Fish, a stream in what is now Marion County. They found it did not meet their requirements. So they again petitioned, asking to extend their lands to meet their needs. This petition stated the lands were not suitable for planting hemp and flax, and requested a more favorable location. Griffith John first settled on Catfish, as well as John Jones and wife and William Jones and wife. The petition to extend their lands was signed by Daniel James, David Lewis, and Samuel Wild as representatives. John Jones and William Jones later had land on the Catawba River.

The Hon. Thomas Broughton, Esqr., Lt. Governor and Commander In Chief In & Over his Majesty's Province of South Carolina answered with this Proclamation:

"Whereas, I have this day received information in Council, from Danl. James that the Lands which David Lewis, Saml. Wild, and the said Danl. James, prayed for in their petition of 13th August last, to be set apart for the Welch Families mentioned therein, were the vacant Lands they viewed, and desired might be reserved for them, lying on each side of Great Pedee River, and up to the two Main branches thereof, and that the Lands set forth, and prescribed in the order of Council of the 21st January last, are not the Lands they desired, and were assigned them agreeable to the said Petition; nor will these Lands suit their intention of planting Hemp and Flax; and whereas I have also received information from the said Danl. James that several of the said families, on the encouragement they had from the first Order of Council, have sold their Possessions in Pennsylvania, some being arrived, and others on their way to this Province, I have therefore thought fit, by and with the advice and consent of his Majesty's Hon. Council, to issue this, my Proclamation, to give Notice, that I have (with the advice and consent aforesaid) refused the said last order of Council of the 21st of January last, and confirmed the said first order of the 13th of August; and have ordered that the Lines be run parallel, as near as may be, with the course of Great Pedee River; and further to give Notice, that the Surveyor-General is ordered and directed to instruct his Deputies not to survey, (for any other Persons than the said Welch people) any more of the said Lands above Pedee Township, lying within eight miles on each side of the said River, and so up to the Branches aforesaid. Given under my hand and the Great Seal of this his Majesty's Province, this 8th day of February, in the 10th year of his Majesty's reign, Annoque Domini, 1737."

This gave the Welch exclusive rights to a large territory embracing more than a hundred miles by the course of the Pee Dee River. This was said by Gregg in "History Of The Old Cheraws" to have embraced the area twenty five miles above the state line into North Carolina. The area described by Gregg as 'extending down from the branches of the Rocky River and Yadkin River' would have been in what is now Richmond County, N.C., then extending along the Pee Dee River south through Anson Co., N.C., into the S. C. counties of Marlboro, Chesterfield, Darlington and Marion. W. W. Sellers, author of "A History of Marion County" only mentioned the eight miles on each side of the Pee Dee River, as stated above. This was probably because it is where the main Welsh Neck Church group settled near the church.

In "History of Marlboro Co.,"[4] Thomas wrote that 'settlers in 1736 first stopped near the mouth of Catfish Creek, in what is now Marion County; but having much sickness there, they remained but a short time, and most of them removed about fifty miles up the Pee Dee River, and settled in what has ever since been called the "Welsh Neck;" a district embracing the lands on the east side of the river from the mouth of Crooked Creek to the Red Hill or Hunt's Bluff.'

Many of the N. C. grants later found to be in S. C., as documented by Brent Holcomb in several books, were for some of the Welsh from New Castle Co., Del. and are located in several S. C. counties now. Some settled on branches of the Catawba River, with many of the grants on Fishing Creek. Fishing Creek appears to be in the same general area as Catfish Creek named in these grants.

The lands subsequently granted to the Welsh in 1737 were also immediately contiguous to the river that was the main source of transportation at that time. As happened in Pennsylvania, this left a lot of land open for settlement beyond the Welsh Neck Settlement made by the Baptists.

Griffith John's first claim was in Queensborough Township, per research by Leah Townsend in "South Carolina Baptists, p. 78. She showed a claim on Catfish Creek to Griffith John, which read: "Thomas James and wife (650 acres in Queensborough Township on Griffith Johns' land, 1738.)" She also showed "Griffith Jones 300 acres in 1738 in Queensborough Township touching lands of Thomas James." Perhaps Griffith was related to Thomas James. John Jones Jr. had land touching that of David James and Thomas Evans Sr.

Daniel James was one of the sons of James James Esqr., who was probably the wealthiest of the group which arrived. This was the James James, Esqr., who had been a Justice of the Peace in New Castle County. The land owned by James James Esqr. in South Carolina was located on both sides of the Pee Dee River in the area later known as Spark's Ferry. The first public ferry was established there in 1768. The Baptist Church was located in this area also.

The father of James James, Sr. had been the owner of 1244 acres of land granted by William Penn in Delaware, which was located near the Baptist Church on Iron Hill. He gave various amounts of land to his sons, and had sold 250 acres to Thomas John, who died in 1720, and who had wife Rebecca. Most of this group had a familial relationship, as well as religious.

---

[4]History of Marlboro Co., by Rev. J. A. W. Thomas, Atlanta, Ga. The Foote & Davies Co., Printers & Binders 1896.

Philip James, one of James James' sons, was the first Pastor of the Welch Neck Church that was established in 1738. He was born near Pennepek, in Philadelphia Co., in 1701. He had owned land in New Castle Co. near the Baptist Church on Iron Hill. [There was another Philip James there, who was probably a cousin to this Philip.] James James, Esqr., had other sons, James James Jr., Howell James, David James, Thomas James, and Samuel James [who had started up and owned part of Abington Furnace Co., as shown in the deeds in New Castle Co., Del.]

The earliest grants in the upper part of Darlington District were said by Rev. Alexander Gregg in 'History of the Old Cheraws' to go back to 1734, although he was unable to find any grants dating before 1736.

The Welsh Baptist group met in January 1738, and organized the church with the name "Baptist Church of Christ at the Welch-Neck." They erected a house of worship on the east bank of the river, a short distance above the ferry. Gregg stated "James James owned the lands on both sides of the river, at what is now known as Spark's Ferry." 'This is on the road leading from Society Hill to Bennetsville.'

Under one of the Proprietary Acts, although never ratified, religious tolerance was practiced. The main purpose was to get more people of the Protestant faith to settle the area. The earlier settlers were so isolated and surrounded by so many hostile Indians, that they wanted more of their own people to settle.

Even though the Welsh established their Baptist church with no opposition, there was a British act of November 30, 1706 that remained in effect until 1778. This stated the Church of England was the established religion. Taxpayers' money was used to pay their Pastors. The early Acts were written in such a way as to retain power in people of the English and Episcopal religions.

In 1712, an Act was made to nominate yearly Overseers of the poor of the Parish and to exercise civil functions. The Overseers of the poor, along with the Churchwardens, also had the duties of binding out orphan children as apprentices.

After the Act of 1721, it was made the duty of Churchwardens to provide for the election of Members of Assembly. At this time and with the sparse population, these rules were not enforced. The Council Chamber seemed to be the main enforcing agency.

* *

JOHN JONES and ANN:

John was son of David John (ca 1669-1748) and Esther Morgan John (ca 1678-1754.) We estimate his birth date as ca 1695/1700. He was mentioned in his father's will, along with three of his children, Esther Jones, Benjamin Jones, and Enoch Jones. John, with wife Ann, was among those in the early group to settle on the Pee Dee in 1737.

The grants in 1738 showed he had 250 acres on James's Neck west on Peedee in the Welsh Tract or "New Camberarer." This indicates that he had five people in his family at this time, or three children, as fifty acres per person were allowed. Leah Townsend gave his name and William Jones as being among the constituents of Catfish Creek, the first spot chosen as a settlement by the Welsh, but given up because it was not suitable. There were several later grants to John Jones, but it would be hard to differentiate which pertain to this particular one. One grant was made for 100 acres more in 1741 "bordering on his own land." It appears to me from later grants that John and William remained in this lower area.

Their known children were:

1. ESTHER JONES, b. Del.
2. BENJAMIN JONES, b. Del.
3. ENOCH JONES, b. Del.

Had other children, with ones possibly theirs listed below.

4. GRIFFITH JONES*.
5. DAVID JONES*.
6. EDWARD JONES*.
7. THOMAS JONES*.
8. JOHN JONES*.

*Mentioned in Welsh Neck Baptist Church Minutes. We believe Griffith Jones was Griffith John. David Jones was said by some writers as being David James in the Church Minutes.

* *

Several things written by Gregg regarding the location of the house of John Jones seems to indicate it was located near the Welch Neck Baptist Church. The first church services after this group arrived from Delaware were held in the home of John Jones.

Writers quoting Gregg often mention the Welch Concordance of the Bible by Abel Morgan as being in the possession of John Jones. Leah Townsend believed it indicated the use of the Welsh language by these settlers.[5] John Jones (ca 1695), son of David John (ca 1669), was related to Abel Morgan and was probably the one at whose house the first meetings were held, and the one who owned this Bible. This Bible was said to have the had the signature of John Jones on the flyleaf.

Gregg wrote on page 67 in his "History…" that there was "now in the possession of a family descended from the Welch, and living in the neighbourhood of their settlement, a Welch Bible, of the edition of 1676, which is supposed to have belonged to the leader of the colony, as it

[5]South Carolina Baptists, by Leah Townsend, Gen. Pub. Co., Inc., 1974, p. 63.

contains a record of the births, marriages, and deaths of the James family." I have not seen this Bible, but if it was the same one owned by John Jones, it might indicate his wife Ann was a James.

John Jones died Sept. 19, 1759, according to the church records. His widow Ann married a DOUGLASS. The only Douglass in the Church Minutes was Philip Douglass, who died Oct. 17, 1766. Ann died April 12th, 1766. Several Douglas' [spelled several ways] can be found in the grants along the Catawba River.

* *

JOHN JONES:

Son of John Jones and Ann. Came to S.C. with wife Elizabeth in 1741 or 1742. The surname Jones was used for him in the church records. He was dismissed from the Welsh Tract Church in Delaware in 1741 to go to the Pee Dee. Five hundred acres was taken out by John Jones in 1742, an indication 10 people, or 8 children were in the family. Other land grants were later taken out for John Jones'.

Information from other deeds in N.C. mentioning John Jones, some undoubtedly John Jr.:

Anson Co.:

File No. 2211; Bk. 26, p. 92. Plat: April 22, 1756. Surveyed for John McBride land on N. side P.D--beginning in a reedy marsh above his house--- adj. Jacob Lipham; 191 Acres____Heron, Dept. Sur. John Jones, Thos. Morgan, Chainors. Iss. 26 May 1757.

File No. 566, Gr. No. 295, Bk. 17, p. 247, Plat surveyed for Curtis Culwell, 150 A on both sides Bullocks Creek---adj. his own line---Laughlins line. 30 Oct 1765. John Jones, chainbearer.

Anson Co. Wills and Estates Pp. 296-298: Sale of estate of John Hicks, 6 Nov 1772. One of the buyers was John Jones.

Other Jones:

Anson Co. Deeds & Absts.

Pp. 85-86: 11 Feb 1751, Richard Jones of Craven Co., S.C. planter, to John Mark of Beauford Co., N.C. cooper, for L100 proc money, land on E side Pee Dee. Corner of tract laid out for Matthew Creed, 320 a granted to Richard Jones, 174_, Richard Jones (Seal), Wit: Jacob Paul, Saml Burton. [Richard Jones obtained grant of 320 a. N side Pee Dee, 22 May 1741, File #342, Book 5, p. 381.]

Pp. 87-88: 12 Apr 1749: Thomas Jones of Bladen Co., surveyor sold 200 a on E side Pee Dee to Edmund Cartlidge for L 16. Wit: Wm. Phillips, Alex Osburn.

Pp. 88-89: 7 Sept 1751, Andrew Hampton of Anson Co. sold 640 a on SW side of Pee Dee above Buch Creek to Ambrose Stille, which was granted to James Jones 22 May 1741.

P. 240, 1 Nov 1754: Jas MacManus of Anson Co. to John Campbell of Bertie Co.--300 acres on S. side Pee Dee, adj. William Kemps corner. One of the wit: Thomas Jones.

Pp. 257-258, 28 June 1756, mentioned David Jones, Esqr., Sheriff of Rowan Co.

Pp. 294-297: 16 Jan 1753, Edmund Cartiledge of Anson Co., to Wm. Terry.--land on N side Greate Pee Dee---Thomas Jones lower corner---Lick Branch--12 ½ a., part of 200 a. granted to Thos Jones 10 Apr 1745 & conveyed to Edmund Cartiledge 12 Apr 1749.

Pp. 298: 25 Aug 1752, Thomas Jones of Bladen Co., planter, to William Little of Anson Co., for L 40 Va. money. 400 acres on S side Pee Dee, adj. lands of Hezekiah Russ. Thomas Jones (Seal), Wit: Cleb Howell, Jas. Gillespie, Jno Lane.

Pp. 338-339: 27 & 28 Sept 1753, Peter Elliot of Anson Co. to James Davis of Rowan Co.--50 acres. about 3 miles below John Price's. Granted.7 Oct 1749.Wit: Evan Jones, Alex Lewis.

Pp. 52-54: 21 & 22 June 1754, William Jones, Shoemaker, of Anson Co. to James Johnston, planter of Rowan Co., (lease s5, release L20 Va. money). 500 Acres on N side of S branch of Fishing Creek, below Samuel Moore's corner. William Jones (Seal), Wit: William Courtney, Henry Hendry.

John Jones, Mecklenburg Co.:

Vol. 3, Pp. 52-52: 16 Jan 1768, Joseph Jolley of Meck., cooper to John Jones, of same, planter, for s20--land on S side Thicketty Creek, part of tract granted to sd. Jolley 14 Apr 1767. Wit: Henry Clark, Nath. Clark, Henry Kar. No prov. Date.

Vol. 6, Pp. 315-316, 19 Nov 1773, Abraham Caradine of Meck., planter, to Sarah Alexander, widow of Col. Moses Alexander deceased of same, for L 130, land adj. John Alexander, 254 acres. Wit: Adam Alexander, John Jones. Rec Apr term 1773. Proven by Adam Alexander. (John Alexander purchased 123 a. on Coddle Creek on 25 June 1765. V. 1, pp. 171-173.)
*

GRIFFITH JOHN:

Griffith John seems to have arrived with this early group ca 1737 or soon after, even though his name was not shown with those dismissed from the Welsh Tract Baptist Church. He brought his family with him; had wife named Margaret. His children seem to have been very young when he arrived. We estimate his birth date as ca 1710. Records show Griffith Jones and John Jones had surveys before 1743, which they did not take up. These were undoubtedly the ones first made that were found not to be suitable to their needs.

The first survey we found for Griffith John was a survey in 1738 for 300 acres in Queensborough Township touching lands of Thomas James. A note by Leah Townsend in "South Carolina Baptists" shows a survey made by Thomas James for 650 acres on land on [adjoining] Griffith John's land, 1738, and gave them as Catfish constituents. Catfish was in Marion District, later Marion Co. Joseph Jones and his brother John Jones were on Catfish Creek before and during the Revolutionary War. See later.

The Welsh Neck Church Minutes of January 1738 show Griffith Jones and his wife as being among the group which was constituted a Church under the style and title of the "Baptist Church of Christ at the Welch-Neck." His wife's name was not given. He apparently moved with the others and took out other land in 1743. His later land records show his name as Griffith John.

The first time his name was written as "Griffith John" in the church Minutes was when the membership roll was taken at Welsh Neck Church in 1759. Some early land records have Griffith Jones. Later ones have Griffith John. His wife Margaret's name was also on the list of church members taken in 1759. The records of some land later sold by Jonathan John had his father's name as Griffith John.

Griffith had four children at the time of his first grant, as estimated by using the acreage guide of fifty acres allowed per person.

Children of Griffith and Margaret John:
1. ENOCH JOHN, born ca 1730, Del.
2. RACHEL JOHN, b. ca 1732, Del.
3. SARAH JOHN, b. ca. 1734, Del.
4. JONATHAN JOHN, b. ca 1738, Del. Died ca 1795, Marlboro Co., S.C.
5. JESSE JOHN, b. ca 1740, S. C.
6. ABIGAIL JOHN, b. ca 1745, S. C.
7. THOMAS JOHN, b. ca 1751, S. C. Married Elizabeth Pouncey. Died 15 Feb 1817, Marlboro Co., S.C. Buried Parnassus Cemetery.

Probably others.

*William John might have been his son. However, we cannot positively identify William as son of Griffith.

There are very few extant records in the Welsh Neck Church Minutes regarding the years between 1737 and 1759. The Welsh Neck Church seems to have been busy at this time, with the branch church of Catfish Creek being considered a regular part of the Mother Church. Catfish did not have a separate constitution until Saturday, October 3, 1762, at which time it had thirty-one members. Catfish Baptist Church was later in Bethea Township, Marion Co.

Deeds made in 1794 show Griffith's land was then owned by his son Jonathan and Jonathan's wife Mary. They sold this, and other land they owned, to Robert Campbell. Robert Campbell was in the British army, but settled in this area after the Revolutionary War. The lease and release of this land to Campbell was made on two dates, March 31, 1794 and April 1, 1794, as recorded in Marlboro Co. Deed Bk. AA, pp. 387, 388. One deed stated a total of 252 acres leased for rent of 1 peppercorn (after mentioning a number of pounds that each parcel sold for.) The second deed was for 352 acres total and much more in pounds, and was called a release, which means it was sold and not just leased. Jonathan had 100 acres of land which had been granted to Griffith John and surveyed Nov. 12, 1746. This was land that Jonathan lived on, plus 300 acres more that was surveyed to Griffith on Jan. 3, 1743. (See below under Jonathan John.)

Griffith John died Aug. 1, 1765. In the South Carolina Probate Court Records as shown in The Journal of the Court of Ordinary 1771-1775, p. 22: "Dedimus Issued to Alexr. McIntosh and John Alran Esqrs. to prove the Will of Griffith John and qualify the Exors. therein named. Janry 7. 1772."[6] Mary Kathryn Harris found Griffith's Will in the Charleston Mss. Wills, Volume SS, pp. 100-101:

WILL OF GRIFFITH JOHN

In the name of God amen. I Griffith John of South Carolina being very weak but in perfect mind and memory thanks be given unto God calling unto mind the mortality of my body and knowing that it is appointed for all men once to die do make and ordain this my last Will and Testament that is to say principally and first of all I give and recommend my soul unto the hands of almighty God that gave it and my body I recommend to the earth to be buried in decent Christian burial at the discretion of my Executors nothing doubting but at the general resurrection I shall receive the same again by the mighty power of God and as touching such worldly estate wherewith it has pleased God to bless me in this life, I give an devise and dispose of the same in following manner and form.

First I give and bequeath to Margry my well beloved wife all my lands and negroes stocks and household goods of all sorts until her death. Then I give and bequeath to my well beloved son Enuch John 100 acres of land being the upper tract only taking out the swamp field and foley's field also my negro fellow Robin.

Also I give and bequeath to my well beloved son Jonathan John 100 acres of land being the lower tract and the Swamp field and Foley's field.

I do make and ordain [E]nuch John and Jonathan John my hole and sole executors of this my last Will and Testament.

---

[6]Probate Records of South Carolina, by Brent H. Holcomb, G. R. S., p. 18.

Also I give and bequeath to my well beloved daughter Sarah John my negro wench Rose.

Also I give and bequeath to my well beloved daughter Rachel John my negro girl named Lid.

Also I give and bequeath to my well beloved son Thomas John my negro girl named Jud.

Also I give and bequeath to my well beloved son Jesey John my negro boy named Jack.

Also I give and bequeath to my well beloved daughter Abeygirl John my negro girl named Pot.

Also after my wife's death all the rest of my estate not mentioned stocks and household goods of all sorts to be equally divided amongst my children and I do hereby utterly disannul revoke and disalow of all and every other testaments, wills, legacies, bequests and Executors by me in any ways before named will and bequeathed ratyfing and confirming this and no other to be my last Will and Testament in witness whereof I have hereunto set my hand and seal this 7th day of October 1763.

Signed, sealed, published, pronounced and declared

By the said Griffith John as his last Will and Testament in the presence of Us who in his presence and in the presence of each other have hereto Subscribed our names.

William Pouncey
Enoch John
Jonathan John   /s/ Griffith x John
* *

ENOCH JOHN:

1- Son of Griffith John (ca 1710) and Margaret, is estimated to have been born ca 1730. He was in the South Carolina Militia in 1759 and 1760. He was a Private and was shown in the Muster Rolls of Colonel George Gabriel Powell's Battalion of South Carolina in the 1759 Cherokee Expedition, and was shown on the Muster Roll of Captain Philip Pledger's Company, Jan. 15, 1760.[7] I found no later records of him in this vicinity.

He was probably the eldest son of Griffith John (ca 1710) and Margaret, and was born in New Castle Co., Del. He was a small child when his parents moved to the Marlboro area on the Pee Dee River in South Carolina. He appears to have died before 1794, as his brother Jonathan then owned his land by heirship.
* *

JONATHAN JOHN:

Son of Griffith John (ca 1710) and Margaret, was born ca 1738 in New Castle Co., Delaware. His wife Mary was shown in a 1794 deed.

[7]Colonial Soldiers of the South, 1732-1774, pp. 894, 921.

Jonathan and Mary probably had several children. Gregg in his 'History' wrote of an incident regarding Thomas John, a Tory, who went to 'old Jonathan John's' house to spend the night. He also referred to Asal John as being saved by Thomas Ayers who regarded Asal as 'son of his old neighbor, a peaceable man.' The account seemed to imply Asal and Thomas were not brothers, and we believe the wording indicated the "old neighbor" was Jonathan John, and that Asal was son of Jonathan. We believe Thomas was the son of Griffith.

Ayers descendants lived in Marion Co., according to "A History of Marion Co., " an indication that Jonathan and Griffith also lived nearby.

Children of Jonathan:
1. ASAL JOHN.
2. ELIJAH JOHN.
Probably others.

Records regarding JONATHAN JOHN:
Entered land from 1772-1776, according to Index of Plats in the Office of Secretary of State of S.C.
Pp. 170-171: 4 Dec 1787, JONATHAN JOHN of Marlborough Co., planter, to JOHN WILSON of same, planter, for L 200...150 acres which was granted to sd. JOHN 17 Dec 1770 situated in Marlborough Co. on the N. East side of Giant Pee Dee river on Fells Creek, and Odams Branch bounded at the time of being granted on all side by vacant land and hath such forms shape and marks as appears by a plat to the original Grant annexed...JONATHAN JOHN (LS), Wit: MOT PEARSON [or Mos. Pearson], JAMES EASTERLING. Plat included in deed. Rec. 4 Dec 1787.
*

The Jury Lists of South Carolina 1778-1779, p. 43, Cheraws District:
Jonathan John.
*

Marlborough Co. S.C. Minutes of the County Court 1785-99 and Minutes of the Court of Ordinary 1791-1821:
Dec 1786. Petit Juror: Jonathan John.
Sept. 1787: Jonathan John appeared and acknowledged a deed for 150 acres to John Wilson.
Dec. 1788---Petit Juror: Jonathan John.
June 1789: Thomas Evans Esq. Returned a decimus with bonds executed by William Evans and Jesse Douglas administrators of Enoch Luke deceased. Johathan John and James Hodges Securities.
Mar 1 1790: Phillip Hodges vs. John Mayes
Carney Wright vs. Hubbart Stevens.
Jonathan John appeared and acknowledged himself special bail in the above case.

Dec. 1790: Mr. Robert Campbell appeared and proved the last Will and Testament of Robert Blair deceased by oath of Jonathan John. Ordered that Magnis Cargill, Jonathan John, Jethro Moses, Thomas Vining and William Evans be appraisers of said estate.
[Note: Robert Blair was also a Tory.]
Dec. 1790---Petit Juror: Jonathan John.
*

Marlborough Co. S.C. Minutes of the County Court 1785-99 and Minutes of the Court of Ordinary 1791-1821:
March 1791. Ordered that Jonathan John who was empanelled on a Jury do immediately appear in Court on the said Jury.
Sept. 1791. Ordered that a process do issue vs. Jonathan John empanelled as a Juror at the last Court in a trial the State vs. William Nichols who absented himself before returning the verdict without leave of the Court.
March 1792. Executors of John Mitchell vs. Mathew Whitfield. Ordered that Tristram Thomas Esq. do take Jonathan Johns's examination in this case.
Sept. 1794---Petit Juror: Jonathan John.
31 Mar 1794, Marlboro Co. Deed Bk. AA, p. 387: Jonathan John and wife Mary conveyed to Robert Campbell for 10 pounds sterling, 150 acres of land which was granted to Griffith John, surveyed 12 Nov 1745, whereon Jonathan lately lived; another containing 100 acres, originally surveyed to Griffith John and surveyed for him 3 Jan 1743, adjoining the above tract; a tract of 40 acres originally granted to Anthony Pouncey and joining the before mentioned tract; and 12 acres between the first two tracts and the river, originally granted to Jonathan Asbury 22 Nov 1771. Total 252 acres. Lease for rent of 1 peppercorn. Witnesses: Peter Coggeshall, George Beasely. Signed Jonathan John and Mary x John.
April 1, 1794, Marlboro Co. Deed Book AA, p. 388: Jonathan and Mary Johns to Robert Campbell, for 210 pounds sterling. Release. Tract of 100 acres originally granted to Griffith Johns being the tract whereon Jonathan Johns lately lived. A tract of 200 acres adjoining the tract before mentioned originally granted to Griffith Johns and for him surveyed Jan. 3, 1743. Also 40 acres being part of a tract originally granted to Anthony Pouncey and sold by William Pouncy son of said Anthony to Enoch John. Also tract of 12 acres originally granted to Jonathan Ashberry Nov. 22, 1771, and conveyed by said Ashberry to Anthony Pouncy and then conveyed by said Pouncy to Jonathan John bounded SW by land out to Griffith NW by lands laid out to John Robertson and eastward by Pee Dee River. Witnesses: Peter Coggeshall and George Beasley. Signed: Jonathan John, Mary x John.
* *

ASAL JOHN,

1-son of Jonathan John (ca 1738) and Mary, was born ca 1760 in Cheraws District, Marlboro Co., S.C. He was married and had children, but we are not sure of their names. He must have been the Asal John who was involved in the incident of the capture of Thomas Ayers by the Tories. Asal would have been killed by the Patriots if Thomas Ayers had not "protected him with his own body because he was the son of his old neighbour, who was a peaceable man."[8] He later served in the Revolutionary War as a Private in Benton's Regiment in 1782. (Gregg, History). Shown in 1790 S.C. Census with 2 females and 3 males under 16.

* *

ELIJAH JOHN,

2-son of Jonathan John and Mary, was b. ca 1765 in Cheraws District, Marlboro Co., S.C. Shown in Cheraws District, S.C. in 1790 Census; one male under 16, two females. Records show "Alley John" was a juror in 1792, and "Aley John" was juror in 1794. [This was probably misspelling for "Eli."] Robert Campbell sued Aley and Jesse John in 1796; the same year he sued Thomas John. Oct 10 1793, Aley John gave Peter and Nathaniel Coggeshall, Merchants, a chattel mortgage on "one chestnut sorrel mare and other livestock." Jonathan John and wife Mary sold their land to Robert Campbell.

In his History, Gregg mentioned Azel, Jesse and Thomas John as being Privates in Benton's Regiment. [Azel was probably a nickname for Ezekiel.]

In the 1827 Land Lottery of Georgia was an Eli Johns, Revolutionary Soldier, resident of Burke Co.; drew Lot #125 in District 25, Section 1 (now Lee Co.).

* *

WILLIAM JOHN:

Possibly a son of Griffith John (ca 1710) and Margaret. He was b. ca 1735 in Del. He was a Sargent in the South Carolinia Militia in 1760 from Nov 3 to Dec 31, as shown in the records of the South Carolina Militia. He was on the Muster Roll of Captain John Hitchcock's Company, Jan. 15, 1760, and under Remarks: from Nov 3 to Dec 31. He was also listed on the Muster Rolls of Colonel George Gabriel Powell's Battalion of South Carolina Militia in the 1759 Cherokee Expedition.

* *

JESSE JOHN:

5- Born ca 1740, S. C., son of Griffith John (ca 1710) and Margaret. He was married to Sarah _____ and had at least seven children. He was a private in Benton's South Carolina Regiment in 1783, during the Revolutionary War. (Gregg, History...) In 1802 Deed he lists slaves beginning with negro man Jack and followed by Jen, Jude, Rose and Deannah.

---

[8]ibid, pp. 310-311.

Some records regarding Jesse John:

<u>Marlborough Co. Court Deeds</u>:

<u>Page 41</u>: 4 Sept 1786 George Trayweak of Marlborough Co., planter, to William Townshend son of John Townshend of same, planter, for L 5 sterling...150 A, part of 640 A granted to sd. Trayweak 5 June 1786, by William Moultrie...George Traweak (LS), Wit: Wm. Whitfield, John Hillson, Jesse John, Rec. 4 Sept 1786.

<u>Page 42</u>: George Trayweek, planter, to Benjamin Townshen of same, planter, for L 5 sterling...150 A, part of 640 A granted to sd. Trayweek 5 June 1786...George Traweak (LS), Wit: John Willson, JESSE JOHN, William Whitfield. Rec. 4 Sept 1786.

<u>Page 81</u>: 16 Jan 1787, George Traweck of Marlborough Co., to Lucy Blair, for L 30 sterling...200 A on E side Three Creeks, part of 1000 A granted to William Pouncy, 17 Dec 1772...George Traweek (LS), Wit: Robert Blair, Samuel Sparks, Jesse John. Rec. 5 Mar 1787.[9]

<u>Pp. 101-102</u>: 6 Mar 1787, Anthony POUNCY of Charleston Dist., to JESSE JOHN of Cheraw Dist., Marlborough Co., for Pounds 200 sterling...100 A, the SW part of tract of 200 A on NE side Pee Dee, granted to Andrew Slann 7 Jun 1751 by James Glen...Anthony Pouncy the Elder (Father of the within named Anthony Pouncy); sd. Anthony Pouncy the younger is Exr., at Court held at Long Bluff 15 Apr 1777...Anthony Pouncy (LS), Wit: Edwd Feagin, Benj. David, Wm. Branham. Plat included in deed showing adj. to Joseph Brown, Roger Pouncey and P. D. River. Rec 6 Mar 1787.[10] [Note: This name was probably Anthony Pouncey; see next entry. Holcomb had Powney.]

<u>Page 133</u>: 3 Mar 1787, Aaron Pearson of Marlborough Co., to Jesse John of same, for s20 sterling...100A, part of 405 A adjacent John Waring, John Hodges, Anthony Pouncey, John Westfield, Isham Elliss, William Pouncey and vacant land granted to William Henry Mills and conveyed to Aaron Pearson by L & R 17 & 18 Nov 1775...Aaron Pearson (LS) of Great Pee Dee, Wit: Edwd Feagin, Aaron Pearson, Jonathan Meekins (X). Rec. 4 June 1787.[11]

    In 1795, Jesse John made bill of sale to William and Anny John. (Book B, p. 1, Marlboro).

    In 1796, Robert Campbell vs. Aley and Jesse John. Campbell received judgment of $100 and costs. Suit discontinued in 1799. See below regarding Robert Campbell.

---

[9]Some South Carolina County Records, Vol. 1 Abstd. by Brent Holcomb, CRS, Pub. by So. Historical Press, p. 16.
[10]Ibid, p. 20.
[11]Ibid, p. 22.

A deed made in 1802 by Jesse John listed 150 acres and slaves beginning with negro man Jack and followed by Jen, Jude, Rose and Deannah. They were given to William John, son of Jesse John, by Jesse's brother Thomas John on 29 Aug 1775. This deed conveyed them back to Thomas John. (Book F, p. 315, Marlboro Co.)

Jesse made will 1 Aug 1803; left one shilling each to sons William and Henry; left 275 acres of land and other property to wife Sarah. At her death, to go to "my five younger children." Estate sued in 1806 by Robert McDairmaid. [McDermott ?] Judgment of $30.13 allowed in fall term 1806.

Children of Jesse and Sarah:

1. WILLIAM JOHN, b. ca 1760. Married Agnes, separated and made settlement 5 Oct 1814. John Miles was her trustee, and possibly a relation. On Aug 29 1775, Thomas John gave his nephew William John 150 acres of land and five negroes in fee simple "for and in consideration of the love and good will and affection I have and do bear towards my loving nephew, William John, son of Jesse John." Jesse conveyed this back to Thomas Jan 23 1802. (Bk. F, p. 315, Marlboro.) William John on 22 Apr 1813 conveyed property to three sons Jesse, Thomas & Elijah.
2. HENRY JOHN, named in father's will.
3. JESSE JOHN, one of five younger children. In 1828, John Miles sold 600 acres to Jesse and Francis John, land granted to John Miles.
4. FRANCIS JOHN, one of five younger children. In Index to Land Book N, p. 532, 1833, "Francis John to William Miles;" written by it "Error."

* *

THOMAS JOHN:

6- Born ca 1751, S.C., son of Griffith John (ca 1710) and Margaret. He married Elizabeth Brown Pouncey 6 Jan 1793. He died 15 Feb 1817 in Marlboro County. After his death, his widow Elizabeth married Peter Monroe and moved to Florida.

Thomas, along with Azel (Asal) and Jesse John, was listed as a private in Benton's Regiment that fought in the Revolutionary War.[12] In his "History...," Gregg wrote of an incident which involved a Tom John and Asal John with the Tories, and mentioned Tom and another Tory sleeping at 'old Jonathan's' house.' Thomas Ayer, who protected Asal, did not appear to be concerned about Thomas John, leading me to believe he was not the brother of Asal. He probably was related to Jonathan, as he slept at Jonathan's house. Apparently since Asal was so young when this happened, and later served in the Revolutionary Army, he was not further punished for this. From the above account, one can see Asal's father, probably Jonathan, was held in high esteem by his neighbors.

---

[12]iGregg's "History...", p. 409.

Military men of the area wrote communiques regarding efforts made to get Tories to lay down their arms and fight with the Patriots.

Some former Tories remained in this area after the War. But many of both sides in the War moved away. Robert Campbell, who was a soldier of the British, actually returned and became a prominent citizen of the area. Conflicts occurred, but much effort was made by officials to still animosities left over from the War.

Thomas John was in the 1790 South Carolina Census, Cheraw District, with four females. On 2 Nov 1784, he entered 200 acres of land; on 21 Jan 1785, he was granted 150 acres. He conveyed the 150 acres to nephew, William John. It was conveyed back to him in 1802. Robert Campbell sued Thomas in 1796, with the decision in favor of defendant. Thomas' son Daniel was administrator of his estate at his death. Estate settlement was in Court records from 1817 to 1824.

Thomas' children:

1. SUSANNA JOHN, was deceased in 1817.
2. PETER JOHN, was deceased in 1817.
3. THOMAS JOHN.
4. DANIEL JOHN, b. 11 Jul 1796; d. 29 Jul 1876.

Had other daughters, per census.
* *

THOMAS JOHN,
3-son of Thomas John (1751) and Elizabeth Brown Pouncey, was born ca 1780. In 1824 or 1825, he went to Georgia, then on to Florida. He lived in Leon County, near Tallahassee. Was said to have been in Indian wars and to have had his horse shot from under him. Had daughter MARY JOHN. Mary had daughter ANNIE who married Dr. Parks and lived in Atlanta, Ga. in 1903.[13]
*

A deed in early S. C. records, dated 23 & 24 June 1771, Samuel Wise of St. David's Parish, SC to Joseph Pledger, same, for 300 A on Naked Creek, adj. Philip Pledger, Burgess Williams, Thos. Bingham, has witnesses: Thomas Jones, Thos. Ellerbe, Jesse Councell. Proven before William Pegues 11 Nov 1775 by Thomas Elerby. Rec. 7 June 1787.[14]

Daniel John was said to have been one of the prominent members of Parnassus Methodist Church "in the long ago", along with Thomas Barnett, James Galloway, John L. McRae, Thomas Kinney, James Spears and W. R. Smith.[15]

---

[13]Journal of the John Family, by Cole.
[14]Anson Co., S.C..
[15]History of Marlboro County, by Thomas, p. 244.

Daniel administered his father's estate. Later he purchased the shares in the estate owned by his brother Thomas and his mother.

Daniel John was mentioned several times in "The History of Marlboro County" by Thomas, as an example of the early settlers who worked hard and inspired their children to do so. Examples:

"Some of those who emigrated from provinces further north are said to have driven their domestic animals across the country to their new homes, where abundant pasturage was found in the lowlands upon which their stock could graze. Large droves of cattle and horses ran wild through the forests and stock raising was at once a profitable business...Across the public road leading from Bennettsville to Blenheim, and a mile above the latter place, there flows a branch called "Horse Pen," which according to the statement of the late venerable Daniel John, who was born, lived and died near its confluence with the Three Creeks, got its name from a pen which was located at the fork and used for the purpose of entrapping wild horses in those early days."[16]

"Forty years ago, living in the locality of Blenheim, and on both sides of the creek, were a class of honest, honorable, intelligent and industrious men, who did not cringe and beg the world for a living, but by hard and well-directed licks made their own living...Daniel John taught his sons the possibilities of the Marlboro soil, and they yet know how to make big crops of big potatoes, heavy corn and heavy hogs, and plenty of cotton as a surplus crop."[17]

Daniel died 29 Jul 1876 and was buried in Parnassus Cemetery. For more on this family, see The John Family Journal, by Joada John Cole, available on microfilm at Mormon Libraries.
* *

Regarding EDWARD JONES:

He was also listed, along with William Johns, as being a 'Serjeant' in the South Carolina Militia in 1760, and was shown as a 'Serjeant' on the Muster Rolls of Col. George Gabriel Powell's Battalion of S. C. Militia in the 1759 Cherokee Expedition. He was shown in the Muster Roll of Captain Philip Pledger's Company. Also on these rolls for 1759/1760 were THOMAS JONES, ABRAHAM JONES, FREDERICK JONES, and JAMES JONES.

Anson Co. records show deed dated 10 June 1775 from JOHN MIKELL of Cheraws Dist., Craven Co., SC, planter, to AARON DANIEL for 200 a. in Welch tract, on Muddy Creek adj. Daniel James, Peter Smith, & vacant

---

[16]ibid, p. 50.
[17]ibid, p. 192.

land that was granted 13 Sept 1775 to John Mikell. Witnesses were: Edward Jones, Edward Feagin. Proven before Philip Pledger, J. P. by Edward Jones. 10 June (year not given). No rec. date.[18]

Anson Co. Deed Abstracts, V. 1: 1749-1757 show grants for Richard Jones in 174_ on 320 a. on E side Pee Dee; James Jones 640 a. on S side P. Don Beech Creek, granted 22 May 1741; Thomas Jones 200 a. on E side Pee Dee (sold 12 Apr 1749); and William Jones, shoemaker, 500 a. on N side of S branch of Fishing Creek.

* *

HISTORY:

In order to understand the events affecting the John's and other Welsh in the Pee Dee area, it is necessary to go back to recap events which took place before and during the Revolutionary War.

After 1737 when a committee was set up to see that no private contracts for land were made with the Indians, "the tide of immigration had now set in, and constant additions were made to the population on the Peedee."

On 11th May 1739, the following order was signed by the Council Chamber:

"That the Term for reserving the Welch Tract upon Peedee River for the sole benefit of the Welch and Pennsylvanians, be prolonged for the space of two years from the expiration thereof, in the month of August next, and all Persons are required to take Notice thereof at their Peril. By order of his Honour the Leut. Governor, and his Majesty's Honl. Council. ALEXR. CRAMAHE, C. C."

The sentiments regarding settlement by the Welch were favorable, and this led to immigration directly from Wales. An announcement was made in the Gazette 7th to 14th of July, [1739] stating that "Six Thousand Pounds shall be reserved out of the Township Fund as bounty for the first two hundred People above twelve years of age (two under twelve years…to be deemed as one) who shall arrive here from the Principality of Wales, and become settlers upon the Welch Tract upon Pedee, within the Space of Two Years from hence…"

Some of the people neglected to comply with the requirements of the laws respecting the Township Settlers. A list of them taken from Gazette of Aug 1743, and "whose neglect operated to the prejudice of others who might wish to come in"… (Pp. 56-57, History…Gregg.):

A List of Township Plots (on the Bounty) in the Surveyor-General's Office, August 15th, 1743:--
Queensborough Township.
Thomas James   650 acres   Oct 3, 1738.

---

[18]Anson Co., N.C. early deeds.

Name	Acres	Date	Year
Griffith Jones	300	Oct 4	
Griffith John	100	Sept 1	
William James	400	1	
John Newberry	350	2	
Henry Oldacre	50	4	
Hasker Newberry	300	5	
Evan Harry	100	30	
William Eynon	500	Aug. 23	
James Roger	50	26	
David James	400	27	
Thomas Evans	400	"	
Daniel Dousnal	200	"	
John Jones	250	Aug. 28	
Saml. Sarance	100	29	
Richard Barrow	150	"	
Evan Vaughn	350	30	
Abel James	300	31	
William Tarell	200	"	
Thomas Walley	50	May 18, 1740	
Philip James	250	21	
Sampson Thomas	400	23	
Jacob Buckles	250	24	
Peter Kishley	400	June 2	
John Evans	200	Feb 6	
John Newberry	100	Nov 22	1741
Wm. Tarell	100	Dec 9	
Thos. Evans	250	10	
Thos Evans	75	14	
Abel Evans	100	11	
John Evans'	100	"	
Mary Evans	300	13	
John Jones	100	Dec 1	
Jeremiah Rowell	150	16	
James Rowland	150	14	
Evan Vaughn	100	17	
John Westfield	300	"	
Thomas Elleby	250	"	
Simon Parsons	100	18	
John Carter	100	22	
Wm. Evans	50	23	
Job Edwards	200	28	
Daniel James	350	24	1742
John Jones	500	Dec 24	
David Harry	125	23	

237

David Harry	125	"
Philip James	100	27
Philip Douglas	300	29
William Carey	300	31
Mary Evans	200	Jan 1, 1743
David Malahan	150	4
Thomas Moses	220	5
William Jones	400	Jan 5
Nicholas Rogers	350	6
Thomas Evans	100	15
Thomas Evans	125	28
William James	200	29

"Upon perusing and considering the Memorial of George Hunter, Esq., Surveyor-General, relating to several Plots of land returned into and now lying in the Office of the said Surveyor-General, and which have remained in the said Office for many years, without any applications from the Persons in whose names the same are run, to have them taken out of the said Office, whereby other Persons are prevented from taking up the said Lands, and becoming tenants to his Majesty for the same: It is Ordered that the said List be published in the Gazette, to the intent that the several Persons interested in or claiming the same may apply for, and take out the said Plots, on or before the 1st day of January next; and in case of their neglecting so to do, their failure therein will be taken as a Disclaimer of their Rights to the said Lands; and the same Lands may and shall be granted to any other persons who shall duly apply for the same. A true copy. ALEXANDER GORDON, C.C."

These seem to be the claims they first took out, then abandoned when they moved up the river. However, there did seem to be other problems, as shown in the following Petition. [Gregg, p. 59.]

In the Council Journals was this record from Jan. 26, 1742/43.

"The Petition of part of the Inhabitants of the Welch Tract humbly sheweth: That we have left Pennsylvania and have transported ourselves to this Province by the encouragement given to settle this aforesaid Tract of land; but as some of us had our lands run out, and the Plots put into the Surveyor-General's office 4 years ago, and as we are so poor that we cannot get money to pay the charge of surveying and granting it, has discouraged many from coming over; and we are afraid the discouragement being so great, we not being sure of our grants, by reason of our poverty, that some that have come over will return from us again. So we, your Humble Petitioners, hope your Honr. and Honls. will take it into your serious consideration, what satisfaction it is to every man to have his titles to land secure, and will fulfill the encouragement given us that we should have our

238

lands granted us free from all charge of surveying and granting; and, as we are in duty bound, we shall ever pray, &c.

"Philip James	Abel James	Peter Roblyn
Jeremiah Rowell	Thos. Evans	Creen Vaughn
Philip Douglass	John Evans	Nicholas Rogers
Daniel Devonald	John Evans	Simon Parson
David Harry	John Carter	David Lewis
Thos. Evans	Wm. Kirby	Saml. Sorrency
Thos. Moses	Griffith John	Wm. Terrell
Mary Evans	Danl. Honchorn	John Jones
Jobe Edwards	Walter Downe	Abel Evans
Nathanl. Evans	David James	Wm. James.

The answer to this was:

"And upon reading and considering the Petition of Philip James, Abel James, Thos. Evans, and others, settlers in the whole Tract, praying that the charge of surveying and granting their lands might be all defrayed to them; it was the opinion of the Board, upon considering the Prayer of the Petition, as it appeared to the Board that they had desired the lands only to be reserved for a Term to them, which was accordingly done, and which term had been further enlarged for their benefit, but was not to have their survey of land carried through the offices at the publick expense, that being only for such Welch as should come from the Principality of Wales--that, as this Prayer of the Petitioners is what they had not before asked, nor had any reason to expect from this Government, it could not be regularly granted; but, for a further encouragement of the Settlers of the said Tract, it was the opinion of the Board, and so ordered, that for the first twenty barrels of good and merchantable white flour, of 200 lbs. weight neat each, which shall be made in the said Tract, and brought to the markets in Charles-town, there shall be paid to the makers thereof, upon proof of its being bona fide the produce of the said Tract, a bounty of 5 pounds currency for each barrel. Ordered, that the Clerk of this Board give a copy of the above minute to the Petitioners and the same to the Commissary."

Settlers largely increased between 1740 and 1743, with many being directly from Wales. Records showed an increase in people from other places, including some from England, Ireland and Germany. 'With main body of Welch or soon after came John Brown. He was born near Burlington, N.J. and brought up at Frankfort, in neighbourhood of Philadelphia. He was ordained May 7th 1750, and succeeded Rev. Philip James in charge of Welch Neck Church, briefly...continued to preach in different places. In 1738-39 came Robert Williams, b. Northampton, N.C. in 1717. In 1752, he was ordained, and became pastor for only a short time.'

As happens today, there was criticism regarding other religions. There was a rather disparaging account written by an Anglican missionary in 1745 of finding an "ignorant set of Anabaptists" in the Cheraws settlement, who, were "so possessed of the spirit of enthusiasm that there are about as many ignorant preachers as there were in Oliver's Camp."[19] [The Olivers were Quakers.] The laws of South Carolina were made to favor political power by people of the English or Episcopal Church. This was not changed by the Revolutionary War; in fact, not until after the Civil War.

The Acts of 1710 and 1712 stated no one should be employed as a teacher or schoolmaster in the public schools of the province unless he belonged to the English or Episcopal Church. These acts remained in effect until 1811. [History of Marion Co., by Sellers, pp. 33-38.] The Baptists set up their own schools in a few places, but education was sadly lacking in many areas.

Thomas Elerby [Ellerbee] came directly from England to Virginia, then to South Carolina. He was induced to settle in the Welch Neck. Gregg wrote that he was given permission by Daniel James to settle in the Welch Neck, where he first obtained two hundred and fifty acres, then later obtained a great deal more. He still had descendants there in Gregg's time.

Among grantees of land in Welch Neck in 1743 was Nicholas Rogers. He was one of the Welsh settlers. He had a son, Benjamin, who was the father of Col. Benjamin Rogers of Marlborough. Nicholas died in 1759.

About this same time, settlements were made lower down the river in what was afterwards called the Liberty Precinct, and then the Marion District, later Marion County. John Godbold, an Englishman who had long been a sailor in the British service, was among the first to settle there. He settled in 1735 near what later became the village of Marion. He married Elizabeth M'Gurney, and had John, James, Thomas, Elizabeth and Anne. His eldest son John married Priscilla Jones, and they had three sons, Zachariah, John and Jesse. Zachariah was a Captain in the Revolution. The elder John Godbold was a member of the Church of England, and died in 1765. The early writers were uncertain if Priscilla was daughter of John or Joseph Jones, brothers.

When the Welsh people first arrived, they had expected to raise hemp and flax. Indigo and rice were grown, and became very profitable. However, the most profitable business was stock raising, and many wild horses were rounded up. Cattle grew and flourished on the ample grass and plentiful supply of acorns. Gregg wrote that many of the early settlers drove their stock to market as far as Philadelphia. "Charles-town" provided a good market for the stock.

---

[19]Quoted by Leah Townsend in "South Carolina Baptists", p. 63. Quote taken from "Fordyce to the SPG, Dec. 2, 1742, Oct. 23, 1743, Nov. 4, 1745, quoted in Harvey Toliver Cook, Rambles in the Pee Dee Basin, South Carolina (Columbia, 1926), p. 157.

* *

JOHN TOWNSEND, whose grandfather, a miller, came to Pa. in the same ship as William Penn, wrote an account of a journey made in 1752 from Chester Co. to North Carolina that showed the difficulty of this journey.[20] The transcriber was an Archivist of the Chester Co. Historical Society. She transcribed this from Townsend's "Travels from Goshen in Chester County Pennsylvania To North Carolina, " and left the original spelling and punctuation. I put a few familiar names in brackets for clarity and aid in genealogical research.

"A Trip from Goshen to North Carolina in 1751
by John Townsend (transcribed by Dorothy Lapp)

Here follows a short memmerandom of some pertecular Accorrancies which happened to me John Townsend and Thomas Duglos [Douglas] and Anoch Eachus [Eichus] in our Travels from Goshon in Chester County pennsylvenia To North Caralinia (viz) Eachus and I set out from Goshon on ye third day of Febrary 1752 and Rid to the house of Aachl Duglas on picquay Creek being by Computation about 24 miles where we met with Thomas Duglas and all three Intend to persue our Jorney on tye morrow We had a blustring North-West Wind to face and Icey Rhods to travel but did not suffer much this day with ye Cold met with good Entertainment and hope for better Weather---I might have observed that the snow was a Considerable debth and Conjected to that degree that it would bare a man and almost a Horse—

The 4 day we only Rid about Ten miles to the House of one Patrick Carigan where we was Kindly Entertained the Rhoad full of Ice this place is mill Creek The 5th We Crossed Susquahanh, on the Ice and put up at John Wrights where we got good Hay for our Horses the Rhoads here are not so full of Ice; Very good Riding and moderate weather We left Thos Duglas this day at Lancaster Expecting every minnuet that he would overtake us 9 O'Clock no news of him yet The 6th Came to York Town about 10 o Waited there for Tho Duglas With much Impatiance till almost sun-set when he Came into Town and Informed us that business detained him at Lancaster till one O'Clock We are glad to meet and all Intend to persue our Jorney on the morros in Earnest. The great Rain we had before we set out which Caused so much Ice in the Roads never Reached here; for there is only a dry hard snow here and good Riding The 7th get out from York and Rid about fifty miles to the house of Joseph Wood in Fredricks County in Maryland; Where our Horses was well used and We paid well for it We past over good Land well Tembered for ye first 18 miles to Adon Furness; then barroney

---

[20]Chester County Historical Society, West Chester, Pa., Journal of, Vol. 1, No. 2, Spring 1976, p. 17. Permission to publish all or part of this trip granted Apr 28, 1998, by Jeffrey Rollison, Director of Collections.

and some pines untill We came nere to the pipe Creeks being Two bold streams of Water about two mile apart both Runing into Menockecy; then better Land untill we Came to ye sd. Woods Who is a smart Intellegable man he Informs me that their next seaport is the head of petapscicoa being between 40 and 50 miles and that it is about 80 to Anopulas; he has a good minde and lives plentifully.

The 8th Rid to Fredricks Town a pritty little Cuntry Villidge very Well set out with Taversn (but we Crossd Menockecy three miles before We Came to Town being a fine large stream Runing south-ward to Potomuck) we made but a short stay here then Rid to George Matthews es where we put up being 7th day we mean to make some stay here We rid in all but about 18 miles this day gloryous good Land here; we are got almost past ye show and have had fine level Rhoads all ye way from Lancaster---Our Main Corse S W nere st s

The 9th went to Pataumoc found it inpassable Came back and must Wate tho Impatiiante we know not how long

The 10 took a Walk to one of the highest Round heads on ye blue Mountain which shews one of the finest Landscapes I Ever saw we saw the Locke of ye two Ridges at Twenty Miles distance and the sugar loaf on the other side and Wished for a good spy-glass To have seen Philadelphia

The 11th did nothing but saunter and go to see Esquire Darnal---

12th; I went on foot down to Potomoc to vew ye River & found it no better; nither fit to Foard Ferry nor go on ye Ice all Ragged and full of holes and no Sighn of Clearing this makes our case look desperate but We must bear it; no going back for we foresee that Susquehannah is in ye same bad pickle

When Enterprising methods faile and all thy strength is try.d

Lay by thy Oar and slack thy sails

Let patiance be thy guide

Ye 13th We Resolved to try again so we Cross'd the mountain and Came to ye River on the back side and found it opne in divers places but most on ye East Side at going on at Length we found a place where we got onto ye Ice on foot and tried it all ye way over with handspikes and the farther We went the firmer it was; Came back and striped our horses and took them on at a point of Ice that Came to the shore not above 6 or 8 foot wide; it bent under our horses some distance from ye shour but proved strong Enugh to bear them onto ye strong Ice so we got them all over one at a time then Carryed our Luggage on our backs and after Crossing 6 or 8 times we landed all our treasure Without receiving any hurt for which We have Cause to be very thankfull to our great Deliveror who is the auther and preserver of our being.

Well We are now to proseed down the River to find our main Road again which we did in five miles Riding and happyly Came to the house of ye Widdow Stear a pensylvenia Women who let us have good hay for our

Horses and stableing and a good bed for ourselves; this day we got forwards about 12 miles This is Farefax County-

ye 14th set forwards and got about 30 miles with much difficulty the Roads being very bad the frost braking and the Ice in the Creeke will neither bear us over nor readyly brake but sometimes thros us in; we Crossed several stout Creeks this Day; first Goos Creek then broad Run and several others less it Rained some this day and looks like a thaw We put up this night With a new settler in farefax County Can git nothing for our Horses but fed them with some Oats we had With us and hobbled them and bded them and turned them in the Woods

Ye 15th we got our horses Just by gave them some more oats and set out; it Rained all this day and the Roads are as bad as well Can be Duglas fell into Bull Run (which dives farefax from prince Williams County) and got much wet, it was Cold and very Uncomfertable; we had another Broad Run to cross this day wch runs to rappahannack as the formor did to Potomock then we Crossd Ceder Creek & some others and with much fetague we got to ye Garmain [German] town being about 28 miles Where we put up for second day Morning got some oats and hay for our horses and are likely to fare pritty well all the way from potomoc to this place our main Corse is very near south some what westwardly. the Widdow tells us she is within a days Journey of the Landing below the falls of Potomoc

The man at our next Lodgings talks of 25 miles to his next Landing at Occoquan from the Widdows to the Jarman [German] Town the Land is mostly Barrony Covered with Low scrubby White Oake mostly; the soyl is Redish and marly but thin low flat and Leavel and this settled mostly With Neagro Quarters whose Children go as naked a they Came into ye world and look as Black as minks and as slick as moles and are hung like stallions

the 16th; this Jerman Town is a small settlement of antiant [ancient] Honest Dutch men from whom the place took the name they are now Increased to 10 or 12 famelyes. We put up with one Peter Hits a chearfull old Chap and his Wife is as harty as he so we like our Lodging Very Well which is Very soft and Warm---

Ye 17th Set out and Rid about 10 miles through a dissolate baron untile we Came to the north branch of Rappahanneck River which is a Large rapped stream and now a smart fresh hoever we forded it; there is very good Land near ye River side; Thence we Came near 20 miles to ye south Branch most of ye way pritty good Land mixt with white oaks and Lofty pines this is also a large stream and full; we got over Just before dark and put up near the old Cort House after having Rid near thirty miles this day we git nothing but Corn for our Horses here This is in Orrange County but the Court is now Removed at 12 miles distance from here They tell me that we are now Thirty miles Distance from ye Tide water on rapahannack which is their nearest Landing Fredrecksburgh

We had a Crooked Road this 4 day but our main Couce was S W nearest south---

the 18th; We rid some miles up ye side of ye south branch of Rappa;k and are very pleased with the Beauty of the River and goodness of ye Land But mis like the Extortion of the people who make us pay 8d for an armfull of fodder and 6d for abed and one shilling for a supper on Hoe Cake and Rashers and turkey too

It is twelve miles from the old to the new Orange Court House which I like the best of any Land I yet saw in vergency it's a little hilley with pleasant Riseings and fallings and ye Land looks good from thence we went about 18 miles through fine Lofty groves of Pines and ye Land looks firtal too we put up at an audenary in Levicey County and got fodder for our horses:

If I had Room and time I would discribe something that pertends to be a smith he set a shoe for Duglas and make us of his pockit knif for a Butris his tongs for pincers his shoeing hammer Came of in his Work his hand Hammer and sledg was Battered to ye Eye and looked as If they had been seven years battering down stone walls.

We crossed no Large Water this day it is very good Riding agane &c frost is out and ye ground setled and the Frogs begin to Croak—

Our main Corse S-W-nearst t S –

Ye 19th We find it 9 miles from McCawleys where we put up to ye N Branch of James River Secutarys foard a fine bould stream and Rapid we thence Rid by Computation 25 miles to Albamarl Court-house upon ye south Branch which is a large River we ferryed over in a little Rottne Boat and Rid about a mile untill we Came to high Land and then pitched out Tent fed our horses Hobbled and Belled them made a fine fire of pine knots Rosted a Phesent With some Neats Tongue and made a good supper then made our Beds and lay down to sleep and Rested very well; we think this is better and Cheaper than their Ordanarys and Intend (God Willing) to follow this way for ye futer, our Roads this day were very much Up and down hill mostly Covered with Pine trees; Our Cours S by W fine warm weather Birds singing and frogs Croaking merryly

The 20th; can't find our Horses they are gone out of hearing we unted until ye middle of ye afternoon Can hear nor see nothing of them at length we saw their Tracks in a Path that leads down to the moidl of Slate River Conclude that T D shall persue them; but by the Way he had got a little horse in a swap Just before and Lest he should run away we tyed him to a sapling so that he was now ready to persue the rest with; we fear they are stolen agree that he shall follow them untill he gits word of them; we yet the mean time are to Carry our Luggage to ye next House and then make farther sarch. It hapned that Just after he was gon we met a nagro who told us they were at a house 2 or 3 miles down James River we went directly and had ye lock to git them by sun-set; I took one of them and persueded – after Riding

244

12 miles through a dissolate pine barron without a house I Came to the place where he put up. we got his hors and about mid-night got back to the house where we had Carryed our things This sarch after our houses [horses] gave me an oppertynity of seing the land about the River which is all hils and vales; as the river here makes a Neck, there it Draughts, In almost Every two forlongs making towards it each way and seems only a ridge in ye middle for ye Road; these are so preseppetous that I dare say some of them are an hundred foot deep and the tops of the hils on Each side not above 100 Yards apart there is Excellent Rich Bottoms on the River side and ye largest and farest white-Oaks I ever saw our horses had followed ye path aforesd 4 or 5 miles and then took through ye road to ye place we found them in

The 21 we set out Early and in 12 miles Crossed the slate River highup many miles from where we Was the night before then took a smale path for a near Way and after Riding about 21 Miles over pine barrons and hilly Ways Came to Stephen Sanders his mill Could git no fodder so resolve to go on till we Come to a Conveniant piece of Woods and Camp again that our horses may have ye benefit of ye Wood grass did so and Douglass Was to keep a wake a while to mind their motions: Just after We fell aslep he Caled and told us they were going off we followed as faxt as we Could but they ran so that we Could not overtake them I run through the Bushes sometimes upe some times down untile I Catched Ds new horse he not being so much used to hobbles as ours and when they Came to me Ds mounted him and with much ado got before ye rest we Caught them and then Could not find ye way back to our fire; we went many miles back and forward and after midnight found a house Within a mile of them; the man Was sivel and after staying with him untill day light he With our discription took us to our things

22nd; Rid about 26 ms this day Came to the house of David Immanuel [Emanuel] in ye County of Luningburg where we intend to spend the first day of ye Week but by the way We foarded Appamattock which devides Albamarl from Amelia County which we Crossed a part of and so came in ye afore sd; Luningburg; it rained verry hard some part of this day and we very wet we are now got past ye pine trees for ye present the Land here is hilly and well watered our Corse ye same as before

23rd Rested our selves and horses- and went to ye Widow Verners and spent ye day and night with her She made us very welcom they tell us here they are about 80 ms from the Navegable part of James River at Worwick; or Appamattock point their Land here seems then and sanddy not Well timbered Cheifly short Oaks and scrubs

24 went 10 miles to Jonathan Vernons and liked his Entertainment so well that we are prevailed on to stay all night and towards evening took a Walk with him about a mile to Stanton River which is ye N branch of Rhon Oak a beautiful stream about 100 yards Wide abounding with good bottoms and fine Timber on its banks

The 25th Rid to Richards Dogons [Dougan] and forded the Cub Creek thence foarded Stanton River so on over Terrable and Diffecult untill we Crossed Bannester River on a high Bridg that I thought haxerded our Lives; so on to the jouse of Patrick Boyd on Dan River in all about 30 miles where We propose to stay abd Rest our Horses

The 26th; took a walk to see Tho Douglass his Land there which lyes on Dan River where I saw Oaks Poplar sweet gum Birch Ash Grape-vines Big Enugh for Cables for a first Rate Man of War Button wood popp au pines and divers others sorts of Wood all growing together on as good Land as any under ye Cannapeys; we Live well here and so dos our horses and Costs us nothing but we must not expect such Quarters much longer they filed our Bottle with good Rum here when we went away all on free Cost; our Land Lord Patrick is a harty Pensylvenia Irish Man who Usecs us with much Civillety and we Receive his kindness with Greatitude

I forgot to mention that among ye rest here is the tellest Hickery, and Largest Walnuts I Ever Saw some of them 3 ½ foot over and more- here We saw Mary Buckley a Woman formerly Noted in Pennsylvenia by the name of Woolven

The 27 Went up Dan R about three miles and ferryd over at John Boyds Where we Intend to stay one night the people here live on the banks of a pleasant River land have as good Land as hart Could Wish; have great plenty of Corn and Beef and poark and might be happy but that they have a Certain Kanker among them Which (if they Cannot provide an Antedote for) Will Infailablely Distroy some of them; it is know by the name of a Stile and the People are so far from distroying it; that they seem Rather to pay it a kind of Hommage and make it their boosom friend by which means it arives at their Interiors and so feeds on their Intrails in a distroctive manner; when we we reflect seriously it is shocking to think that Reasonable Creatures should provide means for the support of ye Body and that them very Means should prove distroctive booth of body and soul; and at the same time so benumb their Reactional faculty as to bring those things Insenceablely upon them; it shows how much need we have to be dayly subdueing our Lusts and Passions: and (according to the directions of our great Redeemer) overcoming Evle with good. We are here about 110 miles from appamattock point where is a good markit for Beef and Poark skins and Furs and where they are Supplyed with what Commodetyes they want at Reasonable rates.

When I behold the Warmness of ye Weather ye forwardness of ye Trees the springing of ye Grass & Pleasentrey of ye season all kinds Rejoyceing it puts me in mind of dateing my memmores

May the first---

The 28th set out sometime this forenoon and Rid about 20 miles and at night Camped in ye Woods Cross hobbled our Horses to prevent their leaving os Made a fire of pine Knots and slept well by the way We Crost ye waters of Highcho Where is a good Bottom Land and Timber but poor up-Land Chefly scrubby Pines and Oaks

The 29 Rid about 25 miles to the House of James Taylor on the Yeano by ye Way Crost flat River which together with little River make Nooce R where within 70 miles of this place ye people Expects soon to have a place of Trade they say ye River is passable so far for Barges &C. althp it is not much of a poart yet they have been oblidged to goto the Navegable part of Roan Oak heretofore; which is 100 miles from the aforesd heads of Nooce [Neuse] River here is ye best and longest body of Upland I have seen in my Travels sence I Left pennsylvenia finely situated with pleasant Hills and veals and abboundance of Hickery Trees

March ye 1st; We stay this first day of ye week With James Taylor took severall Walks and like ye Land very Well but see no good Low Lands for meadowing but I see the Climate is so warm that there is no great need of them this day I saw Peach Tree Buds full Blown ye 2nd; went through ye plane fields which is as good Up Land as any I have seen here so on in about fifteen miles Riding we Crossed the Yearno River which makes the Cape fear inlet 200 ms from here on which stands Willmington. I should observe that we went near ye same Cores S by W untill We Came to Yearno thence to the Haw R near due West; Now We intend to Look about us Conclude to apay a Visset to Kane Creek so turn to the left Cross ye almance branch and stear S E over most horrable Bearons where ye black Oaks Looks like an old Decayed Orchard about as high as an old dead apple-tree and as scrubby for 12 or 14 miles where we Came to ye house of James Willimes [Williams] on Kane Creek who has ye best Grice mill have have seen Either in Vergeny or Carolina; he declared to us that it would gring 10 Bl of Corn in 24 hours and that ye Mill-well and mill-House stones Iron and Dam and all other Cost his own labour Included Cost him near Ten ponnds and altho this looks alittle Incredeble yet his behaviour to us obledges us to believe him

we stayed here all night and the 3rd; set out down Kane Creek E N E from Hugh McLoghlons [McLaughlin] which we found is 5 miles Riding he was not at home but his Wife and Val; Hollingsworths [Valentine] Wife and Samuel Allins [Allen] Wife were all here and seem very well Pleased with their Change of Climate they have Plenty of Vitling but look new settleors I Saw Garden Pea-Vins Come up Green here and other things Proportionablely forward after some hours stay we set out W N W up Kane Creek for ye trading Path agane and in 6 miles Came to John Wrights and stayed all night We do not like their land here very Well it is somewhat broken and stoney Seems not very timbered and but little of it but what is worse; however it Pleases them and I am satisfied

The 4th set out agane for ye Tradeing path Which we Came into in about 15 m- Riding but by ye Way we are but 23 miles from ye Haw foard Strate on our Cours We Rid near 30 miles this day Crossed deep River and

Camped in ye Woods where we found good picking for our horses; fine pleasent Moderate Weather, I do not Remember to have seen above one frost sence we left Potomock

The first County we Came into in Carolina is Gramwoll County in which are Highcho and Yeano Lands, ye second is Bleaton where in is Kane Creek & c The third is Anston County at Atkin foard &c

The 5th; Rid about 30 miles along ye Trading path Crossed Abbott Creek and at night lay in the Woods. We seem now to be on ye borders of ye Land of promis however I think we have past Enough of ye wilderness for it, I may say safely that the last 40 miles of our Journey has been over such an Inhospetable dessert that it never Can be habbitable for the Human Specise; but we are now eithin 7 miles of Atkin River and Expect to see great mattere soon

The 6 we Crossd Atkin R at ye Trading foard and I Realy do not see such Land yet as I Expcd it may be firtal Enugh and I believe Will produce any sort of Grane very well yet I see nothing so Exterodenary as to Induce me to plant my self in a place so remote from all Trade and Commerce Go which way they Will I Cant find that they Can Come to a good markit in less than 250 miles That is Either Charles Town S Carolina or Appamattock point Vergeny. however we proseeded this day as far as George Cathes [Cathey] in the Atkin Irerish settlement 22 m from where we lay nere abbots Creek we stayd here all night and find they have plenty of stilled Liquar which makes them merry but our Landlord was Civel Enugh

Their Land here is very good and there is plenty of good Meadow ground almost Ready Cleared but the fire Ruens the Timber on Up-Land and makes very hard Grubing but this place is Inviting Enugh if the people Were good Christians and a Seaport Within reach; above all I admire the goodness and Temperature of the Climate and helthfuleness of the place; it is Enugh to fill ye brest of an Emperror With Infutions of Joy and Chear up the Hart of a slave to see such fine Warm Weather at this time of the Year and feel ye pleasant Breeses that seem refreshing to every thing in a Land that lyes in fine high Ridges

The 7th; Went to John Jiles [Giles] and from there to James Cathes [Cathy] and took a View of ye settlement Went to Mr. Carr's and thence to the House of James Elexander [Alexander] where we Intend to stay untile 2nd; day there is plenty of good meadow Ground here but they have the Vanity to ask L150 for a plantation Containing 640 acres

The 8th went to their meeting where we had an opportunity of seing most part of ye Inhabetance Collected in one spot Which I suppose amounted to near an hundred pritty well dressd people; No bad Collection Considering the remote part of ye World We are in

Our mane Corse from the Yeano to this settmt seems to be near West; Well eachus and I begin to think of Turning our Cours towards home accordingly we make some provision for that porpose against the Morrow

Whilst we were at James Elexanders his son Billy gave us a Relation of ye
Ways and Manners of some of his Contrey people one of which in as few
Words as I can Repeat it is as followeth (viz) he knew a man in his way to
ye Landing who was so much of a gentle-man that he used to play all day
long on ye fiddle; whilst the gentleman himself danses to it; they have says
he nine or ten Children who spend their wole time in playing at Cards;
except their oldest son who is oblidged once or Twice in a week to go to the
woods with his gun and kile a Deer which having don they take the skin
directly to the next Convenient place and purchace a Bushel of Corn with it;
which they Eat With the Carkas and so every one to his delight agane whlst
that lasts and when it is gon jack must repeat he futague of ye gun agane; he
added that the old gentlewoman was of such strict Morals that she would
not allow of the least deccimulation in her family; but on ye Contrary if one
of her Children Complained that the other used foul play at cards she would
start from her fiddle and like a Mattron of veracity give ye offender a blow
and with it repremand him in ye following manner D-n you what will you
Cheat your brother I will larn you to Cheat you son of a B-h &c

The 9th about three this afternoon parted with my friend and fellow
Travelor Tho D not without some Concern; he designing for Charls Town
and we for pennsylvenia"
*

In handwriting which appears to be old was written :
"The Names of ye Childen of John and Deborah Townsend of
Thornbury in Chester County with time of their Birth.

John and James Townsend were Born on the 16th day of the ____
[indecif.] in ye year 1756 John about two o'Clock in ye morning and James
about Ten at night the same day.

Rebecca Townsend was born on ye Tenth day of ye Sixth month 1758
near 7 o'Clock in ye Evening

John Townsend of Thornbury Chester County Departed this Life the 7 of
ye 4 month 1759 near 1 [?] o clock in ye afternoon."

Several of the people mentioned in this journal had land grants that can be
found in land grants compiled by Brent Holcomb for Anson and
Mecklenburg, N.C. and in his North and South Carolina deeds.

The "Journal of West Chester" intended that Townsend's return journey
would be published by them at a later date. When I was unable to find a
copy of the Journal with the return journey, I called the Historical Society in
West Chester and learned it was never printed. I was sorry to hear this, as it
was probably also very interesting, and I'd love to read it. There was a John
Townsend in the Welsh Tract Church in New Castle, and I feel sure this one
was a relation. Townsends were Quaker's when they first came to Pa., and

many remained Quakers. Some Townsends migrated to South Carolina, and John Townsend's trip was for the purpose of looking the area over.
* *

The main problem with the Welsh settlement was the floods caused by the river. The settlers built their homes close to the Pee Dee River, so they could be close to transportation, close to each other for social reasons, and for protection from the Indians. The river drained into the bottoms and caused swampy conditions that made an unhealthy environment. It was many years before this condition was improved.

'Welch planted themselves mostly immediately on the river and made locations of lands in small parcels. Being in an isolated wilderness, they selected such quantities as suited their present needs... [this] enabled them to concentrate against the sudden incursions of the Indians, by whom they were surrounded. They met weekly with neighbors to worship. Had no court of justice. They were open and sincere, making no profession of feeling which did not exist. Distinguished for sobriety and moderation."[21]

In his history of this area, Rev. Gregg did not write anything about the interchangeable way the surname Jones and Johns was found in the records, as indicated by earlier writers, and perhaps he did not know. Probably by the time he lived in the area around 1850, the people had settled on either a John or Jones spelling. The way the names were written earlier, both as John and Jones, was considered correct, as previously stated.

The Griffith John written about in these early records was easily the same as Griffith Jones. In cases where some children used John, and the other Jones, it was usually the elder son who used John. As shown in the list of Township plots surveyed in 1738, Gregg listed Griffith Jones for 300 acres, and Griffith John for 100 acres. Griffith John's will showed these amounts still owned by him when he died, with son Enoch inheriting some and son Jonathan the rest. After Enoch died, his land was apparently left to Jonathan.

The land records help to see the number of children these people had, as they were allowed fifty acres for each person. The records show occasions of people applying for more land as their children arrived from Pennsylvania or Delaware, or when they had other children.

Leah Townsend, Ph.D., in "SOUTH CAROLINA BAPTISTS 1670-1805" Genealogical Publishing Co., Inc., Baltimore, 1974, covered a lot of the early land records of the people associated with this church.

Her research covered the land records of Griffith Jones and Thomas Jones, and the surveys before 1743 which they did not take up.

Several records of land grants in the name of David Jones and David Lewis were found in the surrounding areas, but at this date it would be impossible to say just which ones apply to the Baptist group. I didn't find any in the Queensborough District. Joada John Cole wrote there was a land

[21]Paraphrase Gregg, History..., pp. 66, 67.

grant to David Johes in 1740, for land in the Darlington District of S.C., land on the Pee Dee River.[22] (Grant #277, Land Grant Bk. 12, N.C.) It might have been for one of the sons of the Jones'.

A John Jones also took out 100 acres west on Pee Dee north of his own land in the Welsh Track, Prince George Winyah, in 1741; 500 acres in Welsh Tract, Prince George Winyah, in 1742. Townsend also gave references to other surveys at later dates by John Jones, as shown in Plats IV, pp. 145, 188, 190, 191, 198, 199, 200, 201, 204, 206, 207, and p. 435; page 262 in Plat VII; and pages 112, 145, 197, 202, and 471 in Plat IV. Some of these later ones were probably for a John Jones Jr., and possibly Griffith John's son John or Jonathan.

Other information of interest regarding land surveys:
Furman, Charleston Assoc., p. 55, 1752, <u>Catfish Constituents</u>: Thomas James and wife (650 acres in Queensborough Township on Griffith Johns' land, 1738; William Jones (400 acres in Prince Frederick, northeast on Peedee, 1742; 141 acres at Pine Bluff in the Welsh Tract, southwest side Peedee, 1747.
P. 96, ibid. ...William DeLoach and wife Judith, 200 acres on southwest side of Peedee in the Welsh Tract in 1746, bounding east on Peedee, 150 acres northeast side of Peedee in the Welsh Tract in 1746, touching David James, Thomas Evans, Sr., and John Jones Jr.
* *

MINUTES OF THE WELCH NECK BAPTIST CHURCH 1737-1841...

A list of the members was taken in 1759, with notations being made later, so some of interest are shown here:
PHILIP DOUGLASS (died Oct. 17, 1766)
SAMUEL WILDS
JOHN EVANS
THOMAS EVANS (died Jn. 28, 1785)
SARAH JAMES
ELIZABETH WILDS
WILLIAM JAMES
GRIFFITH JOHNS (died Aug. 1, 1765)
ABEL EVANS (died June ?)
PHILIP EVANS (died 5 Dec. 1771)
JAMES HARRY (Dismissed to Cashaway)
EDWARD JONES
ELEANOR EVANS (died Feb. 16, 1765)
MARGARET EVANS
ANNE JONES (now DOUGLASS)
        (Died Apr. 12, 1766)

---

[22]John Family Journal, Joada John Cole.

SARAH JAMES
MARY HOLLINGSWORTH
HOWEL JAMES
MARGARET JOHN
JAMES JAMES (died 21 Nov. 1769)
WILLIAM JONES (died July 2nd)
DAVID EVANS
VALENTINE HOLLINGSWORTH (died
    Aug. 6th)
ELEANOR HARRY (Now JONES)
    (Died Apr. 20, 1745)
MARY JONES (died Dec. 1751)
SARAH JAMES
_____ JONES (now McIntosh) (died Dec. 30th, 1764)
MARTHA ROACH (now EVANS)
SARAH JAMES
THOMAS JAMES
SARAH BOOTH (now WILDS)
MARY WILDS
ELIZABETH EVANS
JAMES ROGERS
[Other names defaced and could not be deciphered.] Excerpts:
1759 April 5 Rev. Mr. NICHOLAS BEDGEGOOD of Charleston called.
SAMUEL REREDON suspended for obscene conversation. The Rev. Mr.
JOHN BROWN & SARAH his wife dismissed to Cashaway Church.
Apr. 15th JAMES JAMES suspended for beating his neighbor. Messengers
to ANNE WILLIAMS for absenting herself from church...
July 1 WILLIAM JAMES baptized & received into full communion.
JACOB D'SURRENCY suspended - letter of admonition, etc.
Aug. 9 DAVID HARRY, SENR. Died. Rev. Mr. WILLIAMS applied to
absend himself, etc.
Sept. 19 Departed the Life JOHN JONES (end of page 3)
1759 Oct. 6 ...Letter to Rev. Mr. WILLIAMS. Three messengers were
appointed to go to Association to meet in Charleston Nov. 12th.
* *

    The people again did as they had when they settled in New Castle, Del.
They moved and set up other churches nearby; they provided ministers for
weak congregations up and down the river, using Welsh Neck as the main
or constituent church. Charleston, or Charles Town as it was called, had the
main Baptist Church, but the Welsh Neck soon became the second center of
Baptist influence in the province. There were churches such as Catfish,
Mars Bluff, Cashaway, Beauty Spot, Lynches Creek, Cheraw Hill, and
many others.

Some excerpts to bring the church activities down to 1766:

Jan. 5th Messengers sent to Mr. WILLIAMS. Letter of admonition to JACOB DE SURRENCY.

Feb. 2nd Mr. WILLIAMS, refused to receive the Letter a second time. JOHN BOOTH publicly suspended.

March 8th RACHEL DAVID, wife of JENKYN DAVID, was baptized. Called Mr. BEDGEGOOD as pastor, he accepted. Admitted a Member from Charleston Church.

March 26th VALENTINE HOLLINGSWORTH departed this life.

April 15th JAMES JAMES suspended for beating his neighbor. Messengers to ANNE WILLIAMS for absenting herself from church (end of page 4.)

1760 June 1st Messengers sent to ANNE WILLIAMS and Mr. WILLIAMS. PHILIP DOUGLASS ordered publicly suspended for drinking to excess and to the public reproach of Religion. WILLIAM JAMES, JUNR. ordered to be publicly suspended for the same crime.

July 1 ....JACOB D'SURRENCY suspended - absenting himself from worship. WALTER DOWNES suspended - letter of admonition, etc.

July 5th Messengers failed to see Mr. WILLIAMS (to try again). Inquiry directed to be made why ELEANOR the wife of ABEL EVANS doth not live with her husband. Let Friday to be kept as a day of public prayer during the present public calamities and war. Ordered that every quarterly meeting Deacons shall receive such donations as God shall be pleased to influence the hearts of the Members to give. Letter to be sent to Mr. WM. ROWEL and his wife living at the Congarees directing them to apply for a Letter of dismission.

Aug. 2nd Church covenant adopted (end of page 5)

Aug. 2nd Church covenant continued. Written in margin: This covenant was signed by the Pastor and the Church. We deem it unnecessary to copy the names as they can be seen by referring to the original. (End of page 6.)

1760 Aug. 2nd THOMAS JONES was baptized and received full communion. JOHN BOOTH asked to be restored.

Sept. 6th PHILIP DOUGLASS appeared before the Church and acknowledged his sin.

Nov. 1st WILLIAM KILLINGSWORTH died.

Dec. 7th Messenger sent to Mr. and Mrs. WILLIAMS.

1761 Jan. 4th Mr. WILLIAMS and his wife ejected Jan. 5th.

Jan. 9th HANNAH EVANS died.

Jan. 26 WILLIAM JAMES, Esq. And MARTHA ROGERS died.

Jan. 28 SARAH JAMES wife of WM. JAMES, Esq. Died.

Jan. 30 DANIEL MONAHON died.

1761 Jan. 31 JAMES JAMES who was suspended Apr. 5, 1760 was this day restored to his place. Messenger sent to JANE POLAND (absenting and selling liquor.)

Feb. 11 ELIZABETH WILDS died (end of p. 7.)

1761 Apr 4 JANE POLAND suspended. JOHN BOOTH - repentence - to take his place tomorrow. MARTHA MARTIN received upon examination and recommendation. ELISHA JAMES baptized and received full communion. Messenger sent to JACOB D'SURRENCY.

June 6 Messenger again to JACOB DE SURRENCY. JAMES HARRY suspended (drinking)…

July 4 JACOB DE SURRENCY made confession - but remained under suspension.

Aug. 1 ELIZABETH SIMONSON (formerly JAMES) was suspended under suspicion of her having been guilty of very abusive language.

Sept. 6 … JAMES HARRY again received. JOSHUA EDWARDS publicly suspended. ... JAMES HARRY, MARY HARRY and ELIZABETH WILDS (the wife of GEORGE) residing near the Church at Cashaway, requesting a letter of dismission; which was granted. ABEL EDWARDS received from Cashaway by letter. (End of p. 9.)

1761 Oct. 3 WILLIAM THOMAS and wife and JOHN BOWEN received by Letters from Church at Cashaway.

Dec. 24 HANNAH HOWEL died.

1762 Jan. 2 Mr. WILLIAMS (under excommunication) made application to join the Association in Charleston, etc. DAVID & MARTHA EVANS guilty of criminal conversation before marriage - suspended. Messenger to JACOB DE SURRENCY.

Feb. 6 Mr. WILLIAMS refuses to comply etc. Messenger to JACOB DE SURRENCY. Messenger to PHILIP HOWEL, and one to WALTER DOWNES. SARAH HICKS received by letter from Cashaway Church.

March 6 PHILIP HOWEL admonished for his faults.

Apr. 3 A messenger of care sent to WILLIAM JAMES under suspension. Another sent to JACOB DE SURRENCY. Same to DAVID EVANS and to MARTHA EVANS. (End p. 10.)

1962 May 1 … MARTHA EVANS repented, admitted to communion. JACOB DE SURRENCY was again sent to.

June 5 WILLIAM JAMES professing repentance was restored…

Aug. 1 MARY HICKS was baptized 31st July.

Sept. 4 TABITHA JAMES was baptized. Complaint against WILLIAM JONES for drinking excess.

Messenger to JANE POLAND and to GRIFFITH JOHN for non-attendance.

Oct. 2 … ELIZABETH COUNSEL examined (was formerly baptized in No. Carolina) and received...

1763 Feb. DAVID EVANS restored to Communion. WILLIAM JONES publicly suspended.

June 4 ELIZABETH SIMONSON suspended (lives in wilful separation from her husband).

July 2 ROBERT HICKS baptized.

1764 Sept. 1. Mr. WILLIAM JAMES suspended (drunkenness). Mr. WILLIAM JONES restored. ELIZABETH SIMONSON restored.

1965. Feb. 16 Concluded public suspension not to be practiced in this church. ROBERT HICKS died Feb. 12th. Mrs. ELEANOR EVANS died Feb. 16th.

Mar 2 Mr. WILLIAM THOMAS suspended (drunkeness). Mrs. POLAND restored. Mr. BEDGEGOOD Letter of Dismission to Church in Charleston.

May 4 Miss HANNAH SUTTON baptized by Rev. Mr. OLIVER HART. Mr. PUGH appointed to write a letter to Mr. PHILIP HOWEL to come to the Church. Also to go to Mr. JOSHUA EDWARDS and to Mr. WILLIAM THOMAS to admonish them. Mr. JOHN BOOTH died Mar. 9th.

June 1 Mr. JOSHUA EDWARDS restored to his place.

July 6 Mr. WILLIAM THOMAS restored to his place.

Aug 3 Call to Rev'd Mr. HART in Charleston come and be minister. GRIFFITH JOHN died.

Oct. 5 ABEL WILDS messenger to JACOB DE SURRENCY & WILLIAM JAMES. SAMUEL WILDS messenger to Mrs. COX. Other names - PHILIP HOWEL, Mr. PUGH, THOMAS EVANS, SAMUEL EVANS, Mrs. MARTIN, DAVID EVANS. Mr. PUGH messenger to the Association.

Dec. 17 Rev'd Mr. HART declined to accept the call of the Church. Mrs. COX appeared and was acquited.

1766 Jan. 4 Rev'd Mr. PUGH became the Church's Pastor.

...Apr. 12 Mrs. ANNE DOUGLASS died. (End of p. 12.)

1766 July 5 ... WILLIAM & MARY THOMAS dismissed by Letter.

Oct. 4 PHILIP HOWEL & WILLIAM JAMES excommunicated. Rev'd PUGH appointed messenger. Rev. BEDGEGOOD dismissed by Letter. His dismission began "The Church of Christ" in the Welch-Neck on Pee-Dee. (Rev'd Mr. NICHOLAS BEDGOOD.)

Oct. 17 PHILIP DOUGLASS died.

Dec. 6 Letter of Dismission (another for Rev. BEDGGOOD). Mr. PUGH asked to leave.

Mar. 7 Mr. BEDGGOOD recalled and accepted.

* *

From the excerpts above, an outline of problems in the church can be seen. Rev. Joshua Edwards, who was ordained in May of 1752, had the care of the church for about six years. Rev. Robert Williams' ministry for the church was contemporary with the time of Mr. Edwards. The church records gave the following information:

On Aug. 9th, 1759, Rev. Williams applied for liberty to absent himself from the Lord's Table and Church Meetings, which the Church officials thought would be irregular to grant. They were then informed that he charged the Church with crimes as to prevent his communion. They sent messengers to him to appear at the church meetings for discussion of the

255

charges, but he would not appear or read their letter. He disowned himself as a member and said the church was not a Church of Christ. They tried to handle him with Kindness, but he was eventually ejected.

In March 1759, while this was still going on, the Church presented a call to Rev. Mr. Nicholas Bedgegood of Charleston to minister to them for a term of one year and he accepted. The call was given again the following year, and he agreed to stay on "for the term of time during which divine Providence may render it his duty to remain among them."

On Aug. 2, 1760, members drew up a covenant of what they believed was their relationship to God and to each other. This involved a careful watchfulness over each other's conduct and chastisements, etc. if the conduct didn't please.

On March 2, 1765, Mr. Bedgegood requested that he be dismissed to return to the Charleston Church. The congregation tried to secure the services of Rev. Oliver Hart as Pastor. They were unable to, and were without a pastor until Jan. 4, 1766, when Rev. Evan Pugh accepted their call. Two members were excommunicated, and many other suspensions, etc. took place.

In 1766, the church was in such a declining state that Brother Abel Wilds asked the opinion of the Church as to the cause of so much declension. Upon consideration, it was the unanimous opinion of the members that the decline was caused by a general dislike of Mr. Pugh. After several days of consideration, they agreed that it was best for Mr. Pugh to be removed. He was dismissed. No reason for this dislike was given. Leah Townsend wrote that it might have been because of his activities with the Regulators. He was also strongly in favor of the Patriots obtaining their freedom from Great Britain.

There was no regular law enforcement in the area, so the Regulators were vigilante type law enforcers. With a background for pacifism due to their religion, many church members did not want any controversy. There was a need for law enforcement, but as sometimes happens, the Regulators soon started committing atrocities themselves and the people turned against them. Also, as we will show later, many of the people in the area were loyal to the British.

Mr. Pugh left an interesting diary, though with brief entries, which tells of much of the troubles in the area during the Revolutionary War. He was an ardent Patriot.

A call was put out for the return of Mr. Bedgegood, which he heeded, and returned to preach on April 12, 1767. He preached there for the next seven years, until his death in 1774. This period was considered a period of prosperity for South Carolina. There was an Indian trade for the southern colonies which was centered in Charleston. This consisted mostly of the trading of pelts [deerskins.] The area was rich in agriculture, and the growing of rice and indigo was expanding. This supplied the economic base for the coast country society of notable intelligence and culture.

However, many people of the area had become used to their freedom and resented any encroachment by Governments in their lives. The Council had almost ceased to have any control over any legislation by 1760. Events were taking shape to lead to the overthrow of British rule.

The Church of England was the established religion of the Carolinas. There was no opposition to the Baptists and other Protestant religions. But the area contained enough people by 1768 that it was decided to set up a new Parish, and many of the Baptists and other church members joined in voting for this Parish. St. David's Parish was established by making a new Parish out of part of the parishes of St. Mark, Prince Frederick, and Prince George. This was done although the church building itself was not opened for worship until 1772 and was not completed until 1774.

Several Welsh attended the public meeting establishing this parish and became members of St. David's Parish. The Commissioners of the Parish met according to public notice, at the house of Charles Bedingfield, in the area later known as Irby's Mills in Marlborough District, on the public road from Cheraw to Bennettsville.

Some of those attending were: Alexander M'Intosh, James James, Robert Allison, Claudius Pegues, Philip Pledger, William Godfrey, Charles Bedingfield, Thomas Lide, Thomas Ellerbe, Thomas Bingham, Alexander Gordon, Benjamin Rogers, Durham Hitts, William Hardwick, Duke Glen, John Mackintosh, John Jenkins, Edward Ellerbe, John Husbands, Thomas Boatwright, Sr., John Pledger, Robert Anderson, Robert Clary, Benjamin Jackson, James Knight, Samuel Wise, James Thorsby, Thomas Williams, Thomas Wade and Leonard Dozier.

Notices were sent out in September 1768, which required the inhabitants of the Parish to 'meet at the home of Mr. John Mackintosh on Tuesday and the home of Mr. Charles Bedingfield's on Wednesday,' the fourth and fifth days of October ensuing for the purpose of electing a Member to represent the Parish in the Commons House of Assembly.

"Likewise, Circular Letters were writ to the Captains, James Knight, James Thomas, Thomas Conner, and Benjamin Jackson; and to Messrs. John Kimbrough, William Watkins, Robert Lide, and Gideon Gibson, with two or three of the Advertisements of the Election enclosed in each, to put up at the most Public Places in the respective Districts, and a desire to bring their Companies, under their proper leaders, to the Places of Election, to prevent confusion."[23]

Apparently one reason for the precaution was the fear that the Regulators would come down from North Carolina and cause trouble.

---

[23] History of the Old Cheraws, Gregg, p. 168.

This election was held Tuesday, October the Fourth, 1768, at the House of Mr. Mackintosh, to elect a Member of Assembly for the Parish of St. David, in Craven County, South Carolina, and the following voted: Bartholomew Ball; Richard Pouder; Simon Holmes; Francis M'Call Jun.; John Renynolds; Thomas Harry; William Reeves; John Mackintosh; John Holley; Charles M'Call; William Lucas; Roderick M'Iver; John Jamieson; John Evans; Robert Clary; Daniel Devonald; Samuel Sparks; Thomas James; Lewis Rowan; Alexander Mackintosh; Charles Strother; Philip Howell; John Davis; Edward Lowther; John Courtney; Francis M'Call; Malachi Newberry; Gideon Parish; Thomas Evans; William Edwards; John M'Call; Daniel Luke; John Cheeseborough; David Harry; Richard Blizard; Joshua Douglass; Nathaniel Douglass; Jacob Lamplugh; Thomas Davidson; Howel James; John Prothero; Joseph Barker; Evans Prothero; Isam Ellis; James Knight; William Tyrrell; James Rogers; Abel Edwards; Joseph Dabbs; James Bruce; Peter Kolb; William Pouncey; John Kimbrough; John Jackson; John Cooper; Joshua Edwards; David Harry; John Brown; William Dewitt; Enoch Luke; William Allen; Jenkin David; Andrew Hunter; Richard Allen; John M'Call; Philip Robland; Christopher Teal; Abel Wilds; George King; Edward Jones; Josiah Evans; Benjamin Wright; Joseph Luke; Gilbert Moody; Samuel Wilds; Thomas Lane; John Rowell; William Megee; Dennis Galphin; Samuel Evans; Benjamin Pruiel; Martin Kolb; Thomas Edwards; Robert Lide; John Griffith; Joseph Alison; John Knight; John Alran; Philip Pledger; John Brown; James James; John Flanagan; Daniel Man; Job Edwards; Magnus Corgill; Richard Mc La More; William James; Anthony Pouncey; John Dyer; Duke Glen; John Marsha; Joshua Hickman; Thomas Levy; David Evans; Robert Blair; Walter Downes; Lewis Blalock; Aaron Daniel; John Bruce; Martin Dewitt; James Dozier; John Darby. Number of Voters this day, 113."

"Wednesday, October 5th, 1768. The Poll for Electing of a Member of Assembly for the Parish of St. David, in Craven County, South Carolina, was opened at the House of Mr. Charles Bedingfield, and the following Persons voted,

"Thomas Boatright; Samuel Hatfield; Lewis Gardiner; John Jones*; William Carter; William Johnson; Benjamin James; Thomas Williams; John Purvis; William Hicks; Charles Bedingfield; John Beverly; Enoch James; George Hicks; Jesse Counsell; John Lyons; William Gardiner; John Sutton; John Pledger; Edward Bryan; John Williams; Benjamin Rogers; John Jenkins; Thomas Bingham; Abraham Colt; William James; William Ellerbe; Thomas Conner; Thomas Ellerbe; Kedar Keaton; Enoch Thomson; William Godfrey; Edward Ellerbe; George Sweeting; Charles Irby; John Moffatt; Alexander Gordon; John Westfield; Peter Heathy; Jonathan Wise; John Frazier; John Shumake; Thomas Sommerlin; John Hicks; John Williams; Thomas Rogers; William Hardwicke; Samuel Williams; Thomas Lide; John Powe; John Husbands; William Hernsworth; Jonathan Williams.

"Number of Voters this Day, 53."

"Claudius Pegues, Esqr. Was unanimously elected a Member of Assembly for the Parish of St. David's...full number of votes 166."

*John Jones. The John Jones who was married to Anne had died before this time. Also Griffith John had died. This would have been John Jones Jr. or Jonathan John, son of Griffith.

Gregg wrote the people voting were a large preponderance of the population in the lower parts of the Parish, which embraced the two principal settlements of the Welsh near Long Bluff and the Sandy Bluff neighborhood below.

The Governor of South Carolina dissolved that Assembly, and another election was called for the following year, with the elections ordered for the 7th and 8th of March. Additional people voted in this who had not voted in the previous election; from lower poll, viz:

"Daniel Saunders; Jordan Gibson jun.; _____ Saunders; Reuben Gibson; John Rothmahler; Nathaniel Hunt; Nicholas Bedgegood; Daniel Sparks; Daniel Monahan; Thomas Avery; John Crawford; Charles Sparks; James Mikell; Walter Owens; Solomon Staples; Harrison Lucas; Robert Moody; Charles Lisenby; Moses Bass; John Hitchcock; Joshua Lucas; John Crews; Malachi Murphy; Blundell Curtis; Arthur Hart; John Mikell; William McTierre; William Floyd; Stephen Sebastian; George Booth; Edward Owens; Jacob Baxter; Samuel Haselton.

At the upper poll 59 names were cast for the first time, and what was most interesting was that several of them were women. Remember, this was 1768! The names were, viz:

" Rebecca Lide; Daniel Lundy; Catharine Little; Benjamin Ladd; Francis Benton; William Lankford; Simon Lundy; Sarah Booth; Cornelius Aemens; Abel Wilds; Robert Westfield; William Crowley; John Perkins; Thomas Wade; Elizabeth Counsell; William Prestwood; Michael Griffith; Soloman Holmes; Samuel Hards; Frederick Kimbell; Wm. Gardiner, jun.; Joel Yarborough; Silas Harandine; William Jackson; Francis Gillespie; Thomas Tomkins; James Salmons; David Davidson; James Lundy; Joseph Parsons; Jacob Johnson; Thomas Williamson; Richard George; William Hayes."

Col. George Gabriel Powell received 154 of the 157 votes cast, and was elected the new member for St. David's. He was in command of the Craven County Regiment. I wonder if the women voted against him?

On April 30th 1770, the Freeholders of the Parish met and elected the following as Church officers:

John Kimbrough, Ely Kershaw, Jesse Counsell, Samuel Wise, Henry William Harrington, John Pledger, and William Ellerbe, Vestrymen; William Godfrey and William Pegues, Wardens."

*

Excerpts of Welsh Neck Church Minutes, continued:
Apr. 16 James James & Thomas Jones have a difference, arbitrators appointed were Thomas James, Howel James & Thomas Evans...

A list of the Members of the Church 1775-1778. ELHANAN WINCHESTER, Pastor.
Included Josiah Pierce, William Jones, Thomas Ayer, Tristram Thomas, Mary Jones, Sarah Pouncey, Sarah Pledger, Ann Peggy Ayer, Elizabeth Lide, Elizabeth Hicks, Elizabeth Thomas, Elizabeth Counsel, Elizabeth Pledger, Mary Wilds, Phebe Pledger, Mary Griffiths, Elizabeth Ayer, et al.
* *

CHAPTER NINE

REVOLUTIONARY WAR:

There was much agitation and turmoil going on in the Pee Dee area during the Revolutionary War period, especially from 1778 to 1783. South Carolina was completely overrun by British troops from 1780 to 1782 and experienced fighting involving more battles, though most were small, than any other state. But in addition, the state had numerous residents who were Loyalists.

In fact, a civil war was fought between the residents of this area who were divided between the Tories and the Whigs. The Whigs or Patriots were on the American side and the Tories or Loyalists were for the British or sympathetic to them. Both sides committed atrocities against the other, and were cruel whenever their side was winning. A lot of bitterness was engendered during this period, especially around 1780 to 1783, and the fallout from this lasted a long time, causing many people to leave the area. Houses were looted and burned, men were shot or hung. Actions by Tories caused Patriot men and sometimes their families to have to hide in the swamps, and vice versa. Many families moved away to safety in parts of North Carolina during the time this was going on. Some of the Tories were driven away after the War, and their land was confiscated. In some areas, the Whigs were the ones who moved away.

A lot of the people who lived in this area are immortalized in our history of this period. Tristram Thomas, from a Welsh family and undoubtedly a connection of the allied group related to our family, was a member of this early Welsh Neck Baptist church and much has been written about him. Thomas Ayer was also a member of this church. He was an Irishman, and very patriotic. [I was surprised more was not written about him.]

D. D. McColl was author of "Sketches of Old Marlboro" in 1916. He went into a lot of history of the Thomas family of Welsh ancestry who lived in the Welsh Tract. He gave some of the records on General Tristram Thomas who fought bravely in the Revolutionary War, and even had a ballad written about his exploits. McColl lamented the lack of effort made to record the exploits of the Pee Dee soldiers until half a century had elapsed, resulting in just the records made by Gregg in "History of the Old Cheraws."

McColl wrote, "History records that the soldiers from the Pee Dee not only marched to the relief of beleagured Charleston, and participated in the pitched battles of Eutaw and Cambden, but that they were also engaged in the dashing forays against the Tories [which were] under Major Gainey in Marion and Captain Campbell in Georgetown." He told of Tristam Thomas being in Hicks' Regiment and in 1780, they marched to help Charleston, but were defeated.

Leah Townsend wrote of the Baptist pastors and their efforts in going through the countryside to rally the people for the cause of freedom. Many had to flee the area because of efforts to kill them.

The settlement of this area was not just of Welsh Baptists. About the same time as the Welsh emigrated to the Pee Dee, settlements were made lower down the river in what was then called Liberty Precinct, which is now in Marion County. John Godbolt was an Englishman, and was among the first to settle in 1735. Other families who came directly from England were the families of Britton, Graves, Fladger, Davis, Tyler, Giles, Hunter, and others. Two important settlements were made in this region. One was in Britton's Neck, twenty miles below Mars Bluff, and forty miles above Georgetown. Colonel Hugh Giles came from this area.

Another settlement was made at a point on the east bank of the river, called Sandy Bluff, located two and a half miles above Mars Bluff. The community there was composed of the families of Crawford, Saunders, Murfee, Crosby, Keighly, Berry, and the Gibson's. They came from England and Ireland, and landed at Charles-town. They were Church of England, and erected churches in both communities.

In 1780 the inhabitants of South Carolina were very apprehensive of the increased approach of the enemy. When the call came from 'Charles-town' for help, all the available troops from the Pee Dee were promptly dispatched, as were those from other parts of the state. The first division of Col. Hicks's Regiment under command of Lieut.-Col. Abel Kolb, marched to the aid of Charleston. The second division under Col. Hicks, with Tristram Thomas as major, John Andrews, adjutant, set forth in February. Also commanding companies were Edmund Irby, Thomas Ellerbe, Stephen Jackson, James Gregg, and Maurice Murphy. There were a lot of Scotch and Irish people from this area, as well as the Welch.

Capt. James Gregg's company formed part of a detachment under Major Thornby. They stayed at the Ten Mile House near Charleston for about two months, when their term expired. When they heard Sir Henry Clinton was approaching the city, Major Thornby and other officers proposed the men volunteer for Charleston's defense. They were unanimous in doing so, and marched into the city and remained until the city was lost.

One of the members of this group mentioned by Gregg was George M'Call, of the Darlington District. "During the Revolution, or about a generation after the first settlement, the "Company which mustered at the M'Call old field," numbered from 130 to 140, all of them said to be Welch."[1]

Many from the Pee Dee area had marched to the defense of Charleston, so their families were very alarmed regarding their fate and that of their loved ones after the Americans were defeated. Gregg wrote, "Major

---

[1] History Of The Old Cheraws, by Gregg, pp. 51-52.

Wemys of the 63rd Regiment marched, soon after the fall of Charlestown, from George-town to Cheraw, on the west side of the river, destroying property of every description, and treating the inhabitants with relentless cruelty." [P.303.]

"After the fall of Charleston in May 1780, the British sent officers through the countryside and compelled the conquered males to swear allegiance to King George III."[2] Apparently after that loss, the Tories (the British soldiers and their local sympathizers) had this North and South Carolina area, including parts of Georgia, under their control. "The British conceived themselves in possession of the rights of sovereignty over a conquered country, and that therefore the efforts of the citizens to assert their independence any further, was chargeable with the complicated guilt of ingratitude, treason, and rebellion."

There were already many Tories in the area. McColl wrote, "First a detachment of Light Horse, under the infamous Wemys, fell upon the Pee Dee and ravaged its patriotic inhabitants with fire and sword. Immediately afterwards a battalion of the Seventh-first Regiment, composed of the flower of the Highland Clans, was stationed on the Pee Dee to over-awe the Whigs and reanimate to desperate deeds the drooping spirits of the Tories. The presence of this historic British Regiment, which had been famous in military annals for over a hundred years, naturally encouraged the Tories to renew their bloody expeditions and to revenge, by unspeakable outrages, the crushing defeats they had already suffered at the hands of their Whig neighbors. In these dark and unhappy days Major Thomas was a tower of strength to his distressed countrymen, and by his unremitting and successful efforts for their relief, he won that strong public affection..." Gregg wrote of the atrocious deeds that reflected disgrace on their arms. Major Wemys of the 63rd Regiment marched from Georgetown to Cheraw, destroying property and inflicting cruelties on the inhabitants. Houses were burned, people were hung, as they put out the call for the people to submit. Mr. Pugh, the pastor, wrote in his diary of going in and taking the oath to the King at Dr. Mills' house. An entry from his diary: "Saturday, July 2. Went to preach at Cashway, began my sermon, but the congregation broke up by the re(bels) taking the horses."

They were forced to take this oath: "I, _____, do hereby acknowledge and declare myself to be a true and faithful subject to his Majesty, the King of Great Britain, and that I will at all times hereafter be obedient to his government; and that whenever I shall be thereunto required, I will be ready to maintain and defend the same against all persons whatsoever."

[2]THE BAXTERS OF THE CAROLINAS AND GEORGIA, by Elmer O. Parker, Columbia, SC. In Ga. Genealogical Magazine, Vol. 32, No. 4 (126) p. 281.

Wemys troops burned Dr. Wilson's house at Long Bluff. The dwelling of Capt. William Dewitt on Cedar Creek was destroyed. Some of these people took their families to North Carolina and elsewhere to safety, then returned to repel the enemy. Many inhabitants submitted, while others only yielded nominally because of the force, but with plans to resist at the first opportunity. This latter group did not consider the Oath as binding since it was under duress. Capt. Dewitt did not submit to the Oath, nor did Thomas Ayer. John Wilson and James Gillespie went to Cheraw and swore allegiance, but did not consider it meant anything.

Sir Henry Clinton wrote a letter dated 4th June 1780, to Hon. George Gervain, in which he gloats of the way they have subjugated the people. "In many instances they have brought in as prisoners their former oppressors or leaders; and I may venture to assert, that there are few men in South Carolina who are not either our prisoners or in arms with us."

The Tories on Lynche's Creek committed many murders and indignities. They were led by two of the Harrisons. M'Arthur with his troops reached the Cheraws in June, and he promptly requisitioned the parish church for the use of part of his force. The soldiers were not restrained, and they plundered and did as they pleased.

The following account given in "History of The Old Cheraws" by Gregg[3], shows that some of the John's at this time were involved with the Tories:

"Soon after M'Arthur's [British army Major with the 71st Regiment (Highlanders)] arrival at Cheraw, he went down the river with a detachment, and made his headquarters for a short time at Long Bluff. His force was large enough to admit of division, and to keep the country in awe.

While at Long Bluff, he offered a handsome reward for the capture of Thomas Ayer. Ayer became known a short time before as the leader of a company that had been sent out to take some bold and mischievous persons, who had rendered themselves obnoxious to the inhabitants by their lawless depredations. Having succeeded in capturing a portion of the band, he secured the country against any more of their ravages by hanging them all.

The effect of the reward offered for Ayer was his capture by a party of Tory neighbors. They kept vigilant watch for him, and caught him while on a brief and cautious visit to his family. He came up at night, and keeping close during the day, intended to leave for camp the following night; but late in the afternoon, sixteen Tories galloped up to the house and secured him. They tied him with buckskin strings, furnished by old Magnus Corgill* for the purpose, and hurried him off toward the river, intending to take him immediately to M'Arthur. But, by the time they reached Hunt's Bluff, a terrific thunderstorm had blown up, and fearing to cross the river and prosecute their journey through the swamp in the darkness of such a

[3]Gregg's History...", pp. 309-312.

night, they concluded to keep their prisoner in an old unoccupied house on the bank until morning. George Manderson, the leader of the party, apprehending no danger from any quarter, left Ayer in charge of the others, and went down with one of his companions, Tom John, to get supper and sleep at old Jonathan John's. Relief was soon to overtake the now despairing Ayer. A few hours after the Tories left his residence, his elder brother, Hartwell, with five Georgians, rode up very unexpectedly to the family. The names of these timely visitors were -- William Cooper, James Nephew, Charles Tharp, John Tharp, and Joseph Plummer.

Upon being informed of what had occurred, Hartwell Ayer and his companions set out in immediate pursuit, and took the Tory party completely by surprise. They approached under cover of the darkness and tempest, and were at the door before being discovered. Most of the party within were asleep. Shooting first those who were up, they continued to fire and dispatch with the sabre and bayonet until all were killed, except Asal John. Being a son of his old neighbour, who was a peaceable man, Thomas Ayer protected him with his own body, and induced the captors to spare his life. Then mounting the horse of Dick Owen, one of the Tories just killed, he returned with all possible speed to his family, not knowing what might have befallen them. Upon learning the whereabouts of George Manderson and Tom John, Hartwell Ayer and his companions went off in pursuit. Riding up cautiously to old John's residence, they civilly inquired for Captain Manderson, who, as he appeared at the door, was saluted with a shower of bullets. Though struck by several balls, the wounds inflicted were slight; and springing through the back door of the house, he made his escape to the swamp, which was near at hand. Tom John was not so fortunate. He was knocked down with the butt of an old musket, and then pinned to the floor with the bayonet, remaining in that condition as the gun was jerked off, and supposed to be dead. But, on the bayonet being removed, he arose, and proved to be not seriously injured. He lived several years afterwards. When informed of the rescue of Ayer, and the slaughter of the Tories, M'Arthur was more enraged than ever. He determined to go in person and take vengeance. Crossing the river with a strong party, he came very near surprising the family, then at home, consisting of Mrs. Ayer and her sons, Lewis Malone and Zacceus, both of whom were lads. They made a timely escape, however, to the swamp, which was near by, and there remained in concealment several weeks, being supplied with food by their good neighbour, James Sweat. M'Arthur took possession of the deserted premises, killed the stock, destroyed most of the fencing, and burned all the buildings except a large crib, which he spared on account of the corn it contained, meaning to appropriate it to the use of his troops. It was, however, subsequently taken off and secured by the friends of the family. Every valuable negro was carried away, with others belonging to different persons in the neighbourhood. The now empty crib became the dwelling of the family to the close of the war."

*Magnus Cargill was a member of St. David's Parish. He had warned Thomas Ayer that the British would confiscate his property if he didn't take the Oath of Allegiance, but Thomas Ayer was said to have warmly replied "the question was not one of property, but liberty!"

NOTE: In this account, Thomas Ayer does not seem concerned about Thomas John, but was about Asal John. This leads me to believe that the Thomas John involved here was probably not the brother of Asal.
*

One of the places plundered by M'Arthurs marauding troops was north in Richmond County, N.C. The home of General Harrington was located there, and was severely looted. The Negroes were carried off with the livestock to the Cheraw. The overseer was made to accompany them. Mrs. Harrington managed to escape on a horse she had secreted in an out-building. She followed M'Arthur, and asked for the return of her servants. Only one woman and her family agreed to return with her.

Captain Thomas Ellerby, a Whig who lived a few miles below Cheraw, also suffered severely from losses of horses taken by the British, and some of his slaves. Claudius Pegues also had a number of Negroes taken, with one treated cruelly by the British. He managed to escape and return home, and eventually recovered. Philip Pledger lost eight horses. Jonathan John lost at least one horse, as a claim was later found for this. People with Whig sympathies were kidnapped, and several were taken prisoner and carried to Camden.

The Tories joined with the British in committing such atrocities they finally drove the Whigs to desperation. Mr. Pugh wrote in his diary on 25th of July, "The people in arms against the English."

McColl wrote of the events that took place in 1780 when Major Tristram Thomas captured a British detachment at Hunt's Bluff. He wrote that the British Seventy-first Regiment, which was under Major McArthur was camped at Cheraw upon the banks of the Pee Dee River which was unhealthy, and a lot of the soldiers sickened and died. Knowing there were no Patriot soldiers around, British Maj. McArthur sent about a hundred of the sick men in boats down the Pee Dee to Georgetown. He placed them under the care of Lord Nairne and a detachment of the Royal militia under the new British Col. William Henry Mills. Col. Mills was a physician from the Pee Dee area who had previously been in the revolutionary movement and had been sent as a delegate to the Provincial Congress in 1776. But after the British success, he joined up with them and 'became a determined foe to the American cause.' Most of the people in the river settlements remained true to the cause of liberty.

When the Whigs heard of M'Arthur's projected expedition of men down the river, a group of them gathered at Beding's Fields, afterwards Irby's Mills, to stop it. James Gillespie was their leader. Their numbers increased and Major Tristram Thomas was put in command. When the boats departed, Maj. McArthur retreated toward Black Creek. The Whigs chose to intercept them at Hunt's Bluff, which was about twenty-five miles below Cheraw, between Darlington and Marlborough Counties. [The John's lived at Hunt's Bluff.] The Whigs placed a battery of wooden guns in a bend of the river, and when the slow moving boats began to pass, they made "a most imposing demonstration" against the flotilla, and demanded unconditional surrender. Some of the men in the Loyalist party mutinied against Col. Mills, who escaped to Georgetown, and they joined the fight against the flotilla. This flotilla was captured, with one hundred British soldiers. The Patriots also captured a large boat that was then coming down the river with supplies for the Loyalists.[4] This was their first victory, and revived their spirits.

In another account of this, Gregg wrote the 100 British prisoners taken by Major Thomas were carried into North Carolina. This increased the alarm of the British, who were already upset by the movement of the North Carolina troops which had taken to the field and agreed to rendezvous at Anson Court House on the 20th of July, so they could be ready to cooperate with the Continental army. Anson Court House was about thirty miles above Cheraw on the river. General Gates arrived in the American camp on the 24th of July. His arrival set off feelings of jubilation in those people wanting to be rid of the Tories and British.

The inhabitants of the area were ripe for a revolt, so McArthur was ordered to move his troops from the Pee Dee. He was ordered to draw nearer to Camden. From accounts written by the British regarding this, they treated it as a revolt of the people of the area against the British. They felt it was unwise of Gen. Miles to have had so many untried troops under his command.

They also referred to the sickness suffered by the British troops. They were not used to this southern climate, and many sickened and died. Gregg wrote of a perceptible sink in the earth in front of the parish church of St. David where many British soldiers were buried in one common grave. The British 71st Regiment returned to Camden on the 15th of August, the eve of the battle, about three weeks after it left Cheraw. Its ranks were thinned by the deaths of many of the soldiers, caused by illness.

When the Americans heard of Gen. Gates' approach to the Pee Dee, they were elated. Several youths from the Welsh Tract area went south to Giles' Bluff some distance below, to join Col. Giles when they heard he was raising a volunteer army. After two weeks, Col. Marion's force joined up

---

[4]Sketches of Old Marlboro, by D. D. McColl, 1916.

with it. Col. Giles received orders to march with his volunteer force to join Col. Kolb at Long Bluff.

The Americans went into the Battle of Camden under Gen. Gates with high hopes. They were thoroughly routed by the British, and Gates had to make a hasty escape into North Carolina. The populace was again overcome with fear and consternation, but many became more determined to win against the British. The most devoted Whigs moved their families to North Carolina and Virginia, and returned to fight again.

The emboldened Tories came forth from Drowning Creek and the Little Pedee, from Lynche's Creek, and parts lower down to plunder and raid. On Catfish Creek lower down, lived Joseph Jones and his brother John. Joseph moved there from Fishing Creek in Anson Co., N.C. Joseph became a notorious Captain under the Tories. He was a Surveyor and had made an important contribution to the field of surveying in Marion by inventing a compass used in surveying. His brother John apparently fought for the British in Col. David Fannings Regiment from 1 Mar 1781 to 24 Aug 1782.[5] He was here referred to as Jno. Johnes.

Mrs. Harrington, wife of the General, was sent a message by her husband to flee to Maryland, and to take as much property as she could. He had an excellent library, and asked her to take his books with her. Her party was intercepted at Mountain Creek in Richmond County by Captain John Leggett, a noted Tory of Bladen County. They plundered her possessions, destroying what they could not take with them. Gen. Harrington's books and valuable papers were strewn along the road, and were lost or destroyed. Their horses were all taken. Mrs. Harrington made her way to her father's house in Anson County. He was Major James Auld. Her brothers, John and Michael quickly gathered a group of men and took off after the Tories, but were unable to catch them.

The Whigs were overcome with feelings of unsparing revenge, and those from the border of North Carolina above to the upper limits of Marion below responded in kind to the Tories. Col. Kolb had his home with his family in the Welsh Tract neighborhood, and he remained there for the protection of the lives and property of the inhabitants against the Tories. Col. Hicks left to take his family to Virginia. He left Lieut. Col. Kolb as acting commander of the forces on the Pee Dee. The warfare extended up into the neighboring counties of North Carolina.

Gen. Marion was also in the area and was actively engaged with the enemy for several months. A dispatch from him to Gen. Harrington read:

"Blackmingo, 17th Novr., 1780.
"Sir,

---

[5] The Loyalists in North Carolina During The Revolution, by Robert O. DeMond, Baltimore, Gen. Pub. Co., Inc., 1979, p. 230.

Since my last to you, Colonel Tarleton retreated to Camden, after destroying all the houses and provisions in his way. By information, I was made there was but fifty British in George-town, and no militia, which induced me to attempt taking that place. But, unluckily, the day before I got there they received a reinforcement of two hundred Tories under Captains Barfield and Lewis from Pedee. The next day the Tories came out and we scummaged with them.

Part I cut off from the town, and drove the rest in, except the two men killed, and twelve taken prisoners. Our loss was Lieutenant Gabriel Marion, and one private killed. These two men were killed after they surrendered. We had three or four wounded, one since dead of his wound.

Captain Barfield was wounded in his head and body, but got off. Captain James Lewis, commonly called "Otter Skin Lewis,' was one killed. I stayed two days within three miles of the town, in which time most of the Tories left their friends and went home. [Note: This referred to a propensity for wearing garments made of otter skin.]

Finding the regulars in the town to be eighty men, besides militia, strongly entrenched in a redoubt, with swivels and cohorns on their parapet, I withdrew my men, as I had not six rounds per man, and shall not be able to proceed on any operations without a supply of ammunition, which I will be obliged to you to furnish me with by Captain Potts, who commands a detachment to guard the prisoners taken. I have not heard anything from General Gates since the letter you sent me.

A man from the high hills of Santee, within eight miles of Camden, says that Washington's Horse is at Rugely's Mill, one mile from there. I beg to know where our army is, and what news from them.

I am, with esteem, your most obedient Servant,

Francis Marion.

Hon. Brig.-General Harrington, Pedee."

* *

The British became more emboldened after the victory at Camden, and Major Wemys again made his presence felt. Houses were burned of the men who joined up with Col. Marion and Col. Peter Horry. Many Whigs were taken away by the British. The American troops were still in various places in the area, and ranged about against the Tories in an attempt to "keep the Tories in awe." From letters written during this period by General Gates, Gen. Harrington and others, the Whigs were now performing excellently against the Tories.

Col. Kolb visited Gen. Gates and urged he have Gen. Harrington remain on the Pee Dee. They were in urgent need of more provisions, especially cattle. Col. Brown received permission from the Governor to collect all the cattle on or near Pee Dee and have them driven to the interior of the state. He remained on the Pee Dee, and was able to render service against the Tories. In October, he wrote that he had killed Miles Barfield, wounded two others of the Barfields, and they possibly had shot Jesse Barfield through the hand. He had captured four of the Barfields and had them as prisoners. The Barfields had slowed him down in collecting cattle, but he had 259 head that he was taking to Headquarters. Major Barfield had been in the American army, but because of some slight, he became angered and joined the Tories and became a notorious leader. His force was well organized and was difficult to capture. However, he contracted smallpox and died during the war. Other letters tell of other people coming in to pledge their loyalty to the American side.

Gen. Smallwood wrote Nov. 15th, 1780, of daily expecting Gen. Gates to arrive. He stated they were now getting their supplies of forage and provision from the upper part of Lynche's Creek and the Tory part of the Waxsaw settlement. He stated he was extending this lower down and across the Catawbas. He believed Cornwallis was inactive at Wynsborough, and Tarleton was below on the Santee, where he was wasting and destroying all before him. He figured this indicated they would soon evacuate Camden, unless they were reinforced. He mentioned Major Wemys was wounded and some twenty more were taken prisoners.

Col. Kolb was in Long Bluff, and the acknowledged leader on the Upper Pee Dee. He wrote he had only 233 men, but would send some of them to Gen. Harrington.

Col. Marion caused so much trouble to the British that they sent Tarleton's troops after him. They pursued him for several days and chased them into the swamps. Marion returned and carried on a partisan warfare.

On the 18th of Nov 1780, Gen. Alexander M'Intosh, a patriotic and honored man who was the first senator elected for St. David's, died. His funeral was preached by Mr. Pugh at the Welsh Neck Church.

In December, Gen. Harrington moved up the river to Grassey Creek in Richmond County, N.C. where he had command on both sides of the Pee Dee. It was about this time that Col. Marion began to be referred to as Gen. Marion. An extant account records articles of pork, bundles of corn blades, and bushels of corn that George Hicks furnished Gen. Harrington.

Gen. Green was sent to take charge of the Southern Department, and arrived at Charlotte, N.C. on December 2nd. He marched on the 20th of December for Pee Dee. He had no more than one thousand Continentals, and about as many militia. He was bare of ammunition and clothing, and had no money. He pitched his camp on the southern bank of Husband's Creek, three miles from Cheraw. He moved soon to a position on Hick's Creek, a mile higher up.

The year opened with Gen. Green's presence inspiring confidence in the Patriot inhabitants. Col. Kolb was held in high esteem. Col. Murphy was active in the parts lower down on the east, and Maj. Benton had his post west of the river. Marion was busily engaged from Lynche's Creek to George-town.

John Wilson was appointed captain of a small company called the "Munchausen Corps." They were to scour the country during Green's sojourn. Green was able to stay only a month, however. Cornwallis pursued Morgan, and upon learning this Gen. Green left to join Morgan. James Gillespie resided near Green's Camp, and acted as guide to the general on his march from the Pee Dee.

This again caused the Whigs of the Cheraw District to rely on themselves for protection. The warfare with the Tories renewed with "unsparing ferocity."

Col. Kolb took a party of men, which included Maj. Lemuel Benton, Capt. Joseph Dabbs, and John Cox, below to Cat Fish Creek to rout some of the notorious Tories who were in that area. John Deer was shot, and received a broken arm. Deer was killed. Caleb Williams, who was known to burn houses of the Whigs, was taken and hung. Others were captured and punished. After this, Col. Kolb returned to his home, thinking he would be able to rest.

This did not happen. The Tories were furious and decided to go after Col. Kolb. About fifty of them gathered at Tart's Mill, six miles above Marion Court House. Their leader was Capt. Joseph Jones, who lived in the neighborhood. They rode rapidly under cover of darkness, to surprise Col. Kolb. On this night, the 28th of Apr 1781, Col. Kolb was at home with Mrs. Kolb, his daughter Anne (who later married Maj. James Pouncey of Marlborough), and two sisters. The sisters were Ann James, who married Joshua Edwards, and Sarah, who married Evander M'Iver. Two young Evans brothers were also there. A resistance was made, and several Tories were killed.

The Tories threatened to burn the house if Col. Kolb did not surrender. Some accounts state the house was actually set on fire. He agreed to surrender as a prisoner of war, and came out with his wife and sisters. As he was preparing to present his sword, he was shot by Mike Goings who was a private in the Tory ranks, and who went against Capt. Jones' orders. Thomas Evans tried to escape, but was shot and later died of his wound. His brother was also killed. The dwellings were plundered and burned before the Tories rode away. Later accounts told of Capt. Joseph Jones' brother John being seen riding Col. Kolb's horse and saddle, with a feather bed tied before him.

Col. Kolb was well liked by the people of the Pee Dee, and his death caused much melancholy in the area. He had an able successor, however. Maj. Lemuel Benton, as Lt. Colonial, assumed his command and held it until the end of the War.

The Tory who led the raid, Capt. Jones, was said by Gregg to be a man of some note and "ingenious to a remarkable degree." He continued to live on Cat Fish Creek until about 1802, when he moved to Colleton District where he later died.

The fortunes of Cornwallis declined after losing the Battle of Guilford Courthouse in North Carolina. Cornwallis withdrew into South Carolina after the end of the winter campaign in North Carolina. He wrote from Wilmington to Lord George Germaine: "The distance from hence to Camden, the want of forage and subsistence on the greatest part of the road, and the difficulty of passing the Pedee, when opposed by an enemy, render it utterly impossible for me to give immediate assistance, and I apprehend a possibility of the utmost hazard to this little corps, without the chance of a benefit in the attempt; for, if we are so unlucky as to suffer a severe blow in South Carolina, the spirit of revolt in that Province would become very general, and the numerous rebels in this Province be encouraged to be more than ever active and violent...."

Broken in spirit, and feeling threatened on all sides, Cornwallis made a decision which led to his ruin. He withdrew, heading towards Duplin Court House, then Hillsborough in the vain hopes of drawing Gen. Green after him. Virginia became the scene of his final overthrow.

Partisan warfare now raged. Col. Benton proved able in his command. Col. Murphy battled on the eastern side of the river below. Major Thomas, Capt. Sparks, Capt. Pledger, Capt. Council, Capt. M'Intosh, Capt. Ellerbe, Capt. Pegues, Capt. Jackson, and others were noted by Gregg as being gallant in service to the cause of freedom. Capt. Edward Jones was mentioned as commanding an important point on the river at Kolb's Ferry.

Whigs noted by Glenn were Charles Evans of Lynche's Creek, Capt. Duke Glen of St. David's parish, Col. Benjamin Rogers of Marlborough, William Pratt on Anson Co., Daniel Hicks, Col. John Donaldson, William Pegues, John Lucas, Maj. John Mikell and many others. He wrote of John Wilson being captured by the Tories, but being able to escape. Many exploits were told of Capt. Alex. M'Intosh, a Whig commander.

On Lynche's Creek were many Tories. Incidents regarding a Dubose, a Bradley, a man named Snowden, and Capt. Jeff Butler. Marion had to shelter Butler later when he surrendered, to keep him from being killed by Whigs who hated him for the suffering he had inflicted on them. Fanning of Drowning Creek was especially notorious.

In June 1782, a treaty was signed at Burch's Mill on Pee Dee, by which the Tories would agree to lay down their arms, to behave afterwards as peaceable citizens, etc. Micajah Gainey continued to violate the Treaty until the governors of both North and South Carolina agreed to send a party under the command of Marion to subdue him. From this treaty, Gibson, who killed Col. Kolb, and Fanning and his party were excepted, but they escaped. Feeling was so strong against Maj. Micajah Gainey that he moved to Richmond County, N.C.

The Battle of Eutaw was fought on the 8th of Sept, and militia from Pee Dee took part. Capt. Claudius Pegues' company was among them. Capt.

Pegues was wounded in the leg, and saved by Thomas Quick, a private. Joshua David, a private, was badly wounded and permanently disabled.

On the 17th of Sept, Benton's regiment was assigned to Gen. Marion's brigade. They held this position until the end of the war. Several of the John's were under Benton's command. Records show most of the militia from Pee Dee were more or less in constant service under Marion.

On the 23rd of Nov, Gov. Rutledge sent to Marion writs of election for Members of the Senate and House of Representatives. Because of the uncertainty of the times, the Governor left it to Marion to determine the places of election. Tristram Thomas, Philip Pledger, William Dewitt, and William Pegues were four of the six representatives later elected for St. David's and took their seats in the House at Jacksonborough on the following 18th of January, 1782. William Dewitt was elected Sheriff.

In 1782, Azel John, Thomas John, Abel Wilds and Samuel Wilds were privates in Benton's Regiment. Alexander James was a Lieutenant in Kolb's Regiment. George James and James James were privates in Kolb's Regiment. William Miles was a private in Marion's Brigade. Jesse Wilds was a Lieutenant in Benton's Regiment. And Jesse John was a private in Benton's Regiment in 1783.

In 1783, after the end of the Revolution, feelings were strong for confiscating property of Tories and getting other revenge in general. When the first court was held at Long Bluff on 15th Nov 1783, Judge Grimke appeared for the first time on the Northern Circuit and gave expression to some very wise and sage advice which changed the minds of many bent on revenge. Gregg wrote of Judge Grimke's eloquent address to the Grand Jury. He spoke of the need for laws to be obeyed, and for a feeling of forgiveness to prevail in order to maintain peace and harmony. He desired the distinction of Tory no longer be used, and all regarded as citizens of the new country. It is an address worth reading.

Some property was confiscated, but many claims of family members were heard and much leniency shown.
* *

CAPT. ROBERT CAMPBELL

Capt. Robert Henry Campbell settled in this area on the banks of the Pee Dee near Hunt's Bluff, after the Revolutionary War. He was a Capt. in the British Army. He was from Scotland, and was in the Seventy First Regiment of Scotish Highlanders, which was stationed on the banks of the Pee Dee near Cheraw about 1780-81. They occupied Cheraw and held the entire area near the Pee Dee in subjection by frequent and bloody forays. After the Battle of Camden, a large number of American prisoners fell into the hands of the British, and for some time Capt. Campbell had charge of these. Capt. Andrew Jackson, who was a prisoner under him, was said to have later written a letter thanking Campbell for his humane treatment of prisoners.

Campbell married Lucia Blair, daughter of Robert Blair, a Tory who lived in Redhill Township, which furnished a great many active Tories. After the war, Blair's property was ordered confiscated, and he paid a large fine.

After he settled on the Pee Dee, Campbell soon acquired large amounts of land, and was a man of considerable wealth when he died in 1820.[6] His sons Robert and John were very well liked and became members of Congress from the Pee Dee District.

*

---

[6]Sketches of Old Marlboro, by D. D. McColl, 1916, Bennettsville, S.C.

CHAPTER TEN

NORTH CAROLINA AND GEORGIA:

When the group of Welsh Baptists from New Castle County, Del., received the right to settle on the large survey of land granted to the Welsh on the Pee Dee River in South Carolina in 1737 and 1738, final surveys for the boundary between the Carolinas had not yet been made. The survey of the South Carolina line was not made until 24 Sept 1764. Some of this land was located in what is now North Carolina. As well, surveys then in North Carolina were later found to be in South Carolina.

The Welsh were given rights to a large territory embracing more than a hundred miles by the course of the Pee Dee River, according to the Rev. Gregg, who wrote "History of the Old Cheraws." Gregg's belief from reading the documents was that the territory given the Welsh extended over an area of twenty-five miles above the state line of South and North Carolina. The northern part of the description of the survey was described as "extending down from the branches of the Rocky River and Yadkin River..." However, a later book by W. W. Sellers, Esq., "A History of Marion County," written in 1899, stated this grant dated 8 Feb 1737 extended the Welsh area up to the North Carolina line, eight miles on each side of Pee Dee River.

Other settlers also left Pennsylvania and Delaware. Some took out land in Virginia; some only stopped briefly in Virginia before moving on to North Carolina. In North Carolina, many of their grants were on creeks and rivers located northwest of the Welsh Tract. These grants were in Anson Co., N.C. at the time, but were later found to be in S.C. Some would have been located in part of the Welsh Tract as laid out in its entirety per Gregg.

The original group of Welsh Baptists that filed for this land settled on the east side of the Pee Dee River in a small (approx. seven miles) area that extended from the mouth of Crooked Creek to Hunt's Bluff in South Carolina. It was later located opposite of Society Hill. They called this Welsh Neck because of the bend in the river.

Some of the grants given to these constituents in the early 1740's were in Anson County, indicating settlements away from the main body of Welsh Baptists. Many Anson County grants and deeds were made in the early 1750's. Some deeds show land purchased from settlers who had received grants during the early 1740's. These early Anson Co. deeds also included the Germans who settled in the western area of North Carolina.

Anson was formed in 1748 or 1749 from Bladen County. The northern boundary was the Virginia line until Rowan County was formed in 1753. It had no western boundary until Mecklenburg County was formed 1 Feb 1762. Its southern boundary was not determined until the survey made to determine the South Carolina line 24 Sept 1764.

Anson County included all or part of the South Carolina Counties of Marlboro, Chesterfield, Lancaster, York, Chester, Cherokee, Union, Spartanburg, Greenville, Laurens, and Newberry until Mecklenburg County was formed and the South Carolina border surveyed. Brent Holcomb has published several books covering deeds granted in this territory. The deeds have excerpts that are helpful. With the immense territory Anson County covered then, it is easy to see the difficulty now of locating all the grants designated as being in Anson Co.

* *

DAVID JOHN:

I estimate he was born ca 1720, in New Castle Co., Del. I believe he was the son of Griffith John (d. 1749) of New Castle Co., Del. A marriage record in Philadelphia at the First Presbyterian Church was for David John who married Mary Davis 28 Sep 1740. A neighbor of Griffith's was Henry Davis. All of Griffith John's land, said to be located in diverse places, was left to David. David was the only son mentioned in the will. I believe this was because he was the youngest, or the only one who did not have land of his own.

David continued to live in Delaware until 1754. On May 17, 1754, he received a Crown grant of 210 acres in Anson County, N. C. See later.

There is a good possibility that Griffith John (ca 1710) who went to the Pee Dee area of S. C. in 1737 was a brother of David (ca 1720), and son of Griffith (d.1749.) Griffith (ca 1710) apparently arrived with the group of church members of the Welsh Tract Baptist Church.

We were unable to ascertain the mother of David John (ca 1720.) Since his birth date is estimated, his mother might have been the Mary John, wife of a Griffith, who died in 1715, as shown in the Welsh Tract Church Minutes in Delaware.

Family researchers believe David's first wife died, and he married again. This appears to be based on David only mentioning his older sons David and Joseph in his will. This lead to the belief by some family historians that these elder children had a different mother. From accounts regarding wills of the Welsh, he might have only mentioned them because they were older. We do not know if Mary was a second wife.

He called her "More" in his will, and "Moire" is the Irish name for Mary, and I have been unable to find how Mary is pronounced in the Welsh language. In receiving a grant in Georgia, she was called "Moore John" and later, in her Will, she called herself "Mary" John. An entry in 1749 in land records regarding "Henry Boykin and wife More" showed More as a given name in this area. Henry Boykin was shown in Leah Townsend's 'History of Baptists in South Carolina' as being one of the Deacons in the first

Baptist Church of Lynches Creek, in an area where John Jones Jr. owned land.

Joada John Cole wrote[1] that a statement was repeated in 1918 by great-grandchildren of Mary John that their mother was very proud of her lineage and claimed she had royal blood in her veins. This might refer to the Welsh royal blood from the Princes of Wales. It is interesting to note the way Mary worded, in her will, the part about her funeral, as if she expected to be treated in a royal way. "As for my burial, I desire it may be without pomp or state but decent at the discretion of my executors and children."

Joada Cole wrote other family members believed Mary's surname was Moore, and this was the reason she was called Moore. Moore's were checked, and we found several Moore's who were from Ireland. George Moore, who was earlier mentioned with the Jones' in several deeds in New Castle Co., Del. was from Ireland. And of course, there are stories of the Moore children who were sent to the New World by one of the English royal members who thought they were not his legitimate children.

Lacking any definite record of her surname, there are several others to consider in North Carolina. The name Roger was given to their youngest son, which might be an indication that Mary's surname was Rogers. Another name soon to be used in the family line was Brice. There were Rodgers, Rogers, and Brice's living in the area, but no marriage records have been found to reflect a marriage with them. One reason could be the scarcity of records.

The Welsh Baptists were criticized by members of the Episcopalian religion for performing marriages, as they felt this should be left to those designated by the English. This might account for the sparse records of marriages performed by the Baptists.

David was a blacksmith, and he must have taken his family with him as he journeyed across the Carolinas and Georgia. There was a large market for livestock, and a good demand for the services of a blacksmith. Horses were rounded up, held in pens, then driven to Charleston for sale. Stock raising was considered the number one money making occupation. Stock was driven to market as far as away as Philadelphia.

David was made a Captain in the Georgia Militia in April 1764, replacing David Emanuel who resigned. The officers in the state militia had to supply their own uniforms, horses, etc., so only those able to afford it could take on these positions. David Emanuel's son was later a Captain in the state Militia, and the resignation here of David Emanuel Sr. was probably due to his age.

We found no record of David John being a member of any of the Baptist Churches in the area. He seems to have settled in a very isolated area at first. Later records indicate the Lewis and John families were Baptists.

---

[1]A Journal of the John Family 1701-1960, Cole.

David John died in November 1764 in St. George's Parish, Burke Co., Ga. His will was probated 5 Mar 1765, Parish of St. George, Ga. In his will, only two children, David and Joseph, were mentioned, and the balance of his estate was left to his wife "More." The way this will was written probably indicated an understanding that the younger children would be looked after by Mary. He must have known he was dying, as Mary promptly filed for more land and appears to have put important plans into action, probably with the help of the Lewis' and David Emanuel. At this time, David Emanuel was a Justice of the Peace in Georgia.

David's known children were:

1. JOSEPH JOHN, b. ca 1744, Del.
2. DAVID JOHN [Jr.], b. ca 1745, Del.
3. BENJAMIN JOHN, b. ca 1748, Del, died ca 1777.
4. DANIEL JOHN, b. ca 1749, Del.
5. ZEPHANIAH JOHN, b. ca 1750, Del.
6. ROGER JOHN, b. ca 1755, Del. or possibly S.C.

(Birthdates are estimates only.)

Possibly other children.

ELIZABETH JOHN was mentioned in the will of Mary John. She was believed to have been a daughter-in-law, Elizabeth McLendon, wife of Daniel. A near neighbor of the John family in the late 1770's was Roger Cunningham.
* *

From his Will indicating his two elder children were underage when he died, we are estimating that David John was born ca 1720 in New Castle Co., Del. From his Will and a deed, we learned he was a blacksmith.

An ASSESSMENT LIST OF PENCADER HUNDRED, New Castle Co., Del. made by Thomas James, not dated, showed the following:

David John 18 L; <u>David John, smith 8 L</u>; Rachel Griffith, widow 8 L; John Griffith 8 L; Richard Griffith 20 L; John Griffith 10 L; Thomas Lewis 14 L; Daniel Griffith 8 L; Jonathan John 8 L; Jacob John 8 L; David John 8 L; et al. (Scharf, History of Delaware, Vol. II, p. 952.)

This record showed there were three David John's living in Pencader Hundred of an age to be taxed. One of the David John's named was a smith, or blacksmith.

From the account by Morgan Edward, [see Chapter Five] Esther Morgan was married to a David John (d. 1748) who came to Pennsylvania with her in 1710. They lived in Pencader Hundred, where Esther was a member of the Welsh Tract Baptist Church. That David (d. 1748) had a son David Jr. He lived on land owned by his father David and died early. There was another David mentioned in the will of David, husband of Esther. That was his grandson David, who was his son Morgan's child. David, son of Morgan, later became a Baptist Minister and never lived in the Pee Dee area. The above tax entry also had Jonathan John's name followed by Jacob and David John. The son of David (d. 1748) might have been on the tax roll, but it is doubtful that the son of Morgan was on there.

From the will of Griffith John (d. 1749) of Pencader Hundred we know there was a David John who was his son, and Executor of his will. This David also inherited his father's real estate, and quite possibly had not taken any land out in his own name. We found no record of any connection between Griffith John (d. 1749) and David John (d. 1748) who had wife Esther. That David John arrived from Wales in 1710, and Griffith had taken out land in 1703/4.

A newspaper account from the Pennsylvania Gazette showed this:

John Fitzgerald, Irish servant, age c. 20, runaway from Daniel Howell, living in the Welsh Tract, Newcastle Co.; a shipmate, age c. 23, of said Fitzgerald, runaway from <u>David John</u> of the Welsh Tract (4 May).[2]
* *

DAVID JOHN'S CAROLINA LAND

On May 17, 1754, David John received a Crown grant of 210 acres in Anson County, N.C., on branch of Mountain Creek, adjoining Alexander McCarel's [McConnel's] corner.[3] When he sold this land it was described as follows:

Mecklenburg Co. Deed Abstracts 1763-1779, pp. 566-568:
26 & 27 Oct 1763, David John of Parish of St. George, Ga., Blacksmith, to John Walker of Mecklenburg (lease s5, release L-) ---land on Mountain Creek, adj. Alexander McConnels, 210 a...David John (Seal). Wit: Thomas Irwin, Jacob Coburn.
Georgia, Parish of St. George: 27 Oct 1763, appeared before me David Emanuel, Thomas Irwin of the parish aforesaid, proved deed...David Emanuel, J.P.

Mecklenburg Co. Deeds, John Walker to William Berry:
<u>V. 3, Pp. 40-43: 12 & 13 Jan 1767</u>, John Walker of Meck., gent., to <u>William Berry</u> of same, (lease, release L25)...250 A on a branch of Mountain Creek, adj. Alexander McConnel, granted to David John 17 May 1754 & deeded to

[2]ABSTRACTS FROM THE PA. GAZETTE, 1748-1755, By Kenneth Scott & Janet R. Clarke, Geneal. Publ. Co., Inc., Baltimore, 1977, p. 47.
[3]Vol. 1, entry No. 4473, NC Patent Bk. 15, p. 10, as abstracted in Colony of NC Land Patents Vols. 7 and 2, by Margaret M. Hoffman.

Walker, 26 & 27 Oct 1763. John Walker (Seal), Wit: Jacob Coburn, Benj.
Grubb, Alexander Gilleland. Proven Jan. term 1768.
* *

Deeds mentioning William Berry, Leonard Killion, Jacob Forney, Robert
Leeper, George Brown:

V. 4, Page 313: 20 July 1767, Jacob Forney & wf Mary of Meck., to Karot
Will of same for L119 NC money. Land on S side Cataba River, on middle
fork of Killions Creek above Wm. Berrys Land whereon he now lives,
formerly belonging to Leonard Killion, 320 Acres...Jacob Forney (Seal),
Mary Froney (X) (Seal). Wit: Leonard Saylor (LS), James Abernathy. Prov.
July term 1767.

V. 2, Pp. 324-328: 14 & 15 Mar 1764, George Potts of Meck., cooper, to
Jacob Forney, Distiller, of same (lease L50). Land on S side Cataba, both
sides Killions Creek, 300 A adj. Killion, granted to Michael Miller 28 Feb
1754 & sold to Devault Potts, 13 Oct 1756. George Potts (Seal), Wit: Charles
Moore, Leonard Killian, ____[German signature.] 15 Mar 1764, Mary Potts,
widow & relict of Devault Potts, release of dower--Mary Pots (x) (Seal).

V. 1, Pp. 482-486: 24 Mar 1764, Peter Club of Meck., to Jacob Sights [Sides]
of same, (lease s5, release L25). 250 Acres on S side Cataba, both sides
Killions Creek--between Killions line and Robert Leepers old survey. Granted
to Samuel More 1 Sept 1753. Peter Club (Seal), Wit: Francis Beatey, James
Beatey.

V. 4, Pp. 77-79: 22 & 23 Sept. 1766, George Brown & wf Eve of York Co.,
Pa., to Robert Watkins & Francis Coot of Frederick Co., Md. (lease s5,
release ___) 950 A on S side Katawba River and on Killians Creek, granted to
Leonard Killian 30 Sept 1749, conveyed to sd. Brown by L & R 1 & 2 Jan.
1754. George Brown (Seal), Eve Brown (E) (Seal). Wit: Absolem Bonham,
_____ (German signature), Thomas Hill. Rec. Jan. term 1767.

V. 2, Pp. 560-563: 25 Oct 1764, John Watkins & wf Rachel sell part of 250 A
granted to Leonard Killion 30 Sept 1749, conveyed by Killion & wf Margaret
to George Brown 1 Jan 1754, then to Watkins 20 Jul 1757.
* *

ALEXANDER MCCONNELL:
ANSON CO. NC WILL BK. 1, pp. 7-8: Will of Alexander McConnell of
Anson Co., written June 2, 1760. Mentioned cousin Andw McConnell of
Roan County: his cousin's son John McConnell; his cousin John McConnell
of Roan Co., his son John McConnell Jr.; his step-children Thos. & Jane
Black; "my man Alex Henderson to serve out the rest of his time to my wife

Catherine McConnell;" his wife Catherine McConnell; daughter Agness McConnell. Wit: Charles Moore, Charles McPeters, James Sharp.

Anson Co. Deeds, pp. 200-204: 19 & 20 March 1755, Thomas Irwin & Rebecca his wife of Anson Co., to John McDowell of same (Lease s5, release L16 s3 Va. money). 200 Acres on a branch of McDowell Creek, adj. John Kallers line, McCullochs line. Granted to Irwin 23 Feb 1754. Thomas Irwin (Seal), Rebecca Irwin (Seal), Wit: John Thomas, Allexander McConel, Robt. Denney.

Mecklenburg Co. Deeds, V. 2, Pp. 188-290: 7 & 8 June 1765, John McDowell & wife Ann of Meck., to James Moore of Stevensburg, Va., taylor (lease s5, release L70 proc. Money). 204 A on McDowells Cr., part of 725 A conveyed from Henry Eustace McCulloh to sd. McDowell. John McDowell, Ann McDowell. Wit: Richard Barry, Charles Moore, William Barry [Berry].

V. 1, pp. 188-189: 6 May 1766: Henry Eustace McCulloh of Chowan Co., NC to George Cathey, for L85 sterling. Land on McDowel's Creek...adj. John McDowel & John Potts land. 710 Acres. H. E. McCulloh (Seal), Wit: John Frohock, J. McKnitt Alexander.

Mecklenburg Co. Deed, V. 1, pp. 55-59, has mention of McDowell's Creek being on the south side Cataba on Crowder's Creek adj. Allisons survey, granted John McDowell 30 Aug 1753. Another deed, V. 1, Pp. 404-405, 6 Sept 1766 Richard Barry, son & heir to Andrew Barry, decd. & wf Ann of Meck., to Hugh Barry of same, planter. Land on N side Cataba, S side McDowell's Creek, where sd. Hugh Barry now lives. 428 a, adj. Samuel Wilsons, granted to sd. Andrew Barry 23 Feb 1754.
[Some later records have the name as Berry.]

Another deed showed Samuel Wilson's land on north side Cataba adj. George Cathey Sr. George Cathey's land was granted to him on 7 Oct 1749. The description was given in a deed in Anson Co., Pp. 308-309, 22 & 23 June 1753: George Renick & Mary his wife to John Willson. 350 Acres on S side Cataba, below place George Cathey claims, adj. Joseph Clarks, John Davis. Granted to Renick 21 Mar 1753.

George Renick & Mary also sold land 10 & 11 Feb 1758, Anson Deeds, pp. 385-388: to Adam Meek, 300 acres on north side Catabo, about a mile and a half from the river, including the forks of Renicks run. Granted to Renicks 31 Mar 1753. Also 100 acres adj. sd. Tract granted 30 Aug 1753. Wit: Saml. Willson, John Price, Alexander Lewis.

There is a map made by Elmer Oris Parker in 1977, found in Anson County, N.C. Deed Abstracts, Volume I: 1749-1747, by Brent Holcomb 1974, which showed the location of Adam Meek's land which he conveyed to

Samuel Watson in 1802. Next to this is notation of several transactions, then one from Danl. McClary and his wife Mary Stephenson McClary to Mrs. Jane Meek 1793 –willed to her sons James & Adam Meek 1797. This might not be the same land Adam Sr. had from the Renicks. Some of the other names shown on this map are the same as those in the area where Adam Sr. had land. The description of the land shown on this map states "North Carolina Land Grants on the Headwaters of Bullocks and Allison's Creeks in present York County, S.C." [There was an Adam Meek in Knox Co., Tn. in the early 1800's.]

A deed from George Cathey Jr. & Sarah his wife to Charles McPetters, pp. 361-362, 14 & 15 Jul 1753, described land on S side Cataba, opposite Robert Rennixs land. 325 A granted to sd. Cathey 7 Oct 1749. Signed George Cathey, Sarah Cathey, Wit: Alex. McConnell, George Renick.

Anson Co. Deed, pp. 298-302: 16 & 17 Jul 1755, George Cathey & Sarah his wife Anson Co. to William Alexander of Rowan Co. 130 acres on south side Cattawba, adj. James Armor. Granted to George Cathey 29 Mar 1753.

A deed from George Cathey to Martin Pfifer made 16 & 17 May 1758 gave a description "300 a. on south side Catabo, adj. Samuel Corbon [sic] and the Dutchmans Island, including the place where Andrew Cathey formerly lived…"
* *

JACOB COBURN:

Jacob Coburn was also a neighbor from this area, and was apparently German, as in several deeds he witnessed his signature was referred to as a German signature. He witnessed deeds, but we were unable to find any grants for him before 6 Nov 1764.

We believe Jacob was son of Samuel and Margaret Coburn.

Anson Co.

 Deeds, pp. 364-365, 11 & 13 Jan 1753, Samuel Coborn [sic] & Margret his wife of Anson Co., to Henery Johnston of same, (lease s5, release L20 Va. money). Land on S side Cataba, 260 Acres, granted to Coborn 29 Sept 1750. Samuel Coborn (X) (Seal), Margt. Coborn (X) (Seal), Wit: Jon. Betty [sic - probably Beaty], Alex. Osburn, Henry Hendry. (Note: Henery Hendry witnessed several deeds mentioning south side Cataba, N fork Fishing Creek.)

One deed for Samuel Coburn, Pp. 294-296, Anson Co. Deeds, dated 28 & 29 Dec 1755, had sale from John Clement & Judith his wife to Samuel Coburn of Anson Co., 378 A on South side Catawba above Saml. Cobruns land on the Tuckaseged path. Granted to Judith Coburn, now wife of John Clement, 30 Aug 1755. This deed was witnessed by Alex. Lewis, Jacob Coburn, Wm. Card.

Samuel Cobron [sic] and Margaret his wife sold land 1 & 2 Apr 1757 to James Kuykendal, 319 A on Leepers creek on the Indian path about two miles from Jacob Kuykendalls, granted to Cobron 1 Mar 1753. (Pp. 365-367.) [Note: Leepers Creek was named for Robert Leeper, wife Catherine, 'land on S side Catawba, Leeper's Creek, 300 A granted to Leeper 8 Oct 1751,' Anson Deeds, pp. 538-539.]

Samuel and Margaret made another deed on the same day, Anson Co., Deeds, pp. 368-371, to James Kuykendall for 132 A on Beaver Dam Branch, S side Catabo, adj. Samuel Coborns line. Granted 23 Feb 1754 to Charles Beaty, then conveyed to Cobron 25 Mar 1754.

On a map by Elmer O. Parker, 1978, showing the boundaries of Mecklenburg County in 1763-1769, Kuykendall's Creek was located in Gaston County. Leepers Creek was in Lincoln and Gaston. The northern end of Crowder's Creek was in Gaston Co., with the southern end in York County. [S.C.] Allison's Creek, Bullock's Creek, Turkey Creek, and the north end of Fishing Creek were in York Co. The southeast part of Fishing Creek was in Chester Co.

[Another record stated David John's was Grant #1633.[4]]

Mention of Mountain Creek in deeds:
V. 2, Pp. 51-53: 12 Apr 1765, Jacob Cook of Meck., to Michael Hoil of same, (lease s5, release L20 N.C. money). 200 A on waters of Beaver Dam Creek and a cattail branch of Mountain Creek, S waters of the S fork of Cataba adj. Jacob Mauneys line Granted to Jacob Cook 21 Dec 1763. Jacob Cook (Seal), [appears to be a German signature under his], Wit: Christian Simmerman (C S_, and a German signature, Ernst____.
[Several deeds mention Beaver Dam Creek as being a south branch of south fork of Catawba.]

Page 284: 4 Sept 1756, Stephen Brown of Anson Co., to Morgan Brown, for L30 proc. Money, 170 A on N side Great Pee Dee, below mouth of Mountain creek, granted to John Tamer 29 Sept 1750. S. Brown (Seal), Wit: Jno. Tamer [Hamer ?], Saml. Firth. [Anson Co., N.C. Deed Abstracts, V. I: 1749-1757].

David John witnessed a deed made 24 & 25 Oct 1755 by Evan Lewis and his wife Mary of Anson Co. to John Moore. Land on S side Catawba, S side Indian Creek, 600 Acres granted to Evan Lewis 10 Apr 1752.

NOTE: This land was shown by Brent Holcomb to be in South Carolina now. David John probably lived near the area of land that was located on the south

---

[4]ANSON CO. NC ABSTRACTS OF EARLY RECORDS, The May Wilson McBee Collection, Vol. 1, 1950, p. 11.

side of the Catawba, near Indian Creek and Beaver Dam Creek. His land appears to have been north, possibly northwest, of the Lewis'.

An early Mountain Creek Baptist Church was mentioned by Leah Townsend in her History of the Baptists in S. C. This was near, probably south of, Boiling Springs, N.C. A Mountain Island is shown on the map west of Charlotte, N.C.

* *

DAVID LEWIS:

He took out a grant the same day as David John, May 17 1754. Also on this date, Rees Thomas took out a grant. David Lewis might be one of the sons of Thomas Lewis, Pencader Hundred, New Castle Co., Del. Thomas' will was written 13 Jun 1749 and probated 27 Jun 1749. From Thomas Lewis' Will, Will Bk. G, p. 323:

Eldest son was Evan Lewis; second son was Alexander Lewis; third son was James Lewis; fourth son was David Lewis. Mentioned son in law Reec Thomas and my daughter Elizabeth his wife. Executor: Son in law Reec Thomas. David was the youngest son of Thomas Lewis.

* *

CHILDREN OF THOMAS LEWIS:

1. Evan Lewis, b. ca 1719. Wife Mary. Died Aug-Dec 1766, St. Georges Parish, Ga. Had son Thomas Lewis (land grant in 1766), and six other children. See will.
2. Alexander Lewis, b. ca 1721. Wife was Hannah. Died Mecklenburg Co., N.C. (Will 1784.) Children: Benjamin, Sarah, Dinah, Hannah, Josiah, Joseph.
3. Elizabeth Lewis, b. ca 1723, m. Reece Thomas.
4. James Lewis, b. ca 1725.
5. David Lewis, b. ca 1727.

[Estimated birthdates.]

* *

There was also a David Lewis who was the son of John Lewis and wife Elizabeth. There were several Lewis' of New Castle Co., Del. Elizabeth was sister of David John (ca 1720.) This was mentioned in the will of Griffith John (d. 1749), whose daughter was married to John Lewis. A grant was made to a David Lewis for 500 acres on the Broad River, possibly the one who came to the Pee Dee area in 1737.

[South Carolina Records: Petitions for Warrants of Survey, and Certifying of Platts: David Lewis 500 acres on Waters Broad River.[5]]

Indications are that the Lewis' mentioned as living near this David John were descendants of Thomas Lewis of Pencader Hundred. However, there is

---

[5]South Carolina.

certainly room for more proof. Rees Thomas was married to Elizabeth Lewis, daughter of Thomas Lewis. His widow was Joanna, as shown in a later deed, possibly a second wife. They all came to the area where Evan Lewis was settled, described as "south side Catawba, south side Fishing Creek." Evan was the name of the eldest son of Thomas Lewis. His wife was named Mary. David Lewis and Rees Thomas took out grants on the same day as David John. We found no Baptist records of the sons of Thomas Lewis.

<u>David Lewis, Grant #1164, 17 May 1754</u>.
<u>Bk. 15, p. 21, #4525, May 17, 1754</u>: David Lewis 600 acres Anson Co. on North side of the South Fork of Fishing Creek.[6]

<u>Anson Co. File No. 1238 (1740); Bk. 13, p. 42</u>: Alexander Brown, 320 a. on S. fork Fishing Creek above David Lewis land. 24 Sept 1754 Matt Rowan.
* *

Brent Holcomb in his book of Anson Co. deeds points out that Fishing Creek is now in South Carolina. There are a number of deeds of land on Fishing Creek stating [when the land was sold later] it was 'formerly in Anson Co., but now in Craven Co.' Later some deeds mention Fishing Creek that 'now be in Chester Co., S.C.' There is a small town named Lewis in Chester Co., southwest of Fishing Creek.. Northwest of Lewis is a town named McConnells in York Co., S.C. Fishing Creek appears to be the same creek called Catfish Creek by Gregg in his "History…" or was at least in the same general area. He mentioned Joseph Jones as living on Catfish.

<u>Mecklenburg Co. Deeds,</u>:
<u>File No. 2508; Gr. No. 474; Bk. 23, p. 294</u>. Plat: Surv. for Alexander Brown 200 acres on both sides S. fork Fishing Creek between lines of George Craig, Henry Culp, William Miller, Joseph Boyd, <u>David Lewis</u>. 11 Mar 1768 Wm. Dickson, Sur. Iss. 29 Apr 1768. William Henry & James Henry, C.C.

<u>File No. 0203, Anson Co</u>.:
Warrant: Unto Townsend Robinson, 600 a. on N. side S. fork Fishing Creek below the Indian path to Sandy River. Formerly <u>David Lewis…17 Nov 1753.</u> Matt:Rowan.

<u>V. 2, Pp. 356-359: 24 & 25 Nov. 1763</u>, Evan Lewis & wf Mary of Parish of St. George, Prov. of Georgia, to Hugh Shannon of Meck., (lease s5, release L63). 600 A on N side first branch of <u>S fork Cataba, S side of sd. Fork</u>…Evan Lewis (Seal), Mary Lewis (M) (Seal), Wit: David Emanuel, <u>David Lewis</u>, Josiah Lewis.

---

[6] Colonial Records of N. C. 1735-64 Abstracts of Land Patents.

Deed of Conveyance
Page 260. 29 Jan 1791,:
Joseph Lyon, yeoman to Robert Harper, yeoman, both of Chester Co. whereas
290 acres granted 29 Apr 1768 to Alexander Brown Sr. in Mecklenburg Co.,
N.C. at the time of survey now in Chester Co., S.C. on both sides of the south
fork of Fishing Creek, joining and between lines of George Craig, Henry
Culp, William Miller, John Boyd & David Lewis--including his (Brown's)
plantation,-- plat attached to grant recorded in sec'ys office of that province
(N.C.) Part of grant sold to Joseph Lyon by attorney of Alexander Brown,
recorded in clerk's office in Chester Co.; now in consideration of 100 pds.
sterling Joseph Lyon conveyed to Robert Harper 160 acres of sd plantation on
south side of the south fork of Fishing creek. Signed: Joseph Lyon. Dated 29
Jan 1791. Wit: William Wilson, William Jack..

P. 62: Indenture dated 22 Oct. 1783 bet. Archibald Elliott and Sarah his wife
of one part, planter and Rev. John Simpson of the other part V.D.M. for sum
of 100 pds. pd. Archibald and Sarah Elliott by John Simpson, --cause is their
unto moving.-- Archibald and Sarah his wife do convey unto John Simpson
269 acres lying on waters of the south fork of Fishing Creek, co. of Craven
joining Alexander Brown by patent dated 1772 from David Lewis. Signed:
Archibald (X) Elliott, Sarah (S) Elliott. Wit: William Elliott, Daniel Cooke.
Proved 15 Nov 1783.

P. 38. Indenture made 6 Oct 1785 bet. James Neely and his wife Martha of
Chester Co., planter. 100 acres on waters of Fishing creek in Craven Co. now
Chester Co.
[A David Lewis apparently had land granted to him on Indian Creek 17 Apr
1764. Evan Lewis already had land there.]

Pp. 323-325: Jacob Lewis, planter of State of Georgia, to David Mayson of
Laurens Co., SC, planter for L20 5 sh., 200 acres on Indian Creek, bounded
by John Mayson. Land orig. granted to David Lewis 17 Apr 1764, and
conveyed by him to Benjamin Lewis and conveyed to John Lewis by heirship
and conveyed by him to Jacob Lewis by power of attorney. Wit: James
Millwee, David Collior & Money Sherell. Probate was made at Pendleton
Co., SC by David Collior bef. William Halbert.

[NOTE: The Lewis' mentioned here, Benjamin, Jacob and John were
probably sons of David Lewis. We know from a later deed that he had a son
named David.]

<u>Benjamin Lewis 200 acres in Berkley Co.</u> Remarks: New Grant to David Lewis April 17, 1764.[7]

<u>Rees Thomas: Grant #1118, 17 May 1754.</u>

<u>Bk. 15, p. 10, #4472, May 17, 1754</u>: Rees Thomas 200 acres in Anson Co. on the <u>South side</u> of the <u>South Fork of Fishing Creek</u>.

Other grants:
Joseph Jones, Grant #1134, 1754, Little River.
Another deed shows his grant was 17 May 1754.

<u>Joseph Davies Grant 17 May 1754</u>: <u>V. 2, pp. 378-381: 24 & 25 Mar 1764</u>, Joseph Davies of Rowan Co., planter, to Robert Armstrong of Meck., (lease S5, release L30). Land on S side Catawa, land granted to sd. Davies <u>17 May 1754.</u> 280 Acres. Joseph Davies (Seal), Wit: James Beaty, Arthur Patterson.
* *

EVAN LEWIS:

He arrived in North Carolina from New Castle Co., Pa. in 1752, with a large family. One of his brothers was Alexander Lewis, who later was a surveyor, J. P. and Sheriff of Mecklenburg Co., N.C. He seems to have taken out land before David John in several areas, with David John soon following.

<u>Bk. 2, p. 14, #67, Apr 7 1752</u>: Evan Lewis 600 acres in Anson Co. on N. side of the First Branch next to the South Fork of the Cataba River and (on the) South Side of the said Fork.
<u>Evan Lewis, #852, 10 Apr 1752, Indian Cr. (S.C.)</u>

<u>Bk. 2, p. 14, #68, 10 Apr 1752</u>: Evan Lewis 600 acres in Anson Co. joining the S. side of Indian Creek and S. side of Cataba River.

<u>Mecklenburg Co., pp. 273-275: 24 & 25 Oct 1755.</u> Evan Lewis of Anson Co., & Mary his wife to John Moore for L 30 Va. money. Land on <u>S side Catawba</u>, S side Indian Creek, 600 acres granted to Evan Lewis 10 Apr 1752. Evan Lewis (Seal), Mary Lewis (M), (Seal), Wit: Alexander Lewis, <u>David John</u>.

<u>V. 2, Pp. 356-359: 24 & 25 Nov 1763</u>, Evan Lewis & wf Mary of Parish of St. George, Prov. of Georgia, to Hugh Shannon of Meck., (lease s5, release L63) 600 Acres on N side first branch of S fork Cataba, S side of sd. Fork. Evan Lewis (Seal), Mary Lewis (M) (Seal), Wit: David Emanuel, Davis Lewis, Josiah Lewis.

---

[7]Anson Co., N.C. records.

* *

ALEXANDER LEWIS:

He was a surveyor, a Justice of the Peace and later a Sheriff in Mecklenburg Co. He was probably brother of Evan, James, and David. He was probably son of Thomas Lewis, of New Castle Co., Del. He did not take out land in N. C. until 1753, but he was there in 1752. After his initial survey, there were several deeds for him. He was a witness to many deeds.

Anson Co.: SAMUEL MOORE, File no. 0394. Plat: Surveyed for Samuel Moore on N side S fork Fishing Creek. Dec 15 1752 Alexr Lewis (surv.)

Alexander Lewis, #753, 9 Apr 1753, File No. 120; Bk. 2, p. 40. 400 a. on E. side Fishing Creek below Cobus Kirkendalls. 9 Apr 1753 Matt Rowan.

Bk. 2, p. 40, #211, Apr 9 1753: Alexander Lewis 400 acres Anson Co. on E. side Fishing Creek by a small branch about 2 miles below Cabas Kirkendall.

B, 2, p. 32, #162, Apr 3 1753: Alexander Lewis 300 acres Anson Co. joining (a point) near Zebulon Brevard's corner, McCulloch's line and David Davis.

Deed Book 1, Page 294. Dec 29, 1755. John & Judith Clement, of Halifax Co., Va. to Sam'l Coburn, of Anson Co., N.C., for 5 shillings, land on South side of the Catawba above Sam Coburn's corner of Tuckaseged path, granted Judith Coburn, now wife of John Clement, 29 Aug 1753. (S.C.) Wit: Alexander Lewis; Jacob Coburn, Wm. Card.

Meck. Co., Vol. 1, pp. 476-480: Peter Elliott of Parish of St. George, Province of Georgia; Indian Trader. Land on Cataba River in Meck., to Alexander Lewis to sell 19 Jan 1764. Peter Elliot (P) (Seal), Wit: David Emanuel JP, Benj. Lewis.

Anson Co. Deeds, pp. 338-339: 27 & 28 Sept 1753, Peter Elliot (Ellet) of Anson Co., to James Davis of Rowan Co., (lease s5, release L9 Va. money). 150 A about 3 miles below John Price's granted to Ellet 7 Oct 1749. Peter Ellet (P) Wit: Evan Jones, Alex. Lewis.

23 & 24 April 1764. Peter Elliott to John Miller of Meck., (Lease s5, release L___). 150 acres on N. side Cataba, granted by George II, 7 Oct 1749 - about 3 miles below Price's land...Alexander Lewis for Peter Elliott (Seal), Wit: Richd Barry, Hugh Barry, John McDowell.

V. 2, Pp. 163-166: 11 & 12 July 1765, Alexander Lewis & wf. Hannah of Meck., to Samuel Neally, planter, of same (lease s5, release L40). -400 Acres formerly in Anson Co., now Meck., on E side Fishing Creek about 2 miles below Cobus Kirkendalls land- granted to sd Lewis 9 Apr 1753- Alexander Lewis (Seal), Hannah Lewis (Seal), Wit: John Thompson, James Harris, Benj. Lewis.

V. 2, Pp. 715-717: ___ 1765, Alexander Lewis, Sheriff of Meck., to Abraham Alexander. On 15 Oct 1763(?) at Superior Court of Wilmington for L119 s16 proc. Money...against James Carter, good & chattles--667 A on S fork Catawba. Alexander Lewis Sheriff (Seal), Wit: Nathl. Alexander, Adam Alexander.

New Patent 6 Apr 1765: [Land near Mary Lewis' grant in Mecklenburg Co.]
* *
MECKLENBURG CO. N.C. DEEDS, Vol. 1, Bk. 2, July 15, 1765, Alexander Lewis of Mecklenburg Co. and Hannah his wife, to James Lynn of same for 5 shillings sterling, 470 acres on Six Mile Creek between David Houston's and Jonathan Lewis's surveys. Lease for 6 months... Alexander Lewis (Seal). Wit: Benj. Lewis, Jas. Beaird.

July 15, 1765: Alexander Lewis and Hannah, his wife, to James Lynn. Release of land, patented to sd. Lewis April 6, 1765. Signed Alexander Lewis. Wit: Benj. Lewis, Jas. Beaird.
* *
BENJAMIN LEWIS:
He was a son of Alexander Lewis. (Per will.)
Benjamin Lewis, #678, 31 May 1753, File No. 678 (53); Bk. 10, p. 331 (2,23). 450 A on head of S. fork Fishing Creek Metias (sic) Clements corner--31 Mar 1753 Matt Rowan.

V. 2, pp. 722-724: 22 & 23 _____ 1765, Benjamin Alexander & wf Susannah to Andrew Meek of _____ Prov. of Maryland, (lease s5, release L37)-- Land on __ side Cataba, on Fishing Creek, adj. Benjamin Lewis, granted 9 Nov 1764.Benjamin Alexander, Susannah Alexander (L) Wit: Nathaniel Alexander, Moses Fergus___, ___ses Meek.

Note: Peter Elliott seems to have a familial connection with the Lewis'. Benjamin Lewis, son of Alexander, took out land in Georgia joining Peter Elliott's:

"Col. Records of Ga." Vol. IX, May 1764:
Read a petition of Benjamin Lewis setting forth that he had several years in the Province had had no land granted him and was desirous to obtain a piece

of land therefore praying for 50 acres in Hallifax District at a place called Walnut Branch joining South land granted Peter Elliott, North land of Joanna Thomas and West land of Evan Lewis.

V. 3, Pp. 30-33: 1 & 2 Dec 1767: Benjamin Lewis of Meck., Gent. To James Murphy of same (lease s5, release L102 s10)--450 Acres in Meck. & perhaps falling into SC. -On head of S fork Fishing Creek, adj. Mathew Clement-- Granted to sd. Lewis, 31 Mar 1753; Benj. Lewis (Seal), Wit: James Hannah, John Martin, Richard Saddler. Proven Jan. term 1768. (This land wholly in present SC.)
* *

JAMES LEWIS:
There was a Capt. James Lewis who was mentioned as a Tory. (See chapter of Rev. War.)
CRAWFORD, OLIVER File No. 236 (858); Gr. No. 354; Bk. 2, p. 70. 455 A on N side Broad River on Turkey Creek above James Lewis survey--30 Aug 1753 Matt Rowan.
[Remember, there was an early grant to David Lewis on the Broad River.]

V. 4, Pp. 863-865: 7 Jan 1769, David Davis of Mecklenburg, to Nathaniel Miller of same, for L 35 proc. Money, 200 Acres on S. branch of N. Fork of Tygar River above Robert Millers land, patented to David Davis 25 Sept. 1766. David Davis (Seal). Wit: James Lewis, Jonathan Potts. Rec. Jan. term 1769.

CHAPTER ELEVEN

POSSIBLE CONNECTIONS:
DAVID DAVIS:

David John is believed to have first married Mary Davis. David Davis lived near the Lewis' and probably near David John in S.C. He might have been a relation. Alexander Lewis, brother of Evan, etc. took out land in 1753 near David Davis' line. David Davis was a neighbor of Joseph Jones, and was also listed as a surveyor on several deeds.

File No. 2079, Meck. Co., Gr. No. 49; Bk. 23, p. 90. David Davis---200 A on both sides N fork Tyger Adj. Jonathan Newmans line. 26 Oct 1767 Wm Tryon.

File No. 1380; Gr. No. 53, Bk. 18, p. 260 (17,285). David Davis..200 A on S branch N. fork Tygar above Robert Millers land, 25 Sept 1766 Wm. Tryon.

V. 2, Pp. 569-570: 16 Nov 1764, Dobbs & wf to John McKnitt Alexander of Meck., for L13 s2 proc. Money. 131 A on head branches of Rocky River, where David Davis did live. Wit: Richd Barry, Martin Phifer.

P. 43, Mecklenburg Co. 28 Apr 1768, David Davis shown as Surv. with Joseph Jones.

P. 54, Meck. Co., 29 Apr 1768, shown with Joseph Jones.

P. 71, Meck. Co., 4 May 1769, shown with Joseph Jones.

P. 77, Joseph Kelly surv. Jul 7 1766, adj. Josh Millers Mill Seat, David Davis...

P. 82, File No. 0238, 9 Jan 1768, John McCarter--- Surv. James Reynolds, David Davis, CB.

P. 99, . File No. 0296; Entry No. 404. Samuel Nesbet--- Warrant 200 Acres on main fork of Tygar Riv. adj. his own, Joseph Jones, David Davis, Robert Millar. 26 Apr 1768. Wm. Tryon.

Similar entry, except Samuel Neisbett, File No. 895; Gr. No. 136; Bk. 17, p. 403. Survey for 200 Acres on both sides S branch N fork Tyger adj. David Davis, Robert Miller. 18 Mar 1766. Wm Dickson, Surv. Joseph Jones, Thomas Penny, CB Iss. 25 Apr 1767.

File No. 2435, Gr. No. 301; Bk. 23, p. 242. Elisha Thompson survey 200 A on N branch Tyger River adj. David Davis. By Wm. Sharp, Surv. 9 Jan 1768, Joseph Jones, David Davis, CB Iss. 29 Apr 1768.

Other deeds for David Davis go to 1777:

Vol. 7, Pp. 140-142: 13 Aug 1777, John Beats [Beaty?] & wf Margrat of Meck. to William McDowel of same, for P 150. 130 A on waters of Kings Branch, adj. Margrat Donelson, David Davis, granted to sd. John Beats [sic]

by deed from George Selwyn, 19 Jan 1767. John Bates, (Mark), (Seal), Margaret Bates, mark, (Seal), Wit: Will Reed, Robert Campbell. No rec. date.
* *

MOORE'S:

Samuel Moore, File No. 0394. Plat: Surveyed for Samuel Moore. N side S fork Fishing Creek. Dec 15, 1752 Alexr Lewis [surv.]
John Moore, #2135, 26 Mar 1755, N. of Turkey Cr.
V. 2563-564: 4 Jan 1765, John Moore & wf Ann of Meck., to John Garvin for L60, 580 A granted to sd. Moore 26 Mar 1755. On N side of a branch called by some Moores Creek. John Moore (Seal), Ann Moore (A) (Seal), Wit: William Dunlop, John Thomas, James McCord.
Wm. Moore, File no. 0548, Plat: April 8 1754, Surveyed for William Moore, 300 A on ye South fork of fishing Creek adj. Branches of turkie creek. Pr Saml Young, Dep. Sur. Jas. Kukindal & Samuel Young, Ch.Ca.
Tryon Co.:
Moore, James, File No. 166, Grant No. 461, Bk. 20, p. 488. Plat: Surveyed for James Moore 300 A in Mecklenburg (striken) Tryon County on the waters of the south fork of Fishing Creek on Laccys spring branch and on both sides of the Waggon Road. John Prices corner--Edward Laceys corner--Thomas Raineys line--John Walkers line--16 Feby 1767 Wm. Dickson Sur. Samuel Rainey & Joshua Lacey, Cha. Bear. Grant issued 6 May 1769.

Tryon Co. had a grant surveyed for Charles Moore in 1772. He witnessed several deeds in Mecklenburg Co. during the latter part of the 1760's.
File No. 456; Grant No. 75; Bk. 22, p. 19. Plat: Surveyed for Charles Moore 200 A on So. Side of Tygar River--John Foard's line--near Neallys Corner--16th Jany 1772. Jno. Kirkconell Sur. Andrew Berry, Alexander Barron CB Grant issued 15 May 1772.
*

There was a John Moore in this area that was a Baptist Preacher. He was from Virginia, according to the records given in Morgan Edward's "Materials...." However, there was also a John Moore who lived in New Castle Co., Del. He might have gone to Virginia, then to South Carolina. Moore was granted 580 acres on North side of a Branch of Turkey Creek, called Moores Creek. [File no. 2135, Grant no. 78, Book 23, p. 81.] One John Moore had brother Moses Moore, who had a son named John. Moses Moore was a Colonel in the military, and he & his son were Tories.

One John Moore was killed by Indians in 1760. He left a noncupative will, given by Peter Kuykendall. He left his land to John, son of his brother Moses.

Mecklenburg County Deeds: PP. 579-581: 23 Nov 1762, Moses Moore of Anson Co., to Valentine Mauney of Anson Co., (lease s5, release L35)

370 A on N side Indian Creek, adj. land on Joseph Cloud, decd--170 A granted to John Moore decd, then conveyed to Jeremiah Potts, then to Moses Moore, and 200 A granted to Moses Moore 10 Apr 1761. Moses Moore (Seal), Wit: Thomas Robinson, Francis Beaty.

Pp. 581-584: 24 Nov 1762, Moses Moore of Anson Co., to Thomas Robinson, planter, of same, for L55 NC money--300 A on both sides Indian Creek, a branch of S fork Cataba, part of 600 A where sd. Moses Moore now dwells, granted 28 Mar 1755.Moses Moore (Seal), Wit: Valentine Mauney, Frances Beatey.

"North Carolina Land Grants in South Carolina", by Brent Holcomb, lists these grants as being in Anson Co. There were several grants to Guyan Moore, one being for 800 acres on both sides of Broad River 3 Apr 1752.

Mention was made of Beaverdam Creek, Loves Creek, and Clark's Creek.

Another Moore receiving an early grant in N.C. was Samuel Moore, file No. 0394, land on the North side of the South Fork of Fishing Creek, Dec. 15, 1752. The surveyor was Alexander Lewis.

Fishing Creek figured prominently in several of the deeds from North Carolina. A map by Elmer O. Parker included by Holcomb has a Fishing Creek in Chester Co., S.C. A deed showing Fishing Creek notes it was formerly in Craven Co., S.C. but now in Chester Co.

William Moore received 300 acres on the South fork of Fishing Creek adjoining branches of Turkey Creek, File no. 0548, April 8, 1754.

Some of the records for the same land were found in files of Anson Co., Mecklenburg Co., and Tryon Co. Brent Holcomb, who has recorded and published many of the North and South Carolina early land grants, wrote that North Carolina issued land grants that were later found to be in South Carolina. The counties issuing these grants were Bladen, Anson, Mecklenburg and Tryon. [Review: Bladen was formed in 1734; Anson was formed from Bladen in 1748 or 1749; Mecklenburg from Anson in 1763; and Tryon from Mecklenburg in 1769.]

The map made by Elmer O. Parker in 1978 shows a small creek in Gaston County as Kirkendall's Creek. Just north of where this enters the Catawba River in Lincoln County regular maps show a large body of water called Mountain Creek. It is impossible to say how far south this creek ran in 1754. It appears to be part of the Catawba River.

Mary Kathryn Harris, who has done a lot of investigating of the John's land records, believes the Mountain Creek mentioned in David John's grant was in what is now Lincoln County. Some of her reasoning: David John was a witness when Evan Lewis sold land (his 1752 grant) to John Moore in 1755. This was located on S. side of Indian Creek. There was an Indian Creek in Lincoln Co. In his (John Moore's) noncupative will, his land was 'bought of Jeremiah Potts.' This land was later sold to Moses Moore, who sold it to Valentine Mauney, "land on Indian Creek granted to John Moore deceased, then conveyed to Jeremiah Potts,..." in 1762. Potts Creek is located a little north and east of Indian Creek in Lincoln County.

From the reference made in a deed to a cattail branch of Mountain Creek, it is possible that the John's land was located farther south than Lincoln Co. Brent Holcomb seems sure the land on Indian Creek as shown above was in Craven Co., then in Chester Co., S.C.

The Mountain Creek on the Pee Dee River, now in Richmond Co., N.C., was shown on a map in Gregg's History. This showed it to be in South Carolina near the border of North Carolina at the time the Pee Dee area was settled. It was located on the Pee Dee River, and several old deeds have reference to the Pee Dee and Mountain Creek. However, the records of David John's land nearly all reference Catawba River, and not the Pee Dee River. The Catawba is west of the Pee Dee.

MECKLENBURG COUNTY HISTORY:

Mecklenburg County was taken from Anson County in 1762. It included northern part of Lancaster and York Counties, S. C. Mecklenburg was divided into Tryon Co. in 1767, Cabarrus in 1792, and Union in 1842. Name of Tryon Co. was changed to Lincoln Co. in 1776. From it, Gaston Co. was formed in 1846.

Charlotte is county seat and records are kept there. South of Mecklenburg Co., N.C. border is the area that was Craven Co., N.C. It is now Marlborough County, S.C.

Other Land Records helping to locate David John's land:

MECKLENBURG COUNTY.

V. 2, Entry No. 880, NC Pat. Bk. 18, P. 303: John Gullick 26 Sep 1766, to John Walker--300 a., Mecklenburg Co., N.C., south side Little Catawba River, between David John and Samuel Gingle. [Our David John died in Nov 1765.]
Vol. 3, Pp. 50, 51, 52: 16 Jul 1767, John Walker of Meck., planter to Alexander Gilleland, for L20--202 a. granted to sd. Walker 26 Sept 1766 on a branch of Crowder's Creek at Coburn's corner. John Walker (Seal), Wit: James Gordon, Robert Spurlock, John Robertson. Proven Jan term 1768.
Pp. 50-51: 21 Dec 1767, Samuel Cobrun [Coburn] of Meck., to William Ray of same, for L50--272 a. granted to sd. Cobrun 16 Nov 1764 on both sides N. fork Crowders Creek--adj. Jacob Coburn. Samuel Coburn, Mark, (Seal). Wit: Richd Barry, Jacob Coburn, Hugh Barry. Proven Jan term 1768.
V. 2, Pp. 51-53: 12 Apr 1765 Jacob Cook of Meck., to Michael Hoil of same, (lease s5, release L20 N.C. money).--200 A on waters of Beaver Dam Creek and a cattail branch of Mountain Creek, s waters of the S fork of Cataba adj. Jacob Mauneys line--Granted to Jacob Cook 21 Dec 1763...Jacob Cook

(Seal), [appears to be a German signature under his], Wit: Christian Simmerman (C I_, and a German signature, Ernst _____.

V. 2, Pp. 418-421: John Campbell of Bertie Co., is possessed of a tract in the back of this province, granted 3 Mar 1745, to Jeremiah Joy, 1000 A on Anson County on S side S fork Catawba, formerly granted to Elias Lagardere 3 Apr 1753, & another tract of 1000 A on S side Pedee, lower side of Browns Creek, granted to George Gould ___ Mar 1747, & 640 A in the fork of Mountain Creek to sd. Gould on Jones Creek, a tract granted to Gould 25 Mar 1748...& 300 A on S side Pedee, adj. William Henry, granted 6 Apr 1750 to James McManus--Power of attorney to Henry Eustace McCulloh, 10 Aug 1762. John Campbell (Seal), Wit: Robert Aarney (?), Alexr. Ford.
*

JACOB COBURN:

Deeds, Bk. 1, Anson Co., p. 294: Dec 29 1755: John & Judith Clement of Halifax Co., Ga. (Va.) to Sam'l Coburn, of Anson Co. N.C. for 5 shillings, land on S. side of the Catawba above Sam Coburn's corner of Tuckaseged path, granted Judith Coburn, now wife of John Clement, 29 Aug 1753 (S.C.) Wit: Alxr. Lewis, Jacob Coburn, Wm. Cord (McCord?)
*

ANSON COUNTY grants with reference to Mountain Creek and Pee Dee:

#1309 William Terry (Esq.) 27 Sep 1756; 300 acres north of Peedee, on south fork of Mountain Creek, surveyed Feb 23, 1756.
Surv. 20 Sep 1771, adj. widow Franklin's line--John Jarmin's line--on Buffalo & Mountain creeks--.

Secy. of State Papers (SS884) Dept. of Archives & History, Raleigh, N.C.
"northeast of Peedee on North fork of Mountain Creek, adj. Wm. Coleman, granted Wm. Ferrill 1756..."
"N.E. of Peedee, on Mountain Creek, adj--- pat. to Wm. Terrell 27 Sep 1756..."
P. 470. 20 Aug 1774. Wm. Coleman & James Pickett, of Anson, to Geo. Jefferson, of Lunenburg Co., Colony of Va. for 60 pounds 200 acres on NE side of Peedee, lower side of Mountain Creek on small branch that enters the Grassy Islands. John Chiles, John Cartright.
" 50 acres on north side of the Peedee near Mountain Creek."
"150 a. on northeast side of Peedee, N side of Mountain Creek, which land was granted to Wm. Thomas & John Coleman 27 Sep 1756."
14 Apr 1772, p. 78. "lands between Mountain Creek & Drowning Creek as high as Anson Co. line and as low as Patrick Sanderson's work same."
"many who received these land grants were from Augusta Co., Va. See: The Expansion of Upper S.C. by Robert L. Meriwether."

Some names listed as receiving grants and being on Fishing Creek at this time were David Lewis, Peter Kuykendal, Abraham Kuykendall, Alexander Lewis, Benjamin Lewis, Samuel Neely, Thomas Neely, Andrew Wood, George Carthy [Cathy], Benjamin Alexander, Thomas Morgan, James Murphey, Jonathan Kirkkendall, and Thomas Walker.

[George Robison had survey 13 Oct 1756 for 310 acres on the South side of Broad River. (File No. 1349, Bk. 13, p. 138.)]

Tryon County had records of many of the surveys shown in Mecklenburg Co. --John Moore's land on Fishing Creek; Moses Moore's land on N. side Indian Creek, etc. There was mention of Peter Keykendalls line on branch of Fishing Creek, corner of the Indian Land (claimed by the Catawba), in a grant of Martin Armstrong's, File No. 812, Grant No. 88, Bk. 23, p. 329, 22 Dec 1768. Daniel Brice and Samuel Brice had grants mentioning Tygar River in 1769. Samuel Brice's grant had mention of 'about 2 miles below Jones' old place.' Several grants located here mentioned Turkey Creek and Thicketty Creek.
* *

JOSEPH JONES:
We believe he was son of John Jones and Ann, and grandson of David John, who died in Del. in 1748. [The eldest son of our David John was named Joseph, but nothing was found regarding a Joseph John in Burke Co., Ga. or Mecklenburg Co., N.C.] During the Revolutionary War, one of the notorious Tory Captains was Capt. Joseph Jones, a surveyor, probably this Joseph who was grandson of David (d. 1748.) He led the raiders when Col. Kolb was killed. We believe this Joseph was too old to be son of our David (who d. Ga. 1765.)

Joseph Jones had a grant on Little River in 1752, probably the Little River running into Greater Pee Dee. He was described as exceptionally intelligent, having made a compass in Marion District that greatly assisted in surveying the land. Gregg did not know his parentage. He had a brother named John Jones, and at that time Gregg wrote they lived on Catfish Creek in the Marion area. This was undoubtedly the same person whose name was shown in a number of grants on or near Fishing Creek, as a surveyor or witness, etc. John Jones, his brother, was also in the area.

Some of the deeds with his name were given with David Davis, as previously shown. Other records are:
1763: V. 2, pp. 364-366: 10 Dec 1763, Mathew Bigar of Meck., to Robert Elliot of same for L35 or L40, land on N branch of McAlpins [McAlpine] Creek, 200 Acres. Mathew Bigar (Seal), Wit: Samuel Coningham [Cunningham], Joseph Jones, Adam Allexander.

1765: File No. 1511, Mecklenburg Co., Gr. No. 464, Bk. 18, p. 339. Warrant unto John McRee, 640 Acres on middle fork Tyger above Joseph Jones. 24 Oct 1765 Wm. Tryon.

File No. 791, Mecklenburg Co., Gr. No. 466; Bk. 18, p. 339. Warrant unto David McRee, 200 acres on N. branch Tyger adj. Place where Joseph Jones lives. 24 Oct 1765...Wm Tryon.

1766: A survey for Robert McMurdie File No. 0258. 300 acres on S. side Lawsons fork of Packolet, Jones Waggon Road--John Millers--14 Dec 1766.

1767: Another survey for Samuel Neisbett dated 25 April 1767 was made showing Surv. Joseph Jones and Thomas Penny.

File No. 2285; Gr. No. 195; Bk. 23, p. 181. Joseph Jones---200 Acres on both sides N fork Tygar river. 26 Oct 1767 Wm. Tryon.

File No. 2207; Gr. No. 361; Bk. 23, p. 148. Jean Knox---300 Acres on middle fork of Tygar---path from Joseph Jones to his old plantation---Joseph Alexander. 26 Oct 1767. Wm. Tryon.

File No. 1657 (936); Gr. No. 183; Bk. 18, p. 378 : John Laycock---Tyger River adj. where Joseph Jones now lives and David Davis line. 22 Sept 1766 Wm. Tryon. Plat: surveyed for Robert McRee, 300 Acres on SW branch of N fork Tyger adj. David Davis. 2 Dec 1766 Peter Johnston, Surv. William Dickson, David McRee, D Bear.Iss 26 Oct 1767.

File No. 2289; Gr. No. 204; Bk. 23, p. 182. Warrant unto James Miller 200 a. on N. side main fork of Tygar on both sides the Waggon Road leading from Robert Millers to Charles Town. 27 Sept 1766 Wm. Tryon. Plat surveyd for James Miller 200 Acres on both sides ye S fork Tygar on both sides the Waggon road from Robert Millers to Charles Town. By William Sharp, Sur. John Nichols, John Miller, CB Iss. 26 Oct 1767.

File No. 0279. Warrant unto James Millar, 300 a. on N. fork Tyger above Francis Wilsons, on the wagon road from Joseph Jones to Alexander Varners--Robert Millers land--18 Apr 1767. Wm. Tryon.

File No. 2276; Gr. No. 90, Bk. 23, p. 180. Warrant unto John Miller, 100 A. on N side N fork of Tyger River on Wards branch abt. A mile above Wards land & near or Joining Robert Millers land--on both sides of the waggon Road--22 Sept 1766. Plat surveyed for John Miller 100 a. on N side N fork Tyger on Wards Branch adj. Charles Moore--17 Dec 1766 Wm. Dickson, Surv. Nathaniel Miller, Martin Oats or Cates, CB Iss. 26 Oct 1767.

Another survey same date for John Orr File No. 2151. S branch of N fork Tyger adj. Alexander Vernon, John Miller, James Miller...

File No. 2273; Gr. No. 73; Bk. 23, p. 179. Warrant for John Miller, 2— A on branch of Tyger River. 29 Oct 1765 Wm. Tryon.

Plat surveyed for John Miller, 200 a. on N. side N. fork Tyger adj. Joseph Jones plantation--Jonathan Newmans line--6 Mar 1766 William Dickson, Surv. Joseph Jones, Alexander Ray, CB Iss. 26 Oct 1767.

File No. 854 (1575); Gr. No. 87; Bk. 17, p. 393: John Moore---

300 acres on waters of S fork Fishing Creek adj. Edward Lacey, James Moor on both sides Waggon Road 25 Apr 1767 Wm. Tryon.

File No. 1679 (958); Gr. No. 216; Bk. 18, p. 383. Plat: Surveyed for John Brandon, 200 a. on waters of Turkey Creek on head of Titus branch on both sides Waggon Road including Wm Hillhouses Great Cowpen. 27 July 1765 William Dickson, Surv. John Brandon, John Smith, C.B.Iss. 25 Apr 1767.

1768: Plat surveyed for James Miller, 180 a. on S. side N. fork Tygar on Jemmeys Creek, adj. Vernons, Penneys, & Leeches dated 7 Jan 1768. Wm Sharp, Surv. Thos Collins, Alexander Ray, CB.

Mecklenburg Co.:, File No. 2431; Gr. No. 297; Bk. 23, p. 241. Plat: Survey'd for John Alexander 200 a. on both sides of Lawsons fork of Packelet above John Wottens (?) Land. 5th Jany 1768 by Wm. Sharp, Survr. Jos. Jones & David Davis, C: Bear. Iss. 28 Apr 1768.

TRYON COUNTY, File No. 873; Grant No. 274; Bk. 23, p. 362. Plat: Surveyed for Hugh Barney 200 acres in _____ County on the Middle fork of Tygar River joining the lower line of Jos. Jones place--near Alexander McCarters line on the No. side of sd. Fork 12th Sepr 1768 by Wm. Sharp Survr. (No CB). Gr. Issued 26 Dec 1768.

File No. 874; Grant No. 275; Bk. 23, p. 362. 150 acres on N. side of the Middle fork of Tygar River on a branch falling at the upper end of Jones land--22d December 1768 Wm. Tryon.

NOTE: This also showed David Davis as a surveyor. Later deeds show their land adjoining. [David John's will was witnessed by Phoebe Davie.]

File No. 0208. Plat: Feb 26 1768.
Surveyed for Joseph Jones 200 a. on N fork Tygar--McRee line---Zach Bullock Joseph Jones, Joseph Thompson, CB.

1769:
File No. 0296; Entry No. 404.
Warrant: Unto Samuel Neisbet, 200 acres on Main fork of Tygar River adj. his own, Joseph Jones, David Davis, Robert Millar--26 Apr 1768 Wm. Tryon.
Plat: Surveyed for Samuel Neisbet, 200 Acres in Tryon County on N fork Tyger including the improvement he lives on 9 Feb 1769 Peter Johnston, Surv. Thomas Penny, James Neisbet, CB. (Another survey for James Neisbet has Surv. Daniel Brice and Samuel Brice.)

File No. 853; Grant No. 192; Bk. 23; p. 348 200 acres on the middle fork of Tygar river about a mile and a half below the Indian path---about 2 miles below Jones' old place---22d Dec 1769 Wm. Tryon.

Joseph Jones was one of the people signing statement that they had known Major Martin Fifer for two years and that the charges and aspersions against him were false.

There were other Jones' deeds in Mecklenburg & Anson Counties:
Vol. 3, Mecklenburg Co. Deeds, pp. 52-53:
16 Jan 1768, Joseph Jolley of Mecklenburg, cooper, to John Jones of same, planter, for s20. Land on S. side Thicketty Creek, part of tract granted to said Jolley 14 Apr 1767. Joseph Jolley (Seal). Wit: Henry Clark, Nath. Clark, Henry Kar.
John Nuckols File No. 2375, Gr. No. 135; Bk. 23, p. 205. Plat Survey'd for John Nuchols 400 Acres on both sides Thicketty, Stephen Jones line--David Robertsons line--Zach Bullock Joab Mitchell, Stephen Jones, CB Iss. 28 Apr 1768.
Anson Co. Abstracts, Pp. 16-17: 26 Sept 1749, James Jones of Craven Co., S.C., planter, to Andrew Hamton of Anson Co., planter, for L500 proc. money---640 Acres granted to sd. Jones 22 May 1741--on S side P. D. --Beech Creek--James Jones, Wit: Wm. Bedingfield, Wm Kemp, Jo Staffard.
*

GEORGIA

David John [ca 1720] owned land on Mountain Creek in N. C. for a period of nine years. He sold this land 26/27 Oct 1763.[1] He was using land in Georgia during at least part of this time, although he apparently had failed to finalize his title. Records show his Georgia deed was not Registered until May 22, 1765. This was either done by Mary John, or his son David Jr.

He did not complete the 1758 grant, which was as follows:

"On Tuesday, Dec. 5, 1758, David John petitioned for land in the Province of Georgia:

Read a petition of David John setting forth that he had been four months in the Province and had no Lands therein, and was desirous to obtain a Grant of Lands for Cultivation Therefore Praying for One hundred Acres in the Fork of Briar Creek about a Mile from Land of William Champ which if granted he engaged to improve the same.

GRANTED: That on Condition only that the Petitioner doth take out a Grant for the said Land within Seven Months from the Date, And that he doth also register the said Grant in the Register's Office of the Province within Six Months from the Date thereof that his Majesty may not be

---

[1]Mecklenburg Co. Deed Abstracts by Holcomb, PP. 566-588, 26 & 27 Oct 1763. Land on Mountain Creek, adj. Alexander McConnels, 210 acres...

defrauded of his Quit Rents, Then the Prayer of the said Petition is granted."[2]

*

Evan Lewis sold his land in Mecklenburg Co. 24 & 25 1763, and was then living in St. George Parish, Ga.:

Deed Abstrs., V. 2, pp. 356-359: 24 & 25 Nov 1763, Evan Lewis & wf Parish of Parish of St. George, Prov. of Georgia, to Hugh Shannon of Meck., (lease s 5, release L63)--600 A on N side first branch of S fork Cataba, S side of sd. Fork. Evan Lewis (Seal), Mary Lewis (M) (Seal), Wit: David Emanuel, Davis Lewis, Josiah Lewis.

Apparently Evan Lewis had taken out a land grant on Briar Creek in Feb., prior to David John taking his out in Dec. 1758:

"The Colonial Records of Georgia...Vol. VII, Feb. 1758: Petition of Evan Lewis that he was settled in this province having a family consisting of a wife and six children and was desirous of obtaining land - - - praying for 350 acres at the Head of a Branch of Briar Creek called Walnut Branch already settled by the petitioner."

Benjamin Lewis also took out land in Georgia, as did Joanna Thomas, widow of Rees Thomas.

Col. Records of Ga., Vol. IX, May 1764:

Read a petition of Benjamin Lewis setting forth that he had several years in the Province had had no land granted him and was desirous to obtain a piece of land therefore praying for 50 acres in Hallifax District at a place called Walnut Branch joining south land granted Peter Elliott, North land of Joanna Thomas and West land of Evan Lewis.

The Col. Records of Ga., Vol. 7, Feb 1759: Read a petition of Joanna Thomas Widow setting forth that she was settled in the Province, had no lands therein and was desirous to obtain land for cultivation having 3 children therefore praying for 200 acres on a Branch of Briar Creek the South side thereof joining lands granted David Emanuel.

As written previously, it was common practice for the Welsh to maintain two places of abode. The John's and Lewis' seemed to have homes in both Georgia and North Carolina for a few years.

These records were found:

---

[2]The Rev. George White, M.A., Historical Collections of Ga. (New York; Pudney & Russell, 1855), Vol. VII, p. 850.) Also shown in "English Crown Grants in St. George Parish in Ga. 1755-1775, by Pat Bryant, Surveyor Gen. Dept., State of Ga., St. Printing Office, Atlanta, p. 100. Surveyed on March 12, 1759, Plat Book C, p. 96. Granted on Apr 2, 1765, Grant Book E, p. 157.

"The early Cymric land-holder had always two places of abode. One of these, built high up on the mountain side, was called the "Vottai," or summer residence. The other house was his "Hendre," or "Permanent Home," erected in some spot in the low-lands which was sufficiently sheltered from the winter blasts...in the early spring the wealthy farmer left his Hendre, taking with him his family, servants, his cattle and his sheep. The sheep would be sent to the higher mountains but the cattle would be grazed on the joint pasture lands belonging to the different Hendres. ...in August the farmer would return with his cattle to his Hendre, bringing with him the summer product of cheese and butter, to gather his harvest. Later in the season the sheep would be brought from the hills and secured in comfortable quarters for the winter...women oversaw the dairy, ...poultry and...spinning and knitting...At the time of their removal to Pennsylvania, in 1682, the Cymric Quakers farmed their places in much this manner..."[3]
* *

"History of Marlboro County" [S.C.], Rev. J. A. W. Thomas, Atlanta, Ga., The Foote & Davies Co., Printers & Binders 1896, Page 50, gave an account of Daniel John, son of Thomas John and Elizabeth Pouncey of Marlboro County, telling of entrapping wild horses in the early days. Thomas told of driving domestic animals across the county to their new homes.

David John took out a land grant again in April 1764 in Georgia. ["Bryar Creek" was "Briar Creek", on which he had petitioned for land.]
This petition for land follows[4]:
"APRIL, 1764.
Petition of David John for 100 acres
Read a Petition of David John setting forth that some years since he had one hundred Acres of Land ordered him in <u>Hallifax district</u> for which he had omitted to take out a Grant and the same was afterwards included in a Tract of five hundred Acres ordered <u>David Douglass</u>[5] deceased. That he had a family consisting of a Wife and four Children and having no Land was desirous to obtain Land for Cultivation Therefore praying for One Hundred Acres in Hallifax district aforesaid adjoining Land there granted <u>David Lewis</u>--
RESOLVED That on Condition only that the Petitioner doth take out a Grant for the said Land within seven Months from this date and that he doth also register the said Grant in the register's office of this province within Six

---

[3]Merion In The Welsh Tract, by Thomas Allen Glenn, Baltimore, Genealogical Publishing Co. 1970, pp. 188-189.
[4]The Colonial Records of the State of Georgia. Compiled and published under Authority of The Legislature By Allen D. Candler Partly from State Archives and Partly from Manuscripts in the British Public Record Office, London. Volume IX 56487. PROCEEDINGS AND MINUTES OF THE GOVERNOR AND COUNCIL From January 4, 1763, to December 2, 1766. Atlanta, Ga. The Franklin-Turner Co., Printers, Publishers, Binders 1907" (Found in McClung Collection Lawson McGhee Library, Knoxville, Tn.) P. 153, April 1764.
[5]There was a David Douglass in New Castle Co., probably this one.

Months from the date thereof that his Majesty may not be defrauded of his Quit rents then the prayer of the said petition is granted--"

There was also a petition of David Lewis in 1765, as follows:
"Page 314.
Petition of David Lewis for 150 Acres read.
Read a Petition of David Lewis setting forth that he had been many Years settled in the Province had had Two hundred Acres of Land granted him and was desirous to obtain an additional Tract having a Wife and Six Children Therefore praying for One hundred and fifty Acres upon a Branch of Lambert's big Creek on the south side thereof near Land lately ordered David Emanuel---
RESOLVED That on Condition only that the Petitioner doth take out a Grant for the said Land within seven Months from this Date and that he doth also register the said Grant in the Register's Office of the said Province within Six Months from the Date thereof that his Majesty may not be defrauded of his quit Rents the prayer of the said Petition is granted--"
*

In Ga. Roster of the Revolution, Abner Bickham used this as bounds for his land in Burke Co.: Survey General Book "I", p. 95, indicates 287 1/2 a. "bounded North by David Lewis, and other sides vacant....
* *

DAVID EMANUEL:
David Emanuel, who had lived in Chester Co., Pa. and Lunenberg Co., Va., received a grant in North Carolina which was obtained the year prior to David John's, and was also sold to John Walker.
This grant was found in 'Some S.C. County Records Vol. 2,' The Rev. Silas Emmett Lucas Jr., Editor, p. 245, Southern Historical Press, Inc. 1989:

Deed Abstracts, V. 4, Pp. 403-406: 21 & 22 _____ 1766, John Walker of Meck., to Nathl Henderson of same, (lease s 5, release L15)...530 A on W side North fork of Fishing Creek, granted to David Emanuel 31 Mar. 1753, and conveyed to John Walker 11 Jan. _____ John Walker (Seal). Wit: Jno Muckols, Adam Baird. Prov. Jan. term 1768.

[This land now in S.C.)

David Emanuel (d. ca 1769) had taken out a grant in Georgia prior to David Lewis and registered it in 1765[6]. Historians have written that he arrived from Lunenburg, Va. at this time. We know he came from Wales to Philadelphia Co., and lived in Chester Co., Pa., and then Lunenburg Co., Va.

---

[6]Colonial Records of the State of Ga., Vol. 28, Part II, by Kenneth Coleman and Milton Ready.

before living in N.C. He witnessed several deeds in Mecklenburg Co., N.C. His grant in Georgia:

Page 145: Grant dated 7th May 1765.
To David Emanuel for 200 acres of Land in the Parish of St. George.
Registred 22d May 1765.

In an account written by John Townsend[7] of Chester Co., Pa. of his trip from Goshen to North Carolina in 1752, he told of stopping to visit with David Immanuel in Lunenburg Co., Va.

"A History of Burke Co. (Ga.) 1777-1950," by Albert M. Hillhouse, Magnolia Press, 1985, had a lot about David Lewis and David Emanuel [Jr.], son of the above David Emanuel. He gave the account of David Lewis being killed by Tories while he was with David Emanuel Jr. (See later.)

David Emanuel [Sr.] was found in the early records of Chester Co., Pa. named as Executor of estate of John Jones, which he refused. He was in Lunenburg County, Va. in 1752 when John Townsend reported stopping by his house for a visit on his way to North Carolina. He seems to have been a friend of the David John's family, and several things document this, such as his witnessing David John's will, and the following document appointing David John a Captain in the Georgia militia. David Lewis and David John probably knew David Emanuel Sr. when they lived in Delaware.

David Emanuel Jr. became a very prominent person in the history of Georgia. Emanuel County was named for him. He was Governor- Pro- Tem, and a prominent officer during the Revolutionary War.

"Colonial Soldiers of the South, 1732-1774, by Murtie June Clark" contains the following records:

P. 954, Georgia Militia, Captain David John, commission dated 3 Apr 1764, Company of Foot Militia at Bryer [Brier?] creek, Augusta Division (in room of David Emanuel who resigned.)
[Note: David's son David John Jr. probably was too young for this.]

Military Commissions issued by the State of Ga., 1754-1774:
Capt. David Emanuel comm. Oct 6, 1762
Bryer Creek Regiment, Augusts Division
Same for David Lewis, except Lieutenant.
*

Capt. David John comm. Apr 3, 1764.
Company of Foot Militia at Bryer Creek, Augusts Division (in room of David Emanuel, who resigned)
Under an account of the Officers of the N. C. Militia, undated Craven Co. Regiment:
13 Captain   Lewis, David

---

[7]Chester Co. History, Chester Co. Historical Society, 1976, p. 17.

David Lewis took out grant for more land [150 a.] in St. George's Parish, Burke Co., Ga. "upon a Branch of Lambert's Big Creek on the south side thereof near land lately ordered Davis Emanuel."

* *

David John's will was made in November 1764, and was not probated until March 1765. His land grant was finalized in March, as shown in one account. Other accounts gave a date in April. Some of these early Welsh have a record of not completing their grants on time.

David John, Blacksmith, of the Parish of St. George, Province of Georgia, "being sick and weak in Body but of perfect mind and memory," made his will October 11, 1764[8]:

DAVID JOHN'S WILL

For the Name of God Amen. This Eleventh day of October One thousand Seven hundred sixty and four I David John of the Parish of Saint George in the Province of Georgia Blacksmith being sick and weak in Body but of Perfect mind and Memory thanks be to Almighty God for all his mercies, calling to mind the mortality of my Body and that is Ordained for all men once to Die; do make and ordain this my last will of testament in manner and form following, principally of first of all I recommend my soul into the hands of Almighty God my Saviour & redeemer by whose merits alone I hope to be saved, and as for my body I commit to the earth to be buried in a Christian like and Decent Manner at the Discretion of my Executors, nothing doubting but at the General Resurrection I shall receive the same by the mighty power of God, and as touching such worldly Estate wherewith it hath pleased God to Bless me in this Life I give devise and dispose in manner & form following viz

Imprimus I give to my Son David John the plantation & tract of land whereon I now live with the hereditaments & appurtenances to him and his heirs & Assigns forever, from the time that he arrives to one & Twenty years of age.

Item I give and bequeath to my Son Joseph the sum of five shillings to be paid him when he arrives to one & Twenty years of age.

Item All the rest of my Estate Moveable & Immoveable I Give & Bequeath to my loving wife More John; whom I likewise constitute make & Appoint Sole Executrix of this My last Will and testament And I do hereby revoke disallow & disanul all other & former Wills Legacies & Executors by me in anywise named made & Ordained or bequeathed. Ratifying and confirming this and no other to be my last will & testament. In Witness Whereof I have hereunto set my hand & Seal the day & Year above written.

/signed/ DAVID JOHN (Seal)

Signed Sealed & Declared by the

Testator to be his last will & Testament
In the presence of us
David Emanuel Senr.
David Lewis
Phoebe Davie
GEORGIA Before his Excellency James Wright Esquire Captain General and
Governor in Chief of His Majesty's said Province and Ordinary of the Same
Personally appeared David Emanuel and David Lewis two of the subscribing
witnesses to the last Will and Testament of David John late of the Parish of
St. George in the Province aforesaid Blacksmith and being duly sworn on the
holy Evangelists made oath that they were present and did see the Testator
sign seal Publish pronounce & declare the same to be and contain his last will
of testament and that he was of sound and disposing mind and mory to the
best of their knowledge and belief and that they with Phebe Davie subscribed
their names as witnesses to the said will at the request and in the presence of
the Testator and in each others presence.
At the same time More John named Executrix qualified before me.
Given under my hand the fifth day of March 1765.
                    JA: WRIGHT
Recorded 5 Mar 1765.
(Georgia, Secretary's Office, Recorded in Book A, folios 131 and 132. On
reverse: "The Last Will and Testament of David John")
(Note: Who was Phoebe Davie, who witnessed his will? Could she be this
Mary's mother, or mother of his first wife, if he was married twice?)
*

Another entry on p. 251, "Some S.C. Co. Records, Vol. 1," by Lucas, was
for Benjamin Lewis' 200 acres in Berkley Co. Under Remarks, it has "New
Grant to David Lewis April 17, 1764." This would indicate this grant was
taken out in Berkley Co. around the time Mary took out the one in
Mecklenburg Co. They both still had land in Burke Co., Ga. at this time.

Alexander Lewis & Mary John were Administrators of David John's estate
in N.C. in 1764, per Joada John Cole, from information she gathered from a
descendant. I was unable to find this, although I have searched. I hoped to
find the exact date of his death. I also asked Mr. William Skinner, a
genealogist of Charlotte, N.C., to obtain a copy of this settlement, but he also
couldn't find it, although he found other records which helped.

The grant Mary took out in November 1764 in Mecklenburg Co., N. C.,
stated she was a widow then. It seems obvious David was ill and dying when
he wrote his will in November, and perhaps died right away, although his will
was not probated until the following March. Mary seems to have wasted no
time in taking this grant out.

Mar 1765 Moore John took out land [150 acres] in Ga. "upon a Branch
of Lambert's big Creek near Lands this day petitioned for by David Lewis
---" She was granted this in May 1767.

Records show Mary Jones was granted 400 acres of land in Mecklenburg Co., N.C. on the waters of McAlpine Creek, "including Aaron Smith's improvements," on 16 Nov 1764, stating she was a widow with four children.[9] [Several Smith's had land on Fishing Creek.]

The Lewis' also took out grants for land in North Carolina after they had grants in Georgia. They sold their previously held land in North Carolina. Alexander Lewis owned land on Six Mile Creek, which was near McAlpine Creek. He patented 470 acres there 6 Apr 1765 located between David Houston's and Jonathan Lewis's surveys. He sold this to James Lynn on 15 July 1765. (Pp. 146-149.)

In July 1766: "Petition of Evan Lewis setting forth that he had 350 acres granted him and was desirous to obtain an additional tract having a wife and seven children therefore praying for 150 acres in Briar Creek at the mouth of a Branch called Stalking Head Branch about two miles above land granted to Thomas Lewis" [probably his son.]

McAlpine Creek can still be found in Mecklenburg County, N.C., southeast of Charlotte. McAlpine Creek joins Campbell Creek near Hwy. 74, then continues on to join Fourmile Creek. Branches of Sixmile Creek and Twelvemile Creek do not extend all the way to McAlpine Creek, but might have at an earlier period. Both Sixmile Creek and Twelvemile Creek are large creeks farther southeast in Lancaster Co., S.C. Both have branches shown on a topographical map as extending from Lancaster Co. northeast up into the area near McAlpine and Fourmile Creek in Mecklenburg Co. Sixmile Creek is on the boundary of Mecklenburg and Union Counties, with a branch extending almost to Fourmile Creek.

Twelvemile Creek is farther southeast and has a branch extending northeast almost up to Sixmile Creek. Southeast, Twelvemile extends into Lancaster Co., S.C.

LAND RECORDS helping to identify location of land held by MARY JOHN:

V. 2, Entry No. 6083, NC Pat. Bk., p. 124: John Willson, 26 Oct. 1767, 100 a., Mecklenburg Co., NC, east sd. Catawba, waters of Six Mile Cr., between Brice Miller, William Donaldson and John Neal, joining a point near Mary John.

V. 2, Entry No. 2329, NC Pat. Bk. 20, P. 549: Benjamin John 9 Apr 1770, 62 acres, Mecklenburg Co., N.C., head waters Clems Branch of Sugar Cr., joining Brice Miller, a branch and the Indian line.

V. 7, Pp. 359-361: 11 Aug 1778: Elizabeth Lusk and John Lusk of Meck., to George Harkness, for L 300 proc. Money--land on McAlpins Creek adj.

---

[9]Raleigh (N.C.) Land Grant Bk. 17, p. 137.

Surveys formerly made for Smith and Critenden 137 a. adj. John Lusk, John Sloane, John Wilson, Brice Miller. Elizabeth Lusk (Seal), John Lusk (Seal). Wit: Henry Downs, George Hogans, Daniel John. No rec. date.
* *

SAMUEL LOFTON:

Mecklenburg Co. N.C. Deeds, V. 2, Entry No. 1900, N.C. Pat. Bk. 20, P. 485: Samuel Lofton, 5 May 1769, 160 a. Mecklenburg Co., NC, east side Catawba River, west branch Six Mile Cr., jng. Donaldson's line, McClure's line, Alexander's line and Mary John's.

Mecklenburg Co. Deeds, N.C., 30th Book. PP. 103-104: 19 Feb 17--, Samuel Lofton & wife Sarah of Meck., to Aaron McWhorter of same, for L____proc. money, land on waters of Twelve Mile Creek, adj. Donalson, Alexander _____ & Mary Johns lines, 160 Acres granted to said Samuel Lofton. Saml Lofton (Seal), Sarah Lofton (S) (Seal), Wit: Andrew Crocket, William Robison, Hugh Barnet, Jurate. Rec. July term 1772.
*

"Moore John" in Mar 1765 took out her land grant for 150 acres in St. George's Parish in Georgia, located "upon a Branch of Lambert's big Creek near Lands this Day petitioned for by David Lewis--." She was granted this petition, but did not complete the registration, and had to re-apply. She was granted this land in May 1767.

Mary's actual petition read[10]:

"Read a Petition of Moore John Widow setting forth that she was settled in this Province had a family of four Children & was desirous to obtain Land for Cultivation Therefore praying for One Hundred and fifty acres upon a Branch of Lambert's big Creek near Lands this day petitioned for by David Lewis. April 1767. Granted. Read a Petition of Moore John Widow setting forth that she had ordered her One hundred and fifty Acres of Land in St. George's Parish which had been surveyed and returned and a Fiat passed by the Attorney general but the time was elapsed in which a Grant ought to have been taken out Therefore praying that not withstanding the lapse of time, she might be permitted to take out his Majesty's Grant for the said Land and that the Secretary be ordered to prepare the Same.
(Historical Coll. of Ga., Vol. X, p. 142.)

May 1767. Grant was signed by His Excellency the Governor. [11]"
* *

Granted on May 5, 1767   Grant Book F, page 235
150 acres bounded on all sides by vacant land.[12]

---

[10]Historical Collections of Ga., Vol. IX, p. 314.
[11]Ibid, p. 187.

* *

"Moire," pronounced "More," was the Irish word for Mary. "More" in Irish means "Greater." Indications that make us believe Mary and Moore were the same person was the later use of the John name in Mary's will, the mention of bringing the horses from Georgia, and her taking out land near David Lewis.

WILL OF EVAN LEWIS

Evan Lewis, St. George's Parish, planter. Son: Thomas, tract of land, containing 150 acres in St. George's Parish at the mouth of Stalking Head Branch. Dau: Ann, two cows and calves, two breeding sows, six pounds and five shillings Sterling. Son: Jacob, 125 acres of land, being part of a tract I now live on; all the shoemaker's tools I now have. Son: Evan, 100 acres of land, being part of the tract I now live on; all my cooper's tools. Dau: <u>Mary</u>, one grey two year old horse colt, a cow and a calf. Wife: Mary, mare called Fly, she shall be maintained by my son, Joseph, during her widowhood. Exors: wife and son, Jacob. Wit: David Lewis; David Emanuel; Thomas Lewis, Jr.

D: 23 Aug 1766. P: 16 Dec. 1766. R: 16 Dec. 1766. pp. 180-181 WBA. [Abstracts of Colonial Wills of the State of Georgia 1733-1777, Published by the Atlanta Town Committee of the National Society Colonial Dames of America in the State of Georgia for the Department of Archives and History in the Office of Secretary of State of Georgia 1962. Page 77.]

* *

WILL OF DAVID EMANUEL

David Emanuel was one of the witnesses to David John's will in Ga. "John Journal" by Cole has: P. 17: "David Emanuel was Governor ex-officio for a short time. He and his father John Emanuel settled on Breas [Brier] Creek in 1756. Both died in 1768, leaving wills in the Parish of St. George, Georgia. (Historical Collections of the Joseph Habersham Chapter of D.A.R. (1902), Vol. II, p. 343)."

This statement regarding the father of David Emanuel was incorrect as copies of these two wills reveal that John Emanuel was son of David Emanuel (Sr.) and apparently was not married. This David Emanuel (Sr.) had a son named David, who was the David Emanuel Jr. who was sixth Governor of Georgia, serving about one and a half years as Governor-Pro-Tem.

David Emanuel Sr. died after will written 22 Nov 1768, probated 6 Mar 1769 (see below.) He left sons Amos, David, Levi, and Asa. Daughters were Elizabeth, Rebeckah, Martha, and Ruth. His 200 acres were located in St. George's Parish on a creek called Chevis's Creek. Wit: David Lewis;

---

[12]English Crown Grants in St. Geo. Parish in Ga. 1755-1775 by Pat Bryant, Surveyor Gen. Dept., St. of Ga., St. Printing Office, Atlanta, 1974.

Thomas Lewis; Thomas Lewis, Jr. [NOTE: Son John Emanuel had died before this will was written.]

John Emanuel's will was written 21 Mar 1768, probated 16 Jun 1768. Mentioned brothers: Levi, Amos, David, Asa; sisters: Elizabeth [K]Nowland, Rebecca Walker, Martha Duehart, Ruth. Exor: father, David Emmanuel. Wit: David Lewis, Jacob Lewis, Evan Davis, his mark.

Note: Phoebe Davis was witness to David John's will, and Evan was possibly a connection. Jacob Lewis was son of Evan Lewis.

*

On July 25, 1777, Mary John, of Mecklenburg County, North Carolina, made her will. The original will is on file in the North Carolina Historical Commission, Raleigh, North Carolina, and a copy is in the County Court House, Charlotte, North Carolina. She only names the younger children in the will.

MARY JOHN'S WILL

In the name of God, Amen. I, Mary John of Mecklenburg County, North Carolina being weak in body, of sound judgment and memory, do make and ordain, this as my last will and Testament, and decree it may be received by all as such. I most humbly bequeath my soul to God, my Maker, and my body to the earth, from which it was taken. In full assurance of its resurrection, at the last day, through the Almighty power and goodness of God, my Maker. As for my burial, I desire it may be without pomp or state but decent at the discretion of my executors and children. As to my worldly estate, after just debts and funeral expenses paid, I desire it may be as follows, viz:

ITEM I give and bequeath to my beloved children, Zephaniah John, Benjamin John, Daniel John, and Roger John, my tract of land I now live on, to be equally divided, as follows: Zephaniah John to have his equal number of acres including his plantation where he now lives, and Benjamin John his number of acres including his clear field, and Daniel John and Roger John to have their number of acres, including the plantation where I now live, as they agree between them two selves.

ITEM I give unto my son Daniel John, one cow, his choice of my stock of cattle about this plantation and the remainder of the cattle to be divided equally as they can agree, to Zephaniah John, Daniel John and Roger John. I likewise give to my son, Daniel John, a large brown horse, three years old, which was raised in Georgia, and the remainder of my stock of horses about this range I give to be equally divided between my sons, Daniel John and Roger John, as they can agree.

ITEM I give to my beloved son Benjamin John all my cattle and horses in the Province of Georgia, that was left there last Spring, when the others were brought away. I give to my son Zephaniah John one weather and ewe, and the rest of the sheep to be divided between my sons Daniel and Roger John. I give and bequeath to my son Zephaniah John one bed quilt and one big pot. I give to my sons Daniel and Roger John all my money which is due me by note. I give to my beloved daughter-in-law Elizabeth John, my saddle and the remainder of my estate to be equally divided between my two sons Daniel John and Roger John, and I do hereby constitute and appoint my beloved sons, Daniel John and Roger John as Executors of this my last Will and Testament. In witness whereby I have here unto set my hand and Seal, this 27th day of July, 1777. Signed, sealed and pronounced as the last Will and Testament of the subscriber in the presence of

Henry Downs	/signed/	MARY JOHN
John Springs		(Seal)

* *

In Mary John's will, she wrote:

"I likewise give to my son Daniel John a large brown horse three years old which was <u>raised in Georgia</u> and the remainder of my stock of horses that is about in this range I give to be equally divided between my sons Daniel John, & Roger John as they can agree. Item, I give to my beloved son Benjamin John all my cattle and horses in the Province of George that was left there last spring when the others were brought away."

This appears to confirm they kept the Welsh practice of maintaining two places of residence.

*

Miscellaneous COURT RECORDS from Mecklenburg Co. N.C. Court
July '75: P. 34 C52:R52

Court adjourned until an hour.

Court met according to adjournment.

Present the worshipful_____
Same Justices

Andrew Reignhart)	Proven	
vs.)	Petit Jury	
Godfrey Uder)		
Jacob Egner (Agner)	John Hone	James Scott
Isaac Breden	<u>Benjamin John</u>	James Martin
Hugh Merran	James Jack	Chas. Fisher
Joshua Hall	Thomas Gribble	Christoph.Horlocker

Jury impannelled and sworn (assess) the plaintiff's damage to L/12" and 6 d Costs.

1775___C56:R56   P. 36

Samuel Lashley)		
vs.)		
William Franklen)	Petit Jury	
Andrew Greer	James Sloan	Daniel McNear
Thomas Gribble	_____ John	Edward Sharp

| Henry Vernor | Joseph Mitchell | Phenias Alexander |
| John Allen | David Robinson | Thomas Barnett |

Verdt. a Non suit

*_____

James Andrews)
vs.) Paiment Same Jury
John Higgins) Verdt. L/14" 17" 10 & Costs.
James Dnaffen)

_____

William Miller) Same Jury
vs.) Verdt. for Plaintiff 6d Damage &
James Stafford) 1d Costs.

1777: P. 71 C118:R118

The last will & testament of Mary John was proven in open court by the oath of Henry Downs a subscribing witness thereto. Ordered by the court that Letters Testamentary issue to Daniel John one of the Executors.

C119:R119:

_____ nominated in said Will who came into Court & took the oath of an Executor.

1778: P. 110:

List of the Grand Jury:

James Bradshaw	Mathias Mitchell	James Harris
James Stafford	James Wallace	John Wylie
Moses Alexander	Samuel Harris	Reese Price
William Holland	Hugh Barnett	John Springs*

Constable Hugh McCain

_____

*Witnessed Mary's will.

*Henry Downs and John Springs were witnesses to Mary's will. They owned land near Mary John. Henry Downs had land on Four Mile Creek.
[John Downes was mentioned by Gregg in giving an account of the killing of Col. Kolb during the Rev. War, p. 362.]

REVOLUTIONARY WAR:

The Revolutionary War was a trying time for the residents of Georgia, as well as North and South Carolina. Many in the area were sympathetic to the British, and a civil war was carried on. A previous chapter has an account of this.

We found some records pertinent to this area, as follows:

"A HISTORY OF BURKE CO., [Ga.] 1777-1850, Albert M. Hillhous, Reprint Co., Magnolia Press, 1985 contains this factual information:

P. 4: David Emanuel, Sr. and his four daughters and five sons, including David, Jr. came from Pa. in the 1760's.

Mentioned John Twiggs, as a young boy of fifteen, came from Maryland about 1765; settled in St. George and learned the millwright's trade. He became a leading patriot and officer in the Revolutionary War like David Emanuel, Jr., his brother-in-law. After the war, he moved to Augusta in Richmond County.

P. 15: Among the Justices of the Peace Appointed for St. George Parish: David Emanuel, David Lewis. Mentioned two of the deputy surveyors, and Benjamin Lewis.

P. 28: Although it was isolated in the back country from the coast, St. George Parish responded right away to the Patriots' call. In January 1775, St. George sent Henry Jones, William Lord and David Lewis to Savannah.
St. George sent eight delegates to the July meeting, which took place a year before the Declaration of Independence. Delegates: Henry Jones, William Lord, David Lewis, John Green, Thomas Burton, Benjamin Lewis, James Pugh and John Fulton.

NOTE: This Thomas Lewis was probably son of Evan Lewis Sr.:
Pp. 29-30: Between May and September 1776 militia officers were commissioned, and assigned to specific districts in the parish. These included Thomas Lewis, 1st Lt.; Levi Emanuel, 2nd Lt. [brother of David Emanuel Jr.]

P. 31: (Courts were set up in various parishes. The Council appointed magistrates: District of Queensborough, included Thomas Lewis.
Three Justices of the Peace were listed: David Lewis, Daniel McMurphy and Francis Stringer.
Mentioned Col. John Jones in Aug 1776 sent to the Council in Savannah affidavits that established that Henry Sharp of St. George was an active Tory.
Mentions the two clashes between Tory and Patriot forces that occurred in Burke County. One was at the county jail located about a mile from the center of present Waynesboro and on the south side of McIntosh Creek.. Col. John Twiggs and his mounted forces joined the Patriots who were under Lt. Col. Ingram and Col. Pugh.
    Col. Campbell and his British force of about 1000 men were at that time heading toward Augusta. To stop any interference, Campbell sent Col. Thomas Brown, a Tory leader, with a troop of mounted men to make a forced

march to the jail in Burke Co. and join forces with Col. John Thomas and his Tories. Col. John Thomas was a Burke planter. They attacked the American force of about 250-350 men, but were defeated.

Col. Brown and Col. Thomas gathered their men, and attacked again the next day with reinforcements from South Carolina under two Tory majors, plus a detachment led by Tory Major Henry Sharp. The Tories were again defeated. Capt. Joshua Inman became a hero when he cut down three of the enemy.

Accounts were given of the exploits of Col. John Jones of Burke, who was said to be from Virginia. Col. John Twiggs was also one of the Georgia leaders.

I found two accounts in the History of Burke Co. regarding David Emanuel Jr.'s exploits during the Revolutionary War in 1781. An account was written regarding David Emanuel and one of the Lewis'. They were riding their horses, when they were overtaken and captured by some Tories. Lewis was shot and killed. The author didn't know the name of which one it was. Another account said David Emanuel was with David Lewis and Myrick Davies when they were captured. David Emanuel managed to jump on his horse and escaped, but both David Lewis and Myrick Davies were killed.

This was undoubtedly the David Lewis who had some kinship with the David John, who died in 1764. This might explain why there was no will for him in Burke Co.

Myrick Davies was then President of the Executive Council and a man of some note. [He was probably the Myrick Davies who was in New Castle Co., or his son.] On p. 48, was an account of conveying the body of the late Myrick Davies, Esq., president of the Executive Council, to Augusta, Ga. on Dec 11, 1781. David Lewis had been a Member of the Executive Council from Burke Co. in 1778, but the author did not mention his funeral.

Members of the Executive Council from Burke, from 1777 through 1782, included:

- 1778 John Fulton and David Lewis.
- 1781 James Jones and Myrick Davies.
- 1782 Thomas Lewis, Sr. (res.)
- 1782 Benjamin Lewis (elec. May 4.) [P. 50]

Other Lewis' listed as Patriot officers were Thomas Lewis and Josiah Lewis. The author stated there were several Lewis' who were officers. He was unable to sort them out. Henry Jones was a Patriot Colonel.

There were concentrations of Tories in the Queensborough township area, and one in the general area that is now Girard. Col. John Jones was elected Speaker of the House of Assembly in 1781.

After the war, several Tory estates were sold. Eestates of Major Henry Sharp and Col. John Thomas, Sr. were among those sold. Hillhouse wrote that the "Sharp estate comprised 1,572 acres and the Thomas property some 600 acres, 50 head of cattle and one slave. The latter property was bid in by William McIntosh, Jr., but by 1795, had been acquired by James Jones. It became the Jones family's old Canaan plantation. The beautiful Burkehaven subdivision in present Waynesboro was developed on part of the confiscated Thomas estate."

The County of Burke was created on 5 Feb. 1777, and the county seat was laid out after the war. This was authorized by an Act of the General Assembly, 31 July 1783. Thomas Lewis, Sr., Thomas Lewis, Jr., John Duhart, Edward Telfair, and Col. John Jones were appointed commissioners to oversee the sale of one acre lots. (P. 53, History of Burke Co.)

The site chosen for the town of Waynesboro was at the juncture of the Quaker Road and the main road to Augusta. It was most convenient for the people who had served as Patriots in the war: Col. Thomas Lewis, Sr., Col. John Jones, Henry Jones, Hugh Lawson, Edward Telfair, John Green, the Whiteheads, the Emanuels and others. During the post-war years, David Emanuel [Jr.] held office in the State Executive Department. He was Commissary General in 1787.

Members of the Executive Council from Burke included:
1783 John Fulton and Benjamin Lewis; 1786 Thomas Lewis, John Green, David Emanuel, (Feb. 14) and Isaac Perry (Aug. 15.) These were undoubtedly connections of the Lewis' previously mentioned.

Names of other Burke officials for 1786-1788 were:
Assistant Justice, Superior Court: David Emanuel [Jr.], Thomas Lewis, John Jones, Hugh Lawson.
Clerk of Land Court: Levi Emanuel.
Sheriff: James Lewis
Receiver of Tax, district: Included Jacob Lewis, Batt Jones, James Jones.
County Surveyor: Thomas Lewis, Sr.
Collector of the Specific Tax: James Lewis, John Jones.
Foreman of Grand Jury: James Jones.
Capt. of militia districts included a Lewis, first name not given.

The churches in the area were badly disrupted by the war, especially during the worst part of the struggle from 1779 to 1782. Only one old Baptist minister, David Marshall, remained in Georgia. Rev. Matthew Moore at Dipping Ford was a Tory sympathizer. Rev. Botsford moved back to S. C.

Rev. Josiah Lewis of the Presbyterian Church, served full time with the American military forces. He was said to be from Virginia. I wonder if the Lewis' and John's were previously in Lunenberg, Va., as was David Emanuel. This Josiah might have been son of Evan.

Rev. John Holes, Rector of St. George Episcopal Church, became chaplain in the Patriot forces in 1778.

*

DAVID JOHN, [JR.],
1-son of David John (ca 1715) and Mary, was born ca 1744 in Del. He was
the heir to the "plantation and tract of land" which his father had in Burke
Co., Ga., "when he is twenty one years of age." [Will was made 11 Oct 1764.
Land grant to David Sr. said this land was 100 acres in the Halifax District.]
His mother Mary took out a land grant for herself and four children in March
1765, after David Sr.'s will was probated. We do not know what happened to
this land.

[NOTE: Notation under David John from Ga. Archives: "d. prior to Mch 6,
1786.* *Land in Burke Co. 1786. (Lewis, Thezia.)

Information regarding David and Mary's grants:

From "English Crown Grants in St. George Parish in Ga. 1755-1775" by Pat
Bryant, Surveyor Gen. Dept., State of Ga., St. Printing Office, Atlanta, 1974:
David John, April 1764: 100 acres in Halifax District..adjoining Land there
granted David Lewis… [This was located on Brier Creek.]

Moore John grant: One hundred and fifty acres upon a Branch of Lambert's
big Creek near Lands this Day petitioned for by David Lewis—
The County seat was Waynesboro, and Brier Creek ran nearby, northwest to
southeast across county.
*

JOSEPH JOHN,
2-son of David John (ca 1720) and Mary, was born ca 1745 in Del. He
inherited five shillings Sterling "when he is twenty one years of age." We
were unable to find any further record of Joseph in this area using the
surname John. The Joseph Jones mentioned had a brother named John. At
the same time David John (Sr.) received his land grant in Anson Co., N.C. 17
May 1754, there was a grant for a Joseph Jones, #1134, on Little River.
There is always the possibility this was the son of David.

ROGER JOHN,
youngest son of David John (ca 1715) and Mary, was born ca 1750 in Burke
Co., Ga. or Mecklenburg Co., N.C. Very few records were found regarding
him. In one of the deeds where he sold land, the name Roger was changed to
"Robert." Note in the deed below, he was of Chesterfield Co., S.C.

Research by William Skinner: Mecklenburg Co., N.C. Deed Bk 15, p. 223.
Says completely faded out. From Index: Roger and Zephaniah John to Jessie
Neel and Daniel John 2 Dec 1796, 133 acres, McAlpine Creek, Mecklenburg
Co.

Page 24:

1793: July 30, Roger John, of the County of <u>Chesterfield</u>, State of S.C., sold to Jessey Neel, of the county of Mecklenburg, State of North Carolina, for fifty pounds N.C. currency, 133 acres of land, this being Roger's one-third part of the 400 acre tract granted to Mary John in 1764. This land joined the land of Loftin and that of Downs. (Alexander Bk. 14, p. 223.)

(Henry Downs had land on Six Mile Creek.)

Other land records sent by Mr. Skinner showed the purchase of this land after death of Mary.

*

The William Johns of Burke Co., Ga., who was issued a passport, see below, in 1803, might have been a son of David John Jr. or Joseph John.

"State of Georgia, Burke Co.

Bearer her[e] of <u>William Johns</u> Being about to leave this State and go as fare as the Natches or als-ware We Certify that he has being long an Inhabetant of this County and has always behaved him Selve Candidly as a good Peaceable Subject and good Neighbour it is there fore Requested that he may pass unmolested; from under our hands this 26 day of April 1803. Signed: Daniel Evans, J.P., Thomas Jones, Thomas Gabard, Philip Jones, Richard Hines, J.P., David Robinson J.I.C. recommendation for a passport granted the 28th April 1803."

"Georgia   By his Excellency John Milledge Governor and Commander in Chief of the Army and Navy of this State and of the Militia thereof.

To all to whom these presents may come or whom the same may concern Greeting

Know ye that I have granted the bearer hereof William Johns my permission to travel through the Creek Nation to the Mississippi Territory, he taking special care to conduct himself peaceably toward the Indians and agreeably to the laws of the State and of the United States.

Given under my hand and the Executive Seal at the State House in Louisville the twenty eight day of April in the year of our Lord eighteen hundred and three and of American Independence the twenty seventh.

By the Governor

Geo. R. Clayton

Secy. E. D.

On back:

Pass Port for Wm. Johns returned & another granted the 24th April 1804 recommendations on which the first was granted filed. 28th April 1803. (Photocopy From: File II: William Johns, Dept. of Archives & History.)

*

Other Passports Issued by Governors of Ga. 1810-1820:
19th January 1797

I this day signed passports for James Lewis, Prior Hardiman and James Foster, of the district of Natches, to go into the State of Georgia. James Lewis is a native of North Carolina, born near the shallow ford of the Yadkin, he at present lives on Coles Creek 13 miles from the Mississippi, and 30 from the Natches.

James Foster is a native of South Carolina, and he has resided in the Natches since he was a boy.

I have been for several days confined to the house with dul cloudy rainy weather. was only able to make short excursions up the river. I have been visited frequently by the few Indians who are in town or who arrive from the woods.
*

Page 103--Monday 13th May 1811
On application
ORDERED
That a passport be prepared for Mr. James Lewis with his wife and six children from the County of Burke in this State to travel through the Creek Nation of Indians--Which was presented and signed--
* *

Page 106--Thursday 31st Oct. 1816. On application of Fauntleroy Lewis and John Moreland, it is,
ORDERED
That a passport in the words following be granted, to wit--Colonel John Lewis of this place desiring again to renew his efforts to recover some absconded negroes, who he has reason to believe, are lurking in some part of the Province of East Florida, at this time, under the Command of his Excellency Josef Coppinger--Two persons have been appointed by him, the said Col. Lewis to go in quest of the said negroes, viz. Fauntleroy Lewis, his son, and Mr. John Morland, who are charged with this recommendation to his Excellency the said Coppinger, whose friendly aid in assisting the said persons to secure their said absconding slaves, if within the Government of East Florida is respectfully solicited.
Given in the executive Office Milledgeville Under my hand
D. B. Mitchell.
To his Excellency
Josef Coppinger
Governor
East Florida
St. Augustine.
*

317

JESSE JOHN:

There was a Jesse John who was in Burke Co., Ga. Census of 1830. He might have been descended from Elijah, a son of Griffith John of Craven & Marlboro Co. He married Sarah _____, and they lived in Burke Co. Ga. In 1830, he was 40/50, had 1 female 30/40, and 1 female 5/10. There was a Jonathan Johns, 20/30, probably his son.

A deed was made in Burke Co. from George Oliver to Jesse John on the 10th day of Nov 1837 for six acres of land, for the sum of Twenty Dollars. Land was "granted to Joseph Attaway and adjoining lands of the Estate of Carter Benjamin Oliver Henry Lewis & Caleb Botley." Witnesses: Joseph Cates and John Saxon J.P.

The land was sold by Sarah Johns to Edmund Kidd on the 13th day of Aug 1855 for Twenty Seven Dollars. It was described as "adjoining land of John Applewhite, Henry Drake and others...and containing six acres." Witnesses were John Applewhite, Augustus A. Saxon and Joseph Saxon, J.P.
*

CHAPTER TWELVE

DAVID JOHN'S CHILDREN, Continued...
DANIEL JOHN,
son of David John (ca 1720) and Mary, was born ca 1749[1] in New Castle Co.,
Del. He married Elizabeth McLendon, daughter of Dennis and Martha Dunn
McLendon. They remained in the area where Daniel had inherited land from
Mary, his mother. Daniel died 22 Nov 1807. Elizabeth died 9 Oct 1802.
Both are buried in Providence graveyard, about ten miles from Charlotte,
Mecklenburg Co., N.C.[2]
Children:
1. ABEL JOHN, b.1786, Mecklenburg Co., N.C.
2. MARGARET BRICE JOHN, b. 1788. Died 1863. Married John
   McLaughlon, and had at least one son.
3. WILLIAM JOHN, b. ca 1790.
4. ZEPHANIAH JOHN, b. ca 1800. (Per 1800 Census.)
* *

NOTE: Much of this information was found in a letter in the Verticle
file, Charlotte Mecklenburg Public Library, Charlotte, N.C. Marked on file is
*from letters of E.M. Sharpe - 1968. Thru the courtesy of Mrs. John
Matthews. * William Vaughn Montgomery. More information on this family
was also found in Mrs. Joada John Cole's "Journal of the John Family 1701-
1960."
* *

The Johns and McLendons were both Baptists, but since there was no
Baptist church there, they attended the Presbyterian Church. The McLendon's
lived in Anson County that adjoined Mecklenburg County.

The will of Mary John, on file in Mecklenburg Co., N. C. left Daniel 133
acres of land and other items when she died. Her will was written 27 Jul
1777, Mecklenburg, N.C. His brother Benjamin had died by the time this will
was probated. Daniel fought in the Revolutionary War, and Joada John Cole
wrote that tradition was that Daniel fought at the Battle of Guilford
Courthouse, which appears likely. We obtained a copy of his voucher for
service:

Salisbury District, Voucher #2708, issued 7-14-1781. Paid L15.10.6.
(Revolutionary War Accounts, Bk. VI, p. 272.)

---

[1] Taken from tombstone inscription.
[2] The Johns Journal, by Joada Cole.

Other records regarding Daniel:

In 1785: MECKLENBURG CO. N.C. COURT MINUTES: 23. March term 1785, page 526:

Ordered that Daniel John be appointed Overseer of the Road in Cap. Flenniker's Company in the room of James Johnstone.

1790 CENSUS MECKLENBURG CO., N.C.:

Daniel John
  1 M over 16
  1 M under 16
  3 Females
  1 Slave
* *

The land records from Mecklenburg Co., N.C. show this:

Jan. 2, 1796, Daniel John bought from his brother Zephaniah John, of Hancock Co., Ga., 133 acres of land, ...being Zephaniah's third part of the 400 acre tract granted Mary John in 1764. (Raleigh Land Grant Bk. 17, p. 137.) The 400 acres granted to Mary 16 Nov. 1764 was described as being on the waters of McAlpine Creek, "including Aaron Smith's improvements."

This adjoined the land of Samuel Loftin and William Donaldson, and others, as previously shown.

In an 1802 deed from Zephaniah John to Daniel John, there was this additional information: "joining next to Roger Cunningham's land and lying on the north side of the aforesaid tract..."(Alexander Bk. 14, p. 223.)

Dec. 30, 1802, Daniel John witnessed the deed of his brother, Zephaniah John for 62 acres of land to David Neel Ray, being the tract of land granted to Benjamin John in 1769 and which fell to Zephaniah by heirship. (Alexander Bk. 19, p. 69.)

Nov. 28, 1805, Daniel John received a state grant of 40 acres in Mecklenburg Co., N.C. on the waters of McAlpine's Creek. (Raleigh State Grants, File 4898, Bk. 119, p. 252.)

Nov. 29, 1806, Daniel John received state grant of 22 acres on McAlpine's Creek. (Raleigh State Grants, File 4945, Bk. 119, p. 252.)
* *

McAlpine Creek is located southeast of Charlotte, N.C. It appears Daniel remained in the area where he had lived with his Mother Mary and his brothers. Daniel left his estate to be divided between his four children, Abel John, Margaret B. John McLaughlin, Zephaniah John, and William John. (Estate papers in Raleigh, N. C.)
* *

ABEL JOHN,

1- son on Daniel John (1749) and Elizabeth McLendon John, was born in the spring of 1786, in Mecklenburg Co., N.C. He remained there until his death 28 Sept 1825, aged 39 yrs., 6 mos. He was buried in Providence Graveyard in Mecklenburg Co. A descendant said he was killed by a timber falling from a wagon while it was being loaded. He married Isabella Reed, daughter of Joseph Reed and Isabella Nelson. She was born 24 Jan 1784 in N. C. She moved to Alabama in 1839 after her son Joseph moved there. She died 29 Jan 1855 at Uniontown, Ala.

(Per records left by W. V. Montgomery, Selma, Ala.)

Children:

1. JOSEPH REED JOHN, b. 16 Mar 1814.
2. ELIZABETH McLENDON JOHN, b. 15 Nov 1815; died unmarried Coltharp, Tex., 22 Jul 1906.
3. JANE NELSON JOHN, b. 4 May 1818; died Uniontown, Ala. Married Jesse Ezell.
4. ZEPHANIAH BRICE JOHN, b. 13 Jan 1822; died 1899 Coltharp, Houston Co., Tx.. Married Frances Craddock 1850 at Uniontown, Ala.
5. SAMUEL WILLIAMSON JOHN, b. 6 Dec 1823; died 1859 at Marion, Ala. Married Mary Billingslea.

* *

Abel lived on land that adjoined land of his brother William. William sold his land 22 Oct 1821 to Miles J. Robeson that consisted of 88 acres which were "part of a tract formerly belonging to the estate of Daniel John."

On 8 Jan 1823, Abel John and his brother Zephaniah sold to William Black 216 acres on Four Mile Creek..[3]

On 30 Dec 1824 Abel John sold to John Arnold 11 1/2 acres on McAlpine Creek.[4]

Abel John died 28 Sept 1825, and left his estate to his widow Isabella Nelson John and five minor children: Joseph Reed John, Elizabeth McLendon John, Jane Nelson John, Zephaniah Brice John, and Samuel Williamson John.

On 15 Jan 1839, Isabella John, who was guardian for Z. B. John, S. W. John, Elizabeth M. John, Jane N. John, and Joseph R. John, sold to Francious E. Ferguson 60 acres in Mecklenburg Co., N.C. adjoining lands of James Kerr and John Arnold on McAlpine...being part of the estate of Abel John, deceased.[5]

* *

---

[3]Alexander Bk. 23, p. 41.
[4]Alexander Bk. 22, p. 148.
[5]Alexander Bk. 27, p. 96.

JOSEPH REED JOHN,

1- son of Abel John (1786), was born in Mecklenburg Co., N.C. 16 Mar 1814; died 17 Jan 1890 Selma, Ala. He was oldest of five children and became head of family when his father was killed by fallen timber when he was 11. He married Rosanna Jane Smith, 7 Mar 1837, Mecklenburg Co., N.C. She was daughter of David Smith and Sarah Black, and granddaughter of James Black and Rosanna McCluen. She was born in Providence Settlement 2 Aug 1810 and died at Selma Ala. 4 Dec 1899.

One month after their marriage in 1837 the young couple left N.C. in a spring wagon for Alabama. In 1839, he returned to N.C. to bring his mother and her family to Alabama. They settled at Uniontown, Perry Co., where they lived until 1855, when he moved to Selma, Dallas Co., Ala. He was a lawyer; was Chancellor of the Middle Division Ala.; Mayor of Selma during the Civil War; and organizer of the public school system of Uniontown and Selma, Ala.[6] (Courtesy records of W. V. Montgomery.) Census records show he was quite wealthy for that time.

Their children were:

1. ISABELLA MARGARET ELIZABETH JOHN, b. 30 Apr 1838.
    Married John Wirt Blandin, had children:
    1) JOHN J. BLANDIN, b. 1863, Ala.
    2) MARY BLANDIN, b. 1864, Ala.
    3) JENNIFER BELLE BLANDIN, b. 1866, Ala.
        She was a schoolteacher, and was widowed and living at home with her parents and her children in 1870.[7] Isabella (Belle) died in Houston, Tx. 24 Jun 1912.[8]
2. SARAH HARRIET JANE JOHN, b. 5 Jun 1840. Married Rev. Jeremiah McCartha Boland, Methodist Minister, at Selma, Ala. 1882. No children[9].
3. FRANCES JEFFRIES JOHN, b. 11 Nov 1843, Uniontown. She married (1) Samuel Freeman Hobbs. He was born ca 1824 in Maine, and was a Merchant.[10] They had one child, SAM HOBBS, Jr. b. 1887. He was Judge of Fourth Judicial District Circuit Court of Ala.. 1920; later elected to Congress from Fourth District. Sam Jr. married Sarah Ellen Green of Birmingham. Mr. Montgomery wrote Frances married (2) Edward H. Hobbs, who was shown in 1880 census as Merchant and was living next door to them. Her second husband was E. H. Harris.
4. SAMUEL WILLIAMS JOHN, b. 29 Jun 1845, Uniontown Ala.
5. JOSEPH FRANKLIN JOHN, b. 5 Jun 1847, Uniontown, Ala. Married Sarah Matilda Davis, Marion, Perry Co., Ala. He died in Clearfield, Pa..

---

[6]1880 Census Dallas Co., Ala., p. 13, Supv. Distr. 3, En. Dist. 71.
[7]1870 Census, Dallas Co., Ala., L. 18.
[8]Ibid, she & her children living with her parents.
[9]Ibid, living with her parents; she was age 36.
[10]1880 Census Selma, Dallas Co., Ala.

in 1930. Was an Episcopal Minister, and ministered in Ala., Ill. & Pa. during his career. Had son: (1) SAMUEL WILLIAMSON JOHN IV. Lived in New England.

6. MARY AMELIA JOHN, b. 3 Mar 1850. Married Frederic Watson of Selma, Ala. Lived in Cincinnati, Ohio in 1929, had children.

7. ANNIE GODDEN JOHN, b. 22 Oct 1853 at Uniontown, Ala.
* *

SAMUEL WILLIAMSON JOHN,
4-son of Joseph Reed John (1814) and Rosanna, was born 29 Jun 1845 in Uniontown, Ala. He married (1) Susan Woolsy, who died without children.[11]
He married (2) Estelle C. Carson, b. 1849 Ala. They had:

1. ESTELLE C. JOHN, b. 1878, Ala.[12]
2. JOSEPH WILLIAMSON JOHN, who did not marry. He lived in Florida."[13]
* *

Samuel W. John died in Selma, Ala. 29 Jul 1921. He practiced law in Selma and Birmingham, Ala. Per writings of W. V. Montgomery, he organized the Department of Archives and History in Montgomery, Ala. Mr. Montgomery referred to him as "Colonel Samuel Williamson John," which perhaps was an honorary title, often given in the South to distinguished men.
* *

ANNIE GODDEN JOHN,
7-dau of Joseph Reed John (1814) and Rosanna, was born 22 Oct 1853 at Uniontown, Ala. She married Lawrence Harvey Montgomery (Sr.) at Selma, Ala., son of John Harvey and Hannah Emeline Moore Montgomery. He was born May 26, 1849, at Summerfield, Dallas Co., Ala. He died Dec. 30, 1906, at West Greene, Ala. Buried at Pineville, Ky. They lived in Pineville, Knox Co., Ky. many years. Joada John Cole wrote Annie was 89 years old and blind in 1942, but used a typewriter to correspond with Mr. W. V. Montgomery, Mr. Maxcy John, and others.

Children:

1. LAWRENCE HARVEY MONTGOMERY Jr., b. 1874.
2. WILLIAM VAUGHN MONTGOMERY, b. 28 May 1876.
3. ROSA BELLE MONTGOMERY, b. 1880.
4. EVELYN MOORE MONTGOMERY, b. 1883. Married: William Ray Wood. Lived in Pineville, Knox Co., Ky.

---

[11]1870 Census, Selma, 2d Ward, Dallas Co. Was living with his wife Susie, age 20, in home of her parents Benjamin and Lucinda. Benjamin was a Cotton Factor.
[12]Ibid.
[13]P. 109, Journal of John Family, by Cole.

5. CHARLES GAMEWELL MONTGOMERY, b. 1886. Died: 1906, Las Vegas, N.M. Unmarried.

6. ANNIE JOHN MONTGOMERY, b. 1888. In 1942, lived in London, England. Married: (1) Kaurie Weston Gwyn and (2) Herbert Somerville Smith. Mr. Somerville-Smith worked in the English Foreign Office, and they lived in Turkey in 1942. They had a daughter, who married F. F. Wicks, a Commander in the R.A.F. The Wicks had two children who lived with W. V. Montgomery in Selma, Ala. in 1942.

* *

WILLIAM VAUGHN MONTGOMERY,

2-son of Annie Godden John (1853) and Lawrence Harvey Montgomery Sr., was born 28 May 1876. He married Etta May Hamilton 1895. No children. He worked on John family history for many years, and left several records of his work which he so generously shared. Lived in NYC for 35 years, then returned to Selma, Ala.. Joada Cole mentioned in her "Journal of the John Family" two little English grandchildren of his sister who lived with them during WW II.

* *

ZEPHANIAH BRICE JOHN,

4- second son of Abel John (1786), b. 13 Jan 1822, married Frances C. Craddock. After Civil war, he moved to Colthrop, Houston Co., Tx. They had children:

1. THOMAS FRANKLIN JOHN.
2. SAMUEL WILLIAMSON JOHN.
3. JOSEPH DRAYTON JOHN.
4. ISABELLA SUSAN JOHN.
5. MARY ALABAMA JOHN.

* *

WILLIAM JOHN,

3- second son of Daniel John (1749) and Elizabeth McLendon John, was b. ca 1790. He married Elizabeth Stevens, daughter of Dr. John Stevens of South Carolina.

William served in the War of 1812 as a 3rd Cpl., 8th Co., under Capt. Robert Wood, and as 3rd Lt. in 2nd Regt. under Capt. David Moore, Mecklenburg Detached Troops (Aug 1814). Received grant in Cherokee lands. He died near Dalton, Ga.

Children:

1. ZACHARIAH JOHN. In 1820 Wilkinson Co., Ga. census, age 26/45; wife was 26/45; two males under 10; one male 10/16; one female under 10.

2. STEVENS JOHN, b. 1813.

* *

LAND RECORDS concerning children of Daniel John (1749):
Mecklenburg NC, 19/352, 22 Oct. 1821:
This Indenture made this 22d day of October AD 1821 between <u>Wm. John</u> of
the County of Mecklenburg & State of NC of the one part & Miles Jay
Robison of the other part ...that for & in consideration of the sum of $1100
dollars to the sd Wm. John in hand paid by the said Miles J Robison at or
before the sealing & delivery & thereto payunto the rest & payment whereof
is hereby acknowledged hath given granted Bargained & sold [alined] in fee
& a conveyance & confirmed & by [this] fee [ ] [ ] give grant bargain & sell
& absolutely convey & confirm unto the said Miles J. Robison his heirs &
assigns & issues a certain tract of land lying & being on the Waters of
McAlpine Creek containing 88 acres be the same more or less Beginning at a
line Able Johns corner & running thence sd. 36[ ] 215 poles to a [ ] thence at
45[ ] 60 poles to a [M.C.] thence N E 6[ ] 196 poles to a [ ] thence to the
beginning being part of a tract formerly belonging to the Estate of Danl. John
& laid off by the Admr. by order of Court lying & being as [ ] with all the
appurtenances rights & numbers of all & [singular?] the said lands Tenements
[thereto] himself & promises hereby grants or intended to be granted & of
every part & parcel thereof & all rights [?] issues services & proffits or any of
them incident[ ] & all rights [tilles] claims of the said Wm. John unto the said
land to the said Miles J. Robison his heirs assigns to this only profess ask & of
the said Miles J. Robison his heirs assigns forever & the said Wm. John for
himself his heirs Excdr. & Admr. doth hereby covenant promise & agree that
he shall & will at all times Warrant & defend forever the sd. land & premises
unto the sd Miles J. Robeson his heirs & assigns against all lawful claims &
demands whatsoever whereby the sd or person is as may be or may be
affected or incumbered contrary to the [ ] interest & [ ] purposes. Witness
whereof the sd Wm. John hath hereunto set his hand & seal the day & year
above written   Wm. John
Signed Sealed & delivered in presence of
Andrew Dunn & David [Protter] Mecklenburg County Nov term 1821
Thereby certify that the Execution of this deed was proven in Court by David
Poitter & recorded & ordered to be registered
Capt Isaac Alexander C.C.
Feb 2 1822.

* *

<u>MECKLENBURG CO., N.C. 21/275, Jan 8 1821</u>:
Zepheniah John and Abel John sold 216 acres on Fourmile Creek ...on the
branch Jack Wilies corner...to William Black for $600.00.
<u>Alexander Book 22, p. 148</u>:

325

On Dec 30 1824, Abel John sold 11 1/2 acres on McAlpine Creek to John Arnold.

Alexander Book 27, p. 96:

Jan 15, 1839, Isabella John, ...guardian for Z. B. John, S. W. John, Elizabeth M. John, Jane N. John and Joseph R. John sold 60 acres in Mecklenburg Co. adjoining lands of James Kerr and John Arnold on McAlpine Creek, to Francious E. Ferguson. [This was described as being part of the estate of Abel John, deceased.]

NOTE: W. V. Montgomery wrote that the entire family of Abel John, deceased, moved to Alabama in Feb. 1839.
* *

STEVENS JOHN,

2-son of William John (1790) and Elizabeth Stevens John, was born in 1813. He married Nancy Ann Hamilton Hood, daughter of Lazarus Hood. She was b. 1827 in Greenville, S.C. and died 15 Dec 1885 near Fort Worth, Tx. He was a private in "Salacca Silver Grays", Co. F with Army in Tn. (28th Regiment of Cherokee (Ga.) Mountaineers). Died 18 Sept 1900 in Waxahachie, Tx. They lived at Ft. Payne, Ala. from 1869 to 1879, then moved to Texas. They lived for a time at Midlothian, Tx. They had five children:

1. RACHEL JOHN, died young.
2. SUSAN JOHN. Married Marshall Stephens or Stevens. One son, FRANK.
3. JOHN JOHN, died 1895. Had two daughters.
4. ELIZABETH JOHN, b. 1855. Married Robert Kiker, Walker Co., Ga. She lived and died in Sulphur Springs, Tx. Had several sons, one being FRANK KIKER, who had a daughter, MEDIA KIKER.
5. REBECCA MALINDA JOHN, b. 25 Dec 1863, Gordon, Ga. Died 8 Dec 1937, Dallas, Tx. Married Belford Franklin Thompson, son of Bernard Thompson, b. 12 Oct 1859, Ga. He d. 11 Sep 1905 Dallas, Tx., killed in the Battle of Seven Pines. Had daughter: FRANCES MAI THOMPSON, Dallas, Tx. (1954), per Joada Cole, p. 113.
* *

ZEPHANIAH JOHN,

4-son of Daniel John (ca 1749) and Elizabeth McLendon, was born ca. 1800 in Mecklenburg Co., N.C. He married Margaret Sharp 22 Dec 1824 in Mecklenburg Co. He purchased 216 acres of land on Four Mile Creek from Tunnis Hood, 22 Oct 1819. He sold this 8 Jan 1823 to William Black. He moved to Montgomery Co., Ala., and was living there in 1830. He was a farmer, and in 1850, was working as a carpenter.

Their children were:

1. WILLIAM A.. JOHN, b. ca 1827, Ala.
2. ELIZABETH JOHN, b. ca 1830, Ala.
3. MARGARET E. JOHN, b. ca. 1833, Ala.
4. ANDREW JOHN, b. ca 1835, Ala.
5. ELIZA JOHN, b. ca 1836, Ala.
6. BARNEY JOHN, b. ca. 1842, Ala.[14]
* *

ZEPHANIAH JOHN (Sr.),
son of David John (ca 1720) and Mary, was born ca 1750 in New Castle Co.,
Del. We are uncertain as to his wife's name, but some family genealogists
have said records indicate it was Elizabeth Loftin. We found no record. Their
children were:
1. EZEKIEL JOHN, b. ca 1668, Mecklenburg Co., N.C.
2. JONATHAN JOHN, b. ca 1769, Mecklenburg Co., N.C. Died ca 1802.
3. WILLIAM JOHN, b. ca 1770, Mecklenburg Co., N.C. Married Mary
   Hall.
4. DANIEL JOHN, b. ca 1772, Mecklenburg Co., N. C.
5. SAMUEL JOHN, b. ca 1774, Mecklenburg Co., N. C. Married Nancy

   _____.
6. MARY JOHN, b. ca 1778, Mecklenburg Co., N.C.
7. ZEPHANIAH JOHN Jr., b. ca 1780 Mecklenburg Co., N.C., m. Lydia
   Nunn abt 1810.
Probably others.
* *

   Zephaniah's (ca 1750) family, along with his mother, brothers and servants
had brought horses from their home in Georgia to N.C. during the spring, as
mentioned in Mary's will of 1777. From this fact, it appears she still had the
land she was granted in Georgia. Both of Zephaniah's parents, David and
Mary, received land simply by filing claims for it, living on it and paying a
small fee. They seemed to have been slow in confirming their claims, as were
the Welsh in Pennsylvania and those first settling in the Welsh Tract on the
Pee Dee. Perhaps this was because of a desire not to pay the taxes required,
as money was scarce.
   There was "government land" still available which could be obtained
cheaply as late as the 1930's, and I have heard my mother say a lot of people
were reluctant to clear new land and own it, as they were usually taxed a lot
and sometimes lost it through taxes. I don't know if this was just her opinion,
or a view handed down. There seems to be a universal dislike of paying taxes.
   Zephaniah was already living on the land which Mary left him in her will
in 1777. Joada John Cole, who wrote about the Johns, believed Zephaniah's
wife was a Lofton or Loftin. Samuel Lofton and wife Sarah sold 160 acres to

[14]1850 Census Montgomery Co., Ala, #138.

Aaron McWhorter, land located on waters of Twelve Mile Creek, adj. Donalson, Alexander _____ & Mary Johns lines, which was recorded July term 1772.[15] Zephaniah's land was also adjoining land owned by Roger Cunningham. Mary John, his mother, named one of her sons Roger.

We found a deed for 62 acres of land which Zephaniah had inherited from the estate of his brother, Benjamin John, deceased, in 1778.[16]

LAND RECORDS:

MECKLENBURG CO., N.C. BOOK 19/522, No. 16:

Dec 30 1802...Zephania John of <u>Hancock Co. in Ga</u>... & David Ness Rea of Mecklenburg Co. [62] acres ...on the Indian line... "being a tract originally granted to Benjamin John in 1769 and fell to Zepheneah John by kinship in the year 1778."...Witnesses: Simon Clymore, Daniel John, Mary Clymore. Isaac Alexander, Clerk.

* *

Events leading up to the Revolutionary War had been slowly evolving for over a decade. The men in this area, as elsewhere, differed in their outlook on the ideas of an independent nation. Many just wanted to be left alone to build and maintain their estates, but there were some very zealous people who resented the demands from England and others just as zealous in supporting the British. A large group of Germans living nearby in North Carolina were pacifists, but some fought in the war and many furnished supplies to the Patriots.

One of the Baptist churches in the area voted to excommunicate any man who joined the Regulators, but this order was later rescinded. The Regulators had been set up because there was no law and order in the area. However, as often happens, they became overzealous and began to be feared and hated by a lot of people living there.

Most Baptist preachers in the area were strong Patriots and went about the area rallying people to the Patriot cause. Because of this, they had to flee the territory, and there was not much church activity during the early 1780's.

Many Scots-Irish in the area were Loyalists, sympathetic to the British. Leah Townsend in her History of the Baptists in South Carolina wrote that many who were neutral at first, or leaned towards the British, finally became so angry at the atrocities of the British and their sympathizers, that they took or sent their families out of the area. They then returned to join in the fighting against the British. Both sides committed atrocities, and events forced people to choose sides.

It must have been a terrible time, with the control of the territory changing often among these varying factions. This area was near the Pee Dee region,

---

[15]Mecklenburg Co., N.C. Deed Abstracts 1763-1779, by Brent H. Holcomb, p. 237, taken from 30th Book, pp. 103-104.
[16]Alexander, Book 19, P. 69.

and after the loss of Charleston, the Tories hung people, burned their homes and committed so many atrocities that a civil war was waged. The British sent troops through the countryside forcing the men to sign loyalty oaths to the British King under threats of death otherwise.

The John's were regular churchgoers and were peaceable people. They lived in an area that did not have many people, and they worked hard and lived quiet lives. Zephaniah's father David was a blacksmith, a profession which was in demand in the new land, as well as being a planter. They had family connections in the territory. David's work as a blacksmith and stock raiser caused him to maintain two homes. He took his family with him when he stayed in Georgia. After David died, they still maintained a home during the winter in Georgia and returned to Mecklenburg Co., N.C. in the spring, bringing many of their horses with them.

The John family had many relatives and friends still living in the Welsh Tract area in the Cheraw area, in what later became Marlboro County, S.C. This area was not very far from their home in N. C., which was located about twelve miles south of Raleigh near the South Carolina border.

The events of the Revolutionary War were very distressing to the people of this entire area, and they suffered unimaginable hardships. There was no escaping the events taking shape. Men were already in the Militias that had been organized for mutual protection, mostly from hostile Indians. David John was a Captain in the Georgia State Militia until his death. The majority of the Johns seem to have sided with the Patriots, especially by 1781. Once the Welsh blood was aroused enough to fight, they proved to be good soldiers. Several battles were fought in the immediate vicinity of Zephaniah's home, but unfortunately many records are lost, so we are unable to tell if he actually participated in any fighting. The Battle for Charleston, which was lost, and several others were fought in the area. The Battle of Kings Mountain had drawn a lot of men from the area. Guilford Courthouse was not far away.

Records show Zephaniah sold beef, sheep, etc. to the Patriot army. History books indicate the cattle and livestock in this area were rounded up by the soldiers and held for their use. In South Carolina there was even talk of shipping them out of the state to keep the British from getting them. This alarmed the residents, who raised protests. The record of the sale of sheep and other things to the State Militia by Zephaniah is shown here:

22 Oct 1780: REVOLUTIONARY WAR:
Zephaniah received Voucher #43 in Mecklenburg Co., N.C. for beef sold to the Revolutionary Army, dated Oct. 22, 1780. He also received Voucher #6 in Mecklenburg Co., N.C. for unspecified claim from the Revolutionary Army, dated Nov. 1780. We also received a copy of the following record from the N.C. Archives:

"This verifies that the following information is recorded in a manuscript volume in the custody of the State Archives titled "Revolutionary Army Accounts" (Volume A, Page 139):

Heading: The United States of America To the State of North Carolina Dr. For Sundries furnished the Militia of North Carolina, Virginia and South Carolina as allowed by Wilson and Cathey Auditors Salisbury District as per their Report No. 36.
Number: 4268
To whom and for what paid: Zephaniah John, for 2 sheep &c
Number of voucher: 3567
Amount: 7 pounds, 7 shillings, Specie
Other information: (Reports numbered 34 through 39 are not dated. Report number 32 is dated May, June 1781 on page 119 (report number 33 is lacking) and report number 40 is dated September, November 1781 on page 172, 181 and January 1782 on page 192.)
Raleigh, North Carolina   Jesse R. Lankford Jr.
August 13, 1991   Chief, Archives and Records"
* *

Daniel John, brother of Zephaniah, received Voucher #2708, issued July 14, 1781, paid L 15.10.6. Salisbury District.[17]

Benjamin John, brother of Zephaniah Sr., served on the jury in July 1775: "Proven Petit Jury": Jacob Egner (Agner), Isaac Breden, Hugh Merran, Joshua Hall, Jone Hone [John John?], Benjamin John, James Jack, Thomas Gribble, James Scott, James Martin, Chas. Fisher, Christopher Horlocker.
(Mecklenburg Co. N.C. Court Records, July 75 P. 34 C52:R52.)

Another of the John's served on the jury three times in 1775, but the first name is just underlined: _____ John, with the other jurors listed: "Petit Jury": "Andrew Greer, Thomas Gribble, Henry Vernor, John Allen, James Sloan, _____ John, Joseph Mitchell, David Robinson, Daniel McNear, Edward Sharp, Phenias Alexander, Thomas Barnett." After the first listing of the jurors, it just says "Paiment Same Jury" after the defendants name, and "Same Jury" after the next time.
(Mecklenburg Co. N.C. Court Records, 1775_____, C56:R56, p. 36.)
* *

In 1787, Zephaniah John received a grant of 200 acres in Washington Co., Ga. as shown in Land Office records, Georgia Archives, Atlanta, Ga.[18] He seems to have moved there with his family at this time. Hancock County was made from parts of Washington and Greene Counties in 1793, and after this division, Zephaniah lived in Hancock County. Records show he was

---

[17]Revolutionary War Accounts, Book VI, p. 272.
[18]Ga. Land Grants, Grant Book 000, p. 531.

330

designated as "of Hancock County" in the deeds thereafter. Further proof of the relationships and the names of his children are found from the Hancock Co. records. The 1794 Tax List of Hancock Co., Ga., Kirk Militia District, p. 7, had listed Ezekiel John and Zefeniah John. Page 8 has Daniel, Samuel and William John. The 1795 Hancock Tax List had Daniel, Ezekiel, Samuel, William and Zepheniah John.

The 1796 Hancock Tax List, Kirk Militia District, p. 23 had Z. John, p. 24, William John and Zepheniah John.

Zephaniah and his brother Roger sold their land in Mecklenburg Co., N.C. in 1796, as indicated by the following records:

Dec. 2, 1796: Mecklenburg Co., N.C. Deed Bk. 15, P. 223. "COMPLETELY FADED OUT!"

From Index: Roger and Zephaniah John to Jessie Neel and Daniel Johns 2 Dec 1796, 133 acres, McAlpine Creek, Mecklenburg Co. We don't know what this deed said, but it must have been Roger's share of the land inherited in his mother's will.

The following record seems to be regarding the land owned by Zephaniah:

On Jan. 2, 1796, a deed was made by Zephaniah John, of the County of Hancock, state of Georgia. In this deed, Zephaniah sold to his brother, Daniel John of the County of Mecklenburg, State of North Carolina, for fifty pounds currency, a certain tract of land, being a third part of a large tract of 400 acres granted to Mary John by patent dated 16th Nov. 1764, recorded in Office Book No. 12, and left by will to be equally divided among her three sons, Zephaniah, Daniel, and Roger, it being Zephaniah John's third part of the aforesaid land and joining next to Roger Cunningham's land and lying on the north side of the aforesaid tract, and containing 133 acres. It was duly proven in open court and admitted to record in order to be registered in Mecklenburg County, North Carolina, October session of 1796.[19]

In 1796 and 1798, Zephaniah John served as a Juror in Hancock County, Ga.[20]

In 1800, Zephaniah John was living in Hancock Co., Ga. Also living there were his sons William John and Daniel John.

On Dec. 30, 1802, Zephaniah John of Hancock Co., Ga. sold to David Neel Rea 62 acres, part of a tract of land granted Benjamin John in 1769, and which fell to Zephaniah by heirship in 1778. The deed was witnessed by brother Daniel John, Simon Clymon and Mary Clymon (or Clymore).[21] This was probably the same person Roger sold his land to.

---

[19]Alexander Bk. 14, p. 223.
[20]Minutes of the Superior Court, Hancock Co., Ga.
[21]Mecklenburg Co., N.C. Deeds, Book 19, p. 523.

In 1803, Zephaniah John was granted land in Hancock Co., Ga.. in the Land Lottery.[22]

In 1812, the Tax Lists of Hancock Co., Ga., show Robert McCook was paying taxes on land granted to Z. John.[23] This was possibly a son-in-law.
* *

TENNESSEE

Zephaniah was probably in his 50's by the time he moved to Knox Co., Tn. around 1805 or 1806. Several of his sons and their families made this move with him. He did not die until around 1832 when he was in his 80's.

In 1806, Zephaniah John was a member of Captain Price's Company, Knox Co., Tn., and was paying taxes on 295 acres.[24] This could have been his son Zephaniah Jr.

This deed was found:

31 Mar 1810: KNOX CO. TN. DEED BK. P-1, P. 83:

This indenture made this 31st day of March 1810 between Jane John of Knox County and the State of Tennessee of the one part and Thomas Lyon of the County and State aforesaid of the other part. Witnesseth that the said <u>Jane John</u> for and in consideration of the sum of $200 to her in hand paid the receipt whereof is hereby acknowledged hath and by these presents doth grant, bargain, sell, alien and enforce and confirm unto the said Thomas Lyon his heirs and assigns forever a certain tract or parcel of land it being part of the tract Zephaniah John Senr now lives on. Beginning on a pine and hickory near the top of a ridge on Adam Meek's line --- 100 acres...

In witness whereof the said Jane Robinson hath hereunto set her hand and seal the day and date before written here.

Wit: Joseph Jackson, Edward Epps, John Robinson

Date filed: June 22 1815   /s/ Jane x John
* *

Note: Remember there was an Adam Meek who was in the area of Mecklenburg County at the time David John received his first grant there. Also, a point of interest, William John, son of Daniel, sold land to Miles J. Robison in Mecklenburg, N.C. in Oct. 1821. There might be some connection between him and John Robinson.

This was in the 1812 TAX LIST of KNOX CO. TN.:

Capt. Jackson's Company

Zephaniah John (Probably Zephaniah Jr.)

---

[22]Court of Ordinary, Hancock Co., Ga.

[23]Tax Lists of Hancock Co., Georgia Archives, Atlanta, Ga.

[24]East Tn. Historical Society Publication, No. 26, (1954). 1806 Taxpayers in Knox Co., Tn., Captain Price's Co., Zephaniah John ---295 acres.

Ezekiel John.

The records show Ezekiel and Zephania purchased items from the estate
sale of William Carter in 1815:
(1815) KNOX CO. ESTATE BOOK, VOL. 2, 1812-1819, p. 206:
Estate settlement of William Carter, (undated, with preceding entry dated 3d
day of October 1815):
Additional Inventory of the estate of William Carter deceased was returned to
Court by the administrator and admitted to record, to wit,
Notes of hand:

Thomas Keys	$	2.75
Ezekiel John		4.75
Reuben Longwith		15.83
Adan Nipp		10.75
Zephaniah John		3.75
Adam Little		25.12 1/2
Edward Epps		7.00
John Wilkinson		13.25
Nathan B. Markland		10.00
John Meek		27.10
Mitchel Harper		8.25
Benjamin Beall		1.37
Elipalet Baker		.68
Joseph Reed		6.52 1/2
John Cook		3.86 1/2
Richard Thompson		18.35
Mark Bean		1.00
Samuel Coys		1.50
Receipt from Captain Kirk for 88 rations of flour & 3 bushes of corn		11.27 3/4
Obligation on George Waddington & Wm. Fablet for 280 bushels corn, Book accounts on the following persons		
Edward Epps		17.83

Page 2 cont.:

Ezekiel John	.63 1/2
Adam Little	.75
Robert Cepher	1.62 1/2
Binford Colyar	2.04 1/3
Felix Brown	1.35
Reuben Longwith	5.50
Markham Fristoe	1.35

John Wilkinson	3.45
David Black	.75
George Snipe	11.52
Robert Meek	5.25
William Harralson	10.75
Thomas Wilkinson	1.75
Wm I. Cobb	19.24
Adam Nipp	.37 1/2
John Craighead	39.51
Mark Parker	.55 2/3
Thomas Carter	.12 1/2
John Mays	1.12 1/2
Nathaniel Robison	4.18 1/4
John Cook	2.25
Edward Price	29.35
Nathaniel Lyon	7.54 1/4
John Wills	2.45 1/4
John Keys	.62 1/2
John Reed	2.41
Wm. Davis	2.75
Isham Epps	1.62 1/2
John Robison	1.75
George Wadlington	.12 1/2
William Spence	1.00
Edward Hankins	.37 1/2
James Carter	.62 1/2
James Keys	3.25
Wm Lea	4.68
Amos Carter	4.18 3/4
Wm. Bridges	2.16 2/3
Wm. Beard	.12 1/2
Major Wilkinson	18.62 1/2
Wm. Robison	33.33 1/3

P. 207:

Charles Carter	1.50
John Boyd	52.62 1/2
Robert Duncan	.37 1/2
Eli King	.25
Henry Lowry	1.87 1/2
John Chamlea	.50
Samuel John	.25
Adam Snipe	.12 1/2
Joseph Steward	.31 1/4
Turner Branham	2.75

Henderson Thatch	4.12 1/2
William Wilkerson	2.50
Thomas Davis	5.75
John Davis	4.16 2/3
James Hunter	.12 1/4

1816: Estate of William Carter, (undated but after date of George Witt estate sale 20th day of March 1816, page 276):
1 Heifer   Zephaniah John   3.00

NOTE: A list of Buyers at this Estate Sale of William Carter as well as Ezekiel and Zephaniah John included:

Robert Chandler	Shadrick Kellum	Moses Smith
Thomas Wilkerson	Wm Beard	Wm Tabler
William A. Campbell	Jas McMillan	Malaiki Tabler
Daniel Price	Wm Mitchell	Jas. Rutherford
Westley Legg	John Dodd	James Hines
Amam M. Kenady	John Ingram	Rich'd Mynatt
Joseph Reed	Moses Lisby	Stephen Harris
Charles Price	Edward Eppes	Rob't Armstrong
Pleasant Forguson	Randolph Carter	Joseph Stewart
Winston Carter	George Peery	Abel Hankins
Richard Morrow	Nathaniel Lyon	Adam Shipe
Martin B. Carter	George Grove	Hiram Mitchell
John Carpenter	John Cook	Jane Carter
Markham Fristoe	John Nelson	Richard Fristoe
Daniel Meek	Alexr McMillan	
Thomas Douglass	John McMillan	Jacob Pearson
James Hull	James Legg	Henry Shipe
Isaac Walker	Alexr McMillan Jr.	

The 1820 census records are missing for Knox Co.

1830: CENSUS KNOX CO. TN., p. 64.
Zephaniah Johns m   80/90
                       f   70/80
*

    Zephaniah was last found listed in the 1832 Tax records of Knox Co., Tn. We believe he died shortly afterwards, as we have been unable to find any further records for him. The Jane John who sold the land was probably his daughter or daughter-in-law.

    The people involved in the estate of William Carter were among those we found associated with records of the John family in Knox County.

Jane John sold the 100 acres of land to Thomas Lyon, and Nathaniel Lyon is listed there. Edward Epps and John Robinson witnessed this deed.

Zephaniah John Jr. was in Price's Company in 1806, and several Prices were listed.

Ezekiel John was one of the buyers at the estate of Thomas Davis in 1816.

In 1832 Henry Keys sold land to Samuel John.

In 1833 Samuel John was involved in a deed with William Taylor and Felix Brown, which was witnessed by William McMillan.

* *

CHAPTER THIRTEEN

EZEKIEL JOHN:
1-son of Zephaniah John (Sr.) (ca 1750) and Elizabeth, was born ca 1768, Mecklenburg Co., N.C. He moved to Washington County, Ga., at the same time as his father around 1787. The part of Washington County in which they lived became Hancock County in 1793. He moved to Buncombe County, N. C. around 1800. He owned 266 acres near the county lines of Madison and Buncombe Counties, 166 acres on Turkey Creek and 100 acres on Sandymush Creek, west of the French Broad River.

He married Lydia _____, who was born ca 1778 in N.C.

Their children were:
1. DANIEL JOHN. Came with Ezekiel to Tennessee.
2. THOMAS JOHN, b. ca 1797, Buncombe Co., N.C. Married Margaret _____. Died ca 1853 McMinn Co., Tn.
3. SAMUEL JOHN, b. ca 1801, Buncombe Co., N.C. Married Jane Harris, July 13, 1825 Grainger Co. Tn.. Died 1852 Knox Co., Tn.
4. WILLIAM A. JOHN, b. 25 Aug 1806, Buncombe Co., N.C. Married (1) Nancy Smith Sept. 30, 1830; (2) Rebecca Deatherage Mar. 21, 1838 McMinn Co. Tn.
5. EZEKIEL JOHN, b. ca 1808, Buncombe Co., N.C. Married (1) Jane F. English 1830 Roane Co. Tn.; (2) Adaline Richards Dec. 11 1856 McMinn Co. Tn.
6. ROBERT JOHN, b. ca 1809, Buncombe Co., N.C. Married Sarah Southard.
7. ELEANOR JOHN, b. ca 1812 Knox Co. Tn. Married William Southard Apr. 14, 1836.
8. JONATHAN JOHNS, b. ca 1815 Knox Co. Tn.
9. MARY H. JOHN, b. ca 1819 probably Knox Co. Tn. Married William C. Robinson.
10. LYDIA JOHN, b. ca 1824 Tn., Knox or McMinn Co.
* *

Ezekiel lived in North Carolina until about 1809, when he moved to Knox County, near Grainger County and the area called Strawberry Plains. A Jane Johns, probably a relation of Ezekiel and of John Robinson, sold land on which his father Zephaniah lived. His father Zephaniah and his brother Samuel had moved to Knox County in late 1805 or early 1806.

Ezekiel moved to McMinn County after it was opened up for settlement in the early 1820's. This territory had been owned by the Cherokee Indians until 1819, when they ceded it to the white man by treaty. The territory was almost solid timberland, mostly oaks but with many kinds of trees. The high hills and mountains on the east provided clear streams. Great herds of wild animals came down to the fertile valleys from these hills. It was considered ideal hunting grounds by the Indians, and had been used by them for that purpose for many years.

On the 27th of February, 1819, a number of Cherokee Chiefs, John Ross, Lewis Ross, John Martin, James Brown, George Lowery, Gideon Morgan, Cobbin Smith, Sleeping Rabbit, Small Wood, Hicks, John Walker and Carohee Dick, met in then Washington City with John C. Calhoun, Secretary of War. There they made the treaty which surrendered this desired territory. Under the terms of this treaty, 640 acres of land was offered to all Indians who chose to become citizens of the United States, and 'if they were capable of managing their affairs intelligently,' a grant of 640 acres in fee simple was made. 'Very few accepted the former privileges, and the latter grants soon fell into the hands of speculators.'[1]

The Cumberland Mountains, a ridge nearly 30 miles wide, divided the state of Tennessee into two divisions, called East and West Tennessee. Nashville and Knoxville were the principal towns. Murfreesborough, in West Tennessee, was the seat of government. The legislature there passed the act for the organization of McMinn County on 13 Nov 1819, and the county court was organized at the house of Maj. John Walker, of Calhoun.

The Cherokees inhabited the southeast corner of the state of Tennessee, and there was established a missionary station, named Brainerd. John Ross and other Cherokees obtained land grants and had homes in the area nearby.

Some pioneers had already purchased land from the Indians and settled in the territory, which was called the Hiwassee District. After the treaty was signed, many more rushed in to take advantage of the fertile land.

A temporary log courthouse had been erected at Calhoun, and was occupied until Dec 1823, when the courts were transferred to Athens. Later a brick building was erected on the town square and completed in June 1828. This was used until 1851 when another brick building was completed.

Ezekiel John died sometime between 1830/1840, in McMinn Co. His wife Lydia was living with daughter Mary Robinson in Jefferson County, Iowa in 1850. She probably died in Iowa.
* *

Early records from Georgia regarding Ezekiel:
"Georgia Tax Digests 1789-1799,"
1794 Tax List Hancock County Georgia - - Kirk Militia District,
Page 7: Ezekiel John, Zefeniah John.
Page 8: Daniel John, Samuel John, William John.

"They Were Here", Georgia Genealogical Records, Dec. 1966, P. 375:
1795 Hancock County Georgia Tax List:

---

[1] From an old newspaper article telling of the early history of McMinn Co. Author unknown.

Daniel John, Ezekiel John, Samuel John, William John, Zepheniah John.

"Georgia Tax Digests 1789-1799":
1796 Tax List Hancock County Georgia -- Kirk Militia District:
P. 23: Z. John.
P. 24: William John, Zepheniah John.

The "Z" John must refer to Ezekiel John. The Ezekiel Johns in the John family were commonly called "Zeke". The only other Zephaniah John (besides his father) in the family in this generation was Zephaniah John Jr. born in ca 1787. In 1796, he would have been only 9 years old.

We believe Ezekiel moved to North Carolina around 1800. On the extant 1804 tax list of Hancock County, Ga., Ezekiel John does not appear.

Some early records from BUNCOMBE Co., North Carolina:
Buncombe Co. North Carolina Deed Bk D, p 259:
Dec. 19, 1800. State Grant to Ezekiel John.
Buncombe Co. North Carolina Deed Bk 7, p. 240-242:
Aug. 5, 1801--: Ezekiel John to Joseph Philpott both of Buncombe Co., N.C., paid 50 pounds - - - 160 acres "on the waters of Turkey Creek on the west side of the French Broad River."
Beginning at a red oak John Dillar's corner - - - including the improvement where William Ramsay lived - - - - part of a tract originally granted to Mark Mitchel, Thomas Davidson and Co. and sold for taxes.
Wit: Robert Harrison, William Ramsay.
Registered during the January session 1803.
Buncombe Co., North Carolina Deed Bk D, p 259.
27 Nov 1804--Ezekiel John witnessed a deed in which Thomas Harrison sold 100 acres on North Turkey Creek to Joseph Harrison. Deed proved in open court 20 Nov 1809. Registered in Buncombe County, N.C. Deed Book B, pp. 222-223.
Jan. 19, 1808: Ezekiel John to John Harrison "...a certain piece of land on the waters of Turkey Creek and part of the tract said Ezekiel John now lives on...containing by estimation fifty acres, more or less..." The amount paid is left blank in deed book. Registered 19 Mar 1808 Buncombe County, N.C. Deed Book 7, p. 654.
12 May 1808--For 50 shillings, the State of North Carolina granted Ezekiel John 100 acres "on the waters of Sandy Mush Creek, beginning at a three-forked beach near the head of a hollow in Nathan Harrison's old line and running west..." Registered 7 Apr 1813 Buncombe County, NC Deed Book D, p. 259.
Oct. 25, 1809 - Ezekiel John of Buncombe Co. granted to John Morrow of Buncombe Co. for...75 pounds - - "a certain piece of land on the waters of Turkey Creek...containing 116 acres more or less...John Dillard's corner".

Wit: James Gudger, George Black Jurat /s/ Ezekiel John. Registered 30 Oct 1810 Buncombe Co., N.C. Deed Book C, pp.133-134.

Note: Ezekiel John does not appear in the 1810 Census of Buncombe County, N.C. He seems to have sold all of his land in Buncombe County by Oct. 1809. Probably about that time he moved to Knox County, Tn. Census records show that Ezekiel John Jr. was born in North Carolina about 1808. Ezekiel must have returned to Buncombe Co. to sell his land in 1809.

15 Dec 1813--John Harrison sold to Joseph Wilson "...a certain piece or parcel of land on a branch of Turkey Creek...beginning at a stake at the northeast corner of a tract of land formerly granted to Ezekiel John..." Registered 12 Apr 1838 by N. Harrison, Clerk, Buncombe Co., N.C. Deed Book 21, p. 212.

18 March 1819--Nathan Harrison sold to Jeremiah Davis for $50 "a certain tract or part of a tract of land originally granted to Ezekiel John on Sandy Mush Creek...containing seventy-six acres more or less..." Registered 24 Mar 1820 Buncombe Co., N.C. Deed Book 11, pp.540-541.

KNOX CO., TN. Records:
1816: KNOX COUNTY Tn. Court Estate Bk. 8, p. 199, 1813-1816.
Thurs. Apr. 4, 1816:
Ezekiel John produced to court an Execution issued by William Carter Esq. in his favor against Joshua L. Jackson for Dos. 48.40
with Interest from the 9 day of February 1816 & costs. A return is made in these words "I find no goods & chateles belonging to the said Joshua L. Jackson. I therefore have levied on a tract of land the property of said Jackson containing twenty five acres more or less lying on the waters of Dale's branch joining Mrs. Armstrong between the big ridge and house [?] mountain* this 9 day of Feby. 1816 Markham Fristoe Const."
It is therefore ordered that the Sheriff sell the tract of land levied on or so much thereof as will be sufficient to satisfy the Judgment aforesaid & the costs of this motion.
* *

   *House Mountain is located across the Holston River from Strawberry Plains, and northwest of the mountain is Chestnut Ridge. Flat Creek is nearby, but we have not yet located Dale's Branch.
   An old map of early Knox County shows Little Flat Creek Baptist Church in this area, in what was then Grainger County until 1850.
   There are several records of the Johns, including Ezekiel, having made purchases from estates that were settled and the records of the sales presented to the court in Knox County. Also shown in some estate settlements were notes owed by some of the John's. One marked "doubtful" was owed by

Daniel. He seems to have either died or moved away by this time, as we found no further record of him.

Knox Co. Estate Book, Vol. 2, 1812-1819, p. 206:
Estate of William Carter:
(This was undated, but preceding estate settlement was dated 3d day of October 1815.)
Notes of hand

Thomas Keys for	2.75
Ezekiel John	4.75
Reuben Longwith	15.83
Adam Nipp	10.75
Zephaniah John	3.75
et al.	

Book accounts on the following persons

Edward Epps	17.83
Ezekiel John	.63 1/2
et al.	

p. 207:

Samuel John	.25
et al.	

Estate of Thomas Davis, undated, included following account of sales of estate of George Witt dated 20th day of March 1816, p. 276:
1 Handsaw   To Ezekiel John   1.50

Estate of William Carter, undated, page 276:
1 Heifer   Zephaniah John 3.00
[Note: Complete list of names in Chapter 12.]

Knox County Estate Book No. 4, 1824-1830, p. 46:
Estate of David B. Ayers, under Notes on hand unpaid...
One note: Daniel John to Thos. Johnston doubt, 2nd April 1825 25.00.
* *

MCMINN COUNTY, Tn. Minute Book 1825-31, P. 83:
Thursday June 9, 1825
The State vs. James H. Bridges
Peace Warrant. This day came Ezekiel Johns who craves the peace against the defendant...
[See this under Samuel John, Sr.]
* *

Note that the name John begins to be spelled with an s, as Johns, with more frequency about this period in time. This referred to Samuel, the brother of Ezekiel, and Samuel's children, Andrew and Hugh. According to the census records, Hugh would be age 12 and Andrew age 7 or 8. Andrew was listed later as a Minister of the Gospel who performed several of the marriages in McMinn Co. in the 1850's. In the list, was B. A. John, Benjamin A. John, and Andrew John.

According to the census records, Ezekiel was living in McMinn County, Tn., in 1830.

1830 Census of McMinn County, Tn., p. 174:
Ezekiel Johns: 1 Male 10/15; 1 Male 60/70; 2 Female 5/10; 1 F 10/15; 1 F 50/60.

Living nearby was son Robert Johns age 20 to 30, and wife age 15 to 20. In the household nearest him lived son William Johns, age 20 to 30, and his wife, age 15 to 20.

The family of Gilliam Southard lived nearby. Lydia John married Aaron Southard, Mar. 2, 1843. (By Justus Steed, J.P.)

We believe Ezekiel died after the 1830 census and before the 1840 census. In 1850, Ezekiel's wife was still alive and living with her daughter Mary's family in Jefferson County, Iowa. Later, Mary and her family moved to Maries Co., Mo., but apparently Lydia had died by this time.

1850 Census Jefferson Co., Iowa - Locust Grove. Twp. p 121, No. 136-140.

William C. Robison	33	m	Tn
Mary H. Robison	31	f	Tn
Mary E. Robison	11	f	Tn
Martha L. Robison	9	f	Tn
John W. Robison	6	m	Iowa
William M. Robison	4	m	Iowa
Nathaniel Robison	1	m	Iowa
Lydia Johns	72	f	NC

* *

JONATHAN JOHN,
son of Zephaniah John (Sr.) (ca 1750), was b. ca 1769 in N.C. He married and had children, but little was found regarding him. He died before 25 Feb 1802. Apparently his brothers went to Washington Co., Ga. at the time their father Zephaniah moved there, but Jonathan seems to have remained in Mecklenburg Co. until the 1790's.

Not sure if this pertains to the above Jonathan John:

HANCOCK CO., GA., DEED BOOK C, 1798-1800:
P. 317: 'JOHN JOHNES of Hancock County, Georgia, to his son ALLEN

342

JOHNES, his right title and claim of the 100 acres of land he now possesses and lives on. This 4th August 1799. Wit: JOHN WILSON and AJONADAB READ. Reg: 22nd April 1800.'[2]

Other records show he lived in Hancock Co., and died there.

HANCOCK CO. GA. MINUTE BOOK 1797-1817,

P. 55. 25 Feb 1802: Anthony Butts appointed administrator of estate of Jonathan Johns, dec'd.

P. 59. 24 Apr 1802. Letters of administration granted to Anthony Butts on estate of Jonathan Johns, dec'd.

P. 61. 24 Apr 1802. George Gray, George Williams, David Phelps, and William Hill, or any three of them, appointed to appraise the personal estate of Jonathan Johns.

P. 93. Appraisal list of Jonathan Johns Dec'd 12th Jun 1802.

Appraised for $1648.76 1/4, with a list; list of items sold, same day for $2163.57. George Gray, George Williams, and William Hill appraisers, Anthony Butts Administrator. See below.

* *

HANCOCK CO. GA. MINUTE BOOK 1797-1817:

P. 93. An appraisement of the estate of Jonathan Johns Dec'd 12th June 1802.

14 head of cattle	70.00
Plow and other old Iron	14.00
2 old chains and old weeding hoes	7.00
1 cross cut saw and saw set	5.00
1 hand saw & 2 small do	1.50
A parcel of carpenter's & Turner's Tools	6.50
Cooper's . do . and 3 clevises	1.62 1/2
A parcel old irons	1.25
1 Carrying Knife	1.00
1 bell and collar	.50
1 Razor & case. and hone	1.00
Parcel Shoe tools & Tea canister	.75
2 drawing knives	1.00
1 pr. Steelyards	1.50
A parcel of old hainspring	1.50
4 old axes	2.50
2 Jugs	1.50
A parcel of pot metal	7.50
1 Iron pot rack	1.00
A parcel of Cooper's Ware	3.50

[2]Georgia Genealogical Magazine, Vol. 35, No. 1-2, (Issue 135-136), Winter/Spring 1995, pp. 19-20.

1 Saddle and bridle	4.00
1 flat iron	.12 1/2
2 Looms and gears	15.00
3 old Cotton Wheels	2.50
1 pair cotton cards	.75
4 chears [chairs] and 2 Tables	5.00
2 chests $6..22 pewter $3.25	14.25
A parcel crokery ware	4.66 1/4
Knives and forks 50 c. 1 looking glass $2.	2.50
Amt. carried forward	$ 178.91 1/4

94.

Amt. Brot. forward	$ 178.91 1/4
1 pr. Sheep shears	.50
2 Shot Guns and Shot bag	16.00
4 feather beds and furnature & 2 bedsteads	80.00
3 head of horse creatures	170.00
1 Negroe Woman and 3 children	850.00
1 Negroe man	350.00
3 pr. Lancets 1 Do horse flumes	1.00
3 books and 1 meal Sifter	1.25
1 pr. spectacles	.50
Whole Amt	$1648.16 1/4

Anthony Butts, Administrator) Geo. Gray, Geo. Williams, William Hill, appraisers

An account Sales; the estate of Jonathan Johns decd as pr. statement returned in Office.

1 lot of pewter, sold for	7.00
5 earthen plates	.50
Earthen Ware	.52
two axes	2.50
One meal sifter	.37 1/2
five earthen bowles	1.37 1/2
Three " do	.56 1/4
one set cups and saucers	.51
two muggs	.50
four books	1.00
1 Razor case and hone	.69
1 pr. horse flumes & 3 do Lancets	.81 1/4
one pr. spectacles	.26
two axes 1.6-- 4 weeding hoes 1.75	2.81 1/4
three weeking hoes $2.8	2.08
Amt carried forward	$ 21.49 3/4
95. Amount Brought Over	$ 21.49 3/4

1 lot Iron hooks	1.00
7 Waggon boxes	.87 1/2
One prae and Wedge	1.50
One Currying Knife	2.50
two bear shear plows and 1 coulter	2.50
One cross cut Saw	5.00
two plow hoes	1.31 1/4
One Dutch Oven	2.50
One bell and 3 pr. traces	1.62 1/2
One lock chain	1.62 1/2
One pot and hooks	1.00
One " " do	.43 3/4
One Spider	1.06 1/4
One lock chain	.43 3/4
One Washing tub	1.20
One half bushel	.75
1 Water pail	.50
One Chum	.50
One Milk Piggin	.30
One lot clevers	.68 3/4
One pr. Steelyards	1.62
One Saddle	4.75
One lot Turner's Tools	.50
One lot Augers	.75
two corking Irons	.12
One Set bridle bits	.56 1/4
One hand saw	1.12
One Sett farming tools	1.02
One drawing Knife	.63
One Looking glass	2.53
One Spinning Wheel	.76
One do.. do..	2.75
One do.. do..	1.00
Amt. carried forward	$ 66.93 3/4
96. Amt. Brot. forward	$ 66.93 3/4
1 Loom and geer	9.25
1 feather bed and furnature	25.00
1 do--- do " do	30.25
1 do-- do " do	33.50
1 do-- do " do	19.13 1/4
4 chears	3.00
1 Jug	.46
1 do..	.82 1/4
1 Shot gun - - - - - -	10.30

1 do do	6.25
1 Table	.75
1 do	2.31 1/4
1 chest $3.	3.00
1 do $2.62 One bull $9.50	12.12
1 cow and calf	15.52
1 do do	9.75
1 do do	13.02
1 do do	10.50
1 do do	10.64
1 do do	13.64
1 Loom and geer	3.00
1 young bay mare	90.00
One stud Colt	50.00
One Sorrel mare	77.00
One negroe Wench and child	601.00
One do boy	430.00
One do girl	386.12
One do do	230.00
Whole Amt.	$2163.58

Anthony Butts, Qualified Administrator.

Draw for orphans of Jonathan Johns, 1805 Lottery Hancock Co., Ga. This draw was a blank, which means they did not receive any land. There are no further records on this.

We do not know for sure the names of the wife and children of Jonathan John. But we estimate he would have married about 1780, and had children, possibly several, born in that era to 1802. We are including information on some Johns who were of an age to be his children. Please keep in mind that the different spelling of names is caused by endeavoring to record them as they are found in the records.

This information was found on a Zepheniah Johns who might be his child as the age was right:

Illinois Historical Collections, p. 198: Census of White County, 1818
(137) Zepheniah Johns; m. 21/up .....1; all other.....4.
* *

1860 CENSUS IOWA 29 day of June WAYNE COUNTY, Union Township, Bethlehem. P. O., P. 447, #458-422:

Micajah Cross	41	Farmer	6,000	3923	Ky.
Elenor	43				Ill.
Zephaniah	17				"
Solomon	13				"
James H.	9				"
Mary E.	5				"

Zephaniah Johns	75		S.C.
Delphy	69		S.C.

P. 449, #480-452:

Zepheniah Johns	27	Farmer	Ill.
Leona	18		Ohio
Mariah Johnston	15		Ohio

* *

Could this elder Zephaniah be Jonathan's son? Could Eleanor Cross be this elder Zephaniah's daughter? In 1860, age 75, this Zepheniah [sic] would have been born ca 1785, or perhaps earlier. It certainly is possible.
* *

JAMES JOHNS,
was issued a pass to travel through the Creek Nation as follows:
PASSPORTS ISSUED BY GOVERNORS OF GEORGIA 1810-1820
"Page. 107-Monday 9th April 1810
On applications ORDERED
That passports be prepared for the following persons to travel through the Creek Nation of Indians, to wit--one for David Mizell with his wife four children and two negroes--one for James Mizell with his wife, and four children--one for David Mizell with his wife and one child all from the County of Bullock--one for John Dunford with his wife and two children from Burke County--one for Holiday Haley--one for Robert Curry, one for Giddings Kellum and one for James Johns all from Washington County-- which was severally presented and signed."

Per records received from Archives in Ga., "James Johns: Private, 2d Co., F.C.M., 13th Regt. (Wash Co.), July 30, 1814. (M.R. 1784-1815- Wash. Co.)
* *

THOMAS JOHNS,
was possibly a son of Jonathan John (ca 1766). This was in the records from the Ga. Archives: Thomas Johns: Priv., 2d Co., F.C.M., 13th Regt. (Wash. Co.) -July 30, 1814-(M.R. 1784-1815-Wash. Co.).
* *

WILLIAM JOHN,
son of Zephaniah John (Sr.) (ca 1750), was born ca 1770, in North Carolina. He moved to Hancock County, Ga. with his father in 1787. He married Mary Hall. Mary Hall was born in Ireland[3] ca 1770. It is said she did not come to

---

[3]Wilkinson Co. Ga. 1850 census, the Ninety-third Subdivision, p. 368B, #390.

this country until after the Revolutionary War, when she was 15 years old. William was shown in the records of Hancock Co. until around 1812, when records show him living in Wilkinson Co. His Hancock Co. land was partly in or near Wilkinson Co. then. He died between 1853 and 1857.[4]

Children:

1. JAMES HALL JOHN, b. 4 Jul 1797, Hancock Co., Ga.
2. WILLIAM LOFTIN JOHN, b. ca 1799
3. ZEPHANIAH JOHN, b. ca 1803. Died before 1850 Wilkinson census.
4. REBECCA JOHN, b. ca 1806, married Thomas Jones. They had son, Joseph T. Jones, b. ca. 1841.[5]
5. MARY JOHN, b. ca 1808.
6. ELIZABETH "Betty" ANN JOHN, married Stephen Lord 31 Jan 1823, (by Daniel M. Hall, J.P., Wilkinson Co.) Their son Stephen M. Lord was discharged from the Confederate Army in 1863.[6]

* *

On Feb. 7, 1801, William John of Hancock Co., Ga. bought from Noah Woodward for $100.00, 230 acres on Buffalo Creek, bounded by Powell, Long and Broughton.[7]

On March 12, 1802, William John of Hancock Co., Ga. bought from William Montgomery of Hancock Co. 143 3/4 acres bounded by Witcher and Rushing and lying on Buffalo Creek. Tract was originally to John Accord, 2 Aug 1786. Wit. Daniel John, Wm. Gilliland, J.P.[8]

In 1803: Dated 26 Jan 1803, Inventory & Appraisement of estate of Nathaniel Parham dec'd...appraised by William John, Greenberry Pinkston & William Gilliland. Notes on Edmond Beard, Abel Johnston, Elisha Roberts, John Nielay, James Parham, John Woodyar (sic), Lewis Parham, John Henry, James Walker, Richard Gary (?). Total appraisal $862.50. Tanzy Parham, Benj. Th-----, Admrs.

In 1804, William John (one eye) drew Lot #700 and had two draws (wife and self) in the Land Lottery.[9]

"EARLY RECORDS OF GEORGIA,
WILKES COUNTY LAND LOTTERY OF 1806 - EXPLANATORY"

'The land given out in this lottery was obtained from the Creek Nation, in a treaty in Washington, Nov. 14, 1805, and was added to the counties of Baldwin and Wilkinson. The lots consisted of 202 1/2 acres each.

---

[4]V. Davidson, History of Wilkinson (Co., Ga.), Wills and Estates 1853-1858.
[5]ibid, #386.
[6]Wilkinson Co., Ga. Historical Collections, by Maddox, p. 96.
[7]Hancock Co. Ga. Deed Bk. E, p. 106.
[8]Hancock Co. Ga. Deed Bk. F, p. 312.
[9]Hancock Co. Land Lottery, p. 9.

Those entitled to draw: free white males, twenty-one years of age and upwards, citizen of the United States, and an inhabitant of this date three years immediately preceding the passage of this act and who paid said tax, entitled to one draw; every free white male of like description having a wife and legitimate child or children under twenty-one years of age, entitled to two draws; all widows with like residence, all free white females, all families of orphans, under twenty-one years, whose father is dead, one draw; those having neither father or mother living, two draws, provided the persons did not draw a prize in the late land lottery.' No mention was made regarding providing land for soldiers of any military service.

Maj. J. Patter's Batt. Capt Jos. Hendersons Dist.

Included: John Johns, 2 draws; William Johns, 1 draw[10]

* *

In the 1806 Georgia Land Lottery, William John received one draw, 202 1/2 acres each Baldwin and Wilkinson County.[11]

In 1812, William John had two slaves and was paying taxes on 143 3/4 acres in Hancock Co. on Buffalo Creek, land adjoining Green, originally granted Acord; 200 acres in Hancock on L.C. (sic.), land adjoining Blount, originally granted to Loftin; and 202 1/2 acres in Jones County on Walnut Creek, adjoining #123.[12]

William John was living in Wilkinson Co., Ga. by 1812. This was probably in the same place, but the boundaries changed by addition of a new county.

In 1812, William John was a Militia Captain in Wilkinson County of the 327th District, Capt. Johnston's District. (now Irwinton District.) [See below.] William John had drawn 202 1/2 acres in 1806, and his Hancock Co. land on Buffalo Creek appears to have been near the county of Wilkinson.

In 1812, there were eight militia districts in Wilkinson Co., Ga. According to the report of John Hatcher, Jr., R. T. P. of the Georgia Journal, Oct 21, 1812:

"Agreeable to the returns made to me by the Captains commanding the several company districts in the county of Wilkinson, the following is a list for the year eighteen hundred and twelve." There follows a list of the different Captains with their districts, including:

Capt. Johnston's District (327)

---

[10]"Chronicles of Wilkes County, Georgia from Washington's Newspapers 1889-1898. Articles of Eliza A. Bowen, Rev. F. T. Simpson, S. A. Wooten, and others. Transcribed and edited by Mary Bondurant Warren. 1978, by Mary Bondurant Warren, Heritage Papers, Danielsville, Ga. 39633, pp. 320-321.

[11]G. G. Davidson, Early Records of Ga., Wilkes Co. (1932), Vol. I, p. 321.

[12]Blair, Some Early Tax Digests of Ga., p. 71.

William Davis, <u>William John</u>, Hector Bowie, Ebenezer Dunham, Wilson Williams, Adam Kimbrough, Thomas W. Mitchell, Colson Copeland, Jonas Mathis.[13]

In 1820, William John Sr. of Wilkinson County, drew Lot 174, District 8 of Irwin County.[14] (Some of his records have "John" and some "Johns.")
1820 Census Wilkinson Co. Ga., p. 350:
William John: 1 M over 45; 1 M 10/16; 1 F 26/45; 1 F 16/24.
* *

On <u>November 19, 1823</u>, William Johns of Wilkinson County, Ga., sold to James Spy 142 3/4 acres on Buffalo Creek bounded by Mrs. Minton's land and Wilkins land originally granted Jno. Acord. Wit.: Curry Dickson, Daniel M. Hall, J.P.[15]
1830 Census Wilkinson Co., Ga., p. 354. [William Loftin Johns.]
William Johns: 1 M 30/40; 1 M under 5; 2 F 20/30; 1 F 60/70.
* *

1850 Census Wilkinson Co., Ga., the ninety third Subdivision, #390
William Johns 83 M N.C.; wife Mary Johns 80 F Ireland.

HH #391:
William L. Johns 51 M Ga.; William 8 M Ga.; James 4 M Ga.
(Living at household No. 392 was James C. Shinholster, age 47, wife Mary, age 52; and children. This might be William's daughter Mary.)

William died between 1853/57, in Wilkinson Co., Ga.
* *

JAMES HALL JOHN,

1- son of William John (ca 1770) and Mary Hall, was born 4 Jul 1797, probably in Hancock Co., Ga. He married Leah Wingate. She was born 9 Feb 1801, the daughter of Isaac Hall (1765-1813) and Polly Nelson (1770-1838.)
Their children were:
1. WILLIAM LOFTIN JOHN, died young.
2. ZEPHANIAH JOHN, d. young.
3. JAMES HALL JOHN Jr., b. 17 Nov 1828, Wilkinson Co., Ga. Married Elizabeth Jane McGlonn Aug 1852, Henry Co., Ala. She was b. 15 Apr 1832. He died 17 Jun 1863 serving in Civil War. He was buried in Shelbyville, Tn. She died 28 Aug 1875, Henry Co., Ala.

---

[13]History of Wilkinson Co. By Victor Davidson Reprint 1976. Published By the John Ball Chapter, Daughters Of The American Revolution. Copyright expired 1958. Press of The J. W. Burke Company, Macon, Ga.
[14]1820 Land Lottery, Georgia Archives, Atlanta, Ga.
[15]Hancock Co. Deed Book N, p. 72.

Their children were:
1) JOHN LUTHER JOHN. Married Ella Horne.
2) WILLIAM HOLLINGER JOHN, b. 22 Oct 1855. Married Emma E. Gaskin. Child: i) ANNIE LEORA JOHN, b. 4 Jul 1880. Married Benjamin Myles Davidson 20 Oct 1897; lived in Dawson, Ga.
3) LEORA JOHN. Married Ed McSwain.
4. DANIEL LUTHER JOHN. Married Elizabeth Cole. Was a physician during Civil War.
Two sons:
1) WILLIAM JOHN.
2) JAMES JOHN.
5. MARY HALL JOHN. Married: (1) John Ratliff Boone. M. (2) Edmund Dillard, and (3) Wilson Deshaze.
6. MARTHA JANE JOHN. Married Nathaniel Nicholson. Lived near Pineville, Ga.
Their children were:
1) JAMES NICHOLSON.
2) SAMUEL NICHOLSON.
3) NELSON NICHOLSON.
4) MARTHA NICHOLSON.
7. ELIZABETH JOHN. Married David Gasken McGlonn.
Their children were:
1) EUGENIA McGLONN.
2) ED McGLONN.
3) LEAH McGLONN.
4) CHARLES McGLONN.
5) JASPER McGLONN.
6) ANDREW McGLONN.
8. REBECCA JOHN, died young.
9. LEAH LOVIE JOHN. Married John Perry. No children.
* *

WILLIAM LOFTIN JOHN,
2- son of William John (1770) and Mary Hall, was born ca 1799 in N.C.
He was married, but we have not been able to identify his wife. His wife died before 1850 census. In 1860, he was still unmarried, age 62, and his two sons were at home. Living next door was James Council, age 28, farmer. In 1870 census, William was identified as "W. L. Johns Sr." and his daughter Mary Council was keeping house for him, and she and her five children lived with him.
His children were:
1. MARY JOHN, b. ca 1832.
2. WILLIAM L. JOHN, b. 1842.

3. JAMES L. JOHN, b. 1846.
**

MARY JOHN,

1- dau of William Loftin John Sr. (ca 1799), was born ca 1832. Married James Council, 18 Dec 1856. (By B. B. Shepherd, M.G. Wilkinson Co.) He was born 1832, the son of George Council and Lovie Jackson.[16] He probably died before 1870, possibly in the Civil War, as Mary was keeping house for her father in 1870.

Children:

1. UNITY COUNCIL, b. ca 1857, m. Daniel M. Eady. He was son of John Eady Sr. and first wife Mary Weatherby. John's third wife was Martha Lindsey Johns.[17]
2. ROBERT M. COUNCIL, b. ca 1861, m. America Jones, b. 1861.
3. LYDIA COUNCIL, b. ca 1863, m. I. W. Price.
4. WILLIAM L. COUNCIL, b. ca 1865, m. Janie Davis.
5. JAMES COUNCIL, b. ca 1867.[18]
**

ZEPHANIAH JOHN,

2- son of William John (ca 1770) and Mary Hall, was b. ca 1803. He married Martha Lindsey 7 Nov 1833. (George Shinholster, J.P.) Died before 1850 Wilkinson Co., Ga. census when wife shown as "Head of Household."[19] She married John Eady Jr., son of John Eady Sr. and Frances Murphy, 4 Sep 1853. The only one of her children still living at home with her and John Eady in 1860 was Isaac. There were six Eady children living with them. (Family began spelling name Johns.)

Children of Zephaniah and Martha were:

1. JOHN JOHNS. Not in 1850 census. Only record found was being named in estate settlement of his father.
2. WILLIAM L. JOHNS, b. 6 Feb 1835.
3. SARAH A. E. JOHNS, b. 1837.
4. MARY J. JOHNS, b. ca 1841. Shown living with mother in 1850.
5. ISAAC L. JOHN, b. 10 Oct 1843, d. 7 Sep 1921.
**

WILLIAM L. "Billy" JOHNS,

2- child of Zephaniah John (1803) and Martha Lindsey, was born 6 Feb 1835. Married Phoebe Smith 8 May 1865. (By E. E. Etheridge, J. P. Wilkinson

---

[16]History of Wilkinson Co., by Davidson.
[17]Wilkinson Co. Ga. Historical Collections, by Maddox.
[18]Dates of birth from 1870 Wilkinson Co. Ga. Census, p. 479.
[19]ibid, #385.

Co.) She was b. 7 Dec 1840, the daughter of John Gabriel Smith and Malinda Underwood, and died 7 May 1910. William died 15 May 1915. Buried Nunn-Wheeler Cem. (See below for directions.)
Children:
1. ARCHIE T. JOHNS, b. 1869. No date of death. Buried Nunn-Wheeler Cem.
2. JOHN GARLAND JOHNS, b. 2 Mar 1870; d. 15 Jan 1903, buried Nunn-Wheeler Cemetery. Married Susan E. Jeanes, daughter of William Jeanes and Camilla Golden. She was b. 2 Sep 1869, and died 20 Sep 1893; buried Golden Family Cemetery.
3. LOVIE H. JOHNS, b. 1875. Died 1896, b. Nunn-Wheeler Cem.
4. JOSEPH SAMUEL JOHNS, b. 1877. Married Lula P. Patterson, b. 1888, daughter of Andrew Patterson and Pricilla Batchelor. She died 1950. (Sam lived in McIntyre, Ga. 1922).[20] He died 1962, both buried Nunn-Wheeler Cem. Son: JOSEPH WILLIAM JOHNS, b. 14 Mar 1914; d. 26 Nov 1962.[21]

Possibly other children.
[To reach Nunn-Wheeler Cemetery take U.S. 441 from Irwinton, Ga. Go nine miles until you pass Macedonia Church on right, continue five miles and turn right on paved Hayward Smith Road. Keep right, the road changes to Nunn-Wheeler. Cemetery is on left.]
* *

SARAH A. E. JOHNS,
3- child of Zephaniah John (1803) and Martha Lindsey, was born 1837. Married Robert N. "Bob" Parker 13 May 1852. (By Daniel McCook, J.P., Wilkinson Co.) He was son of Thomas Parker and Nancy.
Children:
1. MATTIE PARKER, b. 1857. Married _____ Lindsey.
2. SARA PARKER, b. 1857.
3. MARY PARKER, b. 1859. Married _____ Stephens.
Family lived in Indiana.
* *

ISAAC L. JOHNS,
5- son of Zephaniah John (ca 1803) and Martha Lindsey, was b. 10 Oct 1843. He married (1) Shady Meadows, 5 Feb 1865, (by A. Pennington, J.P. Wilkinson Co.) She was born 14 Sep 1846, the daughter of Joseph Meadows and Nancy Pilgrim. She died 19 May 1914. He married (2) Mary Bell Simpson, b. 1 Apr 1880, and died 1 Mar 1923. She was from Baldwin Co., Ga. Isaac L. died 7 Sep 1921. All buried Nunn-Wheeler Cem.

---

[20] 1922 Voters List, Ga.
[21] Nunn-Wheeler Cem.

Children of Isaac and Shady:

1. CHARLES CLEMENT JOHNS, b. 12 Feb 1865.
2. LEILA JOHNS, b. 15 May 1868, did not marry. Died 4 Jun 1886.[22]
3. CLARENCE H. JOHNS, b. 15 Jul 1878, d. 7 Mar 1888.
4. CLIFTON W. JOHNS, b. 6 Mar 1873, did not marry. Died 24 Feb 1914.[23]
5. ANNIE JOHNS, b. 1876. Married Iverson Carr.
6. INEZ JOHNS, b. 1879.
7. HIRAM LAWSON JOHNS, b. 7 Mar 1882. Married (1) Lucile Barnes, b. 4 Oct 1883; d. 25 May 1927; daughter of Gus Barnes and Mattie Butts. Married (2) Willie Belle McCullar. Lived in Milledgeville, Ga. 1922.[24] Died 12 Sep 1962.[25]
8. LIZZIE JOHNS, b. 22 Aug 1884. Married Levi L. Smith. He was son of Archibald M. Smith and Mary McCullar.
9. EDDIE M. JOHNS, b. 29 Jul 1887; died 1 May 1946. Buried Mt. Carmel Cem., Wilkinson Co., Ga.

* *

CHARLES CLEMENT JOHNS,

1- son of Isaac L. Johns (1843) and Shady Meadows, was born 12 Feb 1865. (Some records refer to him as Clement C. Johns.) He married (1) Mary Arrington, b. 13 Dec 1868, daughter of Jesse K. Arrington and Frances Smith. She died 10 Aug 1892. He married (2) Clifford J. Jeanes, 6 Nov 1892, daughter of Vinson Sanford Jeanes and Laurenia Golden. She was born 3 Dec 1875, died 11 Jun 1961. Clement died 3 May 1939. All are buried Nunn-Wheeler Cemetery.

Their children:

1. CORA JEANS JOHNS, b. 25 Dec 1890. Married (1) Oliver Barton Pennington 10 Aug 1908; and (2) Morris Harrington.
2. OLA LEE JOHNS, b. 24 Oct 1891. Married Benjamin Ivey Pennington. She died in 1950.
3. ESSIE JOHNS, b. 1892. Died infancy.
4. DESSIE JOHNS, b. 1892. Died infancy.

Children of Clement and Clifford:

1. ERBY COIL JOHNS, b. 11 Mar 1896; d. 24 Feb 1914. Buried Nunn-Wheeler Cem.

---

[22]ibid.
[23]Buried Nunn-Wheeler Cemetery, Wilkinson Co., Ga.
[24]1922 Ga. Voters List.
[25]Nunn Wheeler Cem.

2. CHARLES ROYCE JOHNS, b. 4 Aug 1900. Married Eva Lee Carr, b. 15 Jan 1905; d. 11 May 1960.[26] She was daughter of John Carr and Alice Kingery.
3. VERNER CONE JOHNS, b. 10 Aug 1906; m. Annie Lou Dunn. D. 6 Jul 1963; buried Nunn-Wheeler Cem. Child: 1) VERNA MARIE JOHN.
4. ALICE RUTH JOHNS, b. 2 Sep 1908. Married Thomas Hugh Pennington. Children: 1) CLEMENT JOHNS PENNINGTON and 2) CLIFFORD AUGUSTUS Pennington. Lived in Milledgeville, Ga.

* *

LIZZIE JOHNS,
8- daughter of Isaac L. John (1843) and Shady Meadows, was born 22 Aug 1884. She married Levi L. Smith, who was son of Archibald M. Smith and Mary McCullar.
Their children:
1. H. V. SMITH. Married Carrie Bell Bloodworth.
2. IMA SMITH. Married Mirabeau Council.
3. I. T. SMITH. Married Adaye Mae Aycock.
4. VIRGINIA SMITH.
5. LAWSON SMITH.
6. HELEN SMITH.

* *

REBECCA JOHN,
5- daughter of William John (ca 1770) and Mary Hall, was born ca 1806. She married Thomas Jones, son of Joseph Jones and Sarah Anderson. They had one son, JOSEPH THOMAS JONES, born ca 1841, who married Priscilla Council, born 1842, daughter of George Council.

In 1850 per Wilkinson Co. census, Rebecca lived alone with her nine year old son Joseph T. In the 1850 census their surname was given as "Johns." Nearby lived Carlton C. Johns (son of Zephaniah and Lydia Nunn) and his family, and in the next house to Rebecca, lived Martha (Lindsey) Johns, widow of Zephaniah Johns (1813). (Census has the "s" on Johns.)

* *

WILL OF THOMAS JONES

In the name of God, amen. I, Thomas Jones, make, publish and declare this my last will and testament, viz:

FIRST. I desire all my debts be paid without the sale of any part of my property, except my Executors deem it necessary in which case they are

---

[26]ibid.

authorized to sell so much and make it necessary in a manner they deem best in the interest of my heirs.

SECONDLY. I bequeath an equal part to my beloved wife Rebecca, and my only son, Joseph Thomas, and should my wife bear no other children, she is to have the one-half and my child the other half in equal parts.

THIRDLY. I wish my estate to be kept together under the management of my wife who is hereby authorized to support herself and family from the proceeds thereof without request to make an returns to Court or to my Executors, but should a surplus remain in her hands after defraying the necessary expense, it is to become a part of my estate.

FOURTHLY. The estate is to be kept together until my son, Joseph Thomas, becomes of age, unless my wife shall again intermarry in which part of her estate is to be settled and turned over to her. For the execution of this my last will and testament, I hereby appoint my wife, Rebecca, and my brother Gabriel Jones, (wives Malinda Underwood and Mariah Carr), and my friend Dr. T. Ford of Milledgeville. And it is my will my Executors shall be separately accountable for so much of my estate as may come through their hands and more; and it is especially my will and desire that the guardianship of my son be in the hands of my wife and Dr. Ford jointly, except on the intermarriage of my wife, that the guardian-ship be placed in the hands of Dr. Ford alone. And it is moreover my will that should he not qualify for Executor, it be my will at the early days, he may at anytime during the minority of my son qualify as guardian to fulfill my intention of the education of my son, to educate and support him during his minority and such guardingship my estate shall be liable. 1845. signed Thomas Jones Recorded in Estate Accounts 1838-50. Page 414.[27]

* *

MARY JOHN,
daughter of Zephaniah John (Sr.) (ca 1750), was born in N.C. She married John Hall, b. 1780, d. ca 1850. Mary died 1855.
Their children were:
1. LYDIA HALL, b. 1810, never married.
2. MARY JANE HALL, m. George Shinholster. George was a Justice of the Peace and performed many marriages as shown in records.
3. JAMES M. HALL, b. 1820. Married Jincey Hughs.[28]
4. SARAH BELLE HALL. Married Daniel Thomas.
5. PERMELIA HALL, m. Levi Ezell.

* *

---

[27]Wills and Cemeteries of Wilkinson Co., Ga., by Jos. T. Maddox, Section One, pp. 193-194.
[28]Wilkinson County, Georgia Historical Collections ---- Compiled and Mimeographed In the United States of America by Joseph T. Maddox, Irwinton, Georgia 31042, 1973.

WILL of JOHN HALL, 1780-1850 [notes inserted]

I, John Hall, of the County of Wilkinson and State of Georgia, do make and publish this my last will and testament, hereby revoking and making void all former wills by me at any time heretofore made.

FIRST. I direct that all my debts be paid as soon after my decease as possible, also I direct that my wife, Mary, and my daughters, Lydia [did not marry], and Mary Jane [married Geo. Shinholster] and son, James M. Hall, [married Jincey Hughs] are the joint owners of the teams and carriages to carry out the business of the plantation; and I further direct that my man Peter, with the entire stock of cattle and sheep, breeding mare and colt, be given to my wife, Mary, during her lifetime and for the benefit of herself and family generally and after her death, to our daughter, Lydia, solely as to another division of my slaves, property and for the present. I give to my daughter, Sarah L. Hall, the following Negroes, namely: Minnie Miley and her two youngest children, Isaac and Ephriam; to my daughter, Mary Jane Shinholster, I give Simon and Charlotte, his wife, to my daughter, Lydia Hall. I give Ransom and Mariah to my daughter, Permelia Hall. I give little James and David to my son, James M. Hall. I give Caroline and her children and Ben, I give to Mary, my wife, also old Charlotte and her family after the decease of my wife to equally be divided between my children aforenamed. The whole remainder of my slave property to be left together and worked under the direction of my son, James M. Hall, and the profits over and above the support of the family, be turned over to my wife Mary, and at her death to be equally divided between my five children aforementioned. I also direct that all my estate, lands, etc. ... be divided equally between my three children; Lydia Hall, Mary Jane Shinholster, James M. Hall, upon the payment of $500 out of the estate to each of my daughters, Sarah Belle Hall and Permelia Ezelle. (signed John Hall in the year 1850.) Recorded in Record of Returns, 1820-1850, p. 381, Probated July 1850.[29]

* *

SAMUEL JOHN Sr.
son of Zephaniah John (ca 1750) and Elizabeth, was born ca 1774 N. C., probably Mecklenburg Co. He married Nancy _____. She was born ca 1790 Pa. and died 1850-60 Bradley Co. Tn. Samuel died 1850-60 Bradley Co., Tn. He probably came to Knox Co., Tn. in 1805 or 1806 with his father Zephaniah. Their children were:
1. ANDREW JOHNS, born: ca 1808 Tn., probably Knox Co.
   Married: Catherine _____.

---

[29]Wills And Cemeteries of Wilkinson County, Georgia by Jos. T. Maddox, Section One, pp. 138-139.

2. HUGH K. JOHNS, born ca 1813 Tn., probably Knox Co.
   Married: Sarah A. Prather Mar. 16, 1842, McMinn, Tn.
3. WILLIAM JOHNS, born: ca 1815 Tn., probably Knox Co.
   Married: Jane Armstrong, Dec. 31, 1839, McMinn, Tn.
4. SAMUEL JOHNS, Jr., born: ca 1817 Tn., probably Knox Co.
   Married: Rebecca Frazier June 24, 1841, McMinn, Tn.
5. BENJAMIN JOHNS, born ca 1820 Tn., probably Knox Co.
   Married: Mary Baker, Jul. 27, 1843, McMinn, Tn.

They probably had daughters born between 1808 and 1813.

In 1805, Samuel (ca 1774) was single, 21 years of age, living in Georgia, when he had "1 blank draw" in the land lottery.
Other records from Georgia:
"GEORGIA TAX DIGESTS 1789-1799":
Hancock County 1794 Tax List, Kirk Militia District, P. 8: Samuel John.
"THEY WERE HERE", Georgia Genealogical Records, Dec. 1966, P. 375.

1795 Hancock County Tax List: Samuel John.

"GEORGIA TAX DIGESTS 1789-1799": 1796--Not listed.

"GEORGIA TAX DIGESTS 1804-1806":
Hancock County 1804 Tax List---Barksdale Militia District, P. 86, Samuel John.

"1805 General Land Lottery" by Virginia S. Wood and Ralph V. Wood
Hancock County: Samuel John---Serial No. 413
1 Blank draw indicating a bachelor 21 years old.
* *

After moving to Tennessee, Samuel John (Sr.) first lived in Knox Co. Later court records indicate he lived in McMinn County and was living in Bradley County at the time of his death. During the time he lived in Knox County, the documents identified him as "of Knox County." He had a son named Samuel who moved to McMinn County, and his brother Ezekiel had a son named Samuel who lived in Knox Co. This makes the records difficult to determine to which Samuel they pertain. Also, some of the land transactions of this Samuel were conducted in the courts at McMinn County, as shown by the identification as "of Knox County."

There seems to have been a family relationship between Samuel and the Taylors. It is possible his wife Nancy was a Taylor, although we have not ascertained this. In 1833 Samuel John and William Taylor jointly sold 100 acres of land which adjoined land of Eli King.

Related records:

TENNESSEE RECORDS:
Knox County Tennessee Will Bk. 2, P. 242.
The last Will and Testament of Andrew Taylor deceased was produced to Court for probate whereupon Eli King and Samuel John, the subscribing witnesses thereto made oath that they saw the said Andrew Taylor sign seal and heard him pronounce, publish and declare the same to be his last Will and testament and that he was at the time of publishing the same of sound mind and memory to the best of their knowledge and belief, which Will is ordered to be recorded and in these words to wit,
In the name of God Amen. I, Andrew Taylor, weak in body yet of perfect mind and considering the mortality of men, make and ordain this my last Will and Testament.
First, I resign my soul into the hands of God who gave it.
Secondly, I leave to my beloved wife, Sarah my land, one bed and furniture and all the household furniture except one large kettle, I leave 1 cow which is to be hers during her life, then the land to be sold and one third of the price of said land to be given to my son William and the kettle at her death and to my daughter Ann I leave one third of the price of my land, one cow and calf, one bed and furniture, only twenty dollars in cash to be kept out of her part for schooling her child, left in the executors hands. And to my daughter, Margaret, I leave one third of the price of my land, one cow and calf, one bed and furniture and to each one of the rest of my children, I leave one dollar and my farming utensils to be kept for the use of the place. My Look I leave equally between my two daughters, Ann and Margaret.
In witness I have set my hand this 22nd day of April 1815. I leave Robert Martin and William Taylor Executors.
Test: Eli King, Samuel John   /s/ Andrew Taylor; /s/ Robert Martin; /s/ William Taylor

KNOX CO. TN. ESTATE BK. Vol. 2, P. 206, 1812-1819:
October 1815, Inventory of the estate of William Carter deceased:
Notes on hand (included): Felix Brown; Eli King; Samuel John.
Knox Co., Tn. Wills, Estate & Guardian Book "O" 1792-1803.
Guardians 1792-1821
Book 2, p. 242, April sessions, 1816.
Andrew Taylor, April 22, 1815.
Wife, Sarah, son William, dau. Ann, dau. Margaret.
Signed: Andrew Taylor.
Executors: Robert Martin & Wm Taylor. Test.: Eli King & Samuel John.
WILL BOOK D, P. 254-255, McMinn Co., Tn.:
HURST, ELIJAH Will executed 12 Dec. 1844; ...Witnesses: Justus Steed, Andrew John.

"A History of Mars Hill Presbyterian Church" by Boyer and Duncan, pp. 81-82:

Johns, Andrew T. - rc before 9/20/1832; joined the Baptists (before 1850.)

Johns, Betsy Ann - rc before 9/20/1832; died 1842.

Johns, Nancy - rc before 9/20/1832 (from the markings in the 1832 list, it would seem that her name was transferred to the 1850 list, but this name is not in that list.)

Johns, Samuel - rc before 9/20/1832; not in 1850 list.

Johns, Samuel - rc by ex and bap 10/17/1842; not in 1850 list.

Johns, Sarah - rc before 9/20/1832; died May 1838.

KNOX CO., TN. DEEDS:

Samuel John, p. 37

Thomas C. John, p. 21, 327 acres.

P. 10: 1834: A deed from William Taylor & Samuel John to Felix Brown for 100 acres was proven by Wm. McMillan & Samuel Sample fur. witnesses thereto on the 18th July 1835.

April 1832 to April 1836 Book A, Knox Co., Tn. List of taxable Property District No. 4, 1844-1845:

Samuel Johns-------92 acres of land valued at $450.

P. 145: Felix Brown to Samuel Johns, Recorded Vol. 1, p. 479, Filed March 3, Deed Oct. 9, 1835, 100 acres.

From "McMinn County Tennessee Deeds & Other Data 1820-1880" Compiled by Reba Bayless Boyer:

Deed Book B, P. 9,

(307) 31 Dec 1831 Samuel John of Knox Co. to Elias Presnell.

Deed Book E, P. 21,

(133) (numbered 233 in error) 3 Aug 1837 Samuel John to William John; Mortgage of personal property.

MCMINN CO. TN. MINUTES BOOK 1825-31, p. 83.

Thursday, June 9, 1825.

The State vs. James H. Bridges.   Peace Warrant.

This day came Ezekiel Johns who craved the peace against the defendant and the defendant in his proper person and thereupon the said Ezekiel Johns dismissed his Peace Warrant and thereupon the defendant confesses judgment for the costs.

It is therefore considered by the Court that the State recover against the defendant the costs aforesaid in form aforesaid

confessed and that he be taken etc. Whereupon came Samuel Johns and acknowledged himself security for the payment of the costs and agrees that execution issue against with the defendant for the same.

The State vs Andrew Johns and Hugh Johns. Assault.

This day came Thomas J. Campbell esquire who prosecutes for the state as well as <u>Samuel Johns the father of the two defendants</u> who are minors under the age of 21 years and the Bill of Indictment being read to him he says thereof they are guilty and prays the mercy of the court and the said <u>Samuel Johns</u> confesses judgment for the fine and costs. It is therefore considered by the Court that for their offense they be fined six and 1/4 cents, that Ezekiel Johns pay the fine and costs of this prosecution and be taken etc. whereupon came James H. Bridges and acknowledged himself security for the payment of the fine and costs and agrees that execution issue against him together with the defendant for the same.

* *

NOTES: The clerk who wrote this entry had two cross outs. In one place where the entry now reads "Samuel Johns the father of the two defendants", the original shows "Ezekiel Johns the father of the two defendants", Ezekiel being crossed out and Samuel written above. Farther down in the entry, it originally said "Samuel Johns pay the fine" but Samuel was crossed out and Ezekiel written above.

It appears to me that Andrew and Hugh assaulted James H. Bridges, possibly in defense of Ezekiel, as Ezekiel had the Peace Warrant issued against Bridges. Apparently Bridges had the boys arrested. They all seemed to want to get along and be held equally responsible. Samuel made himself Security for the costs assessed to James Bridges, and asks that they be assessed in an equal amount with the defendant Bridges. In the assault charges, Samuel agreed the boys were guilty, etc., and Ezekiel was ordered to pay the small fine (although with the cross outs, this could have been in error.) Whereupon James Bridges acknowledged himself Security for the costs assessed and asks that they be assessed in an equal amount with Samuel.

This record shows the close relationship between Samuel John and Ezekiel John.

* *

We could not determine any relationship with James Bridges, although there were Bridges records, such as the following:

DEED BOOK N, MCMINN CO. TN., (322):

11 Jul 1865 William H. Bridges to father James H. Bridges, aged, almost helpless, and in decline of life, for love and affection, for his lifetime, and then to Horace A. Bridges, for love and affection.

DEED BOOK M, MCMINN CO. TN., (233):

3 Mar 1859 James Gettys of Meigs Co. to Daniel Horton; lots 71, 72, 75 and 76 in Athens, on which John L. Bridges' livery stable is erected.

* *

MCMINN CO. TN. DEED BOOK B, (307). (From McMinn Co. Tn. Deeds and Other Data by Boyer):

31 Dec. 1831 Samuel John of Knox Co. to Elias Presnell.

1832 Tax List McMinn Co. Tn., Capt. Smith's Co.:
William Johns (Probably this was son of Ezekiel John.)
McMinn County Tn. Deed Bk. B, P. 235, 1820-1847: S. John.
McMinn Co. Tn. Deed Book C, P. 357, 1820-1852: S. John.
McMinn Co. Tn. Deed Book K, (429), (Boyer):
7 Dec. 1835 Samuel John of Knox Co. to Ezekiel John; 30 Jan 1854, witness
Jonathan John identifies handwriting of the other witness, Thomas John, who
has departed this life.
McMinn Co. Tn. Deed Book E, (133) (numbered 233 in error--Boyer):
3 Aug 1837 Samuel John to William John; mortgage of personal property.
* *

The following record appears to be for Samuel John, Sr., Nancy John,
Samuel John Jr. and Benjamin John. This shows that they moved to McMinn
County before the 1840 census.
Page 115. McMinn Co., 1840 Census.
Head of household, Samuel John; 1 M 15/20; 1 M 20/30; 1 M 70/80;
1 F 50/60.
Page 116. McMinn Co., 1840 Census:
H. H. of William Johns; 1 M 20/30; 1 F 15/20.

Samuel and William John lived in a different area of McMinn Co. than the
family of Ezekiel John.

[Note: Page 113 of the McMinn County, Tn. 1840 Census has Jonathan W.
John. Have not determined his relationship. Also has: 1 M 10/15; 1 M 50/60;
1 F 15/20; 1 F 50/60.]
*

MCMINN CO. TN. MARRIAGES:
Samuel John to Rebecca Frazier, June 23, 1841. By. A.C. Robeson (June 24,
1841.) [This was Samuel John Jr.]

MCMINN CO. TN. DEED BOOK I, (6) (Boyer):
31 Dec 1845 William John and wife Jane formerly Jane Armstrong, heir of
Thomas Armstrong dec'd late of McMinn Co., to James S. Russell;
land...except three acres laid off to Nancy and Clinton B. Armstrong.

1850 CENSUS BRADLEY CO. TN., P. 382, No. 734.
Samuel Johns   79 M NC Farmer; Nancy Johns   60 F Pa.

1850 CENSUS MCMINN CO. TN., 25TH SUBDIVISION, P. 535:
934-641.

362

Hugh Johns 36 Farmer   Tn.; Parthena 34; Mary E. 8; Parelee 6; Martin 4;
_____ 2.

Page 536, 1153-785:
Andy Johns 42 m Farmer Tn.; Catherine 38 f; Henderson 17 m; Uphania
15 f; William 14 m; Nancy 11 f; Charles 9 m; Martha 3 f; McCampbell 2 m.

1860 CENSUS MCMINN CO. TN., The 8th Civil District, 1st June 1860,
Calhoun. Dwelling 29, Family 29, P. 5.
Hugh Johns 47 m Tn. Farmer $1000 $200; Sarah A. Johns 43 f NC; Phebe
Johns 17 f Tn.; Mary E. Johns 15 f Tn.; Nancy P. Johns 13 f Tn.;
Martin A. Johns 11 m Tn.; Paralee Johns 9 f Tn.; Catharine Johns 5 f
Tn.; James W. Johns 3 m Tn.; Clinton Johns 15 m Tn. Laborer.
(Clinton Johns was son of William who was brother of Hugh; i.e., Clinton
was nephew of Hugh.)

DEED BOOK P, MCMINN CO. TN.:
4 Mar 1870 A. K. Johns to James S. Richards; his undivided interest in land.
[NOTE: There are entries for the Armstrongs, Prathers, Fraziers and Bakers in
McMinn Co. Tn. Deeds and Other Data by Reba Bayless Boyer. These are
probably families of women of that name who married into Samuel John's
family.]

DEED BOOK H, MCMINN TN.:
(209) 1 Jun 1843. John Armstrong to his sisters Jane and Ann Armstrong;
land for their lifetime.
(210) 1 Jun 1843 Jane and Ann Armstrong to brother John Armstrong; Bill of
Sale for slaves; to make fair family settlement.

DEED BOOK I, MCMINN TN.:
(6) 31 Dec 1845 William John and wife Jane formerly Jane Armstrong, heir
of Thomas Armstrong dec'd late of McMinn Co., to James S. Russell;
land...except three acres laid off to Nancy and Clinton B. Armstrong.
* *

ANDREW JOHN,
first son of Samuel John (ca 1772) and Nancy, was born ca 1808 in Knox Co.,
Tn. He married Catherine _____. She was born ca 1820 in Va. Andrew
lived in McMinn Co. for a number of years, then moved to Bradley Co., then
to Rhea Co., and back to Bradley Co. He was a Baptist Minister of the
Gospel, and a farmer. Several marriages were performed by him from 1849 to
1853, according to the records in McMinn Co. In 1860, he lived in Rhea Co.,
Tn., where he was listed on the census as "Baptist Preacher." He moved back
to Bradley Co. by the 1870 census.

Their children were:

1. HENDERSON JOHN, b. ca 1833.
2. UPHEMA JOHN, b. ca 1835. Married George W. Lowry ca 1855. Their children were (1) AUBRIE LOWRY, b. ca 1856 and (2) CETHA C. LOWRY, b. ca 1858.[30]
3. WILLIAM JOHN, b. ca 1837.
4. NANCY H. JOHN, b. ca 1839. Married George F. Wilson ca 1858. Child ALBERT F. WILSON, b. ca 1859.[31]
5. CHARLES P. S. JOHNS, b. ca 1841 in McMinn Co., Tn. Married NANCY K. HENDERSON 27 May 1873 in Monroe Co., Tn.
6. MARTHA E. JOHNS, b. ca 1847, McMinn Co., Tn. Married Lewis Stevenson ca 1850 in Bradley Co., Tn. Child WILLIAM STEVENSON, b. ca 1869, Bradley Co., Tn.[32]
7. McCAMPBELL JOHNS, b. abt 1848, McMinn, Tn. Married Sarah _____ ca 1868. [33] Daughter ANNA A. JOHNS, b. Mar 1870, Bradley Co., Tn.
8. CATHERINE J. JOHNS, b. ca 1850, Bradley Co., Tn. Married Francis M. Barnes 30 Nov 1871, Bradley Co.
9. SAMUEL W. JOHNS, b. ca 1852, Bradley Co., Tn.

* *

1831 Tax List McMinn Co., Tn.
Capt. Trotten's Co.: Andy Johns; Samuel Johns.
Capt. Rothwell's Co.: Andrew John   160 acres.

* *

1840 EAST TENNESSEE CENSUS, VOL. 6, Knox Co., P. 100:
And Johns: 1 M under 5; 1 M 5/10; 1 M 30/40; 1 F under 5; 1 F 30/40.

* *

HUGH K. JOHN,
2nd son of Samuel Johns (ca 1772) and Nancy, was born ca 1813, Knox Co., Tn. He married Sarah A. Prather in McMinn Co., Tn. 16 Mar 1842. She was b. ca 1817 in N.C. He was a farmer in McMinn Co.[34] Their children were:

1. PHOEBE JOHN, b. ca 1843.
2. MARY E. JOHN, b. ca 1844.
3. NANCY P. JOHN, b. ca 1847.

---

[30]1860 Rhea Co., Tn. Census, 442-442, Distr. No. 3, 24th July.
[31]ibid, 441-441.
[32]1870 Bradley Co., Tn. Census, p. 406, 13th Civ. Distr., 10 Jun, Cleveland.
[33]1850 Census McMinn Tn. 25th Subdiv., 1153-785. Says McConnell Johns. 1860 Rhea Co. Tn., Distr. No. 3, Washington, p. 487. says McCampbell. 1870 Bradley Co., Tn., Cleveland, 1st Civ. Distr., 48-45. Says Mack Johns.
[34]1850 Census McMinn Co., Tn., 25th Subdiv., 934-641.
1860 Census McMinn Tn., p. 264, No. 5, The 8th Civ. Distr., 1st Jun, 29-29. Living with them was Clinton Johns, son of William, farm laborer, age 15.

4. MARTIN A. JOHNS, b. ca 1848.
5. PARALEE JOHNS, b. ca 1850.
6. CORNELIA CATHERINE JOHNS, b. ca 1855.
7. JAMES W. JOHNS, b. ca 1857.
8. SAMUEL H. JOHNS, b. ca 1861.
* *

WILLIAM JOHN,
3rd son of Samuel John (ca 1772) and Nancy, was born ca 1815 in Knox Co.,
Tn. He married Jane Armstrong 31 Dec 1839, McMinn Co. Tn. (Performed
by D. Cantrell, J.P.)[35] She was daughter and heir of Thomas Armstrong of
McMinn Co. She was born ca 1820 in Tn. He was a farmer and lived in
Bradley Co. in 1850 and 1860.[36]
Their children were:
1. NANCY JOHN, b. ca 1840.
2. ZEPHENIAH LOFTIN JOHN, b. ca 1842.
3. CLINTON JOHN, b. ca 1844.
4. CHARLES JOHN, b. ca 1847.
5. SAMUEL JOHN, b. ca 1848.
6. MARY E. JOHN, b. ca 1850.
7. SARAH JOHN, b. ca 1852.
8. ISAAC J. JOHN, b. ca 1856.
9. MILDRED S. JOHN, b. ca 1860.
*

Deed Book E. McMinn Co., Tn., No. 133, 3 Aug 1837:
Samuel John to William John: mortgage of personal property.
Deed Book 1, 31 Dec 1845:
William John and wife Jane, formerly Jane Armstrong, heir of Thomas
Armstrong Dec'd late of McMinn Co., To James S. Russell; land....except
three acres laid off to Nancy and Clinton B. Armstrong.
* *

SAMUEL JOHNS Jr.,
4th son of Samuel John (ca 1772) and Nancy, was born abt 1817 in Knox Co.,
Tn. He married Rebecah Frazier June 24, 1841. (By A.C. Robeson, J.P.
(Marriages of McMinn Co...by Whitley, p. 21.) They lived in Bradley Co.,
Tn., where Samuel was a farmer.[37] Living with them in 1850 was Nancy Cry,

---

[35]Marriages of McMinn County, Tn. 1821-1864, Compiled by Edythe Rucker Whitley,
Baltimore, Genealogical Publishing Co., Inc. 1983, p. 15.
[36]1850 Census Bradley Co., Tn., Third Subdiv., E. Delancy, 23 Oct,727-727. 1860
Census Bradley Co., Tn., Third Distr., 2 day Aug, p. 169, 1505-1505.
[37]1850 Census Bradley Co., Tn., Third Subdiv., p. 382, 733-733. 1860 Bradley
Census, p. 164, Second Distr., 1399-1399.

b. ca 1840. In 1860, both she and LIDDIE JOHN lived with them. Liddie
was probably their daughter, b. ca1852.
* *

BENJAMIN JOHN,
5th son of Samuel John (ca 1772) and Nancy, was born ca 1820 in Knox Co.,
Tn. He married Mary Baker 27 Jul 1843 in McMinn Co.
*

CHAPTER FOURTEEN

ZEPHANIAH JOHN Jr.,
5- son of Zephaniah John (Sr.) (ca 1750) and Elizabeth Loftin, was born ca 1787, probably in North Carolina. He married Lydia Nunn about 1810. She was born in 1788 in Chester Co., S.C.,[1] daughter of John Carlton Nunn and Elizabeth Pratt.
Children:

1. JAMES CARLTON JOHN, b. ca 1812; married Rutha Lindsey, 10 Oct 1831. (James John m. to Rutha Lindsey, Oct. 10, 1831, by George Shenholster, J.P. Wilkinson Co.)[2]
2. WILLIAM PETER JOHN, b. 4 Apr 1814.
3. JONATHAN N. JOHN, b. ca 1816.
4. FRANKLIN E. JOHN, (or FRANCIS)* b. ca 1822. Married Elizabeth Bruner, 7 Sep 1843. She was b. 1822, dau of William Bruner. (Marriage record has Francis E., but J. W. John says he is the "Franklin, of Irwinton, Ga.")
5. SAMUEL JOSEPH JOHN, b. ca 1831. (1850 Wilkinson Census.) (Per J. W. John, Ak.: Samuel, who moved to Fla. ca 1857.) Married Martha Moore.[3]
6. ELIZABETH JOHN, b. ca 1832, Wilkinson Co., Ga.
7. MELISSA J. JOHN, b. ca 1833. (1850 Wilkinson Census.) Married James Hancock.

Lydia John was one of thirteen children. Her father, John Carlton Nunn fought in the Revolution. The Nunns lived in Anson Co, N.C., (which was later Chester Co., S. C.) in 1788 as shown by deed, but apparently moved from there to Orange Co., N.C., then to Wilkinson Co., Ga. John Nunn died in Wilkinson Co., Ga. between 1825 and 1828, leaving a number of heirs, one of whom was Zephaniah John. (V. Davidson, History of Wilkinson, Estates 1820-1828.) John C. Nunn was buried in the Nunn and Wheeler Cemetery in Wilkinson Co. The land on which the cemetery is located was land John C. Nunn was granted in the 1805 Georgia Land Lottery.

Lydia's brother, Samuel Nunn, died in Crittenden Co., Ky. and left his estate to his twelve brothers and sisters, with an Affidavit signed by several

---

[1]"Some S. C. County Records, Vol. 2, The Rev. Silas Emmett Lucas Jr., Editor, So. Hist. Press, Inc. 1989." P. 40, shows deed from P. 33 S. C. records: 29 Nov 1788, deed between John Nunn of Chester Co. S.C. and Major Grisham, for 10 pounds sterling for 41 acres on Stones Creek of Sandy River, part of tract containing 241 acres.
[2]V. Davidson, History of Wilkinson Marriages.
[3]Wilkinson Co., Ga. Historical Collections...by Maddox, p. 318.

Nunn's on 25 Jan 1856 attesting to their identification.[4] Lydia Johns was one of the heirs and received one-eleventh of his estate.

There are records in the IGI file of the Mormon Family History Center which indicate some of Zephaniah and Lydia's children were born in Crittenden Co., Kentucky. "John, Edmund H., son of Zephaniah John/Lydia Nunn B. 25 Jan 1842 Crittenden." Genealogical writers give William Peter John and Martha Caroline Hancock as father of Edmund H. John who was born on this date. Another IGI Ky. entry has "John, William Peter, son of Zephaniah John/Lydia Nunn B. 4 Apr 1814 Livingston."

Some of the land records shown under Zephaniah Sr. might have been for his son, as there was no way to distinguish which after the younger became of age. Both are probably buried in unmarked graves in Nunn-Wheeler Cemetery. Both the spelling "John" and "Johns" were found in these records, as in most found in Wilkinson Co., Ga.

* *

1820 CENSUS WILKINSON CO., GA., p. 358.
Zephaniah John, one male 26/45, 3 males under 10. One female 26/45, one female under 10.
The 1830 Wilkinson Co., Ga. Census had Zephaniah age 40/50, Lydia age 30/40. One male age 10/15; one male 15/20. Two females under 5.

* *

"On 5 Sep 1836 John Brooks, a son in law, was appointed Administrator of John's [John C. Nunn] estate. On 9 Jun 1837 John Brooks obtained receipts from the following heirs as their "proportionable part in full of said Estate," Carlton Nunn, Zephinoah (sic) John, Timothy Bloodworth, Miles M. Bloodworth, John Nicholson, Samuel Wheeler, John Wheeler for self and Eli Wheeler."[5]
NOTE: This apparently gave the names of the spouses of the Nunn female children.

* *

The 1840 Wilkinson Co. Census has Zepheniah age 50/60; Lydia age 40/50; one male 5/10; one male 10/15. One female 5/10; one female 15/20.

* *

1850 CENSUS WILKINSON CO., GA.: 681-681.

Zepheniah Johns	M	63	Ga.
Lidia	F	62	Ga.
Samuel	M	19	Ga.
Melissa	F	17	Ga.

* *

[4] 25 Jan 1856, Crittendon Co., Ky. Circuit Court.
[5] John Nunn Rev. Soldier, by Delmas C. Nunn, 1993, p. 74.

JAMES CARLTON JOHN,

1- son of Zephaniah John (ca 1787) and Lydia Nunn, was born ca 1812 in Wilkinson Co., Ga. He married Ruth Lindsey 10 Oct 1831, in Wilkinson Co., Ga. He was a farmer. He possibly lived for awhile in Crittenden Co., Ky. The family moved to Covington Co., Alabama about 1857.[6] (Record was found of James Z. Johns buried in Nunn Cem. in Wilkinson Co.) [Some Ga. records have this name as Carlton C. John, with James Carlton in parenthesis, causing confusion.]

Their children were:

1. JAMES Z. JOHN, b. 6 Feb 1835, Wilkinson Co., Ga.; d. 15 May 1915.[7] (Joada Cole gave his name as James H. John.)
2. LYDIA A. JOHN, b. ca 1836, Wilkinson Co., Ga.
3. JOHN F. JOHN, b. ca 1838, Wilkinson Co., Ga.
4. WILLIAM H. JOHN, b. 1841, Wilkinson Co., Ga. Was working as a mechanic in 1860 census.
5. THOMAS L. JOHN, b. ca 1844, Wilkinson Co., Ga. Was working as a mechanic in 1860 census.
6. DANIEL L. JOHN, b. ca 1849[8]Wilkinson Co., Ga.
7. SAMUEL M. JOHN, b. ca 1850 Wilkinson Co., Ga.

* * *

Note: There is a record of: J. G. Johns [who] married Rebecca Granade, b. 1874, daughter of Adam Granade and Elizabeth Bloodworth[9] Wilkinson Co. Not sure who this was.

* *

WILLIAM PETER JOHN,

2- son of Zephaniah John (ca 1787) and Lydia Nunn, was born 4 Apr 1814 in Wilkinson Co., Ga. He married Martha Caroline Hancock 9 Feb 1837. She was b. 27 Sep 1821, Ga., dau of Joseph and Mary Brady Hancock.. Records show they possibly lived in Crittendon Co., Ky. for awhile around 1842.

Their children were:

1. JOSEPH S. JOHN, b. 2 May 1840, Wilkinson Co., Ga. He married Mary _____. "He was killed during the Civil War while serving in an Arkansas CSA regiment. An 1872 family letter stated that he was wounded and captured at Franklin, Tennessee and that they thought he died in prison."[10]

---

[6]ibid, p. 317.
[7]Nunn-Wheeler Cem.
[8]1850 Census Wilkinson Co., Ga., p. 364.
[9]Wilkinson Co., Ga. Historical Collections...by Maddox, p. 294.
[10]John Nunn, Revolutionary Soldier, by Delmas Colmen Nunn, Darby Printing Co., 6215 Purdus Dr., Atlanta, Ga. 30338, 1993, p. 311.

2. EDMUND H. JOHN, b. 25 Jan 1842; died age 13 when thrown from horse, on 7 Jan 1855, at Irwinton, Ga. [He was possibly born in Crittendon Co., Ky.]

3. WILLIAM FRANKLIN JOHN, b. 23 Aug 1845. See following.

4. SAMANTHA LOUISE JOHN, b. 15 Jun 1846 m. J. W. "Bill" Greenlee. Lived and farmed at Calmer, Cleveland Co., Ark. Had eight children. See following.

5. MAXY ANN MISSOURI JOHN, b. 29 Dec 1847. Married 27 Feb 1868 Leonidas (Lee) McLendon. Farmed in Cleveland Co., Ark. See following.

6. JONATHAN TERRELL JOHN, b. 3 Jun 1853. Married Nancy Jane Chambers. Had four sons. Lived in Fordyce, Ark. Jonathan died 18 Mar 1903. See following.

7. JAMES WILLIAM JOHN, b. 15 Jul 1854. Died Cleveland Co., Ark. 4 Apr 1874. Never married.

8. MARTHENA " Betty" ELIZABETH JOHN, b. 3 Nov 1856. Married Will Carithers, a school teacher, at Glendale, Ark. Had one child.

9. MARY LYDIA JOHN, b. 17 Feb 1859, b. Bradley Co., Ark. Married 12 Feb 1877 James Mortimer Clark at Glendale, Ark. Had nine children. See following.

* *

In 1853-1854, William John was Sheriff of Wilkinson Co.[11] In Mar 1858, William P. purchased 133.5 acres in Dooley Co., Ga. for $130.00 from Morgan Kemp. About December 1858, they moved to Bradley Co., Ark. They were shown in the 1860 Census as living in Miller Township, Lehu Post Office. William was 40 years old, had $2500.00 in real estate, and $1,000.00 personal property.

All his children, except Edmond who died in 1855, moved with them to Arkansas. The Civil War began 12 Apr 1861. Joseph S. John, eldest son of William, died during the war. He was a Private in Co. G, 2 Arkansas Infantry.[12]

William died in Glendale, Cleveland Co., Ark. on 7 Oct 1861.[13]Caroline died 16 Aug 1861. Both are buried in Shady Grove Cemetery in Glendale. After they died, their son William F. John raised his siblings.

* *

*A Nancy John was age 14 in the 1860 Bradley Co. Ark. census with this family. Was not shown in family Bible of Jonathan T. John. Do not know if

[11]History of Wilkinson Co., p. 288.
[12]Confederate Vouchers.
[13]Wilkinson Co., Ga. Historical Collections....by Joseph T. Maddox, p. 318.

she was a daughter.[14] Can only surmise that it could have been Samantha who was same age.
* *

1850 Census Wilkinson Co., Ga., #458-458:

William P. Johns	35 M Ga.	
Martha C.	27 F Ga.	
Joseph	10 M Ga.	
Edmond	9 M Ga.	
William	5 M Ga.	
Maxy	3 M Ga.	
Semantha	4 F Ga.	
Louisa P. Stephens	18 F Ga.	

[Louisa Stephens has not been identified.]
* *

WILLIAM FRANKLIN JOHN,
3- son of William Peter John (1814) and Martha Caroline Hancock, was born 23 Aug 1845, Wilkinson Co., Ga. He moved to Arkansas with his parents in 1858. He was married on 9 May 1867 to Mary Jane Chambers, daughter of James Chambers and Mary Hall. She was b. 23 Aug 1848. The Chambers had been friends of the Johns in Georgia, and came together to Arkansas. Three members of this Chamber family intermarried with members of the William P. John family. William Franklin raised his siblings after the deaths of his parents in 1861. He was only sixteen when their deaths occurred. He paid off the mortgage of the homeplace in Bradley Co. (now Cleveland Co.) and became head of the family. He was a member of the Shady Grove Methodist Episcopal Church, and was very active in church affairs for nearly thirty years. He was also an active member of the Masons.

They moved to Fordyce, Ark. in December 1888.

This family was extensively covered in "Journal of The John Family 1701-1960 with Chambers, McLendon, Hall and Willis" by Joada John Cole. Although out of print, it is available on Microfilm at the Mormon Family Libraries

Joada John Cole wrote that she had a photograph of William Franklin John, and that his chin had the characteristic crease of the Johns, a crease that ran perpendicular across the lower part of his face. I've noticed the same in many in our Johns line, and agree that it is a characteristic feature.

He was known for his good moral character, and his devotion to his family. His family all received excellent educations and became real assets to the community.

William F. John died of pneumonia in Fordyce, Ark., 21 Feb 1903. Buried in Oaklawn Cemetery at Fordyce. His wife Mary Jane died in Stuttgart, Ark. 27 Jan 1918, and was buried beside her husband.

---

[14]ibid.

Their children:

1. JAMES WILLIAM JOHN, b. 27 Mar 1868, Cleveland Co., Ark.
2. MARY VIRGINIA JOHN, b. 12 Jan 1869, Cleveland Co., Ark.
3. A child who died in infancy.
4. RUFUS EDGAR JOHN, b. 8 Jul 1873, Cleveland Co., Ark.
5. JOSEPH FRANKLIN JOHN, b. 10 Apr 1875, Cleveland Co., Ark.
6. MILTON CARR JOHN, b. 21 Jul 1877, Cleveland Co., Ark.
7. NANCY MYRTLE JOHN, b. 28 Jul 1879, Cleveland Co., Ark. She m. Frank Meyers. They owned and operated Meyers, Croom Mercantile Co. in Stuttgart, Ark. After her husband died, she moved to Springdale, Ark. Owned a variety store there. No children.

* *

JAMES WILLIAM JOHN,
1- son of William Franklin John (1845) and Mary Jane Chambers, was born 27 Mar 1868. He married Myra Clavering Hall, of China Grove Plantation, near Edwards, Ms. 8 Nov 1898. She was born 7 Apr 1875, the daughter of Benjamin Franklin Hall and wife Amanda Elizabeth Farr. Her father served in the Confederate Army in both the infantry and the cavalry.

James William John attended Jordan's Pine Bluff Academy in Pine Bluff; Hendrix College at Conway; then Memphis Hospital Medical College, Medical School of the University of Tennessee, and became a Medical Doctor 27 Mar 1896. He practiced over forty-one years in Pine Bluff, Ark. He inspired three of his brothers to become doctors. He was a Mason.

He owned a farm of over one thousand acres along the Arkansas River. He kept horses there for his children to ride, and help round up the cattle. He kept dairy cows that supplied milk to the O. K. Dairy in Pine Bluff for many years. He raised cotton and vegetables, and enjoyed having fish fries and cookouts. He was out-going, and enjoyed having large gatherings of the family around him.

James William John died 2 May 1942. His wife Myra Hall John died 18 Oct 1956 in Senatobia, Ms., and was buried in Pine Bluff, Ark.
Their children:

1. ANITA JOHN, b. 24 Jul 1900.
2. WILLIAM HALL JOHN, b. 1902, d. 1906.
3. MYRA LEE JOHN, b. 5 Nov 1905.
4. FRANK JOHN, b. 1907, d. 1909.
5. MARGARET FARR JOHN, b. 29 Oct 1908.
6. MARY WILL JOHN, b. 28 Apr 1913.
7. JAMES WILLIAM JOHN, b. 27 Dec 1916.

* *

ANITA JOHN,
1-dau of James William John (1868) and Myra, was born 24 Jul 1900 in Arkansas. She married Charles Delwin Baughman 24 Feb 1920. She was a

music major and attended Galloway College, Searcy, Ark. Her husband was in the Army during World War I, and they moved to Mississippi in 1937.

Charles Baughman was State Construction Engineer for the Farm Security Admin. Later, they owned Baughman's Cabinet Shop in Senatobia, Ms. Both active in civic and church affairs. Charles was a Rotarian and a Deacon in First Baptist Church. Had son:

1- CHARLES DELWIN BAUGHMAN Jr, b. 4 Sep 1927, b. Pine Bluff, Ark. Graduate of Northwest Junior College and Memphis State College. Served two years during WW II in Army Finance Div. in Korea. Married Kathleen Claus, of Rochester, N.Y. 8 Jul 1951. Lived in Ca.
* *

MYRA LEE JOHN,
3-dau of James William John (1868) and Myra, was born 5 Nov 1905 in Arkansas. She attended Hendrix College, Conway Ark.; married Purser F. Magee 20 Jul 1928. They lost their children at an early age; were active in civic and educational affairs. Lived in Longview, Tx. Children:
1. JOHN PURSER MAGEE, b. 6 Jul 1929, Pine Bluff; d. 16 Nov 1930.
2. PETER FLEET MAGEE, b. 28 Mar 1933, Longview, Tx.; d. 1 Dec 1949.
* *

MARGARET FARR JOHN,
5-dau of James William John (1868) and Myra, was born 29 Oct 1908. She attended Southern Methodist University, Dallas, Tx. Taught classes in dancing in Stuttgart and Pine Bluff. She married (1) Don Mirike; had one child: DON MIRIKE JR., b. 11 Oct 1933; d. 11 Feb 1937.
Margaret m. (2) Russell Tillman McFarland, a retired Army Colonel.; child: MARGARET PHYLLIS MCFARLAND, b. 9 Nov 1943.
* *

MARY WILL JOHN,
6- dau of James William John (1868) and Myra, was born 28 Apr 1913 in Arkansas. Graduate of West Tenn. State Teachers College. Was Assistant County Auditor of Grigg Co., Tx. from 1936 to 1949. She m. William Earl Sharp, attorney, Longview, Tx. 30 Apr 1944. Children:
1. RACHEL SHARP, d. at birth.
2. JOHN EARL SHARP, b. 29 Dec 1950.
3. JAMES WILLIAM SHARP, b. 3 Oct 1952.
* *

JAMES WILLIAM JOHN,
7-son of James William John (1868) and Myra, was born 27 Dec 1916 in Arkansas. Attended Kilgore Jr. College and Monticello A. & M. College, Monticello, Ark. Served in WW I; stationed in South Pacific. Married Ernestine Fogleman 31 Oct 1942. Lived in Rochester, N.Y., and was Lubrication Engineer with Eastman Kodak Co. Their children:

1. PETER JAY JOHN, b. 1 Oct 1956, Rochester, N.Y.
2. MARK WILLIAM JOHN, b. 17 Jun 1958, Rochester, N. Y.
* *

MARY VIRGINIA JOHN,
2-dau of William Franklin John (1845) and Mary Jane Chambers, was born 12
Jan 1869. She married John Thomas Beard 12 Sep 1889 in Cleveland Co.,
Ark. He was b. 5 Dec 1889, son of John Thomas Beard and Susan Collins.
They lived in Miller Township, Ark. until his death in 1902. They had one
son. Mary and her son moved to Fordyce, Ark., where she died 4 Jul 1904 of
smallpox, and was buried in Oaklawn cemetery in Fordyce.
Child: JOHN IVY BEARD, b. 18 Nov 1890.
* *

JOHN IVY BEARD,
1- son of Mary Virginia John (1869) and John Thomas Beard, was born 18
Nov 1890 in Cleveland Co., Tn. John Ivy married Zera Mae Honnoll on 19
Jul 1912 in Verona, Ms. She was b. 12 Mar 1890, Nettleton, Ms., dau of
Moses Hamilton Honnoll and Onaida Hawkins. Zera d. 15 Mar 1963; John d.
7 Jun 1967; both bu. in Lone Tree Cemetery, Stuttgart, Ark.
Children of John Ivy and Zera:
1. JOHN HONNOLL BEARD, b. 1 Aug 1913, Stuttgart, Ark. Married
    Velma Florence Harris, 22 Dec 1935, Stuttgart. She was b. 29 Aug 1914,
    Carlisle, Ark., dau of John Calvin Harris and Hattie Belle Brown. John d.
    25 Jun 1978, bu Lone Tree Cem. Stuttgart.
Children of John Honnoll Beard and Velma:
    1) JOHN HARRIS BEARD, b. 29 Dec 1937, Stuttgart, lived in
       Wilmington, Del. Attended University of Texas.
    2) ROBERT LARRY BEARD, b. 30 Jul 1941, Stuttgart. Married
       Katherine Leigh Vinson, 26 Jan 1969. She was b. 12 Oct 1946,
       Pine Bluff, Ark., dau of Walter Embry Vinson Jr. and Virginia
       Houston. Have two children.
    3) MARY SUE BEARD, b. 30 Oct 1944, Stuttgart. Married
       Donald Ray Kemp 8 Apr 1972, Houston, Tx. He was b. 20 Jul
       1945, Austin, Tx., son of Raymond Lee Kemp and Margaret
       Mary Johnson. Had two children.
    4) THOMAS IVY BEARD, b. 16 Dec 1945, Stuttgart; m. Donna
       Gayle Lucario 16 Dec 1983, Houston. She was b. 4 Oct 1957,
       Houston, dau of Anthony Russell Lucario and Lois Marie
       Rizzo. Lived in Friendswood, Tx.
2. Daughter who died in infancy.
3. VIRGINIA MAE BEARD, b. 5 Mar 1918, Stuttgart. Married Floyd
    Bennett Murrell 12 Jun 1938; son of A. D. Murrell. He was an
    engineer and graduated from the University of Arkansas, School of
    Engineering; worked for Dow Chemical in Lake Jackson, Tx.. Virginia d.

9 Dec 1988, Quitman Tx. Both bu. DeWitt Cemetery, DeWitt, Ark.
Daughter: VIRGINIA JANE MURRELL, b. 19 Dec 1939, m. James Berry
Cowart III 9 Jun 1962, Lake Jackson, Tx. He was b. 12 Jan 1940; they
have two children.
* *

RUFUS EDGAR JOHN,
3-son of William Franklin John (1845) and Mary Jane Chambers, was born 8
Jul 1873, Cleveland Co., Ark. Attended Clary Training School at Fordyce;
then graduated from the School of Dentistry in June 1899 in Atlanta, Ga. He
married 10 Apr 1901 Mary Elizabeth Porter. He was a D.D.S. and practiced
dentistry for four years, then became a businessman and farmer. Supervised
his farms, which mainly grew rice, and was a successful planter. He was a
Director of the Exchange Bank at Stuttgart. Lived in Stuttgart, Ark. Member
of Stuttgart First Methodist Church, and both he and his wife were active in
the church. Mary Elizabeth was pianist and organist of the church for fifty-
seven years.

They were both sociable and their home was the gathering place for
relatives at Christmas and holidays. They were interested in young people,
and helped pay for the education of over a dozen young men and women.
They had three children:
1. MARY IRA JOHN, b. 19 Oct 1905.,
2. FRANKLIN PORTER JOHN, b. 25 Feb 1913, m. (1) Beatrice Knight.
    She d. in auto accident 1957; they had three children. Franklin Porter
    John m. (2) Lucille _____; both died in auto accident 1992.
Children of Franklin and Beatrice:
    1) MARY JOAN JOHN, b. 16 Jan 1938, m. Douglas Stephens; two
       children.
    2) JIM PORTER JOHN, b. 9 Aug 1941.
    3) MARGARET LOUISE JOHN, b. 21 Nov 1949.
3. MARGARET JO JOHN, b. 16 Aug 1918, m. William Henry Dillingham
    19 Jan 1929. They had no children.
* *

MARY IRA JOHN,
1- dau of Rufus Edgar John (1873) and Mary Elizabeth, was born 19 Oct 1905
in Stuttgart, Ark. She attended Galloway College, Searcy, Ark. She married
James Robert Davis 12 Jan 1925. He attended the University of Arkansas.
They lived in Port Arthur, Tx., where James Davis worked for the Gulf Oil
Co. Children:
1. PORTER JOHN DAVIS, b. 13 Aug 1929. Attended University of
    Denver, Denver, Col.; A. B. degree with honors (Bus. Admin.), Oklahoma
    State College, Stillwater, Ok.; M. A. degree with honors (Business
    Admin.) University of Arkansas. In U. S. Marines 1951-1953. Married

Linon Earl Davis, Lake Charles, La. Lived in Shreveport, La. Child: CATHERINE ELIZABETH DAVIS, b. 6 May 1958.

2.   JAMES CARTHEL DAVIS, b. 5 Nov 1934. A. B. degree in Business Admin. Sam Houston State Teachers College, Huntsville, Tx. In Army for six months, then served in Army Reserves. Married 1 Aug 1958 Patricia Ann Tauzin, who was b. 11 Nov 1936, dau of Ted and Nelta Tauzin of Port Arthur, Tx. They lived in Groves, Tx. He was an active Mason, and he and wife were members of the Methodist Church. He worked for Merchants National Bank.

* *

JOSEPH FRANKLIN JOHN,
5-son of William Franklin John (1845) and Mary Jane Chambers, was born 10 Apr 1875 in Cleveland Co., Ark. He married Lilian Ada Leonard 10 Jan 1907, in Petersburg, Tn. She was daughter of Hiram Franklin Leonard and Sarah Jane Forbes. Lilian's father was a highly regarded educator, and Lilian was educated under her father, then attended Elizabeth College in Petersburg, Tn., and Peabody College, Nashville. She taught in Elizabeth College and several other schools.

Joseph Franklin's education was interrupted after his father died, but he persevered with his education and was licensed to practice medicine in May 1904. He was a Medical Doctor and practiced in Eureka Springs, Ark. until he retired in 1953. He kept his medical education up to date, and was an active member of several medical organizations, where he held many elective positions. He was also involved in many civic affairs of the city of Eureka Springs. He was made an honorary member of the Arkansas State Medical Society. He died two weeks before he was to be made a member of the Fifty Year Club. He died 24 Mar 1954 in Eureka Springs, Ark. He was buried in the I. O. O. F. Cemetery. Children:

1.   JOADA JOHN, b. 4 Nov 1912 Eureka Springs.
2.   CLARY LEONARD JOHN, b. 21 Dec 1916
* *

JOADA JOHN COLE,
1-dau of Dr. Joseph Franklin John (1873) and Lilian, was born 4 Nov 1912 in Eureka Springs, Ark. She was graduated with an A. B. degree from the University of Arkansas in 1933; took graduate work at University of Colorado. She taught Latin and English for four years in Eureka Springs, Ark. and Haskell, Ok. She married Charles M. Cole 17 Sep 1938, son of Alva L. and Caroline Ida Robertson of Tahlequah, Ok. He was b. 14 Apr 1909, Akins, Ok. He attended Northeastern College, Tahlequah, Ok. They lived in Oklahoma City. Joada Cole died in 1997.

Joada Cole was the author of "Journal Of The John Family 1701-1760" which has been the definitive genealogical source on the John family. Their children:

1. JOE CHARLES COLE, b. 4 Dec 1940, m. Claudia Leslie Giddens, Oklahoma City, Ok. Joe Charles has a Medical Degree, and is an eye surgeon in Tulsa.

Joe Charles and Leslie's children:
   1) CHARLES MARK COLE, b. 23 Dec 1963.
   2) LAURA DENISE COLE, b. 27 Dec 1965.
   3) ANGELA RENE COLE, b. 29 Dec 1969.
   4) COURTNEY LEE COLE, b. 14 Oct 1974.
2. JUDITH JOHN COLE, b. 6 Oct 1947, m. John Joseph Rownak Jr., a banker in Tulsa.

   Children:
   1) JOHN DAVID ROWNAK, b. 7 Jan 1968, m. Jennifer Leigh Finney.
   2) BRIAN CHRISTOPHER ROWNAK, b. 26 Oct 1970, a Baptist youth and music minister.
   3) JOEL MARK ROWNAK, b. 15 Apr 1975.
* *

CLARY LEONARD JOHN,

2-son of Joseph Franklin John (1875) and Lillian, was born 21 Dec 1916 in Eureka Springs, Ark. He graduated from University of Arkansas; U.S. Hall Naval Academy Preparatory School, Columbia, Mo; graduated from U. S. Naval Academy, Annapolis, Md. in 1940; and graduated from U. S. Submarine School, New London, Conn. in 1943. He served in many WW II Pacific naval battles. He was aboard the destroyer U. S. S. Aylwin during the attack on Pearl Harbor; was in the battle of the Coral Sea; the Battle of Midway; the Aleutian Islands campaign; and the Solomon Islands invasion. In late 1942, entered the Submarine Service and made eight combat war patrols in the U. S. S. Seawolf and the U. S. S. Bowfin. Served on the staff of Commander Submarine Force, Pacific Fleet. Awarded many combat medals. He continued in the submarine service after World War II. He was instructor of Naval Science, Villanova College, Villanova, Pa. He wrote over 150 technical manuals for the U. S. Navy and the U. S. Airforce, and was a Chief Technical Writer and Technical Editor for P. W. Voorhees, Inc. in Hollywood, Ca.

He married Kathrine Reynolds Serat 20 Feb 1944 in New London, Conn. He died 6 Mar 1983.

Their children are:
1. KATHRINE LILIAN JOHN, b. 31 Jul 1945.
2. CLARY LEONARD JOHN JR., b. 25 Apr 1947.
3. EDITH REYNOLDS JOHN, b. 18 May 1948.
* *

MILTON CARR JOHN,

5-son of William Franklin John (1845) and Mary Jane Chambers, was born 21 Jul 1877. Graduated from Clary Training School; the University of the South, Sewanee, Tn.; and University of Nashville. He graduated with his M. D. degree in 1903. He married 3 Jan 1904 Ida Gray Towler in Pine Bluff, Ark. She was born 30 Sept 1877 in Dallas Co., Ark., and was the daughter of George Henry and Viola Dedman Towler. He practiced medicine in Laconia, Moscow, and Stuttgart, Ark.

Milton Carr John was active in civic affairs, medical organizations, as well as the Methodist Church. He was a well loved member of the community. He died in Stuttgart, Ark. 9 Jun 1944.

Had two children:

1. LOUISE JOHN, b. 8 Oct 1905. She attended Randolph Macon Women's College, Lynchburg, Va. and graduated from the University of Arksansas. She m. French Caldwell Roe, 25 Dec 1930. He attended the University of Arkansas School of Medicine.

    Child:

    1) JANE GRAY ROE, b. 28 Feb 1936, m. John Wayne Buckley, M.D.

2. MILTON CARR JOHN Jr., b. 16 Jun 1908, m. Amelia Hoffman. He was a graduate of the University of Arkansas School of Medicine. He practiced medicine with his father, and built the M. C. John Clinic in Stuttgart. Active in medical and civic affairs, as well as the Methodist Church. He was a Flight Surgeon in the Army Air Corps during World War II. Had one adopted child:

    1) MEREDITH LOUISE JOHN, b. 17 Dec 1947.

* *

NANCY MYRTLE JOHN,

7-daughter of William Franklin John (1845) and Mary Jane Chambers John, was born 28 Jul 1879 in Cleveland Co., Ark. Graduated cum laude from the Clary Training School, and attended Vanderbilt University, Nashville, Tn. and Mont Eagle College, Tn. She taught school for several years. She married Frank Myers, who was in the mercantile business. After his death, she moved to Springdale, Ark. She married again in later life. She was active in the Methodist Church, and gave an electric organ to the church just before her death. She died in Aug 1948, and was buried in Springdale, Ark.

* *

SEMANTHA LOUISE JOHN,

4- dau of William Peter John (1814) and Martha Hancock, was b. 15 Jun 1846, Wilkinson Co., Ga. She married J. W. "Bill" Greenlee. They lived in Rison, Ark. and farmed there.

Their children:

1. JOHN LEONIDAS GREENLEE, b. 5 Nov 1872.

2. JOE GREENLEE, b. 29 Oct 1875.
3. LEONA GREENLEE, b. 20 Jan 1877.
4. ALICE GREENLEE, b. 22 Mar 1879.
5. WILLIE GREENLEE, b. 24 Feb 1882; m. Annie Wood; had one son:
   PAUL MICHAEL WOOLEY, b. 9 Nov 1952.
6. ACIE GREENLEE, b. 17 Mar 1887.
7. PEARL GREENLEE, b. 22 Nov 1890. Married Clark Livingston 8 Jun
   1940. No children.
8. HUGHEY GREENLEE, b. 15 Jan 1893.
* *

MAXIE ANN MISSOURI JOHN,
5- dau of William Peter John (1814) and Martha Hancock, was born 20 Dec
1847, Wilkinson Co., Ga. She married Leonidas (Lee) McLendon 27 Feb
1868, who was b. 5 Oct 1846, son of Mack W. McLendon and wife Sarah
Frances Raines. He was a soldier in the Confederate Army during the Civil
War, enlisted in Co. G, First Arkansas Cavalry. After the war, he returned to
farming in Cleveland Co., Ark., east of Rison, Ark. Maxie died 7 Sep 1935;
Lee died Jul 1928. Both are buried at Rison, Ark.
Their children:
1. JULIA FRANCES McLENDON, b. 14 Feb 1869. Married John
   Alexander Walker.
2. MARTHA LUCIAN McLENDON, b. 8 Nov 1870. M. 1 Dec 1887 David
   Solomon Chambers. Lived Rison, Ark.
3. ANNIE ELIZABETH McLENDON, b. 1 Dec 1872. M. Henry Davis
   Sadler, M.D. Lived Rison, Ark. Had three sons.
4. WILLIAM OSCAR McLENDON, b. 16 Jan 1875; m. 19 Feb 1908
   Louise Lee Chase. Had two children.
5. EUGENIA GERTRUDE McLENDON, b. 24 Nov 1876. M. 5 Jul 1900
   John E. Crawford. He was an M.D. and they lived in Bay, Ark. Had four
   daughters.
6. EDGAR LEONIDAS McLENDON, b. 27 Jul 1880. M. 26 Feb 1906
   Delector Rhodes, dau of R. B. Rhodes; lived in Rison, Ark. He was
   County Treasurer six years, then was Circuit Clerk. Had three children.
7. JOHN RAINES McLENDON, b. 10 Dec 1881; m. 23 Dec 1912 Grace
   Ola Fike. Lived near Rison, Ark. Had three children.
8. LILLIAN TOM McLENDON, b. 15 Sep 1884; m. 1 Nov 1908 William
   Walter McCullars who was a banker. Had four children.
* *

JONATHAN TERRELL JOHN,
6-son of William Peter John (1814) and Martha Hancock, was b. 3 Jun 1853
in Wilkinson Co., Ga. He moved with his parents to Bradley Co., Ark. in the
winter of 1858. He married Nancy Jane Chambers, b. 12 May 1856. She was
the sister of Mary Jane Chambers, who m. his brother William Franklin John.

They were the children of James and Mary Ann Hall Chambers, who had moved from Wilkinson Co., Ga. to Ark. in 1851.

They moved to Fordyce in 1888, so their children could attend the J. D. Clary Training school. Jonathan d. 18 Mar 1903 in Fordyce, at the age of fifty one. Nancy Jane moved to Arkadelphia after her children finished the Clary Training School. She became a matron at Henderson-Brown College where the boys continued their education.

Nancy Jane d. 20 Jun 1943 in Tahlequah, Ok., at home of son Guy.
Their children:

1. WINBORNE JOHN, b. 25 Apr 1874; d. 18 Sep 1891.
2. GUY FRANKLIN JOHN, b. 24 Apr 1877. Married (1) May Hopper 28 Nov 1905. Had one child who only lived a short time. He m. (2) Myrtle _____. She died in Okmulgee, Ok. He m. (3) Julia McSpadden. He d. 30 Mar 1948, Tahlequah, Ok.
3. ROY FINCH JOHN. A. B. degree from Henderson-Brown School, Fordyce; M.A. degree Vanderbilt University, Nashville, Tn. Director of Activities at Clemson College, Clemson, S.C. Was overseas Director of Dijon Division of Y.M.C.A. during World War I. Was well educated, highly cultured, artistic. He was divorced, and had no children.
4. KEY RAY JOHN, b. 18 Oct 1892; m. Florine F. Miller of Henryetta, Ok. 3 Aug 1919; had no children. Lived in Okemah, Ok. War service impaired his health. Was a veteran of World War I, and was buried in the National Cemetery, Ft. Gibson, Ok.

* *

MARY LYDIA JOHN,
9-dau of William Peter John (1814) and Martha Hancock, was b. 17 Feb 1859 in Bradley Co., Ark. She was called "Molly." She married James Mortimer Clark 12 Feb 1877 in Bradley Co. (formerly Cleveland Co.), Ark. She died 7 Apr 1935 in Fordyce, Ark., and James M. died 21 Aug 1938. Both buried in Oaklawn Cemetery, Fordyce.
Their children:

1. ARTHUR SABESKER CLARK, b. 3 Jan 1879.
2. JAMES L. CLARK, b. 28 Sep 1880; d. 23 Aug 1883.
3. URBAN R. CLARK, b. 13 May 1883.
4. OPHELIA CLARK, b. 31 Mar 1885.
5. WILLIAM H. CLARK, b. 16 Sep 1886.
6. MARY VIRGINIA CLARK, b. 2 Mar 1889. Died 7 May 1953; bu Oaklawn Cemetery, Fordyce, Ark. Did not marry.
7. HENRY K. CLARK, b. 22 Dec 1892. Married Lucy May Starkey, b. 26 Jun 1900. Two children:
    1) THELMA STARKEY CLARK, b. 13 Aug 1918.
    2) LUCY ANITA CLARK, b. 8 Feb 1921.

8. FLOY M. CLARK, b. 17 Sep 1898. Married Fred Stanley 10 Oct 1922 in Dallas, Tx. Lived in Dallas, Tx. No children.
9. IONE CLARK, b. 16 Jul 1898.
* *

FRANCIS E. JOHN,
4- son of Zephaniah John (ca 1787) and Lydia Nunn, was born ca 1822 in Wilkinson Co., Ga. He married Elizabeth Bruner 7 Sep 1843 in Wilkinson Co. She was born ca 1822, the daughter of William Bruner. They moved to Jackson Co., Fla. by 1856.
Their children were:
1. REBECCA J. JOHN, b. ca 1845, Wilkinson Co., Ga.
2. AMANDA ANN JOHN, b. ca 1847, Wilkinson Co., Ga.
3. JAMES W. JOHN, b. ca 1849, Wilkinson Co., Ga.
* *

JONATHAN N. JOHN,
5- son of Zephaniah John (ca 1787) and Lydia was born ca 1816.[15] Married Elizabeth "Elsy" Ann Hancock 28 Dec 1842.[16] She was born about 1820, the dau of Mary Brady and Joseph Hancock. She was sister of Martha Caroline Hancock who married Jonathan's brother, William Peter John. They moved to Fla. ca 1854, and from there to Alabama about 1861. They lived in Covington Co., Ala. Jonathan was a soldier in the Confederate Army. He was a farmer. He died about 1904.
Their children were:
1. LORETTO F. JOHN, b. ca. 1843, m. John Straughn.
2. ELZEBERY NEWTON JOHN, b. 22 Jan 1847.
3. WILLIAM CICERO JOHN, b. ca 1851 in Ga. He was a farmer. He married Susan Childree.
* *

ELZEBERY NEWTON JOHN,
2- son of JONATHAN N. JOHN (1816) and Elsy Hancock, was born 22 Jan 1847 in Wilkinson Co., Ga. He married (1) Sarah Ann Jones. and (2) Susan Childress. He served in the Confederate Army, enlisting while very young. He died 3 Nov 1883.
His children were:
1. HARMON JOHN; m. Vadie Simms and had eight children.
2. JOSEPH JOHN, m. Emma Reeves and had four children.
3. DORMAN JOHN, m. Cora Hicks and had five children.
4. ARRIE JOHN, m. John Hicks and had one child.
5. WENDEL JOHN, m. Amber Powell and had three children.

---

[15] 1850 Census Wilkinson Co., Ga.
[16] V. Davidson, History of Wilkinson, Marriages. Mar. By Wiley Shepherd, J.P.

6. BECKIE JOHN, m. John W. Chandler and had six children.
7. JOY JOHN, m. Fannie Short. No children.
8. LEE JOHN, m. Donnie Lee Blackman and had seven children.
9. LELA JOHN, m. Grady Powell and had five children.
10. JIM JOHN, m. Esther Tillman and had seven children.
11. MARTHA JOHN, died infancy.
12. AUGUSTA JOHN, died infancy.
* *

ELIZABETH JOHN,
6- dau of Zephaniah John (ca 1787) and Lydia, b. ca 1832. She married
Daniel Bruner in early 1840's. In 1860 was living in Jackson County, Florida.
Daniel was a farmer. He died about 1867-1870 in Fla. In 1870 Jackson Co.
census, Elizabeth was head of household.
Their children were:
1. MARY ANN BRUNER, b. ca 1844, Wilkinson Co., Ga.
2. ARCHIBALD "Archy" F. BRUNER, b. ca 1848, Wilkinson Co., Ga.
3. LOUISA M. BRUNER, b. ca 1850, Wilkinson Co., Ga.
4. DANIEL F. BRUNER, b. ca 1851, Wilkinson Co., Ga.
5. MARTHA BRUNER, b. ca 1858, Jackson Co., Fla.
6. JOHN W. BRUNER, b. ca 1858, Jackson Co., Fla.
7. SAMUEL BRUNER, b. ca 1861, Jackson Co., Fla.
8. WALTER BRUNER, b. ca 1862, Jackson Co., Fla.
9. SARAH F. BRUNER, b. ca 1867, Jackson Co., Fla.
* *

SAMUEL JOSEPH JOHN,
7- son of Zephaniah John (ca 1787) and Lydia, was born ca 1831 in
Wilkinson Co., Ga. He moved with his parents to Jackson Co., Florida.
There he married Martha Jane Moore 12 Jan 1854. She was born ca 1832 in
Georgia. Samuel was a farmer. During the Civil War, he served in the
Confederate Army. He was in both Co. F, 19 Arkansas Infantry and Co. E,
6th Florida Infantry. He died while in service in Dec 1862, in a hospital in
Columbus, Ga. Martha died between 1863 and 1869. Their children were
taken to their aunt, Melissa Hancock, and later to their uncle, Jonathan John,
in Alabama.
Their children were:
1. CARTER M. JOHN, (female), b. ca 1848 in Alabama. In 1870, she was
   living with her uncle Jonathan in Covington Co., Ala.
2. ZANIE ANN JOHN, b. ca 1856 in Florida . She was listed as "Fancy A."
   in the 1860 Jackson Co., Fla. census. She married John Jasper Taylor,
   and lived in Andalusia, Ala.
   Their children were:

1) WILLIAM WASHINGTON TAYLOR, b. ca 1874, m. Lettie Dauphin in Tx.
2) SAMUEL JACKSON TAYLOR, b. ca 1877 Covington Co., Ala. m. Emma High in Tx., had MARY ELIZABETH TAYLOR, who m. William F. Ward.
3) MARTHA ELIZABETH TAYLOR, b. ca 1879, m. Thomas Dauphin in Tx.
4) MALISSA R. TAYLOR, b. ca 1883, m. Bob McMichael, Houston Co., Tx.
5) MARY ADELINE TAYLOR, b. ca 1885, m. Herbert Roe.
6) JAMES DANIEL TAYLOR, b. ca 1887, m. Ouida Reeves, Seattle, Wa.
7) GEORGE LEE TAYLOR, b. ca 1891, did not marry.
8) JOHN ERNEST TAYLOR, b. ca 1893, died in 1918 in WW I service. Never married.
9) WILLIAM EDWARD TAYLOR, b. ca 1897, Houston Co., Tx.
3. BRADLEY J. JOHN, b. ca 1857 in Fla. Was living with uncle Jonathan Johns in 1870 in Covington Co., Ala.
4. ELIZA ELIZABETH JOHN, b. ca 1859 in Jackson Co., Fla. Married John Jackson Jones in Ala.
   Had children: 1) E. K. JONES. 2) NAOMI JONES. 3) DOLLIE JONES, m. _____ Russell.
5. SAMUEL JOSEPH JOHN, Jr., b. ca 1862 Jackson Co., Fla. Married Lou Dicey Humphrey in Tx. Died abt 1931 Trinity, Tx.
   Children:
   1) WILLIAM JOHN.
   2) AVERY JOHN.
   3) DORA JOHN, m. _____ Ramsey.[17]
* *

MELISSA J. JOHNS,
8- dau of Zephaniah Johns (ca 1787) and Lydia, was b. ca 1833 in Wilkinson Co., Ga. She married James Hancock, in the late 1850's. James was born in Ga. The Will of Joseph Hancock in 1840 in Wilkinson Co. names one daughter and five sons, with one of the sons named James. In 1860, they were living in Jackson Co., Fla., where James was listed as a merchant, age 38. In 1870 Polk Co., Fla. census, he was a farmer.
Their children (per census):
1. ROBERT HANCOCK, b. ca 1857, Jackson Co., Fla. Died young.
2. MARTHA HANCOCK, b. ca 1859, Ga.
3. SUSAN HANCOCK, b. ca 1863, Ga.

---

[17]Inf. on Zephaniah John and Lydia Nunn line from "John Nunn, Revolutionary Soldier" by Delmas Colmen Nunn, Darby Printing Co., Atlanta, Ga. 30338, 1993.

4. ROBERT HANCOCK, b. ca 1866 Fla. Was age 4 in 1870 Polk Co., Fla. census.
5. CAROLINE HANCOCK, b. ca 1867, Fla.
*

CHAPTER FIFTEEN

CHILDREN OF EZEKIEL:

THOMAS JOHN,

1st son of Ezekiel John (ca 1770) and Lydia, was born ca 1797, in N.C. He came with his parents as a young child to Knox Co., Tn., then moved with them to McMinn Co. after it opened up for settlement. He married Margaret ____. (Possibly Montgomery.) He owned a farm in McMinn Co., Tn. and lived there the rest of his life. He died ca 1854.

Their children:

1. MARGARET JOHN, b. ca 1834 McMinn Co. Tn.
2. LYDIA H. JOHN, b. Jan. 8, 1835 McMinn Co., Tn. She married James S. Richards May 23, 1861. She died Feb. 25, 1891 McMinn Co., Tn. Buried John Cem., McMinn Co.
3. NANCY JOHN, b. ca 1836 McMinn Co., Tn. Was unmarried in 1880, age 43.
4. ALFRED JOHN, b. 2 Oct 1839 McMinn Co., Tn. Was unmarried in 1880, age 41. He died May 10, 1896. Buried John Cem., McMinn Co., Tn.
5. J. MONTGOMERY JOHN, b. ca 1841 McMinn Co., Tn. Married Melvina ____.
6. EMILY JOHN, b. ca 1843 McMinn Co., Tn. Was unmarried in 1880, age 37.
7. CORNELIA JOHN, b. ca 1845 McMinn Co., Tn. Was unmarried in 1880, age 35.

*

Alfred John was in 39th Mounted Infantry, Co. F, Corporal, in Civil War. Enrolled at Mouse Creek March 17, 1862. Men in this Company were from McMinn Co. Zachary T. John, son of Ezekiel Jr., was also in this Company.

1829 Tax List, McMinn Co., Tn:

Capt. Rathwell's Co. by Benjamin Isbell

Robert John--- 160 acres.

Thomas John--- 220 acres.

William John--- 160 acres.

1830 Tax List of McMinn Co., Tn.:

Capt. Rothwell's Co.

Thomas John---220 acres.

1832 Tax List McMinn Co., Tn.:

Capt. Gonce's Co.

Thomas John---380 acres.

McMinn County Tennessee Deed Bk. B, p. 277, 1820-1847.

Thomas Johns

John Cemetery
Thomas John originated in Buncombe County, North Carolina in 1825, and
entered a tract of land, a part of which this Cemetery is located on for the
relatives of Thomas John. Located two and one half miles south of Niota.
Follow road leading from Niota to Mt. Harmony for about one and one half
miles to the farm of H. B. Johnson, turning right into a lane. There, all roads
turn left until reaching the farm of Mrs. Walter Pardue where this Cemetery is
located. There are about thirty two unmarked graves.
Susan M. Turner, 1863-1923, Mother;
Elizabeth Turner, 1896-1920, "At rest."; , Apr. 6, 1905, June 9, 1916, "She's
safe at Home.";
Mary Evelyn Turner, April 21, 1935, Aged 6 years 6 mos. 28 days;
Adaline John ---;
H. A. John, Oct. 2, 1829, May 10, 1896;
A. A. Addleburg, Oct. 2, 1830, Nov. 18, 1870, "How blest the righteous when
he dies.";
Cynthia V. Addleburg, Wife of A. A. Addleburg, Jan. 6, 1831, Oct. 2, 1895,
"We have loved, but God loved you best; dear Mother, it is He that has given
you rest.";
S. W. Holt, Apr. 8, 1842,
Addie Turner, Sept. 23, 1884, Oct. 18, 1905, "At rest.";
"Asleep in Jesus.", Emma Sue Turner, Daughter of E. J. and Agnes
TurnerMar. 1, 1891, Father;
Lydia H. Richards, Wife of J. S. Richards, Jan. 8, 1835, Feb. 25, 1891;
Addie Dixon, Wife of E. C. Dixon, July 29, 1857, Feb. 1, 1925, "She lived in
a house by the side of the road and was a friend to man.";
E. C. Dixon, Oct. 31, 1855, July 12, 1897, "A place is vacant in our hearts
which never can be filled."

This cemetery record was compiled by the W.P.A.
* *

McMinn County Tennessee Deed Bk. K, P. 429.
Dec. 7, 1835 (Deed Made)
Samuel John of Knox Co., Tn. to Ezekiel John of McMinn Co., Tn.
60 acres beginning at the SE corner of the NE quarter of Section 12,
Township 4, Range first West of the Meridian Hiwassee District.
Wit: Thomas John
     Jonathan x John.

McMinn County Tennessee County Court Minutes:
Oct. 5, 1840---p. 517.

Thomas John was this day appointed administrator of all and singular goods and chattel rights and credits of William John, deceased, who took the oath as administrator and entered into bond with security approved by Court and obtained Letters of Administration.

Census Records:
1840 Census McMinn County, Tn. P. 78.
Thomas John: M under 5--1; M 40-50--1; F 30-40--2; F 5-10--2; F under 5--1.
* *
1850 Census McMinn Co., Tn.-P. 483, No. 281.
Thomas Johns--53--M--NC—Farmer; Margaret Johns--48--F—Tn; Margaret Johns--16--F—Tn; Lydia Johns--15--F—Tn; Nancy Johns--14--F—Tn; Alfred Johns--11--M—Tn; Montgomery Johns--9--M—Tn; Emily Johns--7--F—Tn; Cornelia Johns--5--F—Tn.
* *
Jan. 30, 1854.
Personally appeared before me Thomas Vaughan Clerk of the County Court of McMinn County Jonathan John one of the subscribing witnesses of the foregoing deed and say that he is personally acquainted with Samuel John, the grantor, and that he saw him sign the same the day it bears date and Thomas John, the other subscribing witness having departed this life, the said Jonathan John also depose and say he is acquainted with the hand writing of the said Thomas John and that it is his signature.

"Wills and Estate Records of McMinn County Tennessee 1820-1870", p. 87, Compiled by Reba Bayless Boyer: (Permission to use granted.)
Estate of Thomas John
CR 6---Feb. 6, 1854
Ezekiel John appointed administrator.
Will Bk. E, P. 362---Feb. 23, 1854:
Commissioners John L. Bridges, Isaiah Smith and James Wilson lay off year's support for widow Margaret and family.
"Wills and Estate Records.....", p. 87:
Will Bk. E, P. 365---April 3, 1854. Estate of Thomas John.
Inventory of Sale by Administrator.
"One half of a wind mill to the widow 0.50"
Will Bk. E, P. 494---Feb. 29, 1856.
Settled by same administrator.

1860 Census McMinn Co., Tn. - P. 63 (Handwritten), P. 236 (Printed.) 5th day July 1860, Athens, Tn.: Alfred John--21--M—Tn; Lydia John--24--F—Tn; Nancy John--22--F—Tn; Montgomery John--19--M—Tn; Emily John--17--F—Tn; Cornelia John--14--F—Tn.

* *

1870 Census McMinn Co., Tn.-No. 109-115, Fifth Dist.
J. S. Richards--37--M—SC; Lydia Richards--35--F—Tn; John Richards-- 4--M—Tn; Thomas Richards--2--M—Tn; Noah Richards--9/12--M—Tn; Nancy Johns--32--F—Tn; Emily Johns--24--F—Tn; Cornelia Johns--21--F—Tn; Alfred Johns--30--M—Tn; C. M. Keith--44--M—Tn.
* *

1880 Census McMinn Co., Tn.-ED 65, P. 44, 4th Dist., No. 442-477.
Alfred Johns--41--M--Tn--NC—Tn; Nancy Johns--43--F--Tn--NC--Tn—Sister; Emma Johns--37--F--Tn--NC--Tn—Sister; Cornelia Johns--35--F--Tn--NC--Tn—Sister.
* *

John Cemetery, McMinn Co., Tn.
H. A. John--Oct. 2, 1829--May 10, 1896.

This record may refer to Alfred Johns.
However, Alfred Johns was born 1839, not 1829.
* *

There is an interesting article regarding a cemetery located near the John Cemetery. It appeared in a newspaper article that was in "Scrap-Book History of McMinn County, Tennessee." This was compiled by John Morgan Wooten, Cleveland, Tn. in 1937. Author of article unknown; entitled: "1929
   "OLD CEMETERY AT NIOTA HAS NOTED GRAVES.'
   This tells of an old burying ground located on the M. M. Matlock farm near Niota, on lands once belonging to the Cherokee Indians. Henry Matlock in 1818 purchased land from Betsy McIntosh, a half-breed Cherokee, who was former wife of the great chief George Fallingwater. This purchase consisted of about 2100 acres of land on Big Mouse Creek Valley.
   Mr. Matlock discovered a small grave on a hill a short distance from the log cabin that had been the home of the former owner. His inquiry to the Indians revealed the grave was not of an Indian, but was that of an emigrant child. The child was believed to have lost its life from severe cold while traveling with its parents over the wild and unsettled country.
   Another interesting grave in this cemetery is that of a revolutionary war soldier, Maximilion Rector. He fought in the battles of Brandywine, Germantown, Monmouth and at the Siege of Charleston. He was taken prisoner at this last battle. He was held until the exchange of prisoners after the capture of Lord Cornwallis. His war record revealed the fact that he had been commended for bravery by Washington. The paper mentioned that several people who had died recently [1929] had told of reading letters from General Washington that Rector had. They were destroyed when his house was burned.
   There were also two graves of brothers who fought in the War Between the States, one for the South and the other for the Union.

388

Just a few feet from the old Matlock home, Chief Fallingwater, the Cherokee chief, and his daughter Fannie are buried.

"This historic old cemetery is called the Matlock cemetery because a few years after the land was bought from the Indians, Nancy Matlock was buried there and it has since taken the name of Matlock. All the slaves of this family were buried here also."

* *

SAMUEL JOHN,

2nd son of Ezekiel John (ca 1770) and Lydia, was b. ca 1801 NC.
He married Jane Harris July 13, 1825 in Grainger Co. Tn.. She was born ca 1802 in Tn. He died 1852 in Knox Co., Tn.
Their children:

1. PARTHANA JOHN, b. ca 1828 Knox Co. Tn.
2. MARY A. JOHN, b. ca 1830 Knox Co Tn. Married John H. Howell Nov. 10, 1853 Knox Co. Tn.

Samuel John would have been about seven or eight years of age when his father and mother moved to Tennessee.

We believe the following land records were for this Samuel John and show he was living in Knox County as early as 1830.

KNOX CO. TN. DEED BOOK Y-1, P. 479:
This indenture made this 9th Oct. 1833 between William Taylor of the County of Knox and Samuel John of the County of McMinn of the one part and Felix Brown of Knox County $310 --- 100 acres ---
adjoining Samuel Todd, Hugh Fulton and Eli King.
Wit: William McMillan, Samuel Sample.
Recorded March 3, 1835.

KNOX CO. TN. DEED BOOK A, April 1832 to April 1836. Page 10, 1834:
A deed from William Taylor & Samuel John to Felix Brown for 100 a was proven by Wm. McMillan & Samuel Sample fur. witnesses thereto on the 18th July 1835.

KNOX CO. TN. DEEDS, p. 145:
Felix Brown to Samuel Johns, recorded Vol. 1, p. 479, Files March 3, Deed Oct. 9, 1835, 100 a.

Deed Book K, P. 76, (429) 7 Dec 1835: Samuel John of Knox Co. to Ezekiel John; 30 Jan 1854, witness Jonathan John identifies handwriting of the other witness, Thomas John, who has departed this life.

1830 CENSUS KNOX CO. TN.

Samuel John 1 M 20/30; 2 F under 5; 1 F 20/30.

<u>1840 CENSUS KNOX CO. TN.</u>:
Samuel Johns 1 M 30/40; 1 F 10/15; 1 F 30/40.

<u>KNOX CO. TN. List of taxable Property</u>:
District No. 4, 1844-1845: Samuel Johns-----92 acres of land valued at $450.

<u>1850 CENSUS KNOX CO., TN. -- No. 1310</u>:
Samuel Johns 49 M NC Farmer $600; Jane Johns 47 F Tn; Parthena 19
F Tn; Mary Johns 18 F Tn.

<u>MARRIAGE NOTICES</u>.
XV-754. 6 Mar 1863 T. J. Errickson to Miss Parthena J. Johns, m. 26 Feb
1863 by Rev. M.A. Cass, all of McMinn Co.   ATHENS POST.
Published at Athens, Tn. (P. 169, McMinn Co. Tn. Deeds and Other Data" by
Boyer.)

JOHNS, SAMUEL 1852 Will Book P. 257, (Knox County, Tn.)
"On motion of Benjamin Looney administration is granted to him on the
estate of Samuel Johns, deceased, whereupon the said Benjamin Looney
enters into same with Vivian Ch[amberlain] as his Security in the final sum
of fifteen hundred dollars and was duly cereatifieze [certified] as such said
thereupon letters of Administration were recorded and issued which letters are
in the words and figures following to wit
July Session 1852   258
State of Tennessee
   To Benjamin Looney Greeting,
Whereas, It hath been represented within our County Court, held for the
County of Knox, at the Court house in Knoxville, on the first Monday of July
1852, that <u>Samuel Johns</u>, late of said county had died intestate whilst living,
and at the time of his death, goods and chattels and credits the ordering and
granting administration whereof doth appoint unto us, and we be desirous that
the said goods and chattels, rights and credits, may be well and faithfully
administered do grant unto you the said Benjamin Looney full powers by
these presents well and truly to collect and to take unto your possession all
and singular the goods and chattels, rights and credits which were of the said
Samuel Johns deceased, at the time of his death wheresoever the same may be
found hereby requiring you, to make you to cause to be made and returned
unto our said Court, within ninety days, a true and perfect inventory of said
goods, said chattels, rights, and credits, and also to render a true and clear
account of said administration when thereto required.
   Witness, Geo. W. C. Cox, Clerk of said Court at office in
Knoxville the first Monday of July 1852.

/s/ Geo. W. C. Cox Clerk"

* *

MARY A. JOHN,
2nd child of Samuel John (ca 1801) and Jane Harris, was b. ca 1830, Knox
Co., Tn. She married John H. Howell Nov. 10, 1853, Knox Co. Tn. He was
born ca 1826 Tn.
Children:
1. ARABELLA JANE HOWELL, b. ca 1855 Knox Co. Tn.
2. CORDELIA PARTHENA HOWELL, b. ca 1858 Knox Co. Tn.
3. ELIZABETH A. HOWELL, b. ca 1861 Knox Co. Tn.
4. JAMES S. HOWELL, b. ca 1868 Knox Co. Tn.
5. AMANDA L. HOWELL, b. ca 1872 Knox Co. Tn.

* *

Grainger County Tennessee Marriages:
Samuel Johns to Jane Harris July 13, 1825.
Bondsman: Charles N. Peck . Married by Henry Hawkins, J. P.

Knox Co. Tennessee Marriages:
John H. Howell to Mary A. John, Nov. 10, 1853.

1830 Census Knox Co. Tn.:
Samuel John; M 20-30--1; F under 5—2; F 20-30--1.

1840 Census Knox Co. Tn.:
Samuel Johns M 30-40--1; F 10-15-- 1; F 30-40--1.

1850 Census Knox Co., Tn. ---No. 1310.
Samuel Johns--49--M--NC--Farmer--$600; Jane Johns-- 47--F—Tn; Parthena-
-19--F—Tn; Mary Johns--18--F—Tn.

"Marriage Notices; Page 169:
XV-754, 6 Mar 1863 T. J. Errickson to Miss Parthena J. Johns, m. 26 Feb
1863 by Rev. M.A. Cass, all of McMinn Co.
Athens Republican, published at Athens, Tn."[1]

1860 Census Knox Co. Tn., P. 178 (Hand Written), P. 142 (Printed)
John Howell-- 35--M—Tn; Mary Howell--30--F—Tn; Jane Howell--5--F—
Tn; Cordelia Howell--2--F—Tn.

1870 Census Knox Co., Tn., 4th District, P. 121, No. 106-107.

---

[1]McMinn County, Tennessee Deeds and Other Data 1820-1880 Researched,
Compiled, and Edited by Reba Bayless Boyer. Permission to use granted Dec. 1994.

Jane John--70--F—Tn; Cordela John--12--F—Tn; Arabelle John--10--F—Tn;
James John--3--M--Tn.
(Children with Jane, Mary's mother and their grandmother.)

<u>1880 Census Grainger Co., Tn.</u>--ED 99, P. 8, No. 75-80, 8th Civil District.
John H. Howell--52--M--Tn--Va—Tn; Mary A. Howell--50--F--Tn--Tn--Tn—
Wife; Bella J. Howell--35--F--Tn--Tn--Tn—Dau; (Age should be 25).
Parthena C. Howell--22--F--Tn--Tn--Tn—Dau; Elizabeth A. Howell--19--F--
Tn--Tn--Tn—Dau; James S. Howell--12--M--Tn--Tn--Tn—Son; Amanda L.
Howell--8--F--Tn--Tn--Tn--Dau.

John H. Howell was listed as living next house to Sanders Calloway Johns.
* *

ROBERT JOHN,
3rd son of Ezekiel John Sr. (ca 1770) and Lydia, was born ca 1807 in N.C.
and moved as an infant to Tennessee. He married Sarah Southard, called
"Sallie." She was born ca 1815 in N.C. He was a farmer, and was living in
Hamilton Co., Tn. in 1840, per the census there[2]. Before the next census, he
moved to Crawford Co., Mo. [3] He and his wife both died there ca 1855 of
pneumonia, per family descendants. Crawford is now Maries Co.
Children:
1. WILLIAM JOHN, b. 7 Apr 1836, Tn. Died 4 Apr 1898, Tx.
2. REBECCA JOHN, b. 8 Jan 1839 Tn. Died 10 Apr 1893, Mo.
3. ROBERT JOHN, b. 1 Oct 1841 Tn. Died 27 Feb 1910, Tx.
4. NATHAN HARRISON JOHN, b. 16 Feb 1845 Mo. Died 8 Mar 1929,
   Mo.
5. JAMES M. JOHN, b. ca 1849 Mo. Died 29 Mar 1870, Mo.
6. FRANCIS MARION JOHN (Sr.), b. 15 July 1851 Mo. Died 23 May
   1925, Ok.
* *

LYDIA JOHN,
youngest daughter of Ezekiel John (ca 1770) and Lydia, was born abt 1824 in
Knox or McMinn Co., Tn. She married (1) Aaron Southard 2 Mar 1843[4], and
went to Missouri with her brother Robert's family. Her husband died, and she
married (2) E. J. Spencer. She and Aaron Southard had one child, RICHARD
SOUTHARD, born ca 1844 in Missouri. She and E. J. Spencer had at least
one son, W. T. SPENCER, age 1 in 1850.[5]
* *

---

[2]1840 Hamilton Co., Tn. Robert age 30/40; Sarah, age 20/30; 1 female age 5/10; 1
male under 5; 1 female under 5.
[3]1850 Crawford Co., Mo., p. 409, #221-221.
[4]"Marriages of McMinn Co., Tn., by Whitley, p. 28. (Married by Justus Steed, J.P.)
[5]1850 Census Crawford Co., Mo. Taken 20 day Aug. #222-222. E. T. was age 34 b.
Tn., and a farmer.

WILLIAM JOHN,

1st son of Robert John (ca 1805) and Sarah Southard (ca 1815), was born 7 Apr 1836, McMinn Co., Tn. In the early 1840's, he moved to Missouri with his parents. He married Nancy Lewis Martin, 24 Nov 1859 in Maries Co., Mo. She was born 15 Dec 1842, Mo., daughter of Jackson T. Martin and Clementine Underwood.

William and Nancy moved to Ellis Co., Tx. in the spring of 1860.[6] He began work right away, running a mill for a local man named Ben Watson.[7] After a few months, in January 1862, he enlisted in the Confederate Army, and served under Capt. Carr Forrest and Ben Watson. He was in Company C, 19th Regiment, Texas Cavalry, and was in many skirmishes. He served in Arkansas, Louisiana, Missouri, and Texas. He was in Hempstead, Tx.. at the time Lee surrendered. The group was disbanded at Marlin, Tx., 23 May 1865.[8] After the War, he first worked thrashing wheat, and soon owned half interest in a wheat thrasher. He farmed three years before buying seventy-three acres of raw land. He kept adding to this and by 1892, owned 386 acres outside Avalon, Tx. He had 240 acres of this under cultivation, growing cotton, corn and alfalfa. He was a member of the Baptist Church, and served as a Deacon. He also served as road overseer and school trustee, and was a member of the Alliance. He died 4 Apr 1898, and Nancy died 15 Feb 1913. Both are buried in Hughes Cemetery near Avalon.

Children:

1. WILLIAM L. JOHN, b. 8 Dec 1861, Tx. Died 16 Feb 1865 Tx.
2. CLEMENTINE JOHN, born 27 Feb 1866 Tx. Married Walter B. Hale, 28 Feb 1884 Tx.[9] Died 1938.
3. ROBERT J. JOHN, born 22 Feb 1868 Tx. Married Fannie L. Martin, 2 Apr 1893 Tx.[10] Died 28 Feb 1906, Avalon, Tx.[11]
4. HARVEY JOHN, born 28 Feb 1870 Tx. Married Ida Manning, 17 May 1891. Died 29 Nov 1938 Tx.
5. SALLIE JOHN, born 13 Oct 1872 Tx. Married John Edward Loyd, 18 Oct 1891 Tx.[12]
6. ROBERTA LEE JOHN, born 10 Aug 1878 Tx. Married George Gurley Smith, 20 Oct 1895 Tx.[13] Died 21 June 1965 Tx.

---

[6]Ellen John, Lawton, Ok.
[7]"A Memorial and Biographical History of Ellis County, Texas, Chicago: The Lewis Publishing Company. 1892, pp.447-448.
[8]Texas Gen. Records, Ellis Co. 1850-1950, Vol. XII, compiled by DAR.
[9]Ellis County, Texas Marriage Records 1878-1886 Volume II Compiled by Weldon I. Hudson, p. 45.
[10]Ellis Co. Tx. Marriage Records Volume E Through J January 1887 Through May 1900. Ellis Co. Gen. Society, p. 64.
[11]Co. Death Records Volume 1 1903-1909 Volume 2 1909-1917 of Ellis County, Texas. The Ellis Co. Gen. Society, p. 55.
[12]Ellis County Tx. Mar. Records Volume E Through Volume J January 1887-May 1900, Ellis Co.Gen. Society, p. 46.

7. JOHN, born 1 Apr 1892. Died, probably at birth or as an infant.[14]
* *

REBECCA JOHN,
2nd child and only daughter of Robert John (ca 1805) and Sarah Southard (ca 1815), was born 8 Jan 1839 in McMinn Co., Tn. She moved to Missouri with her parents in the early 1840's. She married (1) Edmond J. Moreland 30 Nov 1854 in Crawford Co., Mo.[15] He was born ca 1833 in Tn.[16] His parents were Thomas Moreland Sr. and Elizabeth "Peggy" James.[17] He was a soldier in the Civil War and died at the Battle of Cane Hill in Arkansas on 28 Nov 1862. Their children were:

1. ROBERT H. MORELAND, b. ca 1858 Mo. Married Judith Anderson.
2. JAMES EDWARD MORELAND, b. ca 1862 Mo. Married Nannie Lou Wimberley 23 Jun 1887, Ellis Co., Tx. Lived in Jack Co., Tx.. He farmed and taught school.

After the Civil War ended, Rebecca and her children, along with her brother Francis Marion John, moved to Ellis County, Tx. and lived with her brothers William and Robert, and their families. She married (2) John W. Shinkle, 24 Mar 1868, in Ellis Co., Tx.[18] He was born 30 Jan 1840 Mo. His parents were Samuel Shinkle and Sarah Lavinia Courtney. He was in the Union Army 1 Jan 1863 to 24 May, 1865. He served as a Private in Regiment Co. C, 99th Ill. Inf. They moved back to Maries Co., Mo. after their marriage. Rebecca died 10 Apr 1893. John W. died 1903, and both are buried in Dillon Cemetery, Maries Co.[19]
Their children were:

1. SARAH LAVINIA SHINKLE, born 6 Sept 1869 Maries Co., Mo. Married Louis E. Strain. They moved to Texas 1894. Sarah d. 3 Mar 1944.
2. SAMUEL F. SHINKLE, born Jan 1872 Maries Co., Mo. Married Lizzie Walker. They moved to Washington. He was a schoolteacher.
3. WALTER GREY SHINKLE, born 17 Jul 1874 Maries Co., Mo. Married Rose Cox. They moved to Gladstone, Or. area. Walter d 3 Dec 1947. Children:
   (1) JAMES SAMUEL "Sam" SHINKLE, b. 4 May 1905 in Safe, Mo. Veteran of World War II, served in U.S. Army's 10th Armored Division from 1942 until 1945. He married Helen Blount 10 Apr 1946 in

---

[13]ibid, p. 103.
[14]Courtesy Ellen John, Lawton, Ok.
[15]Marriage Records of Crawford Co., Mo. Marriage Book A, p. 262. Married by William Curtis, M.E.
[16]Census 1860 Maries Co., Mo.
[17]HISTORY OF MARIES CO., MO., King, 1963.
[18]Marriage Records Ellis Co. Tx., p. 276.
[19]The Cemeteries of Maries County, Mo. A Personal History, p. 356.

Vancouver, Wa. Worked as ground wood superintendent for Publisher's Paper Co. for more than 47 years. Retired in 1970. Died of heart problems 21 Sep 1993. Private entombment in Mountain View Cem. Mausoleum. Son FRED S. SHINKLE of Tacoma, Wa.; daughter, PRUDENCE BLUM of Federal Way, Wa.[20]

    (2) MERLE SHINKLE, m. _____ Hopkins, lived in Oregon City 1993.

    (3) ANITA SHINKLE, m. _____ Aldrich, lived in Portland, Ore. 1993.

    (4) ANNA MAE SHINKLE, m. _____ Rogers, lived in Portland 1993.

4. LAURA BELL SHINKLE, born 19 Nov 1876 Maries Co., Mo. Married James Parrott; moved to Texas.[21] Died 3 Dec 1947.

* *

ROBERT JOHN,

3rd child of Robert John (ca 1805) and Sarah Southard (ca 1815), was born 1 Oct 1841 in McMinn Co., Tn. He moved with his parents to Missouri in the early 1840's. He went with his brother William's family to Ellis Co., Tx. in 1860. He joined the Confederate Army in 1861, and served as a Private in Company E, 12th Regiment, Texas Cavalry. Later he was transferred to Company C, 19th Regiment, Texas Cavalry, and was discharged 23 May 1865. His brother William was also a member of Company C, 19th Regiment.

    After the war, he returned to farming. He married Martha "Mattie" Frances Hardeman, 27 Dec 1868, in Ellis Co.[22] She was born 2 Sept 1850 and was the daughter of John Marr Hardeman and Mary A. Hardeman. Robert was a member of the First Christian Church of Italy, Tx., and served as an Elder. Mattie died 30 June 1906 in Texas. Robert died 27 Feb 1910.[23] Both are buried in Italy Cemetery, Italy, Tx.

    Their children:

1. ROBERT H. JOHN, born 10 Dec 1869, Tx. Died 23 Dec 1871.

2. THOMAS JEFFERSON JOHN, born 2 Jul 1871, Tx. Married Maggie May Arnold, 29 Oct 1891 in Ellis Co., Tx.[24] Died 11 Jun 1942 Tx. Had six children. (Four known):

    (1) ROBERT ALEXANDER JOHN, b. 9 Nov 1892.

    (2) THOMAS JOHN, b. 30 Dec 1907. Married Helen Frances Waldrum 25 Nov 1939. Radio and television engineer until retirement. Member of Central Christian Church, Sherman. Helen died 18 Feb 1991. Thomas died 28 Jul 991, Sherman, Tx.

[20]The John Family Journal, Vol. 4, Dec 1993, No. 9, Obituary. (Ellen John.)

[21]History of Maries Co. Mo., by Everett Marshall King, 1963.

[22]Ellis County, Texas Marriage Records 1850-1878 Volume I Compiled by Weldon I Hudson, p. 32.

[23]Ellis County Texas Cemetery Records Volume One, The Ellis County Gen. Soc., p. 75.

[24]Ellis Co. Tx. Marriage Records Volume E Through Volume J, Jan. 1887 Through May 1900, Ellis Co. Gen. Soc., p. 46.

Children: THOMAS GLENN JOHN, Dallas, and CAROL JOHN WEININGER of Waxahachie.

(3) LEON JOHN, died and his widow Bernice lived in Ft. Worth, Tx.

(4) KATY GLADYS JOHN. [25]

3. WILLIAM MADISON JOHN, born 2 Apr 1873 Tx. Married Sarah E. Smithwick, 30 Aug 1898 Tx. Sarah died 6 Sep 1963, Apache, Ok.[26] William John died 13 Jan 1956, Apache, Okla.[27]

Children:

    (1) JOHN W. JOHN, b. ca 1904 Comanche, Ok.

    (2) OLA M. JOHN, b. ca 1904, Comanche, Ok.

    (3) LOLA FAY JOHN, b. ca 1907, Comanche, Ok.[28]

    (4) HOMER JOHN.

    (5) ROBERT JOHN.

    (6) VAUDENE JOHN.

    (7) ADA JOHN.

4. JOHN MARR JOHN, born Mar 1875 Tx. Married Myrtle Charles, 25 Jan 1899, Tx. John Marr John died 1932 Tx.

Children:

    (1) VALLIE JOHN.

    (2) ROYCE JOHN, b. 28 Apr 1903, d. 15 Aug 1904, Ellis, Tx.

    (3) LOTTIE MAY JOHN, b. 13 Sep 1905, Ellis Co., Tx., married Ray W. Spencer 3 Jul 1924, Perico, Dellam Co., Tx. Children: a) GLEN RAY SPENCER; b) DOROTHY LOUISE SPENCER; c) LOLA JEAN SPENCER; d) LOTTIE JO SPENCER. Lottie May died 31 Dec 1991, Hurst, Tx.

    (4) DOROTHY JOHN.

    (5) RUTH JOHN.

    (6) RUBY JOHN.

    (7) ELIJA S. JOHN, born 5 Dec 1876 Tx. Died 18 Oct 1877 Tx.

5. JAMES EDWARD JOHN, born 27 Feb 1879 Tx. Married Agnes Parker, 22 Oct 1899 Ellis Co., Tx. Had four children. Died 7 Aug 1908 Tx.

6. FRANCIS KNOX JOHN, born 9 Dec 1881 Tx. Married Leila Mae Speer, Ellis Co., Tx. and had one child. Died 6 Aug 1959 Ellis Co. Tx.[29]

7. MARY FRANCES JOHN, born 19 Feb 1885 Tx. Married Daniel Eli Briles 1907 Ellis Co., Tx., and had five children. Died 1976 Tx.

8. FANNIE RANKIN JOHN, born 15 Oct 1889 Tx. Married Charles Benjamin Shannon, 25 Dec 1914 Ellis Co., Tx., and had five children. Died 24 Aug 1958 Ellis Co., Tx.

* *

---

[25] John Family Journal Newsletter, Dec 1989 and Dec 1992. (Ellen John.)

[26] Obituary.

[27] Obituary.

[28] Census 1910 Comanche Ok., McMaster Township, En. Distr. 55, Sheet 7.

[29] Ellis Co. Tx. Cem. Records, Vol. I, The Ellis Co. Gen. Soc.

NATHAN HARRISON JOHN,

4th child of Robert John (ca 1805) and Sarah Southard (ca 1815), was born 16 Feb 1845, in Maries Co., Mo. He was known as "Harrison." He married Mary Matilda James, daughter of George James of Maries Co. She was born 20 May 1849, Maries Co., Mo. and died 29 Dec 1911.

Harrison John lived his entire life in Maries Co., where he was a farmer. He helped build the Broadway Baptist Church, where he served as a Deacon. He died 8 Mar 1929, and he and his wife were buried in the Broadway Baptist Church Cemetery.

Children:

1. CHARLES MADISON JOHN, born 5 Oct 1868 Mo. See Below.
2. IDA LEORA JOHN, born 25 Mar 1872. Married E. Herman Essman, 25 Sept 1895. They had children: (1) BOLEY ESSMAN and (2) GLADYS ESSMAN, who married Fred Kubits. Ida L. Essman died 17 Nov 1936 in Maries Co., Mo.
3. WILLIAM NATHAN JOHN, born 17 Feb 1875. Married Gertha Chambers Barbarick. They had (1) VIRGIL JOHN, (2) ARLEW JOHN, and (3) URSULA JOHN; possibly others. William Nathan John died 10 Dec 1908, and was buried in the Broadway Baptist Church Cemetery.[30]
4. ARTHUR DeLEON JOHN born 5 Jul 1877. Died single, 31 Mar 1896. Buried in Dillon Cemetery, Maries Co.
5. ALVA FRANCIS JOHN, born 16 Aug 1883. See Below.
6. LOLA FLOIDA JOHN, b. 11 Mar 1887. She never married, and cared for her father after the death of her mother Mary Matilda John in 1911, until he died in 1929. She died 17 Apr 1975, and was buried in the Broadway Baptist Church Cemetery.[31]

* *

CHARLES MADISON JOHN,

1st child of Nathan Harrison John (1845) and Mary Matilda James, was b. 5 Oct 1868 in Marries Co., Mo. He married Etta M. Glanville, who was b. 11 Feb 1875. Charles Madison John died 24 Apr 1929. Etta died 4 Aug 1937. Charles and Etta John were both buried in the Broadway Baptist Church Cemetery.

Their children were:

1. LLOYD E. JOHN, b. 22 June 1898. Died 25 Mar 1983.
2. CLARENCE N. JOHN, b. 1 May 1897. Married Dessie _____, who was b. 28 Aug 1908. Died 21 Dec 1988.
3. EARL LEE JOHN, b. 26 Sep 1899. Died 10 May 1955.
4. DAISY JOHN. Born 19 Jul 1905.
5. KERMIT L. JOHN, b. 18 Jun 1915.

* *

---

[30]The Cemeteries of Maries County, Mo., Personal History.
[31]ibid, Broadway.

KERMIT L. JOHN,

5th child of Charles Madison John (1868) and Etta Glanville (1875), was born 18 Jun 1915 at the family farm in Maries Co., near Safe, Mo. After he graduated from High School, he purchased the farm and worked it until his Mother died 4 Aug 1937. He moved to St. Louis, Mo. and married (1) Effie Audrey Waldron on 31 Dec 1937. She was b. 15 Jan 1916. After the war began in 1941, he returned to the farm. Effie became ill and died 13 Jan 1979. She is buried in Broadway Cemetery.

They had one son:

1. GARY KERMIT JOHN, b. 29 Sep 1950. Gary graduated from University of Missouri-Rolla, then purchased John's Firestone in Rolla, Mo. He married (1) Judith Ellen Spurgeon; divorced 20 Mar 1981. Married (2) Cathie Sue Hackney 29 Jun 1985. They live in St. James, Mo.

    Children of Gary and Judith are: (1)) SCOTT A. JOHN, b. 19 Mar 1969. Married Bonnie Fay Schuchmann 29 May 1987. Scott is second class petty officer in U.S. Navy. Two sons: NATHAN TYLER JOHN, b. 30 Nov 1987, and CALEB ANTHONY JOHN, b. 16 Sep 1993. (2) BRIAN G. JOHN, b. 31 Mar 1974. (3) GREGORY A. JOHN, b. 24 Jul 1977.

    Child of Gary and Cathie Sue:
    ERIK R. JOHN, b. 4 Aug 1986.[32]

Kermit John married (2) Emma A. Flaim Crowder, 16 Oct 1982. They still farm the family farm, and have enlarged it with additional land.
* *

ALVA FRANCIS JOHN,

5th child of Nathan Harrison John (1845) and Mary Matilda James (1849), was born 16 Aug 1883 in the Broadway Community of Maries Co., Mo. He married (1) Ida May Scott 7 May 1903. She was b. 13 Dec 1882 in Maries Co., Mo. Alva Francis John moved from Missouri to Lawton, Ok. in 1920. He was a farmer. Ida May died 5 Nov 1956 in Lawton, and is buried in Lawton, Comanche Co., Ok. Alva Francis married 17 Nov 1957 (2) Minnie Lee Wood who was b. 29 Jan 1888. Alva Francis d. 3 May 1968 in Lawton, Ok. Minnie Lee d. 22 Nov 1982.

Children of Alva Francis and Ida May:

1. VERGIE IRENE JOHN, b. 23 Feb1904; d. 16 Nov 1915 in Maries Co., buried Broadway Cemetery.
2. LELAND STANFORD JOHN, b. 13 Nov 1905.
3. LYMAN LEON JOHN, b. 22 Aug 1908.
4. CHLOE MARIE JOHN, b. 11 May 1911 in Broadway.

---

[32]"Maries County, Missouri A County Pictorial/Family History Vol. III, p. 388.

5. EULA LORENE JOHN, b. 7 Jul 1917, Maries Co., Mo.; d. 30 May 1951. Married Paul Wayne Pickett, b. 31 Jul 1917; d. 7 Oct 1958.

Alva Francis' descendants mentioned in the John newsletter were: BENNIE JOHN, MARGIE JOHN McMAHAN, MADGE JOHN, LYMAN JOHN, JENA JOHN, RAMON JOHN, RUSSELL JOHN, DON McMAHAN, RUSSELL KRIZ, WESLEY JOHN, MITCHEL JOHN.
* *

LELAND STANFORD JOHN,
1-son of Alva Francis and Ida May, was b. 13 Nov 1905 in Broadway. Married Carrie Belle Elkins, who was b. 5 Sep 1903 in Lawton, Ok. She died 9 Dec 1989 in Lawton. Dau Margie Mae John, b. 14 Jun 1937 in Lawton; m. Donald Leslie McMahan. Children:
1. JOHN LESLIE MCMAHAN, b. 20 Sep 1958.
2. JOE DONALD MCMAHAN, b. 9 Oct 1960.
* *

LYMAN LEON JOHN,
2- son of Alva Francis and Ida May, was b. 22 Aug 1908 in Broadway, Mo. Came to Lawton in Oct 1920 with his parents. Married (1) Matilda Madge Elkins 8 Sept 1929, Lawton. She was b. 27 Sep 1905 in Lawton, Ok. Lyman was a dairyman from 1929 to 1972, and helped popularize the Holstein cattle in that area. In 1948, he brought Angus cattle into southwest Ok. and was an avid breeder of Angus until his death. Died 22 Feb 1996, Lawton. Survived by his wife, two sons, eight grandchildren and 22 great-grandchildren.[33]
Their children:
1- GEORGE RUSSELL JOHN, b. 6 Feb 1905, Lawton, Ok. Married Bennie Carla Wilson, who was b. 13 Oct 1938. Their children are:
   (1) JOSIE CARLA JOHN, b. 4 Nov 1957.
   (2) GEORGE WESLEY JOHN, b. 26 Sep 1960.
   (3) MITCHELL LYMAN JOHN, B. 17 Jan 1972.
2- RAMON LEON JOHN, b. 28 Mar 1935, Lawton, Ok. Married Vivian Ann Fine, b. 30 Dec 1934. Divorced 1972. Ramon adopted Vivian's children from her previous marriage: (a) Carol Elaine White John, b. 13 Apr 1953; (b) Beverly Denice White John, b. 14 Mar 1954; and (c) Randall Lee White John, b. 24 Dec 1955. Children of Ramon Leon and Vivian:
   (1) RAMON LANCE JOHN, b. 8 Nov 1961, Lawton. Married Loretta Beth Bohl, b. 3 Aug 1963.
   (2) LORI ANN JOHN, b. 21 Sep 1964; m. Daniel Ray Elkouri.
Ramon Leon John m. (2) Hona Janise Friedman, b. 18 Sep 1936; d. 12 Apr 1992 in Lawton. He married (3) JoAn Maloney, Divorced Aug 1996.
* *

---

[33]Info. from Ellen John, Lawton, Ok.

CHLOE MARIE JOHN,
2-dau of Alva Francis John and Ida May, was b. 11 May 1911 in Broadway, Maries Co., Mo. Married (1) Charles Aaron Price, b. 9 Jan 1910. He died 16 Aug 1947. Their children were:
1- IDA ILENE PRICE, b. 23 Feb 1927. Married Hoyse Tommie Moore, b. 23 Feb 1935. Their children: (1) RAY LYNN MOORE, b. 20 Sep 1952; (2) KEVIN WYNN MOORE, b. 26 Jul 1958; and (3) MACHELLE MARIE MOORE, b. 27 Jan 1965.
2- CHARLENE MARIE PRICE, b. 8 Jun 1938; d. Dec 1997.
3- JOHN CHARLES PRICE, b. 12 Apr 1941.

Chloe married (2) James Matthew Gladden, b. 11 Dec 1904.
* *

JAMES M. JOHN,
5th child of Robert John (ca 1805) and Sarah Southard (ca 1815), was born ca 1849 in Crawford Co., Mo. He died 29 Mar 1870 in Maries Co., Mo.
* *

FRANCIS MARION JOHN SR.,
6th child of Robert John (ca 1805) and Sarah Southard (ca 1815), was b. 15 Jul 1851 in Maries Co. [formerly Crawford], Mo. His parents died about 1859, and he and his brother James M. lived for awhile with their sister Rebecca and husband Edmond Moreland. He went with Rebecca's family to Ellis Co., Tx. at the end of the Civil War, where they lived with brothers William and Robert.

He married Jincie Ann Butler, 15 Dec 1875, in Ellis Co. She was born 25 Oct 1857 in Fairmount, Gordon Co., Ga., daughter of Absalom Johnson Butler and Louisa Davis. He farmed in several counties in Tx., among them Scurry, Parker, Ellis, and Borden. About 1892, he moved to Indian Territory, now Oklahoma, settling near Loco in Stephens County.

Francis Marion moved to Comanche County, Ok. in 1901, an area which is located southeast of Lawton, and remained there the rest of his life. He was a member of the Baptist Church. He died 23 May 1925. Jincie died 22 Oct 1924. They are both buried in Flower Mound Cemetery, Lawton.
Children:
1. IDA MAE JOHN, b. 15 Jun 1877 Tx. Married Raleigh McKee. He was b. 7 Oct 1875, Ark.; d. 4 Apr 1955 Lawton, Ok. Ida Mae d. 25 Aug 1921 Ok., and was buried Flower Mound Cem., Lawton, Ok.
Their children:
(1) EMMETT LOWELL McKEE, b. 2 Jun 1904 Lawton; d. 8 Jun 1992, Lawton. M. Gertrude Leota Fink 25 Apr 1929, Grandfield, Ok. She was b. 8 Oct 1900. Their children: i) EMMETT LOWELL McKEE Jr., b. 13 Jan 1930, Grandfield, Tillman Co., Ok.; m. Barbara Lucille Cook. ii) GERTRUDE LEOTA McKEE, b. 31 Jan 1932 in Clinton,

Custer Co., Ok.; m. John Guy Erwin Jr., and iii) JOHN RALEIGH McKEE, b. 12 Apr 1936, Lawton, Ok.

    (2) WILLIE JURHEE McKEE, b. 6 Aug 1910 near Lawton, m. Melvin Price, 24 Sept 1931, who d. 29 Sept 1986. Jurhee d. 28 Jan 1996, Lawton. Jurhee, a homemarker, left children: i) IDA MELVINA PRICE, b. 2 Jun 1936, Lawton; m. (1) Durward Dwayne Thompkins, and m. (2) Daniel Lawrence Frank. ii) ELLA FAY PRICE, b. 23 Aug 1941, Lawton; m. George Gill Hunter III. iii) STELLA MAY PRICE, b. 23 Aug 1941, Lawton; m. Bediah George Naifeh.

2. ROBERT LEE JOHN, b. 4 Dec 1878 Borden Co., Tx. Died 28 Nov 1952 in a fire at his home south of Lawton, Ok. Unmarried. Buried in Flower Mound Cemetery.

3. JOSEPH KINNIE JOHN, b. July 1880 Parker Co., Tx. Married Rosa Lee Hannabass, 10 May 1906. Died 16 Nov 1914 Grandfield, Ok. Sons:

    (1) JUSTIN L. JOHN, b. 30 Aug 1909, d. 3 Nov 1910.

    (2) ROY FRANCIS JOHN, b. 24 Jan 1911, Ok., d. 5 May 1974, Grandfield, Tillman Co., Ok.

    (3) JOSEPH LEE JOHN, b. 26 Aug 1913, Grandfield, Ok., d. 26 Jan 1994, Lawton, Ok. Joseph Lee married Marewaine Evelyn Kelley. Their children: i) JANAY LEEWAINE JOHN, b. 2 Jul 1937; m. Cletus Ray Due. ii) JANITA ANNETTE JOHN, b. 30 Jun 1941; m. Jeremiah Paul Mahoney. iii) JIMIANNE JOHN, b. 5 Jan 1946; m. (1) Meyer Wolfson, and m. (2) Jerry Lewis Wisley.

4. ICIE FRANCES JOHN, b. 22 Feb 1882 Tx.; d. 6 Sep 1956, Plainview, Tx. Married John Louis Galloway 27 Oct 1898. Children:

    (1) HERWIN CLYDE GALLAWAY, b. 29 Sep 1899, Loco, Indian Territory; d. 1 Jul 1984, Duncan, Ok.; Married Imola Butler, b. 26 Sep 1903, d. 15 Feb 1981, Duncan, Ok. Child: WELDON CREIGHTON GALLAWAY, b. 11 Dec 1923.

    (2) MARK YOUNG GALLOWAY, b. 2 Oct 1902, Loco, Indian Territory; d. Jan 1973, Amarillo, Potter Co., Tx. Married Virginia Laird, b. 10 Feb 1907; d. Dec. 1980. Child: ANN GALLAWAY.

    (3) FORREST IRA GALLAWAY, b. 14 May 1908, Mangum, Greer Co., Ok., d. 24 Dec 1970, Plainview, Tx. Married Viva Ruth Findley, b. 24 May 1900; d. 3 Oct 1988, Plainview, Tx.

5. WILLIAM ERNEST JOHN, b. 13 Aug 1884, Parker Co., Tx. Married Hattie Hannabass, 27 Sept 1906 Ok. She was b. 18 Feb 1884, Va.; d. 18 Sep 1965, Walters, Ok. William died 6 Nov 1950, Lawton, Ok.. Children:

    (1) LEON STANLEY JOHN, b. 14 Jun 1908 in Clovis, N.M., married (1) Violet Bell, b. 18 Jun 1913, d. 25 Aug 1930; their child: VIOLET BELL JOHN, b. 23 Aug 1930, Oklahoma City; m. Raymond Earl Sloan. Leon married (2) Cletys Graham.

(2) ERNEST PAUL JOHN, b. 11 Sep 1910, Comanche, Ok., d. 21 Feb 1998, Sulphur, Ok. Married Frances Lorine Trisler, b. 26 May 1914, Harrold, Tx. Children:

    1) JERRY PAUL JOHN, b. 21 Mar 1941 Purcell, Ok., m. Joetta Sheila Castleberry.

    2) JAMES CARL JOHN, b. 19 Aug 1945, Purcell, Ok., m. Kathy Sue Woodell.

(3) HAROLD EUGENE JOHN, b. 4 Jul 1915, Lawton, Ok. M. Cleta Lucille Baker, b. 29 Aug 1920, Oologah, Ok., Children:

    1) WILLIAM KEITH JOHN, b. 13 Jan 1949, Sulphur; and

    2) CHERYL ANN JOHN, b. 11 Feb 1952, Sulphur; m. Larry Judson Caldwell Jr.

6. FRANCIS MARION JOHN Jr., b. 12 Feb 1886, Parker Co. Tx.; died 23 Jul 1951, Lawton, Ok.. Married Rosa Lee Lewis, 24 Jun 1908. Children:

(1) MARVIN LEWIS JOHN b. 2 Mar 1909, Taiban, N.M.; d. 10 Jun 1963, Lawton, Ok. M. Wilma Fay Stephenson. Child: KAREN SUE JOHN, b. 11 Oct 1941, Lawton. M. James A. Frame.

(2) JEWEL ALTA JOHN, b. 1 Apr 1911, Lawton, Ok.; d. 15 Aug 1970, Oklahoma City. M. Glenn Daniel Bundy. Child:

    1) BRENT GLENN BUNDY, b. 7 Nov 1946, Oklahoma City; m. (1) Janyth Klopfenstein; divorced; m. (2) Pamela Susan Rhodes.

(3) FRANCIS EDMOND JOHN, b. 25 Nov 1915, Lawton; d. 3 Sep 1962, Lawton; m. Erma Louise Fawley. Children:

    1) ELLEN LOUISE JOHN, b. 24 Oct 1943, Lawton; m. (1) Bobby Glenn Hooper; div. 14 Oct 1974; and m. (2) John Wilbur Hood, div. 8 Sep 1981. Retained John's name.

    2) ELISABETH LUCILLE JOHN, b. 5 Aug 1947, Lawton, d. 4 Jul 1991, Guthrie, Ok. M. Daniel Fred Schroeder.

(4) LEONA FAYE JOHN, b. 17 Sep 1927, Lawton; d. 10 Dec 1981. M. (1) Harold Eugene Evans; children:

    1) MARILYN KAYE EVANS, b. 27 May 1947, Lawton; m. Miguel Luis Rodriguez;

    2) JEANNINE JANE EVANS, b. 2 Aug 1952, Lawton; m. Spencer Houghton.

    LEONA FAYE JOHN m. (2) Russell Vincent John Fisher.

7. CHARLES EARL JOHN, b. Nov 1887, Poolville, Parker Co., Tx.. D. 28 Dec 1980, Ca. Married Elizabeth Kuykendall. Children:

(1) LEWIS M. JOHN, b. 5 Sep 1908, d. 10 Jul 1910, Lawton.

(2) EARL CARMEN JOHN, b. 16 May 1910, Ok.; d. 14 Jun 1980, Ca.; m. Nora Harper. Children: i) EARL ROSS JOHN, b. 6 Nov 1931, and ii) RONALD GENE JOHN, b. 4 May 1933; d. 11 Feb 1990, Ca.

(3) HARVEY CLIFTON JOHN, b. 7 Sept 1912, near Lawton; m. (1) Evelyn Haviland. Son: CLAYTON LOUIS JOHN, b. 30 Jun 1943.

Harvey married (2) Daisy Bolendar. Children: i) LINDA SUE JOHN, b. 28 Jun 1950; and ii) SHARON ANN JOHN, b. 2 Mar 1953. HARVEY died 30 Mar 1996 in Parker, Ariz.

8. DEE LEON JOHN, b. 7 Nov 1889, Tx. Died 13 Dec 1911, Lawton, Ok.

9. ILLIE MONROE JOHN, b. 9 Apr 1891, Tx. Married Lillie G. Duncan 19 Jun 1911. Illie was a farmer southeast of Lawton, Ok. He died 17 Apr 1941.

Their children:

(1) JOHN FRANCIS JOHN, b. 22 Apr 1912, Woodlawn Community, Ok. M. Ruthie May Preece. Children: i) MARLENE P. JOHN, b. 8 Jul 1938; m. Glenn Rippee. ii) LINDA M. JOHN, b. 26 Mar 1942; m. George Pavletich, b. 17 Jun 1940. iii) DERRYAL L. JOHN, b. 13 Sep 1948; m. Claire Underhill, b. 4 Nov 1951. iv) RALPH KENDRICK JOHN, b. 25 Feb 1950, Delano, Kern Co., Ca. M. Jeanna Gay Johnson.

(2) GOLDIE VIVIAN JOHN, b. 16 May 1916, Woodlawn Community, Ok.; d. 15 Nov 1982, Lawton, Ok. M. (a) Sircy Clemmons. GOLDIE m. (b) Malcolm Oswalt. Children: i) GENESE J. OSWALT, b. 27 Jul 1937, Lawton; d. 31 May 1998, Oklahoma City. ii) GAYLON LEON OSWALT, b. 12 Dec 1940. Gaylon m. Lynda Lee Freeman.

(4) OLLIE LEE JOHN, b. 9 Oct 1918; d. 15 Mar 1932 in fall from his pony, in Lawton, Ok.

(5) CLAUDE CALVIN JOHN, b. 24 May 1924, Woodlawn Comm., Ok.; d. 11 Jun 1995, Lawton, Ok. Married Lavona Gwendolyn Robertson. Child: LEONARD DALE JOHN, b. 21 Jun 1960, Lawton.

(6) DON WALTER JOHN, b. 6 Aug 1931, Lawton, Ok. Married Evelyn Joyce McCarty. Children: i) RANDY DON JOHN, b. 28 Aug 1954, Lawton; ii) CINDY LYNN JOHN, b. 3 Jul 1957, Lawton; iii) STEPHANIE RENEE JOHN, b. 9 Oct 1961, Lawton; iv) DERRIN BRENT JOHN, b. 20 Dec 1962, Lawton.

10. BESSIE ANN JOHN, b. Jan 1893 Ok. Married Clint T. Smith, Ok.

11. LOYD JOHN, b. 27 Feb 1895 Ok. Died 4 Aug 1909, Lawton, Ok.

12. CLYDE FOY JOHN, b. 18 Jun 1897 Loco, Ok. Died 3 Jun 1915, Ok.

13. MANVILLE RENZO JOHN, b. Feb 1899, Loco, Ok.. D. Ca 1960, Fresno, Ca.

14. MAURICE EDGAR JOHN, b. 12 Dec 1904, Lawton, Ok. Died 15 Feb 1965, Sulphur, Ok.

The "John Family Journal," had the following regarding J. L. John, son of Joseph Kinnie John (1880) in 1997:

"J. L. JOHN NOW IMPROVED FOLLOWING RECENT STROKE

J. L. John, Grandfield, Okla., one of the real patriarchs of the Francis Marion John Sr., branch of the farflung John family, is reported to be improving from a stroke which he sustained on October 13.

His wife, Mariwane John, reports he was hospitalized for a time and then dismissed to a care center in Grandfield where he responded to treatment. Mariwane reports that J. L. is now walking and eats well on regular food.

J. L. is one of the real success stories in his branch of the John family. Born on a farm southwest of Grandfield in 1912, his father, Joseph Kinnie John, died a year or two later, he was left only with his mother Rosa Lee John, and an older brother, Roy, who was physically handicapped.

On sheer determination and grit, the family prevailed through the years, taking the bad years with the good, and when he retired a few years ago, he was one of the largest wheat farmers in southwest Oklahoma, farming several quarter sections of his own land.

His wife, Mariwane, and three daughters, had a big part in the family's success.

J. L. has been taking it easy in recent years. They like to travel and have done so extensively. Mariwaine has been accorded many honors in library work at Grandfield and also in the Methodist Church there. J. L. has a number of hobbies, which include wood carving, restoring vintage vehicles, making ornamental jewelry and other energy outlets.

Their daughter, Janay and husband, Cletus Due, handle the large farming interests now and the family continues to be one of the building blocks of southwest Oklahoma.

John families, over the years, have been known for their perseverance in bad times as well as good times and J. L. John is one of the best examples of this wonderful trait."

"Marewaine John of Grandfield Oklahoma, was instrumental in getting the black swallowtail named as Oklahoma's official state butterfly."[34]
* *

WILLIAM A. JOHN,

4th son of Ezekiel John (ca 1770) and Lydia, was born 25 Aug 1806 in North Carolina. He was an infant when his parents moved to Tennessee. They lived many years in Knox County, then moved to McMinn County after it was opened for settlement. He married (1) Nancy Smith Sept. 30, 1830. Nancy died 12 Jan 1832. They had no children. He married (2) Rebecca Deatherage March 21, 1838, in McMinn Co. She was born 22 Jan 1819. They had one child, Marcus Bierden John, who was born 3 Jan 1839, McMinn Tn.

William died 24 Sep 1838, said to have been killed by Indians.[35] His estate was settled by his brother Thomas John. His father Ezekiel was appointed Guardian of Marcus.

---

[34]From "Bits 'n Pieces" by Ellen John. The John Family Journal, Aug. 1997.

Rebecca Deatherage John married (2) William Southard, 13 Oct 1842. William had been married twice before, first to Eleanor John on 14 Apr 1836, in McMinn Co. Eleanor was born ca 1812, the daughter of Ezekiel John (ca 1770) and Lydia. Eleanor and William Southard had one child, Mary Ann Southard who was born 21 May 1837. Eleanor died 12 Jun 1838. He married Catherine Trout 12 Dec 1839 (By Russell Lane, J.P.)[36] She died, and in 1842, he married Rebecca John. Rebecca and William Southard moved to Crawford Co., Mo., taking Marcus with them. William Southard was appointed guardian to Marcus 7 Dec 1857. There are several court records regarding the settlement of William John's estate in McMinn Co.

County Court Minutes of McMinn Co., Tn., by Reba Bayless Boyer[37]:
JOHN, WILLIAM
CR4 516, (Co. Ct. Min 1821-41), 5 Oct 1840. Comm. app. to lay off year's support for widow.
WB C 293, 2 Nov. 1840. Comm. Tandy S. Rice, Justus and Henry Steed, sworn before J. H. Benton, J.P., set apart year's support for widow Rebecca and one child, Marcus.
WB C 294-296, no date; 114, 7 Dec 1842; 132, 3 Apr 1843; 171, 7 Dec 1843; 217, no date. Invt., Sett., Add. Invt., and Sett. by Thomas John, Adm.
WB D 88, 4 Jul 1842; 217, no date; 363, 21 Feb 1846; 485, 19 Oct 1847; WB E 50, 7 Jul 1849; 412, Feb 1855. Reports by Ezekiel John, Gdn. to Marcus B. John, minor heir.
CR7, 78, (Co. Ct. Min 1857-61), 7 Dec. 1857. Wm. Suthard of Crawford Co., Mo., is regularly app. Gdn. of Marcus B. John.
WB F 102, 22 Dec 1857. Final sett. by Ezekiel John, Gdn.; balance paid to Wm. Suthard, Gdn.

DEED BOOK J, McMinn Co., Tn.:
(185) 15 Jul 1848 Christian Peters, Sheriff, to William Key; land of Rebecca and William Southard sold in 1843 to satisfy judgments, one of which was rendered to Ezekiel John, Gdn. of Marcus B. John, and Thomas John, Adm. of William John dec'd.

(281) 10 Apr 1860 Marcus B. John and wife Mary Ann to James Willson; land except mother's dower; acknowledged in Maries Co., Mo., on same date. DEED BOOK N, MCMINN CO. TN. (Boyer)
* *

McMinn Co. Tennessee Marriages:

---

[35]Family History.
[36]Marriages of McMinn Co., Tn. 1821-1864, by Edythe Rucker Whitley, Baltimore, Genealogical Pub. Co., Inc., 1983, p. 12.
[37]Perm. granted Dec 1994.

William Johns to Rebecca Deatherage Mar. 21, 1838.
Married March 21, 1838 by Russell Lane, J.P. Bk. C2, P. 149.
William Southard to Rebecca R. N. John Oct. 13, 1842, by Justus Steed, J.P.

<u>1840 Census McMinn Co. Tenn. P. 103</u>:
Will Suthard----M 20/30; 1 F 30/40; 1 F und 5-10.
* *
<u>1850 Census Crawford Co. Missouri----No. 989-989</u>:
William Southard----35--M--NC; R. M. Southard----32--F--Ky; M. A.
Southard----13--F--Tn; S. J. Southard-----7--F--Tn; H. J. Southard----5—F--
Mo; A. A. Southard----2—F--Mo; R. A. Southard----2/12—F--Mo; M. B.
John----11-M--Tn; A. Hart--23-M--NC; J. Beekham----42-- F—Va.

Note: M. A. Southard was Mary Ann, daughter of William Southard and
Eleanor John. M. B. John was Marcus B., son of Rebecca Deatherage John
and William John.
* *

ELEANOR JOHN,
6th child of Ezekiel John (ca 1770) and Lydia, was born ca 1812 Knox Co.
Tn. She married William Southard April 14, 1836. He was born Dec. 10,
1814, Tn. Eleanor died 12 Jun 1838 in McMinn Co.
    William Southard married (2) Catherine Frost Trout Dec. 10, 1839. She
only lived a month after the marriage. He married (3) Rebecca R. N.
Deatherage Oct. 13, 1842, McMinn Co., Tn. (He was married later to (4)
Mary Anderson 1865.)
Child of Eleanor John and William:
1. Mary Ann Southard, b. 21May 21, 1837 McMinn Co. Tn. Married
    William H. Cox. He was born in Tn. Nov. 13, 1829, and died in Maries
    Co. Mo. Jul. 11 1912. Mary Ann died April 13, 1900 Maries Co. Mo.

<u>Historical information from "History of Maries County Missouri"</u>:
    'The Southard family came to Maries Co. from Tennessee about 1840, and
settled on the west side of Spanish Needle Prairie near present Johnathan
Scott place. The parents and five of the children spent the remainder of lives
here. These children were: William, Edward, Rebecca wife of William
Hicks, who died childless, and the mother of Harrison John. The remaining
children, John, George and the wife of James Hinton, lived there but later all
moved to Laclede County where they spent the remainder of their lives.
    William Southard was believed to be the oldest child of the family. He
died June 6, 1881. He came to Maries Co. with the other members of the
family and his third wife, Rebecca, nee Deatherage, widow of William John
in 1839.

He was father of one child, Mary Ann, by first marriage to a sister of William John. His second wife was Catherine Frost, who only lived about a month after the marriage. He spent balance of his life in the southeastern part of Maries Co., where he farmed and raised stock. His third wife died, and he married Mary Davault, nee Anderson, who survived him. Thirteen of his children of his 3 marriages survived him.

Mary Ann Southard, only child of her father's first marriage, was born in Tn. May 21, 1837, and died in Maries Co. April 13, 1900. She came as infant with her father and his third wife. Mary Ann married William H. Cox, born in Tennessee Nov. 13, 1829. He died July 11, 1912. They spent all their married life in Maries and Phelps Counties.'

1860 Census Maries Co. Missouri---Johnson twp, No. 776-768:
W. Southard--46--M—NC; Rebecca Southard--39--F—Tn; Sarah Southard--16--F—Tn; Marenvia Southard--15--F—Mo; Martha Southard--12--F—Mo; Angeline Southard--10--F—Mo; Eliza Southard--7--F—Mo; Margaret Southard--5--F—Mo; William Southard--1--M—Mo.
* *

Rebecca Deatherage John Southard died in 1863.
* *

1870 Census Maries Co. Missouri--Johnson Twp. No. 90-90:
William Southard--55--M—NC; Mary Southard--23--F—Mo; Martha Southard--22--F—Mo; Eliza Southard--17--F—Mo; Margret Southard--14--F—Mo; Theodocia Southard--4--F—Mo; William Southard--11--M—Mo; Walter Southard--3--M—Mo; Andrew Garland--12--M—Mo; James Anderson--7--M—Mo; Mary Anderson--10--F—Mo.
* *

MARCUS BIERDEN JOHN,
only son of William A. John (1806) and Rebecca Detherage, was born 3 Jan 1839 in McMinn Co., Tn. After his father died, his mother remarried and they moved before 1850 to Crawford Co., Mo., now Maries Co. From historical accounts, we know this journey by wagon took about six weeks. He grew up as part of a large, close knit family.

He married Mary Ann Moreland 28 Oct 1858. Her family had also migrated to Missouri from East Tennessee. After their marriage, they built their home near Bourbeuse Creek. Marcus became an active member of the community. He served as judge of the County Court in Vienna in the 1890's.[38] "He deeded land for the church and cemetery. He and his sons built the village of Broadway, its store, post office, and church, and strongly supported the one room Star School." (Submitted by Walter John.)

Mary Ann John died 21 Oct 1902, and Marcus died 29 Mar 1909. Their children were:

---

[38]Maries County, Mo. A County/Family History. Volume II.

1. WILLIAM T. JOHN, b. 8 Apr 1860. See Below.
2. ALBERT F. JOHN, married Josephine Chambers. Had seven children:
(1) Everett H. John; (2) George B. John; (3) Troy F. John; (4) Vertie O.
John, f; (5) Boley D. John; (6) Ora C. John; and (7) Anabelle John. Died
25 Mar 1932.
3. A. HAMILTON "Ham" JOHN, b. 4 Sep 1866. Married Lola V. Martin.
Had eight children: (1) Dorothy I. John, who married George Gerber; (2)
Alma John, who married S. A. Fritts; (4) Robert John; (4) Sylvia John,
who married N. R. Fritts; (5) Florence John, who married Ray Kroner; (6)
Alton H. John; (7) Lula V. John; (8) Audra A. John.
4. ROBERT E. JOHN. Married (1) Ramie Wheeler; and (2) Preshia Hattan.
5. EDWARD LEE JOHN, b. 17 Apr 1872, Broadway, Mo. See Below.
6. CHRISTOPHER D. JOHN. Married Josephine Dillon.
7. LULA JOHN, m. George Cox.
8. & 9. Died before adulthood.
**

WILLIAM T. JOHN,
1st son of Marcus Bierden John (1839) and Mary Moreland, was. b. 8 Apr
1860 in Maries Co., Mo. William married Emma Barringer. They had eight
children:[39]
1. WILLIAM.T. JOHN JR., lived in Springfield, Mo., 1963.
2. _____ John, married R. E. Matlock.
3. ERNEST JOHN. In 1963, lived in Brooklyn, N.Y., was "Major Ernest
John."
4. _____ JOHN, married Mark A. Moreland, lived in St. James, Mo. 1963.
5. GEORGE JOHN, who became a Doctor, and lived in Belot, Wis. 1963.
6. FRANK JOHN, lived in St. Louis, Mo. 1963.
7. ELLSWORTH JOHN, who became a Doctor, and lived in Brownsville,
Ky. 1963.
8. HELEN JOHN, lived in St. Louis, Mo. 1963.
**

ALFRED F. JOHN,
2-son of Marcus Bierden John (1839) and Mary A. Moreland, was b. ca 1862
in Missouri. He married Josephine Chambers. He died 25 Mar 1932. Their
children were:
1. EVERETT H. JOHN.
2. GEORGE B. JOHN.
3. TROY F. JOHN.
4. VERTIE O. JOHN.
5. BOLEY D. JOHN.
6. ORA C. JOHN.
7. ANNABELLE JOHN.

---

[39]History of Maries Co., Mo., by King, 1963.

* *

A. HAMILTON 'HAM' JOHN,

3-Son of Marcus Bierden John (1839) and Mary Moreland, was b. 4 Sept 1866 in Maries Co., Mo. He married Lola V. Martin, daughter of Dr. David Martin. He died 14 May 1914 at Broadway, Maries Co., Mo.

Their children were:

1. DOROTHY I. JOHN. Married George Gerber. Lived in Texas.
2. ALMA JOHN. Married S. A. Fritts. Lived in Belle, Mo.
3. ROBERT JOHN.
4. SYLVIA JOHN. Married N. R. Fritts. Lived in Lebanon, Mo.
5. FLORENCE JOHN. Married Ray Kroner.
6. ALTON H. JOHN. Lived in Phelps Co. in 1963.
7. LULA V. JOHN. Lived in Nebraska.
8. AUDRA A. JOHN. Lived in St. Louis in 1963.

* *

EDWARD LEE JOHN,

5th son of Marcus Bierden John (1839) and Mary Moreland, was born 17 Apr 1872, at Broadway, Maries Co., Mo. He married Ollie Jane Travis 28 Jun 1899. She was born 20 May 1875, the daughter of William James Travis and Elizabeth Hull. They had a large double wedding at Ollie's home, with her sister Della, who married Dr. Enoch Ferrell. Edward and Mollie lived most of their married lives at Broadway. Edward ran the store and post office at Broadway, then later farmed except when he was a Clerk in the House of Representatives at Jefferson City in 1912 and 1913. He was a breeder of Berkshire hogs and Shorthorn cattle. He was very active in community affairs, and served as President and a member of the Star School Board.

In the late 1920's, they moved to Columbia, Mo. where they encouraged their children to attend college.

Ollie died 23 Oct 1952 and Edward died 27 Apr 1954.[40]

Their children were:

1. TRAVIS EARL JOHN, b. 21 May 1900.
2. GERALD AUBURN JOHN, b. 28 Nov 1901.
3. OPAL LEE JOHN, b. 5 Apr 1903. Received B. S. Degree in Home Economics in 1927, taught high school home economics until 1934. Became home demonstration agent for Missouri University. Never married. Died in automobile accident 10 Apr 1937.
4. OREL EDWARD JOHN, b. 18 Aug 1905. Graduated from University of Missouri with B. S. in Agriculture. Taught school 20 years; and operated farm in Randolph Co. Married Ruth Limerick in Kansas City, Mo. 21 Dec 1929. Two children: (1) PEARL IRENE JOHN, and (2) RUSSELL EDWARD JOHN.
5. WALTER WELTON JOHN, b. 11 Mar 1909. See below.

---

[40]ibid, p. 299.

6. HURST TRUSTIN JOHN, b. 30 Aug 1911. Attended University of Missouri in Columbia. Worked from his office in Columbia as an architect from 1937 on, designing and remodeling buildings throughout central Missouri. He married Martha Burr Bates in Boonville 5 Oct 1940. They had four children: (1) SUSAN LEE JOHN; (2) LAWRENCE EDWARD JOHN; (3) MARTHA KINNAN JOHN; and (4) JOHN JOHN. Hurst died 3 Feb 1979.

* *

TRAVIS EARL JOHN,
1st son of Edward Lee John (1872) and Ollie Travis, was born 21 May 1900 at Broadway, Mo. He married Grace L. Manhenke 5 Apr 1922, Rolla, Mo. He taught school in Maries County for 15 years. He was an ordained Baptist Minister, and was active in community affairs. During the Great Depression, he worked for the Government Food Relief Program, and for Triple A. From 1939 until 1968, he worked at the Maries County Bank. He served as Presiding Judge eight years. He farmed at Broadway until he died 16 Feb 1984.

Their children:
1. TRAVIS EARL JOHN JR.
2. MAX WELTON JOHN, born 11 Jul 1928, Safe, Mo.
3. DONALD GENE JOHN.

* *

MAX WELTON JOHN,
son of Travis Earl John (1900) and Grace, was b. 11 Jul 1928, Safe, Mo. Attended University of Missouri in Columbia three years, then taught Veterans Farm Training at Vienna two years. He was drafted into the U. S. Army during the Korean conflict. He married Irene M. Murphy, daughter of J. Boone and Jewel M. Murphy, at the Vienna Methodist Church 15 Nov 1952. She was born in Freeburg 5 Aug 1930.

Max returned to school at the University of Missouri in 1953. He graduated in June 1957 from the School of Veterinary Medicine. After graduation, they returned to Maries County and he began his veterinary practice. In 1975 he was involved in establishing the South Central Livestock Market in Vienna. Irene was an employee of the Division of Welfare until 1953. They are members of the United Methodist Church.

Their children are:
1. BETH JOHN, b. 15 Oct 1953. Graduated from University of Mo. 1975. Married Roger Bullock 2 Aug 1975. Two children: (1) Laura Bullock, b. 27 Aug 1979; and (2) Rachel John, b. 13 Feb 1981. Roger died in tractor accident on 10 Aug 1981. Beth taught school, then went to work at the Maries County Bank.
2. BRENDA JOHN, b. 26 Feb 1957. Graduated from University of Mo. 1979; was employed at Stix, Baer and Fuller in Kansas City, and at

School of Veterinary Medicine in Columbia. Married John Stafford 11 May 1985. Daughter Joan Stafford b. 28 Feb 1988. They live and work in Columbia, but own land in the Paydown community of Maries Co.
3. CHRISTOPHER JOHN, b. 30 Oct 1959. Graduated from University of Mo. in 1981. Worked for Continental Tel. Co. in Wentzville until 1983, then returned to Vienna and went to work at Maries Co. Bank. Lives on a farm south of Vienna.
4. REBECCA "Becky" JOHN, b. 28 Feb 1967. Graduated from Central Mo. State University at Warrensbury, 1989, where she pitched for the CMSU softball team for four years. Is a teacher at Fatima High School in Westphalia. Lives in Vienna.
* *

GERALD AUBURN JOHN,
2nd son of Edward Lee John (1872) and Ollie, was born 28 Nov 1901. He taught school in Boone and Callaway Counties four years. He married Nellie W. Jones 17 May 1925.

He worked as Administrative Assistant for the Production Marketing Administration for 12 years, receiving honors from Secretary of Agriculture Oriville Freeman for his contribution to American agriculture. He worked later as an MFA agent, and then became a Real Estate broker.

Their children are:
1. JUSTIN AUBURN JOHN
2. AUSTIN DAVIS JOHN
3. ILA SUSAN JOHN.
* *

WALTER WELTON JOHN,
5th child of Edward Lee John (1872) and Ollie, was born 11 Mar 1909. He received a B.S. degree in Agriculture in 1933, and a B.A. degree in journalism in 1934. He married Mary Lou McCallister on 14 Oct 1934 in Columbia. He joined the Soil Conservation Service, and worked in Illinois, Iowa and Wisconsin until 1945. He then transferred to USDA's Production and Marketing Administration in Chicago. In 1950, he moved to their Washington, D.C. National Office, and in 1964 was named Director of the Information Division in the USDA Federal Extension Service.

Had son:
1. RICHARD JOHN.
* *

MARY ANN SOUTHARD,
only daughter of Eleanor John (ca 1812) and William Southard, was born May 21, 1837 McMinn Co. Tn. She came to Crawford Co., Mo. with her father and stepmother about 1849. She married William H. Cox. He was born Nov. 13, 1829 Ky. and died July 11, 1912. Mary Ann died April 13, 1900 Maries Co., Mo. Lived in Phelps Co. and Maries Co., Mo.

Children:
1. JOHN WESLEY COX, b. Oct. 29, 1856 Phelps Co., Mo. Never married. Died Nov. 21, 1881.
2. W. COX. ca 1859 Phelps Co. Mo. (Possibly twin to James Napoleon.) Died infancy.
3. JAMES NAPOLEON COX, b. Dec. 7, 1858 Phelps Co., Mo. Married Maggie Crimmons. Died Jan. 26, 1937. Children: 1) MARGARET "Maggie" Cox; 2) JAMES COX; 3) JULIA COX, m. Frank Verkamp of St. James, Mo.; and 4) TIMOTHY COX, m. Ruth Wilson. Son: CARL COX.
4. WILLIAM JACKSON COX, b. Feb. 14, 1860 Phelps Co., Mo. Married: Bertha Jahns. Died March 8, 1898. Their children: 1) FANNIE COX; 2) CLARENCE COX, lived in St. Louis; 3) WILLIAM COX, lived in Ca. in 1963; 4) EVERETT COX, lived in Ca. 1963; and 5) AMY COX, m. _____ Roland, lived in Ca. 1963.
5. JEFFERSON D. COX, b. Dec. 13, 1861 Phelps Co., Mo.
6. MARTHA/VICTORIA COX, b. Sept. 7, 1867 Phelps Co., Mo. Married William Davault. Died Dec. 12, 1924. Children 1) RAINEY DEVAULT, lived in Gasconade Co., Mo. 1963; 2) JACOB DEVAULT, lived in Crawford Co., Mo. 1963; 3) DORSEY DEVAULT, lived in St. Louis; and 4) EFFIE DEVAULT, m. Jesse Scott of St. Louis.
7. ANNA COX, b. March 28, 1869 Phelps Co., Mo. Married William Vaughn.
8. ALBERTINE COX, b. Aug. 18, 1872. Married Joseph Crimmons. Died 24 Jun 1902. Lived in Okla. Children: 1) PERCY CRIMMONS; 2) CHARLES CRIMMONS; 3) MARY CRIMMONS, m. Frank Orr; and 4) NANNY CRIMMONS, m. John Farrell.
9. ELLA COX, b. May 21, 1874. Married (1) Samuel Emerson; (2) Samuel Gosset; (3) Samuel Anderson.
10. GEORGE COX, b. April 11, 1875. Married (1) Lula C. John, dau Marcus B. John, and (2) Eva Clinton. Died Jan. 19, 1919.

Historical info from "History of Maries County Missouri."

1860 Census Phelps Co. Mo.----Rolla Twp., P. 5, No. 33-33.
William Cox--30--M—Ky; M. A. Cox--22--F—Tn; J. W. Cox--2--M--Mo; J. B. Cox--1--M—Mo; William J. Cox--4/12--M—Mo; John K. Moreland--18--M—Mo; J. Southhard--18--F—Mo.

Little River Twp., P. 96, No. 625-625:
W. H. Cox--30--M—Ky; M. A. Cox--22--F—Tn; J. W. Cox--2--M—Mo; T. W. Cox--1--M—Mo; J. N. Cox--1--M—Mo; W. J. Cox-- 4/12--M—Mo; T. Moreland--19--M—Mo; J. Southard--15--F—Mo.

William Cox--40--M—Ky; Mary A. Cox--33--F—Tn; John W. Cox--14--M—
Mo; James W. Cox--11--M—Mo; William J. Cox--11--M—Mo; Jeff L. Cox--
9--M—Mo; Martha A. Cox--7--F—Mo; Annanias Cox--1--F—Mo.
* *

EZEKIEL JOHN Jr.,
5-son of Ezekiel John (ca 1770) and Lydia, was born about 1808 in
Buncombe County, N. C. He came to Knox Co., Tn. around 1809 with his
family. He became a blacksmith by trade, a profession probably learned from
his father. Later, he was also one of the owners of Blair, John & Co. of
Mouse Creek Station. He was a member of the Missionary Baptist Church.
He was considered one of the chief builders of Mouse Creek and Niota.

He married: (1) Jane F. English in 1830 in Roane Co., Tn. She was born
ca 1807 Bledsoe Co., Tn. and died 1856 McMinn Co., Tn. (2) Adaline
Richards Dec. 11, 1856 McMinn Co., Tn. She was born ca 1828 Tn. or SC.
She was buried in the John Cemetery, McMinn Co. Ezekiel Jr. died March
1883 in McMinn County.
Children by Jane English:
1. THOMAS JOHN, b. ca 1834 McMinn Co. Tn.
2. RANDOLPH JOHN, b. ca 1837 McMinn Co. Tn.
3. SAMUEL JOHN, b. ca 1840 McMinn Co. Tn.
4. MARY A. JOHN, b. ca 1843 McMinn Co. Tn.
   Married Robert Hamilton Nov. 28, 1867 McMinn Co. Tn.
5. ZACHARIAH TAYLOR JOHN, b. Jan. 9, 1846 McMinn Co. Tn.
   Married (1) Mary "Mollie" E. Quarles July 11, 1878; and (2) Callie J.
   Parkey Oct. 6, 1886.
6. LYDIA F. JOHN, b. ca 1849 McMinn Co. Tn.

Children by second wife Adeline Richards:
7. JANE JOHN, b. ca 1861 McMinn Co. Tn.
8. SUSAN JOHN, b. ca 1864 McMinn Co. Tn.

"Ezekiel John was born in North Carolina and came to Roane County,
where he was a blacksmith and married Jane English in that county in 1830.
They came to McMinn County and remained for the balance of their lives.
He was a member of the firm of Blair, John & Co. with his son Zachary T.
John. The Blair in this firm was S. P. Blair, born in Monroe, but raised at
Morganton, in Loudon County. Zach John married Mary E. Quarles, of a
Jefferson County family."

"Tennessee Cousins" by Worth S. Ray, page 512.

The following is taken from an account of Ezekiel Jr.'s son Zachery, but also
included this information on Ezekiel Jr.:

GOODSPEED'S HISTORY OF EAST TENNESSEE 1887. McMinn Co., P. 1021:

"The father was of Welsh origin, born in North Carolina, in 1805. He was a blacksmith and farmer, and a decided Democrat. He was married in Roane County in 1830, and passed the remainder of his life in McMinn County, where he died in March, 1883, a devout member of the Missionary Baptist Church. His wife was born in Bledsoe County, Tenn. in 1800, of English-Irish descent. She departed this life in McMinn County, in 1856, a consistent and respected member of the Cumberland Presbyterian Church."
* *

DEATH NOTICES MCMINN TN.
VIII-401, 30 May 1856 :[41]....<u>Mrs. Jane F. John</u>, 50 yrs. 10 mos. 25 days, consort of Ezekiel John, d. in McMinn Co. 19th May; left husband and five children.
<u>McMinn Co., Tn. Marriages, Bk. D, p. 121</u>:
Ezekiel Johns married Adeline Richards, 11 Dec. 1856. By James Forest, J. P. (Dec. 11, 1856.)

From old newspaper clipping:[42] "Riceville and Mouse Creek are both thriving villages and stations on the East Tennessee, Virginia and Georgia Railroad. The former is situated about midway between Athens and Calhoun. It was established upon land owned by Charles W. Rice soon after the completion of the railroad to that point. The business men of the present are: W. M. Long, Gibbins & Emerson, John W. Matlock, G. W. Orton & Co., C. C. Parkinson, L. W. Garlock and Vickers & Co. About 1877 a large woolen mill was erected three miles south of the town by Gettys Bros. and a little village known as Sanford has sprung up around it. The mill is now operated by the Knoxville Woolen Mill Company. (1887.)

The first house built on the site of Mouse Creek was erected by J. H. Gill in 1855; he also opened the first store. The other merchants previous to the war were Stephens & Browder, J. N. Delzell, A. Forrest and F. Cate. John F. Sherman, L. R. Hurst, J. L. Hurst, H. L. Schultz, Greenbury Cate and James Wilson were early settlers in the vicinity. Upon the completion of the railroad a large depot building was erected by the citizens, and an eating house was opened by J. H. Magill. About 1857 Mouse Creek Male and Female Academy was established and soon after similar institution known as Fountain Hill Academy, was established within half a mile of the first. A great rivalry sprung up between them, and the attendance at each became large. About 1860 Fountain Hill succeeded in obtaining the post office, and retained it until the close of the war. During the war the first named Academy

---

[41]McMinn Co. Tn. Deeds and Other Data...by Reba Bayless Boyer, p. 174.
[42]In 'Scrapbook History of McMinn Co. Tn.' Compiled by John Morgan Wooten, Cleveland, Tn. 1937, p. 45.

was burned, and a short time after Fountain Hill was also destroyed. The former has since been rebuilt with a Masonic Hall above it. The business of Mouse Creek now consists of three stores conducted by Blair, John & Co., W. C. Blair, and Thompson & Varnell, respectively, and a tanner opened by S. P. Blair."

Old newspaper clipping[43]: "NIOTA, Formerly Mouse Creek, Dates Back to 1854 As Railroad Gives Lift

Mouse Creek, now Niota, dates back to 1854 or before. The railroad had been extended from Dalton, Ga. to the Hiwassee, McMinn County, in 1852, after much planning and controversy. The first builder, Gene Duff Green, surrendered his contract and J. G. Dent and Co. built the road from Hiwassee to Loudon in 1852.

The people of Mouse Creek community had been blessed with good crops of wheat, to be transported by wagon so they rejoiced when the railroad was built through the community. Residents of Little Mouse Creek, Big Mouse Creek, Sowie, Eastanallee and Chestnut Valleys were instrumental in the erection of the depot at Mouse Creek in 1854 which was the real beginning of Mouse Creek, now Niota. The depot, two stores, two blacksmith shops, one doctor's office, constituted the business section.

Among the chief builders of Niota have passed away, of Mouse Creek, H. L. Shultz, J. Harvey Magill, Samuel P. Blair, the Johns Brothers, Pryor N. Shulez. As Mouse Creek and Niota, John Boggess, as Niota, Dr. W. H. Buttram, J. L. Burns, Sr., H. M. Wilson, W. L. Forrest.

In 1855, the town of Mouse Creek was laid out.

In the same year J. Harvey Magill built the first frame dwelling just across the railroad from the depot. It was later owned by Henry Hurst from whom Walter L. Forrest bought it in 1903.

In 1856 J. Harvey Magill built a hotel where the Matheny house now stands. This hotel was known far and wide. A hack line ran from Mouse Creek to White Cliff. Visitors would get off the train at Mouse Creek, go to the Magill Hotel for a good meal and then go to White Cliff for a rest. J. Harvey Magill also opened the first store in Mouse Creek.

Other merchants previous to the war were Stephens and Browder; C. N. Dalzell, A. C. (Alhartus) Forrest, and E. Cate.

... In 1877 Samuel P. Blair came to Mouse Creek from Loudon County. He bought the tan yard from H. L. Cate, who acted as real estate dealer for Sam Chestnut, who was in Texas at the time.

In August, 1884, the merchandizing firm of Blair, John & Co. was formed, composed of Samuel P. Blair, Z. T. John and A. K. John.

In February, 1885, a revival was conducted in the brick school building by Evangelist N. B. Goforth and C. C. Brown, sent out by the State Baptist

---

[43]ibid, p. 265.

Board. This revival aroused a desire for a place of worship for The Missionary Baptists of the community. The church which is still used was dedicated in October, 1885.

Charter members were John F. Sherman, John C. Cate Sr., James C. Wilson, Robert S. Wilson, William H. Sherman, Zachary T. John, who was the first clerk, Hugh M. Wilson, Henry L. Cate, Thomas N. Sherman, Dr. Russell S. Love, Charles P. Sherman, Mintie Wilson, Ellie M. Wilson, Jane Denton, Sarah R. Wilson, Lannie Cate.

The first pastor was T. C. David, for a short time, then N. B. Goforth.

The business section of Mouse Creek in 1887 consisted of three stores operated by Blair-John & Co., W. C. Blair, and Thompson and Varnell, respectively, and the tannery of S. P. Blair.

When a young man Walter L. Forrest, of the Mt. Harmony community, came to Mouse Creek to work with Blair John & Co.

In 1890 the above firm became Blair-Forrest, composed of Samuel P. Blair and Walter L. Forrest.

In 1895 the Cumberland Presbyterian church was built directly across the railroad from the Baptist church.

Mail for Mouse Creek and Mossy Creek (now Jefferson City) was often mixed. Postmaster John Boggess knew something had to be done so he suggested the name of Mouse Creek be changed. He and some other citizens sent in proposed names to the Post Office Department. Mr. Boggess' name Niota was selected in 1897.

...In 1912 work began on a pike road connecting Athens and Sweetwater." (No date or identification on newspaper clipping.)
* *

McMINN COUNTY TN. TAX RECORDS:

(1831) Capt. Rothwell's Co.: Ezekiel John Jr.--0 acres.

(1832) Capt. Gonce's Co.: Ezekiel John--0 acres.

McMinn Co. Tn. Deed Bk. K, p. 429:

"This indenture made this the 7th day of Dec. 1835 between <u>Samuel John</u> of the Co. of Knox and State of Tn. and <u>Ezekiel John</u> of the Co. of McMinn and State aforesaid of the other part Witnesseth that the said Samuel John for and in consideration of the sum of $100 to him in hand paid, the receipt of which is hereby acknowledged doth bargain and sell and by these presents, doth convey and confirm to the said <u>Ezekiel John</u>, his heirs and Assigns forever a certain tract of land situated in McMinn County. Beginning at the South east corner of the Northeast quarter of Section 12, Township 4, Range first West of the Meridian Hiwassee District running with the sectional lines N 60 poles to a stake thence W 160 to a stake thence 60 poles S to a stake, thence 160 to the beginning. Containing 60 acres more or less which tract of land together with the heriditiments and appurtenances thereto belonging to the said Samuel John, for himself and his heirs to the said <u>Ezekiel John</u>, his heirs and assigns

416

will warrant and forever defend against the lawful claim of all persons whatever as an indefeasible inheritance in fee simple. In witness whereof, I the said <u>Samuel John,</u> have set my hand and seal, the day and year above written. Signed, sealed and delivered in presence of:
<u>Thomas John</u>
<u>Jonathan x John</u>   No signature."

<u>MCMINN CO. TN. WILL BOOK D, PART 1, 1841-1848, p. 88</u>: William John deceased. Ezekiel John guardian to Marcus B. John, son of William John---July 4, 1842.
<u>P. 217:</u> Ezekiel John guardian for Marcus B. John.

<u>DEED BOOK J, MCMINN COUNTY, TN.</u>:
<u>(P. 185) 15 July 1848</u>. Christian Peters, Sheriff, to William Key; land of Rebecca and William Southard sold in 1843 to satisfy judgments, one of which was rendered to <u>Ezekiel John</u>, Guardian of <u>Marcus B. John</u>, and <u>Thomas John</u>, Adm. of <u>William John</u> dec'd.

<u>MCMINN CO. TN. DEED BK. K, P. 429</u>:
"State of Tn., McMinn Co.
Personally appeared before me Thomas Vaughan clerk of the County Court for the County and State aforesaid <u>Jonathan John</u> one of the subscribing witnesses to the foregoing deed of conveyance and after being duly sworn depose and say that he is personally acquainted with <u>Samuel John,</u> the grantor and that he saw him sign the same on the day it bears date and for the purposes therein expressed and <u>Thomas John,</u> the other subscribing witness having departed this life, the said <u>Jonathan John</u> also depose and say he is acquainted with the hand writing of the said <u>Thomas John</u> and that it is his signature. Given under my hand at office in Athens this 30th day of Jan. 1854.   T. Vaughan Clerk

State of Tennessee, McMinn County----Jan. 30, 1854, ... noted in Book A, P 84 and registered in my office in Book K, P 429. /s/ Cornelius Brown, Register."

McMinn Co. Tn. Deed Bk B, 1820-1847, p. 235---S. John.
McMinn Co. Tn. Deed Bk C, 1820-1852, pp. 357 and 393---S. John.

"Wills and Estate Records of McMinn County Tn. 1820-1870"
Court record Bk. 6--Feb. 6, 1854.
<u>Ezekiel John</u> appointed Administrator of <u>Thomas John</u>.

<u>Will Bk. F., P. 102----Dec. 22, 1857</u>:

Final settlement by Ezekiel John, Guardian of Marcus B. John. Balance paid to William Suthard [Southard] Guardian.

"McMinn Co. Tn. Tombstone Inscriptions", Vol. l, p. 339:
John Cemetery: Adaline John--no dates.

McMinn Co. Tn. Marriages:
Robert Hamilton to Mary John Nov. 28, 1867.

1840 Census McMinn Co. Tn. Page 78:
Ezekiel John: M 5/10—1; M 20/30—1; M 30/40—1; F 10/15--1; F 30/40—1.

1850 Census McMinn Co. Tn., p. 482, No. 278:
Z. Johns 42—M—NC—Farmer--$500; Jane Johns—43—F--Tn; Thomas Johns—16—M--Tn; Samuel Johns – 11—M--Tn; Mary A. Johns-- 9--F Tn; Taylor Johns—6—M--Tn; Lydia Johns—1—F-- Tn.

1860 Census McMinn Co. Tn. P. 63 (Handwritten), P. 236 (Printed):
Ezekiel John--51--M—NC; Adaline John-- 32--F—Tn; Samuel John--20--M—Tn; Mary John--17--F—Tn; Taylor John--13--M—Tn; Lydia F. John--11--F—Tn.

1870 Census McMinn Co. Tn. Fifth Dist., P. 43, No. 94-104:
Ezekiel Johns--63--M—NC; Adaline Johns--41--F—SC; Lydia Johns-- 20--F—Tn; Jane Johns--9--F—Tn; Susan Johns--6--F—Tn; Lenora Richards-- 62--F—SC.

1880 Census McMinn Co. Tn. ED 65, P. 44, 4th Dist., No. 440-475.
Ezekiel Johns--71--M—NC--GA—GA; Addie Johns--52--F--Tn--SC—SC; Susan Johns--16--F--Tn--NC—Tn; Onor Richards--73--F--NC--NC--NC--Mother-in-law.

Ezekiel John died March 1883 McMinn Co. Tn. He was probably buried in one of the unmarked graves in the John Cemetery.
* *

MARY A. JOHN,
dau. of Ezekiel John Jr. (ca 1808) and Jane English, born ca 1843 McMinn Co., Tn. She married Robert Hamilton Nov. 28, 1867 McMinn Co. Tn. He was born ca. 1840 Tn. She died between 1870-1880 in McMinn County, as Robert was married to (2) Margaret _____ in 1880.
Children: ALLICE HAMILTON, born ca 1869 McMinn Co. Tn.

We believe Alice was only child of Mary & Robert Hamilton; see below:

1880 Census McMinn Co. Tn. ED 45, 9th Dist., P. 72, No. 767-798:
Robert Hamilton--40--M--Tn--Tn—Tn; Margrett Hamilton--33--F--Tn--Tn--Tn—Wife; Bell Hamilton--4-- F-- Tn--Tn--Tn—Dau; James Hamilton--1--M--Tn--Tn--Tn—Son; Allice Hamilton--11--F--Tn--Tn--Tn—Dau.
* *

ZACHARIAH TAYLOR JOHN,
5-son of Ezekiel John Jr. (ca 1808) and Jane English, was born 9 Jan 1846, McMinn Co. Tn. He married (1) Mary "Mollie" E. Quarles July 11, 1878. She was daughter of N. W. and R. E. Quarles. She was born 1860 Jefferson Co. Tn., and died Sept. 1883 McMinn Co. Tn. Zachary married (2) Callie J. Parkey Oct. 6, 1886. She was born July 1861 Hancock Co. Tn.
  Child by first wife:
1. NELLIE J. JOHN, born: Oct. 1881 McMinn Co. Tn.
  Child by second wife:
2. MAGGIE JOHN, born Nov 1887 McMinn Co. Tn.
* *

1900 Census Roane Co. Tn.--Ed 125, P. 12, L. 22, town of Harriman, Trenton St.: Zachay T. John--Jun 1846—M—54--Tn; Callie J. John--Jul 1861—F—38—Tn—Wife; Nellie J. John--Oct -- F 19 Tn Dau; Maggie John--Nov 1887—F—12—Tn--Dau.

Excerpts from Goodspeeds "History of East Tennessee" 1887, p. 1021:
  'Zachary T. John was a member of the enterprising firm of Blair, John & Co., of Mouse Creek Station. He was born in McMinn County January 9, 1846. He was 5th of 6 children born to Ezekiel and Jane F. (English) John. He received fine educational advantages, and graduated at Mossy Creek (then Carson) College, Jefferson Co. Taught school 8 yrs. in McMinn and Meigs Cos., Tn., and in Lee County, Va. In 1880 he began the study of law; abandoned this for the mercantile business. In 1883, he came to Mouse Creek Station. Was engaged in the grocery and produce trade for a year. In 1884, became a partner in above mentioned firm. Was a member of the Missionary Baptist Church, "a Democrat, and worthy citizen." July 11, 1878, married Mary E.Quarles, daughter of N. W. and R. E. Quarles. Mary was born in Jefferson Co., Tn. in 1860, died in Sept 1883; was a member of the Missionary Baptist Church. She had three children, two of whom were deceased. October 6, 1886, Zachary married Callie J. Parkey, who was born in Hancock County in 1861. She was also connected with the Missionary Baptist Church.'
  Zachary John died in 1906 in Knoxville, Tn., and was buried in New Gray Cemetery.

Zachariah T. John, 39th Mounted Infantry, Co. F, Private.

Men enrolled March 19, 1862 at Mouse Creek, from McMinn County.
[Note: Alfred John, son of Thomas John, was in same company.]
* *

MARY H. JOHN,
8th child of Ezekiel John (ca 1770) and Lydia, was b. ca 1819, Knox Co. Tn.
She married William C. Robinson about 1839. They lived in Locust Grove
Township, Jefferson Co., Iowa in 1850. Living with them was her mother,
Lydia. They later moved to Maries County, Mo., and joined the families of
Mary's brother Robert, and the Southard and Morelands.[44]
Their children were:
1. MARY E. ROBINSON, b. ca 1839, Tn.
2. MARTHA LUCINDA ROBINSON, b. ca 1841, Tn. Married J. R.
   Moreland.
3. JOHN WESLEY ROBINSON, b. ca 1844, Jefferson Co. Ia. Married
   Jennie Frost.
4. WILLIAM M. ROBINSON, b. ca 1846, Jefferson Co., Ia. Married
   Malinda Moreland.
5. NATHANIEL ROBINSON, b. ca 1849, Jefferson Co., Ia.
6. THOMAS ROBINSON. Married Minnie Moreland.
7. GEORGE ROBINSON.
8. LAURA ROBINSON. Married Charles Glenn.
9. MAY ROBINSON. Married Alex Glenn.
* *

1850 Census Jefferson County, Iowa----Locust Grove. Twp., P. 121, No. 136-
140.
William C. Robison---------33--M--Tn
Mary H. Robison------------31--F--Tn
Mary E. Robison------------11--F--Tn
Martha L. Robison--------- 9--F--Tn
John W. Robison------------ 6--M--Iowa
William M. Robison---------4--M--Iowa
Nathaniel Robison---------- 1--M--Iowa
Lydia Johns------------------72--F--NC
*

---

[44]The History of Maries Co. Mo., by Everett Marshal King, 1963.

CHAPTER SIXTEEN

CONFEDERATE CIVIL WAR VOUCHERS
JOHN:
Adam, Co. I 1 Cherokee Mounted Rifles, Pvt.-Pvt.
Alfred K., Co. F, 39 Tn. Mtd. Inf., Cpl.-Cpl.
August, Co. C, 1 (Symon's) Ga. Reserve, Sgt.-Sgt.
August, Co. F, Griffin's Battn. Tex. Inf., Pvt.-Pvt.
B., Co. I, 4 Fla. Inf. Pvt.-Pvt., Orig. Jones, John B.
B. H., Co. D, 6 N.C. Sen. Reserves, Pvt.-Pvt.
Calhoun, Co. B, Inf. Reg., Thomas' Legion, N.C., Pvt.-Pvt., Orig. Calhoun, John.
Caslie, Co. E, 1st S.C. Inf. See also John, Cartes.
Charles H., Hamilton's Co., Shaw's Battn., Tn. Cav. Pvt.-Pvt.
Daniel, Co. K, 8 S.C. Inf., Cpl.-Cpl. See also Hampton Legion Daniel S., Co. K, 5 Fla. Inf., Pvt.-Pvt., Orig. Johns, Daniel S.
David G., Co. E, 57 Ga. Inf., Pvt.-Pvt.
David H., Co. A, 36 Va. Inf., Pvt.-Pvt.
D. C., Co. K, 8 S.C. Inf., Cpl.-Cpl., Orig. John, Daniel.
D. C., Co. H., Inf. Reg., Hampton Leg. S. C., Pvt.-Pvt.
D. H., Co. A., 36 Va. Inf., Pvt.-Pvt.
D. H., Co. A, 36 Va. Inf., Pvt.-Pvt., orig. John, D. H.
D. S., Co. B, Cobb's Leg., Ga., Pvt.-2 St. Orig Jones, Daniel S.
D. S., Co. G, 23 S.C. Inf., Sgt.-Pvt.
E. D., Co. H, 8 Tex. Cav., P.-Cpl.
Edward, Co. D, 7 N.C. Inf., Pvt.-Pvt. Orig John, Edward.
Elias, Co. C-D, 39 N.C. Inf., Pvt.-Pvt., Orig. Johnson, Elias J.
Elijah, Co. I, 3 Tex. Cav., Pvt.-Pvt.E. M., Co. G, 63 Ala. Inf., Pvt.-Pvt., Orig Johns, E. N.
Enoch, Co. -, 1 (Reserves) Fla. Inf., Pvt.-Pvt., Orig. Johns, Enoch.
F., Co. A, 3 (Kirby's) Battn. Tex. Vols., Pvt.-Pvt.
Impson, 2 Co. I, 1 Choctaw & Chickasaw Mounted Rifles, P.-P., orig. John, Simpson.
J. A. C., John Oden's Co., Ala. Mtd. Cav., P.-P.
James, 2 Co. H, 1 Choctaw & Chickasaw Mtd. Rif., P.-P.
James, 3 Co. E., Orig. James, John.
James E., Co. I, 20 Miss. Inf., P-P.
James F., Co. E, 3 Confed. Eng. Troops, P-P.
James P., Co. I, 28 N.C. Inf., P-P.
James R., Co. K, 54 Va. Inf., P-P.
J. C., Co. R (or E?), 16 Ala. Inf., P-Cpl., Orig. Johns, John C.
J. J., Co. -, Crump's Regt. Tex. Cav., P-P.
J. N., Co., B, 10 Ark. Inf., P.-P., Orig Johns, J. N.

John, Co. B K, 26 Tn. Inf. (3 E. Tn. Vols.) P-P, Orig. Johnson, John.

Jonathan, Co. I, 4 Ala. Res., P-P.

Joseph, Co. K, 54 Va. Inf., P.-Sgt.

J. S., Co. G, 2 Ark. Inf., P-P.

J. S., Co. -, 2 S. C. Reserves, --, See 20 Regt.

J. T., Co. N, 20 S.C. Inf., P-P.

J. T., Co. H, Inf. Reg., Hampton Leg. S.C., P-P.

L. B., Co. E, 1 Battn., Hilliard's Leg., Ala. Vols., P-P, orig. Johns, L. B.

Levi, Co. G, 59 Ala. Inf., P-P.

Josaih, 2d. Co. A, Inf. Reg., Thomas Leg., N.C., P-P.

M., Co. A, 28 Ala. Inf.

Marcus B., Co. E, 10 Mo. Inf., P-Sgt., Orig. John, Marquis.

Marquis, Co. E, 10 Mo. Inf., P-Sgt.

Marshal R., Co. E, 42 Ala. Inf., P-P.

Martin L., Co. B, 12 Battn. (Day's) P-P, Orig. Johns, Martin L.

Nathan Z., Co. B., 35 Ga. Inf., P-P, Orig. Johnson, Nathan Z.

N. M., Co. E, 3 Battn. Tn. Inf. (Memphis Battn.), P-P.

N. H., Co. -, Galveston Rifles Texas (Misc.).

Peter, Co. E, 19 Battn., S. C. Cav., P-P.

Peter, Co. L. - N. 20 S. C. Inf., P-P.

Peyton T., Co. E, 7 Va. Cav. (Ashby's Cav.), P-P.

P. M., Co. G, 35 N.C. Inf., P-P, Orig, Jones, Pinkney.

P. T., Co. H., Inf. Reg., Hampton Leg. S. C., P-P.

Randol, Co. E, 2 Creek Mounted Vols., P-P.

R. C., Stapleton's Co., 12 (Wrights) Ga. Cav. (State Guards), P-P
    Orig. Johnson, Ruhesa C.

R. J., Co. F & G, 42 Ga. Inf., 1 Lt. & A2M/1Lt. & A2M.

R. J., Co. D, Timmon's Regt. Tx. Inf., Lt./Lt., See also Wauls Tex. Leg.

R. J., Co. F, Waul's Tex. Leg., 9 Nichols) Tex. Inf., Sr.2Lt./1 Lt., See also
    Timmons Reg. Tex. Leg.

R. N., Co. D, 21 Ala. Inf., P-P.

Robert, Co. A, 47 Tex. Inf., P-P, Orig. Roberts, John.

Ruben, Co. E, 42 Ala. Inf., P-P.

S., Co. A, 15 Ala. Inf., P-P.

S., Fla. Home Guards, P-P, Orig. Johns, Shadrick.

Sam, 2 Co. K, 1 Choctaw & Chickasaw Mtd. Rif., P-P.

Samuel, Co. E, 6 Fla. Inf., P-P.

Samuel W., Co. F, 3 Ala. Cav., P-P.

Shadrack, Co. H, 24 Ala. Inf., P-PSimpson, 2 Co. I, 1 Choctaw & Chick.
    Mtd. Rif., P-P.

S. W., Co. B, Ala. Cadet Corps., Capt.-Capt.

T. H., Co. I, 22 Ala. Inf..

Thomas H., Co. G, 30 Ga. Inf. Cpl./Cpl.

W., Co. B, 21 (Wilson's) Tenn. Cav., P-P.

Warren G., Co. E, 42 Ala. Inf., P-P.

W. C., Co. H., 40 Ms. Inf., P-P, orig. Johnson, W.C.

W. D., Co. E, 31 Tn. Inf. (Col. A. H. Bradford), P-P, orig. Johnson, W. D.

Wesley, Co. C, Densale's Reg., Choctaw Warriors, P-P.

W. A., New Co. F, 6 Ark. Inf., P-P

W. G., Co. G, 12 Ark. Inf., P.-P.

William, Co. B, 7 Ms. Inf., P.-P.

William, Co. C, 19 Tex. Cav., P-P.

William, Co. C, 26 Tex. Cav., P-P.

William, Co. A, Baird's Regt. Tex. Cav., P-P.

William, Co. N.C. S, Timmon's Regt. Tex. Inf., 2MSgt.-2M.Sgt.

William, Co. S (or F), Waul's Tex. Leg., P/1MSgt.

William, Co. 3, 3 Confed. Eng. Troops, P-P.

William G., Co. E, 42 Ala. Inf., P-P.

William H., 2 Co. E, 6 S. C. Inf., P-P.

William H., Co. G, 9 S. C. Inf., P-P.

William Lewis, Co. D, 3 Cav. & Inf. Va. St. Line, P-P.
    See also William L. John, 19 Va. Cav.

Willis, 2 Co. C, 1 Choctaw & Chick. Mtd. Reg., P-P, Orig. Jones, Willis.

W. W., New Co. B, 5 Ala. Inf., P-P, Orig. Johns, William Warren.

W. W. Co. D, 59 Ala. Inf., P-P, Orig. Johns, W. W.

Zachaniah J., Co. F, 39 Tn. Mounted Inf., (Col. W.M. Bradford's Reg. Vols.
    31 Tn. Inf.) P-P.

Zepheniah L., Co. D, 36 Tn. Inf., P-P.
*

JOHNES:

Amos, Co. C, 60 Ala. Inf., Sgt./Sgt., Orig. Jones, Amos.

A. T., Co. F, 14 N. C. Inf., P-P, Orig. Jones, A. T.

Charles, Co. G, 21 (Pattens) La. Inf., P-P, Orig. Jones, Charles.

C. P. 2 Co. E, 18 Va. Cav., P-P, Orig. Jones, C. P.

J. A., Co. A, 60 N.C. Inf., P-P, Orig. Jones, James A.

Jakers, Pendergrast Co., 23 Battn. Ga. Inf., P-P.

James, Co. D, 10 S.C. Inf., P-P, Orig. Jones, James.

James J., Co. C. F., 30 Ga. Inf., P-P, Orig. Johns, Jackson J.

Jasper, Co. B, 39 Tn. Mtd. Inf., P-P, Orig. Jones, Jasper.

Jeremiah, Co. C, 1 Fla. Cav., P-P, Orig. Johns, Jeremiah.

J. H., Co. C, 36 Ark. Inf., Sgt./Pvt., Orig. Jones, J. H.

J. J., Co. E or N, Phillips Legion, P.-P, Orig. Jones, J. T.

Joel, Co. E, 35 Ark. Inf. P-P.

John, Co. G, 21 (Patton's) La. Inf., P.-P., Orig. Jones.

John, Co. H, Clarkson's Battn., Confed Cav., Indep. Rangers, P-:, Orig.
    Jones, John S.

John B., Co. D, 7 Ky. Cav., P-P, Orig, Jones, John Beverly

John J., Co. B, 4 Ala. Inf., P-P, Orig. Jones.

John J., Co. D, 10 S.C. Inf., P.-P., Orig. Jones.

John P., Co. C, 9 Fla. Inf. P-P, Orig. Johns, John P.

John P., Co. A, 32 Battn. Va. Cav., P-P, Orig. Jones.

J. S., Co., F, 13 Va. Inf., P-P, Orig. Johns, John S.

K. B., Co. E, 2 S. C. Rifles, P-P, Orig. Jones.

Luke, Co. C, 1 Fla. Cav., P-P, Orig. Johns, Luke.

S., Co. E, 14 Ms. Inf., P-P, Orig. Jones, Stephen.

Samuel, Co. H., 2 (Duke's) Ky. Cav., P-P.

Shelby W., Co. H, 4 Ms. Inf., Musc./Musc., Orig. Jones, S. W., also Co. F & S.

Thomas D., Co. C, 28 (Gray's) La. Inf., P-P.

William H., Co. C, 28 Ala. Inf., P-P, Orig. Jones, William H.

John, esse, Co. M, 1 Creek Mtd. Vol., P-P

Ochee, Co. -, 1 Seminole Mtd. Vols, P.-P.

* *

JOHNS:

, Co. F, 22 Ala. Inf., P-P.

, Co. E, 25 Tex. Cav., P-P.

A., Co. 2, 1 Chasseurs a pied, La., P-P.

A., Co. K, 15 N. C. Inf., P-P, Orig. Jones, Allen.

A., Co. A, 3 S. C. Cav., P-P.

A. B., Co. B, 14 Tex. Inf., P-P.

A. B., Gen. & Staff Off., Corps, Div. & Brigade Staffs, Non-Comm. staffs & Bands, Enlisted Men, Staff Depts. Asst. Surg.

Absolem, Co. E, 12 Battn. (Day's) Tn. Cav., P-P.

A. J., Co. K, 1 Ala. Cav., P.-P.

A. J., Co. G & B, 7 Ala. Cav., Sgt./P.

A. J. Clanton's Batty. Ala. Art., P-P.

A. J., Co. H, 2 Fla. Cav., P-P.

A. J., Co. I, 2 Fla. Cav., P-P.

A. J., Co. A, 3 La. Inf., P-P.

A. J., Co. H., Consold. Crescent Regt., La. Inf., P-P, Orig. Johns, Andrew.

A. J., Co. H., 46 Ms. Inf., P-P.

A., Co. D, 3 (Clack's) Tn. Inf., P-P.

Albert, Co. I, 16 Ms. Inf., P.-P.

Albert F., Co. -, Orleans Guards Regt. La. Militia, P-P.

Alf, Co. I, 18 Miss. Inf., P-P, Orig. Albert Johns.

Alfred, Co. A, 1 Miss. Lt. Artillery., P-P.

Alfred K., Co. F, 39 Tenn. Mtd. Inf., Cpl.-Cpl., Orig. John, Alfred K.

Allen, Co. G, 5 Tex. Cav., Cpl.-Pvt., Orig. Jones, Allen B.

A. N., Co. G, Va. Cav. (Johnson's Regt.), P-P.

Andrew, Capt. King's Batty., La. Artillery., P-P, See also Consold. Crescent Regt. La. Inf.

Andrew J., Co. H., Consold. Cresc. Reg. La. Inf., P-P.

Andrew J., Co. I, 14 Va. Cav., P-P.

Anthony B. Jr., Co. H, 13 N.C. Inf., Sgt./Capt.

Anthony B., Co. F & S, 45 N.C. Inf., Asst. Sarg./Asst. Sgt.

A. P., Co. K, 11 S. C. Inf., P-Sgt.

A. R., Co. H, 146 Va. Militia.

August, Capt. Hughes' Co., Tex. Lt. Artillery, P-P.

Azer, - - Ala. Conscripts, P-P.

B., Co. A., 10 (Johnson's) Ky. Cav., P-P.

B., Co. C., 19 Battn. S. C. Cav., P-P.

B., Capt. Kirk's Co., Partisan Rangers S. C., P-P.

Barney, Co. F & K, 2 Ala. Cav., Pvt/, Orig. Johns, B. J.

Benjamin, Co. F, 17th (Griffith's) Ark. Inf., P-P.

Benjamin F., Co. C, F & S, 7 Ms. Inf., Capt./Lt. Col.

Benjoh M., Co. D, 21 Ga. Inf., P-P.

Berry, Co. B, 26 Ga. Inf., P-P.

Beverly, Co. C, 18 Tn. Cav., P-P.

B. F., Co. B, 16 Ga. Inf., P-P.

B. F., Co. b, 26 Ga. Inf., P-P, Orig. Johns, Berry.

B. F., Co. G, 12 (Green's) Tn. Cav., P-P.

B. F., Co. K, 5 Tn. Inf., P-P.

B. F., Co. I, 47 Tn. Inf., P-P.

B. H., Co. I, Nixon's Regt. Tn. Cav., P-P.

B. H., Co. C, 18 Tn. Inf., P-P, Orig. Johns, Beverly.

B. H., Co. F, 28 Tn. Inf., (2 Mtd. Regt. Tn. Vols.), P-P. See also 28 (Consold.) Tn. Inf.

B. H., Co. B, 28 Consold. Tn. Inf., P-P, See 28 Tn. Inf.

Berb, Co. E, 10 Fla. Inf., P-P.

B. J., Co. F & K, 2 Ala. Cav., P-P.

B. L., Co. B, 1 (Reserves) Fla. Inf., P-P. Orig. Johns, R. L.

Bluford H., Co. B, 28 (Consold.) Tn. Inf., P-P, Orig. Johns, B. H.

B. M., Co. A, 1 Ga. Cav., P-P.

B. M., Co. E, 2 Battn. Tn. Inf. (Memphis Battn.), P-P.

Branch J., Co. G, 9 Va. Cav., P-P.

Burr, Co. I, 10 Ms. Cav., P-P.

Burrell S., Co. C, 3 Battn. Ms. Cav., P-P.

C., Co. K, 12 (Consold.) Tn. Inf., P-P, Orig. J. C. Johns.

C., 3 Co. F, 59 Va. Inf., P-P, Orig. Jones, Charles.

Cal., Old Co. A, 10 Ms. Inf., P-P.

Calvert, Co. A, 1 Miss. L. Arty., P-P, Orig. Vt Calvert Johns.

Calvin, Co. G, 1 (Reserves) Fla. Inf., P-P.

Calvin, Capt. Hendry's Co., Mtd. Inf. (Pierce Mtd. Vols.) Ga., P-P.

Calvin, Co. I, 39 Ms. Inf., P-P.

Calvin, Co. K, 20 Tn. Inf., P-P.

Calvit, Co. A, 1 Ms. Light Arty, P-P.

Cary F., Co. A, 53 Va. Inf., P-P.

C. C., Co. E, 10 Fla. Inf., P-P., Navy & M. Mitchell.

C. C., Co. K, Crescent Regt., La. Inf., P-P.

C. D., Co. F, 39 Ga. Inf., P-P, 56 Ga. Inf.

C. D., Co. H, 56 Ga. Inf., P-P.

C. H., Co. H, 13 Ga. Inf., P-P.

Ch., Co. A, Fire Battn., La Militia.

C. H., Co. F, 13 Va. Inf., P-P, Orig. Henry C. Johns.

Charles, Co. E, 53 Ala. (Partisan Rangers), P-P.

Charles, Co. B, 12 Ky. Cav., P-P.

Charles, Co. E, 5/35 Tn. Inf.

Charles, Co. B, 5 Tex. Artillery, P-P.

Charles C., Co. B, 10 Confed. Cav., P-P, Orig. Johnson, C. A.

Christopher C., Co. C, 3 Battn. Ms. Cav., P-P.

Clement R., Co. B, 1 (McCulloch's) Texas Cav. 2 Lt./2 Lt.

Clement R., Co. G, 16 Texas Inf., P-P.

Clinton, Co. L, 35 Tn. Inf., P-P.

Colonel A., Co. A, 7 Fla. Inf., P-P.

Columbus, Co. C, 3 Battn. Ms. Cav., P-P, Orig. Christopher C. Johns.

Cornealious, Co. E, 10 Fla. Inf., Cpl./P.

Cornelius, Co. C, 3 (Forrests) Tn. Cav., P-P.

C. P., Chisolms' Co., Ala. Cav., P-P.

C. P., Co. I, 5 Battn. Fla. Cav., P-P.

C. P. S., Co. A, 1 (Carter's) Tn. Cav., Cpl./Cpl.

C. R. Jr., Sub. Dept., Gen. & Staff Offrs., Corps, Div. & Brig. Staffs, Agent/Agent.

C. S., Co. E, 53 Ala. (Partisan Rangers), P-P. Orig. Charles Johns.

D., Cameron's Co., 1 Battn. (Montgomery's) State Troops, Ms. Cav., P-P.

D., Capt. Montgomerys Indpt. Co., St. Trps., (Herndon Rngrs.) Ms., P- P.

Daniel, Co. A, 33 Ala. Inf., P-P.

Daniel, Co. B, 18 S. C. Inf., P-P.

Daniel F., - Schnabels' Battn., Ms. Cav.

Daniel R., Co. G, 21 S. C. Inf., P-P.

Daniel S., Co. K, 5 Fla. Inf., PP.

Daniel W., Co. D, 7 Ga. Inf., Sgt./P.

Dave, Co. F, 28 Ms. Cav., P-P.

David, Co. H, 9 Fla. Inf., P-P.

David, Co. D, 4 Battn. La. Inf., P-Sgt.

David, Ives Co., 54 Tn. Inf., P-P.

David F., Co. F, 2 Partisan Rangers, Ms., P-P.

David M., 2 Co. K, 25 Va. Inf., P-P.

D. C., Co. G, 7 Ga. Inf., (St. Guards), P-P.

Decatur, 2 Co. F, 25 Tn. Inf., P-P.

D. G., Co. I, 32 Ala. Inf., P-P.

D. G., Co. C, 12 (Robinson's) Ga. Cav. (St. Gds.), P-P.

E., Co. A, 25 La. Inf., P-P.

E., Co. I, 3 Texas Cav., P-P, Orig. John, Elijah.

E., Co. F, 5 Va. Cav., P-P.

E., Capt. St. Martin's Co., Va. Mtd. Riflemen, P-P.

E. B., Co. F, 3 S. C. Cav., P-P, See 11 S. C. Inf.

E. B., Co. K, 11 S. C. Inf., P-P.

E. D., Co. H, 8 Tex. Cav., P-Cpl., Orig, John, E. D.

Edward, Co. F, 5 Va. Inf., P-P.

Edward W., Co. C, 41 Ala. Inf., P-P, Orig. Johns, Eli W.

E. E., Co. M, Phillips' Legion, Ga., P-P. Orig. Johns, Elijah.

E. F., Co. A., 17 Va. Inf., P-P.

E. G., Co. C, 18 Tn. Inf., P-P.

E. H., Co. B, Palmetto Sharp Shooters, S.C., P-P.

E. J., Co. D, 6 Ala. Cav., P-P, Orig. Jerome E.

E. J., Co. E, 48 Ga. Inf., P-P.

Eli W., Co. C, 41 Ala. Inf., P-P.

Elias H., Co. E, 4 S. C. Inf., P-P.

Eliph, Co. A, Phillips Legn. Ga., P-P.

E. N., Co. G, 63 Ala. Inf., P-P.

Enoch, New - 1 (Reserves) Fla. Inf., P-P.

E. R., Co. D, 14 (Neely's) Tn. Cav., P-P.

Ervin, Co. H, 2 Fla. Cav., P-P.

E. S., Co. - 3 Ga. Inf., P-P.

E. W., - Gen. & Staff Offcrs. etc., Surg./Surg.

F. M., Co. E, 1 Battn., Hilliard's Lgn. Ala. Vols., P-P.
     Orig. T. M. Johns.

F. M., Co. C, 11 Fla. Inf., P-P.

F. W., Co. G, 20 Battn. Ga. Cav., P-P., Orig. George W. Johns.

F. M., Co. E, 26 Tn. Inf., P-P. Orig. Marion.

Francis M., Co. H, 5 Fla. Inf., P-P.

Francis M., Co. D, 59 Tn. Mts. Inf., P-P. Orig. Jones.

Francis F., Co. I, 1 (Fannin's) Ga. Res., P-P.

Frank, Co. K, Cocke's Reg., Ark. Cav., P-P, Orig. Jones, Franklin.

Frederick William, Co. A, 1 Ms. Lt. Artillery, P-P.

Freeman, Co. K, 13 Ala. Inf., P-P.

F. W., Co. K, 18 Ms. Inf., P-P.

F. W., Ms. (Miss. File) Act. A.D.C. to Gov. of Miss.

G., Capt. Clinch's Batty., Ga. Lt. Artillery, P-P, Orig. Johns, J.

G., Co. 7, 7 Ms. Inf., P-P.

G. D., Co. I, 32 Ala. Inf., P-P., Orig. P. G. Johns.

George, Capt. Fernandez's Mtd. Co. Fla. (Supply Force), P-P.

George, Co. G, 26 Ga. Inf., P-P.

George, Co. K, 11 S. C. Inf., P-P.

George A., Co. F, 2 N. C. Cav., Cpl/Sgt.

George D., Co. E, 30 Battn. Va. Sharpshooters, P-P.

George T., Co. F, 4 Fla. Inf., P-P.

George W., Co. G, 20 Battn. Ga. Cav., P-P.

George W., Co. D, 21 Battn. Ga. Cav., P-P.

George W., Co. A & H, 59 Ga. Inf., 1 Lt./Capt., Orig. Jones.

G. F., Co. F, 4 Fla. Inf., P-P, Orig. Johns, George T.

G. H., Co. E, 13 Battn. Ala. Partisan Rangers, P-P, See also 56 Ala. P.R.

G. H. Co. I, 56 Ala. Partisan Rangers, P-P. See also 13 Battn. Ala. P. R.

G. J., Co. D, E, 42 Ga. Inf., P-P. See also Joseph G.

Granberry, Co. C, 1 Ga. Cav., P-P.

Greer D., Co. I, 32 Ala. Inf., P-P, See also D. G.

G. W., Co. H, 2 Ga. Cav., Bugler-Bugler.

G. W., - . 10 Ga. Cav., P-P.

H, Co. H, 1 (Butlers') S. C. Inf., P-P.

H. Alburtus, Co. B, 2 Fla. Cav. Cpl.-P.

Harris, Co. K, 46 Ala. Inf., P-P.

Harry, Co. C, 18 Tenn. Inf., P-P.

Henry, Co. B, 1 (Reserves) Fla. Inf., P-P.

Henry, Co. G, 17 Va. Inf., P-P.

Henry C., Co. F, 13 Va. Inf. P-P.

Henry H., Co. B, 2 Miss. Inf., P-P.

Hezekiah, Co. F, 9 Fla. Inf., P-P.

Hubbard J., Co. G, 1 Confed. Reg. Troops, Cpl.-Cpl.

I. J., Co. A, 3 S. C. Cav., P-P.

I. S., Co. K, 16 Miss. Inf., P-Sgt. Orig. Jones, Joseph.

Isaac, Co. C, 1 Fla. Cav., P-P.

Isaac, Co. B, 2 Battn. Fla. Inf., P-P.

Isaac, Co. F, 2 Battn. Fla. Inf., P-P.

Isaac, Co. G, 10 Fla. Inf., P-P.

Isaac, Co. D, 11 Fla. Inf., P-P.

Isaac B., Co. I, 13 Ga. Inf., P-P.

Isaac S., Co. C, 3 Ga. Inf., P-P.

J. W., - , 10 Ga. Cav. P-P. See G. W. Johns.

Izrael J., Co. F, 17 (Griffith's) Ark. Inf., P-P.

J., Co. A, 33 Ala. Inf., Cpl-Cpl.

J., Co. F, 8 Ark. Inf., P-P.

J., Capt. Clinch's Batter., Ga. Lt. Artillery, P-P.

J., Co. G, Ogden's La. Cav., P-P.

J., Gen. & Staff Officers, etc., Lt. & Insp. Fd/Transp. - Lt. & A. A. C.S.

J. A., Co. G, 7 Miss. Cav., P-P. Orig. Jerry J.

J. A., Co. A, 2 Battn. S. Car. Sharp Shooters, P-P.
J. A., Co. E, 15 S. C. Inf., P-P. Orig. Joseph.
Jack A., Co. D, 3 (Clack's) Tenn. Inf., P-P. Orig. A. J.
Jackson, Co. A, 10 Fla. Inf., P-P.
Jackson, Co. D, 23 Ga. Inf., P-P.
Jackson, Co. D, 23 Va. Inf., P-P.
Jackson J., Co. C, F, 30 Ga. Inf., P-P.
Jacob, Co. C, 1 Fla. Cav., 2 Lt./2 Lt.
Jacob, Co. H, 2 Fla. Cav., P-P, See also. W. Tillis (Sub.)
Jacob J., Co. G, 20 Battn. Ga. Cav., Sgt.-Sgt.
Jacob J., Co. D, 21 Battn. Ga. Cav., P-P.
Jacob B., 1 Co. F, 1 (Hagood's) S.C. Inf.
Jacob B., 2 Co. G, 1 (Hagood's) S. C. Inf., P-Sgt. See also J.S.
James, Co. L, 1 Ga. Regulars, P-P. See Statement of Service Ref. slip. only.
James, Co. D, 26 Ga. Inf., P-P.
James, Co. I, 42 Ga. Inf., P-P.
James, Co. E, 5 Ky. Mtd. Inf., P-P.
James, Co. A, 9 La. Inf., P-P.
James, - , Coleman's Regt. Mo. Cav. Orig. Jones, James.
James Sr., Co. F, 1 (Orr's) S. C. Rifles, Sgt.-Sgt. See also 2 S.C. Rifles.
James Jr., Co. C, 2 S. C. Rifles, 3 Lt./1 Lt.
James, Co. F, 26 Texas Cav., P-P.
James, Co. I, 31 Va. Inf., P-P.
James A., Co. C, 57 Ala. Inf., P-P.
James A., Co. F, 1 (Orr's) S. C. Rifles, 2 Lt./1 Lt.
James B., Co. F, 5 Fla. Inf., P-P.
James B., Co. C, 3 (Ashby's) Tenn. Cav., P-P. Orig. J. B.
James C., Co. C, 2 Battn. Ga. Inf., P-P.
James C., Co. B, 22 Va. Inf., Sgt.-Capt.
James C. L, Capt. Fields' Co. (Partisan Rangers) Ky., P-P.
          Orig. Johnson, James C.
James D., Co. G, 6 Tex. Cav., P-P.
James F., Co. B, 23 Tex. Cav. P-P., See also 34 (Alexander's) Tex. Cav.
James F., Co. G, 23 Va. Inf., P-P.
James H., Co. H, 39 Ala. Inf., P-P.
James H., Co. G, 17 N. C. Inf., P.-P. See also Johnson, James H.
James Howard, Co. H. 46 Miss. Inf., P-P, See also J. H.
James J., Co. C, 30 Ga. Inf., P-P. Orig. Jackson J.
James M., Co. F & G, 5 Fla. Inf., P-P.
James M., Co. C, 6 Ga. Inf., P-P.
James M., Co. A, 12 Ga. Militia, P-P.
James K., Co. A, 7 Fla. Inf., P-P.
James R., Co. H, 47 Ga. Inf., P-P.
James S., Co. I, 44 Ala. Inf., Cpl.-P.

James S., Capt. Carrington's Co. Va. Lt. Artillery, P-P.
James T., Co. F, 6 Ga. Inf., P-Music.
James W., Co. I, 1 Fla. Cav., P-P.
James W., Co. H, H, 55 Ga. Inf., P-P.
J. B., Co. F & K, 2 Ala. Cav. P-P. See also B. J.
J. B., Co. D, 11 Ala. Inf., Sgt.-Sgt.
J. B., Co. H, 2 Ga. Cav., Bugler-Bugler.
J. B., Co. A, 24 Battn. Ga. Cav., P-P.
J. B., Co. D, 21 Battn. Ga. Inf., Cpl-Sgt. See Jeremiah R.
J. B., Co. E, 2 La. Cav., P-P.
J. B., - , 3 La. Inf., P-P.
J. B., Co. F & S, 45 N.C. Inf., Asst. Surg./Asst. Surg.
    Orig. Johns, Anthony B.
J. B., Co. C, 2 (Ashby's) Tenn. Cav., P-P.
J. B., Co. G, 6 Tenn. Inf., P-P.
J. B., Co. C, 18 Tenn. Inf., P-P.
J. C., Co. H, 2 Ala. Cav., P-P.
J. C., Co. H, 47 Ga. Inf., P-P.
J. C., Co. E, 15 S. C. Inf., P-P. See also Joseph.
J. C., Co. K, 12 (Consol.) Tenn. Inf., P-P. see also 47 Tn. Inf.
J. C., Co. G, 47 Tenn. Inf., 12 Consold.) Tn. Inf.
J. D., Co. L, 8 Ark. Cav., P-P.
J. E., Co. E, 37 Ark. Inf., P-P.
J. E., Capt. Barnwell's Battery., Ga. Lt. Arty., P-P.
J. E., Co. E, 15 S. C. Inf. P-P. Orig. Joseph.
Jeremiah, Co. C, 1 Fla. Cav., P-P.
Jeremiah, Co. K, 3 Fla. Inf., P-P.
Jeremiah, Capt. Clinch's Batty., Ga. Lt. Arty., P-P.
Jeremiah, Co. I, 14 Va. Cav., P-P, Orig. J. Johns.
Jeremiah E., Co. A, 50 Ga. Inf., Capt.-Sgt.
Jeremiah J., Co. F, 4 Fla. Inf., P-P.
Jeremiah J., Co. G, 20 Batt. Ga. Cav., P-P.
Jeremiah J., Co. D, 21 Battn. Ga. Inf., Cpl-Sgt.
Jerry, Co. H, 2 Fla. Cav., P-P.
Jerry J., Co. G, 7 Miss. Cav., P-P.
Jesse, Hamptons Co., 3 (Forrests') Tenn. Cav., P-P.
Jesse L., Co. B, 5 Battn. Ala. Vols., P-P.
Jesse L., Co. E, 13 Ala. Inf., P-P. See Jesse Jones.
Jesse L., Co. A. 7 Fla. Inf. P-P.
J. F., Hurts' Battn., Ala. Lt. Arty., P-P. See also John Johns.
J. F., Co. K, 41 Ala. Inf., P-P., See also John F. Johnson.
J. F., Co. A, 21 Carter's) Tenn. Cav., Sgt.-Sgt.
J. G., Co. M, 5 S. C. State Troops, P-P.
J. H., Co. H & C, 1 Ms. Inf., P-P.

J. H., Co. K, 16 Miss. Inf., P-Sgt. See also Jones, Joseph.

J. H., Co. H, 46 Miss. Inf., P-P.

J. H., Co. A, 36 Va. Inf., P-P.

J. J., Co. F, 22 Ala. Inf., P-P.

J. J., Co. K, 23 Miss. Cav., P-P.

J. J., Co. B, Ford's Battn. Mo. Cav. P-P.

J. J., Co. A, 3 S. C. Cav., P-P. See J. J. Johns.

J. J., Co. B, 7 Confed. Cav., P-P. See John J. Johns.
     J. J., Va. Inf.

J. L., Co. K, 3 Fla. Inf., P-P., See Johns, Jeremiah.

J. M., Co. H, 2 Fla. Cav., P-P.

J. M., Co. D, 4 Fla. Inf., P-P. see John Johns.

J. M., Capt. Clinch's Batty. Ga. Lt. Arty., P-P.

J. M., - , 2 Ga. Inf., P-P.

J. M., Co. E, 50 Ga. Inf., P-P, See Jones, Joshua M.

J. M. C., Co. A, 10 Fla. Inf., P-P.

J. N., Co. I & B, 10 Ark. Inf., P-P.

Joel, Co. E, 35 Ark. Inf., P-P. See Joel Johnes.

John, Hurt's Batty. Ala. Lt. Arty., P-P.

John, Co. D, 4 Fla. Inf., P-P.

John, Co. D, 1 S. C. Arty., P-P.

John, Co. O, 1 S. C. Inf., P-P.

John, Co. K, 11 S. C. Inf., P-P.

John, Co. E, 33 Va. Inf., P-P. See John Jones.

John, Inf. Gen. & Staff, etc. 1st Lt.

John A., Co. D, 26 Ga. Inf., P-P.

John A., Co. F, 1 Confed. Eng. Troops., D Class Pvt. 1/2s Class Pvt.

John B., Co. B & F, 17 Ala. Inf., Jr. 2 Lt./1st Lt.

John B., Co. F, 1 (Orr's) S. C. Rifles, P-Sgt.

John B., Co. C, 18 Tenn. Inf., P-P. See J. B. Johns.

John C., Co. K & E, 18 Ala. Inf., P-Cpl.

John C., Co. K, 12 (Consol.) Tenn. Inf., P-P., See J. C. Johns.

John D., Co. A, 7 Fla. Inf., P-P.

John H., Co. B, 2 Ala. Cav. Blacksmith/Blacksmith.

John H., Co. B, 5 Battn. Ala. Vol., P-P.

John J., Co. B, 18 Va. Inf., P-P. See 7 C. S. Cav.

John L., Co. E, 3 Miss. Inf., P-P.

John M., Co. C, 14 Tenn. Inf., P-P, See Jones, John M.

John P., Co. C, 9 Fla. Inf., P-P.

John R., Co. A, 24 Battn. Miss. Cav., Sgt.-Sgt.

John R., Co. C, 7 Miss. Inf., P-P.

John S., Co. G, 2 Ark. Inf., P-P, See John, J. S.

John S., Co. D, 1 N. C. Jr. Res., P-P.

John S., Co. F, 13 Va. Inf., P-P.

John S., - , 47 Va. Militia, P-P.
John W., Kolbs' Batty, Ala. Light Arty., P-P.
John W., Co. I, 3 Va. Reserves, Capt./Capt.
John W. , Allen's Co., Barks' Regt., Va. Local Def., P-P.
    See John W. Jones.
John W., Gen. & Staff Off., etc. Asst. Surg.
Jonas P., Co. K, 29 Ala. Inf., P.-P. See Johns, Jones P.
Jones P., Co. K, 29 Ala. Inf., P-P.
Joseph, Co. K, 16 Miss. Inf., Pvt.-Sgt. See Jones, Joseph.
Joseph, Co. C, 26 Battn. Ga. Inf., P-P.
Joseph, Co. K, 7 S. C. Reserves, P-P.
Joseph, Co. E, 15 S. C. Inf., P-P.
Joseph, Co. B, 18 S. C. Inf., P-P.
Joseph, Co. I, 14 Va. Cav., P-P.
Joseph, Co. E, 31 Va. Inf., P-Sgt. See Joseph Jones.
Joseph D., Co. A, 33 Tex. Cav., P-P.
Joseph F., Co. B, 11 Tenn. Cav., P-P.
Joseph G., Co. D, E, 42 Ga. Inf., P-P.
Joseph M., Co. G, 20 Battn. Ga. Cav., P-P.
Joseph M., Co. D, 21 Battn. Ga. Cav., P-P.
Joseph S., Co. G, 2 Ark. Inf., P-P. See John, J. S.
Joseph S., Co. K, 16 Miss. Inf., P-Sgt. see Jones, Joseph.
Joseph S., Co. A, 17 Miss. Inf., P-P.
Joshua O., Co. E, 8 La. Inf., P-P, see also Richardson's Battn. Cav.
Joshua O., Co. C, 39 Battn. Va. Cav., P.-P.
J. P., Co. B, 4 (McLemore's) Tenn. Cav., P-P.
J. P., Co. C, 18 Tenn. Inf., P-P.
J. R., Camp Guard Miss., P-P.
J. S., Co. K, 14 Ga. Inf., Cpl.-P. See Jones, J. Samuel.
J. S., Co. D & E, 42 Ga. Inf., P-P. See Johns, Joseph G.
J. S., Co. K, 5 La. Inf., P-P, See Thomas Jones.
J. G., 1 Co. F, 1 (Hagood's) S. C. Inf., P-Sgt.
Julian, Co. D, 23 Va. Inf., P-P.
J. W., Co. C, 6 Ga. Inf., P-P. See Johns, James M.
J. W., Co. D, 7 ga. Inf., Sgt.-Pvt. See Daniel W. Johns.
J. W. Co. D, 48 Miss. Inf., P-Cpt., See Jones, John W.
J. W., Co. G, 1 Va. Cav., P-P.
Kerasy, Gen. & Staff, etc. Major Q.M.
L. B., Co. E, 1 Battn. Hilliards Lgn., Ala. Vol., P-P.
L. B., Co. C, 2 (Ashby's) Tenn. Cav., P-P. See Johns, J. B.
Levi, Co. D, 2 Battn. Hill. Lgn. Ala. Vol., P-P.
Levi, Co. G, 59 Ala. Inf., P-P. See John, Levi.
Levi, Co. B, 1 (Reserves) Fla. Inf., P-P.
Levi, Co. A, 10 Fla. Inf., P-P.

Levi, Co. C, Waul's tex. Leg., P-P.

Levi, Band Finegan's Brig., Gen. & Staff, etc. Music./Musc. See also 10 Fla. Inf.

Levy, Co. A., 10 Fla. Inf., P-P., See Levi Johns.

Lewis, Co. H, 2 Fla. Cav., P-P. See Luke Johns.

Lewis, Co. F, 9 Battn. Miss. Sharp Shooters, P-P.

Lewis, Co. C, 19 Va. Cav., P-P.

Lewis J., Co. I, 1 Fla. Cav., P-P. See Louis J.

L. J., Co. B, 15 Ala. Inf., P-P.

L. J., Co. E, 10 Ga. Cav., P-P.

L. M., Conscripts, Fla., P-P.

L. M., Connsn's. Dept., Gen. & Staff etc. 2 Lt./2 Lt.

Louis J., Co. I, 1 Fla. Cav., P-P.

Luke, Co. C, 1 Fla. Cav. P-P.

Luke, Co. H, 2 Fla. Cav., P-P.

Malachi, Co. G, 5 Ga. Cav., P-P.

Marion, Dodson's Co., 1 Ala. Cav., P-P. See Co. E., 12 Ala. Cav.

Marion, Co. E, 12 Ala. Cav., P-P.

Marion, Co. E, 51 Ala. (Partisan Rangers), P-P.

Marion, Co. E, 26 Tenn. Inf., P-P.

Marshall, Co. E, 42 Ala. Inf., P-P., See John, Marshall R.

Martin L., Co. B, 12 Battn. (Day's) Tenn. Cav., P-P.

Matthew, Co. H, 10 Fla. Inf., Cpl-Pvt.

Matthew, Co. C, 2 Battn. Fla. Inf., P-P.

M. D., Co. H, 1 (Symon's) Ga. Res., P-P.

M. H., Co. H, 1 S. C. St. Troops, P-P.

Morgan, Co. G, 1 Va. Cav., P-P.

Morgan, Co. C, 17 Va. Cav., P-P.

W. R., Co. D, 21 Ga. Inf., P-P. see Benjoh M. Johns.

N. D., Swope's Co., Herberts Battn. Arizona Cav., P-P.

N. D., Co. E, Saufley's Scouting Battn., Tex. Cav., P-P.

Newton H., Co. G, 3 Ala. Cav., P-P.

N. H., Co. G, 51 Ala. (Partisan Rangers), P-P. See 3d Ala. Cav. as Newton H. Johns.

N. M., Co. E, 3 Battn. Tenn. Inf., P-P. See N. M. John.

O. B., Co. E, 2 Battn. Ga. Cav., P-P. See Obediah Johns.

O. B., Co. D, 22 Battn. Ga. Arty., P-P. See Obediah Johns.

Obediah, Co. D., 22 Battn. Ga. Arty., P-P.

Obediah, Co. F, 1 Regt. Ala. Inf., P-P.

Obediah, Co. A, 5 Ala. Inf., P-Cpl.

Obediah, Co. E, 2 Batt. Ga. Cav., P-P. See 22nd Battn. Ga. Hvy. Arty.

Orlando, Co. F, 26 Tex. Cav., P-P.

Oscar, Co. I, 12 Mo. cav., P-P.

P., Co. H, 2 Fla. Cav., P-P.

Paul, Co. C, 18 Tenn. Inf., P-P.

P. B., Co. B, 2 (Walker's) Tenn. Inf., P-P.

Philip, Co. B, 2 (Robison's) Tenn. Inf. (Walker Legion), P-P.

Phillip, Co. H, 3 Texas Inf., P-P.

P. R., Co. H, 36 Texas Cav., P-P, See P. R. Jones.

R., Co. H, 23 S.C. Inf., P-P.

R. A., Gen. & Staff, etc. A.A.Q.M. See also Johns, Reuben A. 2 Lt. 35 Tenn. Inf.

R. C. C., Co. K, 9 Texas Cav., P-P.

R. Dudley, Co. G, 3 Miss. Cav. Res., P-P.

R. Dudley, Co. G, 20 Miss. Inf., P-P, See James Barton (Sub.)

Reuben A., Co. C, 33 Tenn. Inf. 2 Lt./2 Lt.

Reuben H., Co. D, 1 Fla. Cav., P-P.

R. F., Capt. Peneck's Co., Va. Lt. Arty., P-P.

R. H., Co. B, 14 Tex. Inf., P-P.

Richard D., Co. G, 1 Va. Cav., P-2 Lt.

Richard M., Co. H, 55 Ga. Inf., P-P.

Richard W., Co. C, 18 Tn. Inf., P-P.

Riley, Co. D, 1 Fla. Cav., P-P.

Riley, Co. F, 9 Fla. Inf., P-P., See Wm. R. Johns.

R. J., Co. F, 9 (Nichols) Tex. Inf. F. S. 2 Lt./2Lt. See Waul's Tx. Leg.

R. J., Co. D, Timmons Regt.Tex. Inf. 1 Lt./1 Lt. See R. J. John.

R. J., Co. F, Waul's Tex. Legion, Sr. 2 Lt./1 Lt. See R. J. John.

R. L., Co. B, 1 (Reserves) Fla. Inf., P-P.

Robert, Co. M, 5 S. C. State Troops, P-P. See J. G.

Robert, Co. M, 5 S. C. St. Troops, P-P.

Robert, Co. E, 12 Tex. Cav., P-P.

Robert, Co. C, 51 Va. Cav., Cpl./Sgt. See Jones, Robt. C.

Robert B., Co. D, 1 (McCulloch's) Tex. Cav., P-Sgt.

Robert B., Co. G, 16 Tex. Inf., P-P.

Robert N., Co. I, 2 Mtd. Rifs., Ark., P-P.

Robert S., Co. G, 1 (Olmstead's) Ga. Inf., P-P.

Robert W., Co. F, 13 Va. Inf., P-P.

Russell, Co. G, 25 N.C. Inf., P-P. See Jones, Russell M.

R. W., Co. F, 19 & 20 Consol. Tn. Cav., P-P.

R. W., Co. A, 20 (Russells) Tn. Cav., P-P.

S., Co. K, 24 Ala. Inf., P-P.

Sam. J., Co. 15, 19 Ark. Inf., P-P.

Samuel, Co. E, 6 Fla. Inf., P-P. See John,

Samuel, 3 Batty. Mo. Lt. Arty., P-P. M.S.G.

Samuel, Co. A, 162 Va. Militia, P-P.

Samuel S., Co. A, 52 Va. Inf., P-P.

Sander C., Co. C., 2 Battn. (Capt. Dortch's) Ky. Cav., P-P.

Sanders C., Co. C, 2 (Ashby's) Tenn. Cav., P-P. See S. C. Johns.

Sanford T., Co. A, 25 Battn. Ga. Inf. (Provost Guard), P-P. - 1 Battn.
     Confed. Inf. See also 5 Ga. Reg. S. T. Johns.
Sanford T., 2 Co. A, 1 Battn. Confed. Cav. P-P. Also 25 Battn. Ga. Inf.
     Provost Guard St. Johns 5 Ga. Inf.
S. C., Co. C, 2 (Ashby's) Tn. Cav., P-P.
S. C., Co. B, 23 Consold. Tenn. Inf., Cpl-Cpl. See also Stephen C. Johns
     28 Tn. Inf.
S. D., Capt. Maxwell's Co., St. Troops (Peach Creek Rangers) Miss., P-P.
S. H., Co. G, 7 S. C. Cav., P-P.
Shadrick, Fla. Home Guards, P-P.
S. K., Co. B, 18 S. C. Inf., P-P. See Stark Johns.
S. K., Co. H, 23 S. C. Inf., P-P.
S. M., Co. K, 5 Ga. Inf., P-P.
S. M., Co. G, 7 So. Car. Cav., P-P. See S. H. Johns.
S. R., Co. H, 22 S. C. Inf., P-P. See S. K. Johns.
S. T., Co. K, 5 Ga. Inf., P-P. See Sanford T. Johns, 25 Battn. Ga. Inf. (P.
     G.) 1 Battn. Confed. Inf.
Stark, Co. B, 18 S. C. Inf., P-P.
St. Clair, Co. G, 5 La. Inf., P-Capt.
Stephen, Co. C, 1 Ga. Inf. (St. Guards), P-P.
Stephen, Co. D, 8 Battn. Ga. Inf., P-P.
Stephen C., Co. F, 28 Tn. Inf., P-Cpl. See S. C. Johns 28 (Consd.) Tn Inf.
Stewart J., Co. I, 44 Ala. Inf., Cpl-P. See James S. Johns.
S. W., Co. G, 7 S.C. Cav., P-P. See G. H. Johns.
T. T., Co. B, 18 S. C. Inf., P-P.
T. H., Co. E, 10 Fla. Inf., P-P.
Thomas, Co. B, 34 Ga. Inf., P-P.
Thomas, Co. H, 9 Ky. Cav., P-P.
Thomas, Co. I, 3 N.C. Cav. (41 St. Troops), P-P.
Thomas, Co. I, 5 (McKenzie's) Tn. Cav., P-P. See T. J. Johns.
Thomas, Co. H, 5 Va. Inf., P-P.
Thomas, Gen. & Staff, etc. Major A.Q.M.
Thomas E., Co. F, 17 Tex. Cav., P-P.
Thomas F., Co. G, 47 Ala. Inf., P-P.
Thomas J., Co. C, 36 Va. Inf., P-P.
Thomas L., Hurt's Batty., Ala. Lt. Arty., P-P.
Thomas W., Co. C, 7 Miss. Inf., P-P.
T. J., Co. D, 31 N.C. Inf., P-P. See 41 N.C. Inf.
T. L., Co. H, 16 La. Inf., P-P.
T. M., Co. E, 1 Battn. Hilliards Lgn., Ala. Vol., P-P.
T. J., Co. G, 30 Ala. Inf., P-P. See T. F. Johns 47 Ala.
W., Co. E., 51 Ala. (Partisan Rangers), P-P. See Marion Johns.
W., Co. G, 7 Ga. Cav., P-P.
W. A., Co. C, 8 (Livingston's) Ala. Cav., P-P.

W. A., Logan's Co., Ala. Mtd. Reserves, P-P.

W. B., Co. I, 4 Fla. Inf., P-P. See William Johns.

W. B., Co. F, 18 Tn. Inf., P-P. See Johnson, W.B.

W. C., Shepherd's Co., Randolph Co. Reserves Ala., Cpl-Cpl.

W. C., Op. of Insov. Talladega Ala.

W. C., Co. G, 44 Ga. Inf., P-P.

W. C., Co. D, 25 Battn. Va. Inf., P-P.

Wesley, 26 S. C. Inf., P-P.

Wesley, Co. F, 26 S. C. Inf., P-P.

W. G., New Co. F, 6 Ark. Inf., P-P. See W. G. John.

W. H., Co. B, 29 Ala. Inf., P-P. See William A. Jones.

W. H., Co. G, 21 S. C. Inf., P-Cpl.

W. I., Co. G, 3 Ala. Cav., P-P.

W. I., Co. I, 13 Ala. Inf., P-P. see William A. Johns.

William, Co. I, 4 Fla. Inf., P-P.

William, Co. A, 10 Fla. Inf., P.-P.

William, Co. A, 24 Battn. Ga. Cav., P-P.

William, Co. C, 38 Ga. Inf., P-P.

William, Co. B, 60 Ga. Inf., P-P.

William, Co. H, 9 Ky. Cav., P-P.

William, Co. 4, Battn. Wash. Art. 11 La. P-P., See Jones, Wm. W.

William, Co. C, C. S. Zouave Battn. La., P-P. See Wm. Jones.

William, Co. F, 9 Batt. Mo. Sharp Shooters, P-P.

William, Co. G, 3 Batt. S. C. Inf., P-P.

William, Co. K, 11 S. C. Inf. (9 S.C. Vols.), P-Lt.

William, Co. F, 7 Tenn. Inf. P-P. See Jones, Wm. N.

William, Co. L, 35 Tn. Inf., P-P.

William, Co. D, 3 (Yager's) Batt. Tex. Cav., P-P.

William, Co. - , Timmon's Regt. Texas Inf. N.C.S, 2mSgt./2mSgt. See John, Wm.

William, Capt. St. Martin's Co., Va. Mounted Riflemen, P-P.

William, Co. H, 5 Va. Inf., P-P.

William, Co. E, 22 Va. Inf., P-P. Engr. Corps.

William A., Co. I, 13 Ala. Inf., P-P.

William A., Co. I, 30 Texas Cav., P-Cpl.

William B., Co. D, 1 Fla. Cav., P-P.

William C., Co. D, 25 Battn. Va. Inf., P-P. See W. C. Johns.

William D., Co. G, 7 Tn. Inf., P-P.

William F., Co. G, 26 Ga. Inf., Cpl-Pvt.

William W., Co. G, 20 Ga. Inf., P-P.

William H., Co. C, Well's Regt. Tex. Cav., P-P.

William H. K., Co. H, 4 Fla. Inf., P-P.

William J., Co. I, 25 Ga. Inf., P-P.

William L., Co. C, 51 Ga. Inf., Lt./2 Lt.

William L., Co. K, 57 Ga. Inf., P-P.

William L., Co. C, 19 Va. Ca., P-P. See Wm. Lewis Johns, Va. St. Line.

William M., Co. G, 8 Fla. Inf., P-P. See also David W. Mizell.

William M., Co. A, 55 Ga. Inf., P-P.

William M. R., Gen. & Staff, etc. Lt. & Enroll. Offcr.

William N., Co. B, 15 Ala. Inf. Sgt/Sgt. See also W. N. Johns.

William N., Co. C, 1 (Feild's) Tn. Inf., P-P.

William P., Co. C, 7 Miss. Inf., P-P.

William P., - , Mosby's Regt. Va. Cav. P-P

William R., Fla. Conscripts

William R., Co. F, 5 Fla. Inf., P-P. Capt. Mooty's Co.

William R., Co. F, 9 Fla. Inf., P-P.

William R., Co. I, 5 (McKenzie's) Tenn. Cav., P-P.

William R., Co. P, 33 Tenn. Inf., P-P.

William R., Co. C, 3 Va. Lt. Artillery -

William R., Co. G, 12 Va. Inf., P-P.

William S., Co. C, 22 Batt. Ga. Hard Artillery, P-P.

William S., Conscripts Ga. P-P.

William T., Co. E, 22 Miss. Inf., P-P.

William T., Co. I, 1 (McCulloch's) Tex. Cav., P-P.

William W., Co. D, 2 Battn. Hilliard's Legion, Ala. Vol. P-P.

William W., Co. A, 162 Va. Militia, P-P.

William Warren, Co. B (New), 5 Ala. Inf., P-P.

W. J., Co. G, 51 Ala. (Partisan Rangers), P-P. 3rd Ala. Cav.

W. J., Co. F, 5 Fla. Inf. Sgt./Sgt. See Wm. J. Jones.

W. J., Capt. Hopkin's Co., 1 Battn. Ga. Cav., P-P.

W. J., Co. K, 44 Ga. Inf., P-P. See Jones, W.J.

W. L., Co. C, 22 Battn. Ga. H. Arty., P-P. See Wm. S. Johns.

W. L., Co. F, 3 Batt., Ga. (State Guards), P-P.

W. L., Co. I, 25 Ga. Inf., P-P. See Wm. J. Johns.

W. M., Co. G, 11 Fla. Inf., P-P.

W. M., Co. H, 1 Consol. Reg. Tn. Inf., P-P. See William N. Johns, 1 (Feild's) Tenn. Inf.

W. M. R., Co. D, 6 Tn. Inf., Capt./Capt.

W. N., Co. B, 15 Ala. Inf., Sgt-Sgt.

W. P., Co. K, 33 Miss. Inf., P-P.

W. R., Co. G, 8 Fla. Inf. P-P. See William M. Johns.

W. R., Co. I, Nixon's Regt. Tn. Cav., 1st Sgt/Sgt.

W. R., Co. C, 18 Tn. Inf., P-P.

W. S., Capt Pollock's Co., Va. Lt. Artillery, P-P. See Jones, William S.

W. T., Co. C, 7 Miss. Inf. P-P. See Thomas W. Johns.

W. W., Co. B, 15 Ala. Inf., Sgt-Sgt., See W. N. Johns.

W. W., Co. D, 39 Ala. Inf., P-P.

W. W., Co. H, 2 Fla. Cav., P-P.

W. W., Co. I, 10 (DeMoss') Tenn. Cav., P-P.
Zachariah, Co. I, 1 Ga. Regulars, Pvt.
Zac. T., Co. F, 39 Tn. Mounted Inf., P-P. See Zachariah T.
Z. L., Co. L, 35 Tn. Inf., P-P. See 36 Tn. Inf.
Z. L., Co. L, 36 Tn. Inf., P-P. See 35 Tn. Inf.
* *

CHAPTER SEVENTEEN

CHILDREN OF EZEKIEL, cont.

JONATHAN JOHN,

7-son of Ezekiel John and Lydia was born ca 1815 in Knox Co., Tn., married Celia Browder 6 Aug 1838 in McMinn Co., Tn.[1] Celia was daughter of EDMUND BROWDER (ca 1784) and Ruthena Husong[2], b. 14 Nov 1816 in Roane Co.[3], Tn. Jonathan was a Baptist preacher and a farmer.

    Jonathan's grandfather, Zephaniah John (ca 1750), and Zephaniah's son Samuel moved from Hancock Co., Ga. to Knox Co., Tn. around 1806. Zephaniah JOHN was a planter who had inherited land from his mother Mary JOHN (widow of DAVID JOHN, blacksmith) in Mecklinburg Co., N.C. He lived in Mecklenburg Co., N. C. before and during the Revolutionary War. He sold sheep and unspecified other things to the Revolutionary Army.[4] He sold his plantation in N.C. and moved to Georgia after drawing land in the 1803 Ga. Land Lottery. Before leaving Ga. for Tn., Zephaniah sold this land. Jonathan's father Ezekiel JOHN and his family moved from Buncombe Co., N.C. to Knox County, Tn. around 1809 to join Zephaniah and siblings who had arrived earlier. From Knox Co., they moved to McMinn Co. around 1819 or 1820 when it opened for settlement.

    Jonathan's brother, Ezekiel Jr., was a partner in the mercantile company of Blair, John & Co., which was at Mouse Creek Station, now Niota, Tn. Ezekiel Jr. was a blacksmith by profession, but became a merchant with his son Zachary T. JOHN and S. P. Blair.[5] Niota was situated about midway between Athens and Calhoun. Another early store in the area was Stephens & BROWDER. When Jonathan's brother left Buncombe County, N. C. in 1825, he came to McMinn County where Ezekiel and his family lived.

    Thomas John, eldest brother of Jonathan, established the JOHN Cemetery 2 1/2 miles south of Niota.[6] This record states:

---

[1] McMinn Co. Tn. Marriages, Book C, p. 5. Married by A. Slover, M.G.

[2] Deed Bk. H, p. 31, 1726-28, New Castle Co., Del., made 13 Aug 1726 between Andrew Elliot of Red Lyon Hundred and John Hooeuson, weaver, of New Castle Hundred, 385 acres on main branch of Christiana Creek, bounded by lands of William Battells, John Hill, John Harris, Dan Shorts, Benjamin Gibbs and Archibald Nickolls. For the sum of fifty one pounds fifteen shillings, sold part of this land to John Hooeuson. Witnesses Rees Jones and Hugh Hooeuson Jun.

[3] Bible Record found in Case #39, Edmund Browder, McMinn Co., Tn.

[4] Voucher #43 Revolutionary Army, dated 22 Oct 1780, and Voucher #6, Mecklenburg Co., N.C. For sheep and unspecified claim.

[5] Goodspeed's History of East Tn., 1887, McMinn Co., p. 1021.

[6] John Cemetery "McMinn Co. Tn. Tombstone Inscriptions" Vol. 1, p. 339.

"Thomas John originated from Buncombe County North Carolina in 1825 and entered a tract of land, a part of which this Cemetery is located on, for the relatives of Thomas John. Located 2 1/2 miles south of Niota. Follow road leading from Niota to Mt. Harmony for about 1 1/2 mile to the farm of H. B. Johnson, turning right into a lane. There all roads turn left until reaching the farm of Mrs. Walter Pardue where the cemetery is located. There are about 32 unmarked graves."

Jonathan John farmed in this area until around 1853. From the census, it appears he and Celia lived near William Browder's land in Monroe Co. in 1840. William Browder was Celia's uncle, and owned a large dairy farm. About 1853, Jonathan and Celia moved to Jefferson County. This was the area where he had lived earlier. This area was called Strawberry Plains, and was located near the boundaries of Knox, Grainger and Jefferson Counties.[7]

Their sons who were old enough to go to the army during the Civil War fought on the side of the Confederacy. Records indicate some of the Johns connections from the Samuel John (ca 1772) line from Bradley Co., fought on the Union side. J. S. Hurlburt wrote in 1866[8] that among the leading union persons in the Second District were Benjamin John and Samuel John, who had two sons in U.S.A. They mentioned Z. L. John as being pressed into the rebel ranks and died. We found vouchers where Z. L. was in the Confederate Army. This was probably Zephaniah Loftin John, son of William and Jane Armstrong John, who was age 18 in Bradley Co. in the 1860 census.

A picture of Celia John taken around 1862 with son Ezekiel shows a slender, attractive woman with a serious demeanor, wearing typical attire of that era. The picture has been restored, and she appears to me to be originally holding a Bible. She died in late 1870 or early 1871 in Knox Co., Tn. Her father Edmund BROWDER died in 1861, and numerous court records show attempts to locate her, but none of the records indicate she received her share of his estate. We found no record of final settlement and court records indicate the final money was never paid out to the heirs.

Celia's great-grandfather Edmund Browder (b. ca 1720) of Chatham Co., N.C. fought in the Revolutionary War. In our research on the Revolutionary War in N. C., S. C. and Ga. [an area where a civil war took place between residents who were Tories and Whigs,] several accounts were given of the Chatham Co., N.C. militia fighting in that area.

[7]1850 Census McMinn Co. Tn., H.H. #273.
1860 Census Jefferson Co., Tn., P. 278, H.H. #1963-2001.
1870 Census Knox Co., Tn., Distr. 18, P. 329, H.H. #95-95.
[8]The History Of The Rebellion In Bradley County East Tennessee.

After Celia's death, Jonathan married again, to Mary Elizabeth HICKS Lackey on 10 Aug 1871 in Knox Co. She was the widow of John A. Lackey and had a daughter, Lucinda Lackey, later called Lucinda Johns. Jonathan and Elizabeth, as she was called, moved to Dyer Co., Tn. after their marriage. In 1880, Elizabeth's young half-sister Laura Phillips lived with them, and was called Laura Johns in the census.[9]

Jonathan and Elizabeth had two children: a) LYDIA JOHNS, b. 27 Apr 1875, Dyer Co., Tn., married Samuel Franklin Wallace 17 May 1891; and b) MATTIE [Martha] JOHNS, b. Oct 1880, Dyer Co., Tn., married John Leven Bedwell 24 Nov 1897. (More on this line later.)

Jonathan and his family began using the name JOHNS, even though other family members disapproved of it and tried to talk them out of it.[10] Jonathan's brothers and sisters moved to Ia., Tx., Ky., Okla., Fla. and elsewhere, and some of them retained the name JOHN.

The children of CELIA BROWDER JOHN and Jonathan were:
1. CELINA JOHNS, b. 7 Jul 1839, McMinn Co., Tn.
2. JAMES BRADFORD JOHNS, b. Nov 1840, McMinn Co.
3. SANDERS CALLOWAY JOHNS, b. 8 May 1842, McMinn Co.
4. MARTIN L. JOHNS, b. ca 1843, McMinn Co.
5. NAPOLEON BONAPARTE JOHNS, b. 15 Oct 1844, McMinn Co.
6. PRINCE ALBERT JOHNS, b. Aug 1846, McMinn Co.
7. ZEPHANIAH JOHNS, b. 1847/1848 McMinn Co.
8. RUTH JANE JOHNS, b. ca 1849, McMinn Co.
9. ZADOCK JOHNS, b. ca 1850, McMinn Co.
10. BENJAMIN EDMUND JOHNS, b. Nov 1853, Jefferson Co., Tn.
11. EZEKIEL JOHNS, b. May 1858, Jefferson Co.
* *

The children of Jonathan and Elizabeth were:
1. LYDIA JOHNS, b. 27 Apr 1875, Dyer Co., Tn.
2. MARTHA "Mattie" JOHNS, b. Oct 1880, Dyer Co., Tn.
* *

CELINA JOHNS,

1- dau of Jonathan John (ca 1815) and Celia Browder, b. 7 Jul 1839, married Harrison Davis CLIFT in 1858, in McMinn Co., Tn. He was born 22 Nov 1844 in the Strawberry Plains area, Knox Co., Tn., the son of James Clift and Martha Nipper. He was a Baptist preacher and farmer.[11]

During the Civil War, Harrison Clift enlisted in the Confederate Army on 30 Sep 1862 at Strawberry Plains. He joined as a Private in (2d) Co. D, Walker's Battalion, Thomas' Legion, N. C. Troops. He was assigned to duty with Capt. Hardy's Co. E, Phipps Battalion, Tn. Cavalry Dec. 31,

---

[9]1880 Census Dyer Co., Tn., Ed 5, P. 8, Line 41, District 2.
[10]Per family historian Elbert Johns, Louisville, Ky.
[11]1870 Census Knox Co. Tn., Distr. 18, p. 329, H.H. #97-97.

1862. He was captured at the Battle of Murfreesboro at Stone River while charging the enemy's Cavalry. He was taken to a prison camp, Camp Douglas, located on Lake Michigan at Chicago, Ill. in Jan 1863 and held there until a $50 bounty was paid for his release.

He was released at City Point, Va. 4 Apr 1863. He returned and reported for duty in Hardy's Co. E on May 15, 1863.[12] The 12th Battalion, Tn. Cavalry that he served in was also known as Adrian's Battalion Partisan Rangers and as Phipps' Battalion Tn. Cavalry.

Harrison Clift and Celina moved to West Tennessee and lived in Dyer County, where they remained in the general area. He was pastor of Springhill Baptist Church near Dyersburg, as well as pastor of Antioch Church, Beech Grove Church, South Fork Church, and Woodville Church in Edith, Tn. on alternating Sundays. They later moved to Lauderdale County before 1900.[13] Celina died 31 Aug 1907 of tuberculosis [14] in Dyer Co., and was buried in East View/Fairview Cemetery, Newbern, Dyer Co.

After her death, Harrison married (2) Mattie May Sneed 10 Mar 1908. They lived in Crockett Co., Tn.[15] Harrison died 12 Nov 1920 in Dyer Co., Tn. He was buried in East View/Fairview Cemetery, Newbern, Dyer Co., Tn.[16] Mattie Clift died 1968 in Dyer Co., Tn.

Mary Kathryn Harris of Ft. Worth, Tx., whose husband is a descendent of this line, gave me a copy of an interesting letter written by Mattie Sneed Clift to one of Harrison Clift's grandsons, excerpts below.

Children of Celina Johns Clift and Harrison:
1. MARTHA MILANDA CLIFT, b. 11 Sep 1860, Knox, Tn.
2. JAMES OBEDIAH CLIFT, b. 21 Aug 1861, Knox Co., Tn.
3. WILLIAM HARRISON CLIFT, b. 30 Nov 1862, Knox Co. Died 1 Jul 1863.
4. SEALEY [Celia] CORDELIA CLIFT, b. 20 May 1864, Knox Co., Tn.
5. HARRIET RUTHENA CLIFT, b. 13 Aug 1867, Knox Co., Tn.
* *

EXCERPTS OF LETTER FROM MATTIE M. CLIFT, second wife of HARRISON DAVIS CLIFT, to ROY B. PARKS:
"Dear Roy,
How are you all. O.K. I hope. I don't know where you get the Clift and Parks History. It is all mixed up.
Your oldest brother was named William Harrison Park after his father and grandfather. Your grandfather married at 14 years, weighed 160 pounds big was he.

---

[12]Confederate Army Records.
[13]1900 Census Lauderdale Co. Tn., ED 88, p. 11, Line 93, Distr. 14, H.H. #195-199.
[14]See letter from Mattie Clift.
[15]1910 Census Crockett Co., Tn., ED 9, p. 13.
[16]Inf. rcd. from Mary Kathryn Harris of Ft. Worth, Tx.

Your grandmother was 21 and a <u>Baptist preacher daughter</u>. Four children before he was 20 years in Knox County East Tennessee. A Dr. Snead delivered your Aunt Hattie.

Roy your mother was buried in East View Cemetery, Newbern, Tennessee. The town keep[s] it up.

I think your brother Carl was buried there. He died with T. B. So did your grandmother Clift. Your grandfather Bright Disease. Your Aunt Delia married A. A. Troy..."

* *

MARTHA MILANDA CLIFT,

1- dau of Celina Clift (1839) and Harrison, b. 11 Sep 1860, m. William Benjamin Parks. He was b. 6 May 1856 in Jackson Co., Ga., the son of Benjamin F. Parks and Emily B. Brown. William was a very strict, perhaps cruel man, who was fanatically religious and a poor provider. After he found and gave to the church all the money Martha had saved up to buy a piece of land, Martha took the children and went to live with her parents, and divorced William about 1899. His cruelty and beatings embittered the children, and some did not make it to adulthood due to hardship. James went so far as to change his name to Harris. Martha died 25 Sep 1901 and was buried in Fairview Cem., Newbern, Tn.[17]

Their children were:
1. WILLIAM HARRISON PARKS, b. 11 Jan 1880, Crockett Co., Tn. Married Birdie White.[18] He died Jul 1946 at Halls, Lauderdale Co., Tn.
2. JAMES LAFAYETTE PARKS, later changed to HARRIS. B. 8 May 1882, Crockett Co., Tn. Married 1) Anna M. Hodge, (divorced) and married 2) Sarah Berger, 17 Jun 1917 in NYC. He died 11 Sep 1973 in San Diego, Ca. and was buried in Mount Hope Cemetery, San Diego. Mary Kathryn Harris' husband William Harris is his son.
3. EDWARD/EDGAR PARKS, b. 4 Jun 1884, Crockett Co., Tn. Married Geraldine Reed. He died 1917 or 1918 while in the U. S. Army on a ship going overseas, and was buried at sea.
4. CARL PARKS, b. 28 Feb 1886, Crockett Co. Tn. Died 1910, Edith, Lauderdale Co., Tn. Did not marry.
5. VIRGIL PARKS, b. 8 Jul 1888, Crockett Co., Tn. Died bef 1900, Tn.
6. LILLIAN PARKS, b. 5 Aug 1889, Crockett Co. Died bef 1900, Tn.
7. LULA MAY PARKS, b. 5 Oct 1891, Crockett Co., Tn. Married Loren DeWitt. Died in Hammond, In.
8. CLIFT PARKS, b. 25 May 1893, Crockett Co., Tn. Died 24 May 1915, Memphis, Shelby Co., Tn. of tuberculosis. Buried Elmwood Cemetery, Memphis, Tn. Did not marry.

---

[17]Info from Mary K. Harris.
[18]1900 Census Lauderdale Co., Tn., ED 88, p. 11, L. 93, Dist. 14, No. 195-199.

9. ROY BOWMAN PARKS, b. 9 Jul 1895, Crockett Co., Tn. Married Leona Horstman 11 Apr 1914. Lived in Carbondale, Jackson Co., Ill. [Recipient of above letter.]
10. IRMA PARKS, b. 5 Aug 1897, Crockett Co., Tn. Died 1897/1900.
11. WILLIE EUGENE PARKS, b. 1 Apr 1895, Crockett Co., Tn. Died 1917 in Eagle Pass, Tx. Buried Memphis, Tn. Did not marry.

* *

JAMES OBEDIAH CLIFT,

2- son of CELINA CLIFT (1839) and Harrison, b. 21 Aug 1861, married Amanda Blankenship abt 1895, in Tn.[19] She was b. Nov 1877, Tn. He died 11 Apr 1899 in Dyer Co., Tn. of cancer of the stomach or liver. They are buried in Church Grove Cemetery, located just over one mi. from Newbern, Tn.

Their children were:
1. JAMES LEE CLIFT, b. 18 Aug 1896, Dyer Co. He m. Mollie Sue Gelzer 30 Mar 1930 in Dyer Co. She was born 12 Apr 1908. He served in France in W.W. I in U.S. Army. Was a farmer; a deacon at Emmaus Baptist Church. He d.14 Jul 1973, and was bu. Church Grove Cemetery in Dyer Co.

Their children were:
1) ELLA MAE CLIFT, b. 16 Sep 1930, m. Paul Decateau Poplin 27 Jun 1954, Dyer Co., Tn.
2) ANNIE SUE CLIFT, b. 29 Nov 1931. See Following.
3) RUBY LEE CLIFT, b. 2 Jun 1935, Newbern. Married Bobby Kim Harman 30 Dec 1965 in Dyer Co. She was a school teacher. Children: (i) TIMOTHY HARMAN, and (ii) TERESA HARMAN.
4) JAMES CRAFTON CLIFT, b. 7 Nov 1937, Dyer Co. Did not marry.
5) BETTY DEAN CLIFT, b. 31 Jan 1940, Newbern, Dyer Co., Tn. Married Thomas Larry McClarty, 30 May 1963, Dyer Co., Tn.
6) HARRY ALLEN CLIFT, b. 28 Jul 1941, Dyer Co., Tn. Married Linda Jane Crews 24 Sep 1977.
2. JOHN NEWTON CLIFT, b. 8 Jan 1898, Newbern, Dyer Co., Tn. Married Myrtle McDonald. He died Oct 1972; buried Fairview Cemetery, Newbern, Tn. Children:
1) JAMES NEWTON CLIFT Jr., b. 11 Feb 1925; married Sue Autry.
2) MARCELLA CLIFT, b. 18 Apr 192-, m. (1) J. W. Hilliard, divorced, m. (2) Charles Eskridge.
3) RONNIE CLIFT, b. 9 Sep 1945, m. Dottie Sewell 1967.

* *

---

[19]1900 Census Dyer Co. Tn., ED 19, p. 9, L. 75, Distr. 6.
1910 Census Dyer Co. Tn., ED 23, p. 10.

ANNIE SUE CLIFT,

2-dau of James Lee Clift (1896) and Mollie Sue Gelzer, was born 29 Nov 1931 in Newbern, Dyer Co., Tn. Annie Sue was a nurse who was honored by the Tennessee Nurses Association for her outstanding dedication and leadership in the field of nursing.[20] She went as a missionary to Japan in 1961, where she attended two years of language school and worked in the Japan Baptist Hospital, Kyoto, Japan. She taught in their School of Nursing, worked in the hospital and worked in the church. She spent a year and a half following this, working in Yemen in the Jibla Baptist Hospital. She left this and returned to Japan where she worked until her father became ill and she returned to help nurse him, then cared for her mother when she became ill. She then began teaching nursing at the University of Tennessee, Martin in 1973.

In July 1991, she was returning from a vacation with her sister Ruby and Ruby's family when a tire blew out on their van, causing an accident that left Annie Sue paralyzed from the neck down. She has had a brave and remarkable rehabilitation. Through the love and support of her many friends, she keeps her spirits up. Through exercise, she has regained use of her arms. Dr. Jim Lenninger, who designed the special computerized hospital bed, valued at $40,000.00, which she was using, let her use it free of charge for as long as she needs it. A voice-activated IBM computer and printer were purchased and given to Annie Sue by her church, First Baptist Church of Martin. Her nephew Tim Harmon, was also seriously injured in the accident, and has recovered quite well.

Annie Sue loves using the computer, and has been doing a lot of writing. She has many friends who visit and enjoy being with her. She still has much to offer and is an inspiration to others.
* *

SEALEY [CELIA] CORDELIA CLIFT,

4- daughter of Celina Clift (1839) and Harrison, born 29 May 1864, married Adolphus A. Troy.[21] He was born Jan 1869, and died in 1931 in Gibson, Tn.; was buried there in Rutherford Cemetery. [Has Woodman of the World Memorial.][22] Sealey died in 1950, and was buried in Rutherford Cemetery.

Their children were:
1. TAYLOR CLIFT TROY, b. Nov 1889, Dyer Co., Tn; m. Robbie Kerr, b. 1893, d. 1952. They lived in Memphis, Tn. Taylor died in 1958; both buried Rutherford Cem.

---

[20]State Gazette, Newbern, Tn., Wednesday, May 11, 1994.
[21]1900 Census Dyer Co., Tn. ED 19, p. 8, L. 28, Distr. 6.
1910 Census Gibson Co. Tn., ED 49, p. 2.
[22]Rutherford Cem., Gibson Co., Tn. Records.

2. MABEL TROY, b. Sep 1897, Dyer Co., Tn. Married Wright Norman;
    she was a school teacher and lived at Rutherford, Gibson Co., Tn.
* *

HARRIET RUTHENA CLIFT,

5- dau of Celina Clift (1839) and Harrison, b. 13 Aug 1867, married 1) John
Murray. He was b.Mar 1861, Tn. She married 2) George Carter. She d.18
Sep 1932 at Hornbeak, Obion Co., Tn. of cancer of bladder; buried there.
    Children of Harriet Murray and John:
1. OGDEN MURRAY, b. Apr 1886, Lauderdale Co., Tn., m. Lena Brown.
2. HELEN MURRAY, b. Apr 1891, Lauderdale Co., Tn., m. 3 times.
3. ELNORA MURRAY, b. May 1895, Lauderdale Co., Tn., m. 1)
    _____Jones, 2) _____ Newman, 3) _____ Rice.
4. ROBERT L. MURRAY, b. Jan 1898, Lauderdale Co., Tn., d.
    1900/1910.
5. EVERETT MURRAY, b. ca 1901, Lauderdale Co., Tn.
6. BESSIE MURRAY, b. ca 1906, Lauderdale Co., Tn.
* *

JAMES BRADFORD JOHNS,

2- son of Jonathan (ca 1815) and Celia Browder, b. Nov 1840, was living in
Jefferson Co., Tn. near Roseberry in the Strawberry Plains area when the
Civil War started. He enlisted in the Confederate Army and served in Co.
C, 2 (Ashby's) Tennessee Cavalry. [23]

    He was captured and force-marched through Jessamine County, Ky.,
crossing the Kentucky River near Camp Nelson. He liked the country so
well that he made up his mind to return there if ever he was freed. [24]

    After the war, he returned to his family in Knox Co. There he married
Mary Hester Sterling 14 Feb 1867 .[25] She was b. Mar 1850, Tn. He was a
farmer and farmed there for a few years .[26] He told stories of the country he
had seen in Jessamine County, Ky., and those stories inspired his brothers
to move later to Ky.

    About 1871 or 1872, after his mother Celia died, his father moved to
West Tennessee. His father died in 1880/1881 in Crockett Co., Tn.

    About 1883 or 1884, James Bradford Johns moved with his family to
Jessamine County, Ky. near Nicholasville. He died there after 1920.
    Their children were:
1. SAMUEL JOHNS, b. Feb 1868, Grainger Co., Tn.
2. AGNES JOHNS, b. ca 1873, Grainger Co., Tn.; m. John T. Cobb, 12
    Feb 1891. He was b. ca 1856 in Madison Co., Ky.[27]

---

[23]Confederate Vouchers.
[24]Info. from Elbert Johns, Louisville, Ky.
[25]Knox Co. Tn. Marriages. Married by R. M. Miller.
[26]1870 Census Knox Co., Tn., Distr. 18, p. 329, H.H. #96-96.
[27]Marriages of Jessamine Co. Ky. 1851-1899. Compiled by: Bill and Kathy Vockery,
p. 16, undated.

3. JAMES F. JOHNS, b. Jan 1876, Grainger Co., Tn.[28]
4. ZEPHANIAH JOHNS, b. Mar 1878, Grainger Co., Tn., m. Bertha _____
   1906, Jessamine Co., Ky.
5. SARAH BELLE JOHNS, b. May 1882, Grainger Co., Tn. Married
   Samuel Tilton King, 6 Oct 1898, Jessamine Co., Ky. He was born ca
   1885, Garrard Co. Ky. He was a farmer.[29] [Marriage Bond: J. B. Johns.]
6. NORA JOHNS, b. Nov 1883, Jessamine Co., Ky.
7. ZACHARIAH T. JOHNS, b. Aug 1889, Jessamine Co., Ky.

* *

SAMUEL JOHNS,
1- son of James Bradford Johns (1840) and Mary Hester, b. Feb 1868,
Grainger Co., Tn., married Belle Massie 3 Feb 1888 in Jessamine Co., Ky.
She was b. Aug 1867, Grainger Co., Tn.[30] [Consent was given by James
Bradford Johns for the marriage. Bondsman was William Brock.] He was a
farmer.

   Their children were:
1. ADALINE JOHNS, b. Oct 1888, Jessamine Co., Ky.
2. MINNIE JOHNS, b. Aug 1893, Jessamine Co., Ky.
3. PEARL JOHNS, b. May 1896, Jessamine Co., Ky.
4. STANLEY JOHNS, b. Feb 1898, Jessamine Co., Ky.
5. MARY E. JOHNS, b. ca 1901, Jessamine Co., Ky.
6. GEORGIA JOHNS, b. ca 1906, Jessamine Co., Ky.[31]

* *

AGNES JOHNS,
2- daughter of James Bradford Johns (1840) and Mary Hester, b. May 1872,
married John Cobb 12 Feb 1891 in Jessamine Co. He was a farmer, and
was born Oct 1855 in Madison Co., Ky.[32] [Martin L. Johns Bondsman.][33]

   Their children were:
1. MANFORD COBB, b. Jul 1883, Jessamine Co., Ky.
2. STUDY COBB, b. Jul 1885, Jessamine Co., Ky.
3. ERNEST COBB, b. Feb 1892, Jessamine Co., Ky.
4. MARY COBB. Aug 1894, Jessamine Co., Ky.
5. SHIRLEY COBB (m.), b. Jun 1897, Jessamine Co., Ky.
6. BRADFORD COBB.[34]

---

[28]Was single, age 34, in 1910.
[29]Marriages of Jess. Co., Ky. 1851-1899, by Vockery, undated, p. 47.
[30]Marr. of Jess. Co., Ky. 1851-1899, by Vockery, undated, p. 44.
[31]Inf. from 1900 Census Jessamine Co., Ky., ED 26, p. 7, L. 93, Distr. 2, H.H. #134-136.
1910 Census Jessamine Co., Ky., ED 44, P. 4, H.H. #102-102, N. Keene Pct., Distr. 3.
1920 Census Jessamine Co., Ky., ED 66, H.H. #121-144.
[32]1900 Census Jessamine Co., Ky., ED 30, H.H. #250.
[33]Marriage Records, Jessamine Co., Ky.
[34]Info on Bradford and Herbert from Elbert Johns, Louisville, Ky.

7. HERBERT COBB.
*

ZEPHANIAH JOHNS,

4- son of James Bradford Johns (1840) and Mary Hester, b. Mar 1878, married Bertha _____ about 1906 in Jessamine Co., Ky. He farmed in the Wilmore Precinct.[35]

Their children were:
1. WESLEY JOHNS, b. ca1907, Jessamine Co., Ky.
2. JACKSON JOHNS, b. ca 1909, Jessamine Co., Ky. Died 1910/1920.
3. MANUEL JOHNS, b. ca 1910, Jessamine Co., Ky.
4. WILLIAM JOHNS, b. ca 1912, Jessamine Co., Ky.
5. CHARLES JOHNS, b. ca 1914, Jessamine Co., Ky.
6. WOODROW JOHNS, b. ca 1917, Jessamine Co., Ky.
7. ROSA MAE JOHNS, b. ca 1919, Jessamine Co., Ky.
* *

SANDERS CALLOWAY JOHNS,

3- son of Jonathan John (ca 1815) and Celia, b. 8 May 1842 in McMinn Co., Tn.[36] He was called Calloway, and some records indicate he used the surname JOHN. In the Sanders Calloway Johns family Bible, the name was spelled JOHN. [37] However, as his children used "JOHNS', we will also use it. He joined the Confederate Army after the Civil War began and served as a Private in Co. C, 2 (Ashby's) Tenn. Cavalry.[38] He was taken prisoner by the Yankees and held at Richmond, Va. until 17 May 1865, at which time he was given a Certificate of Parole.

He married Agnes Forbes 10 May 1870, Knox Co. She was born 20 Aug 1842, Fife-Shire, Scotland.[39] He was a farmer [40], and around 1883/1884, moved with his brothers to Jessamine Co., Ky. From there he moved across the Kentucky River to Madison Co., to an area known as the "Bent", which was a big bend of the Kentucky River. His son Robert Lee JOHNS was born there 10 Oct 1885. About 1900, he moved across the river to Mt. Lebanon, Ky.[41] The family has a Church Letter dated Oct 7 1883, when he changed church membership because of the move. He moved back to Jessamine Co. before 1910.[42] He died 30 Aug 1912. Agnes

---

[35]1910 Census Jessamine Co., Ky., ED 40, p. 14, H.H. #278-280, Wilmore.
1920 Census Jessamine Co., Ky., ED 68, H.H. #127-128, Wilmore Pct.
[36]Inf. from Elbert Johns, Louisville, Ky; and Morris K. DeWitt, Indianapolis, In. 1985 via Lillie Prichard of Friendship, Tn.
[37]Owned by Elbert Johns, Louisville, Ky.
[38]Vouchers of Confederate Army.
[39]Sanders C. and Agnes' Bible , owned by Elbert Johns, Louisville, Ky. Bible has name as "John".
[40]1880 Census Grainger Co., Tn. ED 99, p. 8, L. 42, Distr. 8.
[41]1900 Census Madison Co., Ky., Million Pct., ED 55, p. 2, H.H. #24-24.
[42]1910 Census Jessamine Co. Ky., ED 46, H.H. #218-219, Distr. 5, Plaquemines.

died 29 Apr 1934. They are both buried in Maple Grove Cemetery, Nicholasville, Ky.

Their children were:
1. CELINA ISABELLA JOHNS, b. 27 Aug 1871, P. O. Roseberry, Strawberry Plains, Knox Co., Tn.
2. PHILLIP FORBES JOHNS, b. 24 Jun 1873, Strawberry Plains, Knox Co., Tn.
3. SANDERS CALLOWAY JOHNS Jr., b. 20 Feb 1876, Strawberry Plains, Knox Co., Tn. He was a farmer. Never married. Died 27 Nov 1961; buried Maple Grove Cem., Nicholasville, Ky.
4. GRACE ADALINE JOHNS b. 15 Aug 1878, Grainger Co., Tn.
5. CHARLES EZEKIEL JOHNS, b. 1 Mar 1881, Grainger Co., Tn. He was a farmer. Married (1) Myrtle Johns. She was a first cousin. They had no children. He married (2) Alice Comley Hunter, who had two children: Luvenia Hunter and Nellie Hunter from previous marriage.
Children of Charles Ezekiel Johns and Alice were:
   a) CALLOWAY JOHNS.
   b) CHARLES JOHNS, m. Mary Ruth Cassity.
Charles Ezekiel died 1923 and was buried in Maple Grove Cem., Nicholasville, Ky.
6. JAMES MARTIN JOHNS, b. 13 Mar 1883, Grainger Co., Tn. He was a farmer. Did not marry. Died 1960, and was buried in Maple Grove Cem., Nicholasville, Ky.
7. ROBERT E. LEE JOHNS, b. 10 Oct 1885, "Bent" section of Madison Co., Ky.
* *

CELINA ISABELLA JOHNS,
1- daughter of Sanders Calloway Johns (1842) and Agnes, b. 27 Aug 1871, married Harry Morton DeWitt 23 Nov 1892. Harry M. was born 25 Jan 1868 in Perkinsville, In. He was a railroadman. Celina died 20 May 1912 in Nicholasville, Jessamine Co., Ky. and was buried in Maple Grove Cemetery. Harry died Feb 1943 in Indianapolis, In. and was buried there in Floral Park Cemetery, located at 3659 Cossell Rd., Indianapolis.
Their children were:
1. MORTON CALLOWAY DEWITT, b. 23 Aug 1900, Nicholasville.
2. CHRISTINE MAY DEWITT, b. 18 Oct 1903, Nicholasville.
3. MARY FORBES DEWITT, b. Nov 1905, Nicholasville,
4. MORRIS KEMPER DEWITT, b. 11 Sep 1909, Nicholasville.
* *

MORTON CALLOWAY DEWITT,
1-son of Celina Isabella Johns DeWitt (1871) and Harry M., b. 23 Aug 1900, married Mildred Carpenter, who was born in Paw Paw, Mich. Morton and Mildred were divorced in 1931, and had no children.

* *

CHRISTINE MAY DEWITT,

2- dau. of Celina Isabella Johns DeWitt (1871) and Harry M., b. 18 Oct 1903, married Earl Alonzo Weaver 30 Oct 1924, Indianapolis, In. Christine died 29 Apr 1963 in Indianapolis, and was buried there in Washington Park Cemetery.

Their children were:

1. HARRY EARL WEAVER, b. 13 Nov 1925, Indianapolis. Married Joanna _____. He died May 1977 and was buried in Washington Park Cemetery. Their children were: 1) MICHAEL WEAVER, and 2) DAVID WEAVER.
2. CATHERINE EVA WEAVER, b. 17 Nov 1927, Indianapolis; m. Herman WARD. Children: 1) MARTIN WARD; 2) CATHERINE WARD; 3) KEVIN WARD.

* *

MARY FORBES DEWITT,

3- dau of Celina Isabella Johns DeWitt (1871) and Harry M., b. Nov 1905, married Ferdinand Winters 29 Dec 1923, New Albany, In. He was b. Apr 1898, Van Wert, In.; d. 1974, Indianapolis, and was buried in Floral Park Cemetery.

Children:

1. ROSEMARY JEANNE WINTERS, b. 2 Sep 1924, Indianapolis. Married Richard Bennett. Children: 1) JOANNA BENNETT; 2) JAMES BENNETT; 3) ELAINE JOANNA BENNETT.
2. EDWIN WENDALL WINTERS, b. Indianapolis. Married (1) Rosemary Whitehead and (2) Mary _____.

* *

MORRIS KEMPER DEWITT,

4- son of Celina Isabella Johns DeWitt (1871) and Harry M., b. 11 Sep 1909. Married Pearl May Kriel 5 Feb 1934, Franklin, In. She was b. 5 Mar 1915, Indianapolis. He was a sheet metal worker and electrical coordinator for Electric Utility. He and his wife did a lot of genealogical research, which they shared with the family.

Their children:

1. CLIFFORD MORTON DEWITT (Sr.), b. 30 Apr 1937, Indianapolis. He was an attorney in Indianapolis. Married (1) Jacquelyn Sue Myers; their son: CLIFFORD MORTON DEWITT Jr.
Clifford Sr. married (2) Betty Wilson Rice; had son EVAN CHRISTOPHER DEWITT. He had other marriages to (3) Linda Hamm, no children; (4) Joy Faye LAKE, a son: BRADLEY RAY DEWITT. [Not sure of order of marriages.]

2. MORRIS KEMPER DEWITT Jr., b. 1 Feb 1940, Indianapolis. He was
    in Real Estate business. Married (1) Janet Lou Carnes; had daughter:
    ADRIENNA ANN DEWITT. He married (2) Vicki Haywood.
* *

PHILLIP FORBES JOHNS,

2- son of Sanders Calloway Johns (1842) and Agnes, b. 24 Jun 1873,
married Elizabeth Lee "Lizzie" Harvey 29 Jan 1900 in Madison Co., Ky.
She was b. 23 Dec 1880, Ky.[43] Phillip was a farmer.[44] He died 1953 in
Nicholasville, Ky. and was buried in Maple Grove Cemetery, Nicholasville.
Lizzie died in 1940 and was also buried there.
   Their children were:
1. LEWIS M. JOHNS, b. 3 Sep 1900, Jessamine Co. Died 2 Apr 1914,
    Jessamine Co.
2. VERDI LANA JOHNS, b. 9 Sep 1901, Jessamine Co., Ky. Died 28
    Sep 1902, Jessamine Co.
3. LOTTIE LANA JOHNS, b. 13 Mar 1903, Jessamine Co. Married John
    Rhorer 20 Feb 1924, Jessamine Co. They have two children.
4. CHARLES EDWARD JOHNS, b. ca 1905, Jessamine Co. See below.
5. GRACIE A. JOHNS, b. ca 1907, Jessamine Co.
6. IDA ERLENE JOHNS, b. 7 Jul 1910, Jessamine Co. Married J. C.
    Fletcher 4 Feb 1931, Jessamine Co. Lived in W. Virginia in 1993.
7. PHILLIP LEE JOHNS, b. 11 Jul 1911, Jessamine Co. Married Pauline
    _____ 24 Mar 1934, Jessamine Co.
8. SANDERS JOHNS, b. ca 1914, Jessamine Co.. Married Mae WILSON
    12 Oct 1940, Ky.
9. SUSIE AGNES JOHNS, b. ca 1916, Jessamine Co. Married Charles
    Burton 8 May 1937, Ky. Lived in Lexington, Ky. in 1993.
* *

CHARLES EDWARD JOHNS,

4- son of Phillip Forbes Johns (1873) and Lizzie, b. ca 1905, married Mable
English. He was a tobacco farmer and a member of the Burley Tobacco
Association. He also worked in numerous management positions at various
tobacco warehouses and with highway construction jobs throughout the
state. His wife Mable preceded him in death.[45] He was a member of the
Mt. Lebanon Methodist Church since 1926, a former Sunday school
superintendent and the oldest member of the church.
   He died 10 Feb 1993 in Jessamine Co. and was buried in Maple Grove
Cemetery. His obituary mentioned grandchildren: Donna Cobb and
husband Gerald Cobb; Danny Johns and wife Pam; Sue Wireman and

---

[43]1900 Census Madison Co., Ky., Million Pct., ED 55, p. 2, #24-24.
[44]1910 Census Jessamine Co. Ky., ED 46, H.H. #194-195, Distri. 5, Plaquemines.
1920 Jessamine Co. Ky., ED 69, Bethel Pct., H.H. #62-64.
[45]Obituary from local newspaper, Feb. 1993.

husband Jeff Wireman; and Jennifer Sturgill from Nicholasville; Debbie Patrick and husband Ken Patrick; and Terrie Barajas, Dallas; Scott Johns and wife Jenny Johns, from Lancaster; Donald Johns, Versailles; Ronald Johns and wife Leslie Johns, Charlotte Hall, Md.; Angie McBride and husband and Jeff Johns, Lexington; Mary Jo Miner and husband Rick Miner from Louisville.

Great-grandchildren were: Christopher Fields, Stephen Fields, J. R. Barajas, Andrew Barajas, Nicole Miner, Linsay Johns, Tyrel Wireman, Matthew Cobb, Gerri Cobb, Hunter Johns, Heather Johns, Cody McBridge, Nicholas McBridge, John Moore and Suzanne Moore.

Children of Charles Edward Johns and Mable:
1. LEWIS KENNETH JOHNS. Married Minnie ____.
2. JORETTA JOHNS. Married David Grow.
3. CHARLES EDWARD JOHNS Jr., called "Sonny". Married Betty

   ____.
4. BILLY C. JOHNS. Married Alice ____.
5. ARBY G. JOHNS. Married Jane ____.
6. VERDENIA JOHNS. Married Robert Johnson. Died bef 1993.
* *

GRACE ADELINE JOHNS,
4- daughter of Sanders Calloway Johns (1842) and Agnes, b. 15 Aug 1878, married William CASSITY. [46]

Their children were:
1. ARTHUR EDWARD CASSITY.
2. AGNES GENEVA CASSITY. Married Clyde R. Clemm.
3. JESSIE EDNA CASSITY. Married "Sparks" Kirby.
4. ISABELLA McCLURE CASSITY. Married John Lowry.
5. WILLIAM ELMER CASSITY.
6. CHARLES SANDERS CASSITY.
7. JULIA CASSITY. Married ____ Anderson.
8. JULIUS CASSITY.
9. MARGARET ANN CASSITY. Married Frank Botkins.
* *

ROBERT E. LEE JOHNS,
7- son of Sanders Calloway Johns (1842) and Agnes, born 10 Oct 1885 in "Bent" section of Madison Co., Ky., the only one of the children of Calloway and Agnes to be born in Ky. He married Inice Brumfield Dec 1910 in Jessamine Co. She was b. 15 Jul 1891 in Ky. He was a farmer. He came to Kentucky as a young man with his family. He died 8 Nov 1969 and was buried in Maple Grove Cemetery, Nicholasville. Inice died in 1967, and was also buried there.

Their children were:

---

[46] Inf. from Morris K. DeWitt, Indianapolis, Ind., 1985. Given to Lillie Prichard.

1. ELBERT B. JOHNS, b. 5 Apr 1911, Mt. Lebanon, Jessamine Co., Ky. See below.
2. CORNELIA JOHNS, b. ca 1914, Jessamine Co. Married Ralph Clarke. Children: a) RICHARD CLARKE; b) RALPH CLARKE Jr.
3. MARY AGNES JOHNS, b. ca 1916, Jessamine Co., Ky. Married Clyde CORMAN. Children: a) CLORA ANN CORMAN; b) ESTHER CORMAN; c) CLYDE CORMAN Jr.
4. ROBERT LEE JOHNS, b. ca 1918, Jessamine Co., Ky. Never married. Died in France during Battle of Bulge, W.W.II.
5. ESTHER JOHNS. Married Charles Wells. Children: a) JACKIE WELLS; b) ANDREW WELLS.
6. CREED JOHNS. Married Susan Rhinehammer. Children: a) VIRGINIA SUE JOHNS; b) GEORGIA JOHNS; c) ROBERT JOHNS.
7. Lucian JOHNS. Married (1) Susan OGDEN; one daughter Georgia JOHNS, who married Pelster Becker. Lucian married (2) Edith Larison Steele. They had no children.
8. TOM WELCH JOHNS. Married (1) Patty Owens. Children: a) BARBARA JEAN JOHNS; b) CHRISTY JOHNS; c) HARVEY JOHNS.[47] He married (2) Eleanor McCray.

* *

ELBERT B. JOHNS,

1- son of Robert E. Lee Johns (1885) and Inice, born 5 Apr 1911, married (1) Myrtle Metcalf 18 Sep 1937, Berea, Ky. Myrtle, daughter of Charles Metcalf and Mary R. Edmonds, was born 27 Mar 1908, Irasburg, Vermont. She died 27 Nov 1988, Louisville, Jefferson Co., Ky. Elbert married (2) Alberta Murphy Atkinson, born 13 Oct 1917.

Elbert has contributed a great deal to family unity through the years by helping set up the Family Reunions, notifying everyone of the dates and places where held, and sending out a Newsletter each year, with announcements of current family events. As well, he has done an enormous amount of genealogical work. He has allowed himself to be used as a focal point for disbursing this information to others who are also doing research. A modest man, enough praise cannot be heaped upon him. All family members owe him a great debt for helping to keep the family spirit alive. Elbert, with the help of Lillie Prichard, provided the cake at the Family Reunion in 1998 for my husband and my 50th wedding anniversary that we happily celebrated with the family on Aug. 2[nd.] (This was held at Reel Foot Lake, Ky. Our anniversary was Aug. 10th.)

Elbert is a retired Boy Scout Executive. He has served in almost every lay role in the Methodist Church; is a member and Past President of the Ky. Lions Eye Foundation, a 50 year member of Lions International and active in the Louisville Downtown Lions Club. He spearheads the Louisville

---

[47]Inf. from Morris K. DeWitt, Indianapolis, In. 1985, given by Lillie Prichard.

Prayer Breakfast Group; has been active in the Berea College Alumni Association and is a member of the President's Club; as well as other civic organizations.

Elbert was the primary caretaker for his wife Myrtle, who suffered a severe stroke in 1973, for 17 years; "everyone of which was a wonderful one," he maintains.

Children of ELBERT B. JOHNS and Myrtle:

1. CAROLYN INICE JOHNS, b. 7 Oct 1938, Berea, Ky. Married John FRENCH 1966, Paducah, Ky. She has two sons.
2. ELBERT B. JOHNS Jr., b. 14 May 1944, Paducah, Ky. Married Christina Mox 19 Aug 1968 Duke University, N.C. Lives in Bloomington, In. (1994). They have four children: a) CHRISTOPHER JOHNS, b) JENNIFER JOHNS, c) PETER JOHNS, and d) ANN JOHNS.

* *

MARTIN L. JOHNS,

4- son of Jonathan John (ca 1815) and Celia, b. ca 1843, was living in or near the Strawberry Plains area of Knox and Grainger Cos., Tn. when the Civil War began. He joined the Confederate Army and was a Private in Co. B, 12th Battalion (Day's). He married Sarah Belle Wylie 14 Jan 1867in Jessamine Co., Ky.[48] She was born ca 1853 in Ky.

He moved to Jessamine County, Ky. after the Civil War, probably the first of the JOHNS brothers to move there.[49] His brother Ezekiel was living with him in 1880 and it is believed he and brother Zephaniah came to Jessamine Co. with Martin. He was a farmer[50] and a Minister of the Gospel[51] He was on the list of Confederate Veterans in 1890 in Ky. He died about 1895/96 in Jessamine County.

Their children were:

1. WILLIAM HENRY JOHNS, b. Mar 1870, Jessamine Co. Married Cordelia _____ ca 1890. She was b. Nov 1871, Ky. [52]
   Children of William Henry Johns and Cordelia:
   a) CLAY JOHNS, b. Oct 1893, Jessamine Co. Married Laura _____ ca 1914; she was b. ca 1896 in Ky. Children: 1) MABLE JOHNS, b. ca

---

[48]Marr. of Jessamine Co., Ky. 1851-1899, Comp. by Bill and Kathy Vockery, undated, p. 44.

[49]1880 Census Jessamine Co., Ky., ED 112, P. 27, HH #246-246-District #15, Plaquemines.

[50]Ibid.

1900 Census Jessamine Co., Ky., ED 25, p. 1, H.H. #22-20, Lee Pct.

1910 Census Jessamine Co., Ky., ED 41, p. 3, H.H. #58-58.

[51]As shown on records of Marriages, he was MG, and performed the marriage of Celia.

[52]1900 Census Jessamine Co., Ky., ED 30, H.H. #335-340, Plaquamine, Distr. #5.

1910 Census Jessamine, Ky., ED 46, p. 12, H.H. #235-236, Plaq., Dis. #5.

1920 Census Jessamine Co., Ky. ED 74, #242-244, Sulphur Well Pct.

1915, Jessamine Co.; 2) HERBERT JOHNS, b. ca 1916, Jessamine Co.; 3) JULIETTE JOHNS, b. ca 1920, Jessamine Co.[53]

b) VINA JOHNS, b. Jan 1894, Jessamine Co.

c) HERBERT JOHNS, b. Oct 1897, Jessamine Co. Married Mayone _____ 1920.[54]

d) LOLA JOHNS, b. Oct 1899, Jessamine Co.

e) HOMER JOHNS, b. ca 1902, Jessamine Co.

f) ROLAND JOHNS, b. ca 1904, Jessamine Co.

g) ELMER JOHNS, b. ca 1906, Jessamine Co.

2. ZEPHANIAH JOHNS, b. Oct 1871, Jessamine Co.

3. SAMINDA JOHNS, b. ca 1873, Jessamine Co. Married _____ Cobb; no children.

4. ROBERT JOHNS, b. Jan 1876, Jessamine Co. Married Ina _____.[55] She was b. Jun 1881 Ky.

5. CELIA JOHNS, b. ca 1878, Jessamine Co. Married Earnest Sageser 16 Oct 1895 in Jessamine Co. [Marriage was performed by Martin L. Johns, MG, who also gave consent.] Earnest Sageser was b. ca 1874 Garrard Co..

6. GLADYS JOHNS, b. May 1882, Jessamine Co. Married John L. Cagle 1908 in Jessamine Co. Child: a) MARJORIE CAGLE, b. 1910, Ill.[56]

7. MYRTLE MAGGIE JOHNS, b. Mar 1885, Jessamine Co.

8. HORACE JOHNS, b. Jan 1891, Jessamine Co.

9. OSCAR JOHNS, b. Oct 1893, Jessamine Co. Married Mary Elizabeth Surface ca 1917, Jessamine Co., Ky. She was b. 1896, Ky. Children: a) ROBERT M. JOHNS, b. ca 1918, Jessamine Co.; b) MARY E. JOHNS, b. ca 1919, Jessamine Co.[57] Oscar died in Jan 1959 in Indiana.

10. HARRY JOHNS.[58]

* *

NAPOLEON BONAPARTE JOHN,

5- son of Jonathan John (ca 1815) and Celia, b. 15 Oct 1844, was of an age to go to the Civil War, and was probably in the Confederate or Union Army. We were unable to locate his records. He retained the name as JOHN. He married (1) Sarah C. Stevens 10 Feb 1868 in Knox Co., Tn., and lived in Knox Co. in Fourth District in 1870. [59] Their child: ELIZABETH JOHN, b. 1869 in Knox Co. He moved to Grayson County, Texas before 1880.[60]

---

[53] 1920 Census Jessamine, Ky., ED 66, H.H. #162-177.

[54] 1920 Jessamine Co. Ky. ED 74, H.H. #245-247, Sulphur Well Pct.

[55] 1900 Census Jessamine Co., Ky., ED 25, p. 5, L. 78, HH. # 92-96, Lee Pct, Distr. 2.

[56] 1900 Census Jessamine Ky., Ed. 41, p. 3, H.H. #58-58.

[57] 1920 Census Jessamine Co., Ky. Ed. 66, p. 4, H.H. #87-90, Frost Pct.

[58] Inf. from Elbert Johns, Louisville, Ky.

[59] 1870 Census Knox Co., Tn. 4th Distr., H.H.#104-105.

[60] 1880 Census Grayson Co., Tx.Justice Pct. No. 1, p. 40.

He married (2) Sarah Ann "Babe" Nichols. He died 23 Feb 1914 and was buried in Collinsville Cemetery, in Grayson Co.

Children were found in 1880 census, Grayson Co. At this census, his wife Sarah [not sure which] was age 32, born in Virginia, and both her parents were born in Virginia.

Children of NAPOLEON JOHN and Sarah:

1. ELIZABETH MAY JOHN, b. 1869, Knox Co., Tn.
2. SAMUEL JOHN, b. 1871 Tn.
3. CELIA JOHN, b. 1874, Tn. Twin.
4. MARTHA JOHN, b. 1874, Tn. Twin.

* *

PRINCE ALBERT JOHNS,

6- son of Jonathan John (ca 1815) and Celia, b. Aug 1846, married Elizabeth Sterling 1 Apr 1869 in Knox Co., Tn. His name, Prince Albert, was in the 1850 census of McMinn Co., Tn.,[61] but he used the name Albert.

In 1870, he and wife Elizabeth lived in the 4th District in Knox Co. near Church Grove.[62] Elizabeth's mother, also named Elizabeth, age 57, was living with them and their new son, MARION JOHN who was eight months old, born in Oct. Albert was a farmer. In the 1870 census, Albert's surname was recorded as JOHN, although living nearby were other family members who had it listed as JOHNS. Albert moved to Jessamine County, Ky. with his family.

Child of Albert Johns and Elizabeth:

1. MARION JOHNS, b. Oct 1869, Knox Co., Tn.[63]

* *

MARION JOHNS,

1-son of Albert Johns (1846) and Elizabeth, b. Oct 1869, married (1) Saminda Reynolds 12 Jan 1893, Jessamine Co., Ky.[64] She was b. ca 1869 Tn. They had one son BUFORD JOHNS, b. 1896 (see below). Marion married (2) Nancy Hunter Reynolds 24 Nov 1898 Jessamine Co., Ky. She was b. ca 1870; died 1950. Marion died in 1940.

The child of Marion Johns and Saminda:

1. BUFORD JOHNS, b. 1896 in Jessamine Co., Ky. Married Rosa Kestel. He was a barber in Nicholasville, Ky. for over 60 years and was featured in local papers as "the oldest barber in Jessamine County." He was a member of the Nicholasville Christian Church. He died 18 May 1994, and was buried in Maple Grove Cemetery. He left nine grandchildren: JOHNY BROWNELL, Huntsville, Ala., DORIS FRYE, Montgomery,

[61]1850 Census McMinn Co. Tn.,25th Subdiv., H.H. #365-273.
[62]1870 Census Knox Co., Tn., 4th Distr., P.O. Church Grove, H.H. #107-108.
[63]Above Census taken 29 Aug, 1870 has Marion age 8/12, b. Oct.
[64]Marr. of Jessamine Co., Ky. 1851-1899, Compiled by Vockery, p. 44. Bond: Lindsay Reynolds.

Ill., DEBBIE HOURSELT, Geneva, Ill., BOBBY JOHNS, Plantation, Fla., SUE JOHNS and LYNDA JOHNS, Nicholasville, DARELL JOHNS, Wilmore, CINDY OVERLAY, Nicholasville, CHARLOTTE MOSS, Harrodsburg. He left 11 great grandchildren; three great great-grandchildren.

The children of Buford Johns and Rosa were:

a) DORIS LOUISE JOHNS. (deceased bef 1994).
b) WELDON JOHNS. (deceased bef 1994).
c) OSCAR JOHNS. (deceased bef 1994).
d) CAROL JOHNS. (deceased bef 1994).
e) VIRGINIA JOHNS. (deceased bef 1994).
f) OPAL JOHNS, who married _____ Brownell. They lived in Montgomery, Ill. (1994).
g) BUFORD "Harold" JOHNS Jr. Lived in Nicholasville, Ky.
h) WILLIAM Wayne JOHNS. Lived in Nicholasville, Ky.[65]

The children of MARION JOHNS and Nancy:

1. WESLEY JOHNS.
2. ALLLEN JOHNS, b. 15 Aug 1901; d. 25 Jul 1955.
3. CARL JOHNS.
4. LUCY JOHNS. Married _____ Harvey. Lived in Jessamine Co., Ky. 1994.
5. ELIZABETH "Lizzie" JOHNS. Married _____ Burton. Lived in Jessamine Co., Ky. 1994.
6. HUNTER JOHNS.

* *

ALLEN JOHNS,

2- son of Marion Johns (1869) and Nancy, married Nettie Walker 15 Mar 1920. Nettie was born 8 Apr 1905.

Their children were:

1. OBRA D. JOHNS, b. 6 Jan 1922.
2. STEWART P. JOHNS, b. 30 Jun 1926, d. Jul 1959.
3. ELWOOD JOHNS, b. 16 Jul 1932; d. 9 Oct 1993.
4. GLODEAN JOHNS, b. 12 Feb 1945.

* *

OBRA D. JOHNS,

1- son of Allen Johns (1905) and Nettie, b. 1922, married Gloria Francine Cooke 7 Nov 1944. He was a Minister for more than 55 years. He was honored 4 Mar 1990 by the Cairo (Tn.) Church of Christ for having preached the gospel for 50 years. He served congregations in Norwood, Ohio, Dickson, Jackson, Milan, Bolivar, and Bemis in Tn. At that time, he had worked with the Cairo Church for five years.[66]

---

[65]Info. from Obituary, undated, Nicholasville, Ky.
[66]Article in Crockett Times, Tn., undated.

He began his preaching career in Ky., his home state in 1940. He resided in Jackson, Tn. His wife died in July 1998.

Children of Obra Johns and Francine:

1. JAMES D. JOHNS, b. 26 Jan 1948. Lived in Jackson, Tn. 1990.
2. TRINA JOHNS, b. 10 Jan 1956. Married (1) _____ Coffman, and (2) _____ Lilly.[67] Lived in Jackson, Tn. 1990.

In 1990, Obra had five grandchildren and one great-grandchild.

* *

ZEPHANIAH JOHNS,

7- son of Jonathan John (ca 1815) and Celia, was born ca 1848 in McMinn Co., Tn. He moved to Jessamine Co., Ky., with brother Martin L. soon after the Civil War was over. He was Bondsman for the marriage of Miles M. Chandler and Lucinda Wylie 24 Dec 1868 in Jessamine Co., showing he was there by 1868, and also knew the Wileys. [Martin L. JOHNS married Sarah Bell WILEY, and marriage records say "POM -permission of marriage --Lucinda Wiley.] Zephaniah married (1) Sarah A. Hughes 3 Oct 1872 in Jessamine Co., Ky.[68]

Sarah died, and he married (2) Armenia Sterling 8 Jan 1885, Jessamine Co., Ky.[69] She was age 32 and he was 37. Armenia was sister of Elizabeth Sterling, who married Albert John. Zephaniah was a farmer and a Minister of the Gospel. See below for marriage performed as MG.

It is believed he died in Jessamine Co. around 1885/1900.[70]

Children of Zephaniah Johns and Sarah:[71]

1. JONATHAN W. JOHNS, b. Mar 1874, Madison Co., Ky.[72]
2. MARY BELLE JOHNS, b. 7 Apr 1876, Jessamine Co., Ky.[73] Married William Morgan 12 Sep 1893 in Jessamine Co.[74] This was his third marriage; he was born ca 1860 in Garrard Co., Ky. The marriage was performed by Zephaniah Johns, MG; consent by Zephaniah Johns; bond John Brock.
3. DIANA JOHNS, b. abt 1879, Tn. Twin. Zephaniah was Bondsman for the marriage of Diana Johns, age 17, to Joseph Gill, age 24, b. Garrard Co, on 29 May 1897.[75]

---

[67]Inf. from above article, and from Obra JOHNS, May 1994.
[68]Marriages of Jess. Co., Ky. 1851-1899, by Vockery, undated, p. 44. Married by William Hughes,PG. Consent by Wm. A. Hughes, Bond, Thomas Jones.
[69]Ibid. Married by Eli Reynolds, PG. Bond: Ezekiel Johns.
[70]Inf. from Mary Kathryn Harris, Ft. Worth, Tx.
[71]1880 Census Jessamine Co. Ky, Plequemine, P. 27, Sup. Distr. 4, En. 113, H.H. 245-245.
[72]Vital Statistics of Jessamine Co., Ky. Births-Marriages-Deaths 1852-1859 1874-1879, Compiled by Bill and Kathy Vockery, p. 1B.
[73]Vital Statistics...By Vockery.
[74]Marriages of Jessamine Co., Ky. 1851-1899, by Vockery, undated, p. 57.
[75]Ibid. P. 32.

4.   PATSY A. JOHNS, b. ca 1879, Tn. Twin.
* *

RUTH JANE JOHNS,
8- daughter of Jonathan John (ca 1815) and Celia, who was born ca 1849, married James BOSEMAN of Knox Co., Tn. He was a Sheriff there. She died shortly thereafter, and he remarried. They had no children.
* *

ZADOCK "DOCK" J. JOHNS,
9- son of Jonathan John (ca 1815) and Celia, who was born ca 1850, married Ruth Bowls. He was a farmer, and lived in Jessamine Co., Ky. He died in 1940.[76]
    Zadock Johns and Ruth had at least one child:
1.   MARTHA DONELLA JOHNS, b. ca 1877 in Madison Co., Ky. She married John K. Chaney, age 27, farmer, born & residing in Madison Co. 8 Sep 1897 in Jessamine Co. Bondsman was Zadock John, per Jessamine Co. Marriages.
* *

EZEKIEL JOHNS,
11- son of Jonathan John (ca 1815) and Celia, who was born May 1858, married (1) Arabelle Corn 8 Sep 1881, in Jessamine Co., Ky.[77] In 1881, he was a farmer, age 24, born in McMinn Co., Tn. She was age 17, b. Washington Co. POM William Robinson, PG, also Bondsman.

    After Arabelle died, he married (2) Nancy D. Reynolds 10 Mar 1890 in Jessamine Co.[78] Nancy was born May 1865 in Ky. [79] He was only 12 or 13 when his father Jonathan moved to Dyer Co., Tn. He went to Jessamine County, Ky. where he stayed with his brother Martin in 1880.[80] Lived in Texas [ck. Grayson Co.] for several years, from around 1891 to 1898. He moved back to Crockett Co.[81] in West Tennessee, and purchased a farm in May 1898 in the 12th District near Friendship, Tn. He sold land there in Nov 1902. Ezekiel died in Jessamine Co., Ky. 12 Sep 1927.

    Ezekiel Johns and Arabelle had the following children:
1.   MYRTLE JOHNS, b. Jul 1882.
2.   CELINA JOHNS, b. Sep 1884.
3.   FREDERICK JOHNS, b. Apr 1887. See below.

---

[76]Inf. from Morris K. DeWitt, Indianapolis, In., via Lillie Prichard.
[77]Marr. of Jessamine Co., Ky. 1851-1899 Comp. by Vockery, p. 44.
[78]Ibid. Bondsman J. J. Reynolds.
[79]1900 Census Crockett Co., Tn., 12th Distr., H.H. #70. Taken Jun 5.
[80]1880 Census Jessamine Co., Ky., ED 112, p. 27, H.H. #246-246, Distr. #15, Plaquemines.
[81]1900 Census Crockett Co., Tn.,

Children of Ezekiel Johns and Nancy:
1. CORDA [Cordelia] JOHNS, b. Sep 1891 Tx.[82]
2. INEZ JOHNS, b. Jul 1892 Tx.
3. HENRY B. JOHNS, b. May 1895 Tx.
4. CALLOWAY B. JOHNS, b. May 1897, Tx.
5. AGNES JOHNS, b. Jan 1899 Tn.
* *

FREDERICK JOHNS,
3- son of Ezekiel Johns (1858) and Arabelle, b. Apr 1887, married Carrie C. Cobb.

They had the following children:
1. JEAN C. JOHNS, b. 1909, Jessamine Co., Ky.
2. EVANDA C. JOHNS, b. 1911, Jessamine Co.
3. GENEVA WELCH JOHNS, b. 1913, Jessamine Co.
4. MYRTLE HARRIS JOHNS, b. 1917, Nicholasville.
5. SALLY BELL JOHNS, b. 1918, Nelson Co., Ky.
6. FRED WELCH JOHNS, b. 1920, Jessamine Co.
7. ELDON BLACKSTONE JOHNS, b. 1922, Nicholasville.[83]
* *

---

[82]Per Morris K. DeWitt, Indianapolis, In.
[83]Inf. from Jean C. Johns, 216 W. Elm St., Nicholasville, Ky.

CHAPTER EIGHTEEN

BENJAMIN EDMUND JOHNS and descendants:
(Most of the information in this chapter previously appeared in "The Browder Connections" which was published in 1995 by Heritage Books, Inc.)

BENJAMIN EDMUND JOHNS,
10- son of Jonathan Johns (ca 1815) and Celia, b. Nov 1853, married 1) Nancy Janeway 24 Dec 1875 in Gibson Co., Tn.[1] She was born 13 Sep 1860, the daughter of Isaac Janeway and Celina Caroline ("Saliney") Janeway of Knox County, Tn. We believe Isaac descended from Thomas Janeway, a well-known Quaker preacher. Thomas arrived in Philadelphia with his family 27 Sept 1683 on the ship "Endeavor" from Liverpool. He was from Pownall Fee and of Styall, Cheshire, Great Britain. They settled on 300 acres in Bucks Co., Pa.

Isaac Janeway moved from Grainger Co., Tn., and farmed in the 16th District in Knox Co. His brother Joseph was a minister who also settled in this area. Isaac's wife, called "Saliney," died about 1871, and he sold his farm and moved to Knoxville. He married 2) Sarah J. Wright on 3 Sep 1871 in Knox Co. Daughter Nancy went to Alamo, Tn. and stayed about a year with her sister Maggie King. There, she married Ben Edmund.

My Grandmother, Mattie Johns Lovelace, told me that her mother Nancy, whom she called "Nanny", told me this: 'Nanny was very young when the Civil War was going on. Her father Isaac opposed the War, and Federal troops occupied the state. He didn't want to serve in the Federal army [possibly due to his Quaker background] so he and other men in the area hid out in the woods so they wouldn't be taken to serve.

The soldiers from both sides would forage over the countryside taking fodder and livestock. She said once, when she was 4 or 5, the Union soldiers came and searched their house and gathered up their fodder, chickens and livestock. They first searched inside their large eight-day clock, looking for money or valuables. Her mother was afraid they would take all their money, which she had hidden on top of the clock. She called the soldiers in and fed them some pies she had baked. While they were eating, she moved the money inside the clock where they had already searched. They didn't find it, although they went back and looked on top of the clock. As the soldiers left, some hay fell off a wagon, and Nanny ran out and started to pick it up. They saw her, and made her leave it alone, and they took that too.'

---

[1]Marriage Book B, p. 307.

Isaac Janeway filed a claim against the Federal Government after the Civil War, for the livestock, etc. that were taken by these soldiers. And believe it or not, the claim (or most of what he filed for) was paid, although it was after his death and 20 years later, when his estate was settled.

Ben Edmond Johns was a farmer, and owned 175 acres in the 11th Civil District in Crockett Co., Tn. Nancy died 17 Feb 1913 in Crockett Co. She was buried in Mt. Zion Cemetery, Friendship, Tn.

He married (2) Sadie Della Cross Thompson 27 Jan 1914, Crockett Co., Tn.[2] She was widow of Charles Thompson and had three children. Ben Edmond died of pneumonia soon after, on 11 Apr 1914, and was buried in Mt. Zion Cemetery. Sadie received 12 1/2 acres of Ben Edmond's farm as dower rights. She married again, (3) C. M. Greer 31 Dec 1915, and had five Greer children.

Children of Ben Edmond Johns and Nancy:
1. NOAH WALTER JOHNS b. 26 Aug 1877, Dyer Co., Tn.
2. ISABELLE "Belle" JOHNS b. 14 Oct 1879, Dyer Co., Tn.
3. BENJAMIN JOHNS, b. 9 May 1882, Tn. Died 26 Oct 1900.
4. MATTIE [Martha] PEARL JOHNS, b. 23 Oct 1884, Gibson Co., Tn.
5. CARLOS C. JOHNS, b. 22 Jul 1887, Dyer or Crockett Co., Tn.
6. CLARENCE B. JOHNS, b. 11 May 1889, Dyer or Crockett Co., Tn.
7. LOVIE [Lavicey] JOHNS, b. 31 May 1891, Tn. Died 31 Oct 1891.
8. EULA JOHNS, b. 28 Nov 1892, Crockett Co., Tn.
9. LENA JOHNS, b. 17 Oct 1894, Crockett Co., Tn.
* *

Deed Book O, p. 741, Crockett Co., Tn.:
Deed from J. C. Harnlett, Trustee, to B. E. Johns, for 75 acres, Oct. 18, 1902.
Deed Book D, p. 664, Crockett Co., Tn.:
Deed from D. W. Knox & Daisey Knox to B. E. Johns, for 100 acres, Nov. 16, 1905.
Deed Book V, p. 733, Crockett Co., Tn.:
Deed from Walter Johns, et al, to Mrs. Sadie Johns, widow of Ben Edmond Johns, for 12 1/2 acres in 11th Civil District where he was living at the time of his Death.
* *

KNOX CO., TN.
ESTATE BOOK VOL. 20 July 1879-Sept. 1884 Page 554:
Tues June 3rd 1884
J. F. J. Lewis Clerk

Isaac B. Janeway

Inventory of the estate of Isaac B. Janeway dec'd.
One claim against the U. S. Government

---

[2]Bondsman T. A. Privett; married by W. C. James, J.P.

for the sum of one hundred and sixty six
dollars on which I received one hundred
and eighteen dollars and eighty five cents $ 118.85

One note on Wm. H. Doane on which I took
judgment before M. Cate, Esq. on the 20th of
Feb 1879 for the sum of $94.00 but he
have no property subject to execution
I have not been able to make the money.

One note on G. W. Brown on which I took
judgment before M. Cate Esq. on the 20th of
Feb 1879 for the sum of $32.75 which I
have not been able to find any property
subject to execution.
Received on his Fathers estate from G. W.
Pickel Attorney.   50.00

      This 30th of April 1884. A. C. E. Callen Adm.
I do swear that the foregoing is a just true and perfect Inventory
of the goods and chattels belonging to the estate of Isaac B. Janeway
deceased.   A. C. E. Callen
Sworn to before me this
April 30th 1884.   J. F. J. Lewis Clerk
* *

Page 577
July Term 1884.
Isaac B. Janeway
Settlement with A. C. E. Callin Administrator of Isaac B. Janeway.
Admr Dr.
To amt rec'd as per Inventory $ 168.85
Admr Cr.
By paid Clk for Letters of Administration $ 3.00

1. '	J. F. Lewis Clk	.50
2. '	J. M. Hammer	3.00
3. '	Thos. Reeder	2.00
4. '	J. F. J. Lewis Clk.	1.00
5. '	S. C. Janeway	15.00
6. '	S. M. Janeway	15.00
7. '	N.J. Janeway now wife of Be. Johns	15.00
8. '	G. W. Pickell	15.00
9. '	Sarah J. Griffin	15.00
10.'	Callie Janeway	5.50
11.'	Jane Griffin	5.50
12.'	I. D. Janeway	5.50

13.'	Maggie King	5.50	
14.'	Nanie Janeway wife of B.E. Johns	5.50	
15.'	I. D. Janeway	15.00	
'	Allowance to Admnr.	20.00	
'	Paid Clk this a/c & notices	3.00	150.50
	Amt. due estate Apl 30 1884		$ 18.35

Account taken and stated on notices
this April 30, 1884.   J.F.J. Lewis Clk. By M. H. McCerkle
Examined and Confirmed this 17 day of July 1884.

J.M. King,   Chairman.

* *

Nanny's siblings were Sarah, Susannah, Isaac DeWitt, Margaret (Maggie), and Caroline (Callie). Mary E. and Benjamin were in the 1850 Knox census, but not listed afterwards. Sarah Jane married James H. Griffin 31 Dec 1879, Knox; Callie married Richard Leeke 15 Oct 1884; Isaac DeWitt Janeway married Minerva Thompson 7 Dec 1871; Maggie married _____ King, possibly in Gibson Co.

* *

NOAH WALTER JOHNS,

1-son of Ben Edmund Johns (1854) and Nancy, b. 26 Aug 1877, married (1) Lula Griggs 26 Sep 1898 in Crockett Co., Tn.[3] She was born Jul 1882 in Crockett Mills, Tn. He was a farmer in Crockett Co.

Lula died, and he married (2) Lina Espey. Lina died Apr 1915 of pneumonia, and was buried in Nash Cemetery, Dyer Co., located near Friendship, Tn. Walter married (3) Mary Dempsey. Walter Johns died 20 Dec 1937,[4] of kidney failure. Children of Walter Johns and Lula:

1. CALLIE MAY JOHNS, b. 28 Jul 1900, Crockett Co., Tn. She died 15 Jun 1980, and was buried in West Frankfort, Ill.
2. EZEKIEL JOHNS, b. 1902, Crockett Co., Tn. M. Alma Barnard. She was b. ca 1902; the daughter of John W. and Lula C. Barnard. He d. 11 Sep 1977.
3. DEWITT "Dee" JOHNS, b. 1906 Crockett Co. Tn. Never married. He d. 3 Dec 1953 in Memphis of t.b. Buried Sudbury Cemetery.

* *

Children of Walter Johns and Lina:
1. HERSHEL PRESTON JOHNS, b. 12 Jun 1911, Crockett Co., Tn.
2. GLADYS MAYOLA JOHNS, b. 17 Sep 1914, Crockett Co., Tn.

* *

CALLIE MAY JOHNS,

1- dau of Walter Johns (1877) and Lula, married (1) John Trotter. Their children:

---

[3]Married by J.M. Moody, M.G. B.F. Burnett, bondsman.
[4]Inf. from Lillie Prichard of Friendship,Tn.

1. JOHN W. TROTTER. Died age 2.
2. LILY MAY TROTTER. B. 1 Mar 1920, Blytheville, Miss. Co., Ark.
   Married John Rice. Their children: (1) ROBERTA RICE, b. and d. 20
   Sep 1940, and (2) SUSAN RICE, b. 28 Sep 1943.

* *

She married (2) Louis Edgar [George] Smith. Their children were:
1. CHARLES EDGAR SMITH, b. 12 Oct 1923, Charleston, Mo.
2. MYRTLE AILEEN SMITH, b. 3 Jul 1924, Charleston, Mo. Married
   Carl Falk. Their child: CARL FALK. She died ca 1942, Ill.
3. GEORGE EDGAR SMITH Jr., b. 14 Jul 1930, Wyatt, Mo. Married Ceil
   _____. Children: a) LINDA SMITH; b) BARBARA SMITH, and c)
   dau, name unknown. George Edgar Jr. died in 1990 or 1991 in Las
   Vegas, Nv.
4. MARY "Coopie" ERNASTINE SMITH, b. 14 Feb 1925, Bloomington,
   Il. Married: _____ Starsky. Child: CAROL ANN STARSKY. She
   lived in Ca. (1994).
5. HERBERT LEE SMITH, b. 1 Aug 1935, Charleston, Mo. Married Mary
   _____. Lived in Las Vegas, Nv. (1994).
6. ADA ANN SMITH, b. 1 Oct 1939, Thompsonville, Il. Married (1) Glen
   Maddox; child: JEFFREY MADDOX. She married (2) Bud Broman.
   Child: STACY ANN BROMAN.

Callie May Johns Trotter Smith married (3) Hugh Rich.
* *

CHARLES EDGAR SMITH,

1-son of Callie May Smith and George, b. 12 Oct 1923, married (1) Mildred
Marguerite Hefner 9 Nov 1940 at Jackson, Mo. She was b. 22 Feb 1920.
He was a truck driver. He married (2) Maybelle Longmire. He died of
brain cancer 27 Mar 1975. The children of Charles Edgar Smith and
Mildred:
1. KATHERINE ANN SMITH, b. 12 Dec 1941.
2. CHARLES KENNETH SMITH, b. 26 Mar 1944.
3. SHARON SUE SMITH, b. 15 Nov 1945.
4. ROBERT WAYNE SMITH, b. 6 Oct 1947. Married (1) Diane Pattera;
   no children. He married (2) Renee _____. Children: a) ROSALIE
   SMITH, and b) ROSEMARIE SMITH.
5. RICHARD LEROY SMITH, b. 2 Mar 1949. Married Cathleen Frances
   Pattera, sister of Diane Pattera (above). They divorced.
6. FRED EUGENE SMITH, b. 26 Mar 1950. Married Beverly _____.
   Child: a) JESSICA SMITH, who m. _____ Bentley, and her children are:
   1) MONICA RENEE BENTLEY, b. 17 Dec 1987; and 2) BRITTNEY
   BENTLEY, b. 17 Apr 1991.

* *

The children of Charles Edgar Smith and Maybelle:
1. CHARLES EDGAR SMITH Jr.

2. RONALD WAYNE SMITH, b. 17 Nov 1955.

* *

KATHERINE ANN SMITH,

1- dau of Charles Edgar Smith and Mildred Marguerite, b. 12 Dec 1941, married John Ortiz 30 Aug 1958.
Children:

1 - DIANA Lynn ORTIZ, b. 28 Feb 1959, m. (1) Michael Slawson. Their children:

  1) BARBARA ANN SLAWSON, b. 5 Aug 1981.

  2) HOLLY MARIE SLAWSON, b. 24 Sep 1983.

  3) MICHAEL ALAN SLAWSON, b. 22 Jan 1985.

Diana Ortiz married (2) Michael Wittman in 1990.

2 - LAWRENCE "Larry" WAYNE ORTIZ, b. 30 Jun 1960. Married (1) Inez Thomas. Their children:

  1) LAWRENCE WAYNE ORTIZ Jr., b. 12 Jul 1978.

  2) NONA ANN ORTIZ, b. 15 Oct 1980.

  3) JOHN RICHARD WILLIAM ORTIZ, b. 12 Jan 1982.

Lawrence [Larry] Ortiz married (2) Ada Rivera. Their child: Joshua Ortiz, b. 5 Apr 1984.

* *

CHARLES KENNETH SMITH,

2- son of Charles Edgar Smith and Marguerite, b. 26 Mar 1944, married (1) Davina Berg. Child:

1 - GEOFFREY SMITH, b. 11 Jun 1969. Geoffrey married Debbie _____.
Their children are: 1) KELLY KATHLEEN SMITH, b. 15 May 1990, and 2) COURTNEY SMITH, b. 2 Sep 1993.

  Charles Kenneth Smith married (2) Kathleen Frances Marley.
Their children are:

1 - MATTHEW MARLEY SMITH, b. 16 Feb 1980; and

2 - MEGAN KATHLEEN SMITH, b. 17 Apr. 1982.

He adopted Kathleen Frances' daughter Gayle Lynn Grammer, who was b. 11 May 1966.

* *

SHARON SUE SMITH,

3- dau of Charles Edgar Smith and Marguerite, b. 15 Nov 1945, married Dennis Salvatore Rizzo 21 Aug 1965. Sharon works for a travel agency, and does a lot of travelling. Her husband is a Police Officer in Chicago, Il. Their children:

1. CHARLES ANTHONY RIZZO, b. 19 Jul 1966. Married Julie Ann VanEck 28 Oct 1989. Child: MORGAN ELISE RIZZO, b. 22 Dec 1992. They have another child born in 1994. Charles Anthony Rizzo is a chemist at University of Illinois, Chicago campus. He has a Masters

Degree in Public Health and Safety from the University of Illinois. His wife Julie Ann is an advertising executive.
2. WENDY ANN RIZZO, b. 10 Jan 1972. Married Brian Charles Bergman 12 Jun 1993. Child: REBECCA ELIZABETH BERGMANN, b. 19 Jul 1994. Wendy received a degree in Social Work at the University of Illinois, Champaign/Urbana, Il. Brian is a Nuclear Engineer with COM ED.

* *

HERSHEL PRESTON JOHNS,

1- son of Walter Johns (1877) and Lina, b. 12 Jun 1911, married Naomi Ruth Alley 18 Dec 1936. He was a farmer and member of Macedonia Baptist Church.[5] He died at Baptist Memorial Hospital in Ripley, Lauderdale Co., Tn., 21 Feb 1992. He was buried in Ripley Memorial Gardens. Their children:
1. WALTER PRESTON "Wally" JOHNS, b. 29 Dec 1937. Married Bonnie Lee Borik 10 Oct 1959. She was b. 23 Apr 1939. Child: MARILYN ANN JOHNS b. 10 Dec 1961; who married Mark Schmucker 9 Jun 1984. He was b. 14 Dec 1956. Their children: 1) BROOKE LEE SCHMUCKER, b. 24 Sep 1985; and 2) JEREMY JOHNS SCHMUCKER, b. 11 Nov 1987. Lived in Lockport, Ill. 1992.
2. JAMES GARLAND JOHNS, b. 4 Nov 1940. Married Millie Ione Simpson 15 Feb 1963. She was b. 10 May 1941. Their children:
   a) TAMMY MODENE JOHNS, b. 5 Jul 1965; m. Rodney Brent WALKER 28 Mar 1992; he was b. 30 May 1962.
   b) JAMES GREGORY "Greg" JOHNS, b. 15 Jan 1969; m. Jana Lynn Rice 7 Dec 1991; she was b. 12 May 1969.
   c) GARLAND WADE JOHNS, b. 20 Dec 1970.
   Lived in Collierville in 1992.
3. LARRY SAMUEL JOHNS b. 5 Sep 1944. Married Sandra Lee Meade 30 Jan 1967; two children: a) LARRY SAMUEL JOHNS Jr., b. 20 May 1968. b) AMY LEE JOHNS, b. 18 Sep 1971.   Lived in Gates in 1992.
4. ANNIE KARYN JOHNS, b. 30 Mar 1946. Married Jerry Thomas Summar 17 Apr 1965. Children:
   a) JERRY THOMAS SUMMAR Jr., b. 8 Mar 1970; m. Stephanie Leigh Rains 7 Oct 1988. She was b. 27 Aug 1971; Child: STEPHEN THOMAS SUMMAR, b. 20 Sep 1989.
   b) ROSEANNA RUTH SUMMAR, b. 5 Aug 1972.
   c) ROBERT HERSHEL "Robbie" SUMMAR, b. 8 May 1975.
   d) JOHNA KARYN SUMMAR, b. 7 Aug 1986.

* *

GLADYS MAYOLA JOHNS,

---

[5]Obituary The Lauderdale Voice, Wed. Feb 26, 1992.

2- daughter of Walter Johns (1877) and Lina, b. 17 Sep 1914, m. 1) Roscoe
B. Alley Jr. 27 Oct 1934. Roscoe was brother of Naomi Alley who married
Hershel Preston Johns. He died of a heart attack. She m. 2) Gene Forner 22
Feb 1969; divorced. She married (3) Robert Frederick Matile 14 Jun 1973.
He died Jun 1988. Gladys d. 29 May 1994 in Terre Haute, In., of heart
disease. She was bu. in Memorial Gardens Cemetery, Ripley. She had 13
grandchildren and 11 great-grandchildren.[6]
Children of Gladys Mayola Alley and Roscoe:
1. JERRY SCOTT ALLEY, b. 3 Jan 1937. Married Marlene Kopeck Jul
   1955. He died 21 Oct 1984 of enlarged heart.
   Children:
   a) RONNIE SCOTT ALLEY, b. 4 Apr 1956.
   b) PATRICE LEE ALLEY, b. Nov 1957/58.
   c) TRESSA JEAN ALLEY, b. 28 Jul 1964.
   d) LISA MARIE ALLEY, b. 17 Jan 1968.
   e) KEVIN CRAIG ALLEY, b. 23 Oct 1969.
2. ALVIN NOAH ALLEY, b. 16 Dec 1939. Married 1) Phillis Abbot,
   1960; divorced; child: STEVEN ALLEY, b. 14 Feb 1961. Married 2)
   Betty Milton 15 Feb 1965, divorced; child: MICHAEL WAYNE
   ALLEY, b. 21 Nov 1965. Married 3) Betty Bradford 4 Jul 1968.
   Children: a) TONI JANE ALLEY, b. 19 May 1970. b) KERRI LYNN
   ALLEY, b. 22 Jun 1976. Lived near Halls, Tn. 1994.
3. LENNIA "Lynn" MAI ALLEY, b. 28 Aug 1960. Married 1) Leslie
   Leasure 1959; 2) Norm Heiman 1 Jul 1966; 3) _____ _____; divorced;
   4) James Van Hook. Lived in Fontanet, In. 1994.
4. BARBARA ANN ALLEY, b. 9 Sep 1947. Married 1) Stephen James
   "Jim" Lang, 1965, divorced. Children:
   a) KRISTINE MARIE "Kris" LANG, b. 4 Nov 1966.
   b) STEPHEN JAMES LANG, b. 20 Apr 1968.
   Married 2) Dave Hos 16 Dec 1978. No children. Lived Terre Haute, In.
   1994.
* *

ISABELLE "BELLE" JOHNS,
2- daughter of Ben Edmund Johns (1854) and Nancy, b. 14 Oct 1879,
married Turner A. Privett 25 Jan 1902 in Crockett Co., Tn. He was the son
of Samuel Levy Privett and Delilah Frances Ward; was b. 15 Mar 1878, Tn.
He farmed near Friendship in Crockett Co. They moved near Blytheville,
Mississippi Co., Ark., in Jan 1928, because of the 1927 flood. His
daughter, Gracie, said when they moved, there were such huge chunks of
ice on the Mississippi River that the ferry couldn't cross, and they had to

---

[6]Obituary, sent by Elbert Johns, Louisville, Ky. No date or paper name given.
Information on this family compiled by Naomi Johns, 3/94, and received from
Virginia Smith, of Friendship, Tn.

return to Friendship, spend the night, then went to Memphis to cross over the bridge. Turner d. 1 Feb 1943 and was bu. Pond Creek Methodist Cemetery, Alamo. Belle Johns died in 19__ in Hayti, Mo. She was bu. in the Blytheville Cemetery.

Children of Belle Johns Privett and Turner:

1. FRED PRIVETT, b. 9 Jan 1903, Friendship, Tn.
2. FRANK PRIVETT, b. 1905, Crockett Co., Tn. Married Lizzie Pulley. Frank died 19__ in Blytheville, Ark., and was buried there in Chickasaw Cemetery.
3. HERSHEL LEVI PRIVETT, b. 29 Aug 1906, Crockett Co., Tn. Married Leah Ardelia Riley 22 Aug 1922, Brownsville, Haywood Co., Tn. Died 19 Dec 1995, at the age of 89 years.
4. J. C. PRIVETT, b. ca 1909, Crockett Co., Tn. See below.
5. WILLIAM BROWDER PRIVETT, b. 30 Mar 1914, Crockett Co., Tn. Married Berlin _____, in Blytheville, Ark. She was b. in Mt. View, Ark. William Browder Privett died Jan 1993 in Hayti, Pemiscot Co., Mo.
6. GRACE B. PRIVETT, b. 31 May 1915, Chestnut Bluff, Crockett Co., Tn. Married 1) Buddie Cochran, Blytheville, Ark. He was b. 1907/1908. Married 2) Herman Storey, founder of the chain of Storey Markets. He died, and she married (3) Charles Lipford , who also died. Now lives in Rector, Ark. (1993), and reverted to Storey name. No children.
7. PERCY PRIVETT, b. 3 Sep 1922, Crockett Co., Tn. Married Pauline _____.

* *

FRED PRIVETT,

1- son of Belle Johns Privett (1879) and Turner, b. 9 Jan 1903, married Ethel Jones 30 Aug 1921 in Crockett Co., Tn.[7] Ethel was b. 9 Feb 1906, the daughter of James Jones and Rosie Davis. Fred died of cancer 24 Dec 1986 at Halls, Lauderdale Co., Tn. and was buried in Halls Cemetery.

Their children were:

1. MARINE PRIVETT, [pronounced Maureen] b. 16 Nov 1922, Friendship, Crockett Co., Tn.
2. HAZEL PRIVETT, b. 9 Jul 1924, Friendship, Crockett Co., Tn.
3. ESTALLE E. PRIVETT, b. 25 Apr 1926, Friendship, Crockett Co., Tn.
4. WANDA PRIVETT, b. 11 Sep 1929, Friendship, Crockett Co., Tn.
5. FRED PRIVETT Jr., b. 17 Mar 1931, Friendship, Crockett Co., Tn.
6. WILBUR FRANKLIN PRIVETT, b. 3 Apr 1933, Friendship, Crockett Co., Tn.

* *

MARINE PRIVETT,

---

[7]Married by Sam Young, J.P.; J. H. Kee, Bondsman.

1- daughter Fred Privett and Ethel, b. 16 Nov 1922, married (1) Clyde
Lucas. She married (2) James B. Johnson. He was b. 8 Aug 1928, the son
of G. W. & Kathlene Johnson.
The children of Marine Privett Lucas and Clyde were:
1. JUDY ELAINE LUCAS, b. 23 Oct 1944, Memphis, Tn. Married Larry
    Sutton. Child: LEAH SUTTON, b. 22 Aug 1967.
2. DAN CLYDE LUCAS, b. 17 Oct 1950, Memphis, Tn. Married Brenda
    Oakley.
* *

HAZEL PRIVETT,
2- daughter of Fred Privett and Ethel, b. 9 Jul 1924, married Jesse Jones 1
May 1945, Memphis, Tn.
Children:
1. RONNIE JONES, b. 24 Jan 1948, Memphis, Tn. Married Daphne
    Thomas 9 Dec 1967. Children: a) JENNIFER JONES;. b) TIFFANY
    JONES; and c) HEATHER JONES.
2. GARY JONES. Married Judy Simmons 3 May 1970. Children: a)
    HOLLIE JONES; b) MARC JONES.
3. TERRY JONES, b. 15 Oct 1957, Memphis, Tn. Married Pamela Melvin
    6 Feb 1981. Child: JESSICA JONES.
* *

ESTALLE E. PRIVETT,
3- daughter of Fred Privett and Ethel, b. 25 Apr 1926, married D. J. Lumley
31 Dec 1943. He was b. 14 Mar 1925, Friendship, Tn. He died 31 Dec
1986, and was bu in Woodhaven Cemetery, Millington, Tn.
Their child:
1. MICHAEL DAVID LUMLEY, b. 4 Sep 1953, Memphis, Tn. He
    married _____ _____. Their children: a) LORI LUMLEY, b. 9 Oct 1975,
    Memphis, Tn.; b) TINA LUMLEY, b. 23 Jan 1981, Memphis, Tn.; c)
    KRISTEN LUMLEY, b. 24 Jan 1984, Memphis, Tn.
* *

WANDA GERALDINE PRIVETT,
4- daughter of Fred Privett and Ethel, b. 11 Sep 1929, m. David Fennell 12
Jun 1948, Hernando, Ms. He was b. 14 Feb 1927, Crockett Co., Tn., the
son of Neut Fennell and Ada Reece. Wanda lived in Collierville, Tn. She
d. 24 Apr 1995, and was bu. 26 Apr in Forrest Hills Cemetery, Memphis.
Their children are:
1. DAVID MARTIN FENNELL, b. 24 Feb 1957, Memphis, Tn. Married
    Rebecca Cauldwell 6 Feb 1988. Children: a) MELISSA FENNELL, b. 7
    Sep 1979; b) DANA NICOLE FENNELL, b. 2 Sep 1983; c) DAVID
    AUSTIN FENNELL, b. 29 Nov 1989; d) CHELSEA ALANA
    FENNELL, b. 18 Apr 1992.

2. DANA LANG FENNELL, b. 10 Jan 1961, Memphis, Tn. Died 22 Oct 1980, Piperton, Tn.

* *

FRED PRIVETT JR.,

4- son of Fred Privett and Ethel, b. 17 Mar 1931, married 1) Claudean Garner and 2) Ethylene _____ 2 Aug 1989, Memphis, Tn. Ethylene was b. 25 Aug 1930, Itawamba, Ms.

Children of Fred Privett Jr. and Claudean:

1. SHERRY DEAN PRIVETT, b. 28 Oct 1950, Memphis, Tn. Married Richard Bell. He was b. 2 Mar 1947. Children: a) RICHARD BELL II, b. 10 Aug 1973; b) KIM BELL, b. 22 Jun 1976.
2. BETTY LORRAINE PRIVETT, b. 12 Sep 1956, Memphis, Tn. Married Roy Taylor. He was b. 28 Apr 1958. Their children: a) MANDY TAYLOR, b. 8 Apr 1978; b) ROY TAYLOR III, b. 14 May 1979; c) RONNIE TAYLOR, b. 13 Apr 1982; d) JEREMY TAYLOR, b. 3 Jul 1985.
3. FRED PRIVETT III, b. 3 Oct 1957, Memphis, Tn. Married 1) Donna Gail _____. She was b. 25 Feb 1960. Children: a) SHANNON GAIL PRIVETT, b. 12 Mar 1977; b) VANESSA PRIVETT, b. 3 Nov. 1979; c) FRED PRIVETT IV, b. 2 Sep 1983.
   Fred Privett III married 2) Christefer _____ 16 May 1987. Their child: JAMES ALLEN PRIVETT, b. 16 Sep 1988.
4. EDWARD MORRIS PRIVETT, b. 30 Jan 1959, b. 30 Jan 1959, Memphis, Tn. Married Vicky _____. She was b. 21 Jan 1958. Their children: a) HEATHER PRIVETT, b. 18 Jul 1985; b) EDWARD MORRIS PRIVETT Jr., b. 19 Jun 1987.

* *

WILBUR FRANKLIN PRIVETT,

6-son of Fred Privett and Ethel, b. 3 Apr 1933; m. Peggy Jean Robison 23 Sep 1950, Tn. She was b. 24 Mar 1934, Halls, Lauderdale, Tn., the daughter of John Robison and Bertha Reese.

Their children were:

1. PAMELA KAY PRIVETT, b. 12 Oct 1951, Memphis, Tn. Married Thomas Verna. Children: a) MARIA KAY VERNA, b. 20 Mar 1976, Memphis, Tn.; b) THOMAS MARK VERNA, b. 12 Nov 1980, Memphis, Tn.; c) ANTHONY BRIAN VERNA, b. 3 Sep 1982, Memphis, Tn.
2. DEBORAH JEAN PRIVETT, b. Apr 1954, Memphis, Tn. Married Clay M. Dean, 26 Sep 1975. He was b. 26 Sep 1975. Their children: a) CLAY FRANKLIN DEAN, b. 30 Mar 1978, Memphis, Tn.; b) LAURIN McLEOD DEAN, b. 4 Jul 1982, Memphis.
3. SUSAN GAIL PRIVETT, b. 7 Jul 1956, Memphis, Tn. Married 1) Melvin Demuth. Married 2) _____ Cordner. Their children: a)

MATTHEW M. CORDNER, b. 17 Oct 1976, Memphis, Tn.; b) JESSICA NICOLE CORDNER, b. 12 Sep 1978, Memphis, Tn.

* *

J. C. PRIVETT,

4- son of Belle Privett and Turner, b. ca 1909, was drafted as a soldier in the U.S. Army in W.W. II, and was killed during the War in Luxembourg at the Battle of The Bulge in Dec 1944. He was with Gen. Patton's Army. He was married to Rachel COCHRAN and had eight children. They resided in Blytheville, Ark. at the time of his death. Friends and the people of Blytheville built a house for the family and donated it after he was killed. A ten room house was built, furnished and decorated. A garden, orchard and poultryyard were made, and a playground for the children was built.[8] My grandmother Mattie Lovelace had a couple of newspaper articles regarding this [undated], and also a picture of the house. His body was returned and he was buried in Blytheville, Ark.

* *

MATTIE PEARL JOHNS,

4- daughter of BEN EDMUND JOHNS (1854) and Nancy, b. 23 Oct 1884, Crockett Co., Tn., m. Albert LOVELACE 17 Jul 1904, Friendship, Crockett Co., Tn. Albert was b. 26 Dec 1876 at Alamo, Crockett Co., Tn.; he was son of John W. Lovelace and Adeline Taylor. They were descended from a pioneer family that previously lived in South Carolina. His great-grandfather Francis came to Lauderdale County near Ripley, Tn. before 1860. [I don't yet know if they are descendants of the Francis Lovelace who was Penn's Governor in Pa.]

Albert rented a farm on Leggett School House Road near Chestnut Bluff in Crockett Co., Tn.[9] He farmed and also drove to Dyersburg in his wagon once a week and hauled freight back to the stores at Chestnut Bluff. His daughter Lillie said he drove two mules he called Alex and Kate.

They lived in Tn. until the Great Flood of 1927, when the Mississippi River overflowed its banks and devastated a wide area. Their family (including husbands of their daughters) had to flee the area in a wagon. They crossed the river by ferry to Mo., taking Grandma's Bible, and only a small amount of furnishings, such as quilts, a feather mattress, and some of their livestock. Cordie's husband Will HOLMES found an old house with only a cook stove in it to spend the night. The men returned to bring back furniture, which they loaded on to the ferry. The water was swift and the dirt cliff collapsed. This caused the ferry to tip over, spilling everything into the river. They managed to get back across the river, then spent the night camping-out in the old house.

---

[8]Newspaper article, undated, kept by Mattie Lovelace.
[9]1920 Census Crockett Co. Tn., Civil District #13, H.H. #217, Sheet No. 10 B.

Mattie's daughters Reba and Lillie tell of this. Reba says she still remembers the smoky house, as the stove and fireplace were old and the chimney was not drawing properly. Mattie tried to make biscuits on the old stove, and they never cooked properly, but they were so hungry they ate them anyway. Mattie and Albert slept on the floor on the feather mattress, and the rest slept on quilts on the floor. The next day, they all rented a house together in Caruthersville, Mo. for a brief time. Then they moved near Blytheville, Ark., where they leased land at an area called New Liberty. Lillie's husband Bob found a job working in Blytheville. There was no government aid in those days, and they went through a tough time. In their later years, Mattie and Albert moved to Scott Co., Mo., to be near their grown children.

Mattie Johns Lovelace was my maternal grandmother. It has been 31 years since she died, yet I have very vivid memories of her. She inspired a lot of loyalty and love. When she appeared with her sisters, all dressed up wearing their hats and gloves, they always reminded me of the classic version of genteel, Southern ladies. They all enjoyed men and were flirtatious. They seemed to possess all the virtues of womankind. They were excellent cooks, kept a spotless house, made beautiful quilts, could crochet and embroider colorful linen, canned delicious food, trusted in God and were regular churchgoers, and loved to entertain.

They were all dainty, frail women except Aunt Bell. Aunt Bell was small, but in comparison, she seemed stronger. They were all entertaining talkers and loved to tell jokes and funny events. I doubt if any of them ever weighed a hundred pounds. Most people called her "Miss Mattie" in the Southern way, until later in life when she became "Grandma" to most. Grandma had dark brown hair and vivid blue eyes. She said her hair had never been cut, and she wore it in a bun pulled up with pins in back.

Grandma had a few critics, among them my father, who maintained she had a will of iron. She went to the doctor on a frequent basis. My Dad maintained that since he first met them, she could be on her deathbed, but when Albert hitched up the buggy, she was the first one in it. My Dad's comments were a source of amusement to us, but we always loved and respected Grandma. One of the characteristics of the Johns women, it seems to me, is that they have very strong wills, a trait not to be ashamed of.

We spent some of our holidays at her house and at the aunts nearby, as that was where all the connections gathered. At that time, the Christmas holidays lasted for several weeks or so it seemed. Everyone gathered near Grandma's and cooked and consumed large meals for quite some time. Since some of the men farmed, I suppose the women and children could take a few weeks off, or perhaps it just seemed that way because schools were out a couple of weeks for the holidays and it was a more leisurely era.

Grandma had a very strong sense of family, was extremely religious and churchgoing. She was a devout Baptist and enjoyed reading the Bible and discussing it. She never complained about her life, and trusted God to look out for her. She loved people and entertaining. She always had a large group of people at her house for dinner on Sundays after church. She could be found in the kitchen, laughing and talking as she cooked. I remember how happy she was in the 1950's telling me about having 38 people for a recent Sunday dinner. She had a surprising number of young people who visited her and enjoyed being around her. At both their 50th and 60th Wedding Anniversary celebrations, an Open House was held and they entertained hundreds of people. At the time of their 60th Anniversary [July 1964], they had 25 grandchildren and 42 great-grandchildren.

Being interested in family history, I once asked her if her family had fought in the War Between the States. With a sweet smile, she replied in her soft voice, "No, Honey, they all hid out." I found this amusing, and was surprised to find during my research that this seemed to apply only to her Grandfather Janeway (who descended from a Quaker family that arrived in Phila. in 1683.) I suppose she based this belief on stories told to her about him by her mother, Nanny Janeway Johns. Her father Ben Edmund had been too young to be involved in the Civil War.

Grandma was one of the prime movers in starting The Family Reunion. After the crops were laid by in 1922, Grandma and Grandpa visited relatives near Friendship, Tn., travelling there by wagon. A group of them took wagons to Reelfoot Lake and camped out for two nights. They cooked together and spread the food out on tablecloths. They enjoyed this very much, and did this again a few times. This led to the idea of later gatherings for the Family Reunion.

After the Great Flood of 1927 when many of the family left Tn. and settled in Ark. and Mo., it was very difficult to visit each other for some time. Grandma and Aunt Eula exchanged letters and set up a date to meet for a Family Reunion in the fall after crops were laid by. I'm not sure of the exact year this function began as an all-inclusive Family Reunion, although it seems from earliest memories of most to have always occurred, but it was probably around the early 1930's. They continued it each year, writing to each other to set the date and expanding it to include more connections. Some of the relatives were reluctant to cross the Mississippi River, as the nearest way to cross was by ferryboat. Even so, during only a few years was this reunion not held.

As the years passed, more people joined in, and I remember Mother saying that for awhile they alternated each year as to which side of the river they met. I remember reunions in Hayti, Mo. During World War II, the meeting was held at Heloise Landing, west of Dyersburg, Tn. For a number of years now, it has been held at Buford Ellington Hall at Reelfoot Lake around the first Sunday in August. Connections come from Ky., Ill., Mo., Ark., Tenn., Okla., Calif., Mich., In., Fla., Tex. and other states. With plenty of bridges over the Mississippi, crossing the River is no longer a barrier, but it is still hard to maintain family contact, and I hope this Reunion continues. However, I would prefer the date be changed to the 1st Sunday in September, because it would make it easier to drive from Ca. if we could avoid the heat of summer.

Grandma was frail, yet she survived a bad car wreck and an appendectomy in her sixties and lived to be almost 83. She had a malignant tumor in her stomach, and was responding to treatment when I visited her several times in the hospital at Cape Girardeau, Mo. She told me of a dream she had, and her face was radiant as she told me. She said Jesus held out his arms and she ran into them and he held her. I had to return to California and soon after, she had a stroke, then was transferred to the hospital at Sikeston. Grandma Mattie Johns Lovelace died 19 Aug 1967 and was buried in the Garden of Memories Cemetery, Sikeston. My grandfather Albert Lovelace died 12 Jul 1971 at Sikeston, of hypostatic pneumonia and was also buried there.

A young churchgoer and friend, Glenda Duke, of Sikeston, wrote the following and read it at Grandma's funeral:

TRIBUTE TO GRANDMA LOVELACE

Mankind has lost a friend because of Grandma's passing,
Because her heart was big enough to love the world.
She was like the women that fed Elijah - her larder was never empty.
Because of her hospitality people from all walks and positions in life have
sat at her table and tasted her good food.
It was hard to visit Grandma without being gifted with some delicious food.
From feeding the mailman to the doctor was an enjoyment for Grandma
And many times she told of the joy she received in sharing with others.
Any visitor to her home went away feeling cheery and uplifted
Because Grandma's joy was contagious.
The advancement of age never robbed her hands and feet of their
usefulness.
Never did she know an idle moment.
Her smile was a shining light for all to see as part of her Christian witness.
And never did she hesitate to tell others of her saviour, who meant so much
to her.
Rich, yes, Grandma was rich for she had a storehouse of treasures that
money can't buy.
Little and frail; yet she walked with giant steps and it will be hard to follow
her footsteps.
We mourn today; not for Grandma, but for those that will have to live
without her.
Women such as she are few and we need to thank the Lord that we have
been privileged to know her and walk with her through this life.
She was meekness personified, and the Bible calls this Blessed.

*

Children of Mattie Johns Lovelace and Albert:

1. CORDIE BELL LOVELACE, b. 24 Aug 1905, Crockett Mills, Crockett Co., Tn.
2. NETTIE PEARL LOVELACE, b. 19 Apr 1907, Crockett Mills, Crockett Co., Tn.
3. LILLIE MAE LOVELACE, b. 14 Jul 1908, Friendship, Crockett Co.,Tn.
4. RAYMOND LOVELACE, b. 4 Oct 1909, Friendship, Crockett Co.Tn.
5. REBA LOVELACE, b. 5 Dec 1914, Friendship, Crockett Co., Tn.
6. ALVIN H. D. LOVELACE, b. 1 Oct 1916, Friendship, Crockett Co., Tn.

* *

CORDIE BELL LOVELACE,

1-daughter of Mattie Johns Lovelace and Albert, b. 24 Aug 1905, m. 1) William Henry Holmes 7 Jun 1924, Tiptonville, Lake Co., Tn. Will was born 2 May 1891, in Ohio, the son of John Thomas Holmes and Ella Mae McCowan, and his first wife [17 Feb 1917] was Florance Ayers, who died. They had one daughter, Alta, who married J. H. Johns. Will and Cordie were farming on Albert Lovelace's farm when the Great Flood of 1927 caused their move to Blytheville, Ms. Co., Ark.

They later bought land in Sikeston, Scott Co., Mo. In 1948, they moved to an area near Bertrand that long ago was known as the Buckeye area. They sold off one corner of their farm during the Eisenhower administration when the interstate highways were being built [around 1956], and Interstate Highway 55 was built there. Will died of a heart attack 4 Dec 1956[10]. Several of her children built homes on this land, then her son Thomas built and they sold a number of homes on what remained of 80 acres of land. Cordie married again, to 2) Marvin Ralph of Sikeston, Mo. After his death, she married 3) Pete Rogers, and retired at Kentucky Lake, Ky.

Cordie, like most of the women in the family, had a strong character and was always a shrewd businesswoman and capable manager. She accumulated considerable wealth after Will's death. She died 22 April 1996.

The children of Cordie Holmes and Will were:

1. THOMAS EDWARD HOLMES, b. 2 Mar 1926, Blytheville, Ark.
2. J. W. HOLMES, b. 31 Oct 1928, Blytheville, Miss. Co., Ark. Married (1) Mabel Western, and (2) Shirley _____.
3. CLARA MAY HOLMES, b. 10 Apr 1930, Blytheville, Ark.
4. ALBERT RAY "Bo" HOLMES, b. 28 Apr 1932. Married (1) Jean WOODWARD, and (2) Joyce _____.

---

[10]In Bible of Mattie Johns Lovelace.

5. DONALD GENE HOLMES, b. 20 Nov 1940, Sikeston, Mo. Married (1)
    Carolyn Lindley, and (2) Betty _____.
6. DEWEY WAYNE HOLMES, b. 23 Nov 1944, Sikeston, Mo.
* *

THOMAS EDWARD HOLMES,

1-son of Cordie Lovelace Holmes and Will, b. 2 Mar 1926, was in U. S.
Navy during World War II and on a ship in the Southwest Pacific. He
married Linnie Mae Quinn 29 Sep 1947 in Union City, Tn. She was b. 26
Oct 1932, Hornbeak, Tn., the dau of Tennie Milton Quinn and Cora Alice
Miller. They owned and operated a grocery store at East Prairie, Mo.
Thomas recently died, in 1998.
Their children:
1. GEORGIE DALE HOLMES, b. 2 Jan 1950, Sikeston, Scott Co., Mo.
    Died 26 Jun 1966, Sikeston, Scott, Mo. in an accident.
2. DEMETRIA G. HOLMES, b. 26 Aug 1951.
3. BRENDA FAY HOLMES, b. 22 Jul 1952, Troy, Tn. Twin to Glenda.
    M. Terry Gilbert Lee in Dec 1971 in Sikeston, Mo. Terry is the son of
    Mr. & Mrs. J. R. Lee of Morley, Mo. They lived in Sikeston, Mo. 1994.
4. GLENDA K. HOLMES, b. 22 Jul 1952, Troy, Tn. Twin to Brenda.
5. MELODY A. HOLMES, b. 7 Sep 1966, Sikeston, Scott Co., Mo.
* *

CLARA MAY HOLMES,

3- daughter of Cordie Lovelace Holmes and Will, b. 10 Apr 1930, married
John Hubert Williams 15 Jun 1946, Piggott, Clay Co., Ark. John was born
13 Nov 1924, Dardanelle, Yell Co., Ark. He was a Nurse Anesthetist, and
Clara was a Licensed Practical Nurse. They are active members of the
Seventh Day Adventist Church. They lived in Oakland, Ore. for awhile, but
prefered the climate in Tennessee. They now live in Ooltewah, Tn. (1996.)
They recently celebrated their Fiftieth Wedding Anniversay with a Potluck
style dinner.
Their children:
1. JOAN DALE WILLIAMS, b. 29 Sep 1947, Sikeston, Scott Co., Mo.
2. JOHNNIE MARIE WILLIAMS, b. 10 Jan 1949, Sikeston, Mo.
3. PHYLLIS ANN WILLIAMS, b. 19 Mar 1951, Sikeston, Mo.
4. SHAWN FREDERICK WILLIAMS, b. 26 Nov 1965, Madison,
    Davidson Co., Tn.
* *

JOAN DALE WILLIAMS,

1-daughter of Clara Holmes Williams and John, b. 29 Sep 1947, married
Billy Lee Chamberlain 23 Jan 1968 in Ringgold, Catoosa Co., Ga. He was
b. 3 Mar 1947 in Ten Sleep, Washakie Co., Wy. He served in the U.S. Army
Jul 1966 to Jul 1968, with service in Vietnam 1 Jan 1967 to 1 Jan 1968. He
was injured in the leg, and received the Silver Star, Bronze Star, and Purple

Heart. Joan received a college degree in Social Work, and was working as a Social Worker. She returned to college and studied nursing.
Their children:
1. WANDA RENEE CHAMBERLAIN, b. 13 Oct 1968, Walla Walla, Wa. Married Scott Alan Lowder 28 Jul 1990 in College Place, Walla Walla Co., Wa. She received her degree as a Registered Nurse in the Spring of 1994.
2. KEVIN WAYNE CHAMBERLAIN, b. 12 Nov 1971, Walla Walla, Wa. Married Alita Straight 6 Jun 1992 in Pullman, Whitman Co., Wa.
* *

JOHNNIE MARIE WILLIAMS,

2- daughter of Clara Holmes Williams and John, b. 10 Jan 1949, married Terrell Wayne Zollinger 14 Jun 1970 at Port Charlotte, Charlotte Co., Fla. He was born 13 Nov 1948 in Chattanooga, Hamilton Co., Tn. He is the son of George Rollin Zollinger and Dorothy Mae Arnold.

Terry is an Associate Professor at the School of Public and Environmental Affairs, and senior researcher at Bowen Research Center at Indiana University. He received a Ms.Ph. in Biostatistics in 1976, and a Ph.D. in Epidemiology in 1980 from Loma Linda University, Loma Linda, Ca. During 1978 and 1979, he was Assistant Director of Survey Research Service, a research unit at Loma Linda University. Terry has been on the faculty of Indiana University since 1979.

Johnnie is a Registered Nurse, and works as an Administrator at St. Francis Hospital. She does genealogical research as a hobby. She and Terry recently planned and built a new home. She has supplied an invaluable amount of information to help make our family history interesting and informative. She is very quick in analyzing our research data, and her contribution to our family history is enormous.
Their children are:
1. DEREK ALAN ZOLLINGER, b. 24 Jul 1972, Atlanta, Fulton Co., Ga.
2. NICOLE MARIE ZOLLINGER, b. 12 Jan 1974, Atlanta, Fulton Co., Ga.
* *

SHAWN FREDERICK WILLIAMS,

4-son of Clara Holmes Williams and John , b. 26 Nov 1965, married Laura I. Accardo, 29 Aug 1992 McDonald, Bradley Co., Tn. He received his degree in Engineering at Rolla, Mo. He works as an engineer in Chattanooga, Tn. Laura has a degree in Business Administration.
* *

NETTIE PEARL LOVELACE,

2- daughter of Mattie Johns Lovelace and Albert, born 19 Apr 1907,Crockett Co., Tn., married (1) Marvin Crouch 4 Oct 1924, at Lake Co., Tn. They moved to Blytheville, Ark. in 1927. They divorced about

1938, and Nettie married (2) Benjamin Edwin Young 27 Jun 1939. He was born 3 Jul 1903 at Evansville, In., the son of Robert Benjamin Young. They lived in Anna, Ill. Edwin died 24 Oct 1963 in Anna, Ill. and was buried in Villa Ridge, Ill.

Nettie married (3) W. Verlin McArthur 9 Mar 1965 and they lived near Sikeston, Mo. He died in 197_. She died 22 Dec 1986 at Sikeston, Mo., and was buried in Green Lawn Memorial Gardens near Cairo, Ill. She had 12 grandchildren and 12 great grandchildren.

Children of Nettie Lovelace Crouch and Marvin:

1. CHARLES MARVIN CROUCH Jr., called "Junior", was b. 21 Sep 1925, Miston, Tn. A talented musician, he sang and played the guitar on the radio at Blytheville, Ark. Died 11 Oct 1942, Dongola, Ill. of internal injuries after an accident in which he was kicked by a horse.
2. CLYDE WILLIAM CROUCH, b. 21 Aug 1927, Luxora, Miss. Co., Ark. See below.
3. C. M. "Sam" CROUCH, b. 30 Nov 1929. Lived in Denver, Colo. He married Lillian Rhodes from Jonesboro, Ill. They have three daughters, 1) REBECCA CROUCH, b. 12 May 1953. 2) CINDY CROUCH, b. 27 Apr 1958, and 3) AMY CROUCH, b. 16 Sep 1963. He and Lillian divorced. Sam was head of NFL CIO Union for state of Colorado. He retired in Florahome, Fla.
4. JUANITA AILINE CROUCH, b. 15 Jan 1931, Blytheville, Ark. Died 15 Jun 1933.
5. THOMAS HAROLD CROUCH, b. 24 Nov 1933, Blytheville, Ark. Was a career soldier in the U.S. Army. Was a captive of North Koreans for 18 months. Married Rose Checiko of Kobe, Japan. No children. Retired. They lived in Parker, Colo., then moved to Lake Havasu, Az. recently.
6. SHIRLEY GLEAN CROUCH, b. 4 Dec 1937, Blytheville, Ark. Married Clifford Poole. Lived in Charleston, Mo. They had four children:
   a) RITA FAYE POOLE, b. 12 Jun 1955, Sterling, Ill. Married (1) Jim Lyerla, 20 May 1972. Children: i) SHAWN ERIC LYERLA, b. 23 Apr 1973, Carbondale, Ill. ii) JAMES MATTHEW LYERLA, b. 22 May 1979, Sikeston, Mo. They divorced, and she married again.
   b) BOBBY DEWAYNE POOLE, b. 31 Aug 1956, Anna, Ill. Married Karen Katona.
   c) TONI JEAN POOLE, b. 30 Aug 1957, Anna, Ill. Married Sam Cunningham 23 Dec 1971. Children: i) MICHAEL SHANE CUNNINGHAM, b. 7 Jun 1972, Centralia, Ill. ii) RICHARD DANIEL CUNNINGHAM, b. 6 Jun 1976, Sikeston, Mo. iii) HEATHER LYNN CUNNINGHAM, b. 26 Feb 1980. iv) DUSTIN REILEY CUNNINGHAM, b. 7 Jun 1984.
   d) SHERRI LYNN POOLE, b. 9 Aug 1962, Anna, Ill. Married Curtis Lemons 3 Jul 1982. They live in Charleston, Mo. (1994). Their

children: i) JAMES BRANDON LEMONS, b. 15 Dec 1982, Cape Girardeau, Mo. Died 26 Mar 198_. ii) ERIK SCOTT LEMONS, b. 5 Sep 1984, Cape Girardeau, Mo.

*

Children of Nettie Crouch Young and Edwin:
1. JAMES EDWARD YOUNG, born 22 Jun 1945, Anna, Ill. He married Florence Hill; they divorced. Child: JAMIE ELIZABETH YOUNG, b. 27 Mar 1973, Sikeston, Mo. Jim owns Young Construction and lives in Sikeston, Mo.
2. LOUISE PEARL YOUNG, b. 23 Nov 1943, Anna, Ill. M. Rudy Crowell. Two children, LORI ANN CROWELL, b. 1 Nov 1964; and KERI LEA CROWELL, b. 13 Mar 1972. They live in Dunfries, Va.

* *

CLYDE WILLIAM CROUCH,

2-son of Nettie Lovelace Crouch and Marvin, b. 21 Aug 1927, married Zona Lou Loper. He was a career soldier in the U.S. Army, and retired in 1975 as a Master Sergeant after 22 years service. He was a veteran of World War II and the Korean Conflict. He was a helicopter pilot, and saw active duty in Vietnam. He lived 15 years in Florahome, Fla., moving there from Jacksonville, Fla.

He was a member of Elks Lodge 1892 of Green Cove Springs, Veterans of Foreign Wars Post 10164 of Interlachen and the AmVets Post 86 in Keystone Heights. He died 27 Jul 1990 at Gainesville, Alachua Co., Fla. and was buried in Paran Cemetery, Grandin, Putnam Co., Fla. with full military honors by a detachment from the U. S. Navy at Jacksonville.[11] His children are: a) WILLIAM DAVID CROUCH, b. 17 Oct 1959, now of Florahome, Fla. and b) CHARLES STEVEN CROUCH, b. 6 Dec 1960, of Boca Raton, Fla. Clyde had two grandchildren: MICHELLE LEIGH CROUCH and MATTHEW STEVEN CROUCH.

* *

LILLIE MAE LOVELACE,

3- daughter of Mattie Johns Lovelace and Albert, born 14 Jul 1908, married Robert Jewel "Bob" Sides 6 May 1925 at Booths Point, Dyer Co., Tn. He was the son of James Sides and Minnie Robins Sides. Bob's great grandfather five times removed was Henry Sides, who came to America from Germany via Holland, just before the Revolutionary War, and was a soldier in that war.[12] He lived in Anson Co., N.C., then he and his sons became pioneer settlers of Walker Co., Ala., and he was buried there in the Sides Family Cemetery. Bob's great-grandfather Stephen Sides moved from Walker Co., Ala. to Tippah Co., Ms., where he was a miller until his

---

[11]Obituary from Florahome, Fla. newspaper.
[12]History of Walker Co. Ala. by John Martin Dombhart, Cayce Publ. Co., Thornton, Ark. 1937, pp. 342-345.

death shortly before the Civil War. Bob's father, Jim, fought in the Civil War. The family remained in Mississippi until after the Civil War, and later most of them moved to Tennessee.

Lillie Lovelace Sides, my Mother, was always an outdoor person, and could do about anything she put her mind to. They farmed, but were all forced to leave Tn. because of the Great Flood of 1927. They found land to farm at New Liberty community in Arkansas, near Blytheville. As the Great Depression continued, it was not very profitable to farm, and they moved into town at Blytheville, Ark. in 1935.

After World War II began, Bob decided to farm again and moved the family to Puxico, Mo. Near this area, a wildlife refuge was established, and it was left in a primitive state. Their children have happy memories of roaming free in this area after their chores were done.

Bob farmed a few years, then moved to Sikeston, Mo. in 1945, where he built a house, doing most of the work himself. He worked for 16 years hauling milk as an independent trucker to Reiss' Dairy in Sikeston. Then he decided to quit and moved back to the country. As a hobby, he enjoyed walking through the fields looking for Indian artifacts and arrowheads to add to his large collection, which I now have. Later he bought two and a half acres of land close to the town of Sikeston, but still in the country. Bob and Lillie celebrated their 50th Wedding Anniversary in 1975 with their children flying in to attend. He was already ill with leukemia, and he died 3 Nov 1978. He was buried in the Garden of Memories Cemetery at Sikeston, Mo.

After Bob's death, Lillie continued to live alone in the country, raising a garden and canning food for her use and to give to others. She kept her lawn of 2 1/2 acres neatly mowed with a small riding-mower tractor, which she purchased new in her 70's. Her yard with its large trees and flowers were park-like, and she enjoyed watching the squirrels play. In 1993, at the age of 85, she went into a nursing home in Sikeston, Mo. She didn't like this, and went to live with her daughter, Betty and her family.

Children of Lillie Lovelace Sides and Bob:
1. JAMES ALBERT SIDES, b. 20 Nov 1928, Blytheville, Mississippi Co., Ark.
2. HELEN RUTH SIDES, b. 24 Sep 1931, Blytheville, Miss. Co., Ark.
3. BETTY JANE SIDES, b. 22 Apr 1933, Blytheville, Miss. Co., Ark.
* *

JAMES ALBERT SIDES,

1- son of Lillie Lovelace Sides and Bob, b. 20 Nov 1928, went in the U. S. Army Nov 21 1946 for 18 months. He moved to Long Beach, Ca. in 1952, and married (1) Anna Mae Hatman Hunt 16 Dec 1951, Tiajuana, Mx. and 23 Sep 1953, Santa Ana, Ca. They lived in Anaheim, Ca. several years, where Jim was President of the Booster Club for Anaheim High School,

numerous civic and social activities. He is a Thirty Second Degree Mason; a Past General Officer of the Fullerton Commandry; a Night Commander in the Scottish Rite and York Rite; and a Shriner. He was co-owner of Hardin Oldsmobile. They moved to Ventura, Ca. in 1965 where he owned an Oldsmobile Dealership located at 39 W. Main St. for several years. They divorced in 1969. Ann married (3) William Earl Clarke 7 Nov 1969, Sikeston, Scott Co., Mo. She died in 1995.

Jim Sides married (2) Mrs. Jean Plunkett of Glendora, Ca., and they divorced. He married (3) Mrs. Lois Wasley. They lived in Laguna Nigel for several years. They now live in Vista, Ca. near the golf course. [1998]. He enjoys golfing, hunting and fishing. He also enjoys meeting new people and selling, and has worked as a salesman for a Cadillac dealer for several years. He now says he will retire when he's seventy.

Children of James Sides and Ann:
1. CHARLES GUSTAV SIDES, b. 13 Sep 1945, Fresno, Ca.
2. JAMES ALBERT SIDES Jr., b. 22 Apr 1954, San Pedro, L. A. Co., Ca.
3. ROBERT ALLEN SIDES, b. 15 Aug 1958, Orange , Ca.
* *

HELEN RUTH SIDES,

2- daughter of Lillie Lovelace Sides and Bob, b. 24 Sep 1931, married George Elmer "Juddy" Dye of Sikeston, Mo. 10 Aug 1948. He was born 15 May 1927, Sikeston, Mo., the son of George Milburn Dye and Lula Jane Akers, who were both descended from early pioneer families. He was a Radio Officer in the U.S. Merchant Marine at the time of our marriage. He went to sea for eight years, including eighteen months during World War II, then was drafted into the U.S. Army in 1952 and served in Korea in the U. S. Army Signal Corps. He received 13 months training at the Signal Corps School at Fort Monmouth, N.J. before going to Korea. We lived in Long Beach, Ca. in 1951 and 1952, and moved to Ca. permanently in 1955. We owned and operated a franchised Honda Motorcycle Dealership in Glendora, Ca. for over 25 years, until we sold it in 1990 and retired. We continue to own commercial real estate in Glendora.

George was active in civic and political affairs for a number of years. He was President of Azusa Republican Club in the 1960's, and has worked in numerous political campaigns. He was elected and served as a Director for the Glendora Chamber of Commerce from 1968 to 1972. He was elected Vice-President of the Chamber of Commerce and served two terms. He is a member of MENSA with a 99.4 percentile rating. He is a serious golfer, and plays as often as he can.

I have also been active in civic and political affairs. I was involved in the local P.T.A. and held several offices in the 1960's, was a Girl Scout leader, worked as a volunteer in office of Congressman, Hon. John Rousselot, was on numerous political committees. I was in Who's Who in the Republican Party in 1991, and belong to several political organizations, and contribute to many. We attended the inaugural ceremonies for Gov. Pete Wilson in Sacramento in Jan. 1992. I am a member of the Daughters of the American Revolution. I am a Docent at the California State Society DAR Headquarters House and Library, past Secretary of District X, past Operations Vice-Chair and Secretary of CSSDAR Headquarters Admin. Committee, and am now Chairman of this Committee. In my Serrano Chapter, I was Librarian 1996-98, and am now First Vice Regent. I have written a number of children's stories, and the genealogical book, "The Browder Connections."

We have a ranch in Lucerne Valley, Ca. that we have used for the past twenty four years to get away and relax. We enjoy travelling and have enjoyed trips to Egypt, England, Japan, Mexico, Hawaii, and other places. We do a lot of driving as we tour the U.S.. In July and August, 1998, we made a tour of the west and midwest, in commemoration of our 50th wedding anniversary. We were happy to celebrate this anniversary with many family members at the Family Reunion at Reelfoot Lake, Ky. in Aug., 1998. We returned to celebrate the occasion with our children and their families in Ca.

Our children are:
1. REBECCA RUTH DYE, b. 17 Aug 1953, Fort Monmouth, Monmouth Co., N. J.
2. GEORGE ROBERT DYE, b. Mar 1956, Bellflower, L.A. Co., Ca.
3. JEFFREY MARTIN DYE, b. 29 May 1961, Bellflower, L.A. Co., Ca.
* *

REBECCA RUTH DYE,
1- daughter of Helen Sides Dye and George, b. 17 Aug 1953, graduated from Cal State Fullerton in 1981 with a B. A. Degree. She majored in Art History and English. She has toured extensively in Europe, visiting areas of artistic and historic interest. She lived in Hawaii for a year, and enjoyed tours to the Big Island to absorb its historical feel.

She married Gregory Drinkert 7 Apr 1985 in San Dimas, Ca. He was b. 4 Jun 1950 in Detroit, Mich., the son of George William Drinkert and Eleanor Mozak. He is a combat veteran of the Vietnam War. He is Operations Manager for Dolphin Imaging Systems, Santa Clarita, Ca. Greg generously gave his time to teach me to use the computer, and took care of the technical details necessary to prepare "The Browder Connections." He has been a real asset and eased the way when I had computer problems.

Becki stays busy taking care of their two small children. She enjoys shopping, gardening and interior decorating. They reside in Ventura, Ca.

Their children are:
1. ALLISON NICOLE DRINKERT, b. 23 Jul 1987, Glendora, Ca.
2. GARRETT ALEXANDER "Gus" DRINKERT, b. 9 Feb 1990, Glendora, Ca.

GEORGE ROBERT DYE,

2- son of Helen Sides Dye and George, b. 1 Mar 1956, graduated from Cal State San Diego in 1978 with a B. A. Degree. He majored in History. He has driven all over the U. S., and visited Japan, Mexico and Hawaii. He married (1) Marci Grinnell 3 Jan 1986. She has two children, Robert and Cori Grinnell. They were divorced in 1987. He married (2) Deborah Schuler 31 Mar 1990 in San Diego, Ca. They were both Real Estate Brokers in San Diego. Debbie has one child, Denise Schuler, b. 27 Jul 1980, from a previous marriage. Debbie was born 21 Jan 1956. They were divorced in 1998. George is now attending Chapman University for his Masters Degree in Education, and is also teaching in elementary school. George and Debbie have one child:

1.   GEORGE JOSEPH DYE, b. 21 Dec 1995, San Diego, Ca.
* *

JEFFREY MARTIN DYE,

3- son of Helen Sides Dye and George, b. 29 May 1961, graduated from University of Southern California in 1981, with a Bachelor of Science Degree. He majored in Public Affairs, and served an internship in the White House News Summary Office in Washington, D.C. while Ronald Reagan was President. He toured in Japan, France, Germany and Hawaii. He married Lori Beylik 28 Jun 1986 in Claremont, Ca. She is daughter of Calvin Beylik and Betty Beylik, now of Redding, Ca. They were divorced in 1995.

Jeff married Marie-Christine Wiltord January 18, 1997, in Glendora, Ca., where they reside. Marie-Christine is daughter of Georges and Monique Wiltord of Paris, France. Jeff produced public service announcements and broadcast on local TV, along with other video work. He has been a schoolteacher for several years, and now teaches in Glendale.
* *

BETTY JANE SIDES,

3- daughter of Lillie Lovelace Sides and Bob, b. 22 Apr 1933, married Paul Edward Hill 28 Jul 1951. He was born 13 Jul 1931, the son of Sherman Horace Hill and Hazel Belle Hatfield. He was in the U.S. Marine Corps during the Korean War, and was a heavy machine gunner. During service, he was among our troops who were exposed to radiation during close-up tests of the atomic bombs in Nevada. He was stationed in San Diego, Ca. and Japan.

Paul returned from military service and sold farm equipment, then farmed for several years near Sikeston, Mo. He later became an insurance agent before retiring because of a heart condition and surgery. He was a member of the Catholic Church. He fought a valiant battle against cancer, but passed away March 13, 1997 after having a stroke. His daughter Terry was able to administer his chemotherapy and see he received the best care.

Betty has always been interested in political affairs, worked in elections, and once ran for office as a Democratic Committeewoman.

Their children are:
1. DEBORAH LYNNE HILL, b. 11 Sep 1952, Sikeston, Scott Co., Mo.
2. CAMILLA JANE HILL, b. 21 Jul 1955, Sikeston, Mo.
3. TERESA DAWN HILL, b. 23 Feb 1957, Sikeston, Mo.
4. PAUL GREGORY HILL, b. 15 Sep 1961, Sikeston, Mo.
5. STEVEN ROBERT HILL, b. 31 Aug 1964, Sikeston, Mo.
6. DANA MICHELLE HILL, b. 14 Aug 1966, Sikeston, Mo.
7. DAVID MICHAEL HILL, b. 29 Feb 1972, Sikeston, Mo.
8. CATHERINE DIANA HILL, b. 8 Jun 1973, Sikeston, Mo. Died 10 Jun 1973.

* *

DEBORAH LYNN HILL,

1- daughter of Betty Sides Hill and Paul, was born 11 Sep 1952. She married Daniel Schuchart 1978 at the Catholic Church in Sikeston, Mo. Dan was b. 25 May 1941, the son of Sylvester Rudolph Schuchart and Ella Heisserer. He was a dairyman, and owned Schuchart Dairy Farm at Bloomfield, Mo. He has fought a battle with cancer for ten years, and only recently sold his dairy business. They still own 65 acres of the farm, and recently (1997) built a lovely, large home there, which Dan supervised. They enjoy putting on barbeques and hayrides for the family, as well as for Girl Scouts and other organizations.

Debbie is a Registered Nurse and works in dialysis at Missouri Delta Medical Center, at Sikeston. She returned to school, taking night classes, and graduated from Parks College in Kansas City in 1994. She recently received her BS degree, and is still going to school and working. She takes part in school activities with her children, and has attended nursing conferences, conventions and other nursing activities. She is a very busy young lady.

Their children are:
1. DANIEL SCHUCHART Jr., b. 2 Aug 1979, Sikeston, Mo.
2. KRISTIN SCHUCHART, b. 26 Apr 1982, Sikeston, Mo. Twin to Diana.
3. DIANA SCHUCHART, b. 26 Apr 1982, Sikeston, Mo. Twin to Kristin.
4. MATTHEW SCHUCHART, b. 5 Sep 1984, Sikeston, Mo.

* *

CAMILLA JANE HILL,

2- daughter of Betty Sides Hill and Paul, b. 21 Jul 1955, married (1) Michael French 1973. He is the son of Gene French and Lucy Carr. Mike is a career man in the U. S. Navy, and is now a Chief Petty Officer in Florida. They divorced in 1980.

Camilla married (2) Randolph James Grzgbowski 19 Jun 1982. Randy was a career man in the Air Wing of the U. S. Marines. They divorced in

Dec 1992. Camilla returned to school to complete her education, and is now teaching school in Mo. She recently married (3) Jerri Sides.

Children of Camilla Hill French and Mike:

1. ERIC FRENCH, b. 9 Feb 1974, Portsmouth, Va. In U. S. Marines. Eric is the third generation in the Hill line to be in the U.S. Marines. Was serving on a ship in Pacific in 1997.
2. JEREMY FRENCH, b. 11 Jun 1976, Sikeston, Mo. Jeremy also joined the U. S. Marines. In 1997, he was stationed in Okinawa.
3. JUSTIN FRENCH, b. 8 Apr 1979, Millington, Tn. Also joined the U. S. Marines after high school graduation.

* *

TERESA DAWN HILL,

3- daughter of Betty Sides Hill and Paul, b. 23 Feb 1957, called "Terri," married Terrence Trucks 23 Oct 1981. He was born 19 Jan 1957, Malden, Mo., the son of Charles Trucks and Marie Alden. Terri is a radiation therapy technician for Deaconess Hospital in St. Louis. They were divorced in 1997. They live in Festus, Mo.

Their children are:

1. ALEXANDER BENJAMIN TRUCKS, b. 25 Feb 1989, St. Louis, Mo.
2. EMILY CATHERINE TRUCKS, b. 10 Jan 1993, St. Louis, Mo.

* *

PAUL GREGORY HILL,

4- son of Betty Sides Hill and Paul, b. 15 Sep 1961, married Belinda Kay Hunsaker 29 Mar 1979, at Sikeston, Mo. She was born 22 Jun 1960, at Cape Girardeau, Mo., the daughter of Donald Hunsaker and Mildred Driskell. They divorced in 1997.

Greg joined the U.S. Marines and served seven and a half years, and was stationed in Ca. during the latter part of his service. He was in Avionics, the Air Wing of the U. S. Marine Corps. He planned a career in the military, but injured his knee and received an honorable medical discharge in 1987. Greg works as an Electrician for Kagmo at Cape Girardeau. Their children are:

1. CHRISTOPHER PAUL HILL, b. 15 Feb 1982, Blytheville, Ark. Twin.
2. GREGORY SCOTT HILL, b. 15 Feb 1982, Blytheville, Ark. Twin.
3. MEGAN DAWN HILL, b. 9 Jan 1985, Yuma, Ariz.

* *

STEVEN ROBERT HILL,

5- son of Betty Sides Hill and Paul, b. 31 Aug 1964, was in the U.S. Air Force six years, stationed in Fla., during which time he received several awards for outstanding performance. He married Cathy Clark. She was born in 1963, the daughter of William and Phyllis Clark. Steven is a level three, non-destructive engineer. He worked for United Technologies, and was on loan to NASA. He was attached to the NASA Space Launch

Facility on Merritt Island, Cape Canaveral, Fla. He has a B. A. degree in marketing. Cathy also has a B. A. degree. They lived in Titusville, Fla. They now live in Missouri and he is self-employed.

They have two children:
1. ASHLEY ELAINE HILL, b. Oct 1990, Fla.
2. KAITLYNN JAYNE HILL, b. 20 Aug 1994, Titusville, Fla.
* *

DANA MICHELLE HILL,

6- daughter of Betty Sides Hill and Paul, b. 14 Aug 1966, married Brian Alexander 27 Aug 1988 in Sikeston, Mo. Brian was born 16 May 1964, the son of Kenneth Eugene Alexander and Patricia Ryan. He works for AT&T and is headquartered in St. Louis, Mo. They live in Hillsboro, Mo. Their children are
1. JOSHUA HENRY ALEXANDER, b. 24 Aug 1993.
2. KIRSTEN ALEXANDER, b. 24 Aug 1995.
3. ALLISON ALEXANDER, b. 2 Jan 1997.
* *

DAVID MICHAEL HILL,

7-son of Betty Sides Hill and Paul, b. 29 Feb 1972, attended school in Sikeston, Mo. David was born with Downs Syndrome, and with his loving disposition has always been an inspiration to his family. We were visiting and were able to see David happily clutching his lunch box as he boarded the school bus when he was around 12 years old. In recent years, he has been experiencing heart and lung problems, but has bravely accepted this. His mother says "I'm lucky to have him. He's taught me a lot about humility and love and being brave - - because he's all of the beautiful things a human being should be."
* *

RAYMOND LOVELACE,

4- son of Mattie Johns Lovelace (1884) and Albert, b. 4 Oct 1909, married Avril Annette Batchelor 16 Mar 1930 Blytheville, Miss. Co., Ark. Avril was b. 18 Feb 1912, Calhoun Co., Miss., the daughter of Berlin Batchelor and Edna Cook Batchelor. Raymond was a carpenter and building contractor. They lived in Altheimer, Jefferson Co., Ark. Avril died 21 Mar 1985, and was buried in Flat Bayou Cemetery, at Altheimer, Ark. Raymond is now retired. He is a member of the Baptist Church.

Their children are:
1. BILLY RAY LOVELACE, b. 7 Jun 1932, Miss. Co., Ark. Married Joyce Hartzog of Sikeston, Mo. She is daughter of Dowdy and Camilla Hartzog of Memphis, Tn. Dowdy and his brother are founders of the Hart's Bakery chain. Billy was in the U.S. Marine Corps during the Korean War. They have children. They live in Altheimer, Ark., where

Bill owns a retail building materials business. He is a member of the Baptist Church, and several civic organizations.

2. CHARLES LOVELACE, b. 26 Aug 1934, Miss. Co., Ark. Was in the U. S. Marine Corps. He married Janis Scott of Sikeston. He is a construction superintendent, and lives in West Paducah, Ky. (1994).

3. JERRY LEON LOVELACE, b. 23 Oct 1936, Miss. Co., Ark. Married Verblene Sugg, daughter of Mr. & Mrs. Daniel L. Sugg of Sikeston, Mo. in Mar 1961 at United Pentecostal Church in Sikeston. They live in Pine Bluff, Ark.

* *

REBA LOVELACE,

5- daughter of Mattie Johns Lovelace and Albert, b. 5 Dec 1914, married Luther Emmett Hodges 27 Oct 1934 in Blytheville, Miss. Co., Ark. Luther was b. 8 Apr 1912, Poteau Co., Okla., the son of Ellis Perry Hodges and Allie Mae Garrett. He was a salesman, and they lived in Sikeston, Mo. for many years, then moved to Springfield, Mo. and ran a Stuckey's franchise. Luther died 31 Mar 1989, and was buried in Greenlawn Cemetery, Springfield. Reba is an outstanding cook, homemaker and hostess. Luther was a talented musician who organized several bands and played on the radio and various places. Reba is still active in church in Springfield, Mo., although she had to have a pin put in her hip.

Their children are:

1. SHELVA JEAN HODGES, b. 7 Aug 1937, Sikeston, Scott Co., Mo.
2. PATSY ANN HODGES, b. 7 Dec 1944, Sikeston, Scott Co., Mo.

* *

SHELVA JEAN HODGES,

1- daughter of Reba Lovelace Hodges and Luther, b. 7 Aug 1937, married (1) James Leslie Gibson 8 May 1959 at Blytheville, Ark. at Calvary Baptist Church. He is the son of Mr. and Mrs. Carl Gibson of Blytheville. They divorced May 1966 Memphis, Tn. No children.

She married (2) Tilsey Ray Byram 24 Nov 1967, in Holland, Mo. Tilsey was b. 1 Jul 1944, the son of Murel & Eva Byram of Parks, Ark. Shelva works for the Office of Hearings and Appeals, a division of the Social Security Administration. She has been a Hearing Assistant to Administrative Law Judges for the past fifteen years. Tilsey was a fireman in the Air Force, and was a fireman for over 20 yrs. for the City of Fort Smith, Ark. He had to take medical retirement due to severe rheumatoid arthritis. He also worked a second job as a carpenter, and built their house as well as several others. He oversaw the building of a house for their daughter Karen. They live in Van Buren, Ark. They are very active in the First Assembly of God Church in Van Buren, and Shelva sings in the choir.

Their children are:

1. LORI ANN BYRAM, b. 13 Oct 1968, Blytheville, Ark.

2. KAREN JEAN BYRAM, b. 20 Jul 1970, Blytheville, Ark.
3. JULIE RAE BYRAM, b. 9 May 1974, Fort Smith, Ark.
* *

PATSY ANN HODGES,
2- daughter of Reba Lovelace Hodges and Luther, married John Perry
Christoph 22 Mar 1962 in Blytheville, Ark. He was in the U. S. Air Force
for eight years. They lived in Blytheville, Ark. and for five and a half years
in Puerto Rico. They now live in Springfield, Mo.

They have three children:
1. JOHN DOUGLAS CHRISTOPH, b. 16 Dec 1964, Ramey Air Force
Base, Puerto Rico.
2. MICHAEL ALLEN CHRISTOPH, b. 15 Jun 1967, Denver, Colo.
3. KENNETH WAYNE CHRISTOPH, b. 23 Jul 1968, Denver, Colo.
* *

ALVIN H. D. LOVELACE,
6- son of Mattie Johns Lovelace and Albert, b. 1 Oct 1916, married Rozella
Oldham 9 Jul 1938 at Sikeston, Scott Co., Mo. She was b. 1 Oct 1916.

He was a carpenter and building contractor. They lived at Sikeston for
a number of years, then moved to Paducah, McCracken Co., Ky., where he
has retired. Rozella is an exceptionally good cook and homemaker.

Their children are:
1. JANET FAY LOVELACE, b. 27 Sep 1944, Sikeston, Mo.
2. LINDA SUE LOVELACE, b. 23 Jan 1949, Sikeston, Mo.
3. GLORIA JEAN LOVELACE, b. 27 Feb 1952, Sikeston, Mo.
4. SANDRA KAY LOVELACE, b. 15 Jun 1953, Sikeston, Mo. Married
Delbert Fowler. He was b. 21 May 1931, Paducah, Ky.
5. BUSTER LOVELACE, b. 28 Sep 1954, Sikeston, Mo. Married Sherry
_____ 24 Dec 1972 Paducah, McCracken Co., Ky. He is interested in
politics, and ran for the office of Sheriff.
* *

CARLOS C. JOHNS,
5- son of Benjamin Edmund Johns and Nancy, b. 22 Jul 1887 [13], married (1)
Florence Irene Privett 16 Dec 1906, at Friendship, Crockett Co., Tn.[14] She
was b. 26 Dec 1890, Friendship, Tn., and was daughter of Samuel Levi
Privett and Delilah Frances Ward. [15] She was sister of Turner Privett who
married Belle Johns. Carlos was a farmer in Crockett Co., Tn. They moved
to Oakfield, Madison Co., Tn. around 1919. They returned to Friendship,
Tn. about 1921, where Carlos owned and operated a grocery store.
Florence died Sep 1927.

---

[13]Inf. from Mattie Johns Lovelace's Bible and Lillie Prichard.
[14]Crockett Co. Tn. Marriages. By T. N. Love, J.P.; Bondsman: Albert Lovelace.
[15]Inf. on monument Mt. Zion Cem. Samuel b. 28 Oct 1853, d. 1945; Delilah b. 26
Dec 1857, d. 14 Apr 1925. Married Nov 1874.

Carlos Johns married (2) Maureen Shepard 7 Dec 1928. She was born 30 Mar 1912, the daughter of Homer J. Shepard and Lorene Hughes. The Great Depression was going on and they moved to Blytheville, Ark. where he worked for the WPA for awhile. They moved to Minor Switch, Mo., near Sikeston, where he farmed and worked as a carpenter. He and Maureen separated in late 1946 and their divorce was final in March 1947. Maureen died 20 Feb 1989, and was buried in Robertson Cem., Alamo, Tn.

He married (3) Ruth Nunally Snider, and they moved to Steele, Mo., where he died 29 Apr 1966 [16]. He was buried at Mt. Zion Cemetery, Friendship, Tn.[17] Ruth died 10 May 1978, at Mid-South Christian Nursing Home in Memphis.[18] She was buried at Mt. Vernon Gardens, Memphis.

Children of Carlos C. Johns and Florence:
1. EZEKIEL JOHNS, b. 1907, d. 1907, Crockett Co., Tn.
2. LILLIE LYDIA MARIE JOHNS, b. 6 Jun 1909, Friendship, Tn.
3. SANDY LEE JOHNS, b. 29 Mar 1911, Friendship, Crockett Co.
4. IRENE JOHNS.
5. J. H. JOHNS, b. 10 Jul 1915, Crockett Co., Tn.
6. JESSE O'NEAL JOHNS, b. 18 Jan 1918, Maury Junction, Crockett Co.
7. AUBREY C. JOHNS, b. 1920, Friendship, Tn. Died 1921, Oakfield, Madison Co., Tn.
8. KATHERINE PAULINE JOHNS, b. 4 Aug 1921, Friendship, Tn.
9. MAMIE DELIA LAVERNE JOHNS, b. 4 May 1923, Friendship. Died 1938, Minor Switch, Scott Co., Mo., buried Minor Switch Cemetery.
*

Children of CARLOS C. JOHNS and Maureen:
1. JACKSON CARLOS JOHNS, b. 31 Jul 1931; d. 5 Aug 1931.
2. ESTHEL LEE JOHNS, b. 17 Jul 1932, Mo. Married Rev. Howard Ray Anger 30 Oct 1950, Corinth, Ms. He was b. 13 Feb 1925 in Tampa, Fla.; died 24 Dec 1982, Crestview, Fla.; buried there. Esthel died 31 Dec 1974 Bonifay, Fla., was buried Robertson Cem., Alamo, Tn. Daughter: JOE SHEA ANGER, b. 2 Nov 1957, Alamo, Tn. Married Aaron "Buddy" Elkins, and they have two children: a) AARON M. ELKINS, b. 5 May 1979, Tallahassee, Fla. b) RACHEL N. ELKINS, b. 31 Mar 1982, Pensacola, Fla. They have been divorced several years.
3. MATTIE BELL JOHNS, b. 29 Mar 1934, Sikeston, Scott Co., Mo. Married Robert "Bobby" Ray.
4. NANCY LORENA JOHNS, b. 22 Aug 1936, Holland, Mo. See below.
5. WILLIAM O'NEAL "Bill" JOHNS, b. 6 May 1939, Crockett Co., Tn.
6. VERA MAE JOHNS, b. 19 Aug 1941. Married John Brown. Lives in Steele, Mo.

[16]Obituary, Crockett Times, Undated, Friendship, Tn.
[17]Inf. from Lillie Prichard and Virginia Smith, Friendship, Tn.
[18]Obituary, The Commercial Appeal, Memphis, Tn. 11 May 1978.

7. LEE JACKSON JOHNS, b. 30 Mar 1947, after Carlos and Maureen divorced.[19]

* *

LILLIE LYDIA MARIE JOHNS,

2- daughter of Carlos C. Johns (1887) and Florence, b. 6 Jun 1909, married Ellis Eugene Prichard 12 Nov 1929, Blytheville, Miss. Co., Ark. [20] They first lived in Holland, Mo., where they farmed until about 1936, then they bought a farm near Luxora, Ark. In Jan 1942, they bought the old Dr. Griffin place, about 100 acres, east of Friendship, Tn. After they sold this, they bought the Mack Carman place two miles north of Friendship. After Lillie's Uncle Edgar (J. E.) Privett died, they bought out his dairy herd and added dairy operation to their farm. In 1947, they sold their farm and bought the M.V. (Vester) Williams Grocery Store in Friendship, and changed its name to Prichard's Grocery.

Lillie converted a small room of the store into a florist, which she has operated for over 40 years in four locations. The flower shop was Friendship Florist, then in 1960's, it was Friendship Flower & Gift Shop. Eugene sold the grocery, and did carpenter work awhile, then bought Frozen Food Locker. He retired in 1972.

They celebrated their 50th Wedding Anniversary 11 Nov 1979 with a reception at Friendship Baptist Church, which was hosted by their daughters. Eugene helped Lillie operate the florist shop until his death 4 Dec 1985. He was active in civic affairs, serving as Alderman, Mayor (short term), was active in Ruritan & Lion's Club, and was active in Merchant's Association. He was an avid gardner and loved gardening. He left the family many trees for future use---fruit, pecan, English walnut, and black walnut trees. His favorite plants were roses and azaleas and he grew many of these. He was a member of Friendship Church of Christ. He was buried in Bellevernon Cemetery, Friendship, Tn.

Lillie has been active in the florist industry for over forty years, and has regularly attended Allied meetings and state florists' conventions. She was honored in 1993 by the Tennessee State Florists Association which dedicated their 41st annual convention program to her.[21] She was President of Westate Florist Assoc. two years, Secy.-Treas. four years, and was also its Director. She is a member of FTD, AFS, Florafax, SAR and AIFD, and still operates the flower shop.

She is a member of First Baptist Church, and serves as Sunday School Teacher; was President of W.M.U., and Director of Training Union. She is active in Friendship Merchants Assoc. and the local American Association

---

[19]Add'l. info from Lorina Johns, Long Beach, Ca., 1996.
[20]Witnesses Frank & Lizzie Privett. Frank was son of Belle and Turner Privett.
[21]The Crockett Times, Wed., Mar 31, 1993.

of Retired People, as well as Girl Scouts, the 4-H Club, and other organizations.

We were very happy to see her again at the Family Reunion in Aug. 1998. She still looks great, and was very active and alert in organizing the setup for the Reunion. She ordered and brought the cake for Elbert Johns, which he purchased for our 50th Wedding Anniversary. She helped emcee the Reunion program. Both are wonderful people.

Lillie and Gene's children are:
1. VIRGINIA IRENE PRICHARD, b. 23 Sep 1931, Holland, Mo.
2. JEAN MARIE PRICHARD, b. 24 Oct 1932, Holland, Mo.
3. ALVIN ELLIS PRICHARD, b. 10 Aug 1933, Holland, Mo. Died 10 Aug 1933. Buried No. 8 Cemetery, Cooter, Mo.
4. JAMES EDWARD PRICHARD, b. 25 May 1935, Holland, Mo. Died May 1935. Buried No. 8 Cem., Cooter, Mo.

* *

VIRGINIA IRENE PRICHARD,

1- daughter of Lillie Johns Prichard and Eugene, b. 23 Sep 1931, married James Ward Smith 12 Mar 1954 in Fiendship, Crockett Co., Tn. James was b. 9 Feb 1929 in Friendship, in Dyer Co., Tn., and is the son of James Burley Smith and Iva Mattie Ward. They own and farm 315 acres near Friendship; both are active members of Zion Hill Baptist Church. Virginia is a graduate of U. of Tn., Knoxville, has a B.S. degree in home economics and taught school 7 years. She has done a lot of genealogical work as a hobby. She assists Elbert Johns in supplying information for the Newsletter, and has been a lot of help in supplying family information. She has been very active in civic and church work, and helps the Family Reunion continue. Her husband recently had heart surgery.

Their children are:
1. IVA MARIE SMITH, b. 30 Apr 1955, Jackson, Madison Co., Tn. Died 17 Jun 1955, and was buried Zion Hill Cemetery, Dyer Co., Tn.
2. JAMES ELLIS SMITH, b. 26 Aug 1958, Jackson, Tn. M. Cynthia Jane Rice 6 Aug 1978. B. S. in Ag. Bus., U. of Tn. at Martin in 1980. Now Vice Pres. of Bank of Friendship.
3. HARRIET VIRGINIA SMITH, b. 2 Aug 1960, Jackson, Tn. M. Lenard O'Neil Cannon Jr. 31 Dec 1993, Ripley, Tn. B. S. in Ag. Bus. at U. of Tn., Marten, 1982. Works for Farmers Home Admin. in Lauderdale Co. Child: CAROLYN VIRGINIA CANNON, b. 7 Apr 1995.
4. THOMAS PRICHARD SMITH, b. 27 Aug 1962, Jackson, Tn. M. Karen Elizabeth Walker 23 Mar 1990. Attended Dyersburg State Community College, and now farms. Children: (1) GRANT MURPHY SMITH, b. 18 Sept 1993, Jackson, Tn., and (2) MATTHEW THOMAS SMITH, b. 2 Jan 1996, Jackson.
5. VALERIE LOUISE SMITH, b. 15 Feb 1967, Jackson, Tn. M. Terry Wayne Hutchison 16 Jul 1988, Friendship. Graduate of Union

University, Jackson, Tn., B. A. degree. Child: LINDSEY NICOLE HUTCHISON, b. 26 Mar 1993, Jackson.

* *

SANDY LEE JOHNS,

3- son of Carlos Johns (1887) and Florence, b. 29 Mar 1911. M. Minnie Maude Cope 27 Feb 1932 in Mo. She was b. 31 Oct 1912 in Devol, Cotton Co., Okla., the daughter of Willie Everett Cope and Minnie Maude Hill. Sandy and Minnie lived in Steele, Mo. He was a carpenter and Independent Contractor. They were members of the Church of Christ.

Their children:
1. IRIS MAUDE JOHNS, b. 19 Mar 1934, Mo. Married Gene Ladd.
2. CHARLES EDWARD JOHNS, b. 24 Sep 1936, Mo. Married Bonnie Duvoll 1962.
3. BILLY LEE JOHNS, b. 28 Dec 1943, Mo. Married Connie Hicks.
4. ELIZABETH JOHNS, b. 31 Jan 1952, Mo. Married David L. Fry 1972.

* *

JAMES HAROLD JOHNS,

5- son of Carlos Johns (1887) and Florence, b. 10 Jul 1915, married Alta Holmes 11 Aug 1936, Charleston, Mississippi Co., Mo. She was born 29 Aug 1918 in Lake Co., Tn., the daughter of William Henry Holmes and (1) Florance Ayers. They live in Jackson, Mo. They observed their 60th Wedding Anniversary in August 1996.

J. H.'s occupation was in construction work from 1937 until his retirement in 1980. Even after he retired, he continued to build churches. He drew plans and supervised the building of Sunday school classrooms for his church, the Shawnee Hills Baptist in Jackson, Mo., in July 1994, and was almost finished with the project when he fell and broke his arm and had to quit. He is still active in church work, and attended the recent Family Reunion.

Their children:
1. FLORENCE MARIE JOHNS, b. 16 Jul 1937, Bertrand, Mo. Married Louis Gibson. She died in April 1965, in a car wreck at Gatesville, Tx. Her husband was in the army, stationed at Ft. Hood. No children.
2. HAROLD OWEN JOHNS, b. 23 Nov 1940, at Sikeston, Scott Co., Mo. Married Beverly Joyce Hueter 27 Jan 1962, at Scopus, Bollinger Co., Mo. Two children:
   a) CHERYL LYNNETTE JOHNS, b. 29 Dec 1963, Marble Hill, Bollinger Co., Mo. She married John William Martin Jr. 11 Mar 1983. They have three children:
      i) ZACHARY WILLIAM MARTIN, b. 12 Apr 1989.
      ii) MACKENZIE LYNNEE MARTIN, b. 14 Apr 1992.
      iii) AUSTIN JOHNATHAN MARTIN, b. 18 Aug 1994.
   b) JANELLE LEIGH JOHNS, b. 24 Jul 1973.

3. JOYCE ANN JOHNS, b. 9 Mar 1945, Miner Switch, Scott Co., Mo. Married John David Burk 10 Jun 1962. Two children:
   a) ANTHONY JOHN (TONY) BURK, b. 29 Oct 1963, Marble Hill, Bollinger Co., Mo.
   b) SUSAN JO BURK, b. 12 Jun 1968, at O'Fallon, St. Charles Co., Mo. She married Tom Gaskill 15 Mar 1993. They have one child: i) KATLYN NICOLE GASKILL, b. 9 Jan 1994, St. Peters, St. Charles Co., Mo.

* *

JESSE O'NEIL JOHNS,
6- son of Carlos Johns(1887) and Florence, b. 18 Jan 1918, married Marcella Drewery 2 Dec 1939 at Marshal, Ark. Jesse served in World War II in 44th Repair Squadron, 5th Air Force in South Pacific and in the Phillipine Liberation. A letter to his sister, Lillie Prichard, dated Sept. 14, 1944, stated he was in New Guinea cooking in the Officers Mess for about 100 men; he had been helping cook for over 1000 men before the changeover. He had been overseas more than 1 1/2 years then.

Jesse went into farming after the War, near Bragg City, Mo. He and Marcella were members of Church of Christ, Bragg City, Mo. He was a member of the Lions Club. Jesse died 18 Sep 1992 at AMI Lucy Lee Hospital, Poplar Bluff, Mo. He was buried in Memorial Gardens Cemetery, Kennett, Mo. Marcella died 15 Apr 1978 in Memphis, Tn., and was buried in Memorial Gardens Cemetery, Kennett, Mo. They had no children.

* *

KATHERINE PAULINE JOHNS,
8- daughter of Carlos Johns (1887) and Florence, b. 4 Aug 1921, married (1) Henry William Ballard 20 Jul 1937 in Blytheville, Ark. He was b. 13 Dec 1903, Lynn Point, Tn., the son of John Ballard and Nancy Fitzgerald of Middle Tn. Henry died 31 Jan 1984 in Flat Rock, Mich. and was buried in Upper Cooter Cemetery, Blytheville, Ark. Pauline married (2) George Vida 22 Mar 1985 in Flatrock, Mich. The children of Pauline Johns Ballard and Henry:
1. WILLIAM HENRY BALLARD Jr., b. 24 Aug 1938, Holland, Mo. Died 24 Aug 1938; buried No. 8 Cemetery, Cooter, Mo.
2. HAROLD EDWARD BALLARD, b. 10 Jul 1940, Parma, Mo.
3. GERALD WAYNE BALLARD, b. 10 Mar 1943, Friendship, Crockett Co., Tn.
4. JOE CARLTON BALLARD, b. 25 Oct 1944, Minor Switch, Mo.
5. RONNIE RAY BALLARD, b. 8 Feb 1947, Minor Switch, Mo.
6. MICHAEL LEROY BALLARD, 5 Apr 1950, New Survey, Mo.
7. CHRISTOPHER ALAN BALLARD, b. 13 Aug 1959, Kennett, Mo. Married Cynitha Harmon 18 Nov 1978, Southgate, Mi.

* *

NANCY LORENA JOHNS,

4-dau of Carlos C. Johns (1887) and Maureen, was b. 22 Aug 1936, Holland, Mo. Married K. S. Needham, Memphis, Tn 13 Jun 1958. They lived in Little Rock, Ark. and Kingsport, Tn., then in Jan 1960, moved to Rowland Hights, Ca. They divorced 9 Aug 1985. Lorena moved to Santa Barbara, Ca. and had the name of Johns restored. She is now living in Long Beach, Ca., where she is an excess merchandise locator. Their children are:

1. KELLEY NEEDHAM, b. 27 Mar 1959. M. Jessica Lin Morley 17 May1986. She was b. 15 Feb 1961, dau of John and Joan Morley of San Diego. Both have B.A.'s in Architecture. Reside in Upland, Ca.
2. SHEENA KAY NEEDHAM, b. 12 Jun 1960, Los Angeles. Graduated Pepperdine Univ. with B. A. in English. Has her own design and development company, which produces and develops children's books.
3. BARRY JON NEEDHAM, b. 2 May 1961, Pico Rivera, Ca. Attended Orange Coast College in Costa Mesa. Barry is now a computer graphic artist and computer illustrator. Son JACKSON NEEDHAM, b. 6 Jul 1995, Newport Beach, Ca. They reside in Long Beach, Ca.

* *

VERA MAE JOHNS,

6- dau of Carlos C. Johns (1887) and Morene, was b. 19 Aug 1941. M. 6 May 1960 John Lee Brown, son of Cecil Ray Brown and Bessie Agnes Buys. John worked for Texaco, Inc., and now is Sales Admin. for Noranda Aluminum Inc. of New Madrid. Children:

1. KAREN SUZANNE BROWN, b. 9 Mar 1962, Hayti, Mo. M. Steven Lynn Piker 29 Mar 1991. Works for State as a Rehabilitation Counselor for the Blind in Sikeston, Mo.
2. MATTHEW SCOTT BROWN, b. 19 Dec 1965, Hayti, Mo. M. (1) Peggy Ann Jones 28 May 1995. Have two sons. M. (2) Patricia Cantrell Patton 16 Aug 1996.

* *

CLARENCE MARTIN JOHNS,

6- son of Benjamin Edmund Johns (1854) and Nancy, b. 11 May 1889,[22] married Emma Bernard 26 Jul 1910, Crockett Co., Tn. [23] She was b. about 1890 in Tn. [24] She was the daughter of John W. and Lula C. Bernard of Crockett Co.[25] Clarence was a farmer, and farmed in Crockett Co., Tn. He died 13 Aug 1967.[26]

Their daughters were [no sons]:

---

[22]Mattie Johns Lovelace Bible.
[23]Crockett Co. Tn. Marriages. by H.D. Clift, M.G. Also recorded in Mattie Lovelace Bible.
[24]1920 Census Crockett Co. Tn., ED 161, p. 6, L. 68.
[25]Ibid.
[26]Bible of Nettie Lovelace Young, Sikeston, Mo., now owned by son James Young.

Crockett Co.[25] Clarence was a farmer, and farmed in Crockett Co., Tn. He died 13 Aug 1967.[26]

Their daughters were [no sons]:

1. MAGGIE LOU JOHNS, b. 26 Mar 1913, Crockett Co., Tn. Married W. Ray Heath 15 Aug 1929, Crockett Co., Tn. [27] Lived in Halls, Tn.[28] Children: 1) EVELYN HEATH, b. 26 Aug 1930, m. _____ Archibald; 2) VERNON LEE HEATH, b. 8 Jul 1932; 3) WILLIAM (BILL) HEATH, b. 7 Oct 1935; EMMA FRANCIS HEATH, b. 23 Jul 1936, m. _____ Shepard; and 4) RAY DWAYNE HEATH, b. 1 Sept 1941. Maggie Lou died in Nov. 1996; she left 10 grandchildren, 12 great-grandchildren and a great-great-grandchild.

2. EUGENE JOHNS, b. 23 Mar 1915, Crockett Co., Tn. Married Virgil "Red" Ellis. He d. Dec 1996. Children: 1) EMMA MARIE ELLIS, b. 7 Apr 1935, m. _____ Carter, (deceased); 2) BARBARA JEAN ELLIS, b. 30 Oct 1938, m. _____ Mullins; and 3) VIRGIL ELLIS JR., b. 26 Mar 1949 (deceased).

3. GERTRUDE JOHNS, b. 11 Feb 1924, Crockett Co., Tn. Married Ernest Jones. Children: 10 ERNEST JONES JR., b. 19 Dec 1941; 2) JOHN DOUGLAS JONES, b. 7 Mar 1943, (deceased); 3) LUOMA JONES, b. 27 Apr 1955; and 4) DEBBIE ANN JONES, b. 15 May 1973, (dec.)

4. NANNIE B. JOHNS, b. 17 Jan 1926. Married (1) _____ _____, and (2) Eli Ethridge, Paris, Tn.[29] Her children are Jo Ann Sollis, b. 16 Aug 1945; and 2) Linda Faye Lauderdale, b. 2 Dec 1947.

* *

EULA JOHNS,

7- daughter of Ben Edmond Johns (1854) and Nancy, b. 28 Nov 1892,[30] married Walter Fitzhugh 4 Apr 1909, Crockett Co., Tn. He was b. ca 1891 in Tn.[31] They moved to Memphis, Tn. Her husband Walter and son J. B. were very devoted to her. J. B. never married, and always looked after her. Walter died many years before she did. She lived to be 99 years of age, and lived awhile at Resthaven Nursing Home, where J. B. visited often. She d. 22 Mar 1992, and was bu. in Memorial Park Cemetery in Memphis.[32] She was a member of Peabody Baptist Church.

Their child:

1. J. B. WILLIAM FITZHUGH, b. 26 Jan 1913, Friendship, Crockett Co., Tn. Served overseas in the U.S. Army during World War II. Was a

---

[25]Ibid.
[26]Bible of Nettie Lovelace Young, Sikeston, Mo., now owned by son James Young.
[27]Crockett Co. Tn. Marriages. Bondsman: Henry Littles. Married by Sam Young, J.P.
[28]1979 Family Reunion Newsletter.
[29]Inf. Mary Kathryn Harris, Dallas, Tx.
[30] Mattie Lovelace's Bible.
[31]1920 Census Crockett Co., Tn., ED 13, p. 5, L. 19.
[32]Obituary. Crockett Times. Mar 1992.

8- daughter of Ben Edmund Johns (1854) and Nancy, b. 17 Oct 1894[33] married A. Otis Bolling[34] 26 Apr 1914 in Crockett Co., Tn.[35] Otis was born 26 Feb 1897, Crockett Co., Tn., the son of William Bolling and Martha Glisson. [Name spelled as in records.]

Otis Bolling farmed in Crockett County, leaving there for awhile in the 1930's when they farmed in Arkansas. He possibly left Tn. because of the 1927 flood.

They had twin boys who were born and died in Arkansas in 1932, near Blytheville, Ark. They were buried in Big Sandy Cemetery near Blytheville. [36] Otis died 29 May 1963 in Jackson, Madison Co., Tn. and was buried in Highland Memorial Gardens, Jackson, Tn.

Lena died 2 Nov 1989 in Jackson, Tn. and was buried in Highland Memorial Gardens.

Their children are [current spelling]:
1. ALVIE BOLDING, b. 26 Feb 1919, Crockett Co., Tn.
2. J. W. BOLDING, b. 23 Mar 1922, Crockett Co., Tn. Married Nell WILEY. He died Nov 1986 in Paris, Tn. Nell died Nov 1985 in Paris, Tn.
3. OTIS BOLDING Jr., b. 17 Jul 1931, Crockett, Tn. Died 17 Jul 1931.
4. KENNETH BOLDING, b. 23 Jan 1933, Crockett Co., Tn. Married Betty Dodson. They live in Jackson, Tn. and have four children.

* *

ALVIE BOLDING,
1- son of Lena Johns Bolling and Otis, b. 26 Feb 1919, married (1) Faye Daniels 2 Jul 1945 in Blytheville, Ark. She was born 22 Nov 1920 in Crockett Mills, Tn. They lived in Memphis, Tn. Faye and their son Billy died in a car-truck accident 27 Jul 1970 near Dyersburg, Tn., while riding with a neighbor who was also killed. They were both buried in Memorial Gardens Cemetery in Memphis, Tn.[37]

Alvie married (2) Jean Carwyle King 11 Dec 1971. She was b. 2 Mar 1932, Pontotoc, Ms., daughter of Bulon H. Carwyle and Loy Mae Luther. Her first husband was Clifton King. Their daughter: Patricia Ann King, b. 25 Aug 1957. Patricia married Glenn Vance 17 Dec 1958, and has children: a) Rachel Vance, b. 2 Apr 1982, and b) Jessica Vance, b. 27 May 1986.

Children of Alvie Bolding and Faye:
1. JUDY CAROL BOLDING, b. 7 Jun 1949, Dyersburg, Dyer Co., Tn. Married (1) Richard Pinner. Their children: a) JEFFREY NEAL PINNER, b. 5 Jul 1967, Memphis, Tn., and b) CRAIG RICHARD PINNER, b. 29 Jun 1973. Judy Carol married (2) Steve Carroll.

---

[33]Bible, Mattie Lovelace.
[34]Name was written as "Bolling" in 1920 Census, Crockett Co., Tn.
[35]Crockett Co. Tn. Marriages. Inf. from Lillie Prichard, Friendship, Tn.
[36]Per Lillie Prichard, Friendship, Tn..
[37]Newspaper article, undated, rcd. from Lillie Prichard, Friendship, Tn.

2. JULIA COLLEEN BOLDING, b. 30 Apr 1956, Memphis. Died 20 May 1956; buried Providence Cemetery, Crockett Co., Tn.
3. WILLIAM ALVIE "Billy" BOLDING, b. 5 Jul 1957, Memphis, Tn. Died in accident 27 Jul 1970, Dyersburg, Tn. Buried Memorial Park Cemetery, Memphis, Tn.
* *

CHILDREN OF JONATHAN JOHNS (ca 1815) and ELIZABETH:
1. LYDIA JOHNS, b. 27 Apr 1875, Dyer Co., Tn.
2. MARTHA 'Mattie" JOHNS, b. ca 1880 in Dyer Co., Tn.
* *

LYDIA JOHNS,
1-dau of Jonathan Johns (ca 1815) and Elizabeth, was b. 27 Apr 1875 in Dyer Co., Tn. M. Samuel Franklin Wallace 17 May 1891 [by H. B. Owins, M.G. in Crockett Co., Tn.][38] Lydia d. 31 Oct 1961 in Dyer Co. They had nine children:
1. BEATRICE WALLACE, b. Dyer Co., Tn.
2. WILLIAM JAMES WALLACE, b. ca 1896. M. Talitha _____. He died in 1929.
3. EUGENE WALLACE, b. Oct 1900; d. in 1922.
4. RUTH WALLACE, b. 7 Mar 1905, Tn. M. Otis Lee Randle 7 Jul 1929 in Tn. Their children:
    a) WALLACE LEE RANDLE, b. 10 Feb 1935, Tn. Married Carol Trent Aug 1958. Their children were: 1) DEE RANDLE, b. 18 Oct 1959, Tn. and 2) EDDIE RANDLE, b. 9 Feb 1963, Tn.
    b) FRANK HARRIS RANDLE, b. 10 Feb 1935, Tn. Married Virginia Slocum, Nov 1958, Tn. Their children were: 1) CARY RANDLE, b. 14 Feb 1963, Tn. and 2) PHILLIP RANDLE, b. 31 Jan 1965, Tn.
5. MARY EVELYN WALLACE, b. 8 May 1908, Tn. Married Arley Ulric Moore 27 Nov 1937 in Jackson, Tn. She d. 16 Jan 1993 in Jackson, Tn. Child: a) JOHN WALLACE MOORE, b. 24 Jan 1944 Jackson, Tn. M. Wanda Whitfield 24 Nov 1971. Daughter, JENNIFER MOORE.
6. SAM O'DANIEL WALLACE, b. Dec 1910.
7. FRANK CAMERON WALLACE, b. 12 Aug 1912, Tn. M. Mary Crippen Aug 1949. Children: a) JUDITH KAY WALLACE, b. 19 Nov 1950, Tn. M. Kenneth Sassman 2 Oct 1976. b) DEBORAH ANN WALLACE, b. 19 Nov 1950. M. James Pearson 22 Mar 1976.
8. PHILLIP WALLACE.
9. THOMAS RYE WALLACE, b. 2 Nov 1915.

---

[38]Info on this family from Lillie Prichard of Friendship, Tn., who received it from Mary Evelyn Wallace More of Jackson, Tn.

* *

MATTIE JOHNS,

2-dau of Jonathan Johns (ca 1815) and Elizabeth, was b. ca 1880 in Dyer Co., Tn. She married 1) John Leven Bedwell 24 Nov 1897, Crockett Co., Tn. She married 2) Grant Cogburn about 1908 in Crockett Co., Tn.[39] Mattie died 26 Jun 1927 in Friendship, Crockett Co., Tn.

The children of Mattie and John Bedwell:

1. ANDREW LISTON BEDWELL, b. 7 Jan 1899. Married Eunice Miller. They had two adopted sons: a) Joe Bedwell, and b) George Bedwell. George died in 1989-90 in Bonicord, Tn.
2. WILLIAM JONATHAN BEDWELL, b. 19 Feb 1901.
3. LIZZIE MAI BEDWELL, b. 15 Jun 1905, Crockett Co., Tn. Died 1 Nov 1906.

* *

WILLIAM JONATHAN BEDWELL,

2-son of Martha Johns Bedwell and John, was born 19 Feb 1901 in Tn. He married Bertha Eugene Young 12 Nov 1921 in Dyer Co., Tn. He died 3 Nov 1963, Friendship, Tn. Bertha died 14 Jul 1969.

Their children:

1. JAMES DOYLE BEDWELL, b. 29 Aug 1922, Friendship, Tn. Married Mary Margaret Guinn 11 May 1946, Ms. Two daughters:
   a) BARBARA JOYCE BEDWELL. Married _____ Swain.
   b) VICKIE LYNN BEDWELL.
2. LAURA FRANCES BEDWELL, b. 27 Sep 1924, Crockett Co., Tn. Married Thomas Lovan. She died in 1990.
3. W. CORRINE BEDWELL, b. 12 Aug 1926. M. Cleman Bigger.
4. MALCOLM YOUNG BEDWELL, b. 1 Apr 1930, Crockett Co., Tn. Married Dorothy _____. He died 9 Mar 1991 and was buried in Bellevernon Cemetery, Crockett Co., Tn.
5. BILLY EUGENE BEDWELL, b. 12 Jul 1933, Friendship, Tn. Married Nancy _____.
6. JOHNNY ANDREW BEDWELL, b. 4 Feb 1936, Friendship, Tn. Married Peggy Jean Park.
7. JERRY LYNN BEDWELL, b. 23 Nov 1937, Friendship, Tn. Married Doris Levesque.
8. REBECCA JANE BEDWELL, b. 5 Feb 1940. Married Doyle Baker.
9. LINDA SUE BEDWELL, b. 25 Nov 1941. Married Robert Howell.
10. EMMA RUTH BEDWELL. Married Paul King.
11. SAMMIE LEE BEDWELL, b. 18 May 1945. Died 30 Jan 1966 in military service in Vietnam.

* *

---

[39]Info on this family furnished by James Doyle Bedwell, Oxnard, Ca. He now owns the Family Bible of Martha Johns Bedwell Cogburn.

Mattie Johns Bedwell Cogburn and Grant had two children:
1. J. D. COGBURN, b. 28 Mar 1909.
2. ISHAM LEE COGBURN, b. 6 Mar 1911.
*

CHAPTER NINETEEN

EPILOG...

After much work, there are still numerous loose ends to research regarding the Johns connections. This seems to be a recurring theme in genealogical research.

I feel I was able to touch base with many antecedents, and have learned much about the Welsh. I have carried the John/Johns research forward, and discovered many places for additional research. Much earlier information from many sources is contained here for ongoing analysis. I hope family members will use this information and perhaps find things I missed.

I had hoped to prove or disprove beyond doubt whether Thomas John was the husband of the Mary who arrived with the Baptist church group in Pennsylvania in 1701. I have given most available information on the early church history and hope that by bringing this together, new discoveries will be made.

Information is given on the use of the name as Jones, as well as John and Johns. However, in most instances, it appears to me that the John family used the surname John from the earliest times we found them in the records, and perhaps earlier in Wales.

The Griffith John who died in 1749, and was father of our ancestor David who moved to North Carolina in 1754, had property taken out in 1703 that was located next to Thomas John in New Castle Co., Del. There is some reason to believe Griffith was the son of Thomas and Mary John, and arrived with them in 1701. I don't want to fall into the category of assuming too much.

With the numerous progeny of the earlier settlers, the majority of those first Welsh families in the Welsh Tract of Delaware with the John name were probably related. It appears that the Griffith John of South Carolina could have easily been a brother of David John. I found they were much closer in age than previously thought.

I've tried to mention other possibilities to aid researchers in finding more information, or giving a different interpretation to what I found. It was very enlightening to see the close connections with the Quakers, and the intermarriages with them. To me, there seems to be more evidence indicating the possibility of our first Griffith being connected with the Quakers. A more extensive look at Quaker records will undoubtedly reveal more marriages between them and some of the Baptists.

The religious trait in the Johns line seems to still be very strong today. Several I've discussed this with share my belief that this trait is still felt strongly. There still exists an influence to strive to better our souls and live a good, beneficial life, while helping others to do so. Despite current views of relativism held by many, our strong feelings of right and wrong still prevail. We still retain a strong feeling that there is plenty of need to continue good works, honesty, and good character in our families and in our country. Strong beliefs help resist current maxims turning our values upside down.

As in most families of the last few decades, there have been many divorces and remarriages in our families. Before this time, divorces were rare. The Johns, male and female, in the past seemed to have a strong sense of family and remarried soon after the death of a spouse.

We hope the current breakup of families will not continue. Children need the secure feelings derived from stable relationships. With our good heritage and strong family values, I feel confident our family will weather these storms, and continue to retain their values.

It is great to see several of our younger family members so interested in genealogy. Our annual Family Reunion is alive and well, with many young people in attendance. I hope this interest continues, and that my research has helped move the knowledge of our family history forward.

Helen Sides Dye,
Glendora, Ca. 91740

INDEX

C

Curtis, John · 142
Curtis, Mr. · 72

D

D'Haes, Johannes · 88
D'Surrency, Jacob · 252, 253, 254
Dabbs, Capt. Joseph · 271
Dabbs, James · 258, 271
Dabeyns, George · 94
Dafis, Emlon · 160
Dafis, Martha · 160
Dafydd, Elizabeth · 160
Dafydd, Rhichart · 160
Dafydd, Rhys · 159
Dafydd, Shion · 160
Dafydd, Susana · 159
Dafydd, Thomas · 160
Dakeyne, Geo. · 216
Danforth, William · 196
Daniel, Aaron · 236, 258
Daniels, Faye · 497
Darby, John · 258
Davault, William · 412
David, Christian · 90
David, Edward · 46, 47, 76
David, Elishea · 188
David, Henry · 79, 91, 109, 170
David, Hugh · 79, 80, 82, 123
David, James Sr. · 79
David, Jane · 190
David, Jenkin · 258
David, Jennet · 90
David, John · 2, 41, 42, 76, 78, 79, 89, 100, 101, 122, 153, 166, 168, 215, 494
David, Joshua · 273
David, Josiah · 215
David, Lewelin · 90
David, Lewis · 13, 41, 42, 72, 81, 82, 108, 109, 154, 155, 162
David, Lewis ap · 15
David, Llewellyn · 79
David, Margaret · 50, 123
David, Morris · 79
David, Philip · 97, 160, 166, 174, 176
David, Rachel · 202, 214
David, Robert · 9, 43, 49, 56
David, Sarah · 215
David, T. C. · 416
David, Thomas · 30, 79, 89, 124, 158, 160, 162, 258, 339

Davidson, Benjamin Myles · 351
Davidson, David · 259
Davidson, Thomas · 258, 339
Davie, David · 214
Davie, Phoebe · 298, 305
Davies, Joseph · 287
Davies, Margaret · 15, 38
Davies, Myrick · 115, 314
Davies, Richard · 7, 15, 21, 22, 40, 44, 45, 112
Davies, Robert · 72
Davies, Thomas · 20
Davies, Timothy · 79
Davis, Abel · 129
Davis, David · 14, 33, 129, 145, 159, 160, 166, 175, 183, 194, 197, 207, 214, 288, 291, 292, 297, 298, 299
Davis, Ellis · 32
Davis, Emly · 159
Davis, Henry · 94, 95, 98, 99, 100, 199, 276, 379
Davis, James · 198, 225, 289, 375
Davis, James Carthel · 375
Davis, James Robert · 375
Davis, Janie · 352
Davis, Janott · 160
Davis, John · 90, 112, 113, 199, 200, 201, 258, 282, 334
Davis, Jonathan · 218
Davis, Linon Earl · 375
Davis, Louisa · 400
Davis, Margaret · 13, 201
Davis, Peter · 189
Davis, Philip · 189
Davis, Porter John · 375
Davis, Rev. David · 129, 145, 197, 207
Davis, Rev. Jeremiah · 129
Davis, Richard · 13, 188, 189
Davis, Rosie · 469
Davis, Sarah Matilda · 322
Davis, Thomas · 334, 335, 341
Day, Elizabeth · 67
Day, John · 14
De Surrency, Jacob · 253, 254, 255
Deal, Mary · 141
Dean, Clay Franklin · 471
Dean, Clay M. · 471
Dean, Lauren McLeod · 471
Dean, Laurin McLeod · 471
Deatherage, Rebecca · 337, 404, 405, 406, 407
Deer, John · 271
Delap, Peter · 144

Dye, Helen Sides · 1, vii, 483, 484, 502
Dye, Jeffrey Martin · 483, 484
Dye, Rebecca Ruth · 483
Dyer, John · 258
Dyre, Capt. Henry · 196
Dyre, James · 165, 174

E

Eachus, Anoch · 241
Eady, Daniel M. · 352
Eady, John Jr. · 352
Eady, John Sr. · 352
Eaglesfield, George · 204
Eastbarn, Benjamin · 134
Eastburn, Benj. · 133, 136
Eaton, George · 159
Eaton, Gwenllian · 159
Eaton, John · 159, 201
Eaton, Joseph · 159
Eaton, Juan · 159
Eaton, Mary · 159
Eatons · 84, 159, 202
Eckley, John · 71
Edge, Jacob · 33
Edmond, Evan · 90, 114, 154, 155, 183
Edmond, Lewis · 90
Edmond, Lyns · 160
Edmond, Lyws · 182
Edmond, Thomas · 122, 160
Edmonds, Mary R. · 453
Edmund, Thomas · 106
Edward, Arthyr · 160, 182
Edward, Jann · 160
Edward, John · 34, 82, 90, 114, 181, 196, 201, 393
Edward, John ap · 9, 23, 34
Edward, Joshua · 160, 255, 258, 271
Edward, Will · 72
Edward, William ab · 18
Edward, William ap · 9, 22, 24, 34, 47, 56
Edwards, Abel · 258
Edwards, Alexander and Bridget · 114
Edwards, Donald · 99
Edwards, Edward · 91, 98, 160, 181
Edwards, Jaen · 97
Edwards, James · 196, 200
Edwards, Job · 237, 258
Edwards, Jobe · 239

Edwards, John Evan · 16
Edwards, Joshua · 255, 258, 271
Edwards, Margaret · 50
Edwards, Morgan · 11, 92, 102, 109, 122, 126, 129, 146, 161, 162, 192, 197, 200, 201, 204, 218, 219
Edwards, Petter · 44
Edwards, Shan · 160
Edwards, Thomas · 258
Edwards, William · 34, 56, 57, 76, 258
Efan, Ann · 160
Efan, Dafydd · 160
Efan, Hugh · 160
Efans, Lidia · 159
Efans, Samuel · 160
Efans, Shon · 159
Egbertson, Lt. James · 196
Egner, Jacob · 311, 330
Eldridge, Madison · 448, 451
Elexander, James · 248, 249
Elkins, Aaron · 490
Elkins, Aaron M. · 490
Elkins, Carrie Belle · 399
Elkins, Matilda Madge · 399
Elkins, Rachel N. · 490
Elkouri, Daniel Ray · 399
Ellerbe, Edward · 257, 258
Ellerbe, Thomas · 257, 258, 262
Ellerbe, Thos. · 234
Ellerbe, William · 258, 260
Ellerby, Thomas · 266
Elliot, John · 197
Elliot, Peter · 225, 289, 290, 301
Elliot, Robert · 297
Elliott, Archibald · 286
Elliott, Sarah · 286
Elliott, William · 286
Ellis, Andrew · 119
Ellis, Barbara Jean · 496
Ellis, Cadwalader · 22, 76
Ellis, Emma Marie · 496
Ellis, Isam · 258
Ellis, Mary · 31, 81
Ellis, Rowland · 20, 22, 33, 44, 58, 73, 81
Ellis, Rowland Jr. · 20
Ellis, Rowland Sr. · 20
Ellis, Thomas · 13, 22, 42, 73
Ellis, Virgil Jr. · 496
Ellis, William Robert · 89
Elliss, Isham · 232
Emannuel, Howell · 83

F

G

H

John, Gregory A. · 398
John, Griffith · iii, v, vi, 22, 28, 32, 35, 36, 37, 50, 53, 54, 55, 56, 57, 58, 59, 60, 61, 62, 63, 64, 65, 72, 76, 79, 80, 86, 90, 92, 94, 95, 99, 102, 110, 121, 143, 148, 151, 153, 159, 161, 166, 167, 168, 169, 170, 173, 174, 177, 183, 186, 190, 193, 199, 208, 209, 210, 213, 219, 220, 221, 223, 226, 227, 228, 229, 230, 231, 232, 233, 237, 239, 250, 251, 259, 276, 279, 285, 318, 501
John, Gwen · 53, 54, 55, 60, 61, 62, 80
John, Gwen Llian · 122
John, H. A. · 386, 388
John, Harmon · 381
John, Harold Eugene · 402
John, Harrison · 397, 398, 406
John, Harvey · 393, 453
John, Harvey Clifton · 403
John, Heath · 195
John, Helen · 408
John, Henderson · 364
John, Homer · 396, 455
John, Hugh · 9, 23, 24, 35, 361, 363
John, Hurst Trustin · 410
John, Icie Frances · 401
John, Ida Mae · 400
John, Illie Monroe · 403
John, Isabella Nelson · 321
John, J. L. · 403, 404
John, J. Montgomery · 385
John, J. W. · 367
John, Jacob · 147, 185, 195, 259, 278
John, James Carl · 402
John, James Edward · 396
John, James Hall · 348, 350, 351
John, James Hall Jr. · 351
John, James M. · 392, 400
John, James W. · 365, 381
John, James William · 372, 373
John, Janay Leewaine · 401
John, Jane · 60, 65, 122, 332, 335, 337, 390, 391, 392, 418
John, Jane Nelson · 321
John, Jena · 399
John, Jerry Paul · 402
John, Jesey · 228
John, Jesse · 231, 232, 233, 273, 318
John, Jewel Alta · 402
John, Jim · 381
John, Jim Porter · 375
John, Jimianne · 401

John, John · 65, 172, 188, 202, 281, 330, 349, 430, 431
John, John ap · 4, 7, 13, 15, 22, 38, 40
John, John Francis · 403
John, John Luther · 351
John, John Marr · 396
John, John Phillip · 79, 90
John, John W. · 396
John, Jonathan · iv, v, 147, 160, 226, 227, 228, 229, 230, 231, 259, 265, 266, 278, 279, 318, 343, 344, 346, 347, 362, 382, 383, 387, 389, 417, 440, 441, 448, 454, 455, 456, 458, 459, 461, 498, 499
John, Jonathan N. · 367, 381
John, Jonathan Terrell · 370, 379
John, Jonathan W. · 362
John, Joseph · 20, 202, 210, 296, 316
John, Joseph Franklin · 322, 372, 376, 377
John, Joseph Kinnie · 401, 403, 404
John, Joseph Lee · 401
John, Joseph Reed · 321, 323
John, Joseph S. · 370
John, Josie Carla · 399
John, Joy · 381
John, Justin L. · 401
John, Karen Sue · 402
John, Katy Gladys · 396
John, Kermit · 398
John, Kermit L. · 398
John, King of England · 1
John, Lee · 354, 372, 373, 381, 393, 398, 401, 403, 408, 409, 410, 449, 451, 452, 453, 467, 490, 493
John, Lela · 381
John, Leland Stanford · 398, 399
John, Leon · 396, 399, 403
John, Leon Stanley · 401
John, Leona Faye · 402
John, Leonard Dale · 403
John, Leora · 351
John, Lewis M. · 402, 451
John, Liddie · 366
John, Linda M. · 403
John, Lloyd E. · 397
John, Lola Fay · 396
John, Lola Floida · 397
John, Loretto F. · 381
John, Lori Ann · 399
John, Lottie May · 396
John, Loyd · 403
John, Lula · 408
John, Lula C. · 412

K

M

P

S

T

548